# ALLIED ESCORT SHIPS
## OF WORLD WAR II

*Frontispiece.* ESCORT AT SPEED IN A
CHOPPY SEA. A Type I 'Hunt' class destroyer
of the Royal Navy in the Mediterranean.
*(Imperial War Museum)*

# PETER ELLIOTT
# ALLIED ESCORT SHIPS OF WORLD WAR II
## A complete survey

Macdonald and Jane's · London

First published in 1977 by
Macdonald and Jane's Publishers Limited,
Paulton House, 8 Shepherdess Walk,
London N1 7LW

ISBN 0 356 08401 9

Drawings by Alan Raven

Designed by Michael Jarvis

Printed in Great Britain by
REDWOOD BURN LIMITED
Trowbridge & Esher

# Contents

# Foreword

This book is probably the first comprehensive study in one volume of all the classes of Allied escort vessels built during World War II.

The objective is a comparative examination of these classes—of the operational service of the escorts, and the evolving designs resulting from the different theatres of war; of the building programmes in each major country, and the differing production methods and speeds; and of the impressive transition in five years from the simple, pre-war built ships, to the final classes, packed with sophisticated radar and weapons.

Not only is this the first such comparative study of these classes, but a mass of new information is published for the first time. The naval and archive authorities have provided ready co-operation, and the list of acknowledgements reflects this, for which the author is indeed grateful. The contribution of the Ministry of Defence (Navy) in the UK, in its many forms, has been outstanding, as also has been that of Ottawa, but Washington and Melbourne, and some private individuals, too, have been most helpful. A large proportion of the photographs are published for the first time, as also a complete pendant list of all RN and Commonwealth ships built during the war. All the plans have been specially drawn by Alan Raven, with great accuracy.

The Royal Navy section is larger than those of the other navies, not so much because more new material was made available in the United Kingdom, as because the RN built 23 new classes, compared with 11 by the US Navy. Similarly, the Royal Canadian Navy section follows that of the Royal Navy, for ease of comparison, and reflecting, too, the great Canadian shipbuilding effort and the remarkable expansion of the Royal Canadian Navy.

It was found difficult to define the minimum size of escort to be included. Finally, 150 feet overall length became the standard; this includes the steel-hulled PC class of the USN, and the A/S trawlers of the RN, and excludes the wooden-hulled, less important submarine chasers and motor launches. In parallel, only ships completed during the war years, or begun before war's end, have been included. Even so, this book still covers some 4,000 ships, most of them classed as major warships!

It is hoped that the reader will feel that justice has been done to each class; even in a book of this size, space has been a major constraint. For example, further research could have been done on major refit dates, and more technical data included on the differing classes of ships; but this would have made the book less attractive to the more general reader, and the extra research would have made the book too long, or too costly, ever to finish or to publish! But the decision as to where to stop was a very real problem, even over three years work.

PETER ELLIOTT

Magnolia Wharf,
Strand on the Green,
London W4,
England

# Acknowledgements

Grateful acknowledgements for the provision of research facilities, information, plans and photographs, are made to the following:

*Australia*
Australian War Memorial
Evans Deakin Industries Ltd, Brisbane
Lt Cdr R. P. Hall, VRD, RANR
RAN Historical Section, Department of Defence, Melbourne
Paul A. Webb, Williamstown

*Canada*
Canadian Forces Photographic Unit, Ottawa
Director of History, Department of National Defence, Ottawa
Historical Photo Section, Public Archives of Canada, Ottawa

*New Zealand*
Naval Information Section, Ministry of Defence, Wellington

*United Kingdom*
P. W. Hayward, Kirby Cane, Suffolk
Imperial War Museum, London
David MacGregor Plans, London
T. Maskell, Bath
Ministry of Defence (Navy), Bath and London
   Director General Ships, Bath
   Naval Historical Branch, London
   Naval Home Division, London and Bath
   Royal Naval Armament Depot, Priddy's Hard, Gosport
Tom Molland Ltd, Plymouth, Devon
Department of Ships, National Maritime Museum, Greenwich
A. & J. Pavia, Malta
Antony Preston, London
Alan Raven, London
Public Records Office, London
Scottish Records Office, Edinburgh
Smith's Dock Co Ltd, Middlesbrough
P. A. Vicary, Cromer, Norfolk
Wright & Logan, Portsmouth, Hampshire

*United States of America*
Bethlehem Steel Corp Inc.
Naval History Division, Department of the Navy, Washington, DC
Audio-Visual Archives Division, National Archives & Records Service, Washington, DC
Edward H. Wiswesser, Reading, Pa

# Statistical lay-out

In a definitive study of this kind, many statistics are necessary, to highlight the main themes.

Many of those produced for this book are published for the first time, and it is hoped that the reader will find these helpful in comparing the shipbuilding efforts of the various Allied countries, as well as the classes.

The careful reader will find both gaps and conflicting statistics in places in this book. This, in spite of intensive research efforts; but a specialised study of these classes does not appear to have been attempted before, and even after 25 years these gaps and conflicts remain, even in official records, and in some cases it has not proved reasonably possible to eliminate them.

In other places, continuing security classification rules out publication of data on some individual ships, or on equipment that was in use for some time after 1945. These rules, not surprisingly, differ considerably between the United Kingdom, for example, and the United States.

The following will guide the reader in finding any particular set of statistics:

*Chapter 1. Escort Building Programmes* (covering the UK, Canada, and the USA)
Building programmes by years
Comparative specifications of various classes
Overall numbers of ships built, by classes
Overall numbers of ships cancelled, by classes
Overall war losses
Planned growth in escort forces for 1945/46

*Chapter 2. Comparative Production Rates*
Comparison of building times for main escort types
Analysis in detail of each navy and class

*Chapter 3. Allied Escort Vessels in Service*
Analysis of U-boats built and sunk
Analysis of Types XXI and XXIII
U-boats' production plans
Allocation of new escorts to commands
Details of escorts in major operations
War losses by theatres
Details of German U-boats, E-boats, small battle units

*Navy Chapters*
Building Programmes, and ordering dates by classes
Total escorts built for each navy, and distribution
Cumulative total of launches for each navy

*Class Chapters (for each class)*
Specification
Production of ships
Alterations and additions
Conversions
War losses
U-boats sunk by the class
Allocation to commands
Class list

*Armaments and Electronics*
Technical data on guns, radar and A/S weapons

*Combined Pendant List*
Identification of all RN, RCN, RAN, RIN, RNZN and SANF ships by pendant number (USN under USN class lists)

*Index*
covers every ship built, cancelled, or projected (where known)

*Hedingham Castle* in May 1945. She has Type 277 radar, two Type 86M radiotelephone aerials, but still only a trawler's boat! *(Ministry of Defence)*

*Damsay* in October 1942. A professional-looking ship with A/S-M/S configuration. *(Ministry of Defence)*

# CHAPTER ONE

# Escort Building Programmes

IN THIS chapter we take the three main shipbuilding countries, the United Kingdom, Canada, and the United States, and we examine the policies and programmes for the building of new escort classes during the war years in each of those countries, and also the exchange of new escorts between the big countries, which was one of the most impressive aspects of the whole operation.

From the content of this chapter will emerge a picture which will explain how the design and sequence of new classes evolved in each of the three countries, and how, towards the end of the war, the designs of new escorts then evolving were becoming increasingly similar.

Finally, we examine the probable growth in new escorts, had the cutback in the mass-production programmes not been put into effect in late 1943. Admittedly, this has to make certain assumptions, which are carefully listed, but it does give a good idea of the astonishing picture which would have appeared by the end of 1945, if production had carried on to that point at its planned level.

*Acute* in August 1942. A good silhouette of the class, with 4″ without gunshield, standard mast platforms, and prominent rangefinder platform aft. *(Ministry of Defence)*

# UNITED KINGDOM

The design development of the RN escort vessel classes was undoubtedly one of the success stories of the war years. Starting with brilliant improvisation, continuing with new weapons and ships of improved Atlantic seaworthiness, and finishing in the middle of a massive building programme of prefabricated frigates and corvettes, this story reflects the North Atlantic battle itself, as well as those of the Mediterranean and Home waters.

Indeed, for variety and speed of change, these classes were significantly different from the USN classes, where a small number of very good designs were mass-produced, with the basic designs changing little, and the weapons in numbers rather than types. The RN produced no less than 11 major classes, and a total of 24 including sub-classes, whereas the USN produced a total of 6, with 11 including sub-classes. These figures do not include classes of ship built in the USA and transferred to the UK, and vice versa.

## ESCORT DESIGN, 1915-38

*World War I*

During the earlier part of the war, Smith's Dock Company had produced two whaler designs which were adapted for escort duties, the 'Zed' and 'Kil' classes. They were smaller than the 'Flower' class corvettes, based on a whalecatcher design, and originally had a dummy whaling gun in the bow; they were armed with a concealed 12 pounder gun.

A World War I 'Flower' class sloop, *Gentian*. Tall masts, a flimsy bridge, no real close range armament, and minesweeping gallows at the stern. *(Ministry of Defence)*

The original 'Flower' class sloops were constructed during World War I. It is fascinating to look back and see that the original requirement for them was based on a better and more numerous class of minesweeper, which could also serve as general utility ships, for carrying baggage and libertymen, and to perform all the minor services of the fleet! Thus did the 'maid of all work' role of the corvette originally emerge!

They were designed, like their namesake successors, on the mercantile system of construction, and orders were placed with a large number of UK yards not specialised in naval construction. The first 12 were ordered on 1st January 1915, a further 12 the following week, and a third batch of 12 on 4th May. They were completed in an average time of six months from keel-laying, and some in nineteen weeks. They were single-screw ships, with 16½-17 knots maximum speed, 1,210 tons displacement, minesweeping gear, and armed with 2 12 pounder guns and 2 smaller A/A guns.

In July 1915, 36 more, of an improved design, were ordered, and by the end of the war some 106 were in service. The first 36 were then named the 'Acacia' class, and the rest the 'Arabis' class. The latter had a 4″ gun in place of the 12 pounder. Their duties ranged from fleet sweeping round Scapa and in the North Sea, to some 30 based in Western Ireland, in the U-boat danger zone, for convoy escort, and a further 6 were in the Mediterranean.

### Between the Wars

Not until 1928 did the Admiralty start to develop some new designs of sloop. A few were built each year for experimental purposes, and their lines were uniformly pleasing. This programme also maintained a nucleus of sloop

*Lowestoft*, one of the inter-war sloops. Note the twin 4″ mounting forward and aft, and two quadruple 0.5″ machine guns. *(Ministry of Defence)*

building expertise in the yards, against an emergency. These ships were not fast, but they were easy to construct and cheap to operate, and they had improved beam and seakeeping qualities.

By 1939, three types of sloop had developed:

—the large convoy sloops, for ocean escort work, which became the specialised 'Black Swan' class.

—the smaller 'Guillemot' class patrol vessels, later reclassed as corvettes, for use in Home waters, but too specialised, with turbines and warship construction, to be produced in any numbers.

—the minesweeping sloops, which became the 'Halcyon' class, and were developed smoothly into the wartime 'Algerine' class.

But none of these met the need for a mass-produced escort, as the war clouds formed. What was needed was a vessel of moderate speed and cost, seaworthy, manoeuvrable, with good acceleration, watertight sub-divisions, good endurance, good anti-submarine detection capability, a low complement, and, above all, capable of rapid production in shipyards not used to building naval vessels.

## THE EARLY YEARS OF IMPROVISATION

It is easy to forget the time-scale difference between the building programmes (the design stage), through the construction period, to the operational period, reflected in the photographs of the finished ships.

### 'FLOWER' CLASS CORVETTES

So we should recall that the Admiralty and Smith's Dock Company were designing the new corvettes together as early as the spring of 1939, and no less than 60 units were ordered before war broke out.

The ship was a combination of the requirements of the naval staff, as outlined above, and the most suitable design readily available—Smith's Dock Company's large commercial whaler *Southern Pride*. This ship, whose outline we

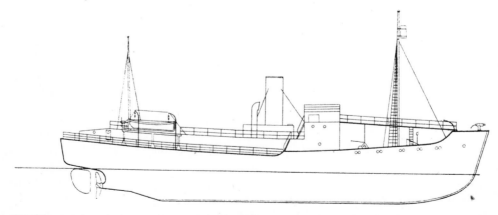

The RN 'Flower' class were developed by Smith's Dock Co from their commercial whaler design, *Southern Pride*, silhouetted here. *(Smith's Dock Co Ltd)*

reproduce here, had been designed by William Reed, now Managing Director of Smith's Dock, who had designed the small patrol vessels for the Admiralty in World War I, and now supervised the new corvette designs. (A contemporary successful whaler design for Norway by Smith's Dock can be seen in the 'Lake' class trawlers, included in this book.)

## ORIGINAL PATROL VESSEL SPECIFICATIONS, APRIL 1939

|  | *'SOUTHERN PRIDE'* | *A/S PATROL VESSEL* | | *ADMIRALTY A/S TRAWLER* |
|---|---|---|---|---|
|  | *(Smith's Dock Whaler)* | *Whalecatcher Type* | | *Coal-fired* |
|  |  | *Oil-fired* | *Coal-fired* |  |
| Displacement, tons | 930 | 1,170 | 1,390 | 680 |
| Dimensions |  |  |  |  |
|   length, pp | 160′0″ | 190′0″ | 210′0″ | 150′0″ |
|   draught, fwd | 11′9″ |  |  | 6′9″ |
|     aft | 15′7″ |  |  | 12′0″ |
|     mean |  | 13′3″ | 13′6″ |  |
| Machinery | 4-cylinder triple expansion | 4-cylinder triple expansion | | triple expansion |
| Boilers | 2 single-ended | 2 single-ended | | 1 single-ended |
| IHP | 2,300 | 2,750 | 2,750 | 850 |
| Speed, knots | 16 | 16 | 15½/16 | 12½ |
| Tons fuel | 250 | 360 |  | 183 |
| Consumption tons pd |  | 31 | 46 | 14 |
| Endurance |  |  |  |  |
|   full speed |  | 3,000 | 3,000 | 3,750 |
|   × 12 knots |  | 4,000 |  |  |
|   no days |  | 7·8 | 7·8 | 13 |
| Complement |  | 29 | 29 |  |
| Armament |  | 1—4″ | | 1—12 pdr |
|  |  | 2 Lewis guns | | 2 Lewis guns |

The table shows how the whaler design was developed into the original 'Flower' class design, and how that compared with the Admiralty coal-fired trawlers, designed at the same time. Originally, there was both a coal-fired and an oil-fired corvette design; the latter proved best for several reasons, not least of which turned out to be the necessity to re-fuel at sea.

The main feature of the adopted design was that it followed merchant shipbuilding practice and classification rules, and thus could easily be built in a number of the smaller yards around the UK; the choice of main propulsive machinery was also made to aid the yards, as well as the reservists who would largely man the corvettes. Yet the design incorporated many of the features necessary for an escort vessel—at first, designed for coastal escort and minesweeping, then revised gradually for North Atlantic mid-ocean work. In this respect, the corvettes fitted into a very different building situation from that of the United States, where very large numbers of new escorts were built by yards not experienced in warship construction.

The further development of the 'Flower' class is covered separately; we will now consider the next major stage in the North Atlantic battle.

## MASS PRODUCTION AND SOPHISTICATED ESCORTS

Again, we see the time gap in new designs and building time. As soon as the 'Flower' class corvettes were switched to mid-ocean work, for which they were never designed, the Admiralty saw the need for a larger escort, more seaworthy, more comfortable for its crew, with more speed to chase U-boats, and with more space to take the extra weapons which were appearing—radar, the Hedgehog, and more close-range weapons.

So the first frigate design, the 'River' class, was produced in short order, again by Smith's Dock; the first 27 were actually ordered under the 1940 Programme, and many more followed. They were known for some time as Twin Screw Corvettes.

When the 'River' class entered North Atlantic service (and we should note that it was the North Atlantic which dictated the evolution of most of the RN escort designs), it was clear that they were basically just what was wanted. Further and more sophisticated equipment, and more crew, could be added within and upon the larger hull, and the extra speed was sufficient for this specialised service.

With the increasing tempo of the Atlantic battle, greater numbers of escorts were increasingly required; so the Admiralty, like the USN, moved into a big programme of mass-produced escorts, with increasingly all-welded hulls and upperworks, and with new equipment built in, as technical progress dictated.

This resulted in 'River' class orders dwindling, and big orders being placed for the new 'Loch' class frigates. This class is described in some detail, under its own chapter. A projected increased production rate, in October 1942, provided for 120 'Loch' class and 80 'Castle' class to be completed by the end of 1944, without going to shipyards not previously used for escort building.

When the European war was clearly going well, in late 1944, a need was seen for escorts with greater A/A firepower to be transferred east for the Pacific war. In Canada, some 20 of the RCN 'River' class were earmarked for re-arming; in the UK, the Admiralty had the opportunity of converting a number of the 'Loch' class on the slips for this duty, resulting in the 'Bay' class of frigates.

## NEW CORVETTES

When the frigates were ordered, the longer hull length precluded a number of the UK (and Canadian) yards from building them; so, to produce the maximum number of new escorts, a new and greatly improved corvette design was produced (once again, by Smith's Dock), in order to keep every slip working at full capacity. But it was clear that, had the naval staff had a clear run, no further

▲ The RCN corvette *Shawinigan* on the slip with two others of her class, less advanced. This was at G.T. Davie & Sons' yard at Lauzon, Quebec, in 1941. *(Public Archives of Canada)*

Launch of RCN *Moosejaw*, 'Flower' class, at Collingwood, Ontario, 9th April 1941. The sideways launch is into a narrow channel. *(Public Archives of Canada)* ▼

corvettes would have been ordered, and all new escort construction would have been of frigates.

In the UK, the Modified 'Flower' class, described under its chapter, had only just started construction, so orders were quickly switched to the new class, designated the 'Castle' class. But in Canada, moving fast on the Modified 'Flower' programme, and with an inevitable lead-time on the design drawings for the 'Castle' class from the UK being available, a large number of Modified 'Flower' units was ordered, the 'Castle' class units to follow.

The 'Castle' class reflected very closely the 'Loch' class design. The revised hull shape is clearly related in the photographs, but the stern was altered, to be more square, with a solid bulwark, due to their smaller size.

A lattice mast was added, as in the 'Loch' class, and the same improved radar, together with a full naval bridge structure (a radical departure from the Modified 'Flower' class), and a single Squid mortar forward, in place of the Hedgehog. The funnel was enlarged, and carried a big Admiralty cap, and full naval boats were progressively added, in gravity davits, as the equipment became available.

## LEND-LEASE US-BUILT SHIPS

The contribution to the RN's escort strength made by these ships is described in this book in some detail.

This was a very different deal from the 50 old 'four-stacker' destroyers transferred early in the war. The Lend-Lease ships were all new, delivered in the yards on completion to RN crews, and reflected the latest USN designs and equipment.

The ships were built to USN standards and, apart from the close-range

The Canadian corvette *Napanee* under construction at Kingston, Ontario, in 1940. She was to be launched sideways. *(Public Archives of Canada)*

weapons and anti-submarine equipment, unfamiliar to RN crews. But specialised training soon overcame this, and much of the equipment was ahead of that available in the UK at the time—radar and radio-telephone equipment were outstanding.

No less than 520 DEs and 150 PCs were ordered by the RN; the effect this would have had on the RN escort forces, had all been built and delivered, is examined later.

## 'HUNT' CLASS DESTROYERS

In parallel with the sloops and corvettes, the Admiralty had foreseen in 1938 the need for a fast escort destroyer. A building programme was put through very quickly, resulting in the 86 ships of this class.

Their development is described in some detail. With good gun armament and fair speed, they were employed in numbers in the Mediterranean, English Channel, and North Sea, and later in the Indian Ocean; apart from the UK-Gibraltar run, they were little used in the North Atlantic battle.

They were built strictly along warship lines, and their numbers were thus restricted, as they had to be produced by warship building yards, and needed the scarce turbine blades.

They provided excellent gun support in the early air/sea battles of the European war, but none of this class carried ahead-throwing A/S weapons. This had its effect in the later, inshore, stages of the U-boat war, in 1944/45. The heavy losses suffered by this class reflect its value.

## FLEET MINESWEEPERS

These are included in this book, as all classes of fleet minesweepers carried anti-submarine equipment. This ranged from restricted depth-charge layouts in the 'Bangor' class, to full Asdic and depth-charge equipment in the 'Algerine' class. The American-built 'Catherine' class, in later years, also carried a Hedgehog. Fleet minesweepers were more often used as escorts in the earlier war years, before new corvettes and frigates were available in sufficient numbers; but this type of employment for the 'Algerine' class continued right through to 1945, on occasion. The 6th MSF (*Ready*, SO) escorted a Russian convoy in 1944, and units earmarked for the East Indies and Pacific Fleets in 1945 received special A/S training.

## ADMIRALTY TRAWLERS

The war-built trawlers, too, deserve their full place in this book. Their numbers were not large, as only the yards specialising in fishery vessel construction usually produced them during the war. Their Asdic equipment was of a simplified type, and their speed was inadequate to chase a surfaced U-boat.

But they made a very significant contribution to local anti-submarine duties, and not least in the Mediterranean and in South Atlantic waters. Especially in the earlier years, they went far afield with ocean convoys, and were prominent in the escorts on the Russian run.

It is interesting to compare their specifications with those of the corvettes, and with the 'Bangor' class fleet minesweepers. The reason for trawler production, rather than for more corvettes, was to use to the maximum the productive capacity of the trawler yards. These yards could cope more easily with the familiar fishing trawler hulls and machinery.

## UK SHIPBUILDING PROGRAMMES

*(as originally ordered—later changes covered under classes)*

|  | 1939 | 1939 War | 1940 | 1941 | 1942 | 1943 |
|---|---|---|---|---|---|---|
| 'Hunt' | 20 | 36 | 30 |  |  |  |
| 'Black Swan' | 2 |  |  |  |  |  |
| Modified 'Black Swan' |  |  | 18 | 10 | 3 | 3 |
| 'River' |  |  | 27 | 19 | 17 |  |
| 'Captain' |  |  |  | 64 | 14 |  |
| 'Colony' |  |  |  |  | 21 |  |
| 'Loch'/'Bay' |  |  |  |  | 5 | 25 |
| 'Flower' | 56 | 60 | 25 | 10 | 4 |  |
| 'Castle' |  |  |  |  | 10 | 17 |
| 'Kil' |  |  |  | 15 |  |  |
| 'Bangor' | 20 | 16 | 12 |  |  |  |
| 'Bathurst' |  |  | 20 |  |  |  |
| 'Algerine' |  |  | 19 | 30 | 35 | 24 |
| 'Catherine' |  |  |  | 22 |  |  |
| 'Guillemot' | 3 |  |  |  |  |  |
| 'Tree' | 20 |  |  |  |  |  |
| 'Lake' |  | 6 |  |  |  |  |
| 'Shakespeare' |  | 12 |  |  |  |  |
| 'Dance' |  | 20 |  |  |  |  |
| 'Isles | |  | 67 | 22 | 38 | 20 |
| 'Hill' |  |  | 8 |  |  |  |
| 'Fish' |  |  | 4 | 4 |  |  |
| 'Military' |  |  |  | 3 | 3 | 3 |

The small escorts suffered in any heavy sea on their mid-ocean duties. This is the Canadian corvette *Barrie*, en route from St John's to Boston in 1945. (*Public Archives of Canada*)

# CANADA

### CORVETTES

Before the war the RCN planned to use Canadian-built escorts based on the RN 'Halcyon' design as its principal A/S escort type. But in mid-September 1939 the Admiralty sent over to Ottawa a set of the first drawings of the new 'Flower' class corvette, as designed in conjunction with Smith's Dock Company in England.

The story of the evolution of the original 'Flower' design has been covered under the RN section; suffice it to say here that the design immediately showed advantages to the Naval Staff in Ottawa. The intention was to use the 'Flower' class units in Canadian coastal waters, just as the Admiralty was at that time planning in UK waters. The reduction in endurance, compared with the 'Halcyon' class, did not therefore seem significant.

The RCN ordered 64 'Flower' class corvettes in all from Canadian shipyards under the 1939/40 Programme, the plan being that those for the RCN would on completion be divided into groups, each of 5 ships, for the defence of Canadian coastal shipping, and of ocean convoys from the mainland assembly points to the open sea. It is fascinating to see how, as the war progressed, the 'Flower' class were very largely employed on ocean escort duties, and their original coastal defence role was taken over by the 'Bangor' class minesweepers, until the 'River' class frigates were available in great numbers.

Canadian 'River' class frigate *New Waterford* building at the yard of Canadian Yarrow Ltd, Esquimalt, BC, on 30th April 1943. *(Public Archives of Canada)*

*New Waterford* at Esquimalt. This was largely the riveted construction method, mass production coming a little later. *(Public Archives of Canada)*

## FLEET MINESWEEPERS

In addition to the 'Halcyon'/'Flower' requirement, the Canadian Naval Staff saw the need for a smaller A/S-M/S vessel, and had ordered four of the 'Basset' class trawlers, sponsored by the Admiralty, in 1938. But the Admiralty also sent out the plans of the new 'Bangor' class fleet of minesweepers, with A/S capability, in 1939, and again the relevance to Canadian requirements seemed clear. The 'Bangor' class were in effect a cut-down version of the 'Halcyon' design, with much of the A/S and M/S equipment and deck space eliminated. Their dimensions were not greatly different from the 'Basset' class, but they promised greater efficiency—the illustrations accompanying this chapter illustrate this clearly. They were quite a bit faster, had greater endurance, being oil-burners, and the Canadian staff saw a saving in building 'Bangor' and 'Flower' class units in place of the larger 'Halcyon' class.

## THE BUILDING PROGRAMME

The RCN programmes, listed separately, show how the orders were progressively placed in 1939, 1940, and 1941 for these two classes. It is interesting to remember that the 64 'Flower' class ships first ordered included not only Canadian requirements but some 20 for the RN, to be exchanged for four 'Tribal' class destroyers, to be built in the UK for Canada. When, in 1940, it was agreed that the destroyers would be paid for in cash, and not in corvettes, some of the latter were transferred to Admiralty account in lieu; they were, however, re-allocated to the RCN after six months, and retained their 'Flower' class names in Canadian service.

The prices of the original 'Flower' class corvettes averaged around $550,000, with the West Coast prices being higher than those on the East Coast. Twelve companies in all participated in their construction, but delivery turned out to be slower than planned, due to the sudden expansion in shipbuilding, with resultant labour and equipment shortages. Canada had a problem, too, very different from the UK situation, in that any ships building in the Great Lakes or Upper St Lawrence River had to be brought out to the sea before the lakes and river froze each winter. In 1940 a number of new corvettes only just made it!

Delays in delivery were also experienced with the initial orders for the 'Bangor' class, but it should be remembered that the shipbuilding effort made in Canada was probably the most remarkable even of the three great naval powers, and delivery delays can take nothing away from the fantastic achievement described in this section.

When the 'Flower' class was switched to ocean escort work, the RCN units followed the alterations suggested by Smith's Dock, and approved by the Admiralty. Thus, of the original 79 corvettes actually built in Canada, no less than 67 were given the lengthened forecastle deck, bridge improvements, and finally extra sheer and flare, that can be seen also in the RN ships.

## 'RIVER' CLASS FRIGATES

During 1941 the RCN followed the RN's lead in going for a larger and faster

Find the 'River' class ship! These two photographs show how similar the refitted Canadian 'River' class ships were to the RN 'Bay' class ships, completing in 1945. *Outremont* (K 322) has a twin 4″ mounting forward, American type SU radar at the masthead, and a new H/F D/F on a high pole mast aft. *Burghead Bay* has the standard 'Bay' class armament for the British Pacific Fleet, and a lattice mast to support her Type 293 radar. Note that Type 291 radar at the topmasthead has displaced the H/F D/F aerial to a pole mast aft also.
*(Public Archives of Canada, and Ministry of Defence)*

escort for mid-ocean work, which was finally called the 'River' class frigate, whose development has been described under the RN section. The plans arrived in Ottawa during the winter of 1940/41, and the RCN decided that, ideally, only frigates should be ordered from that time on. The frigates were, however, too large to pass through the St Lawrence River locks (this was, of course, long before the St Lawrence Seaway—the Lachine Canal, between Lake Ontario and Montreal, was the limiting sector), and so could not be built by the Great Lakes yards; the latter were kept busy with corvette and 'Algerine' class construction, just as the smaller yards in the UK were, and thus the division of escort production between corvettes and frigates was artificially maintained in Canada, as in the UK.

## 'ALGERINE' CLASS ESCORTS

The plans of the 'Algerine' class fleet minesweepers also arrived in this period, and a construction programme was put in hand in Canada. Compared with the 'Bangor' class, they had 45 feet extra length, more speed and endurance, and the larger messdecks and sweep decks were significant. By the end of 1941 the Canadian orders for frigates and 'Algerine' class units were flowing, and no more 'Bangor' class units were ordered.

## THE PEAK SHIPBUILDING EFFORT

The two following years, 1943 and 1944, saw the peak of Canadian escort construction. Apart from ships built under Lend-Lease and for the RN, the commissioning figures listed with this chapter underline the great effort involved—the tailing off of 'Flower' and 'Bangor' completions, and the great increase in 'River' and Modified 'Flower' completions, with the 'Algerine' units thrown in for good measure.

The shipbuilding effort was now settling down to a steady and rapid growth in completions, but it was necessary to keep all slips working flat out, and it was for this reason that the RCN picked up the Modified 'Flower' class design from the UK, and built more of this class than did the RN itself.

Corvettes were still valid for coastal work, where speed was not so essential, and air cover was more continuous. The yards unable to build frigates were, therefore, fully occupied with the Modified 'Flower' class. It so happened that about this time U-boats penetrated the St Lawrence River estuary and torpedoed some ships, which helped the corvette construction programme. The RCN were maintaining, of necessity, operational 'Flower' class escorts as high up the St Lawrence as Quebec.

During 1943 the total building capacity was again increased, and a central berth was created at Quebec for outfitting ships launched in that area. The proportions of classes were altered to give the maximum number of frigates, together with some further Modified 'Flower' class corvettes, and 'Algerine' units were no longer on order. Further efforts were even made to see if frigates could not in fact be built on the Great Lakes; consideration was given to taking them out through the Chicago Drainage Canal and then down the Mississippi River, but limitations on both draught and mast height eventually caused the project to be abandoned.

## MORE 'ALGERINE' CLASS UNITS

In view of the overriding need for fast completions, further units of this class were now ordered on the Lakes. They could be completed more rapidly than Modified 'Flower' class units, although their hull lines made them less satisfactory as ocean escorts.

A remarkable compromise, involving the construction of this class, was agreed at this time between London and Ottawa.

The need for large numbers of this efficient class of fleet minesweeper had been clearly defined by the RN, and at the Harland & Wolff yard in Belfast, for example, the first two had been laid down in June 1943, and two more were then produced every three months. But the need for the new 'Loch' class frigates for the North Atlantic was even more pressing, and a plan was made to turn over this production capacity to the frigates, at the expense of the fleet minesweepers. This would cancel 10 'Algerine' class units, but replace them with 8 extra 'Loch' class frigates by January 1945, the production rate for the Harland & Wolff yard being rated at 12 ships per year in the frigate class alone.

This meant replacing the 10 cancelled 'Algerine' class, and London agreed with Ottawa that these, and more ships of the class besides, would be built in Canada on RN account. The equivalent number of new frigates and corvettes thus displaced in the Canadian yards would be built for the RCN in the UK; this explains the transfer to the RCN of 'Loch' and 'Castle' class units in 1944/45.

One result of this swap was that the RN would have two flotillas of 'Algerine' class ships nearly twelve months earlier than planned, due to the Canadian production capacity. Another result was that the RCN would have 16 more new escorts by mid 1944, in place of the 'Algerine's, which were less efficient as escorts, as the RCN would have used them.

As a matter of interest, the Canadian yards had difficulty in supplying the LL sweep gear, which was accordingly sent from the UK, and the Admiralty agreed to accept 8 of the Canadian-built 'Algerine' class units involved in this swap with Oropesa wire sweeps, and SA gear Mark IV only, and with no LL gear.

6 'Algerine' class units built in Canada for the RN were eventually cancelled, since a pessimistic estimate, as the construction programme slowed down, gave a completion date in 1947. But the RN calculated that by that time it was well supplied with 'Algerine' class units for the Far East, and could pay off the less efficient 'Bangor' class ships. Many of the components for the cancelled 'Algerine' class units were already finished, and pre-fabrication was well under way, so the cancellation charges were unusually high.

## 'CASTLE' CLASS CORVETTES

At the beginning of 1943, the new ships of this class were being ordered in numbers in the UK. They were so clearly a great advance, even on the Modified 'Flower' class, that maximum production was planned. They could be built in the

*Loch Fada,* the prototype frigate of the mass production 'Loch' class, nearing launching at John Brown's yard at Clydebank. The white lettering marks the prefabricated sections brought in from other works. A destroyer is building to traditional methods under cover alongside.
*(Scottish Records Office)*

Great Lakes yards, and in March 1943 the British Admiralty Technical Mission placed orders for 36 to be built in Canada on Admiralty account, for completion between May 1944 and June 1945. These are listed under the RN class section in greater detail, and as the Modified 'Flower' class programme was running late, the last 7 units were switched to 'Castle' class also. Before any of the class had been laid down, however, the Atlantic battle had happily entered a new and more definitive phase, and in December 1943 all 'Castle' class units ordered in Canada were cancelled. Had they been completed, however, they would have represented a most significant addition to the Canadian warship building effort.

*Loch Arkaig* shows the hull form of her class, with the break in sheer to speed mass production. The strength of the lattice mast shows in this picture. *(Ministry of Defence)*

## 'LOCH' CLASS FRIGATES

No details are available, but it is believed that an order for the construction of 'Loch' class units in Canada was placed by the Admiralty in October 1943, but cancelled two months later, in line with the revised policy. The number of ships of this class which would have been built is not known, but it further underlines the accelerating tempo of the Canadian shipbuilding effort, and had the escort building programmes continued, no doubt the RCN would have ordered both 'Loch' and 'Castle' class units in Canada for itself, with a probable end to the 'River' class programme.

## REDUCTION IN NEW BUILDINGS

Towards the end of 1943, with the great improvements in the North Atlantic battle situation, conferences between the three main powers were held to consider the accelerating escort building programme. In the UK a reduction was agreed upon, with no ships due to complete later than October 1944 being laid down. The Canadian Naval Staff were not too happy with any reduction; their target of 354 efficient escorts required by the RCN had by no means been reached, but the growing Allied requirement for more landing craft began to take precedence, and a reduction in the forward programme was agreed. It will be noted that no less than 37 large Landing Ships Tank (Mark 3) were built in Canada as a result of this change of emphasis.

Thus the last 44 'River' class frigates and 12 Modified 'Flower' and 'Castle' class units were cancelled. The RCN agreed to take over 10 frigates already under construction in the UK for the RN, and thus 7 'River' class ships, and the only 3 'Loch' class units commissioned by the RCN, crossed the Atlantic.

## CANADIAN CONSTRUCTION FOR THE USN AND RN

One of the most impressive aspects of the great Canadian wartime shipbuilding effort was that not only were enough new escorts constructed for the rapidly increasing needs of the RCN, but new ships were also made available to the other two great Allied navies, whilst some UK-built ships came to the RCN on a reciprocal basis.

First, 10 of the original 'Flower' class corvettes on order in Canada, and transferred to Admiralty account, were loaned to Canada by the RN for the war years, retaining their RN 'Flower' names; then, on 15th May 1941, 6 'Bangor' class units on order in Canada for the RN were also transferred to the RCN, but 10 other ships of the same class were built in Canada and delivered to the RN.

Next, 8 Modified 'Flower' class units were ordered in Canada by the USN, and delivery taken; then 7 more were ordered, but these were finally allocated to the RN, in fulfilment of numerical US Lend-Lease commitments.

Then, the first two 'River' class frigates launched in Canada were delivered to the USN, and became the prototypes of the USN PF class. A further 8 were ordered from Canada by the USN, but, like the Modified 'Flower' units, were finally allocated to the RN under Lend-Lease.

Then the USN ordered 9 'Algerine' class units from Canada, but these, too, went to the RN under Lend-Lease. It is fascinating to see the large number of further 'Algerine' units ordered by the RN from Canada, making in all as many built in Canada as in the UK for the RN. We have seen that in fact the RCN only retained 12 'Algerine' class units for itself, since the true fleet sweeper role was so largely covered by the RN and USN.

Finally, of 16 'Isles' class trawlers ordered in Canada by the RN, no less than 8 remained on loan to Canada during the war years, for anti-submarine duties.

## ESCORT DESIGN

Throughout the war period, RCN escort vessels followed faithfully RN designs, including alterations and additions, though a few improvements were made separately by the RCN and are listed under the individual classes.

After the war the RCN started on its own escort design programme, which has resulted in some of the most impressive and forward-looking escorts to be seen today.

### RCN BUILDING PROGRAMMES

| Canadian-built | 1939/40 | 1940/41 | 1941/42 | 1942/43 | 1943/44 |
|---|---|---|---|---|---|
| 'Flower' | 64 | 15 | | | |
| Modified 'Flower' | | | | 15 | 12 |
| 'Castle' | | | | | 12 |
| 'River' | | | | 33 | 34 |
| 'Loch' | | | | | 3 |
| 'Algerine' | | | | 10 | 2 |
| 'Bangor' | 24 | 20 | 10 | | |
| 'Isles' | | 8 | | | |

The frigate fitting out base at Quebec, September 1944. *Prestonian*, 'River' class, is ready to commission, and three other ships of the class are nearing completion in the background. *(Public Archives of Canada)*

'River' class frigate *Shelburne* in drydock at Halifax, 13th August 1945. The dock moves up the slip on a railway. The ship has the standard 1945 camouflage scheme of a blue hull band on a white overall base. *(Public Archives of Canada)*

# UNITED STATES OF AMERICA

The USN story is remarkably similar to that of the RN. Before the war, escort design and construction was at a low ebb, but in 1940, a full eighteen months before America entered the war, work was begun on a new destroyer escort (DE) design, and separately the first of the new Patrol Craft (PC) class was commissioned in August 1940.

Then, in the spring of 1941, the first Lend-Lease Act permitted the RN to order escort vessels for construction in the United States. The RN proposed certain dimensions, armament, speed and endurance characteristics, similar to the 'River' class frigates then being ordered in the UK, and by July the first 20 ships were approved, for delivery by about mid-1943. This figure quickly escalated, and in a few months no less than some 300 British Destroyer Escorts (BDEs), later called 'Captain' class frigates, were on order for the RN in American shipyards. They were authorised mainly under the RN's 1941 Building Programme, with some in the 1942 Programme, and 200 should have been delivered to the RN by the end of 1943.

But by this time the USN was deeply interested in new destroyer escorts for itself, and soon after entering the war, at the end of 1941, orders were progressively placed for a total of over 1,000 new DEs in American shipyards.

It was not surprising that, with such a fantastic increase in warship ordering, some delays in completions should be experienced. The 'Captain' class is covered in the RN Section, but USN deliveries, too, were slower than required, and all but 78 of the 300 DEs on order for the RN were taken over by the USN. Then the shipbuilding programme, with some 20 yards participating, got into full swing, and the remarkable DE output shown on the chart was achieved. In spite of production difficulties with main machinery (largely caused by the competing priority for landing craft for the European invasion), and with close-range weapons, the DEs were a most impressive class of ship, efficient, right up-to-date, built on warship lines, and equal to the very best of the RN's escort classes.

In 1942 the USN was short of escorts to combat the German U-Boat drive on the Eastern seaboard and in the Caribbean; the RN transferred 10 corvettes of the original 'Flower' class to the USN (where they were designated Patrol Gunboats (PGs)), and the USN ordered 8 more of the Modified class in Canada; 6 RCN corvettes were loaned, with their crews, to the USN for Caribbean duty, and some two dozen RN A/S trawlers, also with their crews, were loaned for a while.

In the same month, too, the USN, RCN, and RN examined together their shortages in escort vessel requirements at that time. Each needed large numbers of new escorts badly, and it was agreed that all new escorts should be allocated according to need. Hence the reduction in numbers of new escorts available to the RN under Lend-Lease, and the partial make-up of numbers, by allocating ships on order in Canada for the USN to the RN on completion. This was a remarkable exercise in international co-operation.

There were four other new USN escort classes—a much smaller number than those in the RN; concentration on a few designs must have made the building programme much easier to accelerate, but none of these other classes had the same impact as the DEs.

The first was the Patrol Craft (PC) class, of which some 286 were completed. They were found to be less than ideal for ocean work or submarine hunting, but were most useful for inshore work and convoy duty. When they were in service in large numbers they also acted as inshore escort groups, hunting down submarine leads on both seaboards, as well as in the Caribbean. Again, the speed of construction was most impressive.

The succeeding class was the Patrol Craft (Escort) class (PCEs). This design had 10 feet of extra length, with no less than 10 feet of extra beam, and the comparison of the two plans is fascinating. The PCE was designed as a more efficient and seaworthy coastal escort, but appeared in numbers too late in the A/S war to make a significant impact. It will be seen that a large number was cancelled, and many were in addition converted for other duties.

A large number of this same class was completed as Fleet Minesweepers (AM), as the 'Admirable' class. For this duty they must have been excellently suited. It is interesting that the overall hull and upper deck lay-out was so close to the RN's 'Algerine' class.

Originally, some 150 of the PCE class were on order for the RN under Lend-Lease, but in the end only 15 were delivered.

The third class was the Patrol Frigate (PF) class. Based on the RN's 'River' class design, but with USN type bridges and masts, and USN armament, this class does not seem to have been too popular, in part due to hot conditions below decks in the tropics. It may be that transferring a design from one navy, where it was intended for northern service, to another, where tropical conditions were important, was not easy to accomplish successfully. But some 77 were completed for the USN, and they were therefore a significant escort class. Certainly they appear impressive in their photographs, and they must have been efficient escorts. 21 were transferred on completion to the RN, where they were known as the 'Colony' class.

The fourth, and last, class was the 'Raven'/'Auk' class of Fleet Minesweepers (AM). This was a specialised and efficient design, of which some 22 were transferred on completion to the RN under Lend-Lease, where they were known as the 'Catherine' class. About 50 were originally ordered by the RN in this way, but again growing USN requirements changed the delivery picture. These ships did not have much room on their sweep decks for normal escort depth-charge rails and throwers, and the earlier ships followed RN 'Bangor' class arrangements for dropping depth charges; but later ships managed to carry full depth-charge rails, in addition to their minesweeping equipment.

In examining the individual USN escort classes in detail, it is also useful to see the overall numbers in the combined chart; for these numbers of comple-

tions, in a relatively short period of the war, were extremely impressive. They are the more so when it is recalled that the hulls and internal bulkheads were all-welded, the designs were naval, and the equipment advanced—in some ways, ahead of the RN. The enormous industrial strength of the United States made this possible, but the flexibility and imagination which enabled America to mass-produce these efficient escort classes in such a short time is especially noteworthy.

As with the RN and RCN, the escort building programme was sharply cut back at the end of 1943. Had this not been so, the US production would have created, with that of Canada and the UK, a great fleet of up-to-date escorts, which would have eclipsed even the corvette and PC construction programmes of all three navies in the earlier years of the war.

## PLANNED GROWTH IN ESCORT FORCES

This section shows the probable growth in war-built escorts by the end of 1945, if the mass production programmes had not been cut back late in 1943, and the increasing momentum of production had been maintained.

### OVERALL PRODUCTION CHART

Not including fleet minesweepers, or cancelled ships.
By launches in half years, for the three largest navies only.

|  |  | RN | RCN | USN | TOTAL |
|---|---|---|---|---|---|
| 1939 | 1 | 2 |  |  | 2 |
|  | 2 | 17 |  |  | 17 |
| 1940 | 1 | 59 | 4 |  | 63 |
|  | 2 | 92 | 51 |  | 143 |
| 1941 | 1 | 79 | 39 |  | 118 |
|  | 2 | 67 | 27 |  | 94 |
| 1942 | 1 | 65 | 15 | 34 | 114 |
|  | 2 | 62 | 13 | 89 | 164 |
| 1943 | 1 | 63 | 14 | 195 | 274 |
|  | 2 | 144 | 47 | 321 | 512 |
| 1944 | 1 | 61 | 36 | 205 | 302 |
|  | 2 | 40 | 7 | 81 | 128 |
| 1945 | 1 | 22 | 0 | 46 | 68 |
|  | 2 | 7 |  | 1 | 8 |
| TOTALS |  | 780 | 255 | 972 | 2,007 |

A contrast in hull forms. Here is *Kingsmill* an 'Evarts' type US-built DE, serving with the Royal Navy, and in drydock at Portsmouth, UK, in December 1944. Note the finer section, the high sheer forward, and the high bridge structure. *(Lt-Cdr R.P. Hall,* RANR*)*

These figures are a rough calculation, based on orders placed before cancellation, of production rates in 1943, and current rates of war loss. They are probably not accurate, but the trends they show should give an idea of the planned growth. Fleet minesweepers are excluded, as they would have been employed on M/S duties.

| RN | Actually Probable number completed at end of 1945 | |
|---|---|---|
| **Probably Operational** | | |
| 'Black Swan' | 31 | 32 |
| 'Hunt' | 86 | 65 |
| 'River' | 62 | 58 |
| 'Captain' | 78 | 420 |
| 'Colony' | 21 | 20 |
| 'Castle' | 31 | 145 |
| 'Loch'/'Bay' | 44 | 190 |
| TOTALS | 353 | 830 |
| **Probably in Reserve** | | |
| 'Flower' | 115 | 95 |
| 'Kil' | 15 | 148 |
| Admiralty Trawlers | 226 | 210 |
| OVERALL TOTALS | 708 | 1,283 |

| RCN | Actually Probable Number completed at end of 1945 | |
|---|---|---|
| **Probably Operational** | | |
| 'Loch' | 3 | 55 |
| 'River' | 60 | 100 |
| 'Castle' | 15 | 75 |
| TOTALS | 78 | 230 |
| 'Algerine' | 12 | 12 |
| 'Bangor' | 54 | 45 |
| 'Flower' | 106 | 95 |
| Trawlers | 8 | 8 |
| OVERALL TOTALS | 258 | 390 |

NOTES RN

1. In view of the manpower shortage which would then have developed, it would seem probable that the 'Flower' class corvettes would have been placed in reserve, and the balance of the 'Kil' class not taken up. The A/S trawlers would also probably have been phased out, other than those retained for M/S duties.

2. The above figures assume that the full number of DEs originally asked for would have been delivered, once the US building programme reached a production rate able to supply both navies' needs.

3. The alteration in the types of escort employed would have been dramatic. The older, slower, and less ocean-worthy types would have disappeared, and the newer classes, a high proportion armed with the new and more powerful Squid mortars, would have been used against the faster U-boats. Note that some escorts only five years old would probably have fallen short of the new requirements.

NOTES RCN

1. This assumes that 'River' class production planning was switched to 'Loch' class at the end of 1943, and that in the corvette category, only 'Castle' class units were planned from that time.

2. This total would, in fact, have met the Canadian Naval Staff's estimate of the optimum number of escorts required, though the above numbers assume that, unlike the RN, all the war-built escorts were retained in commission. This would not necessarily have been so, in which case the trawlers and 'Bangor' class would probably have been placed in reserve. The 'Flower' class would probably have been retained, especially the relatively high number of Modified units, and mainly on Canadian coastal escort duties.

|  | Actually completed | Probable Number at end of 1945 |
|---|---|---|
| **USN** | | |
| **Probably Operational** | | |
| DE | 381 | 775 |
| PF | 75 | 45 |
| PCE | 48 | 250 |
| PC | 284 | 150 |
| TOTALS | 788 | 1.220 |
| **Probably in Reserve** | | |
| PG | 18 | 18 |
| PC (part) | | 180 |
| OVERALL TOTALS | 806 | 1,418 |

NOTES
1. This assumes that the full DE programme was carried through in this period, which, according to the 1943 actual production figures, should have been possible.

2. This also assumes that, unlike the RN, the USN would probably not have experienced a manpower shortage through this expansion; also that some of the PCs would have been kept in commission. In 1944, for example, a USN DE had a typical complement of 12 officers and 208 ratings, a total of 220; the RN equivalent had 9 officers, 177 men, a total of 186.

3. DEs completed as APDs or in other configurations are not included in the above numbers.

The launch of DE 51 *Buckley* at the Bethlehem-Hingham yard, near Boston. This was one of the very first long-hull DEs, and at the start of a most impressive building programme at this yard. *(US Navy)*

## SHIPS CANCELLED, 1943-45

**RN**

| | | |
|---|---|---|
| 'Flower' | 6 | |
| Modified 'Flower' | 2 | |
| 'Black Swan' | 5 | |
| 'Castle' | 52 | |
| 'Loch'/'Bay' | 57+100? | |
| 'Captain' | 442 | |
| 'Kil' | 135 | |
| Admiralty Trawlers | 24 | |
| 'Algerine' | 12 | |
| 'Catherine' | 26 | TOTAL 761+100? |

**RCN**

| | | |
|---|---|---|
| Modified 'Flower' | 6 | |
| 'River' | 97 | TOTAL 103 |

**RAN**

| | | |
|---|---|---|
| Modified 'River' | 10 | TOTAL 10 |

**USN**

| | | |
|---|---|---|
| PC | 45 | |
| PCE | 70 | |
| PF | 4 | |
| DE | 450 | |
| DEs not completed as escorts | 94 | |
| AM classes—'Raven' | 10 | |
| —'Admirable' | 51 | TOTAL 724 |

GRAND TOTAL
1,598+100?

RN "Hunt" Class.

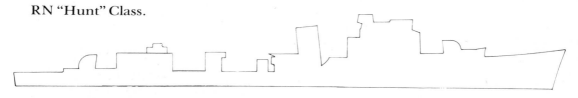

RN/RCN "Castle" Class.

## COMPARATIVE SPECIFICATIONS OF THE LARGER ESCORT CLASSES

|  | USN DE | RN 'Hunt' | RN 'Black 'Swan' | RN/RCN 'River' | RN 'Bay' | RN/RCN 'Castle' |
|---|---|---|---|---|---|---|
| Displacement | 1,400 | 1,015 | 1,350 | 1,445 | 1,600 | 1,100 |
| Dimensions |  |  |  |  |  |  |
|    length oa | 306 | 280 | 299 | 301 | 301 | 252 |
|    breadth | 37 | 31 | 38 | 36 | 38 | 36 |
|    draught | 8 | 7 | 8 | 11 | 10 | 14 |
| Machinery | Turbo-electric | Turbines | Turbines | Triple expan | Triple expan | Triple expan |
| Shafts | 2 | 2 | 2 | 2 | 2 | 1 |
| Speed | 24 | 29 | 20 | 20 | 19 | 16 |
| Endurance (miles) |  | 2,550 | 7,500 | 7,200 | 9,500 | 6,200 |
| Complement | 220 | 170 | 180 | 107 | 157 | 120 |
| Armament |  |  |  |  |  |  |
|    main | 3 3" | 4 4" | 6 4" | 2 4" | 4 4" | 1 4" |
|    close-range | 2 40 | 4 2pdr | 4 40 | 6 20 | 4 40 | 6 20 |
|  | 8 20 | 6 20 | 4 20 |  | 8 20 |  |
| Torpedo tubes | 3 | 2 |  |  |  |  |
| ATW Mortars | HH |  | HH | HH | HH | Squid |

NOTES

1. The above figures are simplified, for quick comparison, by the omission of fractions, and the basic close range armament only is specified, though there were many variations in each class.

2. The USN DE type taken is the 'Buckley', and the RN 'Hunt' is Type III.

3. Comparative numbers of depth charges carried are shown in another table.

*Kingsmill*—a good view of the stern underwater section. Note the shallow draught, twin rudders and twin propellers. *(Lt-Cdr R.P. Hall,* RANR*)*

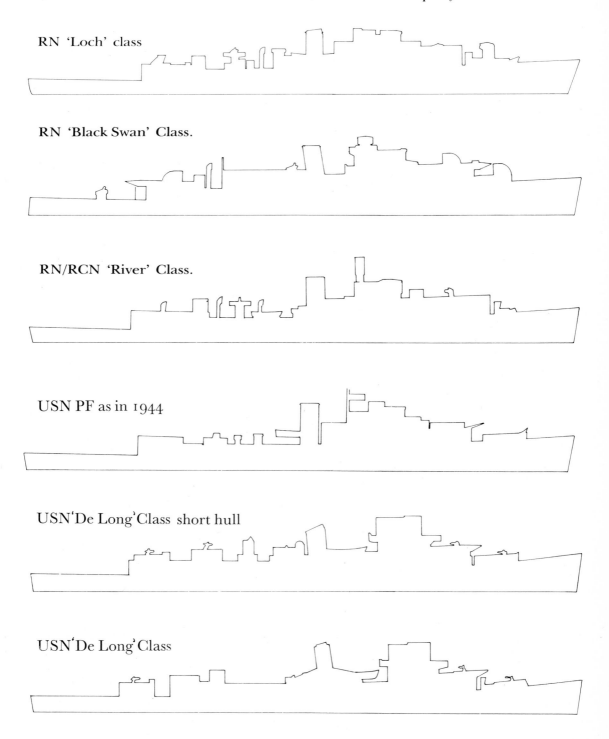

RN 'Loch' class

RN 'Black Swan' Class.

RN/RCN 'River' Class.

USN PF as in 1944

USN 'De Long' Class short hull

USN 'De Long' Class

## COMPARATIVE SPECIFICATIONS OF SOME SMALL ESCORT VESSELS

|  | *TRAWLER* *RN* 'Military' | *CORVETTE* *RN/RCN* 'Flower' | *MINESWEEPER* *RN/RCN* 'Bangor' | *PATROLCRAFT* *USN* *PC* | *USN* *PCE* |
|---|---|---|---|---|---|
| Displacement | 750 | 925 | 670 | 280 | 795 |
| Dimensions |  |  |  |  |  |
|   length pp | 175 | 190 | 171½ | 170 | 180 |
|   breadth | 30 | 33 | 28½ | 23 | 33 |
|   draught | 13 | 11½ | 8½ | 7½ | 9½ |
| Machinery | Recip | Recip | Recip Diesel Turbine | Diesel | Diesel |
| Boilers | 1 | 1 | 0/1 | 0 | 0 |
| Fuel | Coal | Oil | Oil | Oil | Oil |
| Shafts | 1 | 1 | 2 | 2 | 2 |
| Speed | 11 | 16 | 16 | 20 | 16 |
| Complement | 40 | 85 | 60 | 80 | 110 |
| Armament |  |  |  |  |  |
|   main | 1 4″ | 1 4″ | 1 12pdr | 1/2 3″ | 1 3″ |
|   close-range | 4 20mm | 2/6 20mm | 2/3 20mm | 1 40mm 3 20mm | 2 40mm 2/5 20mm |
| A/S Armament |  |  |  |  |  |
|   DCT | 2 | 4 | 2 | 2 | 4 |
|   DC Rails | 2 | 2 | 0 | 2 | 2 |
|   Hedgehog | No | Yes | No | No | Yes |
| Radar, Types | 291 | 271 | 291 | SL | SL |

RN/RCN 'Flower' Class.

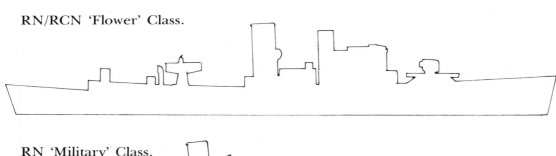

RN 'Military' Class.

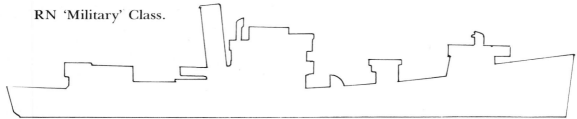

**RN/RCN "Bangor" Class.**

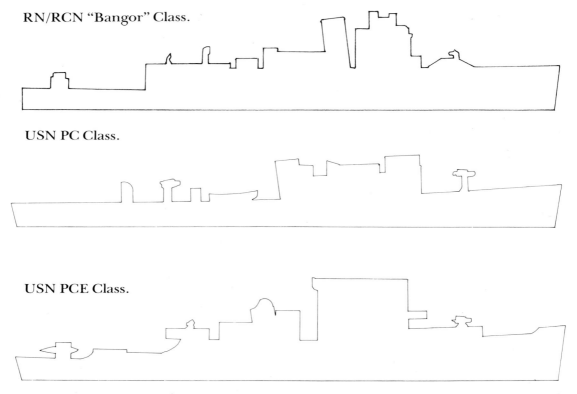

**USN PC Class.**

**USN PCE Class.**

Working-up to a very high degree of efficiency was one of the essentials for every new escort. Here are the new 'Captain' class frigates *Ekins* and *Dakins* exercising off the Bahamas while working-up at the great base at Bermuda. *(P.W. Hayward)*

## OVERALL WAR LOSSES RN, RCN and USN, by classes

| RN | 1940 | 1941 | 1942 | 1943 | 1944 | 1945 | TOTAL |
|---|---|---|---|---|---|---|---|
| 'Black Swan' | | | 1 | 1 | 2 | 2 | 6 |
| 'Hunt' | 0 | 1 | 8 | 6 | 3 | | 18 |
| 'Flower' | 2 | 4 | 6 | 3 | 1 | 2 | 18 |
| 'Castle' | | | | | 1 | 1 | 2 |
| 'Kil' | | | | | | | 0 |
| 'River' | | | | 2 | 2 | | 4 |
| 'Captain' | | | | | 10 | 3 | 13 |
| 'Colony' | | | | | | | 0 |
| 'Loch' | | | | | | | 0 |
| 'Bay' | | | | | | | 0 |
| 'Bangor' | | | 1 | 4 | | | 5 |
| 'Algerine' | | | | 2 | 1 | 4 | 7 |
| 'Catherine' | | | | | 4 | | 4 |
| Trawlers | 3 | 4 | 4 | 7 | 6 | 2 | 26 |
| 'Kingfisher' | | 1 | | | | | 1 |
| Totals | 5 | 10 | 20 | 25 | 30 | 14 | 104 |

| RCN | 1940 | 1941 | 1942 | 1943 | 1944 | 1945 | TOTAL |
|---|---|---|---|---|---|---|---|
| 'Flower' | | 2 | 2 | 2 | 3 | 1 | 10 |
| 'Castle' | | | | | | | 0 |
| 'River' | | | | | 3 | 1 | 4 |
| 'Bangor' | | | | 1 | 2 | 2 | 5 |
| 'Algerine' | | | | | | | 0 |
| Trawlers | | | | | | | 0 |
| Totals | 0 | 2 | 2 | 3 | 8 | 4 | 19 |

| RAN | 1940 | 1941 | 1942 | 1943 | 1944 | 1945 | TOTAL |
|---|---|---|---|---|---|---|---|
| 'Bathurst' | | | 1 | 1 | 1 | | 3 |
| 'River' | | | | | | | 0 |
| Totals | 0 | 0 | 1 | 1 | 1 | 0 | 3 |

| USN | 1940 | 1941 | 1942 | 1943 | 1944 | 1945 | TOTAL |
|---|---|---|---|---|---|---|---|
| PG | | | | | | | 0 |
| PC | | | | 1 | 2 | 2 | 5 |
| PCE | | | | | | | 0 |
| PF | | | | | | | 0 |
| DE | | | | | 8 | 3 | 11 |
| AM | | | | 2 | 4 | 3 | 9 |
| Totals | 0 | 0 | 0 | 3 | 14 | 8 | 25 |

# CHAPTER TWO

# Comparative Production Rates

THIS WOULD appear to be the first attempt to analyse the overall production rates and individual country and yard performances.

This has entailed the calculation of the overall building time, from the laying down date to the completion date, of each warship completed during the war years. It produces a fairly clear pattern of results, but there is a need for caution in several respects:

a) there are undoubtedly some suspect dates, and therefore overall building times, in these statistics; some have been identified, and some left out for this reason—the consistency of the main body of data throws up these anomalies, and the latter do not invalidate the former;

b) some laying down and completion dates are unavailable; where this happens, no overall building time is calculated, but the launching date (which is nearly always available) is quoted, prefaced by the letter 'L', or the completion date is shown alone under its correct heading;

c) the laying down date could be heavily affected, in later years, by the amount of prefabrication done, either in the shipbuilding yard itself or in engineering works far removed; this, too, throws up anomalies;

d) none of the figures quoted in this chapter reflect any discredit on any of the yards; rather do they highlight the very real individual achievements of the many yards involved in these great shipbuilding programmes.

## PEAK PERIODS

Two separate peak periods, of high production rates and quick overall building times, stand out from this study. They also are brought out in the chart of overall launches, included in the Building Policy chapter.

The first was in the second half of 1940, in the UK and Canada, when the 'Flower' and 'Hunt' classes, and fleet minesweepers, were in full swing.

The second was between the second half of 1942 and the first half of 1944, with a maximum production in the second half of 1943, when no less than 512 new escorts were launched.

*Arvida*, an RCN 'Flower' class corvette, shows the contrast of the bluff low bows of the original class. The radar hut offset to the port side is clear here, with the North Atlantic camouflage. This was a March 1944 picture. *(Ministry of Defence)*

All the fastest building times, and highest averages, occur in this period. All three main shipbuilding countries were then geared up to maximum production, concentrating on time rather than cost cutting. Rapid production designs were in full swing, and the prodigious effort made in the United States in 1943 comes through—though the results in the UK and Canada were hardly less impressive, especially bearing in mind the difficulties of supply to the UK over the North Atlantic convoy routes, and of production during the air-raid years.

## RAPID SLOW-DOWN

After it was agreed in December 1943 that the escort building programmes should be slowed down and cut back, the effects quickly became apparent.

The second half of 1944, and the whole of 1945, reflect the run-down, and the overall building times have been distorted in this period—even where fast times were still recorded, the proportion of slow times was rising significantly.

We may note that this slow-down was carried through in the UK, in spite of the tight frigate position in North Atlantic and inshore waters in early 1945, when the need to withdraw frigates for refit before joining the East Indies and British Pacific Fleets was competing with the need to retain the maximum number of effective escorts in those waters.

The list of massive cancellations does show, however, that an even more impressive production rate would have been achieved in all three main countries, had the cut-back not been agreed; and the ships then being produced would not only have been greater in numbers than in the earlier war years, but would also have been faster, and much more sophisticated in weaponry and electronics.

## WAR LOSSES

A word is relevant here about the effect of these losses on the shipbuilding programmes.

In 1944/45 the RN's annual rate of loss of war-built escorts alone was running at about 10% of the new construction rate, and the annual rate of loss was still rising in 1945.

The RCN rate also increased in 1944 and 1945, but the USN did not experience anything like the same rate of loss; the U-boat campaign and the English Channel/North Sea operations in 1944/45 seem to have been more damaging to escorts than the Pacific war.

## AN OVERALL COMPARISON

No easy picture can be drawn from all yards, even in the same country. Fast times can be found to be anomalous where they occur in a yard building only a few units of one class, and most completions were achieved in between the fastest and the slowest times.

In the analysis which follows, fast times can easily be identified, and the most impressive class of all can easily be seen to be the US destroyer escorts. But in all three countries, and in all classes, the slower times, and the average times, were pretty comparable—which may be a surprising conclusion.

In general, the yards with big numbers of one class to build were those most able to gear up for mass-production, and so for fast production rates. The DE types come through clearly on this (note, however, the big slow-down in the last of the six types, in 1945); the original 'Flower' class was fast, and some RN trawler classes, too. Canadian-built 'River' class frigates were in general built faster than their UK-built counterparts, yet we should take note of the Harland & Wolff performance here. The RN 'Loch' class had great mass-production potential, but it was not realised, as the slow-down had started before they began appearing in any numbers.

*Large Escort Types*

Note that the UK-built 'Black Swan' and 'Hunt' classes, on naval specifications, carried comparatively slow building times throughout.

Both UK- and Canadian-built 'River' class frigates came out fairly fast, Canadian ships faster, due to the higher numbers being produced in 1944. The Australian-built ships of the class were few and far between and, not surprisingly, slow in comparison with their sisters intended for the critical A/S battles.

The 'Loch' and 'Bay' classes started off fairly fast, but soon slowed down in the 1944 period. They could have caught up with the faster DE times had the rapid production programme been carried through.

USN PFs were produced at the same speed as Canadian-built 'River's, and rather faster than the UK-built 'River's. The exceptional performance of the Walsh-Kaiser yard for this class should be noted.

The DEs were fastest of all in the fast yards, but the full breakdown included in this chapter does produce a very mixed picture. There were some very remarkable performances by individual yards.

*Small Escort Types*

The RN 'Flower' class showed impressive and consistent production times in 1940/41, but slowed down after that. The slowest times were very much improved during this period.

Canadian-built 'Flower's did not show any great differences from UK-built units, unlike the following 'River' class. The fastest and slowest times kept pretty consistent; but it should be noted that the fastest Canadian-built 'River' class units were consistently produced faster than Canadian-built 'Flower' class units.

US-built PCs were very fast indeed at one end of the scale, through sheer numbers. The slower times, however, fall into the same pattern as other small escort classes.

UK-built 'Isles' class trawlers came out nearly as fast as US-built PCs, in the fast yards, with large numbers. The slowest, again, were very similar.

The US-built PCE class started late, and production times in 1945 were very slow. The fastest time was comparable with a UK-built 'River', but much slower than the larger DEs.

The UK-built 'Castle' class units were built faster than UK-built 'River' class units, and, surprisingly, faster than the earlier 'Loch' class units; but the 'Castle' class slowed down in 1944, following the policy decision, though it had the potential for good production times.

*Fleet Minesweepers*

UK-built 'Bangor' class ships started well, but slowed down in 1942, and were throughout considerably slower than UK-built 'Flower' class units.

Canadian-built 'Bangor's were faster than UK-built ships, faster than RCN 'Flower's, but slower than RCN 'River's—a fascinating picture.

Australian-built 'Bathurst' class units were brought to US speeds of production at their fastest, and on the whole were faster than UK- or Canadian-built 'Bangor' class ships. Canadian-built 'River' class ships were, however, built at the same pace.

UK-built 'Algerine' class ships were produced at a reasonably fast pace, comparable with the UK-built 'River' class; but Canadian-built 'Algerine's were slow, surprisingly, though they had a later start than their UK-built counterparts.

The US-built 'Raven' class started late, had some very fast building times in the early stages, then slowed down. The 'Admirable' class had a good average record, but slowed right down in 1945—a comparable picture, as might be expected, with the PCE class.

## COMPARATIVE BUILDING TIMES

| Large Escort Types | 1940 | 1941 | 1942 | 1943 | 1944 | 1945 |
|---|---|---|---|---|---|---|
| RB 'Black Swan' | | | | | | |
| Fastest | 17m8d | 19m3d | 15m13d | 11m24d | 15m15d | |
| Slowest | 19m6d | 19m10d | | 23m10d | 23m5d | |
| RN 'Hunt' | | | | | | |
| Fastest | 9m0d | 10m25d | 10m16d | | | |
| Slowest | 19m4d | 26m29d | 20m23d | | | |
| RN 'River' | | | | | | |
| Fastest | | | 9m7d | 7m5d | 8m10d | |
| Slowest | | | 16m21d | 22m17d | 24m17d | |
| RCN 'River' | | | | | | |
| Fastest | | | | 5m21d | 5m3d | |
| Slowest | | | | 17m10d | 15m21d | |
| RAN 'River' | | | | | | |
| Fastest | | | | 16m8d | 20m20d | 22m23d |
| Slowest | | | | | 21m27d | 24m15d |
| RN 'Loch'/'Bay' | | | | | | |
| Fastest | | | | 10m1d | 7m25d | 8m25d |
| Slowest | | | | | 13m2d | 17m10d |

| | | | | |
|---|---|---|---|---|
| **USN PF** | | | | |
| Fastest | | 5m0d | 5m14d | 14m5d |
| Slowest | | 9m6d | 18m7d | 21m8d |
| **USN DEs** | | | | |
| 'Evarts' | | | | |
| Fastest | 12m6d | 3m3d | 3m27d | |
| Slowest | | 21m20d | 13m14d | |
| 'Buckley' | | | | |
| Fastest | | 1m23d | 3m2d | |
| Slowest | | 10m20d | 13m21d | |
| 'Edsall' | | | | |
| Fastest | | 3m25d | 3m7d | |
| Slowest | | 11m18d | 4m25d | |
| 'Bostwick' | | | | |
| Fastest | | 3m11d | 3m8d | |
| Slowest | | 11m24d | 15m30d | |
| 'Rudderow' | | | | |
| Fastest | | | 2m7d | |
| Slowest | | | 10m26d | |
| 'J. C. Butler' | | | | |
| Fastest | | 3m17d | 4m18d | 10m6d |
| Slowest | | | 11m27d | 25m6d |

The launch of the first 'Loch' class frigate, *Loch Fada*, at John Brown's yard, at Clydebank, Scotland. Note the difference in hull lines from the US-built destroyer escorts. *(Scottish Records Office)*

H.M.S. "HOME GUARD"
SEPT. 19. 1944.

▲ *Home Guard* in September 1944, showing the final modifications to this class. She has a 4″ gun forward, two tripod masts, Type 290 radar, and the full North Atlantic camouflage.
(*Ministry of Defence*)

*Stevenstone*, Type III, on trials in the Solent, March 1943. Note the twin torpedo tubes amidships, with armoured control position, and bowchaser fitted on completion.
(*Ministry of Defence*) ▼

*Fierce* in January 1946. She was completed as an M/S HQ ship for service in the Far East; she has four single Bofors, extra large boats for communication at sea, Type 268 radar, and the full sweep deck outfit. *(Ministry of Defence)*

*Carnarvon Bay* in September 1945. A fine speed picture, showing her ready for service with the British Pacific Fleet. Radar types 293, 291, 285, and 244. *(Ministry of Defence)*

| Small Escort Types | 1940 | 1941 | 1942 | 1943 | 1944 | 1945 |
|---|---|---|---|---|---|---|
| **RN 'Flower'** | | | | | | |
| Fastest | 4m3d | 5m15d | 10m26d | 10m5d | 10m19d | |
| Slowest | 13m27d | 20m3d | 19m0d | 11m18d | 12m18d | |
| **RCN 'Flower'** | | | | | | |
| Fastest | 7m26d | 8m16d | 10m6d | 8m4d | 8m16d | |
| Slowest | 9m29d | 14m13d | 16m7d | 14m20d | 14m18d | |
| **USN PC** | | | | | | |
| Fastest | | | 3m1d | 3m23d | 4m1d | 6m4d |
| Slowest | | | 17m5d | 18m27d | 16m0d | 25m22d |
| **RN 'Isles'** | | | | | | |
| Fastest | 7m5d | 6m25d | 6m21d | 5m4d | 4m26d | 6m4d |
| Slowest | 9m4d | 11m1d | 21m28d | 9m28d | 17m0d | 6m27d |
| **USN PCE** | | | | | | |
| Fastest | | | | 7m2d | 6m11d | 17m23d |
| Slowest | | | | 11m20d | 23m26d | 27m10d |
| **RN 'Castle'** | | | | | | |
| Fastest | | | | 5m12d | 8m19d | |
| Slowest | | | | 9m5d | 17m24d | |

| FLEET MINESWEEPERS | 1940 | 1941 | 1942 | 1943 | 1944 | 1945 |
|---|---|---|---|---|---|---|
| **RCN 'Bangor'** | | | | | | |
| Fastest | 9m13d | 9m18d | 16m4d | | | |
| Slowest | 16m14d | 25m27d | 29m18d | | | |
| **RCN 'Bangor'** | | | | | | |
| Fastest | | 6m7d | 7m27d | | | |
| Slowest | | 17m25d | 21m5d | | | |
| **RAN 'Bathurst'** | | | | | | |
| Fastest | 9m24d | 7m21d | 5m15d | 7m14d | 6m5d | |
| Slowest | | 15m7d | 18m15d | 14m17d | 14m23d | |
| **RN 'Algerine'** | | | | | | |
| Fastest | | | 9m24d | 7m3d | 8m8d | 8m17d |
| Slowest | | | 14m26d | 16m2d | 20m26d | |
| **RCN 'Algerine'** | | | | | | |
| Fastest | | | | 12m1d | 8m15d | 10m20d |
| Slowest | | | | 19m30d | 17m18d | 12m3d |
| **USN 'Raven'** | | | | | | |
| Fastest | | | 4m16d | 5m26d | 9m5d | 9m5d |
| Slowest | | | 20m0d | 20m13d | 17m6d | 16m1d |
| **USN 'Admirable'** | | | | | | |
| Fastest | | | | 9m8d | 5m28d | 12m19d |
| Slowest | | | | 19m19d | 17m16d | 33m14d |

# CHAPTER THREE

# Allied Escort Vessels in Service

WE COULD not hope, in one section of this book, to cover adequately the war at sea, on a global basis. This has already been done, on such a high professional plane, by the official historians of each of the major Allied navies.

This section has a different objective. It sets out to show how the increasing flow of new escort vessels from the shipbuilding yards affected the war at sea in each ocean. So it starts with the pre-war escorts in service at the outbreak of war; then sketches in the sequence in which the new escort classes appeared, and the impact this had on the war at sea.

It aims to show also the impact on operations of the swift progress in technology, from radar and new A/S weapons to mass-production methods, and of increasingly specialised and highly-trained crews. It does not cover the shipbuilding policy and programmes of the major navies, as these are covered in detail separately.

A further emphasis brought out in this section is the range of types of enemy weapons faced by the escorts in each phase of the war. Thus, we shall see how the RN's 'Hunt' class destroyers, with good speed and gun armament, were largely employed in the narrow seas and in the Mediterranean, but not in the Atlantic; and how the war-built escort classes of the RN and RCN were designed mainly to combat the submarine in tempestuous waters. We see, too, the excellent dual-purpose capability of the USN's destroyer escorts, with their anti-aircraft armament taking precedence for their Pacific operations.

If the North Atlantic takes precedence in this section, it is because it was the critical battle throughout the war, and also because a wealth of operational reports on this battle have recently been released for the first time.

## COMMAND ALLOCATION OF NEW ESCORTS

Before examining the impact of new escorts on each major war theatre, we should first see how the new ships were allocated between the commands.

This shows some surprising trends, which are analysed and commented upon. In particular, it will be seen that although most RN/RCN new escort vessel classes were designed very much with the North Atlantic battle in mind, in fact a surprisingly high proportion of these new escorts had to be deployed overseas.

The contribution of the RCN escorts, in holding the North Atlantic line while the RN covered not only that commitment but many others, comes through very clearly, not only as a remarkable achievement by Canada, but also as a very significant factor in the war against the U-boats.

In the last eighteen months of the war this trend was reversed by the arrival in large numbers of the new RN ships of the 'Captain', 'Loch', and 'Castle' classes. This balance of escorts in the North Atlantic would have altered further, had the production cutbacks in late 1943 not taken effect; but the Canadian contribution still remained significant, in that Allied production could be switched to larger numbers of landing craft.

Another trend which stands out clearly was that the 'Flower' class corvettes were vital in the Atlantic in 1941-43, but as the newer classes, especially the frigates, arrived in increasing numbers, the 'Flower' class was re-deployed, and the RN 'River' class was largely sent to reinforce the East Indies and Pacific escort forces.

## 'FLOWER' CLASS CORVETTES (RN AND RCN)

This class made its greatest contribution in the North Atlantic battle in 1941-43.

In 1941 nearly all new ships of the class were thrown into this critical battle, but even then 10 were diverted to Freetown and the Mediterranean.

In 1942 no less than 24 were needed in the West African area, and 13 more in the Mediterranean; but the overall numbers of completed ships had built up very fast.

In 1943 the peak number of corvettes of the class were in the North Atlantic, some 138, but no less than 40 were diverted away, with the first involvement in the Indian Ocean.

### 'FLOWER' CLASS COMMAND DISTRIBUTION

| Date | Total in Commission RN | RCN | North Atlantic RN | RCN | English Channel RN | RCN | Mediterranean Incl. Gibraltar RN | RCN | West Africa RN | Indian Ocean RN | Pacific RN | RCN |
|------|------|------|------|------|------|------|------|------|------|------|------|------|
| 1.1.40 | | | | | | | | | | | | |
| 1.1.41 | 47 | 13 | 36 | 13 | 1 | | 4 | | 6 | | | |
| 1.1.42 | 110 | 67 | 73 | 67 | | | 13 | | 24 | | | |
| 1.1.43 | 108 | 70 | 74 | 64 | | | 12 | 6 | 15 | 7 | | |
| 1.1.44 | 117 | 79 | 57 | 77 | | | 27 | | 12 | 21 | | 2 |
| 6.6.44 | 117 | 88 | 10 | 67 | 45 | 18 | 27 | | 14 | 21 | | 3 |
| 1.1.45 | 113 | 96 | 37 | 79 | 26 | 13 | 10 | | 9 | 31 | | 4 |
| 7.5.45 | 111 | 95 | 26 | 78 | 43 | 13 | 15 | | 10 | 17 | | 4 |
| 3.8.45 | 23 | 4 | 3 | | 8 | | | | | 12 | | 4 |

In 1944 the Mediterranean and the Indian Ocean between them absorbed nearly 50, and D-Day in June diverted 63 ships of the class to the English Channel. It is remarkable that this left only 10 RN ships of the class in the North

Atlantic, whereas the RCN had 67 in that area. This reflected the RN Support Groups' growing influence in the Western Approaches, and the RCN carrying the North Atlantic burden at that time (though with not too much enemy activity), with close escort groups usually composed of 2 'River's and 5-7 'Flower's.

Early 1945 saw some of the 'Flower's returning to the North Atlantic, but many stayed in the English Channel area, as the U-boats' inshore campaign got under way. The ships of the class in the Indian Ocean reached a peak of 31 at that time. Then, by VE-Day, more ships were diverted from the North Atlantic to inshore waters, while 42 were still needed elsewhere.

After VE-Day there was an astonishingly quick disappearance of both RN and RCN 'Flower' class ships to the Reserve Fleet lists, even as Indian Ocean and Pacific escort needs were rising. Indeed, by VJ-Day, almost the only 'Flower's still in commission were a dozen in the Indian Ocean for air-sea rescue purposes.

## 'River' Class Frigates (RN and RCN)

1943—The first ships in service were all thrown straight into the North Atlantic battle.

1944—There was a dramatic rise in new ships coming into service, both RN and RCN. At D-Day, there were 8 RN ships in the North Atlantic, compared with 29 RCN, but 11 RN ships were in the English Channel, and 18 were in the Indian Ocean, with 20 more based on West Africa and the Mediterranean.

1945—By the beginning of the year, there were 28 RN ships in the Atlantic and inshore areas, as opposed to 63 RCN. But 31 RN ships were still serving overseas, with 17 in West Africa alone.

By VE-Day in May, the RN ships in the Atlantic and Channel had dropped to 22, while the RCN ships remained at 61; 21 RN ships were in the Indian Ocean, and 6 in the Pacific.

By early August, RN ships in the Indian Ocean remained at 21, but in the Pacific there was a dramatic rise of ships already there, or committed, to 18 RN, 36 RCN, plus 6 RIN.

### 'RIVER' CLASS COMMAND DISTRIBUTION

| Date | Total in Commission | | North Atlantic | | English Channel | Mediter-ranean | West Africa | Indian Ocean | Pacific Ocean | | |
|---|---|---|---|---|---|---|---|---|---|---|---|
| | RN | RCN | RN | RCN | RN | RN | RN | RN | RN | RCN | RAN |
| 1.1.43 | 17 | 9 | 17 | 9 | | | | | | | |
| 1.1.44 | 41 | 25 | 18 | 25 | | 11 | 6 | 6 | | | |
| 6.6.44 | 57 | 45 | 8 | 29 | 11 | 13 | 7 | 18 | | | 2 |
| 1.1.45 | 59 | 61 | 22 | 61 | 6 | 2 | 17 | 12 | | | 4 |
| 7.5.45 | 59 | 59 | 16 | 59 | 6 | 2 | 5 | 21 | 9 | | 6 |
| 3.8.45 | 40 | 42 | 1 | 6 | | | | 21 | 18 | 36 | 6 |

*NOTE:* 3.8.45 figures include ships refitting, but not yet on station

The refitting of 'River' class frigates for Far East service is covered in the class chapter, and the relatively high number of RCN 'River' class units is explained under that heading also.

## OTHER NEW ESCORT VESSEL CLASSES

We have analysed the command distribution of the 'Flower' and 'River' classes in detail, to show how far the RN global commitments diluted even the critical North Atlantic escort forces. But the other new escort classes, almost entirely of RN ships, affected this changing picture increasingly from 1944 onwards. This breakdown shows how each new class was used to its best advantage.

The chart shows the dramatic switch in allocation of new North Atlantic escorts for D-Day in June 1944. The RN had more war-built escorts in the English Channel at that time than in the North Atlantic—and the latter figure includes the Western Approaches Support Groups, operating off the western end of the English Channel. 'Hunt' class destroyers, as before, are not included in these figures. The RCN had the same number of new escorts in the North Atlantic as did the RN at that time, with a small number in the invasion area also.

We see, too, that by 1945, the total of new escorts, other than the 'Flower' and 'River' classes, outnumbered both those classes combined. The RN 'Flower's had largely been withdrawn to inshore duties, and the 'River's were widely dispersed,

'Black Swan' class sloop *Woodcock* in rough weather. Note the two twin 4″ mountings forward, the Type 271 radar on a short lattice mast aft. *(Imperial War Museum)*

but the RCN North Atlantic close escort groups, now dominating that part of the battle, were still composed of two 'River' and 5-7 'Flower' class units. The RN Support Groups were now largely made up of 'Captain', 'Loch', and 'Colony' class frigates, and 'Castle' class corvettes. This is in spite of the production cutbacks in late 1943, and shows how important the Squid ATW mortar and extra speed were becoming.

Note, too, the build-up in mid-1945 of the East Indies and British Pacific Fleets. By early August the East Indies Fleet included:

18 'Loch' class frigates
 3 'Captain' class frigates
21 'River' class frigates
 5 'Black Swan' class sloops
12 'Flower' class corvettes on ASR duties.

And the British Pacific Fleet included:
20 'Bay' class frigates
54 RN and RCN 'River' class frigates
27 'Black Swan' class sloops
(some of these ships were allocated, but had not yet arrived).

But most of the 'Captain' class, and all the 'Colony' and 'Kil' classes, had been taken out of service, for return to the USN, and nearly all the 'Flower' class were laid up in the Reserve Fleet, with just a few retained for training duties.

It will be seen that 18 'Loch' class frigates brought the Squid ATW mortar to the Indian Ocean, but all the BPF ships were fitted with Hedgehog. No 'Castle' class corvettes, although Squid-fitted, were allocated to these two areas. A full analysis of the Far East escort forces follows in that section.

## EFFECT OF OTHER NEW ESCORT CLASSES ON THE NORTH ATLANTIC

| | 'Flower' | | 'River' | | 'Loch', 'Captain' 'Castle', 'Black Swan' | Totals | |
|---|---|---|---|---|---|---|---|
| Date | RN | RCN | RN | RCN | | RN | RCN |
| 1.1.41 | 47 | 13 | | | 2 | 49 | 13 |
| 1.1.42 | 110 | 67 | | | 3 | 113 | 70 |
| 1.1.43 | 108 | 70 | 17 | 9 | 7 | 132 | 79 |
| 1.1.44 | 117 | 79 | 41 | 25 | 87 | 245 | 104 |
| 6.6.44 | 117 | 88 | 57 | 45 | 131 | 305 | 133 |
| 1.1.45 | 113 | 96 | 59 | 61 | 144 | 316 | 160 |
| 7.5.45 | 111 | 95 | 59 | 59 | 160 | 330 | 157 |
| 3.8.45 | 23 | 4 | 40 | 42 | 108 | 151 | 50 |

## ON LAST FOUR DATES, SHIPS IN NORTH ATLANTIC WERE (ALL CLASSES):

|         | RN  | RCN | Total |
|---------|-----|-----|-------|
| 1.1.44  | 122 | 102 | 224   |
| 6.6.44  | 96  | 96  | 192   |
| 1.1.45  | 186 | 143 | 329   |
| 7.5.45  | 164 | 140 | 304   |

## AND IN ENGLISH CHANNEL/NORTH SEA, FROM NORTH ATLANTIC:

|         | RN | RCN | Total |
|---------|----|-----|-------|
| 1.1.44  | 0  | 0   | 0     |
| 6.6.44  | 98 | 18  | 116   |
| 1.1.45  | 47 | 13  | 60    |
| 7.5.45  | 64 | 13  | 77    |

## AND IN AREAS OTHER THAN THE ABOVE:

|         | RN  | RCN | Total |
|---------|-----|-----|-------|
| 1.1.44  | 133 | 0   | 133   |
| 6.6.44  | 111 | 2   | 113   |
| 1.1.45  | 87  | 4   | 91    |
| 7.5.45  | 97  | 6   | 103   |
| 3.8.45  | 119 | 40  | 159   |

## NOTE INCREASING TOTALS OF ESCORTS IN NORTH ATLANTIC AND UK INSHORE WATERS:

|         | RN  | RCN | Total |
|---------|-----|-----|-------|
| 6.6.44  | 194 | 114 | 308   |
| 1.1.45  | 231 | 156 | 387   |
| 7.5.45  | 228 | 153 | 381   |

## RN—NUMBERS OF NEW ESCORTS IN SERVICE

(all at 1st January)

*1941*   Western Approaches 46 'Flower'   Channel/North Sea 19 'Hunt'   Mediterranean 4 'Flower'   West Africa 6 'Flower'

*1942*   Western Approaches 3 'Black Swan', 68 'Flower'   Channel/North Sea 27 'Hunt'   Mediterranean 11 'Hunt', 13 'Flower'   West Africa 24 'Flower'

*1943*   Western Approaches 5 'Black Swan', 14 'River', 68 'Flower'   Channel/North Sea 40 'Hunt'   Mediterranean 28 'Hunt', 2 'Black Swan', 18 'Flower'   West Africa 18 'Flower'   East Indies 2 'Hunt', 4 'Flower'

*1944*   Western Approaches 18 'Black Swan', 25 'River', 51 'Captain', 1 'Colony', 2 'Castle', 59 'Flower'   Channel/North Sea 26 'Hunt'   Mediterranean 40 'Hunt', 1 'Black Swan', 11

'River', 27 'Flower'    *West Africa* 9 'River', 3 'Flower'    *East Indies* 1 'Black Swan', 1 'River', 13 'Flower'
*1945    Western Approaches* 14 'Black Swan', 15 'River', 54 'Captain', 16 'Loch', 20 'Colony', 24 'Castle', 27 'Flower'    *Channel/North Sea* 31 'Hunt', 14 'Captain', 1 'Colony', 12 'River', 29 'Flower'    *Mediterranean* 21 'Hunt', 9 'River', 7 'Kil', 10 'Flower'    *West Africa* 18 'River', 7 'Kil', 19 'Flower'    *East Indies* 10 'Black Swan', 16 'Hunt', 22 'River', 25 'Flower'
*1945 (VE Day)    Western Approaches* 12 'Black Swan', 19 'Loch', 44 'Captain', 13 'Colony', 11 'River', 23 'Castle', 23 'Flower'    *Channel/North Sea* 1 'Black Swan', 45 'Hunt', 21 'Captain', 10 'River', 1 'Colony', 44 'Flower'    *Mediterranean* 1 'Black Swan', 12 'Hunt', 2 'River', 7 'Kil', 15 'Flower'    *West Africa* 5 'River', 8 'Kil', 6 'Flower'    *East Indies* 13 'Black Swan', 7 'Hunt', 22 'River', 15 'Flower'    *Pacific* 5 'Black Swan', 9 'River'

# NORTH ATLANTIC

## THE BEGINNING

In the first year of the war, the opening skirmishes of the main battle to come were fought.

Western Approaches escort forces at this time consisted of 32 pre-war destroyers (including many 'V and W's from World War I), organised in four flotillas, while U-boats in operational service varied from 10 to 20. The convoy system was quickly started, but, due to limited range, escorts could only accompany the merchant ships as far as 15 degrees west, or some 250 miles west of Ireland, and a similar distance eastwards from Canada.

So the U-boats concentrated largely on unescorted ships, of which there were still many. In the first four months of the war, of some 115 ships sunk, only 12 were in convoy. Special hunting groups were twice tried, consisting of a fleet carrier with escorting destroyers; in these operations, *Ark Royal* was attacked and missed, but *Courageous* was sunk.

By the end of 1940 nearly one-third of the U-boats in service had been sunk, but there were ominous signs. After the fall of France the south-west approaches to the United Kingdom were closed, as the U-boats moved their bases to Biscay ports. The number of new U-boats entering service was increasing, and they were still successful in picking off stragglers from the convoys and concentrating on the mid-ocean area, where the ships were unescorted. Most convoys still only had one A/S escort with them, since the demands of the Dunkirk evacuation, and of the anti-invasion forces based in the English Channel thereafter, had badly denuded the ocean escort forces, which were still largely composed of pre-war built destroyers.

But the first signs of the future Western Approaches organisation were emerging. The old ex-American destroyers made their contribution at this time, the first of the new 'Flower' class corvettes were entering service, and tactics and training were starting to improve.

The year ended on a crisis note, with the U-boats starting their pack attacks by night on the surface and merchant ship sinkings increasing. The real Battle of the Atlantic had begun.

## 1941—THE ESCORT GROUPS EMERGE

In the spring, Iceland became available as a fuelling base, and the eastern escorts could go halfway across, while the Canadian escorts from the west were also increasing in numbers. The corvettes were making their presence felt (100 were in commission by mid-year), and soon 9 escort groups were operating from Greenock and Liverpool, while some special escort groups of fleet destroyers and fleet minesweepers from Scapa were made available from time to time. The first CAM (fighter catapult ship) appeared in this period, defining the need for large numbers of escort carriers, which were ordered at this time.

This period, too, marked the real beginning of American aid. USN destroyers were escorting Allied convoys as far east as Iceland, and the great Lend-Lease building programme of new escorts was started off. The Admiralty had also defined the need for large numbers of frigates, and had started that programme too, for it was already clear that the escorts in service were operating under a terrific strain. The corvettes were too small and too slow for mid-ocean work, and the escort groups were composed of too many different types of ships to be truly effective.

The U-boats continued to seek out the weak spots. As shore-based air patrols narrowed the mid-Atlantic gap where surface escort could not be given, the escort groups worked hard, especially in the fierce winter gales, to escort the convoys, and some kills against U-boat aces were achieved. The U-boats moved farther afield, to West Africa, the South Atlantic, and the Indian Ocean, seeking unescorted targets.

As the months went by, the flow of new corvettes increased, until there were some 8 escort groups, each composed of 2 pre-war destroyers and 4-6 corvettes, beginning to work together as a team, with the first Support Groups, each of 4-5 destroyers on loan from the Fleet, also appearing.

Great convoy battles were now being fought—in December, HG 76 was fought home by an escort led by the great Captain F. J. Walker, with an early escort carrier *(Audacity)*, 3 sloops, 3 destroyers, and 7 corvettes. 5 U-boats were sunk, and two Focke-Wulfs shot down, for the loss of 2 merchantmen, *Audacity*, and 1 destroyer.

The Liverpool Tactical School, which was to have such a marked effect on the achievements of the escort groups, started to operate, and the great working-up base at Tobermory also got under way, training every new escort under pressure, before she joined the battle.

Escort group tactics were becoming standardised, and ships kept in the same group as far as possible. The first of the Hedgehog ahead-throwing A/S weapons appeared, the depth-charge pattern was increased to 14, by the addition of extra throwers, and the first of the much-improved Type 271 radar sets (then still called RDF) appeared in the Western Approaches, to help ward off the U-boats' surface pack attacks.

The ships and the men of the Western Approaches and Canadian escort forces were building a colourful image, of skill, courage, and endurance, and of new ships and weapons, and service in corvettes, and later in frigates, became a challenging assignment, to be sought after.

## 1942—THE BATTLE ESCALATES

By the year's beginning some 25 escort groups in all were operating, but still largely with pre-war ships and the imperfect but plucky 'Flower' class corvettes. Some long-range ships were going right across the Atlantic, fuelling at sea, and some USN destroyers were operating from Londonderry.

But the first half of the year was dominated by the entry of the USA into the war, and the attack by the U-boats on the unprotected shipping on the eastern seaboard of America, and in the Caribbean. The U-boats called this their 'happy time'; an average of only 10 boats was operating in that area, but their bag was enormous. The North Atlantic convoys were left very largely alone, as a result, and drastic measures were taken to stop the losses on the western side. Two North Atlantic escort groups were sent, some two dozen RN A/S trawlers, and half a dozen RCN corvettes. This, too, was the time when 8 RN corvettes were turned over to the USN on reverse Lend-Lease, and others ordered from Canadian shipyards.

By mid-year the battle was back under control. The U-boats again searched for stragglers, and sought weakly-protected convoys. But the flow of new escorts was beginning to show results; some 150 corvettes were now in service, the frigates were starting to appear, and convoys usually had a close escort of some 6 ships—a great advance over the days of 1940. High Frequency Direction Finding (the famous Huff-Duff, whose birdcage aerial is so prominent in many of our photographs), was also now in service, and with radar and improved Asdic equipment our close escorts were much better able to detect the U-boats.

The rapid advances in technology were really crucial by this stage. Not only was the new Hedgehog ATW fitted in the new 'River' class frigates, but it was being added to pre-war destroyers, sloops, and the war-built corvettes. By June, 168 ships were so fitted, and 12 more were being added to the total every month; and better still, the pilot model of the Squid was at sea, in the old destroyer *Ambuscade*.

But the corvettes were too slow to chase U-boats on the surface, and the pack attacks continued, with serious losses of merchant shipping. The U-boats started a new offensive, and patrolled the North Atlantic in well-organised groups, directed by shore radio, until one of their number sighted a convoy, and homed the others in.

Two other new demands emerged during the year, to keep the North Atlantic escorts working under immense strain.

The first was the Arctic convoys to Russia. These were a true Fleet operation, unlike the North Atlantic; the battleships, carriers, and fleet destroyers hit the headlines, but the escorts were also there, enduring the intense cold, fighting the U-boats, and rescuing survivors. On these convoys especially, fleet minesweepers

augmented the regular escorts; indeed, if we look at the convoy PQ 17 (so well related elsewhere), we find that the initial close escort was 3 fleet minesweepers and 4 trawlers, while the additional long-range escort consisted of 6 destroyers and 4 corvettes.

The following convoy, PQ 18, included the first escort carrier to be used on this run, *Avenger,* and 19 destroyers in the close escort.

The second extra strain came from the invasion convoys for Operation Torch, the invasion of North Africa. Some of the normal North Atlantic convoys were suspended, and 125 escorts were diverted to take the invasion convoys as far as Gibraltar. There were 10 main RN assault convoys, and a typical one consisted of 47 ships, with 18 close escorts.

## 1943—THE ESCORTS TRIUMPH

This year in the North Atlantic was one of grave crisis—the year in which the U-boats came closest to winning the battle of the convoy routes. Both sides threw in all the ships and men at their disposal, and some great battles were fought.

The U-boats fought well and tenaciously, but the RN and RCN escorts fought back in defence of their charges even better, and in the end they triumphed, and the U-boats retreated.

Some of these battles are featured separately in this section, but the fighting was almost continuous.

In March the great battle of convoy HX 228 and SC 122 was fought. 33 merchant ships were lost, and only 1 U-boat was sunk. This was a severe setback, and followed on convoy SC 118 the previous month, in which of 63 ships with 10 escorts 13 ships were lost, though 3 U-boats were sunk.

April passed a little more easily, and convoys were fought through with little loss, but the following month produced the battle of convoy ONS 5, which is described separately. The escorts fought their convoy through against tremendous odds, and triumphed. The combination of radar, H/F D/F, and very long-range aircraft; the appearance in some numbers of the new 'River' class frigates, and the first effective use of support groups, one including the escort carrier *Biter,* all combined with the skill and courage of the escort crews to defeat a large and tenacious pack of U-boats.

Further battles followed, but the escorts were clearly gaining the upper hand; in spite of the use of the German acoustic torpedo, finally the U-boats withdrew from the Atlantic battle, to lick their wounds, and to work out fresh tactics. Convoy battles still took place, as ONS 18/ON 202 featured here, and U-boats operated off the eastern US seaboard, off Brazil, West Africa, and the Cape; but the crisis had passed, and sinkings of our merchant ships declined in the second half of the year to a more acceptable level.

August was the best month of the war to date for the Allies, in terms of merchant ship losses; only 13 ships, of 86,000 tons, were lost, but 20 German and

'Captain' class frigate *Ekins* oiling at sea from the escort oiler in a North Atlantic convoy. This operation became really hazardous in heavy weather. *(P.W. Hayward)*

Italian submarines were sunk, including some of the large tankers. But all was not over; there were 140 U-boats in commission in the Biscay ports, and 200 more under trials and training in the Baltic. The respite was to be temporary.

There were two other important aspects of the battle in this year. First, USN escorts withdrew from the North Atlantic in the spring, due to their increasing commitments elsewhere; though one escort carrier, with destroyer escorts, was operating with North Atlantic convoys from time to time. But the North Atlantic routes became the sole responsibility of the RN and RCN, with the latter assuming its greatly enlarged role, with rapidly expanding numbers of new corvettes and frigates. Thus, in March, the northern convoy escorts were made up of: RN 50%, RCN 46%, and USN 4%; the USN destroyers were based on Iceland, and when they withdrew, the RCN corvettes in the Caribbean also returned to their home station.

From this time until the end of the war, the USN operated Hunter-Killer Groups in the mid-Atlantic, concentrating on the USA-Gibraltar convoy route, and their greatest successes were in the next twelve months.

These Hunter-Killer Groups were composed of an escort carrier (CVE) and between 4 and 12 destroyer escorts. Their original task was to operate in support of US convoys sailing in the build-up for the Sicily invasion, but after that event they had a roving commission in the same area, and were most successful in locating and sinking U-boats. In one period of 100 days no less than 16 were sunk; this series of operations was perhaps the US Navy's greatest operational contribution to the Battle of the Atlantic.

14 CVE Groups of this kind were planned, but 11 CVEs were actually allotted to this duty: *Bogue, Card, Block Island, Core, Croatan, Guadalcanal, Santee, Mission Bay, Solomons, Tripoli,* and *Wake Island.* Of these, 5 were of the 'Bogue' class as supplied to the RN, and the others were of the later, more advanced 'Casablanca' class. One was of the last war-built CVE class, the 'Commencement Bay' group.

By 1944, RN escort carriers were also operating with the North Atlantic and Russian convoys—no less than 8 were on the Russian run in the first half of that year. On occasion, they operated with frigate screens, following the successful USN pattern; but more often they needed to stay with the convoys they were supporting, due to their scarcity of numbers.

The other major aspect was the campaign against the U-boats crossing the Bay of Biscay, to and from their French bases. This battle was largely fought by shore-based aircraft, though with the 2nd Escort Group, led by Captain Walker, composed of sloops, and other escort groups also participating. Many U-boats were sunk in this battle, in spite of their greatly augmented A/A defences.

In the second half of the year the Support Groups began to make their presence felt on a continuing basis. In place of the fleet destroyers on loan from Scapa Flow, groups of the newer and faster escorts were formed, trained intensively together, and then operated on six-week patrols in the North Atlantic.

The most famous of these was still Captain Walker's 2nd Escort Group, composed of 6 new sloops of the 'Black Swan' class; but other similar groups were being formed as ships became available, and this trend was most marked from this point until the end of the war. Captain Walker's Group first demonstrated how careful training, and new and carefully-thought-out tactics, could in nearly every case lead to a U-boat kill. His group was at one stage operating with one or two escort carriers, on the lines of the USN groups farther south; but the escorts needed to be free agents, and did rather better on their own in the stormy northern waters.

There were several battles on the UK-Gibraltar route later in the year, but the wolfpack strategy failed again, as the numbers of escorts in the close screen steadily increased, and the escorts finished the year in a dominant position. In these latter battles the first involvement of the new 'Captain' class frigates showed that they would be as good as the sloops, yet greater in numbers.

## 1944—NORMANDY AND THE SCHNORKEL

The year opened with some 30 U-boats operating in various areas of the North Atlantic, but their efforts were not very successful. Gibraltar convoys were found and attacked, with honours just about even, which was not good enough for the Germans.

The 2nd Escort Group, operating with two escort carriers, had a most successful patrol, supporting several convoys, two of which each had their own escort carrier in company. The 2nd Escort Group sank 6 U-boats in a month, and 5 others were sunk near convoys in the same period; the triumph of ONS 5 in 1943, in fighting off successive attacks by U-boats at night, had been followed by the triumph of the highly-trained Support Groups, operating in support of convoys.

A Canadian escort group carrying out close quarters manoeuvres in calm weather. 'Flower' class corvettes *Collingwood* and *Orillia* with one other, and two pre-war destroyers in foreground. *(Imperial War Museum)*

The 1st Escort Group, composed entirely of the new 'Captain' class frigates, then coming into service in large numbers in a very short period, also had a successful patrol in February/March, and the close escorts of a number of convoys also won successes in their own areas. By May the escorts were sinking a steadily increasing number of U-boats, some after very long hunts of up to 38 hours, and the U-boats were withdrawn, in part for the fitting of Schnorkel breathing tubes, but in part also while new tactics were thought out.

This was important, since by that time many escorts were being withdrawn from the Atlantic in readiness for the invasion of Normandy.

This meant several things for the escorts. First, some 180 frigates, sloops, and corvettes were re-trained and allocated to the English Channel commands; secondly, the Western Approaches Support Groups needed to be re-grouped, mainly at the western end of the English Channel, to prevent U-boats getting at the invasion operations; and thirdly, as a result, the escorts available for North Atlantic convoys had to be drastically cut, and the convoys combined into very large units, to cover the battle area as well as possible.

How difficult this was, in spite of the fast-growing numbers of escorts, is shown in the breakdowns of escort allocation included here.

While the Normandy Invasion will be covered in the English Channel section, we should cover here the operations of the Support Groups in the south-western approaches.

Some 36 U-boats were grouped in the Biscay ports to attack our invasion convoys, and they put to sea, to attempt to penetrate the English Channel, on 6th June itself. Some were fitted with the new Schnorkel, and other boats joined from the Norway bases; few got through to the western Channel, but the Schnorkel largely frustrated aircraft sightings in that area, and the Support Groups were moved into the western Channel area, to hunt the U-boats there.

Two frigates were quickly lost by torpedo, and some 7 U-boats appear to have got through; but while they sank a 'Flower' class corvette off Cherbourg, they achieved few successes. The blanketing of the area by highly-trained escorts, either Support Groups operating on the western fringes of the assault area, or experienced North Atlantic escorts working as close escorts of the assault convoys right through the Channel, was most successful.

After the U-boats had failed to disrupt the Channel invasion traffic, they returned to normal operations. But the arrival of the Schnorkel-fitted U-boats opened an entirely new phase in the battle; for the aircraft patrols now found it very difficult to locate and attack them, either on passage to and from Norway (after France was liberated) or in their patrol areas.

So the U-boat war moved into the inshore waters around the UK, as from September, and the escorts needed to learn a whole new bag of tricks. Some 20 U-boats were on patrol in this area, and the difficulty of locating a submarine among shoals, wrecks and strong tides became apparent; while a U-boat, once attacked, could lie quietly on the bottom until the attackers had gone, and then slip away on the tide. So new searching methods, attacking tactics and skills had to be worked out quickly by the escorts, both the close escorts and the support groups, and this phase lasted until the end of the war, without either side winning a decisive victory.

The number of U-boats in the North Atlantic itself was now small, and they were achieving very little; but the U-boats inshore were tying down large numbers of our newest and best escorts, due to the difficulties in locating them, and this meant that escorts for the big North Atlantic convoys were, in fact, not nearly as strong as before. We can best follow these developments through the first four months of 1945, and remember that large numbers of escorts had been allocated to the Eastern Fleet and the British Pacific Fleet, and were due to refit and move to their new operational areas in the course of that year.

## 1945—VICTORY JUST IN TIME?

Even though the European war was clearly moving towards a successful conclusion on land, and losses at sea were not significant, the year opened with worrying overtones for the escorts.

Over 350 trained escorts were engaged on close escort or support of convoys in coastal waters by this time—the greater part of the North Atlantic escort forces. A breakdown is given of the latter, showing the very impressive improvement in the numbers of escort groups, and the types of frigates and corvettes in them; and the brunt of this work naturally fell on the North Atlantic ships, highly trained in U-boat hunting.

The difficulties of this type of campaign are shown briefly in the story included of a patrol by the 3rd Escort Group. Ships were being damaged or sunk in our own Home waters, off the entrance to the Clyde and Liverpool, and on the northern East Coast. By March some 50 U-boats were working in these waters, and until they attacked it was difficult to detect them; but once they had shown themselves several support groups at a time would be directed at them at full speed, and a highly skilled and detailed search would begin, using new tactics for the shallow waters, which in a number of cases produced a kill. U-boats appeared again in the English Channel, where Western Approaches frigates and corvettes had been retained; for the first time experienced North Atlantic support groups operated in the Portsmouth and Nore Commands. Indeed, one such group swept through the Straits of Dover and up into the southern North Sea in April—for the first time during the war.

The first of the new Type XXI and Type XXIII U-boats were by now actually on patrol in our waters—in the Irish Sea, off the east coast of Scotland, and, more significant still, in the southern North Sea, off the Thames approaches, where U-boats had not appeared since 1940.

The 'Captain' class frigates, operating in 6 separate support groups, made an especially impressive impact during this period, but groups containing the new 'Loch' class frigates and 'Castle' class corvettes were also active close inshore, and Squid kills were increasing rapidly in number.

U-boats also reappeared off Halifax and off Gibraltar, scoring some successes, but it was in the coastal waters of the UK that the final battle was fought. The numbers of U-boats were steadily increasing, and although their successes were relatively small they kept our surface forces fully stretched, with the crews under no less continuous strain than they had been in the tempestuous North Atlantic. As an example, the 21st Escort Group (*Conn*, S0) supported no less than 15 convoys in four weeks early in the year.

## THE THREAT OF THE FAST U-BOATS

In studying the war-built escort classes we must examine the probable trend of the anti-submarine battle, had the war continued for another six or twelve months.

In October 1943 the Germans laid their plans for a new series of U-boats, with much faster underwater speeds and capable of diving to much greater depths. The main design was the Type XXIC, a U-boat with a beautifully streamlined hull and an underwater speed of $17\frac{1}{2}$ knots for an hour, or 110 miles at 10 knots. The U-boat design table shows how great an advance this was on the older war-built boats.

135 construction firms were mobilised to build this type alone, plus another 32 as hull assembly yards. Production began in March 1944 and was up to the scheduled level of 33 boats completed per month by mid-summer. Thus, in 1945 the production programme for this type alone went to 360 boats.

The Type XXIII, for use in coastal waters, was being produced in parallel. Much smaller, with only 2 torpedoes slung externally, it had an underwater speed of $12\frac{1}{2}$ knots—still twice as fast as the older ocean-going boats.

Looking further ahead, a greater threat still lay in the Type XXVI Walter U-boat, operating on hydrogen-peroxide fuel and capable of at least $22\frac{1}{2}$ knots submerged. Three of this type were commissioned before VE-day, but had not got beyond the trials stage. 180 more were already on order.

Some production delays were caused by Allied bombing, but, more importantly, design and construction defects held back the new U-boats from entering service in great numbers before VE-Day. 125 Type XXIC boats were completed, but only 2 were in operational service in UK coastal waters; 60 Type XXIII were completed, but only 3 similarly reached the coastal battlegrounds.

But the situation would have changed very drastically by the end of 1945. How would the escorts have coped with this new threat?

As early as March 1944 the Admiralty was analysing the capabilities of the new U-boats. The Liverpool Tactical School started teaching new search and attack methods from the same time, but realistic exercises at sea were hampered by the lack of fast submarines on the Allied side.

It was expected that the fast U-boats would use their speed to attack a convoy from any angle, rather than mainly from ahead; and that they would move away fast from the scene of the attack, perhaps diving to great depths, when away from coastal waters. This would be particularly to their advantage when a heavy sea was running and the escorts were slowed down, with difficult Asdic conditions.

But not all was on the side of the new boats. They would need to slow down to listen for the attacking escorts, since at high speed they would be both deaf and blind. It was also unlikely that they could fire acoustic torpedoes from great depths.

The US Navy came largely to the same conclusions. In a research study by the US 10th Fleet, Atlantic, in May 1945, the only major difference in search tactics was a proposal that escorts should use their Asdic (sonar) sets more for listening than for sonic search, a tactic largely reversing the practice of the previous war years.

What would have been the tactics of the escorts, and which types of escorts would have been the most effective?

The first problem would be to detect these new U-boats. As with the earlier Schnorkel-fitted boats, detection from the air would be much more difficult, and the surface escorts would bear the brunt of the battle. Further, the last few months of the war, in coastal waters, indicated that the first detection of a U-boat would only come in many cases when it attacked; thus large numbers of escorts, organised into well-trained escort groups, and able to descend at speed onto the attack position, would be vitally important. The new depth-detecting Asdic set, the Type 147B, would become critical in open-water situations, and an increase in its capability from 880 to 1,300 feet was seen as important. The new radar sets, with much greater sensitivity for small objects, would assist in detecting the Schnorkel at longer distances.

The 2nd Escort Group, as re-formed in August 1944. Taken from *Starling*, the Group includes *Loch Fada*, *Wren*, *Dominica* and *Loch Killin*. (*Imperial War Museum*)

Then, in the attack, new tactics would be needed. It was expected that a stern chase would become the norm, and ships would no longer run out between attacks, due to the increased enemy speed.

It was important that the fast U-boat was given no warning of an escort's counter-attack, to avoid her escaping at high speed. This, together with the 'dead' time needed to get ahead of the U-boat before firing depth charges from the stern, seemed to the RN to spell the end of depth charges as an offensive weapon against the U-boat. This, in itself, was a dramatic turn of events. The USN, on the other hand, thought that their new Mark 14 depth charges, with an acoustic proximity fuse, then under development, would be as effective as the Hedgehog against the new U-boats. The Admiralty did not agree with this view. Both navies agreed on the probable difficulties in switching Foxer gear on and off, during the search procedures, and yet maintain protection against Gnat torpedoes.

But, luckily, ahead-throwing weapons had been developed very quickly over the past few years. By this time all support group frigates, and most of the close escort ships, had the Hedgehog, and the new 'Loch' class frigates, with a double Squid mortar, and the 'Castle' class corvettes with a single, were coming into service in increasing numbers in the RN, and in part in the RCN. Indeed, the success rate in U-boat actions for the three main weapons in the RN in the last few months of the war was in itself dramatic evidence:

60% for Squid-fitted ships
28% for Hedgehog-fitted ships
5% for depth-charge attacks

It was the Admiralty view that against the fast U-boats, even the Hedgehog, with a 60-second sinking time to 1,300 feet, would be less effective than the Squid, with a 30-second equivalent. But in coastal waters this difference would have been less serious, though the moral effect of the Squid explosions on a U-boat crew would still be much more significant.

The USN agreed with this view in principle, but did not adopt the Squid. Instead, double Hedgehogs were recommended, and it is interesting to find these in some of the USN postwar DE A/S conversions, as illustrated in this book.

It was expected that attacks would be carried out at slow speeds, once the enemy was detected, using a number of ships in creeping attacks, as developed in the later war years. Highly-trained crews, and close co-ordination by high-frequency radio-telephone, would be essential to success.

The greater speed of the frigates, in arriving at the scene of U-boat attack, and in chasing a fast U-boat after detection, would be important. The turbo-electric 'Captain' class ships could be pushed to 26 knots easily, and the other frigates made a good 20; but the 'Flower' class corvettes, heroic convoy defenders in the early war years, had clearly had their day. Even before war's end they were being earmarked for de-commissioning to reserve, their crews to commission new frigates.

The 'Hunt' class destroyers, in the Channel and North Sea, would hardly have been effective against these fast U-boats. Their speed, of 27 knots, was the highest of the war-built escorts, but they had no ahead-throwing weapons, and, as their class chapter shows, fitting would not have been practical. They were mostly earmarked for the Far East in 1945.

A new development, in the closing months of the war, had been the Sonobuoy, an American device to drop a buoy into the sea from the air, equipped with Asdic detection apparatus, to pick up passing submarines. This could have played a good role in this renewed battle.

Lastly, it is interesting to see that, as the capabilities of the fast U-boats were analysed, not only were new tactics worked out for the existing escort forces, but new weapons were planned as well. Thus as early as March 1944 an RN staff paper was calling for A/S homing torpedoes, fired from an escort, and a development of the Squid as an A/S gun, with a range of 600 yards or more! So the next steps in the war of technology were already under way, a full year before the first Type XXI and Type XXIII boats entered operational service.

But the backbone of the defence against these fast submarines would, in 1945/46, have been the highly-trained support groups of new frigates, and the Squid mortar, backed up by the Hedgehog. We can see that, when the escort building programmes were cut back drastically at the end of 1943, it was the large numbers of the 'Captain', 'Loch' and 'Castle' classes that were cut down. In the event, the extra ships were not needed, but if the war had continued into 1946 it would have been the quality of the new escorts and A/S weapons that would have counted, and not just the numbers of war-built escorts available. We might well have seen a revival of the 'Loch' and 'Castle' class building programmes in 1945.

So the battle would have taken a fresh turn. It would have been increasingly fierce, with higher losses on both sides, and the outcome would have been hard to predict.

## ESCORT CARRIERS

Although this book is mainly concerned with war-built escorts of frigate or corvette type, we should briefly outline also the important wartime building programmes for escort carriers, as they operated in close conjunction with the escorts.

The need for the carriers to operate with convoys outside the effective range of shore-based aircraft was seen early in the North Atlantic battle; and once the escort carriers came into commission their additional value in assault operations, and in fleet operations in the Mediterranean and northern waters, and very widely in the Pacific, was quickly seen.

The full story of the escort carriers has been well told elsewhere; but an outline follows of the role the RN saw them playing, mainly in the anti-submarine battle. For the far greater numbers of CVEs built for the USN the emphasis was in part on the Hunter-Killer groups of the mid-Atlantic areas, in 1943-45, but much more on their employment in every type of operation in the Pacific. The RN, too, had a significant number earmarked for the British Pacific Fleet in 1945.

A table is attached, showing how the first programme of US-built escort carriers was of great benefit to the RN, but when the USN in 1943 refused further ships as a follow-on, due to their Pacific requirements, the RN MAC ship programme became vital, as an alternative method of air protection for convoys.

The Admiralty requirement for escort carriers for trade protection, as opposed to fleet operations, ran between 20 and 30 ships. In effect, there were probably never more than 10-12 escort carriers so employed, as the tables show. But it is interesting to see that, to have achieved the target of 20-30 ships on convoy work, and the second target for assault and fleet operations, and allowing for refits and war losses, the RN were planning for 83 escort carriers in commission!

The first Admiralty plan for employment of escort carriers with convoys, in 1943, allocated 30 ships as follows:

| | |
|---|---|
| West Indies—UK (oil) | 1 |
| West Indies—Mediterranean (oil) | 1 |
| USA—Mediterranean | 4 |
| USA—UK (North Atlantic) | 8 |
| UK—Mediterranean (slow convoys) | 3 |
| UK—Mediterranean (fast convoys) | 2 |
| UK—Freetown | 3 |
| Mid-Ocean Reinforcements | 4 |
| Refits, etc. | 4 |
| TOTAL | 30 |

But before the end of that year the Admiralty had produced an alternative plan, to copy the successful USN CVE group operations then under way in the mid-Atlantic. This would have provided for carrier groups, each of 1 or 2 escort carriers, plus 6 escorts, three of the latter to be free to be detached for hunting.

A preliminary plan would then have allocated escort carriers as follows—and note that this would have required 60 of the latest escorts to be detached for these operations, rather than being in the support groups or close escorts. In fact, shortage of escort carriers dictated that only on a few occasions were these ships attached to escort groups for Hunter-Killer operations, the 2nd and 3rd Escort Groups being among those so involved; but the need for escort carriers to stay with convoys, and the difficult flying conditions in northern waters, especially in winter, produced a different picture from that of the US 10th Fleet.

| | | | | | |
|---|---|---|---|---|---|
| Support in North Atlantic | 6 | carriers | + | 18 | escorts |
| Offensives in, eg, Bay of Biscay | 6 | ,, | + | 18 | ,, |
| West Africa and Brazil | 2 | ,, | + | 6 | ,, |
| S. Africa and Mozambique Channel | 2 | ,, | + | 6 | ,, |
| Arabian Sea | 2 | ,, | + | 6 | ,, |
| Ceylon | 2 | ,, | + | 6 | ,, |
| Totals | 20 | carriers | + | 60 | escorts |

It was noted that further carrier groups would be required for the Gibraltar run, for the Russian convoys (to which some 6 were, in fact, diverted), and possibly the Bay of Bengal.

## ESCORT CARRIERS IN COMMISSION

| | US-BUILT Escort Carriers | Escort Carriers | UK-BUILT MAC Ships | WAR LOSS | TOTAL |
|---|---|---|---|---|---|
| 1.1.43 | 14 | | | 2 | 12 |
| 1.6.43 | 22 | 1 | | 2 | 21 |
| 1.1.44 | 31 | 6 | 12 | 3 | 46 |
| 1.6.44 | 31 | 6 | 15 | 3 | 55 |
| 1.1.45 | 31 | 6 | 18 | 4 | 59 |
| 1.6.45 | 31 | 6 | 18 | 5 | 60 |

NOTES
1. US-built escort carriers totalled 36 for the RN, 78 for USN.
2. 1 escort carrier was manned by the RCN (and was a war loss).
3. No MAC ships were lost.
4. Escort carriers were employed roughly as follows:

| | 1943 | 1944 | 1945 |
|---|---|---|---|
| In commission | 21 | 37 | 35 |
| Lest refitting, etc. | 7 | 13 | 12 |
| Total | 14 | 24 | 23 |
| On fleet operations | 5 | 10 | 23 |
| On trade convoy escort | 9 | 14 | 0 |

Part of the naval piers at Halifax, Nova Scotia, 3rd August 1944. AN RCN frigate support group is just returning from patrol; *La Salle* is alongside, *Charlottetown* and *Kokanee* in the stream. *(Public Archives of Canada)*

## TYPICAL PARTICULARS OF US- BUILT ESCORT CARRIER

Displacement    11,420 tons
Dimensions (feet)492 oa, 69 breadth, 23 depth
Machinery       Geared turbines SHP 9350, 1 shaft
Speed           17 knots
Armament      2 single 4″
                  5-8 twin 40mm Bofors
                  20 single 20mm Oerlikons
                  18-24 aircraft

## GERMAN U-BOATS—THE ESCORTS' MAIN ENEMY

| | | TYPE VIIC | TYPE IXC | TYPE XXIC | TYPE XXIII | TYPE XXVI (WALTER) |
|---|---|---|---|---|---|---|
| Number completed | | 660 | 200 | 125 | 60 | 3 |
| Displacement | surfaced | 769 | 1,120 | 1,621 | 232 | 1,621 |
| | submerged | 871 | 1,232 | 1,819 | 256 | 1,819 |
| Dimensions | length (feet) | 220 | 244 | 252 | 112 | 252 |
| | breadth | 20 | 21 | 22 | 10 | 22 |
| | draught | $15\frac{3}{4}$ | $18\frac{1}{4}$ | 20 | 12 | 20 |
| Machinery | | diesel-electric | diesel-electric | diesel-electric | petrol-electric | hydrogen-peroxide |
| Shafts | | 2 | 2 | 2 | 1 | 2 |
| BHP | | 2,800 | 3,000 | 4,000 | 600 | |
| Fuel, tons | | 114 | 200 | 250 | 18 | 250 |
| Speed | surfaced | 16 | $18\frac{1}{2}$ | $15\frac{1}{2}$ | $9\frac{3}{4}$ | 20 |
| | submerged | $7\frac{1}{2}$ | $7\frac{1}{2}$ | $17\frac{1}{2}$ | $12\frac{1}{2}$ | $22\frac{1}{2}$ |
| Endurance | surfaced | 6,500×12 | 11,000×12 | 11,150×12 | 2,800×8 | |
| | submerged | 80×4 | 63×4 | 285×6 | 113×6 | |
| | | | | 110×10 | 43×10 | |
| Guns | | 1 3.5″ | | | Nil | |
| | | 1 37mm | 1 37mm | 2 twin 30mm | | |
| | | 2 20mm | 2 20mm | | | |
| Torpedo Tubes | | 5 21″ | 6 21″ | 6 21″ | 2 21″ | 6 21″ |
| Torpedoes | | 14 | 19-22 | 20 | 2 | 20 |
| Crew | | 44 | 50 | 57 | 14 | 50? |

## CONVOY ONS 4   WESTBOUND, APRIL 1943

### Close Escort

*B2 Group (RN)*
2 pre-war destroyers   *Hesperus* (SO), *Whitehall*
5 'Flower' class corvettes   *Gentian, Clematis, Campanula, Heather, Sweetbriar*
1 pre-war trawler   *Cape Argona*
2 rescue trawlers

## Support Groups

*5th Escort Group (RN)*
1 escort carrier—*Biter*
3 war-built destroyers  *Opportune, Obdurate, Pathfinder*
*1st Escort Group (RN)*
1 pre-war sloop  *Pelican* (SO)
3 'River' class frigates  *Jed, Spey, Wear*

The convoy was a very slow one, as it included some coasters, not suited to the North Atlantic. It was soon hove-to in a gale, and 2 stragglers returned to the UK. *Whitehall* brought the Iceland section in; she sighted and chased a U-boat, en route.

Next day there was H/F D/F evidence of U-boat activity. A Liberator attacked one 28 miles from the convoy; *Whitehall* was despatched to kill, but could not make contact. The convoy was still only making good 3 knots in a gale. It was diverted north, near Cape Farewell, and the escorts were able to fuel from a tanker in the convoy. The escort carrier *Biter*, with her destroyer escort, joined that day, remaining over the horizon for tactical reasons.

It was clear the convoy was passing through a U-boat patrol line, and a sighting report 20 miles away was intercepted. *Hesperus* swept out at high speed, and sighted and hunted that U-boat to a probable kill.

During the next three days there was much H/F D/F activity. On Easter Day the escorts detected at least one U-boat near *Biter;* she was warned, flew off Swordfish patrols, and a U-boat was attacked nearby. The destroyer *Pathfinder* of her escort despatched it.

An early North Atlantic convoy photograph. The 'Flower' class corvette *Hibiscus* is in the foreground; note no radar yet fitted, the foremast stepped before the bridge, and the short forecastle. *(Imperial War Museum)*

Two days later the 5th Escort Group, *Biter* and her destroyers, left for Newfoundland, and the 1st Escort Group joined. A further sighting report was heard, but a diversion by the convoy threw off the attackers.

Soon they were among icebergs, a most serious menace during the night. 16 days out from Liverpool, B2 escort group, the close escort, was relieved by the Canadian Western Local escort, HMCS *St. Francis* (SO).

This was a typical mild convoy battle of this period. Co-operation between the escorts was improving fast, but this was also one of the first occasions when an escort carrier and her destroyer escort were supporting a convoy, and much needed to be improved in R/T communications, and in agreement on tactics between the commander of the convoy's close escort and the carrier group. In the course of the action *Biter* dropped two depth charges—the first recorded instance in the RN of an escort carrier doing so. There were two escort tankers in the convoy for re-fuelling, with flexible rubber hose, and this difficult man-oeuvre was carried out with increasing success, even in bad weather. Difficulty was found in the flying conditions for the carrier's aircraft in these northern latitudes.

## CONVOY ONS 5—WESTBOUND FROM HALIFAX, APRIL 1943, 43 SHIPS

### Close Escort

*B7 GROUP (RN)*
*Duncan* (SO), *Tay, Sunflower, Loosestrife, Snowflake, Pink, Vidette* (Iceland portion)

### Support Groups

*3RD ESCORT GROUP (RN)*
*Offa* (SO), *Penn, Panther, Oribi, Impulsive.*
*1ST ESCORT GROUP (RN)*
*Pelican* (SO), *Wear, Spey, Jed, Sennen.*

In the opinion of the Admiralty, this was one of the outstanding convoy battles of the war. 5 U-boats were sunk, and the convoy losses (11 ships) avenged. It marked the end of large-scale attacks by U-boats, and the heavy casualties inflicted affected their morale. 45 attacks on U-boats were made by escorts in the vicinity of the convoy, and 340-odd depth charges fired by B7 and 1st Escort Groups, with only 2 failures. The success was seen to be the result of stiff training, showing that a close RDF ring of well-tried escorts around a convoy can defeat U-boats on practically every occasion. 6 attacks in one night were fought off without loss; convoy sinkings only occurred when the screen was reduced to 5, and then to 4 escorts—8 escorts was the minimum for safety. It was imperative that the Asdic equipment of all escorts in the ahead screen should be in very top order, and that escorts should point towards U-boats they were attacking, to escape torpedoes fired in retaliation. Well-tried Western Approaches tactics were again used successfully—Half Raspberries, Artichoke, and Apples.

Huff-Duff was again invaluable in giving warning of attacks, and actually resulted in several day sightings. The convoy went very far north, and hit both ice and gales; air cover was sporadic, but the Liberators gave magnificent performances in flying very long distances in appalling weather.

After departure on 22nd April the convoy had poor weather for a few days, while the Admiralty kept it posted with U-boat reports. On 25th two ships collided in a gale off Iceland, and at midnight there were no less than 7 ships burning the red lights signifying 'not under control'. On 26th, *Vidette* and the Iceland portion joined, but already the Senior Officer of the escort was getting worried about fuel levels. 3 escorts topped up on 27th; the following day a H/F D/F report showed a U-boat reporting another convoy nearby, but *Vidette* was sent to sweep 30 miles out, and passed the contact on to a passing Catalina!

At 1230 *Duncan* and *Tay* received a strong U-boat signal, *Duncan* swept out at high speed in 3 miles visibility, sighted nothing, but the convoy passed safely by the U-boat.

At 1830 a U-boat was sighted close on the port bow of the convoy; *Duncan* and *Tay* swept out at high speed, in a rough sea; the U-boat dived at 3,000 yards, and the Type 271 radar did not pick it up before diving. 10 depth charges were dropped by plot in the heavy sea, and *Tay* left to sit on the U-boat till an hour after sunset.

Then a series of night attacks began. H/F D/F bearings were received in rapid succession from the port bow, beam, quarter, and astern! At 2105, *Sunflower* got one by RDF on the port bow at 3,000 yards; she and *Tay* attacked without result. Then *Duncan* found one by RDF at $3\frac{1}{2}$ miles, lost contact, got it back, and attacked quickly with 10 depth charges. She got another RDF contact while still attacking the first, and dropped depth charges while the spray was flying mast-high, as she steamed into the sea. Returning, she found yet another, dropped charges at 12 knots and saw the U-boat's wake clearly under her port bow. *Snowflake* found another at 0140, dropped two patterns of 10 charges, was narrowly missed by a torpedo, then *Tay* took over and continued the attack.

Next day, several escorts swept for damaged U-boats and in following up bearings; at 0530 a ship in convoy was torpedoed, and the escorts followed their tactics of following up and attacking every contact at high speed, then returning quickly to their stations in the convoy screen.

3-4 U-boats were still in touch, but the weather was bad, all air cover was cancelled, and a full gale was blowing. There was more H/F D/F activity, and *Oribi* was homed in to support by R/T. *Tay* attacked a U-boat 49 miles astern, but no attacks were made that night, though the escorts dropped warning charges on several occasions.

At 0445 next morning Liberators were homed in, but another gale was blowing from ahead. A quiet day was passed, but at 2305 *Snowflake* sighted a U-boat, and drove it off under starshell. *Vidette* sighted a U-boat, and chased it at her maximum speed in that sea, of 9 knots! The convoy was by now badly scattered in the gale, and this continued for several days. The escorts were unable to oil, and the convoy altered course to avoid pack ice.

Next evening the 3rd Escort Group was homed in and formed an extended screen ahead during the night, while *Tay* and *Pink* stayed astern with the stragglers. *Duncan* ran too low on fuel and had to leave, handing over to *Tay*.

On 4th May the battle resumed in earnest. At dusk U-boats were reported on all sides of the convoy, and attacks continued throughout the night. At 2228 a straggler was torpedoed 6 miles astern, and *Loosestrife* attacked; then *Vidette* sighted and attacked, followed by *Snowflake* again. After midnight, *Sunflower* found one on the port bow, and *Snowflake* detected one on the port beam, and could not catch it, so called up the destroyer *Oribi* to take over.

Day attacks were continued throughout the next day, *Sunflower* and *Offa* attacking a U-boat which was firing at the convoy from ahead. By dusk, H/F D/F bearings were being received from all round the convoy.

That night no fewer than 24 attacks were attempted by the U-boat packs, without a stop, right through to 0420. There was a confused situation, but the escorts, by following their tactics of hitting every contact hard and then rejoining at full speed, more than held their own. No ships were torpedoed, but four U-boats were certainly destroyed, with one probable as well. All escorts were reported by the Senior Officer to have worked hard, capably, with intelligence and considerable humour, and the situation was always well in hand.

The following morning the Canadian Local Escort, under *Barrie*, joined from ahead, and some of the escorts were released to proceed to St John's to

A magnificent shot of an RCN 'Flower' class corvette at sea. This was *Battleford* in December 1941, with no radar, short forecastle, tall mainmast, all-grey camouflage and full minesweeping gear. (*Public Archives of Canada*)

refuel. But all was not quite over. At 0200 the next morning *Snowflake* got an RDF contact in poor visibility and sighted a 500-ton U-boat at 100 yards range. All guns that would bear opened fire, but the U-boat was turning inside the corvette's turning circle, and came up alongside her starboard side, with only a few feet separating them. She was in a sinking condition, but the corvette's guns could not depress enough to hit her. The ships drew apart, and the U-boat sank astern. The crew was encouraged to abandon ship by some bursts from the 2 pounder pom pom, plus some intimidation from the 4″ gun, which missed! *Sunflower* also just missed another U-boat by ramming just then, in the low visibility.

Then all was over, and the convoy arrived wearily but safely in harbour.

## CONVOYS ONS 18/ON 202 WESTBOUND, OCTOBER 1943

### ONS 18 Close Escort

**B3 GROUP (RN)**
2 pre-war destroyers *Keppel (SO)*, *Escapade*
1 'River' class frigate *Towy*
5 'Flower' class corvettes *Narcissus, Orchis, Roselys* (FFL), *Lobelia* (FFL), *Renoncule* (FFl)

### ON 202 Close Escort

**C2 GROUP (RCN)**
2 pre-war destroyers *Gatineau* (SO), *Icarus*
1 'River' class frigate *Lagan*
3 'Flower' class corvettes *Drumheller, Kamloops, Polyanthus*

### Support Group

**9th ESCORT GROUP (RCN)**
1 'River' class frigate *Itchen* (SO)
1 ex-American destroyer *St Croix*
3 'Flower' class corvettes *Chambly, Morden, Sackville*

This convoy marked the renewal of U-boat attacks in the North Atlantic, and the introduction of the German acoustic torpedo.

In the early stages the frigate *Lagan* was torpedoed. Then the attempt to join the two convoys together was difficult, due to thick weather and corrupt position signals. As a result, the close escort commander recorded, the two convoys 'gyrated majestically around the ocean, never appearing to get much closer to each other, and watched appreciatively by a growing swarm of U-boats'.

The next day there were four attacks on U-boats by ships of the close escort, and the corvette *Polyanthus* was torpedoed while attacking. During the night *Itchen* and *Narcissus* carried out a spirited action with a number of U-boats, and the following night, in similar conditions, the frigate *Itchen* was torpedoed and blew up, and the destroyer *St Croix* was also torpedoed and lost. There was much fog, and an aircraft from a MAC ship in the convoy, *Clan Macalpine,* made a miraculous landing on the carrier in a visibility of 50 yards.

The interesting aspect of this convoy was that no merchant ships were lost, but there were four successful attacks on the escorts, all at night, and in good conditions. When fog permitted, close air cover was provided to the convoy, and the carefully-rehearsed offensive tactics of the escorts paid off, surprising the U-boats in the fog, by radar detection.

## OPERATION 'GOODWOOD', AUGUST 1944

**Home Fleet, Force 2**

ESCORT CARRIERS
*Trumpeter, Nabob*

*5th ESCORT GROUP*
6 'Captain' class frigates *Bickerton* (SO), *Bligh, Aylmer, Kempthorne, Keats, Goodall*

After five days without incident, *Nabob* and *Bickerton* were torpedoed in quick succession. That night, *Bickerton* had to be sunk by our own forces, while *Nabob*, with three frigates as escort, proceeded at $8\frac{1}{2}$ knots on one engine towards the Faeroe Islands.

Next day, in a moderate gale, they were joined by the escort carrier *Trumpeter*, the Canadian destroyer *Algonquin*, and *Keats*. The 5th Escort Group was relieved by the 27th Destroyer Flotilla, and *Kempthorne*, with the survivors, returned to Scapa Flow with 520 on board.

*Aylmer, Bligh* and *Keats* then operated A/S patrols off the entrances to Thorshavn Roads, while Home Fleet units were refuelling there. Then they screened the fleet carrier *Furious* on return to Scapa Flow. From there they supported a convoy and then returned to Belfast.

This shows 'Captain' class frigates operating as Home Fleet escorts—an unusual situation. The Senior Officer of the escort group commented that diesel-electric frigates of that class were unsuitable for screening the fleet; they were a source of anxiety, since at their best speed they had little in hand for alterations of course. If they suffered a minor breakdown, they were unable to keep up even on a straight course. But groups of either all turbo-electric or all diesel-electric ships could not be organised, due to the difficulties in coping with a whole escort group of diesel-electric ships together in their lay-over period.

No contact with the U-boat responsible was made, due to impossible Asdic conditions. It was thought that *Bickerton* was hit by an acoustic torpedo which was still circling the wreck of *Nabob*—she was actually streaming her CAT gear when it hit.

## A SUPPORT GROUP TO RUSSIA, 1945

*19th ESCORT GROUP*
*Loch Shin, Loch Insh, Cotton, Goodall, Anguilla*

This was a typical Support Group patrol, of some five weeks, with a mixed group, composed of ships of the 'Loch', 'Captain' and 'Colony' classes, all frigates and all new.

The Group sailed from Scapa Flow on 17th April, screening the fast minelayer *Apollo*, and had an uneventful passage to Kola Inlet, along the route of the famous Russian convoys.

On their arrival they saw an aircraft attacking a U-boat in one of the new deep anti-submarine minefields. The ships streamed their Unifoxer gear (against Gnat torpedoes) on the edge of the minefield, and soon *Cotton* and *Loch Insh* gained a contact, which was attacked with the latter's Squid, though without result, a rarity for this new weapon. They observed and supported the arrival of convoy JW 66 on 25th April, with two escort carriers included in its close escort—another sign of increasing escort strength.

On 29th April they swept the Inlet ahead of the departure of convoy RA 66. *Loch Insh* found *U 307*, and destroyed her by Squid, but *Goodall* was torpedoed by a Gnat. 19th Escort Group gained a new submarine contact and had to stay with it, and *Anguilla* and *Loch Shin* attacked and severely damaged the U-boat. The 7th Escort Group (*Farnham Castle,* SO) was coming up astern, and *Honeysuckle* of that Group put her bows to *Goodall*'s quarter to take off the survivors.

Next day, with the convoy clear away to sea, the 19th Escort Group returned to the minefields area for a further sweep. No more U-boats were found, but the wreck of *Goodall*, still afloat, was sunk in a great explosion by *Anguilla*. The Group then caught up with the convoy, and stayed with it until new escorts from Iceland arrived to take over. The Group then returned to harbour.

## 3RD ESCORT GROUP IN THE IRISH SEA, JANUARY 1945

*(Operation CE)*

This was a typical inshore operation against U-boats in the final stages of the European war. The U-boats were using Schnorkel, and aircraft sightings were few and far between. The escort groups needed great care in evaluating wrecks on the bottom, tidal effects and rocks. The battle against the U-boats had entered a new and difficult phase.

The 3rd Escort Group, of 6 'Captain' class frigates, *Duckworth* Senior Officer, one of the crack Western Approaches Support Groups, was near Milford Haven, when a ship in convoy was torpedoed south of the Bishop Rock. In company with a group of 5 fleet destroyers, they carried out a sweep in line abreast down the swept channel, without success.

It appeared that the U-boat might be hiding on the bottom in St Bride's Bay, until he could use the last of the north-going tide to escape. 3 'Flower' class corvettes from Milford Haven, *Clematis, Moosejaw,* and *Roselys* (RN, RCN, and FFL), were detached to search the bay. A frigate and a corvette found a good bottom contact, but it was evaluated as a rock pinnacle, 36 feet high.

Next morning the 2nd Escort Group took over, the frigate *Loch Ruthven* got a resounding contact, and carried out a successful Squid counter-attack.

Then a ship in convoy was torpedoed off Holyhead, and the 3rd Escort Group, together with the 31st and 21st Groups, closed in a gale which reduced their speed to 11 knots. A second ship in the convoy was sunk.

The weather was unfavourable for Schnorkel operations, so it was concluded that this U-boat was bottomed on the ebb, to conserve his batteries, and would then go dead slow with the north-going tide. The 3 groups swept to the U-boat's 'furthest on' position, another group, the 6th, joined in, and each was allocated an area, to ensure radar and Asdic cover. The 3rd Escort Group swept Carnarvon Bay very carefully, and there was an aircraft sighting report, but all their contacts were assessed as 'non-sub'. The 31st Escort Group joined the 3rd at this point.

During the night *Duckworth* got a good echo-sounder contact and a bottom target was attacked. The weather moderated, making Schnorkel operations possible, and the search harder, for the U-boat was no longer forced to creep along in the lee of the land. A sector radar search was carried out, with one ship coast-crawling, to prevent him escaping round the coast.

To show how difficult the search was, *Duckworth* had a very small but very persistent radar contact 800 yards astern of her during the night. It turned out to be a 4 fathom patch, with overfalls! But the radar echo on a calm night was much like that of a U-boat's conning tower, low in the water.

While they were sweeping there was an underwater explosion off Llandudno; two groups raced to the scene, but without result. Then two ships were torpedoed in quick succession in the Clyde. The 3rd and 18th Groups rushed to the scene; the channel was crowded with shipping, and there were many 'non-sub' contacts.

The 3rd Escort Group finished its two-week patrol by helping to create an impassable escort barrier at every bottleneck through which the U-boats could escape, and two ships of the Group were assigned, to their disgust, to escort the Irish Sea ferry!

In this new type of search it was clear that teamwork, as well as escort numbers, was more critical than ever before, and with so many escort groups operating in such a restricted area the shore headquarters had a difficult but important tactical role in trying to co-ordinate their movements. The Group had carried out intensive inshore searches under difficult conditions and made many attacks but without tangible result. U-boats were being sunk in the inshore areas, however, and the very much greater number of escorts, most equipped with sophisticated search sets and attacking weapons, kept this new campaign under control.

## CONVOY HX 336 EASTBOUND, FEBRUARY 1945, 48 SHIPS

### Close Escort

B1 GROUP (RN)
1 'Castle' class corvette *Tintagel Castle* (SO)
1 'Captain' class frigate *Inman*
4 'Flower' class corvettes *Lotus, Poppy, Starwort, Dianella*
1 Mac escort carrier *Empire  Maccabe*

### Support Groups

23rd ESCORT GROUP (RN)
3 'Colony' class frigates *Montserrat* (SO), *Nyasaland, Papua*
1 pre-war destroyer *Montrose*
*19th ESCORT GROUP (part) (RN)*
1 'Loch' class frigate *Loch Shin*
1 'Captain' class frigate *Goodall*
*31st ESCORT GROUP (RN)*
4 'Castle' class corvettes *Berkeley Castle* (SO), *Carisbrooke Castle, Dumbarton Castle, Lancaster   Castle*

The weather was moderate, and there was no enemy activity. A sign of the times—the convoy came in through the South West Approaches, France having

'Flower' class corvette *Borage* at sea with her convoy. She shows many of the modifications installed. (*Ministry of Defence*)

been liberated, and detached sections to the English and Bristol Channels! Note three separate Support Groups, almost entirely of new ships, were in contact, and the close escort, also, was entirely composed of war-built escorts.

## THE FIRST SQUID KILL

Loch Killin *against U 736, 6th August 1944*

The new Squid ATW mortar, fitted in 'Loch' class frigates (double mounting) and 'Castle' class corvettes (single mounting), combined with new Asdic equipment, and especially the depth-finder, Type 147B, came into service in 1944 in some numbers. The crews trained very hard with their new ships, and evolved a smooth and efficient drill, with equipment which operated faultlessly. The rate of kills in Squid attacks soon rose to 80%, compared with 28% with Hedgehog, and 5% with depth charges.

This first successful attack was a dramatic one. *Loch Killin* carried out her Squid drill smoothly, but then things happened fast, after the terrific Squid explosions.

The U-boat fired a Gnat during the attack, and this torpedo exploded less than a second after the Squid projectile, and only 20 yards off the port side of the frigate. It was not known if it was running parallel or on a collision course at the time!

The effect of the Squid pattern on the U-boat was dramatic. It surfaced right under the frigate's stern, as she ran past the attack position, and as it hung there 14 survivors managed to climb out onto the frigate's quarterdeck, before the submarine plunged to its doom almost vertically. The port twin Oerlikon got in a burst on the conning tower as it disappeared.

## TYPICAL COMPOSITION OF ESCORT GROUPS

| | | |
|---|---|---|
| 1.1.40 | *Destroyer Div* | 2 'V' and 'W', or pre-war 'A' to 'I' class |
| 1.1.41 | *2 EG* | 2 destroyers, 4 'Flower' |
| 1.1.42 | *36 EG* | 2 pre-war sloops, 7 'Flower' |
| | *11th Corvette Group (Alex)* | 4 'Flower' |
| 1.1.43 | *42 EG* | 2 destroyers, 4 'River' |
| | *37 EG* | 1 'Black Swan', 10 'Flower' |
| | *B3 EG* | 2 destroyers, 1 'River', 2 'Flower' |
| 1.1.44 | *B5 EG* | 1 'River', 5 'Flower' |
| | *C3 EG (RCN)* | 1 'River', 7 'Flower' |
| | *3 EG* | 6 'Captain' |
| | *37 EG (Algiers)* | 2 pre-war sloops, 1 'River', 2 'Flower' |
| 2.6.44 | *B5 EG* | 1 'River', 5 'Flower' |
| | *6 EG (RCN)* | 6 'River' |
| | *15 EG* | 6 'Captain' |
| | *B3 EG* | 3 'Colony', 3 'Castle' |
| | *C4 EG (RCN)* | 2 'River', 6 'Flower' |

|           | 58 EG (Freetown) | 5 'River'                                      |
|-----------|------------------|------------------------------------------------|
|           | W1 EG (RCN)      | 5 'Flower'                                      |
| 1.1.45    | 9 EG (RCN)       | 1 'Loch', 6 'River'                             |
|           | C4 EG (RCN)      | 2 'River', 6 'Flower'                           |
|           | 2 EG             | 2 'Loch', 1 'Black Swan', 3 'Colony'            |
|           | 7 EG             | 2 'Black Swan', 2 'Castle', 1 'Flower'          |
|           | 3 EG             | 6 'Captain'                                     |
|           | 60 EG (Ceylon)   | 2 'Black Swan', 8 'River'                        |
|           | W2 (RCN)         | 1 'Algerine', 4 'Flower'                         |
| 7.5.45    | B2 EG            | 1 'River', 1 'Captain', 1 'Castle', 4 'Flower'   |
|           | 12 EG            | 2 'Black Swan', 1 'River', 1 'Loch', 3 'Colony' |
|           | 7 EG             | 1 'Black Swan', 4 'Castle', 3 'Flower'          |
|           | 16 EG (RCN)      | 5 'River'                                        |
|           | 3 EG             | 6 'Captain'                                     |
|           | C2 EG (RCN)      | 2 'River', 5 'Flower'                            |
|           | 58 EG (Freetown) | 5 'River'                                        |
|           | 77 EG (Ceylon)   | 4 'River'                                        |
|           | W2 EG (RCN)      | 1 'Algerine', 4 'Flower'                         |
| 3.8.45    | TF 11.2 (BPF)    | 5 'Black Swan', 9 'River'                        |
|           | 31 EF (BPF)      | 5 'Black Swan', 3 'River'                        |

*Atholl*, a Canadian Modified 'Flower' class corvette, coming alongside a consort at sea to exchange papers. Note the paint worn away from the forefoot by constant pounding in heavy seas. (*Canadian Forces Photo Unit*)

## GERMAN U-BOAT SINKINGS

**How the new escorts took over the battle**

| | | Pre-war built ships | War-built ships | Total |
|---|---|---|---|---|
| 1939 | | 6 | 0 | 6 |
| 1940 | | 11 | 3 | 14 |
| 1941 | | 25 | 13 | 38 |
| 1942 | | 25 | 17 | 42 |
| 1943 | | 32 | 45 | 77 |
| 1944 | | 23 | 79 | 102 |
| 1945 | (4 months) | 6 | 43 | 49 |
| | (equivalent for year) | 18 | 129 | 147 |

NOTES
1. The pre-war built ships held the line until 1943, when the flow of new ships reversed the proportionate involvement.
2. In 1944 and 1945, the involvement in kills of pre-war ships was rapidly declining, while that of the new escorts was increasing by some 50% each year.
3. The number of surface vessels involved in kills was increasing rapidly each year, despite the escort production cutbacks at the end of 1943, and the refitting or departure of numbers of new escorts for the Far East.

## POSSIBLE TOTALS OF OPERATIONAL ESCORTS AND U-BOATS AT END 1945

The following numbers are only approximate, but indicate how the situation might have changed, if the European war had not ended in May 1945.

| | *Operational May 1945* North Atlantic and UK inshore only | *Operational End 1945* Total including ships cancelled | *Maximum Possible End 1945* if 1943 escort and 1945 U-boat production speeds kept up | | |
|---|---|---|---|---|---|

### ESCORTS

| | | | Active | Reserves | Total |
|---|---|---|---|---|---|
| RN | 235 | 400 | 830 | 453 | 1283 |
| RCN | 200 | 260 | 225 | 160 | 385 |
| USN (Atlantic) | 50? | 50? | 100? | | 100? |
| Totals | 485 | 710 | 1155 | 613 | 1768 |

### U-BOATS

| | | | | | |
|---|---|---|---|---|---|
| Types VIIC and IX | 260 | | 430 | | |
| Types XXI and XXIII | 6 | | 300 | | |
| Type XXVI | | | | | |
| Total | 266 | Total | 780 | | |
| | | Less est losses | 200 | | |
| | | Total | 580 | | |

*Photo opposite: Kapuskasing,* a Canadian 'Algerine' class escort vessel, at sea with a convoy. The 12 RCN ships of this class were completed for escort duties only, and carried no minesweeping equipment. Note the H/F D/F aerial at the masthead, four twin power-mounted Oerlikons, and full depth charge outfit. (*Public Archives of Canada*)

COMMENTS

1. Note the closing gap between the numbers of U-boats and the numbers of escorts in European waters. In May 1945, some 50 U-boats were tying down some 380 escorts in UK inshore waters, but higher numbers of U-boats in those waters would not necessarily have needed more escorts to contain them.

2. RN escorts had commitments all over the world. When the war in the Mediterranean diminished, there was the increasing demand for escorts in the Indian Ocean and Pacific. But had the European war continued, and the fast U-boats really appeared in numbers, there can be little doubt that fewer escorts would have gone East, and the building programme would have been revived, giving more escorts of the very latest design.

3. The U-boat numbers shown for late 1945 assume that production would have been maintained, but that defects would still have limited the numbers coming into operational service by up to 50%.

## GERMAN U-BOAT CONSTRUCTION, 1939-45
**These figures are thought to be reasonably accurate.**

|  | Completed in period | Sunk in period | Total in commission | Trials and Training | Total | Operational N Atlantic UK coast | Med |
|---|---|---|---|---|---|---|---|
| Sept 1939 | 0 | 0 | 56 | 10 | 46 | 17 | 0 |
| Jan 1940 | 4 | 9 | 56 | 32 | 24 | 15 | 0 |
| Jan 1941 | 50 | 23 | 90 | 22 | 68 | 25 | 15 |
| Jan 1942 | 200 | 35 | 250 | 100 | 150 | 65 | 20 |
| Jan 1943 | 240 | 88 | 400 | 215 | 185 | 80 | 25 |
| Jan 1944 | 270 | 227 | 436 | 170 | 266 | 30 | 15 |
| Jan 1945 | 245 | 240 | 425 | 145 | 280 | 50 | 0 |
| May 1945 | 100 | 151 | 430 | 165 | 265 | 55 | 0 |

### COMMENTS

1. The enormous building programme in 1940/42 produced a very large rise in the number of U-boats in commission in 1942/43. The number under trials and training shows the massive problems the Germans experienced in bringing the boats into operational service; but the growth in U-boat numbers appeared rather sooner than the growth in RN/RCN North Atlantic escorts, and in between were the crisis periods of 1942/43.

2. Notice the comparison between the totals in commission, and the numbers operational in the North Atlantic. The latter figures were affected by the tactical flows of the battle, and the deployment of U-boats in other war theatres is paralleled by the wide spread of the RN frigates and corvettes into the Mediterranean, South Atlantic, and Indian Ocean.

3. Notice, too, how the total of U-boats in commission increased greatly each year, until the losses almost equalled the greatly expanded building programme. After that time, the increase in the total of U-boats was a slow and painful business, and the flow of the battle was largely dictated by changing technology and tactics, reflected in the battle areas, such as:
   —wolf pack attacks against numerically weak escorts, up to 1943
   —advances in RN/RCN radar, Hedgehog, and Squid, and escort and support group tactics, pitched against acoustic torpedoes, the Schnorkel, and the inshore campaign
   —the weapons of the numerous new escorts had not been pitched against the new Type XXI and Type XXIII boats before VE-Day.

4. Of all U-boat kills, 632 were at sea.
   Of these, 206 were by RN/RCN ships, 37 by USN ships.
   48 by ships and aircraft together, and of these, 35 were by RN/RCN ships.
   14 by RN shipborne aircraft, 29 by USN, reflecting the use of escort carriers in the North, as opposed to the calmer South Atlantic.

'Captain' class frigate *Bickerton*, operating with her Support Group in company with the RN cruiser *Kent* and escort carrier *Trumpeter*. She was torpedoed and sunk shortly afterwards. (*Imperial War Museum*)

*Ancon*, a USN landing HQ ship, under way with two USN PCs off the coast of France, 7th June 1944. *(US National Archives)*

## ENGLISH CHANNEL/NORTH SEA

### 1939

War dispositions took immediate effect in this, the closest area to Germany.

A strong squadron from the Home Fleet, called the Channel Force, was based at Portland, to guard the eastern Channel from attack; this included 5 destroyers. A further force of 2 modern cruisers and 8 destroyers was based in the Humber, and a Dover mine barrage was laid in October, which was effective in barring that passage to U-boats. The wartime swept channels arrived in these waters early.

The British Expeditionary Force, of 160,000 men, was safely transported to France, without reaction from the enemy. The ships were escorted by destroyers from the Local Defence Flotillas and from the Western Approaches Force.

### 1940

In the first half of the year there were some surprising German attacks on our coast, made possible by the shortage of destroyers for patrol work. In March a German ship laid a minefield off the North Foreland (in the Thames approaches), a U-boat laid magnetic mines off Portsmouth, and another surface vessel laid a field off the East Coast.

The minesweeping campaign was in full swing, and convoys stretched as far as 20 miles in the narrow swept channels around the coast. Many of the available escorts had to be switched to the Norwegian campaign, and the coastal convoys had very few escorts with them.

To this situation were now added German air attacks on our coastal shipping, along the full length of the south and east coast. The new 'Hunt' class destroyers, just commissioning, with their twin 4″ high-angle guns, took on a critical role in this battle. 19 joined the UK coastal escorts during the year, and, significantly, none as yet went to Plymouth, relatively free from air attack as yet. The old 'V and W' class destroyers were, however, still the backbone of our escort forces at this time, especially the 'Wair' conversions, with twin 4″ guns.

Then the German invasion of the Low Countries in May, leading up to the Dunkirk evacuation, changed the picture again. Reinforcements were sent to the Nore Command from the Home Fleet, including 6 cruisers and 8 destroyers. 41 destroyers were involved in the Dunkirk operation, 6 were lost and 19 damaged. They carried out every possible duty, and were usually able to withstand air attack if at sea, where they could manoeuvre at speed.

After Dunkirk, and the subsequent evacuations from Western France, anti-invasion measures were taken till the end of the year, covering the Wash to Newhaven. 4 destroyer flotillas, totalling 36 ships, plus destroyers and corvettes from the Western approaches, were kept in readiness, and it was accepted that merchant shipping losses in the Atlantic would probably rise as a result. The four main ports at which these destroyer and escort forces were stationed were the Humber, Harwich, Sheerness and Portsmouth.

## *1941*

This was a year of defensive tactics. The coastal convoys needed every protection against air attack, now that the Germans had bases near at hand on the Continent. Channel convoys became particularly hazardous, and the number of ships in a convoy was cut from about 30 to about 12, with 2 'Hunt' class destroyers and some 3 trawlers in each escort. At the beginning of the year there were 5 'Hunt's at Sheerness, 8 at Harwich, and 6 at Portsmouth.

There were also some 15 German E-boats operating against our coastal convoys, with torpedo and mine.

But even at this dark hour we did not entirely lose the initiative. Our destroyers made sweeps at night to the French side of the Channel, but few targets were found. One of our greatest problems at this time was in allocating the efficient new 'Hunt' class ships, now available in increasing numbers, between the narrow seas and the Mediterranean, where air attack was also menacing our shipping.

*1942*

The main event in this year was the passage through the Channel of the German battleships *Scharnhorst* and *Gneisenau* with the cruiser *Prinz Eugen* and escorts.

This has been fully described on many occasions; here, some comments are offered on the destroyer situation at that time.

The only destroyer attack on the German ships was made by 6 old 'V and W' class ships, from the Harwich and Sheerness flotillas. 6 'Hunt' class destroyers, exercising with them outside Harwich at the time, were left behind, as their speed was some 3-5 knots slower (25-27, against 28-30). But the 'V and W's were not 'Wair' conversions, with twin 4″ guns like those of the 'Hunt's, and so their A/A armament was very weak, and they sorely missed the support of the newer ships. Similarly, 12 'Hunt' class ships met the returning 'V and W' class destroyers on the UK side of the mine barrier, to give them A/A protection at that point, some 40 miles east of Harwich.

Three thoughts emerge from this:

1. If the German ships had been detected and reported earlier, the Nore destroyers would have had more time to intercept, the 'V and W' class ships would not have needed their maximum speed, and the 'Hunt' class ships could have gone with them, to give A/A and surface protection in the real battle area, close to the German ships.
2. None of the 'Hunt' class ships at the Nore was of Type III, with 2 torpedo tubes. The latter were just beginning to commission at the time.
3. It may be recalled that the original 'Hunt' class requirement from Director of Naval Operations in 1939 was for a ship capable of doing 30 knots and with 4 torpedo tubes. This is described in the 'Hunt' class chapter; if those 12 'Hunt' class ships had been built to that specification, the outcome, even at that late stage of the German ships' dash, might have been very different!

At the beginning of the year there were 5 'Hunt' class ships at Harwich, 6 at Sheerness, 4 at Portsmouth, and 6 at Plymouth. They were having an increasing influence on the war in these narrow seas.

The Germans were protecting their coastal convoys against them with torpedo boats, though there were in fact few encounters. Some of our destroyers attacked a raider passing down Channel in mid-March, though without result. 4 Type I 'Hunt's were involved in the raid on St Nazaire, and 8 in the raid on Dieppe in August, one, *Berkeley*, being lost (see the photograph). In October, another German raider was attacked, successfully, by 5 'Hunt's from Portsmouth, and 4 from Plymouth, with MTBs.

Finally, the UK shore radar stations were becoming effective in detecting raiding E-boats and directing our defending forces against them; this was a significant step forward, to be taken further by the 'Captain' class frigates in 1944/45.

## 1943

By the beginning of this year the force of 'Hunt' class ships had reached its maximum. There were 4 at Rosyth, 6 at Harwich, 9 at Sheerness, 4 at Portsmouth, and 9 at Plymouth. They were still supplemented by a few old 'V and W's, and by the half dozen 'Puffin' class corvettes at Harwich; but it was the 'Hunt's which increasingly took the offensive in raids across the Channel, and successfully defended our coastal traffic against the E-boats.

By now, air raids against our coastal shipping were rare, and, strangely, the Germans never committed their torpedo boats to cross-Channel raids at this time. They maintained destroyers in the west Channel area, however, and in October a force from Plymouth, including the cruiser *Charybdis*, 2 fleet destroyers, and 4 'Hunt's (3 of them of Type III, carrying torpedoes) engaged a German force off the North Brittany coast. The fight did not go well for our side—the cruiser and *Limbourne*, a Type III ship, were torpedoed and sunk.

Also in October, a force of 28 E-boats based in Holland attacked one of our East Coast convoys off Cromer; but little damage was done to the convoy, and 2 E-boats were sunk. But they continued actively on both coasts.

## 1944

The first five months of the year showed an increasing tempo, as the time for the invasion of Europe was clearly approaching.

Our coastal traffic was growing, and some 36 E-boats were active against it. The German coastal traffic seemed to be decreasing, but in February 4 'Hunt's from Plymouth damaged a German torpedo-boat and drove it ashore off the Brittany coast. 4 'Tribal' class fleet destroyers (3 of them Canadian), operating out of Plymouth, had a similar success. A 'Captain' class frigate and a Type III 'Hunt' unit fought a successful action against E-boats from Boulogne—a forerunner of the fighting to come.

The E-boats kept up their forays against our coastal shipping, and in April attacked a US invasion rehearsal, in Lyme Bay, and sank 2 LSTs and an escorting 'Flower' class corvette.

But it was essential that we had effective control of the English Channel before we committed vulnerable invasion convoys to it; and that control was now ours.

*THE ASSAULT ON NORMANDY*  Here, we can only touch briefly on the escort involvement in this great operation. The chart shows the great number of RN North Atlantic escorts brought into the English Channel for the assault; it will be noted that the Western Approaches Support Groups patrolling against U-boats at the western end of the Channel were in addition to these numbers.

During the assault phase the escorts based on the three Channel Commands were mainly employed as close escorts to the very large numbers and different types of convoys. There were convoys of merchant ships fitted out as motor and troop transports, liners carrying troops, landing craft of all kinds in profusion, and each convoy escorted by 2 or 3 well-experienced frigates, sloops or corvettes.

Extra close-range weapons were added to these ships, and they were alert against U-boats, E-boats, small battle units, flying bombs and, in the Dover Straits, the 15″ long-range guns from Calais. All were active, and many actions took place. Some frigates and destroyers carried out lone patrols in mid-Channel, to intercept E-boats, and some turbo-electric 'Captain' class frigates operated as coastal forces control frigates, taking with them a 'Hunt' class destroyer and some 6 MTBs, to attack E-boats and coastal shipping off Le Havre and Cherbourg, the frigate's superior radar being used to detect enemy forces, and the other ships being vectored in to attack with the frigate by radio-telephone.

The RN escort forces were, naturally, far more numerous than those of the USN. As an example, while 31 RN 'Captain' class ships were directly involved, with most of the other 40 ships of the class in the Support Groups in the west Channel, USN DEs numbered 7, with 28 PCs. RN ships supplemented the USN escorts to the western assault forces, and 3 Type III 'Hunt's carried out bombardments close inshore, during the US assault on the Pointe du Hoc.

The Germans laid large numbers of influence mines throughout the assault area, causing a number of sinkings. At night, German light forces attacked the invasion fleet anchored close inshore, surrounded by a defensive ring of escorts; and in this circle, in three days, 3 RN fleet minesweepers of the Lease-Lend 'Catherine' class were lost by midget submarine torpedoes. A 'Captain' class HQ ship, *Lawford*, was also lost, on 8th June, by German bombing in the assault area, and the USN lost a DE and a PC to ground mines.

RN destroyer and frigate patrols were active at night throughout the eastern Channel area, and the US screen west of the beaches included 3 DEs and 9 PCs. The latter were later involved in repelling German raids down the west coast of the Cherbourg peninsula, launched from the Channel Islands.

There were 36 U-boats in the Biscay bases on 6th June, and more in Norway. All sailed for the assault area, but after many battles only about 7 got through, and the Schnorkel-fitted boats, which could escape the aircraft searches, were the successful ones. They sank 2 frigates, a corvette and a few ships from the invasion convoys; but their own losses were very heavy, and the escorts were relieved that the battle went so well. One convoy off Selsey Bill lost 4 Liberty ships, as an example of what might have happened.

In July there were still U-boats on the invasion convoy routes—and being sunk as far east as Brighton; but their successes were still minimal.

The small battle units, midget submarines and explosive motor boats, were very active on a number of occasions round the assault area in July and August; they were vulnerable to the depth charges and guns of the escorts, and most were sunk, though they in their turn also sank a 'Hunt' class destroyer and some smaller ships.

By the end of August the invading armies had penetrated far enough to take the heat off the convoys in the Channel. U-boats were, however, still being sunk in that month by our frigates and corvettes as far east as Le Havre

The coastal forces control frigates, with their destroyers and MTBs, were in many actions off Cape Barfleur during the German evacuation of Le Havre, and Western Approaches support groups waiting off Brest to catch U-boats were attacked by glider bombs, one Canadian frigate being damaged.

But by September German forces had been driven out of the Channel (though the U-boats were to return a little later); the E-boats retreated to Ostend and Flushing, and the assault on Antwerp was the new focus of the fighting.

The coastal forces frigates, and their attendant destroyers and MTBs, were now operating from Harwich, while the Sheerness and Harwich normal 'Hunt' class units were responsible for the coastal convoys, and later the close escort of the Antwerp convoys, still assisted to the end by some 6 'V and W' class destroyers.

The frigates were operating at night with their units inshore near the Belgian and Dutch coasts for some weeks before Antwerp fell, and when that port was opened up in October fixed patrols were established along the convoy route from the Downs to Flushing, and up the Dutch coast towards Ijmuiden.

These patrols continued the type of fighting started off Normandy; the frigates directing the MTBs against the E-boats, and usually getting involved in gun battles themselves. The midget submarines and explosive motor boats also appeared in large numbers, and V1 flying bombs, as well as V2 rockets, were also much in evidence. The last three months of the year produced frequent actions throughout the area of the southern North Sea.

### 1945

So the picture was set for the final and hectic four months of the naval war in these narrow waters.

The Germans remained very active to the last, and actions were usually fought by all these ships on several nights a week. The winter was a rough one, but the E-boats were out on almost every night in February and March, and many fierce actions were fought, with losses on both sides. Merchant ship losses, mainly to E-boat-laid influence mines, were fairly light, but of the 8 'Captain' class frigates based at Harwich 3 were victims of these mines off Ostend or Holland, and 2 of these were written off as constructive total losses.

The midget submarines were also active, but had few successes. But one caught the Type III 'Hunt' class destroyer *La Combattante*, active under the Free French flag, and sank her; many of these small submarines were themselves sunk. A few blockade-runners trying to get through to Dunkirk, still in German hands, were also intercepted.

During these last months German bombers flew on many nights across the North Sea, carrying V1 flying bombs which they released within range of London. To combat this, *Caicos*, a 'Colony' class frigate converted to Fighter Direction duties for the Far East and fitted with Type 277 radar, anchored some 20 miles east of Harwich on most nights, and with fighters under her control, fought against this new menace.

Finally, U-boats returned to the North Foreland area for the first time since 1940. *U 245*, a Type VIIC boat, made two trips, and *U 2322*, a Type XXIII boat, also came over, and 3 ships in convoy were torpedoed. These U-boats were not detected.

It is surprising that the Germans did not use their destroyers and U-boats more actively in this area at this time, as they could have inflicted much more serious damage and loss on this really vital convoy route. But the escorts in the area were still very strong, as the chart shows, and the control frigate patrols nearest the Dutch bases usually had with them one or two Type III 'Hunt' class units, carrying two torpedoes each. The frigates were fully fitted and trained for A/S warfare, too.

Perhaps the outstanding impression of these few months was of strong escorts and patrols, and excellent use of advanced radar and radio-telephone techniques by the small and highly-specialised group of control frigates, with their destroyers and coastal forces. This was a very different war from that of 1939.

## NORTH ATLANTIC ESCORTS TO THE NORMANDY INVASION

| | *NORE* | *PORTSMOUTH* | *PLYMOUTH* | *TOTAL* |
|---|---|---|---|---|
| **Allocated for the Assault** | | | | |
| War-built fleet destroyers | 3 | 32 | 8 | 43 |
| Pre-war destroyers | 2 | 7 | 7 | 16 |
| TOTALS | 5 | 39 | 15 | 59 |
| 'Hunt' class destroyers | 1 | 3 | 2 | 6 |
| 'Captain' class frigates | 15 | 13 | 3 | 31 |
| 'Black Swan' class sloops | 4 | 4 | 3 | 11 |
| 'River' class frigates | 1 | 5 | 4 | 10 |
| 'Flower' class corvettes | 31 | 13 | 17 | 61 |
| TOTALS | 52 | 38 | 29 | 119 |
| **Permanent Escort Forces** | | | | |
| 'Hunt' class destroyers | 11 | 8 | 5 | 24 |
| 'V and W' class destroyers | 7 | | | 7 |
| 'Guillemot' class corvettes | 6 | | | 6 |
| TOTALS | 24 | 8 | 5 | 37 |
| TOTAL ESCORTS FOR THE ASSAULT | 81 | 85 | 49 | 215 |

NOTES

1. No Squid-fitted 'Loch' or 'Castle' class ships.

2. The permanent escort forces in the three commands represented less than $\frac{1}{4}$ of the total escort forces.

3. Most war-built fleet destroyers were in the centre and west Channel, to guard against German destroyer attacks.

4. The majority of the additional escorts were hard-bitten, experienced A/S ships from the North Atlantic.

5. 7 of the additional ships for Portsmouth were converted as LSH(S), assault headquarters ships.

## THE NEED FOR NEW ESCORTS IN THE NARROW SEAS
How they were retained after the Normandy assault.

| By classes, on dates | HARWICH | SHEERNESS | PORTSMOUTH | PLYMOUTH | TOTAL |
|---|---|---|---|---|---|
| **1st January 1945** | | | | | |
| 'Hunt' class | 10 | 16 | 0 | 4 | 30 |
| 'Captain' class | 11 | 3 | | | 14 |
| 'River' class | | | 5 | 1 | 6 |
| 'Colony' class | 1 | | | | 1 |
| 'Flower' class | | 12 | 9 | 18 | 39 |
| 'V and W' class | 4 | 5 | | | 9 |
| 'Guillemot' class | 6 | | | | 6 |
| TOTALS | 32 | 36 | 14 | 23 | 105 |
| **7th May 1945** | | | | | |
| 'Hunt' class | 15 | 22 | | | 37 |
| 'Captain' class | 8 | | 4 | 4 | 16 |
| 'River' class | | | 1 | | 1 |
| 'Colony' class | 1 | | | | 1 |
| 'Flower' class | | 13 | 14 | 23 | 50 |
| 'V and W' class | 4 | 5 | | | 9 |
| 'Guillemot' class | 6 | | | | 6 |
| TOTALS | 34 | 40 | 19 | 27 | 120 |
| **3rd August 1945** | | | | | |
| 'Hunt' class | 7 | 8 | | | 15 |
| 'Captain' class | 4 | | 4 | 3 | 11 |
| 'Flower' class | 6 | | 1 | 1 | 8 |
| 'Castle' class | | | | 2 | 2 |
| TOTALS | 17 | 8 | 5 | 6 | 36 |

*Opposite top:* The RCN 'River' class frigate *Swansea* preparing to tow another escort, in January 1944. An excellent view of the quarterdeck depth charge equipment, with charges on the throwers.
(*Public Archives of Canada*)

*Opposite below:* The crew of the destroyer escort USS *Fiske* (DE 143) begin to abandon ship after being torpedoed in the Atlantic, 2nd August 1944. (*US National Archives*)

*Overleaf:* A U-boat surrendering to the 'Captain' class frigate *Byron*, in May 1945. A fitting picture, as this class of frigate played such a prominent part in the A/S war in 1944/45. Note *Byron* has spray shields on her single 3″ mountings. (*Imperial War Museum*)

NOTES
1. Harwich and Sheerness carried the bulk of the close escort of convoys to Antwerp, and on the east and south coasts of England.

2. The 'Captain' class frigates at Harwich were the Coastal Forces Control Frigates, working with MTBs as the front line patrols against the enemy in Holland.

3. Note the continuing involvement of the 'Flower' class in close escort in this area.

## THE MEDITERRANEAN

When we examine this theatre of war it probably holds more surprises than the others, in the build-up of new, war-built escort vessels. For the Mediterranean fighting conjures visions of fleet carriers and cruisers fighting fast merchant ships through to Malta, and fleet actions against the Italian Navy.

But behind these fleet operations lay an ever-growing armada of new escorts, with not only nearly half the total ships in the 'Hunt' class of escort destroyer, with high-angle twin 4″ guns, but also a surprising number of new corvettes and frigates—and with Canadian corvettes, Australian A/S—M/S vessels, and Indian sloops fighting side by side with the RN.

The table in this chapter, giving these figures, is worth some study. Note the 'Flower' class corvettes based at Alexandria in the dark days of the Atlantic battle—building up to 27 by 1st January 1944; in the early days, these ships were used as fleet minesweepers ahead of the fleet, as much as they were for anti-submarine work.

There were 11 'River' class frigates there, in 1944, and 5 'Black Swan' class sloops. The Gibraltar Escort Force was largely occupied with the Atlantic approaches, but note that the greater number of frigates and corvettes were well inside the Mediterranean.

The A/S trawlers were also there in large numbers. All the war-built classes were well represented, including the entire 'Fish' class, and 29 of the 'Isles' class. There were 45 of them there in early 1944. Gibraltar had 8 of the 15 'Kil' class auxiliary A/S vessels—the US-built PCEs, which strangely were never classed as corvettes by the RN, though their capability was at least as good as that of the 'Flower'!

The peak of war-built escorts in this sea was reached in 1944, with 129 ships of various classes. At that time there were some 24 pre-war escorts there too, destroyers, sloops and trawlers. By early 1945 the strength was running down rapidly, as escorts were re-allocated to the East Indies and Pacific Fleets, while the A/S war was still raging round the coasts of the UK.

The US Navy, too, made a significant contribution to the strength of the escorts, from 1942 onwards. It is difficult to give accurate figures, as these are not yet available from official sources, but it is probable that about 50 DEs were involved in Mediterranean build-up convoys from the United States—in the spring of 1944 there were 10-12 DEs with each convoy, and some 70 USN escorts were present at the invasion of Southern France. Two USN DEs were operating for some 18 months, in 1943/44, with the RN 'Hunt' class force based on Algiers.

Predictably, the escort strength in the Mediterranean was run down quickly in 1945; by VJ-Day there were only 2 sloops, 7 'Hunt's, and 4 'Castle' class corvettes, the latter working as Air Sea Rescue Vessels, as they were not allocated to the Far East.

RN losses of escorts in the Mediterranean were heavy; 4 sloops (including

RAN), 8 'Hunt' class destroyers, 7 'Flower' class corvettes (including one RCN), and 5 trawlers.

## ESCORTS IN THE MEDITERRANEAN BATTLES

In *1939,* escort vessels in the Mediterranean Fleet numbered only 4, with destroyers in addition.

### 1940

100 Italian submarines were operational, and 46 were sent on patrol—a larger number than the Germans had on station in the North Atlantic. But they accomplished very little, and became easy victims, so that their number was soon reduced to 20.

3 sloops joined the Mediterranean Fleet from the Home Fleet, and 'Hunt's were soon to be seen helping to fight convoys through to Malta, from both ends of the sea.

### 1941

In April the withdrawal from Greece and Crete brought many losses to the Fleet. In addition to the 'Hunt' class destroyers, 3 'Flower' class corvettes from Alexandria were also there, active in both minesweeping and rescue work.

Supply convoys were still being fought through to Malta whenever the opportunity presented itself. One was forced through during this period, and on its arrival at Malta from the west it was led into Grand Harbour by the 'Flower' class corvette *Gloxinia,* the only minesweeper available, and her LL sweep exploded nearly a dozen mines on the way in. In others of this series of convoys, 5 'Flower' class corvettes were included in the close escort.

### 1942

The 'Hunt' class destroyers became an important factor in these battles. At Alexandria there were only 3 destroyer flotillas; 2 each of 8 fleet destroyers, the third, the 5th Flotilla, of 8 ships of the 'Hunt' class. If surface forces attacked a convoy, the fleet destroyers went out to the attack, while the escort destroyers remained with the convoy, for A/A cover and to lay smoke.

They were also involved in surface actions on occasion. In June, convoys were run through to Malta from both ends of the sea, and the eastern one had the A/A cruiser *Coventry* and 7 'Hunt' class ships creating a diversion. Other escorts also were playing their part. The 'Flower' class corvette *Hyacinth* captured the Italian submarine *Perla* off Beirut on 9th July, whilst the 'Isles' class trawler *Islay* sank the Italian submarine *Scire* off Haifa on 10th August.

In August came the great convoy operation 'Pedestal', from Gibraltar through to Malta. This famous convoy started with 14 fast merchantmen, escorted by 3 fleet carriers, 2 battleships, 7 cruisers and all the destroyers available, which, naturally, included a quota of 'Hunt' class units. It sailed from Gibraltar on 10th August 1942.

Almost immediately, the German and Italian attacks started. We cannot retell this famous tale adequately here, but will pick out a highlight or two.

Among all the air and submarine attacks, the destroyers were continually dashing about, keeping the ships roughly in station for maximum protection, providing constant A/A barrages, and picking up survivors from the many ships sunk. One, damaged by air attack and straggling behind, was escorted by the 'Hunt' class destroyer *Bramham*, keeping close to the African shore to escape air attack. But she was found late in the evening and sunk by bombers; *Bramham* picked up the survivors and raced to rejoin the convoy.

There was a successful attack by Italian submarines, while torpedo planes and bombers joined in, and it was in this action that the famous tanker *Ohio* received her first damage from a torpedo. Her compass failed and the 'Hunt' class destroyer *Ledbury* went back to guide her through the narrow channel. Air attacks continued, and when one of the other merchantmen was blown up by bombs, it was *Ledbury* again who rescued the survivors from the burning sea. Yet another ship was disabled, and this time it was *Bramham* who stood by, while *Ledbury* was off searching for the crippled cruiser *Manchester*.

Then the struggle to get the crippled *Ohio* into Malta was carried through to a successful conclusion. The Malta minesweeping squadron of 'Bangor' class fleet sweepers came out to assist, and it was a combined operation, with *Rye* towing, *Ledbury* steering by a stern line, and *Bramham, Speedy, Hebe* and *Hythe*, forming the protective screen.

One convoy from Gibraltar in this period included two tankers with their own escort of 4 corvettes to refuel the escorts en route—forerunner of the Pacific logistic groups.

Two 'River' class frigates of an RCN Support Group at sea, December 1944. *La Salle* in the foreground, with *Coaticook* behind; note the twin 4″ mountings forward, and twin Oerlikon mountings in each ship. The bombs on *La Salle*'s Hedgehog stand out clearly. (*Public Archives of Canada*)

Then came the invasion of North Africa—Operation Torch. There were 6 RN advance convoys, with 42 escorts for 82 ships. A typical escort consisted of 2 sloops and 6 corvettes and A/S trawlers were also included. The 6 RN assault convoys, similarly, had 50 escorts for 158 ships, which included 2 escort carriers. The North Atlantic escort groups were temporarily denuded for these operations.

The 3 USN convoys, impressively, had 75 escorts for 107 ships.

The total escort forces engaged comprised:

*RN*     43 destroyers, including 'Hunt' class.
    5 sloops
   13 corvettes
   20 trawlers
   15 fleet minesweepers
   ─────────────────────
   96 TOTAL

*USN*    38 destroyers
    8 fleet minesweepers
   ─────────────────────
   46 TOTAL

The Algiers assault force included corvettes and trawlers in the close escort to the landing craft, and the USN were using PCs effectively for this same purpose—a practice later widespread in the Pacific operations. Some good A/S work in the convoy phase was done by 'Hunt' class destroyers, including *Wheatland, Easton, Bicester* and *Lamerton.*

German U-boats were by now active in the Mediterranean, and by November 25 were operating there, out of some 200 boats operational in all. 5 were sunk during that month, plus 10 Italian submarines off North Africa. They had few successes, considering the flow of build-up convoys, but they did pick off some valuable troopships, and the escort carrier *Avenger.* The trawler *Lord Nuffield* (pre-war built) had the distinction of sinking one U-boat.

The corvettes *Starwort* and *Lotus* got one, too, in November, then *Lotus* another one, with *Poppy* this time, and using her Hedgehog.

*1943*

During the opening months of the year fast troop convoys were coming into Algiers every three weeks, and slower supply convoys in addition. Landing ships and craft were also convoyed locally, as required. An inshore squadron operated in the western areas, just as one had from Alexandria earlier, and included corvettes.

There were still 23 German U-boats and 12 Italian submarines operating in the western end, but they did surprisingly little harm and suffered heavy losses. 10 German and 8 Italian were sunk in a period of six months, but then reinforcements were not forthcoming to replace the boats lost, and they were down to 12 German boats by the autumn. But a convoy of tankers was badly mauled off the Azores, losing 7 out of 9 ships to a group of 12 U-boats, showing what could have happened with a less efficient escort force. It is interesting to remember that the U-boats were defeated in the Mediterranean some months later than their colleagues in the North Atlantic; during this period losses of merchant ships in the Mediterranean were averaging 12 per month.

The air battles, too, were continuing, as evidenced by the torpedoing of the 'Hunt' *Avon Vale.*

Some of the RAN 'Bathurst' class ships, from the 20 built to RN account but manned by the RAN, arrived in the Eastern Mediterranean in this period, as the Tunisian campaign finished, and the through route was reopened in May.

The 21st MSF was formed in Alexandria in that month, with *Gawler* (SO), *Ipswich, Lismore* and *Maryborough.*

The 22nd MSF was also formed, coming under the Levant Command and comprising *Geraldton* (SO), *Cessnock, Cairns* and *Wollongong.* They were attached individually to escort groups, rather than operating as one group, and were involved in attacks on submarines.

The convoys in the eastern waters were fought through without serious loss in this year, and both German and Italian submarines were sunk. E-boats were also operating against them, and RN 'Hunt's and MTBs were carrying out sweeps against them.

The *invasion of Sicily* in July occupied the escorts heavily, with many convoys building up. The RN and USN convoys joined up at Gibraltar, with mixed escorts, and one convoy, of 130 ships and 19 escorts, was the largest of the war to that time. There were many air attacks, with pitched battles as detachments split off to the various ports.

The RAN 'Bathurst's were active in the invasion, a typical convoy escort comprising 10 escorts, 1 RIN 'Black Swan' class sloop, 5 RN and 4 RAN corvettes. The RAN ships also helped escort the landing craft right in to their release positions, carried out endless chain A/S patrols off the assault anchorage, and swept for mines as well. They were also assisting to escort the long-distance convoys right through the sea, a typical escort of 1 'Hunt', 3 RN 'Flower', and 4 RAN 'Bathurst' being provided for 75 ships, or 5 RN 'Bangor' and 4 RAN 'Bathurst'.

The USN had 14 PCs operating at the Sicily invasion, and *PC 624*, escorting a small convoy from Sicily to Africa, sank *U 375* on 30th July.

Total escort forces for Sicily were:

| | RN | USN | Allied | TOTAL |
|---|---|---|---|---|
| Destroyers | 71 | 48 | 9 | 128 |
| Sloops, frigates | 35 | | 1 | 36 |
| Minesweepers | 34 | 8 | | 42 |
| TOTALS | 140 | 56 | 10 | 206 |

During this period we find 2 'Halcyon' class fleet minesweepers acting throughout as A/S escorts, and the 2 USN DEs operating with the RN 'Hunt's out of Algiers.

RN convoys for the invasion numbered 5 from the UK, of 113 ships, 4 from the Middle East, with 116 ships, and 6 from North Africa and Malta, with 167 ships. USN convoys numbered 7, with 358 ships.

There were heavy losses of submarines by both the Germans and the Italians during the invasion period, but there were notably few kills by newly-built escorts—2 were sunk by MTBs, and 1 by 4 'Bangor' class fleet minesweepers!

Next came the *assault on Salerno* in September 1943. The composition of the escort forces was interesting:

— the RN force, for 7 convoys of 179 ships, included 12 'Hunt's, 12 A/S trawlers, 19 minesweepers, 29 motor launches, and 9 USN PCs.

— the USN force, for 8 convoys of 244 ships, included 20 destroyers, 40 minesweepers, and no less than 37 PCs.

— in addition, the Support Carrier force included 5 escort carriers, 3 cruisers, and 7 'Hunt's as escort.

There were some good examples of inter-Allied co-operation. 'Hunt's were bombarding tanks close inshore, and USN *Wainwright* and RN *Calpe* together sank *U 593* in December, north-west of Algiers.

The German U-boats reacted strongly. 3 went to the assault area, but the escorts were too strong, and they only sank 2 ships. 9 operated against convoys along the North African coast and sank 10 ships, including 1 RN and 1 USN fleet destroyer, and a 'Bangor' class fleet minesweeper.

13 more U-boats were operating from Toulon or Pola, laying mines, but also using acoustic torpedoes with some success; 2 destroyers and a frigate were lost in December. Strong support for the escorts came from shore-based aircraft, due to the great advantage of airfields nearby.

Type I 'Hunt' class destroyer *Garth* with an East Coast convoy. This is an early photo; she has radar Type 286 at the masthead, and semaphores were still in use for communication. Bowchaser pom pom in the eyes of the ship. *(Imperial War Museum)*

The Germans also used glider bombs at Salerno and later, with some success, and some of the escorts, notably including two USN DEs, were active and successful with radio countermeasures.

In the eastern section of the Sea, the Levant Force was active in retaking the Greek Islands. There were some unhappy incidents in this campaign, and the 'Hunt's were prominent—17 of them. 2 were mined, one of them, a Type III Greek-manned ship, being beached, but *Hurworth* was lost. *Rockwood* was sunk by a glider bomb, off Turkey, as was *Dulverton,* and *Belvoir* was hit during a sweep in the Aegean. The 'Hunt' class certainly did manage to remain in the thick of the fighting, and made their mark many a time.

### 1944

The year opened with the *landing at Anzio.* The escort force was much smaller this time:
— RN, 7 'Hunt's, 12 fleet minesweepers, 4 A/S trawlers.
— USN, 10 destroyers, 2 DEs, 27 fleet minesweepers and 11 PCs.

The local convoys were by this time well organised, but they were involved in numerous actions, with glider bombs, U-boats, and air torpedo attacks, with E-boats also operating against them, and some midget submarines. Thus the A/S trawler *Mull* sank *U 343* off Sardinia, and the USN *PC 591* on 21st April destroyed a German Marder-type midget, after detecting it by radar at 6 miles; *PC 558* the same morning got another one, after seeing a small wake off her starboard bow and dropping depth charges. *PCs 528* and *626* shortly afterwards sank another. The pace was still hot. The French DE *Sénégalais* was torpedoed at the end of a long hunt by Allied ships against a U-boat, and the Schnorkel was now also in use in the Mediterranean.

Fighter direction ships were seen to be badly needed in this fighting, and the conversion programme for the RN 'Colony' class probably dated from this time. One convoy alone had 91 air torpedoes launched against it in one attack!

But the remaining U-boats were largely destroyed during this year, either at sea or by air attacks on their bases. By the time the *invasion of Southern France* was mounted only 3 were left, and only 1 was operational, so they could not affect that assault.

The escort forces for Operation Dragoon were as follows:
— RN, 7 escort carriers and 60 escort vessels, of which 21 'Hunt's and 2 'Flower's (with 5 Free French DEs) were attached to the US Task Group 80.6, the A/S and Convoy Control Group.
— USN, 2 escort carriers and 61 escort vessels, including 8 DEs and 16 PCs.

Small battle units were still active at this time, both Marder and Molch types, but they were mainly in the Adriatic, and convoys in the Mediterranean ended in September 1944.

During the Germans' retreat up the Dalmatian coast at the end of the year, 'Hunt' class ships were still in hot coastal actions. The need for fighter direction ships became even more clear. E-boats and small Italian escort vessels, manned by Germans, were also active in this area, together with Linsen explosive motor boats. The Type III 'Hunt' unit *Aldenham* was lost to a mine off Pola in December.

So the Mediterranean war drew to a close, a war in which the war-built escorts had played a prominent part, although the larger fleet units more usually hit the headlines. Then the escorts were re-allocated to the Far East campaign, and after refits moved to the East Indies and Pacific Fleets. These were tough, experienced escorts who would have played an equally important role in those campaigns, had the submarine and air attacks equalled the fury which had been hurled against them in the Mediterranean, as in the North Atlantic.

### The sinking of U 450 off Naples, March 1944

This was a fairly typical Mediterranean anti-submarine action. The sophisticated tactics of the North Atlantic escort groups were absent, and the Allied ships were fleet and 'Hunt' class destroyers; but when the U-boat surfaced, the gunnery, from twin 4″ mountings, was probably more accurate than that of frigates or corvettes. No ahead-throwing weapons were fitted in the ships involved.

On 8th March a U-boat was reported by a patrolling aircraft between Naples and the beachhead at Anzio. The 'Hunt' class destroyers *Exmoor* (Captain (D), 22nd DF), *Blankney* and *Brecon* (Types I, II and IV) were sailed at very short notice from Naples to hunt, under the codeword 'Cushion 324'. They were to rendezvous with two fleet destroyers of the 'T' class, and another 'Hunt', *Blencathra,* and carry out an offshore sweep.

Soon afterwards the weather deteriorated, and all anti-submarine aircraft were withdrawn. Next day the two fleet destroyers left for Naples, and the 'Hunt's carried out a sweep close inshore that night, in case the U-boat attacked the Anzio anchorage or the inshore convoy route.

At 1936 they heard the sound of depth charges not far ahead, from the USN destroyer *Maddison,* who had a good contact, but then lost it. The 'Hunt's formed up for a box search; *Blankney* got a contact at 2207, and *Brecon,* the nearest ship, joined her, while *Exmoor* and *Blencathra* patrolled round them in bright moonlight.

At 2227 *Blankney* dropped a 5-charge pattern, but the others had no contact. Just before *Blankney* dropped her charges she lost her Asdic dome and oscillator, as she hit the U-boat's jumping wire. After the attack, contact was not regained, and a square search yielded no result. *Blencathra* and *Blankney* returned to Naples, but *Exmoor* and *Brecon* remained, and were joined by the new fleet destroyer *Urchin* at 0400.

At 0423, *Brecon* got a contact, and *Exmoor* attacked it with 10 depth charges at 0440, but it sounded like fish. At 0507, *Exmoor* again attacked with 5 depth charges, dropped a calcium flare to mark the spot, but lost contact again. Then distinct hydrophone effect was heard, and *Exmoor* dropped a deep pattern at 0518, set for 500 and 700 feet.

At 0540 the U-boat surfaced 2 miles on *Brecon*'s port quarter, right in the path of the moon. She fired tracer from her pom pom, to indicate the target to

US Navy *PC 611* operating in the Pacific. Note the three single Oerlikons mounted on top of the bridge, and the slim hull form. *(US Navy Official)*

*Exmoor,* increased speed to 20 knots, and engaged with her main armament.

*Exmoor's* range was foul to start with, but she got a hit on the conning tower, and started a fire. *Urchin* and *Blencathra* also engaged the U-boat, and at this point salvos from *Exmoor* were landing very close to *Brecon's* stern, so *Exmoor* was requested to cease fire, which she did! *Brecon* closed, with the intention of finishing off the surfaced U-boat with depth charges, but at 500 yards she saw numbers of survivors in the water.

She launched her whaler, but it was just unable to reach the U-boat's bow before she sank vertically. 24 survivors out of a crew of 56 were picked up.

Points of interest in this action were that the U-boat was making $8\frac{1}{2}$ knots submerged, to the astonishment of the destroyer captains; and that in *Exmoor* the blast from the after 4″ mounting fractured an oil pipe to the after galley and started a fierce fire, which was soon brought under control.

*Urchin* returned to Anzio, but the 3 'Hunt's returned in triumph to Naples, arriving with their prisoners at 1145 on 10th March. Another 'Hunt', *Hambledon,* joined after delivering her convoy to Anzio, but was too late for the kill, so returned with *Urchin.*

## THE BUILD-UP OF NEW ESCORTS IN THE MEDITERRANEAN

| | 'Black Swan' Class | 'Hunt' Class | 'Flower' Class | 'River' Class | 'Kil' Class | Trawlers | Total |
|---|---|---|---|---|---|---|---|
| **1.1.41** | | | | | | | |
| Eastern Med | | | 4 | | | | |
| **1.1.42** | | | | | | | |
| Eastern Med | | 8 | 7 | | | | |
| Gibraltar | 2 | 3 | 6 | | | | |
| Total | 2 | 11 | 17 | | | | 30 |
| **1.1.43** | | | | | | | |
| Eastern Med | | 18 | 6 | | | | |
| Algiers | | | 5 | | | | |
| Gibraltar | 2 | 10 | 7 | | | | |
| Totals | 2 | 28 | 18 | | | | 48 |
| **1.1.44** | | | | | | | |
| Eastern Med | | 12 | | | | | |
| Levant | 1 (RIN) | 4 | | | | 4 | |
| Malta | | 14 | 3 | 1 | | | |
| Algiers | | 11 | 18 | 7 | | | |
| Gibraltar | 4 | | 6 | 3 | 2 | 41 | |
| Total | 5 | 39 | 27 | 11 | 2 | 45 | 129 |
| **2.6.44** | | | | | | | |
| Eastern Med | 1 (RIN) | 11 | | | | | |
| Malta | | 28 | | | | 4 | |
| Algiers | 4 | | 21 | 6 | | | |
| Gibraltar | | | 6 | 5 | 8 | 18 | |
| Total | 5 | 39 | 27 | 11 | 8 | 22 | 112 |
| **1.1.45** | | | | | | | |
| Eastern Med | | 17 | 10 | 1 | | | |
| Gibraltar | 1 (RIN) | | 10 | 1 | 7 | 15 | |
| Total | 1 | 17 | 20 | 2 | 7 | 15 | 62 |
| **7.5.45** | | | | | | | |
| Eastern Med | | 12 | 6 | 1 | | 8 | |
| Gibraltar | 1 (RIN) | | 9 | 1 | 7 | 2 | |
| Total | 1 | 12 | 15 | 2 | 7 | 10 | 47 |
| **3.8.45** | | | | | | | |
| Med. Command | 2 | 7 | 4 | 'Castle' class as ASR | | | |

## GERMAN U-BOATS SUNK IN THE MEDITERRANEAN

Ships were involved as follows:

|  |  | 1941 | 1942 | 1943 | 1944 | 1945 |
|---|---|---|---|---|---|---|
| **Pre-War Ships** | | | | | | |
| Destroyers | | 1 | 3 | 1 | | |
| | Totals | 1 | 3 | 1 | 0 | 0 |
| **War-Built Escorts** | | | | | | |
| Fleet Destroyers | | 1 | 2 | 1 | 3 | |
| 'Hunt' class | | | 3 | 3 | 4 | |
| 'Flower' class | | 1 | 2 | 2 | | |
| RCN 'Flower' class | | | | 1 | | |
| RAN 'Bathurst' class | | | | 1 | | |
| Trawlers | | | | | 1 | |
| MTBs | | | | 2 | | |
| US Navy Ships | | | | 3 | 3 | 1 |
| | Totals | 2 | 7 | 13 | 11 | 1 |

'Hunt' class destroyers returning from a Channel sweep. Type III *Eggesford* is in the lead; note the second ship still has twin yards on her mast. *(Imperial War Museum)*

## ITALIAN SUBMARINES SUNK IN THE MEDITERRANEAN

|                        | 1940 | 1941 | 1942 | 1943 |
|------------------------|------|------|------|------|
| **Pre-War Ships**      |      |      |      |      |
| Destroyers             | 8    | 4    | 2    | 3    |
| Sloops                 | 2    |      | 1    |      |
| Trawlers               | 1    |      | 3    |      |
| ex-USN 4-stackers      |      | 1    |      |      |
| ex-USN cutters         |      |      | 1    |      |
| Totals                 | 11   | 5    | 7    | 3    |
| **War-Built Escorts**  |      |      |      |      |
| Fleet destroyers       | 1    | 1    | 3    | 2    |
| 'Hunt' class           |      | 2    |      | 2    |
| 'River' class          |      |      |      | 1    |
| 'Flower' class         |      | 2    | 1    |      |
| RCN 'Flower' class     |      |      |      | 2    |
| 'Bangor' class         |      |      |      | 1    |
| Trawlers               |      |      |      |      |
| MTBs                   |      |      |      | 2    |
| US Navy Ships          |      |      |      | 1    |
| Totals                 | 1    | 5    | 4    | 11   |

A dramatic shot of the Type I 'Hunt' class destroyer *Berkeley* being hit forward by a bomb from a German aircraft during the 1942 Dieppe raid. She was later sunk by RN forces.
*(Imperial War Museum)*

# THE FAR EAST

As with the North Atlantic, we cannot hope in one chapter to paint a clear picture of the great campaigns in the Indian and Pacific Oceans. Our emphasis will again be on the build-up of new escorts, culminating in the great strength projected for the end of 1945.

## INDIAN OCEAN

In 1939 the escort strength in the Far East for the RN was small—5 escort vessels on the China Station, 4 in the South Atlantic Command, and 7 in the East Indies, of which 5 were RIN ships.

By January 1942 only 2 RN sloops were left in the area, apart from the RIN ships, but the RAN sloop *Yarra* was active in the evacuation from Java, and 3 RAN 'Bathurst' class ships with an old USN destroyer sank a Japanese submarine off North Australia.

But the Eastern Fleet had to retreat from Singapore to Ceylon. The first 'Flower' class corvettes arrived at this time, via the Cape, and while the Japanese Fleet was operating off the east coast of India *Hollyhock,* with other ships, was sunk by air attack 65 miles from Trincomalee. The Eastern Fleet withdrew to Bombay and Mombasa.

The RAN was by this time well into its construction programme of 'Bathurst' class A/S-M/S vessels, and their presence was to be very important in the next two years. Of the 60 building in the class, 20 were for RN account, and on completion, and with RAN crews, these were employed in the South East Asia and Indian Ocean commands. The first two ships actually commissioned in June 1941 for the East Indies. They were based on Aden until the end of the year, then moved to Colombo.

Thus 5 RN 'Bathurst's were in the SE Asia area by April 1942, and 3 more were in the East Indies by September. The 4 RIN units of the class were also a welcome reinforcement. At one time in mid-year the Eastern Fleet possessed 16 sloops and corvettes, of which 3 were 'Bathurst's; 12 were employed on trade protection in the Indian area, the other 4 comprised the Colombo A/S Force.

Surface raiders were also operating in the Indian Ocean in this period, and the epic fight of the RIN 'Bathurst' class *Bengal* in August 1942, to protect the tanker she was escorting, is well recorded.

### 1943

The fortunes of the Eastern Fleet remained at a low ebb. Some 48 ships, including some 'Bathurst' class, were withdrawn to the Mediterranean for the invasion of Sicily, and the remaining escorts were inadequate to provide convoy protection.

By now some 7 German U-boats were operating in the Indian Ocean, together with about the same number of Japanese submarines. 60 merchant ships were lost to them during the year, and while reinforcements, especially A/S trawlers, were brought up from the South Atlantic station (which was quiet at this time) the RIN escorts were critically important in this period, and once again it was seen how a relatively small number of submarines could cause considerable dislocation of traffic in a weak escort situation.

In the early months of the year 4 'Bathurst's were based on the East African coast, to ward off U-boat attacks, and there were notable occasions when a mixed RIN/RAN escort force beat off attacks on convoys. But this was little more than emergency work. The Commander-in-Chief, Eastern Fleet, recorded at this time that 'Bathurst' class ships and 'Bangor' class fleet minesweepers provided only token escort protection and suffered from equipment defects; long-range frigates were seen as the only effective answer.

### 1944

But reinforcements were on the way. In the opening months of the year some 54 extra escorts arrived on the station. But even with this help, many ships were still not sailing in convoy—an interesting comparison with the North Atlantic by this time. 19 U-boats were still active in the Indian Ocean, and 40 ships were lost to them and to Japanese submarines during the year. But by

A rare picture of the Type III 'Hunt' class destroyer *Limbourne*. She was torpedoed and sunk in October 1943 in an action with German forces off the Brittany coast. *(Ministry of Defence)*

year's end the U-boats' fuelling tankers were under attack, Penang had been closed to them by mines, and they had been forced to move to Batavia.

In November the British Pacific Fleet was brought formally into being, and the Eastern Fleet became the East Indies Fleet. But by this time the planned reinforcements were arriving in numbers, and even after the BPF departed the East Indies Fleet had 5 escort carriers and rapidly increasing forces of war-built escorts.

### 1945

The first major event of the year was that the German U-boats were ordered to leave for home by mid-January. 3 were lost on the way (one to a USN submarine in the Java Sea), 3 reached home safely, and 4 were turned over to the Japanese on VE-Day. One was operating off Australia at the turn of the year, and sank 2 ships.

But the result was that all ships except troopers were able to sail independently, and the escorts were freed to support the combined assault operations along the Burma coast.

The first operation was the Arakan assault, and the Akjab landing in January. Force 64 was formed to support the Army, and included 3 'River' class frigates and the 6 RIN 'Black Swan' class sloops.

During the follow-up operations some of the strangest RN actions of the war took place. Enemy craft were using the *chaungs,* or tidal inlets, and frigates and sloops were operating 20 miles up-river, carrying troops, bombarding enemy positions, and taking hits in return. There were Japanese trip wires strung across the rivers and attached to mines, troop ambushes for the ships, and, to ensure continuous entertainment, plentiful supplies of crocodiles, water snakes and mosquitoes.

A photo-reconnaissance group, Force 62, left Trincomalee late in February, including 2 escort carriers and 3 frigates, while Force 61, a tanker group, was escorted by another frigate. Next month a similar mission included a group of no less than 7 escort carriers together, and again the frigates and sloops acted as escorts.

This led up to the assault on Rangoon, with those escort carriers and with numerous escort vessels in attendance, also employed on shore bombardments. 2 flotillas of 'Algerine' class fleet minesweepers were also included, and they had received special A/S training before leaving the UK. The 6th Flotilla, of 8 ships and 2 'Isles' class danlayers, was employed almost entirely on escort duties. During these operations one 'Algerine' was lost on a contact mine, and a second to a Kamikaze suicide plane.

This was the last offensive action by the East Indies Fleet before the Japanese surrender. But note the balanced escort force which was being built up for the assault on Singapore—20 'Hunt' class destroyers, 20 'River' class frigates, 18 'Loch' class frigates (with double Squid mortars, the only such A/S weapons in the Far East), 3 'Captain' class coastal forces control frigates, and 14 'Flower' class corvettes for air-sea rescue duties. 6 assault group headquarters ships, LSH(S), converted from 'River' class frigates, were also allocated, and probably some of the 'Colony' class frigates under conversion to fighter direction ships would also have joined the East Indies Fleet. Details of these conversions are included in depth in the class chapters concerned.

## PACIFIC OCEAN

We will cover the RAN/RN sector first, separately from the USN operations for clarity.

First, in 1942, Japanese submarines raided Sydney, launching reconnaissance aircraft and then midget submarines. The attack caused some damage, and 3 of the early 'Bathurst' class units, including one for the RIN, were there and in action.

Then the Japanese submarines attacked merchant shipping off the Australian east coast, scoring successes against many unescorted ships. Convoys were quickly organised, and typically consisted of about 6 merchant ships, with one destroyer and one 'Bathurst' as escorts. There were many A/S attacks, but no successes.

During the evacuation of Timor and Papua, RAN 'Bathurst' class ships were active in transporting troops and stores, and *Armidale* was lost by air torpedo.

By 1943 the RAN 'Bathurst' strength had reached full peak. There were 3 sloops and 48 of these corvettes employed around Australia on escort work—15 in the north-east, 2 in the north-west, 2 in the south-west, and 14 on the south and south-east coasts.

## BRITISH PACIFIC FLEET

This brings us to the short, but eventful, career of this unique fleet. It was modelled on the highly successful US Fleets in the Pacific at this time, and for the first time in RN history a numerous Fleet Train was used. A large fleet had to be maintained at sea for long periods, and supplied with fuel and stores over vast distances.

Space precludes a full description of this operation, but the fleet itself did not include escort vessels. The latter were fully employed in escorting the large fleet train at sea, and in back-up escort operations, right back to the intermediate bases at Manus and Leyte, and thence to the fleet's main bases at Fremantle and Sydney.

The story of these replenishment operations is in itself a fascinating one—the fleet train and the carrier force meeting at sea in pre-arranged areas, the ships fuelling from tankers, replenishing stores and ammunition from storeships, carrying out exercises, receiving mail, transferring new aircraft from the ferry escort carriers to the fleet carriers, while all around them the escorts maintained the A/S and A/A screen.

It seems incredible that the Japanese submarines did not attack these operations, but they did not. It is not difficult to imagine the battles which would have ensued had a determined pack of German U-boats been operating in the area.

But the balanced fleet, as shown in the chart, was built up on the assumption that such attacks would take place. Thus the Fleet was to include all the 'Black Swan' class sloops in commission, mainly for A/A protection, and all the 'Bay' class frigates similarly, as they were completed in the UK; there were to be no less than 52 'River' class frigates, for A/S escort of the Fleet Train, and 5 'Captain' class frigates for fighter direction duties.

Note that supply distances apparently ruled out the use of Squid-fitted frigates in the greater areas of the Pacific, though not in the East Indies, and that the RCN was slated to play a very full part in the BPF operations, by the allocation of 40 'River' class frigates, though it is believed that none of the latter had arrived on station by VJ-Day.

In looking at ships allocated to the BPF it will be noted that USN war experience had been accepted, and in particular that 20mm Oerlikons were unlikely to stop Kamikaze suicide planes; so the fitting of 40mm Bofors became a real priority, as it did in ships of the East Indies Fleet, to a rather lesser extent. This is also covered in the armaments chapter.

Here are some indications of the steady growth in numbers of ships in the Fleet Train—otherwise known as the Logistic Support Group.

In early March it arrived at Manus, designated Task Force 112. It comprised 27 ships, plus a tanker group, including an escort carrier with replacement

The 'Captain' class frigate *Holmes* at her assembly point before the Normandy invasion, 1944. Her camouflage was of the Channel pattern at that time, and she had a bowchaser pom pom without a spray shield. H/F D/F was fitted at the masthead, with Type 244 interrogator below. Single Oerlikons have been added in lieu of the 40mm gun not fitted aft. *(Imperial War Museum)*

aircraft, and another as fighter escort. The escort vessels included 1 'River' class frigate and 2 'Black Swan' class sloops.

By May the peak of 125 ships had been approached, against a target of some 300 ships by the end of the year. No less than 5 escort maintenance ships were seen to be necessary for the forward bases.

When the Fleet left Leyte for the Okinawa campaign there were 9 tankers and 5 escort carriers in the Fleet Train in the forward area, and some 6 'River' class frigates and the same number of 'Black Swan' class sloops were up with them. A few of the RAN 'Bathurst's also managed to get right up into the forward battle areas. *Arbutus,* an RNZN Modified 'Flower' class corvette, was in use forward as a radio and radar repair ship, carrying electronic spares.

Within the planned escort force shown on the chart, we should remember that a second carrier task force was planned, which would have needed a second Logistic Support Group to supply it. Hence the greatly increased number of escorts, refitting or on passage, allocated to the area for the end of 1945.

There were smaller operations during the last year of the Pacific war, of which we should not lose sight.

As the land forces recaptured the Solomons and New Guinea, the RAN 'River' class frigates and 'Bathurst' class vessels moved up in support. A/S patrols, shore bombardment, combined landing parties with USN PCs, survey work in inshore channels, all were the order of the day. At the end of 1944 3 frigates and 20 corvettes were so employed north of New Guinea, and one of the latter was lost by collision, and another badly damaged by shellfire.

During the surrender and liberation operations after VJ-Day, the light fleet carrier *Glory,* with 2 'Black Swan' class sloops, went to the Bismarcks, the cruiser *Cleopatra,* with RIN *Bengal* and the 6th MSF of 'Algerine's, to Singapore, 8 RAN 'Bathurst's to Hong Kong, and the cruiser *Cumberland* and 2 frigates to Batavia. So the wheel had come full circle since the dark days of 1942.

## THE US NAVY IN THE PACIFIC

Undoubtedly, the greatest story of the escort vessel programme in World War II was the speed of reaction of the great American industrial machine. Even before Pearl Harbour, the RN's orders for new escorts, to be built in the USA under Lend-Lease, were producing the need for a great new production programme; but thereafter the USN's own rapidly increasing needs, for both the Atlantic and Pacific, resulted in the fantastic building programme described in this book.

Again, in one small section, we cannot possibly do justice to the effect this had on USN operations in the Pacific. All we can aim to do is to outline the growing numbers of new DEs, PFs, and PCs arriving in the region and to reflect these in the operations themselves. But the achievements involved—in construction, in manning, in shaking down, and in organisation into the great task forces of the Pacific—cannot be adequately covered here.

There is one overall point to be emphasised. In the war histories, pride of place was of course given to the spearheads, the fast carrier task forces, and the new fleet destroyers that screened them. But just as important were the supply and replenishment operations, stretching all the way back through the advanced bases, back through Pearl Harbour to the Pacific seaboard of the United States. The lack of success of the Japanese submarines takes nothing away from this vast operation; and every logistic support group, every convoy, every base, had its escort screens operating efficiently and faithfully around it.

The landing craft, too, were not only screened by escorts on passage but were guided in by PCs and PCEs, and all the escorts bore their share of the Kamikaze attacks. A look at the DEs damaged at Okinawa alone highlights these operations.

Unfortunately, accurate statistics are not available of the detailed allocation of new escorts in the Pacific; the notes that follow represent a summary of those so far published, and reference to the totals commissioned will show that this summary is, of necessity, incomplete.

## 1942/43

The new destroyer escorts did not come into service in numbers until late in 1943; the main impact of new escorts in the intervening period was largely limited to the numerous PCs. These were useful for inshore work, but were not seaworthy enough, or of great enough endurance, to undertake effectively the longer screening duties. But they performed bravely and efficiently, and played a new part as navigational and control ships, leading the waves of landing craft into the beaches once the leapfrog assaults back across the Pacific began.

*Dacres,* one of three RN 'Captain' class frigates of the 'Evarts' type, converted as assault headquarters ships for the Normandy invasion. Note Type 271 radar added on the bridge, with Type 244 on top, but the American Type SL radar retained. 13 single Oerlikons, a tall pole mast aft for extra communications, the after deckhouse extended, and a skimming dish fast motorboat on the port side, handled by a torpedo davit. *(Ministry of Defence)*

Japanese submarines in this period were largely used for reconnaissance for their main fleet, and for attacks on large warships, where opportunity offered; but it is to be noted that they attacked merchant shipping successfully down the east coast of Australia, and tied down all the available Australian escorts, including the increasing numbers of new ships of the 'Bathurst' class.

In January 1943 the RNZN A/S trawlers *Kiwi* and *Moa* distinguished themselves by sinking the Japanese submarine *I.1* off the Solomon Islands, but on 7th April nearly 200 aircraft attacked the anchorages off Guadalcanal and Tulagi, and *Moa* was sunk.

### 1944/45

We will now comment on the great leapfrogging operations of these two immortal years in the history of the USN.

*GILBERTS AND MARSHALLS (November 1943-July 1944)*   This widespread operation, which included the assaults on Tarawa and Kwajalein, was the first in which the new escorts are recorded as having an impact.

9 of the new destroyer escorts were in the front line of the battles, which meant that many more were either already employed on the supply lines or were on passage after shaking down, in the United States or at the great specialist base at Bermuda.

*NEW GUINEA AND THE MARIANAS (April-August 1944)*   Overlapping this period were the operations in these two areas, and it is clear that the new escorts were beginning to appear in force in this theatre.

During these assaults (which included Guam and Tinian) the landing operations were refined to a level of efficiency never before seen. The attacking forces had to cover a distance of some 1,000 miles from their bases to the landing beaches, and the covering forces were now operating at sea for long periods, and the specialised logistic support groups were beginning to provide the fuel and supplies necessary to maintain them at sea over such vast distances.

During this period no less than 26 destroyer escorts were up with the attack force, accompanied by 3 patrol frigates and a number of patrol craft. A further 15 destroyer escorts were operating with the fuelling group, making a total of 50 in the spearhead of the operation.

It was during these actions that the greatest anti-submarine feat by an individual ship of the entire war was recorded.

Some 25 Japanese submarines had been sent to establish a patrol line, designated 'NA', north of New Guinea and New Ireland, to attack the main US fleet, which was hopefully to pass that way. But the USN detected the presence of these boats, and all available destroyer escorts were sailed to attack them—with great success, no fewer than 17 of the enemy submarines being sunk.

Among these destroyer escorts was a Hunter-Killer Group of 3 ships, one of which was *England,* newly arrived from home only a few weeks before.

She detected and sank a submarine on 19th May, then, moving westwards with her consorts, sank 4 more in the short period from 22nd to 26th May, as they ran up a part of that patrol line. Then, on 31st May, operating in an escort carrier screen, she assisted in the sinking of yet another. In all attacks she made good use of her Hedgehog—a weapon which seems to have been especially effective in Pacific waters.

So, in the space of a few days, *England* sank no less than 6 submarines—a feat never paralleled in the North Atlantic, or elsewhere. Perhaps it was partly luck which placed her in the attacking ship position each time (no matter how the escort commander shuffled his ships!), perhaps the Japanese submarines did not react as swiftly as would have done a German U-boat patrol line at the height of the North Atlantic battle; but nothing can take away from this magnificent achievement by one newly-commissioned ship.

*LEYTE (September-December 1944)*   The return to the Philippines was bound to be bitterly contested, and so it was.

The landings on Leyte were themselves relatively easy, but the follow-up attacks by the Japanese naval forces led to some famous battles.

During the landings themselves 17 destroyer escorts were operating with the attack groups, plus an unspecified number of PCs—and the first PCE(R)s made their appearance in this operation—a type of ship destined to be most useful during the Kamikaze suicide bomber attacks.

The Logistic Support Group, growing all the time, included in its screen 26 destroyer escorts, 10 of the new patrol frigates, and 12 patrol craft. An Australian 'River' class frigate, *Gascoyne,* was also there, operating with Task Group 77.5, a minesweeping and hydrographic survey group.

*Primula* of the original 'Flower' class, arriving in a Mediterranean harbour. Ships of this class were prominent in the fighting in this sea, and due to the heavy air fighting often carried extra A/A guns—she has several showing in this shot. Type SA acoustic minesweeping gear is carried over the bows. *(Ministry of Defence)*

We must pass by the big naval battles, where the new escorts were not directly involved; but we must remember the battle off Samar, on 25th October 1944.

16 USN escort carriers were operating off Leyte Gulf, as Task Group 77.4, in support of the landing forces, while the main US Fleet was off chasing away the main Japanese naval units. This task group was split into 3 units, each covered by 3 destroyers and 4 destroyer escorts.

One of these units, of 6 escort carriers, was surprised in the early morning when it detected by Type SG radar a large Japanese naval force bearing down upon it, composed of 4 battleships, 6 cruisers, and many destroyers!

While the carriers retired at top speed, the destroyers were sent in to attack with torpedoes, while heavy salvoes from the Japanese ships dropped ever closer. The destroyers attacked gallantly, and took very heavy punishment.

Then a second torpedo attack was ordered, carried out by the destroyer escorts! Here was the justification for the heavy torpedo tube mounting on the upper deck. The DEs, too, carried out a courageous attack, taking heavy damage and losing one of their number, *Samuel B. Roberts.*

Only one escort carrier was lost, and the destroyer escorts, trained in A/S work but not in torpedo attacks, had closed the enemy to 6,000 yards, taken 14″ shells from the battleships, and fired individual torpedo spreads at the enemy.

The air and surface attacks from the US force made the Japanese force retire, thinking they had run into a much stronger force, and this action, in which escort vessels closely engaged heavy enemy surface forces, must go down in history as an epic.

Two other types of operation involving the new escorts in this period should be mentioned; they must have been typical of so many other actions, not recorded in detail.

At the end of 1944, 8 Japanese submarines attacked the major USN base at Ulithi. Each launched 2 midget submarines, which attacked the anchored ships; but the patrolling escorts detected them in time, though during the attacks, 3 destroyer escorts were actually dropping depth charges on midget submarines among the ships inside the lagoon.

The 'Flower' class corvette *Peony* arriving in Benghazi harbour shortly after its capture. She is in her original configuration, with strange funnel markings.

In the other, 2 DEs and 2 PCs were engaged in a widespread search for survivors from ships of the US 7th Fleet, following on the far-ranging naval battles of this period.

*LUZON (December 1944-June 1945)* During this follow-up assault the new escorts again increased their forward contribution.

In the attack force in January were 2 PCE(R) and 16 PCs, while 32 DEs were in the reinforcement and service group screens. The RAN supplied the sloop *Warrego* and the frigate *Gascoyne,* while the A/S-fitted 'Bathurst' class ship *Benalla* was also there.

The Logistic Support Group, at sea to replenish the 3rd Fleet, included 25 destroyer escorts in its screen.

Then, in the liberation of the southern Philippines in February to April, 3 DEs and 5 PCs were up in the vanguard, while 6 DEs were with the escort carriers, at the battle for Lingayen Gulf in January. It is worth noting at this point that CVE (escort carrier) Hunter-Killer Groups, with DEs as their A/S screen, were by now operating throughout the Pacific, hunting for Japanese submarines.

Among these liberation assaults, we may pick out one of interest in this narrative. At the attack on Tarakan in May (a relatively small operation), a USN

'Hunt' class destroyers at Algiers in 1943. Note the varying camouflage patterns. *Whaddon*, of Type I, is at the left; the other three are of Type II. *(Imperial War Museum)*

DE, *Formoe,* and an RAN frigate, *Barcoo,* together gave fire support to the troops ashore, while another RAN frigate, *Lachlan,* surveyed the passage in the assault period, to locate hidden obstacles.

*IWOJIMA AND OKINAWA (February-August 1945)*   The assaults on these two islands brought the climax of the USN operations in the Pacific, together with the great battles with the Kamikaze suicide planes.

Iwojima was a strategic point in the US forces' advance toward Japan, and for six weeks, in February and March, the battle raged around it.

Then the assault forces moved on to take Okinawa, and the greatest of the air battles raged. From October 1944 through to March 1945 this had been building up to the D-Day landings of 1st April and the bitter fighting thereafter.

In these battles the new escorts appeared in greater strength yet once more. In the attack groups alone, 78 destroyer escorts were deployed—54 right forward and 24 in the fuelling groups; the number of PFs and PCEs cannot be calculated easily, but some 80 PCs were also present. Once again, we should remember the even greater numbers of escorts employed in the supply lines, all the way back to the main bases.

The PCs were now regularly employed in the very front line. They were destroying floating mines in the wake of the fleet minesweepers (in a way parallel with the RN's use of the 'Isles' class trawlers), and they were also acting as control craft off the landing beaches, flying distinctive banners to guide in the landing craft.

But the major threat at Okinawa was the Kamikaze suicide planes. The big ships and the destroyers on extended radar picket duty bore the brunt; destroyer escorts were not normally used on the latter duty, until they came out with the later armament of 2 5″ and 10 40mm Bofors, plus 10 20mm Oerlikons, but nevertheless 25 DEs were damaged by suicide planes at Okinawa, 6 on one day alone.

*Oberrender,* for example, was hit on 9th May while on A/S patrol; a PCE(R) came alongside and removed all her casualties.

On the same day the famous *England* was operating in the north-west outer A/S screen. 3 planes dived for her, hotly chased by the carrier air patrol; she took evasive action at full speed, and fired back with all guns, but one plane struck her superstructure, the bomb it was carrying exploded, and started serious fires. These were brought under control in 45 minutes, and she was towed in with heavy casualties.

*Underhill* was lost in different circumstances. On 24th July, with 5 PCs, she was escorting some LSTs when she investigated a radar contact. Her captain reported that he was chasing human torpedoes, when a heavy explosion forward ripped off the bow section as far aft as the forward fireroom bulkhead. The bow section sank immediately, but the after section stayed afloat for four hours. It is interesting to note that these human torpedoes had also been launched from parent Japanese submarines.

Figures in the production charts will show the large numbers of new escorts

The 'Flower' class corvette *Amaranthus* at Alexandria in December 1942. The exploits of her unit of corvettes are covered in this chapter; note the awnings, minesweeping gear (frequently used by this unit), and mast before the bridge, although radar is fitted. (*Ministry of Defence*)

One of the latest German E-boats surrendering at Harwich in May 1945. The escort base was at Parkeston Quay, in the background. The frequent battles between frigates and MTBs and these E-boats, are described in this chapter. (*Imperial War Museum*)

of all types, but especially of DEs, that were operating in the Pacific by VJ-Day. We should note, too, how many of the newer DEs then completing or under construction were to be fitted as radar pickets, with heavier armament, to supplement or relieve the valuable fleet destroyers used latterly on these duties.

## JAPANESE SUBMARINES SUNK BY SURFACE FORCES

|                               | 1942 | 1943 | 1944 | 1945 |
|-------------------------------|------|------|------|------|
| **RN**                        |      |      |      |      |
| war-built fleet destroyers    | 1    |      | 1    |      |
| 'Black Swan' class sloops     |      |      | 1    |      |
| **RAN**                       |      |      |      |      |
| war-built fleet destroyers    |      | 1    |      |      |
| 'Bathurst' class A/S-M/S      |      | 1    |      | 1    |
| **RNZN**                      |      |      |      |      |
| 'Kiwi' class trawlers         |      | 2    |      |      |
| **USN**                       |      |      |      |      |
| All classess                  | 13   | 16   | 38   | 25   |
| **Totals**                    | 16   | 18   | 41   | 25   |
| **Ship/air co-operation in sinkings** | | | | |
| Sunk by ships                 | 8    | 8    | 25   | 8    |
| Sunk by ships and shore a/c   | 2    | 2    | 1    | 1    |
| Sunk by ships and carrier a/c |      |      | 2    | 5    |
| Sunk by submarines            | 5    | 3    | 7    | 7    |
| Sunk by other means           | 1    | 5    | 6    | 4    |

*Puckeridge,* Type II 'Hunt' class destroyer, coming up to an aircraft carrier to pick up orders. She was lost in September 1943. *(Imperial War Museum)*

## FAR EAST ESCORTS—SUMMARY OF RN, RIN, AND RNZN FORCES

|  | *Planned for end 1945* | *On Station 3rd August 1945* |
|---|---|---|
| **EAST INDIES FLEET** | | |
| Escort Carriers | ? | 16 |
| 'Hunt' class destroyers | 20 | 9 |
| 'Black Swan' class sloops | 6 (RIN) | 6 (RIN) |
| 'River' class frigates | 20 | 20 |
| 'Loch' class frigates | 18 (3 SANF) | 16 (1 SANF) |
| 'Captain' class frigates (c/forces direction) | 3 | 0 |
| 'Flower' class corvettes (air sea rescue) | 14 (2 RIN) | 15 (3 RIN) |
| 'Algerine' class fleet minesweepers | 16 | 16 |
| 'Bangor' class fleet minesweepers | 13 (RIN) | 13 (RIN) |
| 'Bathurst' class A/S-M/S vessels | 4 (RIN) | 4 (RIN) |
| 'Isles' class trawlers | 26 (24 RIN) | 26 (24 RIN) |
| Totals | 140 | 141 |
| **BRITISH PACIFIC FLEET** | | |
| Escort carriers | ? | 8 |
| 'Hunt' class destroyers | 13 | 0 |
| 'Black Swan' class sloops | 24 | 17 |
| 'Bay' class frigates | 26 | 4 |
| 'River' class frigates | 5 | 9 |
|  | 40(RCN) | 0(RCN) |
| 'Captain' class frigates (fighter direction) | 5 | 0 |
| 'Bathurst' class A/S-M/S vessels (RN account) | 18 | 18 |
| 'Algerine' class fleet minesweepers | 15 | 0 |
| 'Flower' class corvettes (radio repair) | 1 | 1 |
| 'Isles' class trawlers | 2 | 0 |
| Command and HQ Escorts ('Enchantress') | 1 | 1 |
| Command, Logistic Supply Group ('Aire') | 1 | 1 |
| Totals | 151 | 59 |

**NOTE**

1. RAN ships based on Australia are not included in these figures, which relate to the two Fleets only. EIF ships were at greater strength than those of the BPF at VJ-Day, because many of the former were RIN ships on station, while the BPF ships had all to come out from the UK.

Type II 'Hunt' class destroyer *Calpe* at Alexandria, September 1943. Mediterranean camouflage and three twin 4″ gun mountings. *(Ministry of Defence)*

The RIN 'Bathurst' class escort *Bengal* returning in victory after defending her tanker convoy against a surface raider. *(Imperial War Museum)*

'Black Swan' class sloop *Flamingo* operating
many miles up a *chaung*, or inland river, in
Burma, during the 1944 operations.
Ambushes, crocodiles and tripwires were
common in this form of warfare!
*(Imperial War Museum)*

*Punjab,* an RIN 'Bathurst' class escort,
operating with one of the RIN 'Black Swan'
class sloops in the Indian Ocean.
*(Imperial War Museum)*

# War-built Escort Classes

*Martin H. Ray*, DE 338, of the 'Edsall' type, escorting cargo ships in the Pacific. *(US National Archives)*

*Ebert*, DE 768, in drydock at her builder's yard in Tampa, Florida. Her surface radar aerial is fitted low down, between mast and yard—an unusual configuration. *(US National Archives)*

# ROYAL NAVY

## FLEET STATISTICS—UK

### TOTAL ESCORTS BUILT 1939-45

|  | 'Flower' Class | Mod 'Flower' Class | 'Black Swan' Class | 'Hunt' Class | 'River' Class | 'Loch' Class | 'B C |
|---|---|---|---|---|---|---|---|
| **TOTAL BUILT IN UK** | 135 | 10 | 37 | 86 | 57 | 36 | 19 |
| Retained by RN | 102 | 4 | 31 | 72 | 51 | 25 | 19 |
| Received from Canada | 0 | 7 | 0 | 0 | 8 | 0 | 0 |
| Received from USA | 0 | 0 | 0 | 0 | 0 | 0 | |
| Received from Australia | 0 | 0 | 0 | 0 | 0 | 0 | 0 |
| TOTAL RN SHIPS | 102 | 11 | 31 | 75 | 59 | 25 | 19 |
| Transferred to USA | 10 | 0 | 0 | 0 | 0 | 0 | 0 |
| Transferred to Canada | 0 | 4 | 0 | 0 | 8 | 3 | 0 |
| Transferred to India | 1 | 3a | 6 | 0 | 0 | 0 | 0 |
| Transferred to other Allied navies | 22 | 2 | 0 | 14 | 6 | 0 | 0 |
| CANCELLED | 6 | 1 | 5 | 0 | 0 | 56h | |

*NOTES*
(a) Ships transferred in 1945
(b) 5 ships completed as merchant rescue ships
(c) of which 39 were on order in Canada.
(d) including ships built in Canada under Lend-Lease.
(e) 16 were ordered in Canada, but 8 remained there

## CUMULATIVE TOTAL OF NEW ESCORTS LAUNCHED

|  |  | 'Black' Swan | 'Hunt' | 'Flower' | 'Castle' | 'River' | 'Loch' | 'Bay' | 'Capt |
|---|---|---|---|---|---|---|---|---|---|
| 1939 | 1st half | 1 | | | | | | | |
|  | 2nd half | 1 | 3 | | | | | | |
| 1940 | 1st half | | 13 | 30 | | | | | |
|  | 2nd half | 4 | 15 | 47 | | | | | |
| 1941 | 1st half | | 14 | 35 | | 1 | | | |
|  | 2nd half | | 18 | 17 | | 2 | | | |
| 1942 | 1st half | 1 | 18 | 6 | | 7 | | | |
|  | 2nd half | 11 | 4 | 4 | | 20 | | | |
| 1943 | 1st half | 6 | 1 | 7 | 2 | 19 | | | |
|  | 2nd half | 6 | | 5 | 16 | 15 | 2 | | |
| 1944 | 1st half | 2 | | | 20 | 1 | 13 | | |
|  | 2nd half | 2 | | | 6 | | 11 | 7 | |
| 1945 | 1st half | 1 | | | | | 3 | 10 | |
|  | 2nd half | 2 | | | | | 1 | 4 | |
|  | TOTALS | 37 | 86 | 151 | 44 | 62 | 36 | 21 | 78 |

## FLEET STATISTICS—UK

## TOTAL ESCORTS BUILT 1939-45

| 'Castle' Class | 'Algerine' Class | 'Bangor' Class | Admiralty Trawlers | 'Bathurst' Class | 'Captain' Class | 'Colony' Class | 'Catherine' Class | 'Kil' Class | TOTALS |
|---|---|---|---|---|---|---|---|---|---|
| 44 | 48 | 54 | 228 | 0 | 0 | 0 | 0 | 0 | 754 |
| 31 | 48 | 36 | 218 | 0 | 0 | 0 | 0 | 0 | 627 |
| 0 | 49d | 6 | 8 | 0 | 0 | 0 | 0 | 0 | 78 |
| 0 | 0 | 0 | 0 | 0 | 78 | 21 | 22 | 15 | 158 |
| 0 | 0 | 0 | 0 | 13 | 0 | 0 | 0 | 0 | 13 |
| 31b | 97 | 5 | 226 | 13f | 78 | 21 | 22 | 15 | 876 |
| 0 | 0 | 0 | 0 | 0 | 0 | 0 | 0 | 0 | 10 |
| 12 | 0 | 0 | 8e | 0 | 0 | 0 | 0 | 0 | 35 |
| 0 | 0 | 9 | 0 | 0 | 0 | 0 | 0 | 0 | 19 |
| 1 | 0 | 0 | 14 | 0 | 0 | 0 | 0 | 0 | 59 |
| 53c | 12 | 0 | 0 | 0 | 442g | 0 | 26g | 135g | 737 |

(f) Manned by RAN, operated under RN operational control.
(g) Balance to original total agreed under Lend-Lease.
(h) Not including ships scheduled to be built in Canada.

## CUMULATIVE TOTAL OF NEW ESCORTS LAUNCHED

| | | 'Colony' | 'Kil' | 'Guillemot' | Trawlers | 'Bangor' | 'Algerine' | 'Catherine' | Totals |
|---|---|---|---|---|---|---|---|---|---|
| 39 | 1st half | | | 1 | | | | | 2 |
| | 2nd half | | | 2 | 11 | | | | 17 |
| 40 | 1st half | | | | 16 | 4 | | | 63 |
| | 2nd half | | | | 26 | 11 | | | 103 |
| 41 | 1st half | | | | 29 | 12 | | | 91 |
| | 2nd half | | | | 30 | 13 | 1 | | 81 |
| 42 | 1st half | | | | 27 | 2 | 6 | | 69 |
| | 2nd half | | | | 16 | | 17 | 9 | 84 |
| 43 | 1st half | | 5 | | 16 | | 16 | 25 | 112 |
| | 2nd half | 21 | 10 | | 20 | | 19 | | 172 |
| 44 | 1st half | | | | 8 | | 19 | | 63 |
| | 2nd half | | | | 12 | | 18 | | 56 |
| 45 | 1st half | | | | 7 | | 3 | | 24 |
| | 2nd half | | | | | | 1 | | 8 |
| | Totals | 21 | 15 | 3 | 218 | 42 | 100 | 34 | 945 |

## RN ESCORTS IN COMMISSION, BY COMMAND AND YEARS

| *1.1.41* | 'Bird' | 'Hunt' | 'Flower' |
|---|---|---|---|
| **Home** | | | |
| Rosyth | 2 | | |
| Sheerness | | 5 | |
| Harwich | | 6 | |
| Nore Unallocated | | 2 | 1 |
| Portsmouth | | 6 | |
| Londonderry | | | 7 |
| Liverpool | | | 25 |
| Greenock | | | 13 |
| **Mediterranean** | | | 4 |
| **West Africa** | | | 6 |
| Totals | 2 | 19 | 56 |

| *1.1.42* | | | |
|---|---|---|---|
| **Home** | | | |
| Scapa | | 4 | |
| Sheerness | | 6 | |
| Harwich | | 5 | |
| Portsmouth | | 4 | |
| Plymouth | | 6 | |
| Londonderry | 2 | 2 | 19 |
| Liverpool | 1 | | 36 |
| Greenock | | | 13 |
| **Mediterranean** | | | |
| Gibraltar | | 3 | 6 |
| Alexandria | | 8 | 7 |
| **West Africa** | | | 24 |
| **West Indies** | | | 1 |
| Totals | 3 | 38 | 106 |

| 1.1.43 | 'Bird' | 'Hunt' | 'Flower' | 'River' |
|---|---|---|---|---|
| **Home** | | | | |
| Scapa | | 6 | | |
| Rosyth | | 4 | | |
| Harwich | | 6 | | |
| Sheerness | | 9 | | |
| Portsmouth | | 4 | | |
| Plymouth | | 9 | | |
| Londonderry | 4 | 2 | 26 | 13 |
| Liverpool | 1 | | 32 | |
| Greenock | | | 10 | 1 |
| **Mediterranean** | | | | |
| Alexandria | | 20 | 6 | |
| Gibraltar | 2 | 10 | 7 | |
| Algiers | | 1 | 5 | |
| **South Atlantic** | | | 3 | |
| **West Africa** | | | 15 | |
| **Eastern Fleet** | | 2 | 4 | |
| TOTALS | 7 | 73 | 108 | 14 |

'Black Swan' class *Pelican*, August 1942. Completed just at the outbreak of war, she has no less than four twin 4″ gun mountings, with a gunnery director. The quarterdeck mounting has an extensive breakwater. *(Ministry of Defence)*

| 1.1.44 | 'Bird' | 'Hunt' | 'Flower' | 'River' | 'Castle' | 'Captain' | 'Colony' |
|---|---|---|---|---|---|---|---|
| **Home** | | | | | | | |
| Aberdeen | | 1 | | | | | |
| Rosyth | | 1 | | | | | |
| Harwich | | 6 | | | | | |
| Sheerness | | 7 | | | | | |
| Portsmouth | | 5 | | | | | |
| Plymouth | | 5 | | | | | |
| Londonderry | | | 18 | 6 | 2 | | 1 |
| Belfast | | | | | | 51 | |
| Liverpool | 6 | 1 | 16 | 4 | | | |
| Greenock | 12 | | 25 | 15 | | | |
| **Mediterranean** | | | | | | | |
| Algiers | 1 | 28 | 18 | 7 | | | |
| Gibraltar | | | 6 | 3 | | | |
| Malta | | 14 | 3 | 1 | | | |
| Levant | | 4 | | | | | |
| **South Atlantic** | | | 3 | 9 | | | |
| **Eastern Fleet** | 1 | | 13 | 1 | | | |
| Totals | 20 | 72 | 102 | 49 | 2 | 51 | 1 |

*Crane* in a swell. Note the crowded quarterdeck, and the radar Type 272 fitted aft to avoid replacing the pole tripod mast with a lattice. *(Ministry of Defence)*

| 1.1.45 | 'Bird' | 'Hunt' | 'Flower' | 'River' | 'Captain' | 'Castle' | 'Loch' | 'Colony' | 'Kil' |
|---|---|---|---|---|---|---|---|---|---|
| **Home** | | | | | | | | | |
| Rosyth | | | 3 | 2 | | | | | |
| Harwich | | 11 | | | 11 | | | 1 | |
| Sheerness | | 16 | 7 | | 3 | | | | |
| Portsmout. | | | 9 | 3 | | | | | |
| Plymouth | | 4 | 10 | 1 | | | | | 1 |
| Londonderry | | | 6 | 8 | 4 | 6 | 4 | 6 | |
| Liverpool | 2 | | 16 | 1 | 4 | 8 | 2 | 5 | |
| Belfast | | | | | 42 | | | | |
| Greenock | 12 | | 5 | 4 | 4 | 10 | 10 | 8 | |
| **Mediterranean** | | | | | | | | | |
| Alexandria | | 17 | | | | | | | |
| Gibraltar | | 4 | 10 | 1 | | | | | 7 |
| **West Africa** | | | 9 | 8 | | | | | 7 |
| **South Atlantic** | 1 | | 10 | 10 | | | | | |
| **East Indies** | 10 | 16 | 25 | 22 | | | | | |
| Totals | 25 | 68 | 110 | 60 | 68 | 24 | 16 | 20 | 15 |

*Chanticleer*, of the Modified class, in March 1943. She has eight depth charge throwers, four angled aft. A twin Oerlikon mounting is on the quarterdeck, and two more are on the after gundeck. *(Ministry of Defence)*

| 7.5.45 | 'Bird' | 'Hunt' | 'Flower' | 'River' | 'Castle' | 'Captain' | 'Loch' | 'Colony' | 'Kil' |
|---|---|---|---|---|---|---|---|---|---|
| **Home** | | | | | | | | | |
| Campbeltown | | | 3 | | | | | | |
| Rosyth | | 2 | 4 | | 3 | | 1 | | |
| Harwich | | 16 | | | | 11 | | 1 | |
| Sheerness | | 27 | 7 | | | | | | |
| Portsmouth | 1 | | 13 | 7 | | 5 | | | |
| Plymouth | | 1 | 17 | | | 4 | | | |
| Londonderry | | | 4 | 7 | 6 | 3 | 6 | 6 | |
| Belfast | | | | | | 33 | | | |
| Liverpool | 8 | | 16 | 2 | 8 | 2 | 6 | 7 | |
| Greenock | 4 | | 3 | 2 | 9 | 7 | 7 | 6 | |
| **Mediterranean** | | | | | | | | | |
| Alexandria | | 12 | 6 | 1 | | | | | |
| Gibraltar | 1 | | 9 | 1 | | | | | 7 |
| **West Africa** | | | 3 | 5 | | | | | 8 |
| **East Indies** | 13 | 7 | 15 | 22 | | | | | |
| **South Atlantic** | | | 3 | | | | | | |
| **British Pacific Fleet** | 5 | | | 9 | | | | | |
| Totals | 32 | 64 | 103 | 59 | 23 | 65 | 19 | 20 | 15 |

## 'BLACK SWAN' AND MODIFIED 'BLACK SWAN' CLASS SLOOPS
## 37 ships completed

This class of sloop, and the 'Hunt' class escort destroyers, were the only two classes of escort vessels built during the war years to retain full warship specifications and scantlings. Indeed, it is probably not without significance that each of these two classes retained its naval generic title (no other sloops were built), while all other classes, corvettes, frigates, and trawlers followed classification society rules and merchant shipbuilding practice. It is interesting to add that although the US-built DEs and PCEs followed warship practice in their design and construction, they, too, were classified in the RN as frigates and patrol craft respectively!

A further comment is that, at least during the earlier war years, the 'Hunt' and 'Black Swan' classes were largely officered by regular RN men, while the corvettes and frigates were operated by RNR and RNVR; but in the last two years of the war, with the latter so vastly outnumbering the former, this no longer held true.

The 'Black Swan' class was an impressive one, representing the naval staff's specialised thinking on escorts for A/A and A/S protection of ocean convoys. Their armament was proportionately heavier than that of other escort vessels, and their gunnery control and radar was in general more advanced. Conversely, they did not have so much space for ahead-throwing weapons, or depth charges, compared with the frigates.

The sloops' specialised warship construction and main machinery required them to be built by shipyards familiar with naval practice; this inevitably restricted the numbers that could be produced (especially as the vital new fleet destroyers were largely being built in the same yards), and for sheer weight of numbers of escorts produced the emphasis was switched to corvettes and frigates. When the mass-production 'Loch' and 'Castle' classes started appearing this difference became even more marked.

The attached comparative specifications show how the class developed, from the original staff requirement of 1937 through to the full Modified class in 1944.

It will be noted that the main difference between the original class and the Modified was in the minesweeping gear being omitted, the depth-charge armament greatly increased, and the radar and close-range gunnery capabilities being improved. The full boat complement was reduced, to provide more deck space and to reduce topweight, and the complement gradually increased by some 30%.

The naval staff's original hope was to combine the three types of sloop emerging in 1937 into one type for rapid production. It was soon found, however, that it was hardly possible to combine adequate minesweeping and anti-submarine effectiveness in the same hull, and the 'Black Swan' class became the more highly specialised gunnery vessel, while the 'Algerine' class were developed as the minesweeping specialists.

We find, however, that the original 'Black Swan' units had to be capable of minesweeping on occasion, and 1 in every 6 was to be fitted as a minelayer in addition! They were also to be fitted for tropical service, and to aim at a long period of roll, to provide a good gunnery platform.

A quadruple 2 pounder pom pom was included in the original specification, though without its own director, as topweight did not permit. But the main armament carried the 'Hunt' class type director throughout, with Type 285 radar added later. It will be noted that paravanes were not at first specified, but were added, then deleted in later ships, and SA gear against acoustic mines carried instead.

The original class units carried the pre-war high foremast and mainmast; both were soon supported by tripods rather than stays, to give clear fields of fire. In January 1940 the foremast was reduced in height, and the mainmast removed, to provide a clear field for the multiple pom pom. Then the Type 272 radar aerial was added aft, on a lattice mast, until a full lattice foremast replaced the pole, and the main radar aerial was moved forward on to it. The H/F D/F birdcage aerial was sometimes carried at the foremasthead, and sometimes on a pole aft, where the main radar aerial was forward.

During this period of change *Woodcock* and *Wren* of the original class received so many modifications that they were practically indistinguishable from the Modified class.

The later ships had their beam increased by 1 foot at the waterline, to cope with the considerable added topweight; all ships were fitted with Denny-Brown stabilisers, and the extent of welding was progressively increased. A distinctive feature of the class was the large escape port fitted in each side of the forecastle.

It will be seen in the specifications that the 1944 Programme ships were not to carry either a Hedgehog or a Squid, but the 1951 staff requirements for refit included a single Squid, at the expense of one twin 4″ gun mounting. It will also be seen that the cost of that refit approximated to the estimated cost of the original ships in 1937!

The 1951 specification also included two greatly improved radar sets, the Type 293Q, as a surface and low air warning set, with gunnery direction in addition, and the Type 974, a high definition surface warning set.

The 'Black Swan' class were undoubtedly highly efficient ships, which were always welcome in an escort screen. They had high A/A capability, as well as good A/S outfits, and the entire class was allocated in 1945 to the British Pacific Fleet and the East Indies Fleet.

It is noteworthy that the only ships of the class to be transferred during the war years to another Allied navy were the 6 units built directly for the RIN.

## HMS Black Swan

This was the name ship of the class, a sloop authorised under the 1937 programme. She was laid down on 20th June 1938 at Yarrow's yard on the Clyde, launched on 7th July 1939, and completed on 27th January 1940.

After trials she was allocated to the Rosyth Escort Force, and in April she landed a party of Royal Marines and troops at Andalsnes and acted as A/A guard ship at the port. On 28th April, after having brought down at least four enemy aircraft, she was badly damaged by a bomb and had to return to the UK. She was repaired at Falmouth during May, and was then employed on East Coast convoy duties. On 1st November she struck a mine which damaged her main engines, and as a result she was under repair at Dundee until May 1941. In June she joined the Western Approaches Command, but on 24th August, while escorting convoy BB 47, she was badly damaged by low-flying German aircraft off Milford Haven, and was in dock there for six weeks.

At the end of October she was allocated to the 37th Escort Group, and was employed with the Atlantic and Sierra Leone convoys. She refitted at Rosyth in June, and returned to her group. During the North Africa invasion she escorted troop convoys to and from the Mediterranean, until February 1943.

On 2nd April 1943, while escorting convoy OS 45 from the UK to Freetown, she and the corvette *Stonecrop* destroyed *U 124*. In December 1943 she was assigned to the 51st Escort Group of the Mediterranean Fleet, and in January 1944 sailed from the UK with a convoy. She remained in the Mediterranean until September, when she was recalled to UK waters because of the increased U-boat activity.

She refitted at Leith from January to March 1945, and in June sailed to join the British Pacific Fleet, arriving at Shanghai on 27th September, after the end of the war with Japan. She remained on the Far East Station first with the 1st Escort Flotilla, then with the 3rd Frigate Flotilla, until November 1951.

In June 1950, when the Korean War broke out, she was one of the first British ships in the operational area. Her first assignment was with CTG 96.5 off the east coast, where, with the cruiser *Jamaica*, she took part in the first naval action of the war, in which 5 out of 6 North Korean E-boats were sunk. She completed three periods of about three months each off the Korean coast, and steamed some 41,000 miles on operations.

She finally left Singapore for the UK on 26th November 1951, arriving at Devonport on 20th December. She was placed in reserve, and scrapped at Troon on 13th September 1956.

### German U-boats sunk by 'Black Swan' Class

| | | |
|---|---|---|
| U 213 | 31. 7.42 | *Erne* and others |
| U 124 | 2. 4.43 | *Black Swan* and others |
| U 202 | 1. 6.43 | *Starling* |
| U 119 | 4. 6.43 | *Starling* |
| U 449 | 24. 6.43 | *Wren, Woodcock, Kite* and *Wild Goose* |
| U 504 | 30. 7.43 | *Kite, Woodcock, Wren* and *Wild Goose* |
| U 226 | 6.11.43 | *Starling, Woodcock* and *Kite* |
| U 842 | 6.11.43 | *Starling* and *Wild Goose* |
| U 592 | 31. 1.44 | *Starling, Wild Goose* and *Magpie* |
| U 762 | 8. 2.44 | *Woodcock* and *Wild Goose* |
| U 238 | 9. 2.44 | *Kite, Magpie* and *Starling* |
| U 734 | 9. 2.44 | *Wild Goose* and *Starling* |
| U 424 | 11. 2.44 | *Wild Goose* and *Woodpecker* |
| U 264 | 19. 2.44 | *Woodcock* and *Starling* |
| U 653 | 15. 3.44 | *Starling, Wild Goose* and others |
| U 961 | 29. 3.44 | *Starling* |
| U 962 | 8. 4.44 | *Crane* and *Cygnet* |
| U 473 | 5. 5.44 | *Starling, Wren* and *Wild Goose* |
| U 333 | 31. 7.44 | *Starling* and others |
| U 736 | 6. 8.44 | *Starling* and others |
| U 198 | 12. 8.44 | *Godavari* (RIN) and others |
| U 354 | 24. 8.44 | *Mermaid, Peacock* and others |
| U 394 | 2. 9.44 | *Mermaid, Peacock* and others |
| U 482 | 16. 1.45 | *Peacock, Hart, Starling, Amethyst* and others |
| U 425 | 17. 2.45 | *Lark* and others |
| U 1208 | 20. 2.45 | *Amethyst* |
| U 327 | 27.2.45 | *Wild Goose* and others |
| U 683 | 12.3.45 | *Wild Goose* and others |

## 'BLACK SWAN' CLASS COMMAND ALLOCATION
(all at 1st January, except last two)

|  | 1940 | 1941 | 1942 | 1943 | 1944 | 1945 | 7.5.45 | 3.8.45 |
|---|---|---|---|---|---|---|---|---|
| Liverpool |  |  | 1 | 4 | 6 | 2 | 8 | 0 |
| Londonderry |  |  | 2 | 4 | 0 | 0 | 0 | 0 |
| Greenock |  |  |  | 1 | 12 | 12 | 4 | 0 |
| Rosyth |  | 2 |  |  |  |  |  |  |
| Algiers |  |  |  |  | 1 |  |  |  |
| Gibraltar |  |  |  | 2 |  |  | 1 | 2 |
| South Atlantic |  |  |  |  |  | 1 |  |  |
| Far East |  |  |  |  | 1 | 9 | 14 | 23 |
| Totals |  | 2 | 3 | 11 | 20 | 24 | 32 | 25 |

## 'BLACK SWAN' CLASS FOR THE FAR EAST, 1945

|  | East Indies Fleet | British Pacific Fleet |
|---|---|---|
| Planned | 6 RIN | 24 |
| On station, 3rd August 1945 | 6 RIN | 17 |

**British Pacific Fleet,** 3.8.45

*Pheasant, Crane, Redpole, Whimbrel, Woodcock, Alacrity, Amethyst, Black Swan, Erne, Hart, Hind, Cygnet, Flamingo, Opossum, Starling, Stork, Wren.*

## 'BLACK SWAN' CLASS – CLASS LIST

| Name | Pendant No. | Job No. | Builder | Building Time | Completion Date |
|---|---|---|---|---|---|
| **1939 Programme** |  |  |  |  |  |
| *Black Swan* | U 57 |  | Yarrow | 19m6d | 27.1.40 |
| *Flamingo* | U 18 |  | Yarrow | 17m8d | 3.11.39 |
| **1940 Programme** |  |  |  |  |  |
| *Erne* | U 03 | J 4000 | Furness | 19m3d | 26.4.41 |
| *Ibis* | U 99 | J 4047 | Furness | 19m10d | 2.5.41 |
| *Whimbrel* | U 29 | J 1861 | Yarrow | 14m13d | 13.1.43 |
| *Wild Goose* | U 45 | J 1862 | Yarrow | 13m14d | 11.3.43 |
| *Woodcock* | U 90 | J 11702 | Fairfield | 19m8d | 29.5.43 |
| *Woodpecker* | U 08 | J 1259 | Denny | 23m10d | 11.2.43 |
| *Wren* | U 28 | J 1260 | Denny | 23m5d | 4.2.43 |
| *Godavari* (RIN) | U 52 |  | Thornycroft | 19m29d | 28.6.43 |
| *Jumna* (RIN) | U 21 |  | Denny | 14m13d | 13.5.41 |
| *Narbada* (RIN) | U 40 |  | Thornycroft | 20m0d | 29.4.43 |
| *Sutlej* (RIN) | U 95 |  | Denny | 15m19d | 23.4.41 |

## MODIFIED 'BLACK SWAN' CLASS

### 1940 Supplementary War Programme

| | | | | | |
|---|---|---|---|---|---|
| *Chanticleer* | U 05 | J 1263 | Denny | | 29.9.42L |
| *Crane* | U 23 | J 1264 | Denny | 22m27d | 10.5.43 |
| *Cygnet* | U 38 | J 3065 | Cammell Laird | 15m13d | 1.12.42 |
| *Kite* | U 87 | J 3467 | Cammell Laird | | 16.2.43 |
| *Lapwing* | U 62 | J 1131 | Scott | | 10.3.44 |
| *Lark* | U 11 | J 1132 | Scott | 23m5d | 10.4.44 |
| *Magpie* | U 82 | J 6082 | Thornycroft | 20m0d | 30.8.43 |
| *Peacock* | U 96 | J 6196 | Thornycroft | 17m11d | 10.5.44 |
| *Pheasant* | U 49 | J 1880 | Yarrow | 13m26d | 12.5.43 |
| *Redpole* | U 69 | J 1881 | Yarrow | 13m6d | 24.6.43 |
| *Starling* | U 66 | J 11701 | Fairfield | 17m10d | 1.4.43 |
| *Cauvery* (RIN) | U 10 | | Yarrow | 11m24d | 21.10.43 |
| *Kistna* (RIN) | U 46 | | Yarrow | 13m12d | 26.8.43 |

### 1941 Programme

| | | | | | |
|---|---|---|---|---|---|
| *Actaeon* | U 07 | J 6751 | Thornycroft | | 24.7.46 |
| *Amethyst* | U 16 | J 1494 | Stephen | 19m8d | 2.11.43 |
| *Hart* | U 58 | J 1475 | Stephen | 20m16d | 12.12.43 |
| *Hind* | U 39 | J 1274 | Denny | 15m15d | 11.4.44 |
| *Mermaid* | U 30 | J 1275 | Denny | 19m23d | 1.5.44 |
| *Modeste* | U 42 | D 2409 | Chatham | | 3.9.45 |
| *Nereide* | U 64 | D 2410 | Chatham | | 6.5.46 |
| *Opossum* | U 33 | J 1282 | Denny | | 16.6.45 |

### 1942 Programme

| | | | | | |
|---|---|---|---|---|---|
| *Alacrity* | U 60 | J 6750 | Denny | | 13.4.45 |
| *Snipe* | U 20 | D 1162 | Denny | | 9.9.46 |
| *Sparrow* | U 71 | D 1163 | Denny | | 16.12.46 |

## CANCELLED SHIPS

### 1941 Programme

| | | | |
|---|---|---|---|
| *Nonsuch* | U 54 | D 2516 | Portsmouth |
| *Nymphe* | U 84 | D 2517 | Portsmouth |

### 1944 Programme

| | | | |
|---|---|---|---|
| *Partridge* | U 37 | J 6315 | Thornycroft |
| *Waterhen* | U 05 | | Denny |
| *Wryneck* | U 31 | | Denny |

## WAR LOSSES

| | | |
|---|---|---|
| *Ibis* | 10.11.42 | Aircraft, north of Algiers |
| *Kite* | 21.8.44 | Torpedoed by *U 344*, Arctic |
| *Lapwing* | 20.3.45 | Torpedoed by *U 716*, Kola Inlet |
| *Woodpecker* | 20.2.44 | Torpedoed by *U 764*, North Atlantic |

| 'BLACK SWAN' CLASS DISTRIBUTION OF SHIPS | | SHIPBUILDING PROGRAMMES | |
|---|---|---|---|
| Total completed | 37 | 1940 | 7 plus 4 RIN |
| Retained by RN | 31 | 1940 | 11 plus 2 RIN |
| Built for RIN | 6 | Supp | |
| Cancelled ships | 5 | 1941 | 6 |
| All built in UK | | 1942 | 3 |
| | | 1943 | 0 |
| | | 1944 | 3 |

*Sparrow*, the last of the Modified class to be completed, taken soon after commissioning in 1946. She has radar Type 293 and 291 on her lattice mast, and two twin Bofors with directors amidships. *(Ministry of Defence)*

## 'BLACK SWAN' CLASS SPECIFICATION

|  | 1937 Staff Requirement (Modified Egret) | Original 'Black Swan' Class (Flamingo) | Modified 'Black Swan' Class (Amethyst) |
|---|---|---|---|
| Displacement, tons | 1,300 | 1,300 | 1,350 |
| Dimensions |  |  |  |
|   length pp | 283' | 283' | 283' |
|       oa | 299' | 299' | 299' |
|   breadth | 37' 6" | 37' 6" | 38' |
|   draught | 8' 6" | 8' 6" | 8' 9" |
| Machinery | All double reduction geared turbines | | |
| SHP | 4,300 | 3,600 | 4,300 |
| Speed, knots | 20 | $19\frac{1}{4}$ | 20 |
| Boilers | All Admiralty water tube | | |
| Shafts | 2 | 2 | 2 |
| Oil Fuel | 415 | 390 |  |
| Endurance | 7,500×12k |  |  |
| Complement | 172 | 180 | 181 |
| Armament |  |  |  |
|   main | 3 twin 4" HA/LA Mk XVI on Mk XIX mounting | | |
|   director | yes | yes | yes |
|   close-range | 1 quad 2 pdr pom pom Mk VIII | 1 quad 2 pdr pom pom 12 20mm Oerlikons (6×2) | 2 twin 40mm Bofors 3 single 2 pdr QF 2 or 4 twin 20mm Oerlikons Mk V 2 single 20mm Oerlikons Mk IIIa |
| Anti-submarine |  |  | Split Hedgehog Mk II |
|  | 2 DCT | 2 DCT | 8 DCT |
|  | 2 rails | 2 rails | 2 rails |
|  | 40 D/cs | 60 d/cs | 110 d/cs |
|  |  |  | Shark projectiles |
| M/S Gear | Yes, Mk I | Yes, Mk I | No |
| Paravanes | Yes | Yes | No |
| SA Gear | No | No | Yes |
| Radar |  |  | Types 272 (or 271Q) 276 291 285 282 |
| Boats | 1/2 25' Fast motor boat 1 27' whaler 1 16' planing dinghy |  | 1 25' motor boat 1 27' whaler 1 16' planing dinghy |

## 1951 Refit Specification

Complement—220
Main armament—2 twin 4″ RPC guns, with rocket flares
Close-range armament—4 single 40mm Bofors, power mountings
A/S Armament—1 single Squid ATW mortar
Unifoxers, no SA gear
Radar, types 293Q, 275, 974, IFF
SH/F D/F, H/F D/F, M/F D/F

## 'BLACK SWAN' CLASS PRODUCTION TIMETABLE

|      |          | Built | Losses |      |          |    |   |
|------|----------|-------|--------|------|----------|----|---|
| 1939 | 1st half | 1     |        | 1943 | 1st half | 6  |   |
|      | 2nd half | 1     |        |      | 2nd half | 6  |   |
| 1940 | 1st half | 0     |        | 1944 | 1st half | 2  | 1 |
|      | 2nd half | 4     |        |      | 2nd half | 2  | 1 |
| 1941 | 1st half | 0     |        | 1945 | 1st half | 0  | 1 |
|      | 2nd half | 0     |        |      | 2nd half | 2  |   |
| 1942 | 1st half | 1     |        | 1946 | 1st half | 1  |   |
|      | 2nd half | 11    | 1      |      |          |    |   |

## MODIFIED 'BLACK SWAN' CLASS—CLOSE-RANGE ARMAMENT VARIATIONS

The following were typical close-range armaments of individual ships, as officially recorded at VE-Day in 1945; but refits near to that date may have altered this list yet again.

*4 twin Oerlikons, 2 single Oerlikons*
*Mermaid, Peacock, Hind, Lark, Magpie, Pheasant, Crane, Starling, Wild Goose, Wren, Cauvery, Kistna, Chanticleer, Lapwing, Alacrity*

*2 twin Bofors, 2 twin Oerlikons, 2 single Oerlikons*
*Hart, Amethyst, Redpole, Woodcock, Whimbrel, Sparrow*

*2 quadruple 2 pdr pom poms, 4 single Oerlikons*
*Cygnet*

*1 quadruple 2 pdr pom pom, 2 twin Oerlikons, 6 single Oerlikons*
*Erne, Black Swan*

*1 quadruple 2 pdr pom pom, 4 single Oerlikons*
*Flamingo, Pelican*

*2 single 2 pdr pom poms, 1 twin Oerlikon, 2 single Oerlikons*
*Godavari, Narbada*

*6 single Oerlikons only*
*Jumna, Sutlej*

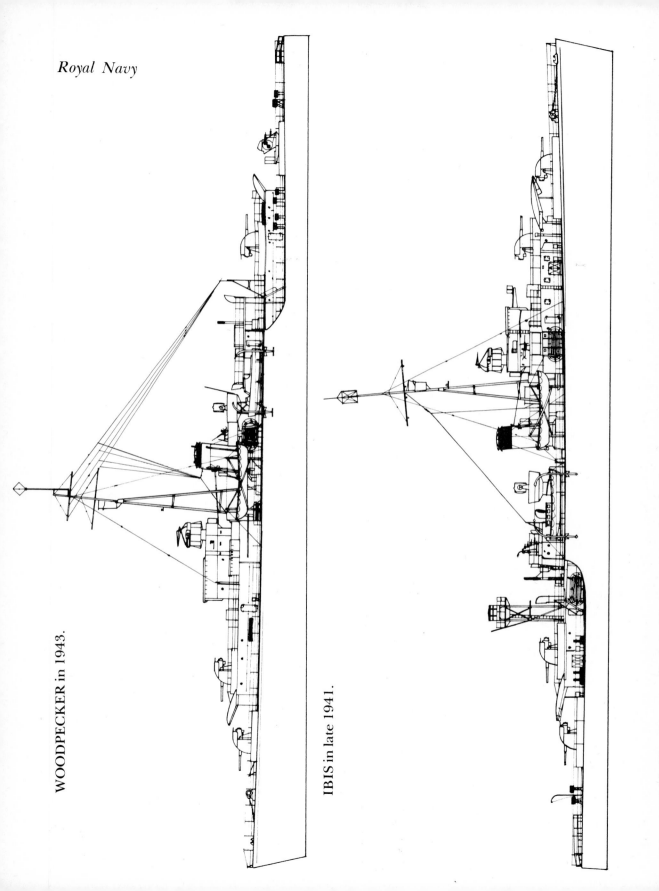

*Royal Navy*

WOODPECKER in 1943.

IBIS in late 1941.

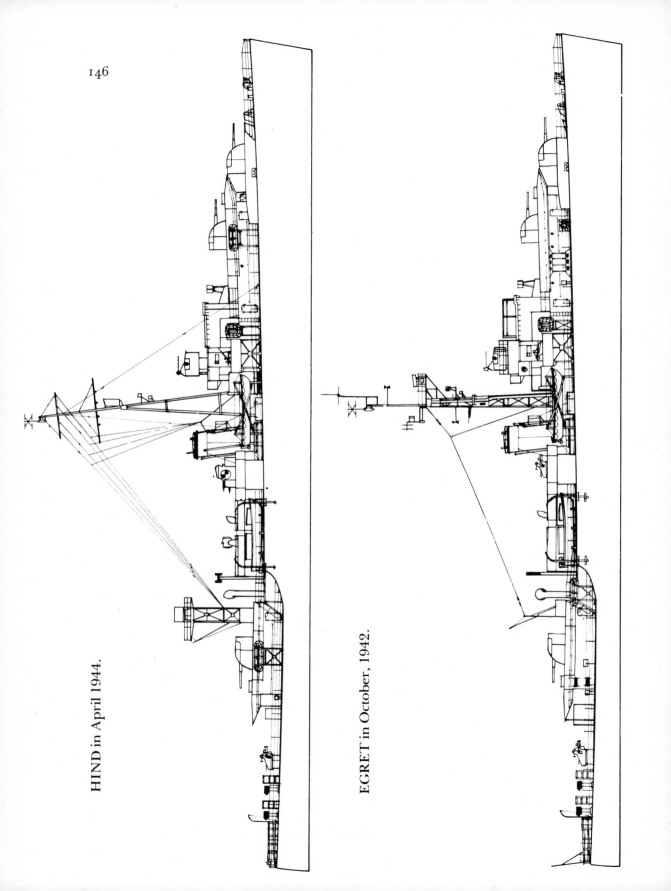

HIND in April 1944.

EGRET in October, 1942.

*Black Swan,* name ship of her class, taken in
May 1945. She still has the quadruple pom pom
on her quarterdeck, with extra depth charge
racks and Foxer equipment.
*(Ministry of Defence)*

*Pheasant,* of the Modified class. She had Type
271 radar on a solid structure aft, with Type
244 on top. She also has 6 twin Oerlikon
mountings. *(Ministry of Defence)*

## 'HUNT' CLASS DESTROYERS
### 86 Ships Completed

This class was, with the 'Black Swan' class sloops, one of the only two RN escort classes built during the war, to warship rather than classification society rules.

A requirement was passed to the Director of Naval Construction on 5th September 1938 for a new design of fast escort vessel. It would be required to perform the work of a modern escort vessel, and be capable of carrying out the manifold duties hitherto allotted to fleet destroyers, with the exception of attendance on a fleet. They were to have the anti-submarine and anti-aircraft armament of an escort vessel, with a speed approaching that of a fleet destroyer. In size and general arrangement they would follow destroyer practice, with certain modifications, to facilitate production and reduce cost.

The tables show how this requirement was turned into a proposed design, with two possible maximum speeds, 25 and 30 knots. Other details were developed: the watertight sub-division of the hull was carefully considered, a good freeboard, and high forecastle were specified, and stabilising equipment for gunnery was seen to be important. The cost was inevitably going to be higher than that estimated for the 'Black Swan' class sloops.

It is interesting to see that a quadruple set of torpedo tubes was originally specified, as two separate sets of twin tubes in the length available was not possible. The ships were to be fitted for minesweeping, and it was clear that a great deal was being expected from one escort vessel hull. The scantlings were increased, to take account of the more complicated specification, and the hull weight was increased in proportion. The engine room would not be sub-divided, but two boiler rooms would be included. The range was seen to be important; and indeed it fell short of the specified requirements in the end.

One of the problems was the size of crew required to work and fight a ship of this sophistication. The minimum complement for the faster ship was seen to be 143 men, plus 7 officers. The converted 'V and W' class destroyer *Whitley*, then commissioning, was to carry 124, with one twin 4″ mounting less, and the hull of the new escort had to be lengthened by 20 feet, to accommodate an extra 30 men.

*Type I*

In December 1938, a remarkably short period, the design had been largely settled, and was approved by the Board of Admiralty; but international treaty limits were still being observed, and although orders were placed for the first 10 ships on 21st March 1939, no keel could be laid before 8th June 1939, to conform with the treaty. Cammell Laird laid the first two keels at Birkenhead that very day! All these ships were to be built by private firms accustomed to building warships, as the naval dockyards were fully occupied at that time with refits and conversions.

From this point the design was steadily developed, while the ships were under construction. In January 1939 it was decided to omit the 0.5″ guns, and substitute a quadruple 2 pounder pom pom, with director. But delivery delays on the pom pom mountings would delay their fitting for a while. The depth-charge armament was to be steadily increased, as far as possible, to 30 in peace and 40 in war. For the first time in British destroyer practice the officers were to be berthed forward, under the bridge, to facilitate access to action stations for the whole crew. There were to be two masts, 60 feet apart, with the mainmast being a 30-feet-high pole.

Throughout this design and construction period it was clear that a very great deal of armament and equipment was being crammed into an escort vessel hull, and much concern was felt by the Director of Naval Construction as to whether the stability of these ships would be sufficient. In June 1939 he advised the Director of Naval Operations that 'there would be no margin for topweight in the design of the fast escorts, and only the inclining experiment on the first vessel of the class as completed, would afford the information required as to the maximum permissible weight'. In January 1940 he expressed his great interest in knowing how the stability was working out, by an inclining experiment on *Atherstone*, the first of the class to be completed.

In the event, though great efforts were made by all concerned to reduce the topweight, the stability was indeed a problem. When the quadruple pom pom was specified, 200 rounds of 4″ ammunition were deleted, together with some amenities; and the quality of steel to be used for various fittings was downgraded. The pom pom director was omitted, and the beam was increased by 9″ while the ships were on the stocks. In March 1939 it was decided to omit the minesweeping equipment, due to slow delivery, and this, too, helped.

*Liddesdale* arriving in the Forth, May 1942. The bowchaser stands out clearly here, as does the lack of armament between the funnel and the pom pom. *(Ministry of Defence)*

But in spite of all this effort it was clear, when the first ship was near completion, that too much had been expected from the one hull, and the following modifications had to be effected in the first group of ships, and the first three ships of the second group, which were too far advanced to be stopped.

a)  No 2 twin 4″ gun mounting omitted.
b)  Pom pom moved aft to No 2 gun position.
c)  No 1 gun bandstand removed, gun fitted on forecastle deck.
d)  After superstructure and blast screen reduced in height.
e)  Rangefinder director tower lowered by 2 feet.
f)  Searchlight platform lowered.
g)  4″ ammunition further reduced.
h)  Night lookout position on bridge removed.
    Bridge and signal deck reduced in size.
i)  Oiling at sea fittings removed.
j)  Funnel reduced 2 feet in height.
k)  16 foot dinghy and davits not fitted.
l)  Accommodation ladder and davit removed.
m) Ammunition derrick aft removed.
n)  Ammunition supply arrangements for No 2 gun omitted.
o)  Deck coverings were lightened.
p)  Direction-finding hut and fittings removed.
q)  Foremast and struts shortened 8 feet where not already fitted.
    Mainmast moved further aft.
r)  Ensign staff and stern boom omitted.
s)  No awning stanchions fitted.
t)  Hot fresh-water system omitted.
u)  No 2 boiler-room vents reduced in height.
v)  Reserve feed tanks omitted in No 1 boiler room.
w)  Electric cables double-banked, carrier plating reduced.
x)  Small breakwater fitted after end of after superstructure, to minimise washing down at No 3 gun.
y)  Some lagging was omitted.
z)  The torpedo tubes were omitted.

In addition, about 50 tons of ballast were fitted, and as a consolation the depth-charge outfit was increased to 50. A second inclining experiment was carried out on *Atherstone*, after modification, and this was found to be entirely satisfactory.

By this time the programme was well under way, and the second 10 ships (ordered in sequence, as shown in the table), followed the modified design of the first group. The elimination of the torpedo tubes in the latter had caused the Chief of Naval Staff to ask if they could not be reinstated in the second group, 'to provide them with a sting, as a means of self-defence, should they be attacked by a superior force at any time, be this by enemy destroyers or light cruisers'. But the design side pointed out that to do so the break of the forecastle would need to be moved 14 feet further forward, and the mizzenmast stepped 7 feet further aft, with the after superstructure being shortened by 4 feet; so that in March 1939 it was decided not to reinstate the torpedo tubes in the second group of 10 ships.

Being designed as regular warships, the boat outfit, as originally specified, comprised:

1 25 ft motor cutter
1 27 ft whaler
1 16 ft fast motor dinghy (the 'skimming dish')
4 life rafts

The fast motor dinghy was deleted in later ships, to obtain the maximum armament outfit.

Delivery for the first group of ships was specified as sixteen months from laying of the keel, but the complicated design caused the shipyards concerned to ask for seventeen to twenty months for the second group of ships.

In July 1939 arrangements were made to fit an early type of RDF set in one in every five of the new fast escort vessels.

On cost, it was estimated that one 'Hunt' could be built for the price of two 'Guillemot' patrol vessels, or 10 Admiralty trawlers.

### Type II

After war started, the programme of construction for this class was greatly expanded; the first 20 ships were ordered under the 1939 Programme, but a further 36 were quickly ordered under the 1939 War Emergency Programme, and as it was possible to modify the design somewhat, to incorporate the changes to date and improve the armament, this group of ships was designated the Type II.

The main differences were that the beam was increased to 31 feet 6 inches, and the third twin 4″ mounting was reinstated. The superstructure was modified, and the bridge was rearranged. Most of the modifications carried out to the Type I ships were carried through to Type II, but ballast was not found to be necessary in the latter.

This type comprised nearly half of the total 'Hunt' class, and many of them served in the Mediterranean.

### Type III

In March 1940, with some war experience in hand, a new version was seen to be necessary for a further 28 ships then to be ordered.

The outward identification signs of this type are distinctive—the funnel upright, with a sharply cutaway top, and the mast vertical also. The main armament reverted to two twin 4″ mountings, in A and X positions, as the third (Y) mounting in the Type II ships had been found difficult to work in bad weather. A twin torpedo tube mounting was reinstated, since it was felt that the only offensive value of these ships against enemy surface ships at night or in low visibility was the torpedo.

It was accepted, for speedy construction, that a speed of 27 knots in deep conditions was the maximum, but it was specified that the depth-charge outfit should be increased to 100, with 3 rails aft, and the greatest possible number of throwers that could be fitted (though 2 a side had to be accepted). Bullet-proof plating was added to the bridge, replacing the rather makeshift look of the padding fitted to the previous ships, and M/F D/F was added. Standard displacement by now had increased to 1,015 tons, and endurance was specified at 2,550 miles at 20 knots.

*Type IV*

In October 1938 Messrs John I. Thornycroft Ltd, at Southampton, a shipyard greatly experienced in destroyer building, and also in designing destroyers, proposed to the Admiralty that they should build 2 units of the 'Hunt' class to their own modified design.

There followed prolonged negotiations with the Admiralty, as to the details of this modified design. The outcome was *Brecon* and *Brissenden*, and although the Admiralty design staff of the time apparently saw aspects of these ships that needed modification, the finished ships seemed very smart and sleek in their appearance.

The basic difference in these two ships was that the forecastle deck was carried aft as far as the after superstructure, as a continuous deck. This gave the great advantage of covered access along the upper deck from forward to aft; in 1940 this was seen as a defect in the 'Hunt' design, though walking ways, weighing about 2 tons, could have been fitted between the tops of the deckhouses. But passage along the upper deck in the earlier types in heavy weather was at best a wet and precarious business.

In the Thornycroft design, a standard 'Hunt' class stem casting was used, with the upper portion raked well forward. The overall length was increased, and the beam also increased by 3". Thus the original stability conditions were maintained, and a set of triple 21" torpedo tubes could be carried, mounted on the upper deck, with their training gear located on the deck below.

Standard displacement was increased again, and the maximum speed fell a little. Endurance was at first calculated at 2,350 miles at 20 knots, including the capacity of the peace tanks; but this was later increased to 2,800 miles, greater than the earlier types.

The reinstatement in this new hull design of the third twin 4" gun mounting on the quarter deck meant a smaller depth-charge outfit than in the Type III ships, and in Type IV it was in fact reduced to 30 charges, handled by 2 rails and 2 throwers.

The table of comparative specifications for this class highlights the essential differences, but not so clearly as the selection of photographs that we have included. The original Thornycroft design proposals are also compared with the Type I design.

In a number of ships of all four types, when employed on the UK east coast or in the English Channel, where surface engagements against E-boats were common, a single manual 2 pounder pom pom was fitted as a bowchaser, right in the eyes of the ship. Sometimes this mounting had spray shields fitted on the ship's side, sometimes not. A few Mediterranean ships also had this bowchaser added later, when E-boats became common in that theatre of war also.

It should be remarked that no ahead-throwing anti-submarine weapons, either Hedgehog or Squid, were fitted in this class, even in the later war years; this was almost certainly due to the topweight problems in this class, though it will be recalled that the USN managed to fit in a Hedgehog, 2 single 3″ guns, and 4 single 20mm Oerlikons forward of the bridge in the DE classes. The 'Hunt' class was the only major RN war-built escort class not to have an ATW mortar at all.

The operational chapter on the Far East shows how the 'Hunt' class were seen as useful A/A escorts for the concluding stages of that war; but their short range made them less suitable than the frigates for the wide spaces of the Pacific. Types III and IV were allocated to the British Pacific Fleet, and Type II ships to the East Indies Fleet.

*Liddesdale*, taken in August 1942 by a Fleet Air Arm plane in the Forth. The deck layout is very clear. *(Ministry of Defence)*

## *Wensleydale*

This was a Type III 'Hunt' class destroyer, of the type which carried a twin torpedo-tube mounting.

She was built by Yarrow and Co Ltd, at Scotstoun on the Clyde, and commissioned in September 1942. She went to Scapa Flow for her initial working-up period, carrying out gunnery and torpedo exercises, and also working in the Home Fleet screen when the battleships went out for gunnery exercises. She then went on to the main escort working-up base, at Tobermory in Western Scotland, where she went through the fiery exercises devised by the famous Admiral Stevenson.

On completion, she joined the 15th Destroyer Flotilla, based at Plymouth. This flotilla of 'Hunt's worked convoys from the UK to Gibraltar and the Mediterranean, and along the western English coast, and also carried out sweeps against enemy shipping from time to time, along the northern and western coasts of Brittany.

*Wensleydale* participated in all of these duties, experiencing a near-hurricane in mid-winter in the Bay of Biscay. In October 1943 she was part of the force from Plymouth which engaged a German force off the French coast; the cruiser *Charybdis* was lost, and a sister Type III 'Hunt' also, *Limbourne*.

During the Normandy assault, in June/September 1944, she worked, with some other RN ships, in the USN Western Naval Task Force, escorting convoys in the western section of the English Channel, and across to the beaches. She also worked with the 'Captain' class coastal forces control frigates off Cape Barfleur, and during this period she took part in the sinking of two U-boats.

When the war moved east into the North Sea she did not join other frigates and 'Hunt' class units at Harwich or Sheerness, but remained on escort duties in the English Channel. Near the end of the European war she was involved in a serious collision, and was written off and scrapped soon after the war ended.

*Lamerton,* of Type II, at speed inshore. The after mounting is trained forward, and Type 286 radar is at the masthead. *(Imperial War Museum)*

## GERMAN U-BOATS SUNK BY 'HUNT' CLASS

| | | |
|---|---|---|
| U 131 | 17.12.41 | *Exmoor, Blankney* and others |
| U 434 | 18.12.41 | *Blankney* and others |
| U 587 | 27.3.42 | *Grove, Aldenham* and others |
| U 568 | 28.5.42 | *Eridge, Hurworth* and others |
| U 372 | 4.8.42 | *Croome, Tetcott* and others |
| U 559 | 30.10.42 | *Dulverton, Hurworth* and others |
| U 562 | 19.2.43 | *Hursley* and others |
| U 443 | 23.2.43 | *Bicester, Lamerton* and *Wheatland* |
| U 458 | 22.8.43 | *Easton* and *Pindos* (Greek) |
| U 593 | 13.12.43 | *Calpe* and others |
| U 450 | 10.3.44 | *Exmoor, Blankney, Blencathra* and *Brecon* |
| U 223 | 30.3.44 | *Hambledon* an d *Blencathra* |
| U 371 | 4.5.44 | *Blankney* and others |
| U 453 | 21.5.44 | *Liddlesdale* and others |
| U 671 | 4.8.44 | *Wensleydale* and others |
| U 413 | 20.8.44 | *Wensleydale* and others |

## ITALIAN SUBMARINES SUNK BY 'HUNT' CLASS DESTROYERS

| | | |
|---|---|---|
| *Maggiori Baracca* | 8.9.41 | *Croome* |
| *Galileo Ferrari* | 25.10.41 | *Lamerton* and others |
| *Amiraglio Caracciolo* | 11.12.41 | *Farndale* |
| *Narvalo* | 14.1.43 | *Hursley* and others |
| *Asteria* | 17.2.43 | *Wheatland* and *Easton* |

## 'HUNT' CLASS COMMAND ALLOCATION
**(all at 1st January, except last)**

| | *1941* | *1942* | *1943* | *1944* | *1945* | *7.5.45* | *3.8.45* |
|---|---|---|---|---|---|---|---|
| Sheerness | 5 | 6 | 9 | 7 | 16 | 27 | 8 |
| Harwich | 8 | 5 | 6 | 6 | 11 | 15 | 7 |
| Portsmouth | 6 | 4 | 4 | 5 | 0 | 0 | 0 |
| Plymouth | 0 | 6 | 9 | 5 | 4 | 1 | 0 |
| Scapa | 0 | 4 | 8 | 0 | 0 | 0 | 0 |
| Londonderry | 0 | 2 | 2 | 1 | 0 | 0 | 2 |
| Rosyth | 0 | 0 | 4 | 2 | 0 | 0 | 0 |
| Mediterranean | 0 | 11 | 29 | 46 | 21 | 12 | 7 |
| Far East | 0 | 0 | 2 | 0 | 16 | 7 | 9 |
| TOTAL | 19 | 38 | 73 | 72 | 68 | 64 | 33 |

**NOTE**
Ships of this class allocated to the Far East in 1945 totalled 33.

## 'HUNT' CLASS FOR THE FAR EAST, 1945

|  | East Indies Fleet | British Pacific Fleet |
|---|---|---|
| Planned | 20 | 13 |
| On station, 3rd August 1945 | 9 | 0 |

### EAST INDIES FLEET, 3.8.45

*Farndale, Bicester, Blackmore, Bleasdale, Brecon, Calpe, Chidding-fold, Cowdray, Eggesford*

*Brissenden*, one of the two Type IV ships completed by Thornycroft to their own design. The knuckle in the bow section, and the well-raked stem, stand out. The covered upper deck has been carried right aft, as in the frigates, and torpedo tubes were carried, as well as 3 4" mountings. (*Ministry of Defence*)

## 'HUNT' CLASS PRODUCTION FIGURES

| | | Type I | Type II | Type III | Type IV |
|---|---|---|---|---|---|
| 1939 | 1st half | | | | |
| | 2nd half | 3 | | | |
| 1940 | 1st half | 13 | | | |
| | 2nd half | 4 | 11 | | |
| 1941 | 1st half | | 14 | | |
| | 2nd half | | 9 | 9 | |
| 1942 | 1st half | | 2 | 15 | 1 |
| | 2nd half | | | 3 | 1 |
| 1943 | 1st half | | | 1 | |

Cancelled Ships—0

## OVERALL NUMBERS

| | |
|---|---|
| Completed | 86 |
| Retained by RN | 72 |
| Transferred to other navies | 14 |
| Cancelled | 0 |
| War losses | 18 plus 3 Allied |

## PLACING OF ORDERS

| | |
|---|---|
| **1st Group** | 1939 Programme. 10 ships, Type 1<br>Tenders out, 20.12.38<br>Orders placed, 21.3.39 |
| **2nd Group** | 1939 Programme. 10 ships, Type I<br>Sketch design, 20.2.39<br>Orders placed, 11.4.39 |
| **3rd Group** | 1939 War Emergency Programme. 20 ships, Type II<br>Tenders out, 9.10.39<br>Orders placed, 30.10.40 |
| **4th Group** | 1939 War Emergency Programme. 16 ships, Type II<br>Orders placed, 10.12.40 |
| **5th Group** | 1940 Programme. 14 ships, Type III |
| **6th Group** | 1940 Programme. 16 ships, Type III<br>2 ships, Type IV |

## 'HUNT' CLASS—FULL SPEED ON TRIALS

| | | |
|---|---|---|
| TYPE I | High 30.25 knots | Low 26.75 knots |
| TYPE II | High 27.1 knots | Low 22.1 knots |
| TYPE III | High 27.91 knots | Low 23.0 knots |
| TYPE IV | High 25.0 knots | Low 24.91 knots |

## 'HUNT' CLASS DESIGN DEVELOPMENT, 1938/39

| | Original DNO Requirements | | DNC Proposal | | Approved Design |
|---|---|---|---|---|---|
| Date | 22.9.38 | 22.9.38 | | | 20.10.38 |
| Ship Type | Destroyer Escort | | Destroyer Escort | | Fast Escort Vessels |
| Speed | 30 | 25 | 30 | 25 | 32 |
| Displacement | | | | 640 | 875 |
| Dimensions | | | | | |
|   length pp | | | 265 | 240 | 272 |
|   breadth | | | 27' | 25'3" | 28'3" |
|   draught | | | 9' | 8'6" | 7'8" |
| Machinery | Single reduction Parsons geared turbines | | | | |
| Shafts | 2 | 2 | 2 | 2 | 2 |
| SHP | | | 17,000 | 8,000 | 18,000 |
| Speed | 28/31 | 20/26 | 31 st | 26 st | 32 st |
| | | | 28 deep | 24 deep | 29 deep |
| Oil Fuel | | | | 150 | 205 |
| Endurance | 3,500× 15 kn | 3,500× 15 kn | | 3,000× 15 kn | 3,100×15 kn 1,280×25 kn |
| Complement | 120 | | 150 | 100 | 135 |
| Armament: | | | | | |
|   main | 4 4" | 4 4" | 4 4" | 4 4" | 6 4" |
|   close-range | 2 0.5" | 2 0.5" | 2 0.5" | 2 0.5" | 2 0.5" |
| Torpedo tubes | 2×2 or 1×4 | None | 1×4 | None | None |
| Searchlight | 1 24" | 1 24" | 1 24" | 1 24" | 1 24" |
| Depth charges | | | | 30 | 20 |
| Minesweeping cap | Yes | Yes | Yes | Yes | Yes |
| Est Cost | | 375,000 | 375,000 | | 390,000 |

A good aerial picture of *Ledbury* at speed in October 1942. The 4″ mounting has the canvas hood extended, as was normal with these guns, due to blast problems. *(Ministry of Defence)*

## COMPARATIVE SPECIFICATIONS OF SHIPS BUILT

| | *Type I* | *Type II* | *Type III* | *Type IV* |
|---|---|---|---|---|
| Displacement | 1,000 | 1,010 | 1,015 | 1,175 |
| Dimensions | | | | |
|   length pp | 264 | 264 | 264 | 276 |
|   length oa | 280 | 280 | 280 | 296 |
|   breadth | 29 | 31'6" | 31'6" | 33'3" |
|   draught | 7'6" | 7'6" | 7'9" | 9' |
| Machinery | Parsons IR single reduction geared turbines, RPM 380 | | | |
| Boilers | 2 Admiralty 3-drum type, 300 lbs/sq in | | | |
| Shafts | 2 | 2 | 2 | 2 |
| SHP | 19,000 | 19,000 | 19,000 | 19,000 |
| Speed, stand cond | 30.5 | 29.7 | 29.6 | 27.0 |
| Highest on trials | 30.25 | 27.50 | 28.30 | 25.0 |
| Lowest on trials | 26.0 | 22.70 | 22.50 | 24.91 |
| OF Capacity | 243 | 277 | 285 | 286 *Brecon* 357 *Briss* |
| Endurance | 2,300×20kn | 2,500×20kn | 2,550×20kn | 2,800×20kn |
| Complement | 133 | 159 | 170 | 170 |
| Armament: | | | | |
|   main | 4 4" QF Mk XVI on Mk XIX mtg. | 6 4" | 4 4" | 6 4" |
|   close-range | 1 quad, 2pdr pom pom | ditto | ditto | ditto |
| | 2 single 20mm Oerlikon MkIIa | 2 ditto | 2-6 ditto | 8 ditto |
| Torpedo tubes | None | None | 2 | 3 |
| Depth charges | 70 | 60 | 70 | 30 |
| Radar | Types 290 285 | 290 285 | 290/272 285 | 290 285 |

*Meynell* on the UK east coast, with barrage balloons flying behind her. She has the early Type 286 radar at her masthead, and anti-splinter mattresses round her bridgework. *(Ministry of Defence)*

## COMPARISON OF THORNYCROFT PROPOSED DESIGN WITH ORIGINAL ADMIRALTY APPROVED DESIGN

|  | Thornycroft Design | | Admiralty Design |
|---|---|---|---|
|  | 35k | 33k |  |
| Displacement | 1,000 | 950 | 875 |
| Dimensions |  |  |  |
| length wl | 268 | 270 | 272 |
| breadth | 31 | 31 | 28'3" |
| depth | 15'6" | 15'6" | 16'6" |
| SHP | 30,000 | 24,000 | 18,000 |
| Speed | 35 | 33 | 32 |
| OF Capacity | 200 | 200 | 205 |
| Endurance | 2,000×20kn | 2,000×20kn | 2,500×20kn |
| Complement |  |  | 176 |

A very early picture of *Holderness* in heavy weather. She has no radar either on her mast or on her gunnery director, and has a tall mainmast as well as two yards on her foremast. The camouflage is still dark grey overall. *(Imperial War Museum)*

*Bleasdale,* in 21st Destroyer Flotilla markings at Sheerness. 1945 camouflage scheme, bowchaser pom pom, Type 271 aft, and Headache on the foremast. She was active in the final operations against E-boats in the North Sea. *(Imperial War Museum)*

*Ledbury* in May 1943. She was probably operating on the Plymouth-Gibraltar run at the time, as she has H/F D/F on a pole aft. Note the canvas blast screens again on the 4″ gun shields. *(Ministry of Defence)*

## 'HUNT' CLASS – CLASS LIST

### TYPE I

| Name | Pendant No. | Job No. | Builder | Building Time | Completion Date |
|------|-------------|---------|---------|---------------|-----------------|
| **1939 Programme** | | | | | |
| *Atherstone* | L 05 | | Cammell Laird | 9m0d | 23.3.40 |
| *Berkeley* | L 17 | | Cammell Laird | 11m28d | 6.6.40 |
| *Cattistock* | L 35 | | Yarrow | 13m22d | 1.8.40 |
| *Cleveland* | L 46 | J 1835 | Yarrow | 14m12d | 18.9.40 |
| *Cotswold* | L 54 | J 1836 | Yarrow | 13m6d | 16.11.40 |
| *Cottesmore* | L 78 | J 1837 | Yarrow | 12m17d | 29.12.40 |
| *Eglinton* | L 87 | | VA, Tyne | 14m20d | 28.8.40 |
| *Exmoor* | L 61 | J 4099 | VA, Tyne | 16m11d | 18.10.40 |
| *Fernie* | L 11 | | J. Brown | 11m21d | 29.5.40 |
| *Garth* | L 20 | | J. Brown | 12m23d | 1.7.40 |
| *Hambledon* | L 37 | | Swan Hunter | 11m30d | 8.6.40 |
| *Holderness* | L 48 | | Swan Hunter | 13m11d | 10.8.40 |
| *Mendip* | L 60 | J 4111 | Swan Hunter | 14m12d | 12.10.40 |
| *Meynell* | L 82 | J 4114 | Swan Hunter | 16m20d | 30.12.40 |
| *Pytchley* | L 92 | J 1111 | Scott | 14m28d | 23.10.40 |
| *Quantock* | L 58 | J 1112 | Scott | 18m11d | 6.2.41 |
| *Southdown* | L 25 | J 6602 | White | 14m17d | 8.11.40 |
| *Tynedale* | L 96 | J 1471 | Stephen | | 5.11.40 |
| *Whaddon* | L 45 | J 1472 | Stephen | 19m4d | 28.2.41 |

### TYPE II

| Name | Pendant No. | Job No. | Builder | Building Time | Completion Date |
|------|-------------|---------|---------|---------------|-----------------|
| **War Emergency Programme** | | | | | |
| *Avon Vale* | L 06 | J 1569 | J. Brown | 12m2d | 17.2.41 |
| *Badsworth* | L 03 | J 3260 | Cammell Laird | 15m3d | 18.8.41 |
| *Beaufort* | L 14 | J 3560 | Cammell Laird | 15m17d | 3.11.41 |
| *Bicester* | L 34 | J 4210 | Hawthorn Leslie | 23m11d | 9.5.42 |
| *Blackmore* | L 43 | J 1479 | Stephen | 14m1d | 14.4.42 |
| *Blankney* | L 30 | J 1570 | J. Brown | 10m25d | 11.4.41 |
| *Blencathra* | L 24 | J 3460 | Cammell Laird | 12m26d | 14.12.40 |
| *Brocklesby* | L 42 | J 3562 | Cammell Laird | 17m21d | 9.5.41 |
| *Calpe* | L 71 | J 4196 | Swan Hunter | 17m29d | 11.12.41 |
| *Chiddingfold* | L 31 | J 1115 | Scott | 19m16d | 16.10.41 |
| *Cowdray* | L 52 | J 1116 | Scott | 26m29d | 29.7.42 |
| *Croome* | L 62 | J 1477 | Stephen | 12m22d | 29.6.41 |
| *Dulverton* | L 63 | J 1478 | Stephen | | 28.9.41 |
| *Eridge* | L 68 | J 4129 | Swan Hunter | | 20.8.40L |
| *Farndale* | L 70 | J 4133 | Swan Hunter | 17m6d | 27.4.41 |

| | | | | | |
|---|---|---|---|---|---|
| *Grove* | L 77 | J 4199 | Swan Hunter | | 29.5.41L |
| *Heythrop* | L 85 | J 4139 | Swan Hunter | | 30.10.40L |
| *Hurworth* | L 28 | J 4207 | VA, Tyne | | 10.4.41L |
| *Lamerton* | L 88 | J 4142 | Swan Hunter | 16m5d | 16.8.41 |
| *Lauderdale* | L 95 | J 6153 | Thornycroft | 24m2d | 23.12.41 |
| *Ledbury* | L 90 | J 6606 | Thornycroft | 24m18d | 11.2.42 |
| *Liddesdale* | L 100 | J 4136 | VA, Tyne | 15m8d | 28.2.41 |
| *Middleton* | L 74 | J 4213 | VA, Tyne | 20m30d | 10.1.42 |
| *Puckeridge* | L 108 | J 6108 | White | | 30.7.41 |
| *Southwold* | L 10 | J 6274 | White | | 9.10.41 |
| *Tetcott* | L 99 | J 6293 | White | 16m13d | 11.12.41 |
| *Oakley*<br>  ex *Tickham* | L 98 | J 4145 | Yarrow | | 7.5.42 |
| *Wheatland* | L 122 | J 1849 | Yarrow | 17m4d | 3.11.41 |
| *Wilton* | L 128 | J 1850 | Yarrow | 20m13d | 18.2.42 |
| *Zetland* | L 59 | J 1854 | Yarrow | 20m26d | 27.6.42 |

## TYPE III

| Name | Pendant No. | Job No. | Builder | Building Time | Completion Date |
|---|---|---|---|---|---|
| **1940 Programme** | | | | | |
| *Airedale* | L 07 | J 1578 | J. Brown | | 31.12.41 |
| *Albrighton* | L 12 | J 1579 | J. Brown | 13m23d | 22.2.42 |
| *Aldenham* | L 22 | J 3766 | Cammell Laird | | 30.1.42 |
| *Belvoir* | L 32 | J 3964 | Cammell Laird | 17m15d | 29.3.42 |
| *Blean* | L 47 | J 4247 | Hawthorn Leslie | | 23.8.42 |
| *Bleasdale* | L 50 | J 4283 | VA, Tyne | 10m16d | 16.4.42 |
| *Derwent* | L 83 | J 3988 | VA, Barrow | 14m5d | 3.4.42 |
| *Easton* | L 09 | J 6061 | White | 20m13d | 7.12.42 |
| *Eggesford* | L 15 | J 6126 | White | 18m28d | 21.1.43 |
| *Goathland* | L 27 | J 1694 | Fairfield | 20m28d | 27.10.42 |
| *Haydon* | L 75 | J 4299 | VA, Tyne | 17m24d | 24.10.42 |
| *Holcombe* | L 56 | J 1489 | Stephen | | 17.9.42 |
| *Limbourne* | L 57 | J 1490 | Stephen | | 23.10.42 |
| *Melbreak* | L 73 | J 4293 | Swan Hunter | 15m16d | 10.10.42 |
| *Penylan* | L 89 | J 3585 | VA, Barrow | | 25.8.42 |
| *Rockwood* | L 39 | J 3989 | VA, Barrow | 13m23d | 21.10.42 |
| *Stevenstone* | L 16 | J 6056 | White | 18m16d | 18.3.43 |
| *Talybont* | L 18 | J 6160 | White | 17m21d | 19.5.43 |
| *Tanatside* | L 69 | J 1869 | Yarrow | 14m11d | 4.9.42 |
| *Wensleydale* | L 86 | J 1870 | Yarrow | 15m2d | 30.10.42 |

## TYPE IV

| | | | | | |
|---|---|---|---|---|---|
| *Brecon* | L 76 | J 6069 | Thornycroft | | 18.12.42 |
| *Brissenden* | L 79 | J 6140 | Thornycroft | | 12.2.43 |

## TRANSFERRED TO OTHER NAVIES

| Name | Pendant No. | Job No. | Builder | Building Time | Completion Date |
|---|---|---|---|---|---|
| **TYPE II** | | | | | |
| **To Greece** | | | | | |
| *Themistocles* ex *Bramham* | L 51 | M 1480 | Stephen | 14m9d | 16.6.42 |
| *Kriti* ex *Hursley* | L 84 | J 4204 | Swan Hunter | 15m12d | 24.4.42 |
| **To Poland** | | | | | |
| *Slazak* ex *Bedale* | L 26 | J 4202 | Hawthorn Leslie | 24m20d | 18.6.42 |
| *Kujawiak* ex *Oakley* | L 72 | J 4145 | VA, Tyne | 20m19d | 7.5.42 |
| *Krakowiak* ex *Silverton* | L 115 | J 6583 | White | 17m23d | 28.5.41 |
| **To Norway** | | | | | |
| *Arendal* ex *Badsworth* | L 03 | | Cammell Laird | | 17.3.41L |
| **TYPE III** | | | | | |
| **To Greece** | | | | | |
| *Pindos* ex *Bolebroke* | L 65 | J 4285 | Swan Hunter | 14m7d | 10.6.42 |
| *Adrias* ex *Border* | L 67 | J 4287 | Swan Hunter | 15m5d | 5.8.42 |
| *Hastings* ex *Catterick* | L 61 | J 3886 | VA, Barrow | 15m6d | 6.6.42 |
| *Canaris* ex *Hatherleigh* | L 53 | J 4295 | VA, Tyne | 19m29d | 10.8.42 |
| *Miaoulis* ex *Modbury* | L 91 | J 4297 | Swan Hunter | 15m21d | 25.11.42 |
| **To Norway** | | | | | |
| *Eskdale* (same name) | L 36 | J 3269 | Cammell Laird | | 16.3.42L |
| *Glaisdale* (same name) | L 44 | J 3367 | Cammell Laird | 16m6d | 12.6.42 |
| **To France** | | | | | |
| *La Combattante* ex *Haldon* | L 19 | J 1695 | Fairfield | | 27.4.42L |

## 'HUNT' CLASS WAR LOSSES

| | | | |
|---|---|---|---|
| *Adrias* | 22.10.43, mine, | CTL | |
| *Airedale* | 15.6.42, aircraft, | E Med | |

| | | |
|---|---|---|
| *Aldenham* | 14.12.44, mine, | NE Adriatic |
| *Berkeley* | 19.8.42, aircraft, | Dieppe landing |
| *Blean* | 11.12.42, U-boat, | off Oran |
| *Dulverton* | 13.11.43, glider | bomb off Kos |
| *Eridge* | 12.42, torpedo, | E-boat, E Med, CTL |
| *Eskdale* | 1943, torpedo, | E-boat, off Lizard |
| *Exmoor* | 25.2.41, torpedo, | E-boat, off Lowestoft |
| *Grove* | 12.6.42, torpedo, | U-boat, E Med |
| *Haldon* (ex) | 23.2.45, mine | or torpedo, N Sea |
| *Heythrop* | 20.3.42, torpedo, | U-boat, E Med |
| *Hurcombe* | 12.12.43, torpedo, | U-boat, W Med |
| *Hurworth* | 22.10.43, mine, | off Kalimno |
| *Kujawiak* | 16.6.42, mine, | off Malta |
| *Limbourne* | 23.10.43. torpedo, | E-boat. English Chan |
| *Penylan* | 3.12.42, torpedo, | E-boat, English Chan |
| *Puckeridge* | 6.9.43, torpedo, | U-boat, W Med |
| *Quorn* | 3.8.44, small | battle unit, Normandy |
| *Southwold* | 24.3.42, mine, | off Malta |
| *Tynedale* | 12.12.43, torpedo, | U-boat, W Med |

Type II *Bicester* in August 1943. This gives a good picture of the wake pattern of an escort at speed. Note the whaler turned out on the port side, as a seaboat. *(Ministry of Defence)*

166

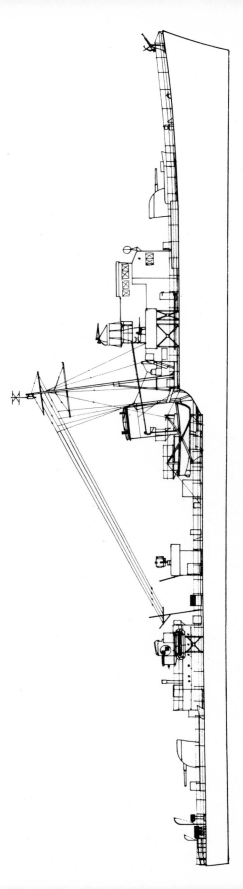

BERKELEY in April, 1942.

COTSWOLD in early 1942.

Royal Navy

BICESTER in June, 1942.

AVON VALE in 1944.

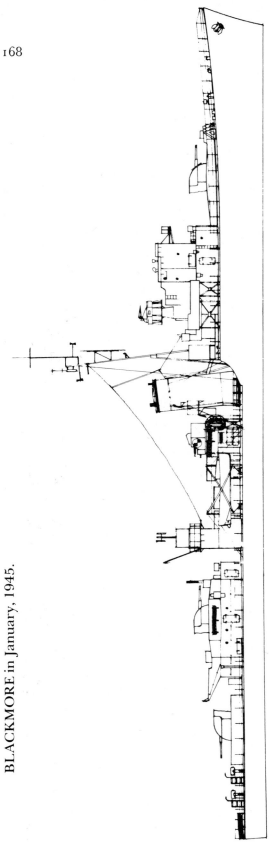

BLACKMORE in January, 1945.

BLEAN in late 1942.

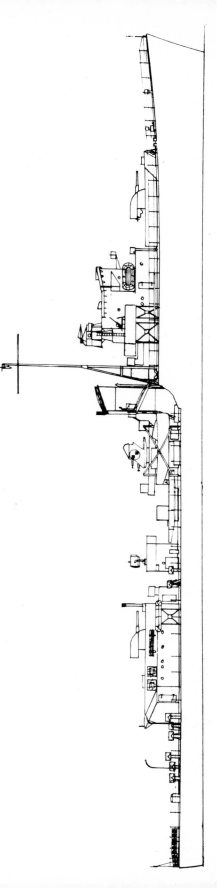

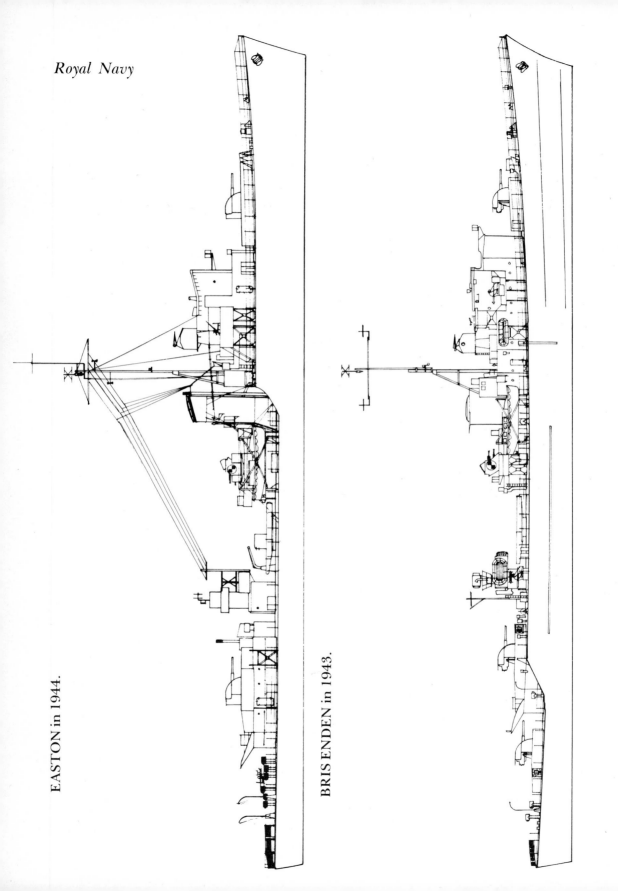

*Royal Navy*

EASTON in 1944.

BRISENDEN in 1943.

*Meadowsweet* in August 1942. The extra sheer is outstanding, and the funnel appears slimmer than usual. The Hedgehog is on the extended platform aft of the 4″ gun, which has been painted out in the camouflage scheme. (*Ministry of Defence*)

*Jonquil* in May 1944, giving a good view of the tumble home aft. She only has one extra Oerlikon aft, despite the late date. (*Ministry of Defence*)

## 'FLOWER' CLASS CORVETTES
## 135 ships completed

The concept and initial design of this class has been explored in the policy chapter; here, we will follow the development of the class. There were many major alterations carried out, as the war progressed, and a study of these is in itself a study of the anti-submarine battle.

Once the Admiralty decided on the initial design, and with war fast approaching, orders were quickly placed—indeed, 60 corvettes were ordered *before* the outbreak of war in 1939. A total of 141 of the original class were ordered, all before the end of 1940, as follows:

```
25.7.39    30
28.8.39    30
20.9.39    30
14.12.39   20=110 by end 1939.
 8.4.40    20
 1.7.40     2
 1.8.40     6
24.10.40    3=31 in 1940, of which 6 were cancelled.
```

The class were originally known, variously, as 'Patrol Vessels, Whaler Type' and as 'A/S-M Patrol Vessels', the 'M' designating merchant-type. The class name was later and happily changed to 'Flower', following on the World War I precedent, and giving a distinctive name to all the ships of the class, which lent itself to some ribaldry.

The first ship was completed in five and a half months from the laying of the keel, and the following vessels were completed at the rate of one every three and a half weeks from the Smith's Dockyard alone. In 1941, Harland & Wolff in Belfast were completing 2 ships a month, and 6-8 ships in all were completing on average each month. The estimated cost of the original ships of this class was some £90,000 per ship—incredible, by today's cost standards.

This production gave some impressive results. By May 1942 some 200 corvettes in all, including RCN ships, were in service, divided as follows:

```
37 UK-based North Atlantic escort groups
78 Canada and Newfoundland-based escort groups
14 UK-Gibraltar escort groups
 6 UK-Russia escort groups
47 Mediterranean, West Africa, South Atlantic, Indian Ocean
10 Transferred to USN
 8 On loan to USN
```

### Minesweeping Corvettes

We have seen that this class was originally intended for coastal work, and not the North Atlantic. With the menace from mines in the early years of the war, and the severe shortage of fleet minesweepers, it was not surprising that in 1940 approval was given for 24 of the 'Flower' class to be fitted for minesweeping with

Oropesa sweeps (against moored mines), and a further 8 (later 16) of the class for minesweeping with LL sweeps (against magnetic mines). The equipment is clearly seen in some of the photographs. It is not clear how far the corvettes were used for minesweeping in Home waters, but certainly they were extensively used as sweepers in the Mediterranean.

In September 1940, Smith's Dock mocked up the first minesweeper corvette, with Mark II Oropesa sweeps, Kites, Otters, davits and winches. There were many difficulties in fitting all this into the restricted space available; the number of depth charges was severely restricted (a minimum of 10), and the displacement went up from 1,180 to 1,203 tons, in the deep-load condition.

Among those fitted with LL sweeps, mark IV, were:
*Delphinium, Erica, Gloxinia, Hyacinth, Peony, Primula, Salvia, Snapdragon, Lotus* (July 1940).
*Borage, Bryony, Buttercup, Hyderabad, Phlox, Pink, Pennywort, Poppy* (November 1940).

In 1941 it was approved that LL fitted corvettes in Home waters should also be fitted with SA gear Type A (against acoustic mines), on a hinged boom fitted over the bows.

The first group of 8 ships fitted with LL sweeps, as shown above, were sent to the Middle or Far East in 1941.

In February 1944, with the supply of new fleet minesweepers steadily increasing, it was approved that LL equipment should be removed from all corvettes so fitted, thus finally recognising their specialised A/S role.

### Improved Hull Form

The 'Flower' class was the only one in which such drastic alterations as these were undertaken, and this resulted from their dramatic switch from their designed coastal role to that of mid-ocean escort. The strain on the ships' companies on this latter service was very great (and when oiling-at-sea facilities became standard was the limiting endurance factor), and it became essential to modify the original 'Flower' class units as refit opportunities presented.

Thus the later ships of the original class appeared with the forecastle deck extended aft to the funnel, and greater sheer and flare built into the bows, thus enabling the ships to ride the seas more easily, and the crews to find better shelter from the freezing spray.

These modifications can be seen in the photographs, and many of the earlier units also received at least a part of these same alterations during refits, at any rate having their forecastle decks extended aft.

But some of the units sent to the Mediterranean in 1940 were not brought home until late in the war, and so did not receive these alterations. An alternative can be seen in the photograph of *Gloxinia,* where additional accommodation, with ship's side plating, was built in amidships, but the original break of the forecastle retained.

It is the hull form, more than any other feature, which distinguishes the Modified 'Flower' class units from the original ships, but the photographs show that the ships completed towards the end of the original programme had been modified to the point where their hull form and bridge structure were almost indistinguishable from the Modified class.

## Tropical Service

Again reflecting the great demand for new escort vessels in the early years of the war, it was approved that first 10 of the 'Flower' class should be fitted for tropical service, then a further 15, and in July 1941 that all should be so fitted, when coming in for refit. Indeed, in that month there were 7 'Flower' class units on foreign service, but not so fitted, reflecting frequent changes in command allocation, as well as great demand for these efficient ships.

## Arctic Service

Surprisingly, it was not found necessary to equip many of this class for Arctic service, and we do not find them heavily involved in Russian convoys. But some, among them *Godetia, Oxlip, Potentilla* and *Saxifrage,* were so fitted, and the photograph of *Lotus* gives a good idea of the variation in weather conditions which the crews of the corvettes had to endure, with spray freezing right over the forward part of the ship, causing serious topweight problems.

## Alterations and Additions

The list of these, as approved, gives a good idea of the increasing sophistication of the Atlantic battle.

The photographs show the original ships with no radar at all, then progressing to an early masthead type aerial, then to the impressive and reliable Type 271, for which 25 units based on Liverpool received high priority, as soon as the sets became available. M/F D/F was fitted in all cases, but it will be noted that this class did not receive H/F D/F, the sets available presumably being reserved to the faster ships, which could run down a bearing on a U-boat's radio transmission.

The armament also developed. The original and old 4″ gun was not changed, due to shortage of new weapons; but the quadruple 0.5″ and the other 0.303″ machine guns gradually gave way, as supply permitted, to a 2 pounder pom pom aft, 2 single 20mm Oerlikons in the bridge wings, and finally to a further 4 single Oerlikons further aft, in bandstands mounted on the ship's side. In some ships, too, the pom pom was moved further aft, and a third single Oerlikon fitted in its old position.

There were, of course, variations to the close-range armament. The photographs show that units in the Mediterranean, being subject to air attack more than those in the Western Approaches, received a variety of extra weapons, and in 1944/45, when the power-mounted twin Oerlikons started to become available, these made their appearance aft in some ships of the class, especially the later Modified class.

When the Atlantic battle was at its height in 1943, and close-range gunfights between escorts and surfaced U-boats became more common, 6 pounder Army Mark II 7cwt guns were fitted in some units, either aft of the 4″ gun, or higher up, on the bridge itself. These guns had a high velocity and penetrating power.

*Anti-submarine equipment*

The original depth-charge outfit for the class was 25 charges, 2 rails, and 2 throwers.

As the Atlantic battle increased in intensity, and the need for units to remain at sea for longer periods increased, this outfit was considerably extended.

In August 1940 it was increased to 50 charges, though not in those ships fitted for minesweeping, where space and weight were already at a premium.

Hedgehogs started to appear in ships of the class from June 1941. The mounting was usually fitted on an extended platform, on the starboard side just aft of the 4″ gun. The weight was balanced, in part, by the addition of the ready-use lockers for the 2″ rocket flares on the port side of the gundeck. In some units the Hedgehog mounting may have been fitted in its 'split' form, with a half mounting on each side, aft of the 4″ gun.

In September 1943 Foxer gear (against acoustic torpedoes) started to be fitted in ships of the class, as in the other escort classes, as a matter of urgency. The depth-charge davits had to suffice for handling for the time being, until better davits could be made and fitted. CSA smoke apparatus was not fitted in this class, due to shortage of space on the quarterdeck, and the fitting of Foxer gear taking precedence. Up to 6 individual smoke floats were, however, fitted in lieu.

Squid mortars were not fitted in this class—it was agreed that the ship's design was not suitable for the addition of these heavy weapons.

*Aubrietia* in July 1941. This was the original configuration—short forecastle, mast forward of the bridge, no radar, and minesweeping gear aft. (*Ministry of Defence*)

*Bridges*

The development of the bridge structure in this class is of particular interest. In no other war-built class were such drastic changes made, with a variety of bridge types being in.service in ships of the class at any one time.

As early as 1940, with units operating in mid-Atlantic, the need to modify the bridges became clear. Following merchant practice, the original ships had wooden enclosed compass platforms and wheelhouses, with many opening windows in them, and the compass platform built up high, to obtain a good view over the 4″ gun.

Then several new requirements produced major alterations. The addition of the Type 271 radar hut, more extensive Asdic (sonar) equipment, 2 single Oerlikons on the bridge wings, protective padding to the bridge guardrails against aircraft attack, and the extension of the forecastle deck under the bridge, all gave rise to several types of bridge. Indeed, by the end of the war the class had discarded their old merchant type appearance round the bridge structure and looked very naval and professional.

The first extended bridges, to take Oerlikons, were fitted in *Buttercup*, *Rockrose* and *Tamarisk,* in late 1941, then to *Genista* and all ships subsequently completed or refitted. In many ships, with the forecastle deck extended, with extra depth charges, and radar, there was too much topweight to give any great margin, and even with an additional 30 tons of permanent ballast in the boiler rooms the bridge extensions could not have steel protection and had to make do with padded mattress squares.

The later standard version of the bridge in this class made its appearance in late 1941, when Smith's Dock did a mock-up on *Freesia,* followed by *Gladiolus* and *Honeysuckle.* Then the last 14 UK-built ships were given the 'open bridge' version, *Samphire, Stonecrop, Vetch, Sweetbriar, Thyme, Zenobia, Phlox, Pink, Lotus, Meadowsweet, Potentilla, Godetia, Tamarisk* and *Balsam.*

*Camellia* in the Mediterranean in 1943. She has a pom pom and six Oerlikons. (*Ministry of Defence*)

*Machinery*

The main propelling machinery of this class was a development of the one fitted in the prototype, *Southern Pride*. Throughout the war, steam reciprocating machinery, designed by Smith's Dock, was used in the new corvettes and frigates, partly for ease of production (turbine blades were at a premium throughout the war), and partly for ease of operation by the reservists and hostilities only crews of the ships.

Similarly, the boilers, almost without exception, were of the Admiralty single-ended cylindrical type.

*Complement*

The original approved complement of officers and ratings in the class was 29, this figure being based on the original coastal escort specification.

It quickly grew to 47 (October 1939), as the corvettes were switched to ocean escort work, and in October 1940 to 53. As armament, electronic and anti-submarine gear increased, this figure neared 80, stretching the accommodation in the ships to its utmost. The requirement for the larger frigates had already become very clear.

*Monkshood* in August 1942. This shows the corvette stern ready to lift to following seas; she is also fitted as a fleet tug. (*Ministry of Defence*)

## 1945 Conversions

Two types of conversion were approved for some units of the class in late 1945.

1. *As Air-Sea Rescue Ships,* with no great change in armament or fittings, and a complement of 76. This was for service with the East Indies Fleet, where 12 ships were on station by VJ-Day.

2. *As Flying-boat Tenders,* for service with the Royal Australian Air Force. In this configuration, they would have an extensive conversion, involving the removal of one boiler. The 4″ and 2 pounder guns would disappear, and one single Bofors be fitted in lieu. The two single Oerlikons on the bridge would remain, but the Hedgehog and all depth-charge fittings would be removed. Their endurance, at 10 knots, would be 5,100 miles.

3. *As Transports in the Pacific.* This further proposal, made earlier in 1945, to use ships of this class in this way, did not go through, due to their fine lines and resulting poor potential cargo space.

4. *As Fleet Tugs.* Due to the great shortage of fleet rescue tugs, especially in the Mediterranean, in the early years of the war, a few units were fitted with towing hooks, and protective rails over the quarterdeck. This can be seen in some of the photographs.

*Campion* in October 1942. The Type 271 radar lantern is of the original type, with wood lattice panels, but she has four extra Oerlikons aft. (*Ministry of Defence*)

*'Flower' class alterations and additions*

| | | |
|---|---|---|
| *1939* | Oct | Complement increased to 47 for ocean escort duties. |
| *1940* | July | Side scuttles cut by half for economy, in ships building. |
| | Sept | Bilge keels modified for greater stability. |
| | Oct | Crow's nest added to mast. |
| | | 20″ searchlight added on bridge. |
| | Dec | 24 ships to fit for Oropesa sweeping. |
| | | Modified bridge fitted to first ship. |
| | | 8 ships to fit for LL sweeps. |
| *1941* | Feb | LL fitted ships in Home waters, to get SA also. |
| | June | Hedgehog to be fitted. |
| | July | All to be fitted for tropical service. |
| | | 2 pounder to move aft, fit third Oerlikon. |
| | Aug | Oiling-at-sea fittings to be added. |
| | Sept | New open bridges, to take Oerlikons in wings. |
| | | Radar Type 271 to be fitted on priority basis. |
| *1943* | Jan | 2″ rocket flare projectors to add to 4″ gunshield. |
| | Mar | 4 extra single Oerlikons to be fitted. |
| | July | Limited fitting of 2 6 pounder guns. |
| | Aug | Foxer to be fitted urgently. |
| *1944* | Feb | LL equipment to be removed. |
| | July | Twin power-mounted Oerlikon to replace 2 pounder. |
| | Sept | No further alterations or additions to ships. Those on foreign service to reserve on return to UK. Western approaches ships —routine refits only. |

*HMS Bluebell*

This was a 'Flower' class corvette, of 900 tons, completed on 19th July 1940 and built and engined by Fleming & Ferguson Ltd, of Paisley in Scotland. She was immediately allocated to Western Approaches, Northern Escort Force, based at Rosyth.

In 1940 she was engaged on all the duties performed by corvettes, escorting convoys, searching for and attacking U-boats which had attacked ships in the convoys, and rescuing survivors. In the last four months of the year she rescued survivors from five incidents, including those from 7 ships in convoy SC 7 from Canada to the UK, which had been attacked by U-boats from 16th to 19th October. She had 203 survivors on board and then rejoined the convoy. Two days earlier she had hunted one of the attacking U-boats, without result. In November 1940 she was allocated to the 5th Escort Group, based at Liverpool. On 6th she assisted in rounding up convoy HX 84 (Halifax to UK), which had been scattered after being attacked by the German pocket battleship *Admiral Scheer*, sinking the armed merchant cruiser *Jervis Bay*.

Early in 1941, *Bluebell* was again hunting a U-boat, with *Westcott*, *Candytuft*, *Scimitar* and *Skate*. Later in January she escorted convoy OGC 51 (UK to

Gibraltar), but was damaged in collision. She sailed to Gibraltar in July with 4 other corvettes, and returned escorting the famous HMS *Breconshire*. In August she was re-allocated to the 37th Escort Group, Western Approaches, still based at Liverpool. She joined in an A/S sweep later that month, after another convoy, OG 71, had lost 10 ships by torpedo. She continued to escort convoys to and from Gibraltar for the rest of that year, and attacked a surfaced U-boat off Cape St Vincent in December.

She continued this work to the end of March 1942, then had a three-month refit on the Tyne. In September she was one of the 4 corvettes escorting convoy PQ 18 to Russia, which lost 13 ships out of 40. About 43 enemy aircraft and 3 U-boats were destroyed. In October she joined the 22nd Escort Group at Liverpool and escorted a further Russian convoy.

In February 1943 a third Russian convoy was escorted, and she returned with *Camellia* in June.

She arrived in Bone, North Africa, on 9th July, as one of the escorts for one of the four assault convoys for the invasion of Sicily. She joined the 22nd Escort Group in the Mediterranean Fleet on 2nd August, then in November escorted a flight of landing craft returning to the UK. She then rejoined the Western Approaches, in the 23rd Escort Group.

After a refit at the turn of the year, she again escorted Russian convoys, then in April joined the preparations for the assault on Normandy. She sailed on D+1 as escort for 31 LSTs, but returned to the Russian convoy run in August. On 3rd February 1945 she sailed with JW 64 from Greenock, and the convoy suffered substantial losses from torpedo bombers on the 10th. The return convoy, RA 64, was less fortunate. The Germans had assembled about 6 U-boats off the entrance to the Kola Inlet, and on 17th February the sloop *Lark*, sweeping ahead of the convoy, was torpedoed, but towed safely into harbour; then a merchant ship was hit by the same U-boat, and sank under tow. Before the day was over, at 1530, *Bluebell* was torpedoed by *U711* and blew up. Only one survivor was picked up.

*Hyderabad* in the Forth, April 1942. She has LL magnetic minesweeping gear aft, and acoustic Type SA over her bows. The mast is still forward of the bridge, although Type 271 radar has been fitted. (*Ministry of Defence*)

*Jonquil*, showing the sturdy build which stood up to mid-ocean escort though only intended for coastal waters. She wears the number of the 38th Escort Group on her funnel. (*Ministry of Defence*)

*Hydrangea*. She has wire sweep gear aft, and only 0.303″ machine guns aft, with a quadruple 0.5″ gun further forward. (*Ministry of Defence*)

## GERMAN U-BOATS SUNK BY 'FLOWER' CLASS

| U 26 | 1.7.40 | *Gladiolus* and others |
|------|--------|------------------------|
| U 104 | 21.11.40 | *Rhododendron* |
| U 70 | 7.3.41 | *Camellia* and *Arbutus* |
| U 65 | 28.4.41 | *Gladiolus* |
| U 110 | 9.5.41 | *Aubrietia* and others |
| U 147 | 2.6.41 | *Periwinkle* and others |
| U 556 | 27.6.41 | *Nasturtium, Celandine* and *Gladiolus* |
| U 651 | 29.6.41 | *Violet, Arabis* and others |
| U 401 | 3.8.41 | *Hydrangea* and others |
| U 204 | 19.10.41 | *Mallow* and others |
| U 433 | 16.11.41 | *Marigold* |
| U 208 | 11.12.41 | *Bluebell* |
| U 131 | 17.12.41 | *Pentstemon* and others |
| U 567 | 21.12.41 | *Samphire* and others |
| U 82 | 6.2.42 | *Tamarisk* and others |
| U 252 | 14.4.42 | *Vetch* and others |
| U 379 | 8.8.42 | *Dianthus* · |
| U 660 | 12.11.42 | *Lotus* and *Starwort* |
| U 605 | 13.11.42 | *Lotus* and *Poppy* |
| U 184 | 20.11.42 | *Pontentilla* (Norwegian) |
| U 609 | 7.2.43 | *Lobelia* (French) |
| U 432 | 11.3.43 | *Aconit* (French) and others |
| U 124 | 2.4.43 | *Stonecrop* and others |
| U 192 | 5.5.43 | *Pink* |
| U 638 | 5.5.43 | *Loosestrife* |
| U 381 | 19.5.43 | *Snowflake* and others |
| U 414 | 25.5.43 | *Vetch* |
| U 436 | 26.5.43 | *Hyderabad* and others |
| U 135 | 15.7.43 | *Mignonette, Balsam* and others |
| U 523 | 25.8.43 | *Wallflower* and others |
| U 634 | 30.8.43 | *Stonecrop* and others |
| U 617 | 11.9.43 | *Hyacinth* and others |
| U 631 | 17.10.43 | *Sunflower* and others |
| U 282 | 29.10.43 | *Sunflower* |
| U 306 | 31.10.43 | *Geranium* and others |
| U 641 | 19.1.44 | *Violet* |
| U 678 | 6.7.44 | *Statice* (Modified 'Flower') and others |
| U 741 | 15.8.44 | *Orchis* |
| U 1199 | 21.1.45 | *Mignonette* and others |

## ITALIAN SUBMARINES SUNK BY 'FLOWER' CLASS CORVETTES

| *Nani* | 7. 1.41 | *Anemone* |
|--------|---------|-----------|
| *Fisalia* | 28. 9.41 | *Hyacinth* |
| *Perla* | 9. 7.42 | *Hyacinth* |

## 'FLOWER CLASS' COMMAND ALLOCATION
### (all at 1st January)

|                        | 1941 | 1942 | 1943 | 1944 | 1945 | 7.5.45 |
|------------------------|------|------|------|------|------|--------|
| Londonderry            | 7    | 19   | 13   | 18   | 6    | 4      |
| Liverpool              | 25   | 36   | 32   | 16   | 16   | 19     |
| Greenock               | 13   | 13   | 10   | 25   | 5    | 3      |
|                        | 45   | 68   | 55   | 59   | 27   | 26     |
| Rosyth                 | 0    | 0    | 0    | 0    | 3    | 4      |
| Nore                   | 1    | 0    | 0    | 0    | 7    | 7      |
| Portsmouth             | 0    | 0    | 0    | 0    | 9    | 13     |
| Plymouth               | 0    | 0    | 0    | 0    | 10   | 17     |
|                        | 1    | 0    | 0    | 0    | 29   | 41     |
| Mediterranean Gib      | 4    | 6    | 12   | 6    | 10   | 9      |
| East                   | 0    | 7    | 6    | 21   | 0    | 6      |
| South Atlantic         | 6    | 25   | 18   | 3    | 19   | 6      |
| Eastern Fleet          | 0    | 0    | 4    | 13   | 25   | 15     |
|                        | 10   | 38   | 40   | 43   | 54   | 36     |
| Totals                 | 56   | 106  | 95   | 102  | 110  | 103    |

NOTES
1. RCN corvettes were based on Londonderry in numbers from time to time; above figures are for RN ships only.
2. Command allocation for Normandy D-Day, 1944, not reflected in above figures.

*Bittersweet* in November 1943. Her bridge is well padded against splinters and a cartoon adorns the side of her 4″ gunshield. (*Ministry of Defence*)

## 'FLOWER' CLASS FOR THE EAST INDIES FLEET IN 1945
### (as Air Sea Rescue Vessels)

*Planned*              12 RN ships,    2 RIN ships
*On station*
*3rd August 1945*      13 RN ships,    3 RIN ships, eg:
*RN ships Freesia, Honesty, Jasmine, Meadowsweet, Monkshood, Nigella, Rockrose,*
*Rosebay, Smilax, Snowflake, Thyme, Tulip, Violet*
*RIN ships (ex-RN Modified 'Flower' Assam, Mahratta, Sind*

## 'FLOWER' CLASS PRODUCTION

|            |          | *UK ORIGINAL* | *UK MODIFIED* |
| ---------- | -------- | ------------- | ------------- |
| 1940       | 1st half | 30            |               |
|            | 2nd half | 47            |               |
| 1941       | 1st half | 35            |               |
|            | 2nd half | 17            |               |
| 1942       | 1st half | 6             |               |
|            | 2nd half |               |               |
| 1943       | 1st half |               | 4             |
|            | 2nd half |               | 5             |
|            | Totals   | 135           | 9             |

TOTAL BUILT   135    Retained by RN 102
Transferred to Allies  33    Cancelled ships  6

*Violet* in September 1942. She has her extra Oerlikons, but the minesweeping gear has not yet been removed. (*Ministry of Defence*)

## 'FLOWER' CLASS SPECIFICATION

| | Original | Revised (long forecastle) |
|---|---|---|
| Programme | 1939-41 | 1940-42 |
| Displacement | | |
| standard | 950 | 1,015 |
| full load | 1,160 | |
| Dimensions | | |
| length pp | 190' | 193' |
| length oa | 205'1" | 208'4" |
| breadth | 33'1" | 33'1" |
| draught forward | 8'3" | 11'10" |
| aft | 13'5" | 15'7" |
| Machinery | steam reciprocating, 4-cylinder triple expansion | |
| Boilers | 2 cylindrical single-ended | |
| IHP | 2,750 | 2,750 |
| Speed, knots | 16 | 16 |
| Shafts | 1 | 1 |
| Oil Fuel, tons | 230 | 230 |
| Endurance | 3,450×12 kn | 3,450×12 kn |
| | 2,630×16 kn | 2,630×16 kn |
| Complement | 25 | 96 |
| | (Later up to 85) | |
| Armament | 1 4" BL Mk IX on on CP1 mtg | 1 4" BL Mk IX on on CP1 mtg |
| | 1 Quad 0·5" MG | 2/6 single 20mm |
| | 2 0·303 Lewis guns | Oerlikons Mk IV |
| A/S | | |
| rails | 2 | 2 |
| throwers | 2 | 4 |
| depth charges | 25/50 | 70 |
| | (1/42 A/S ships, 72 A/S LL, 40 A/S M/S, 62) | |
| Hedgehog | no | yes |
| Radar | no | Types 271Q 242, 253 |
| Boats | 2 17' 6" merchant type lifeboats | 2 16' 0" trawler boats |

NOTE
Original ships received alterations to keep them
up-to-date.

## RN 'FLOWER' CLASS CORVETTES—CLASS LIST

| Name | Pendant No. | Job No. | Builder | Building Time | Completion Date |
|------|-------------|---------|---------|---------------|-----------------|

**UK BUILT**

**1939 Programme**

| Name | Pendant No. | Job No. | Builder | Building Time | Completion Date |
|------|-------------|---------|---------|---------------|-----------------|
| *Anemone* | K 48 | J 4100 | Blyth | 9m17d | 12.10.40 |
| *Arbutus* | K 86 | J 4107 | ,, | 10m12d | 12.10.40 |
| *Asphodel* | K 56 | J 1034 | Brown | 10m12d | 11.9.40 |
| *Aubrietia* | K 96 | J 1035 | ,, | 13m27d | 23.12.40 |
| *Auricula* | K 12 | J 1036 | ,, | 15m9d | 6.3.41 |
| *Azalea* | K 25 | J 2608 | Cook, Welton & Gemmell | 14m12d | 17.1.41 |
| *Begonia* | K 66 | J 2610 | ,, | 10m23d | 8.3.41 |
| *Bluebell* | K 80 | J 1037 | Fleming & Ferguson | 8m25d | 19.7.40 |
| *Campanula* | K 18 | J 1038 | ,, | 10m10d | 6.9.40 |
| *Candytuft* | K 09 | J 1053 | Grangemouth | 11m16d | 16.10.40 |
| *Carnation* | K 00 | J 1054 | ,, | 11m24d | 22.2.41 |
| *Celandine* | K 75 | J 1055 | ,, | 12m0d | 30.4.41 |
| *Clematis* | K 36 | J 6003 | Hill | 9m16d | 27.7.40 |
| *Columbine* | K 94 | J 6067 | ,, | 12m7d | 9.11.40 |
| *Convolvulus* | K 45 | J 6122 | ,, | 13m9d | 26.2.41 |
| *Coreopsis* | K 32 | J 1047 | Inglis | 10m4d | 17.8.41 |
| *Crocus* | K 49 | J 1048 | ,, | 9m25d | 20.10.40 |
| *Cyclamen* | K 83 | J 1056 | Lewis | 10m0d | 20.9.40 |
| *Dianella* | K 07 | J 1057 | ,, | 12m29d | 6.1.41 |
| *Dahlia* | K 59 | J 1058 | ,, | 12m21d | 21.3.41 |
| *Delphinium* | K 77 | J 1049 | Robb | 12m15d | 15.11.40 |
| *Dianthus* | K 95 | J 1050 | ,, | 16m17d | 17.3.41 |
| *Gardenia* | K 99 | J 1041 | Simons | 8m4d | 24.5.40 |
| *Geranium* | K 16 | J 1042 | ,, | 9m3d | 24.6.40 |
| *Gladiolus* | K 34 | J 4103 | Smith's Dock | 5m18d | 6.4.40 |
| *Godetia* | K 72 | J 4110 | ,, | 6m11d | 15.7.40 |
| *Heliotrope* | K 03 | J 4003 | Crown | 10m20d | 12.9.40 |
| *Hollyhock* | K 64 | J 4027 | ,, | 11m22d | 19.11.40 |
| *Honeysuckle* | K 27 | J 1064 | Ferguson | 10m19d | 14.9.40 |
| *Hydrangea* | K 39 | J 1065 | ,, | 13m12d | 3.1.41 |
| *Jasmine* | K 23 | J 1066 | ,, | 16m24d | 16.5.41 |
| *Jonquil* | K 68 | J 1039 | Fleming & Ferguson | 9m24d | 21.10.40 |
| *Larkspur* | K 82 | J 1040 | ,, | 9m9d | 4.1.41 |
| *Lavender* | K 60 | J 1067 | Hall | 12m16d | 16.5.41 |
| *Lobelia* | K 05 | J 1068 | ,, | 12m19d | 16.7.41 |
| *Marguerite* | K 54 | J 1061 | Hall Russell | 10m26d | 20.11.40 |
| *Marigold* | K 87 | J 1062 | ,, | 13m2d | 28.2.41 |
| *Mignonette* | K 38 | J 1063 | ,, | 9m22d | 7.5.41 |

| Name | Pendant No. | Job No. | Builder | Building Time | Completion Date |
|------|-------------|---------|---------|---------------|-----------------|
| *Mimosa* | K 11 | J 6254 | Hill | 12m19d | 11.5.41 |
| *Myosotis* | K 65 | J 1059 | Lewis | 11m6d | 30.5.41 |
| *Narcissus* | K 74 | J 1060 | ,, | 8m8d | 17.7.41 |
| *Nigella* | K 19 | J 6155 | Philip | 14m28d | 25.2.41 |
| *Pentstemon* | K 61 | J 6246 | ,, | 20m3d | 31.7.41 |
| *Polyanthus* | K 47 | J 1052 | Robb | 13m4d | 23.4.41 |
| *Primrose* | K 91 | J 1043 | Simons | 9m23d | 15.7.40 |
| *Salvia* | K 97 | J 1045 | ,, | 11m25d | 20.9.40 |
| *Snapdragon* | K 10 | J 1046 | ,, | 13m1d | 28.10.40 |
| *Snowdrop* | K 67 | J 4002 | Smith's Dock | 9m6d | 16.1.41 |
| *Sunflower* | K 41 | J 4006 | ,, | 8m1d | 25.1.41 |
| *Tulip* | K 29 | J 4009 | ,, | 5m19d | 18.11.40 |
| *Verbena* | K 85 | J 4020 | ,, | 5m12d | 10.12.40 |
| *Veronica* | K 37 | J 4026 | ,, | 7m9d | 18.2.41 |
| *Wallflower* | K 44 | J 4030 | ,, | 7m15d | 7.3.41 |
| *Zinnia* | K 98 | J 4034 | ,, | 7m10d | 30.3.41 |

## Ordered on French account, taken over by RN .

| Name | Pendant No. | Job No. | Builder | Building Time | Completion Date |
|------|-------------|---------|---------|---------------|-----------------|
| *Fleur de Lys* ex French *La Diéppoise* | K 122 | J 4141 | Smith's Dock | 7m27d | 26.8.40 |
| *La Malouine* ex French *La Malouine* | K 46 | J 4142 | ,, | 8m16d | 30.7.40 |
| *Nasturtium* ex French *La Paimpolaise* | K 107 | J 4143 | ,, | 4m3d | 26.9.40 |

## 1939 War Emergency Programme

| Name | Pendant No. | Job No. | Builder | Building Time | Completion Date |
|------|-------------|---------|---------|---------------|-----------------|
| *Acanthus* | K 01 | J 1094 | Ailsa | 9m2d | 1.10.41 |
| *Aconite* | K 58 | J 1095 | ,, | 15m28d | 23.7.41 |
| *Alyssum* | K 100 | J 1159 | Brown | 11m24d | 17.6.41 |
| *Amaranthus* | K 17 | J 1195 | Fleming & Ferguson | 9m8d | 12.2.41 |
| *Arabis* | K 73 | J 3140 | Harland & Wolff | 5m6d | 5.4.40 |
| *Bellwort* | K 114 | J 1160 | Brown | 14m9d | 26.11.41 |
| *Borage* | K 120 | J 1161 | ,, | 17m8d | 29.4.42 |
| *Burdock* | K 126 | J 4208 | Crown | 9m14d | 27.4.41 |
| *Calendula* | K 28 | J 3240 | Harland & Wolff | 6m6d | 6.5.40 |
| *Camellia* | K 31 | J 3340 | ,, | 7m4d | 18.6.40 |
| *Campion* | K 108 | J 4214 | Crown | 9m21d | 6.9.41 |
| *Clarkia* | K 88 | J 3342 | Harland & Wolff | 5m23d | 22.4.40 |
| *Clover* | K 134 | J 1170 | Fleming & Ferguson | 10m2d | 31.5.41 |
| *Coltsfoot* | K 140 | J 1171 | Hall | 12m27d | 1.10.41 |
| *Erica* | K 50 | J 3440 | Harland & Wolff | 6m14d | 7.8.40 |
| *Freesia* | K 43 | J 3442 | ,, | 5m1d | 19.11.40 |
| *Gentian* | K 90 | J 3540 | ,, | 5m0d | 20.9.40 |

| | | | | | | |
|---|---|---|---|---|---|---|
| *Gloxinia* | K 72 | J 3542 | ,, | | 5m1d | 22.8.40 |
| *Heartsease* ex *Pansy* | K 15 | J 3544 | ,, | | 6m21d | 4.6.40 |
| *Heather* | K 69 | J 3640 | ,, | | 5m10d | 1.11.40 |
| *Hibiscus* | K 24 | J 3642 | ,, | | 6m7d | 21.5.40 |
| *Hyacinth* | K 84 | J 3644 | ,, | | 5m14d | 4.10.40 |
| *Coriander* | K 183 | J 1166 | Hall | | 11m28d | 16.9.41 |
| *Kingcup* | K 33 | J 3740 | Harland & Wolff | 5m15d | 3.1.41 |
| *Loosestrife* | K 105 | J 1167 | Hall Russell | | 11m16d | 25.11.41 |
| *Lotus* | K 93 | J 495 | Hill | | 11m27d | 23.5.42 |
| *Lotus* (ii) ex *Phlox* | K 130 | J 1168 | Robb | | 13m13d | 9.5.42 |
| *Mallow* | K 81 | J 3742 | Harland & Wolff | 7m18d | 2.7.40 |
| *Meadowsweet* | K 144 | J 521 | Hill | | 10m26d | 8.7.42 |
| *Orchis* | K 76 | J 3744 | Harland & Wolff | 5m12d | 30.11.40 |
| *Oxlip* | K 123 | J 1164 | Inglis | | 12m19d | 28.12.41 |
| *Pennywort* | K 111 | J 1165 | ,, | | 11m22d | 5.3.42 |
| *Peony* | K 40 | J 3840 | Harland & Wolff | 5m13d | 6.8.40 |
| *Periwinkle* | K 55 | J 3842 | Harland & Wolff | 5m9d | 8.4.40 |
| *Petunia* | K 79 | J 1051 | Robb | | 13m1d | 13.1.41 |
| *Picotee* | K 63 | J 3846 | Harland & Wolff | 5m15d | 5.9.40 |
| *Pimpernel* | K 71 | J 3944 | ,, | | 5m21d | 9.1.41 |
| *Ranunculus* | K 117 | J 1162 | Simons | | 12m9d | 28.7.41 |
| *Rhododendron* | K 78 | J 3946 | Harland & Wolff | 4m26d | 18.10.40 |
| *Rockrose* | K 51 | J 6010 | Hill | | 12m7d | 4.11.41 |
| *Rose* | K 102 | J 1163 | Simons | | 13m28d | 31.10.41 |
| *Samphire* | K 128 | J 4206 | Smith's Dock | | 6m26d | 30.6.41 |
| *Saxifrage* | K 04 | J 6761 | Hill | | 12m5d | 6.2.42 |
| *Spiraea* | K 08 | J 1098 | Inglis | | 8m27d | 27.2.41 |
| *Starwort* | K 20 | J 1099 | ,, | | 11m15d | 26.5.41 |
| *Stonecrop* | K 142 | J 4211 | Smith's Dock | | 5m26d | 30.7.41 |
| *Sundew* | K 57 | J 1093 | Lewis | | 10m8d | 12.9.41 |
| *Violet* | K 35 | J 1096 | Simons | | 10m13d | 3.2.41 |

### 1940 Programme

| | | | | | | |
|---|---|---|---|---|---|---|
| *Abelia* | K 184 | J 3840 | Harland & Wolff | 5m15d | 3.2.41 |
| *Alisma* | K 185 | J 3446 | ,, | | 5m25d | 13.2.41 |
| *Anchusa* | K 186 | J 3346 | ,, | | 5m17d | 6.3.41 |
| *Armeria* | K 187 | J 3444 | ,, | | 6m13d | 30.3.41 |
| *Aster* | K 188 | J 3246 | ,, | | 5m29d | 11.4.41 |
| *Bergamot* | K 189 | J 3648 | ,, | | 6m27d | 12.5.41 |
| *Bryony* | K 192 | J 3646 | ,, | | 19m0d | 16.6.42 |
| *Buttercup* | K 193 | J 3548 | ,, | | 16m7d | 24.4.42 |
| *Chrysanthemum* | K 195 | J 3040 | ,, | | 13m9d | 26.1.42 |
| *Cowslip* | K 196 | J 3148 | ,, | | 6m24d | 9.8.41 |
| *Eglantine* | K 197 | J 3042 | ,, | | 7m11d | 27.8.41 |
| *Fritillary* | K 199 | J 3144 | ,, | | 8m19d | 1.11.41 |
| *Genista* | K 200 | J 3046 | ,, | | 10m7d | 19.12.41 |
| *Vervain* | K 190 | J 3244 | ,, | | 6m24d | 9.6.41 |
| *Vetch* | K 132 | J 4023 | Smith's Dock | | 5m20d | 9.9.41 |

| Name | Pendant No | Job No. | Builder | Building Time | Completion Date |
|------|-----------|---------|---------|---------------|-----------------|
| **1940 Supplementary Programme** | | | | | |
| Balsam | K 72 | J 1405 | Brown | 19m12d | 28.11.42 |
| Godetia (ii) | K 226 | J 4257 | Crown | 12m18d | 23.2.42 |
| Hyderabad ex *Nettle* | K 212 | J 1203 | Hall | 13m30d | 23.2.42 |
| Monkshood | K 207 | J 1188 | Fleming & Ferguson | 9m30d | 31.7.41 |
| Montbretia | K 208 | J 1189 | ,, | 10m13d | 26.9.41 |
| Sweetbriar | K 209 | J 4230 | Smith's Dock | 5m4d | 8.9.41 |
| Tamarisk | K 216 | J 1404 | Fleming & Ferguson | 10m16d | 26.12.41 |
| Thyme | K 210 | J 4286 | Smith's Dock | 5m23d | 23.10.41 |
| Snowflake ex *Zenobia* | K 211 | J 4238 | ,, | 5m14d | 2.11.41 |
| **1941 Supplementary Programme** | | | | | |
| Pink | K 137 | J 1169 | Robb | 13m12d | 2.7.42 |
| Poppy | K 213 | J 1204 | Hall | 14m6d | 12.5.42 |
| Potentilla | K 214 | J 1196 | Simons | 11m0d | 5.2.42 |

## CANCELLED SHIPS

| Name | Pendant No | Job No. | Builder | Building Time | Completion Date |
|------|-----------|---------|---------|---------------|-----------------|
| **1940 Programme** | | | | | |
| Gloriosa | K 201 | J 3448 | Harland & Wolff | Cancelled | 23.1.41 |
| Harebell | K 202 | J 3242 | ,, | ,, | ,, |
| Hemlock | K 203 | J 3748 | ,, | ,, | ,, |
| Ivy | K 204 | J 3546 | ,, | ,, | ,, |
| Ling | K 205 | J 3344 | ,, | ,, | ,, |
| Marjoram | K 206 | J 3048 | ,, | ,, | ,, |

## FOLLOWING SHIPS WERE ORIGINALLY ORDERED BY FRENCH GOVERNMENT

*Abelia, Alisma, Anchusa, Armeria, Aster, Bergamot, Snowdrop, Tulip, Verbena, Veronica, Wallflower, Zinnia.*

## FOLLOWING SHIPS WERE ORDERED IN CANADA BY RN, BUT WERE LOANED TO RCN ON COMPLETION

(Details are in RCN section)

*Arrowhead, Bittersweet, Eyebright, Fennel, Hepatica, Mayflower, Quesnell, Snowberry, Sorel, Spikenard, Trillium, Windflower.*

## TRANSFERRED TO ALLIED NAVIES

### TO USN (after some RN service)

| | | |
|------|------|------|
| Arabis | K 73 | became *Saucy* 1942 |
| Begonia | K 66 | became *Impulse* 1942 |

| | | | |
|---|---|---|---|
| *Calendula* | K 28 | became | *Ready* 1942 |
| *Candytuft* | K 09 | became | *Tenacity* 1942 |
| *Heliotrope* | K 03 | became | *Surprise* 1942 |
| *Hibiscus* | K 24 | became | *Spry* 1942 |
| *Larkspur* | K 82 | became | *Fury* 1942 |
| *Heartsease* | K 15 | became | *Courage* 1942 |
| *Periwinkle* | K 55 | became | *Restless* 1942 |
| *Veronica* | K 37 | became | *Temptress* 1942 |

Details will be found under the USN section

## TO FRANCE

| | | | |
|---|---|---|---|
| *Aconite* | K 58 | became | *Aconit* |
| *Alyssum* | K 100 | became | *Alysse* |
| *Chrysanthemum* | K 195 | became | *Commandant Dragou* |
| *Coriander* | K 183 | became | *Commandant Detroyat* |
| *Lobelia* | K 05 | became | *Lobelia* |
| *Lotus* | K 93 | became | *Commandant D'Estienne D'Orves* |
| *Mimosa* | K 11 | became | *Mimosa* |
| *Ranunculus* | K 117 | became | *Renoncule* |
| *Sundew* | K 57 | became | *Roselys* |
| *La Bastiaise* | — | Smith's Dock | |

(This ship was lost on trials, 22.6.40)
All ships were transferred on completion.
A further 6 ships, building in France to French account, fell into German hands incomplete, in 1940.

## TO THE NETHERLANDS

| | | | |
|---|---|---|---|
| *Carnation* | K 00 | became | *Frisio* 1941 |

## TO NORWAY

| | | | |
|---|---|---|---|
| *Acanthus* | K 01 | became | *Andenes* 1941 |
| *Buttercup* | K 193 | became | *Nordkyn* 1942 |
| *Eglantine* | K 197 | became | *Soroy* 1941 |
| *Montbretia* | K 208 | became | *Montbretia* 1941 |
| *Potentilla* | K 214 | became | *Potentilla* 1942 |
| *Rose* | K 102 | became | *Rose* 1941 |

## TO GREECE

| | | | |
|---|---|---|---|
| *Coreopsis* | K 32 | became | *Kriezis* 1943 |
| *Hyacinth* | K 84 | became | *Apostolis* 1943 |
| *Peony* | K 40 | became | *Sakhtouris* 1943 |
| *Tamarisk* | K 216 | became | *Tompazis* 1943 |

## TO YUGOSLAVIA

| | | | |
|---|---|---|---|
| *Mallow* | K 81 | became | *Nada* 1944 |

GLADIOLUS in 1941.

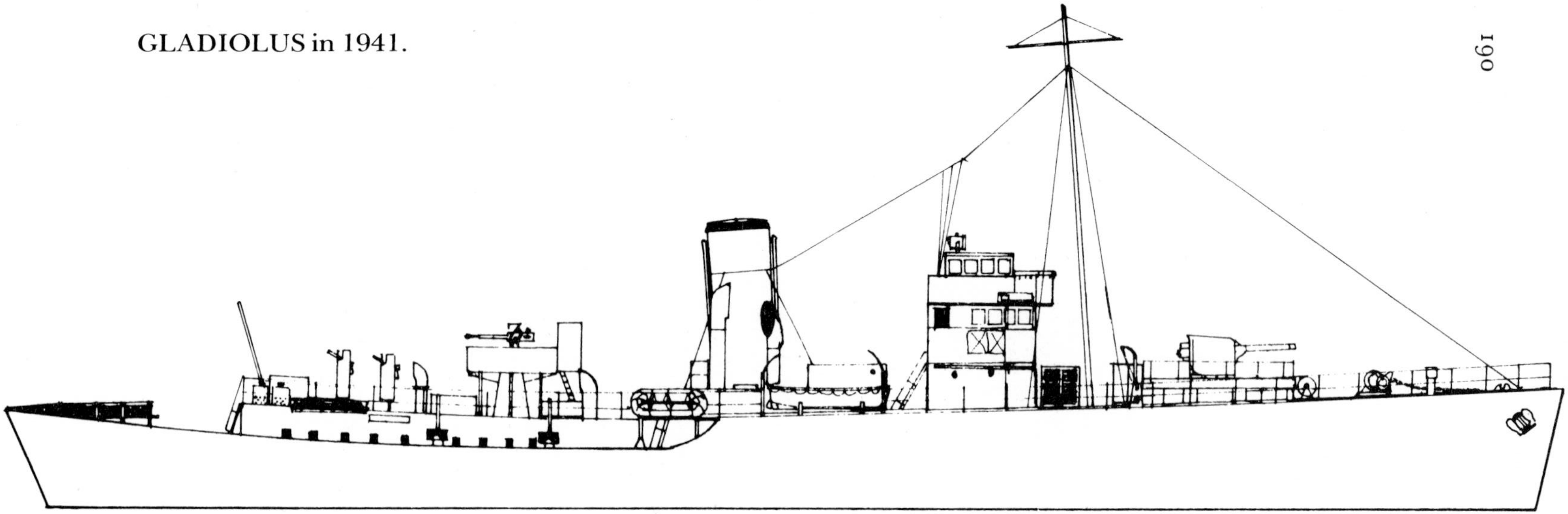

CONVOLVULUS in 1941.

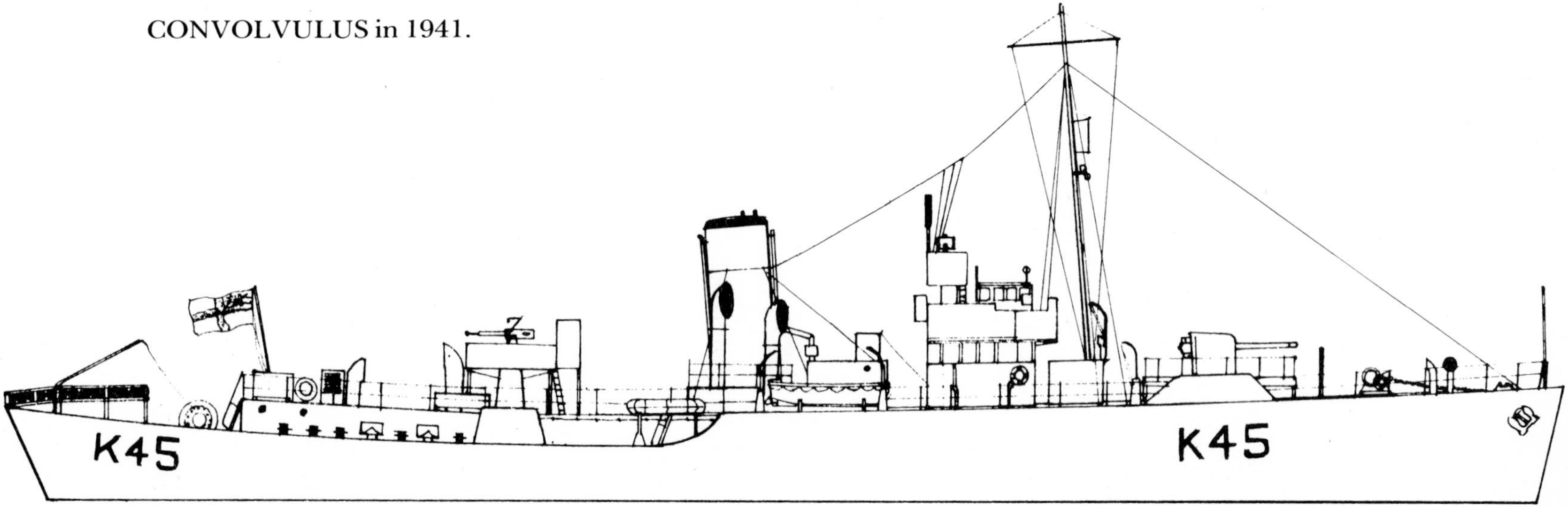

K45

K45

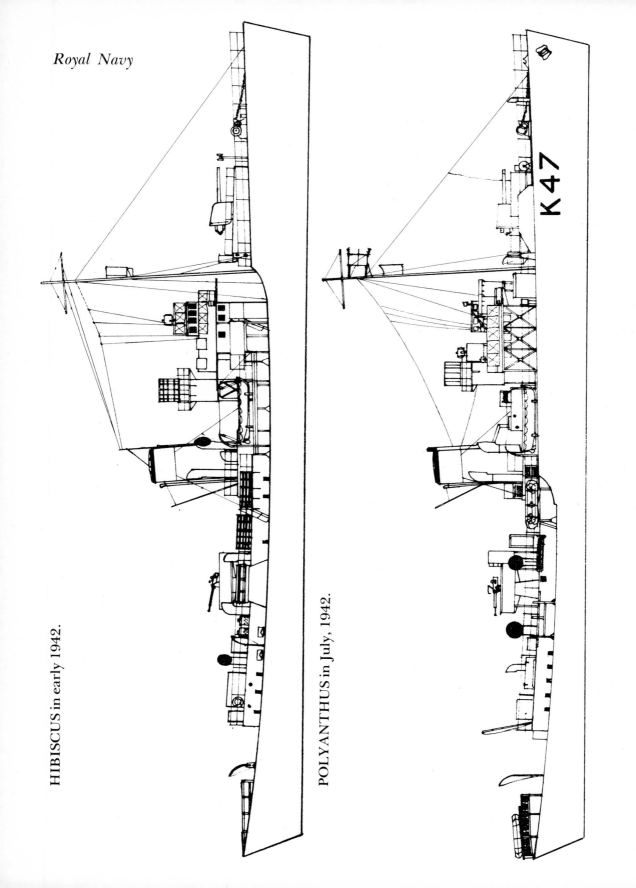

*Royal Navy*

HIBISCUS in early 1942.

POLYANTHUS in July, 1942.

K47

LOTUS in September, 1942.

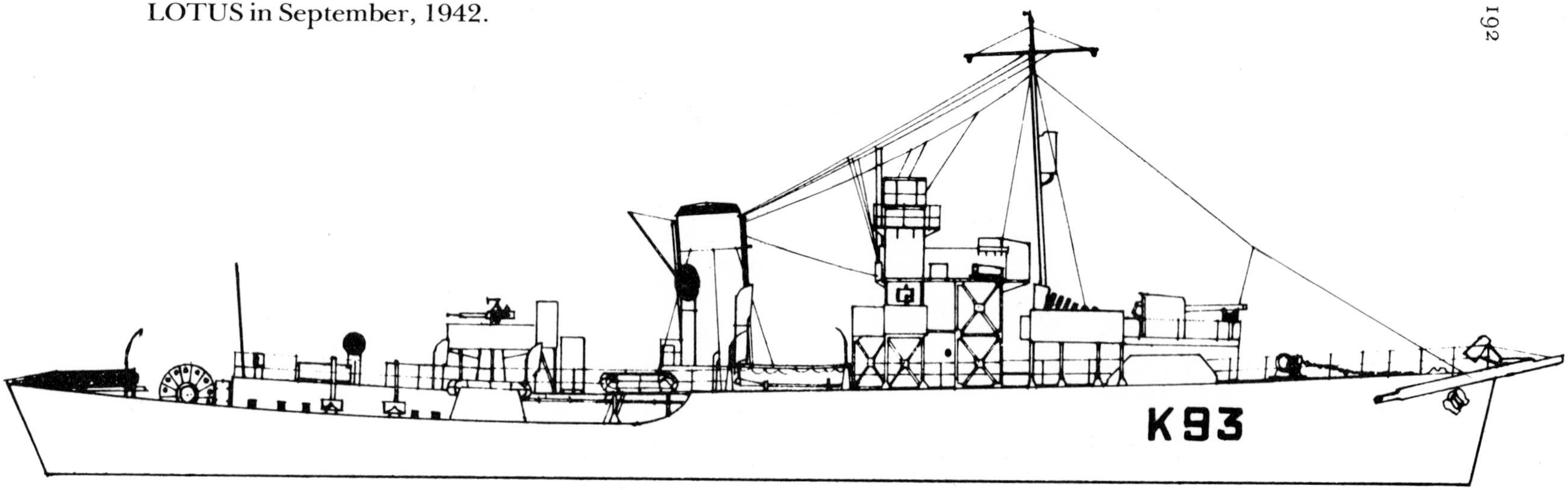

K93

ABELIA in 1942.

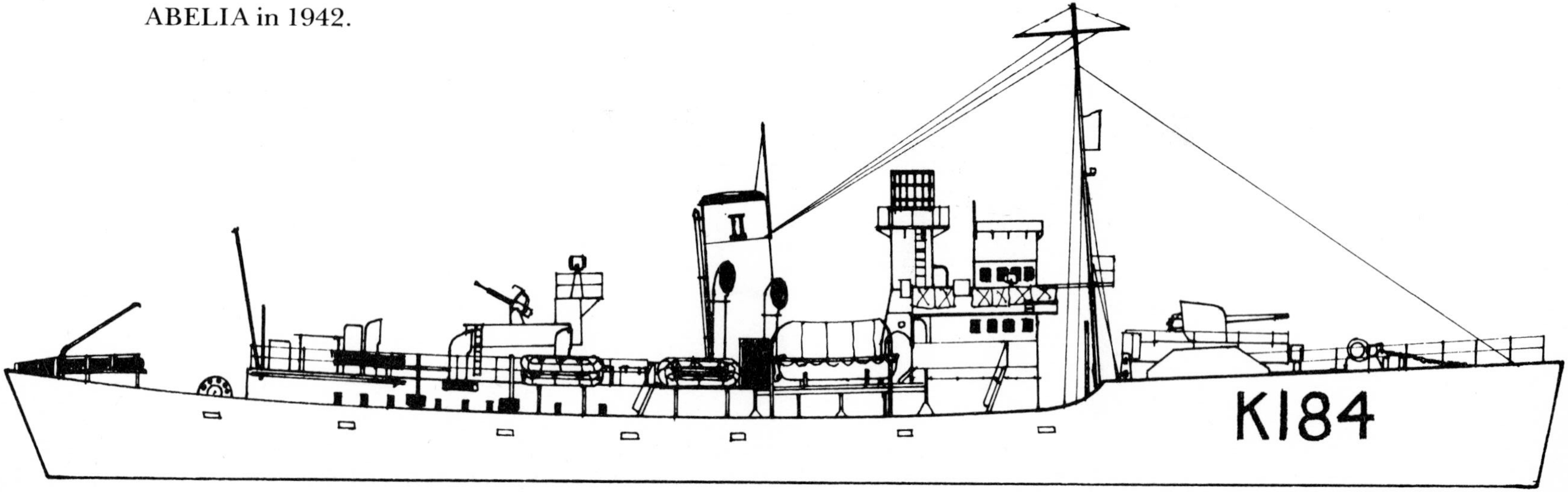

KI84

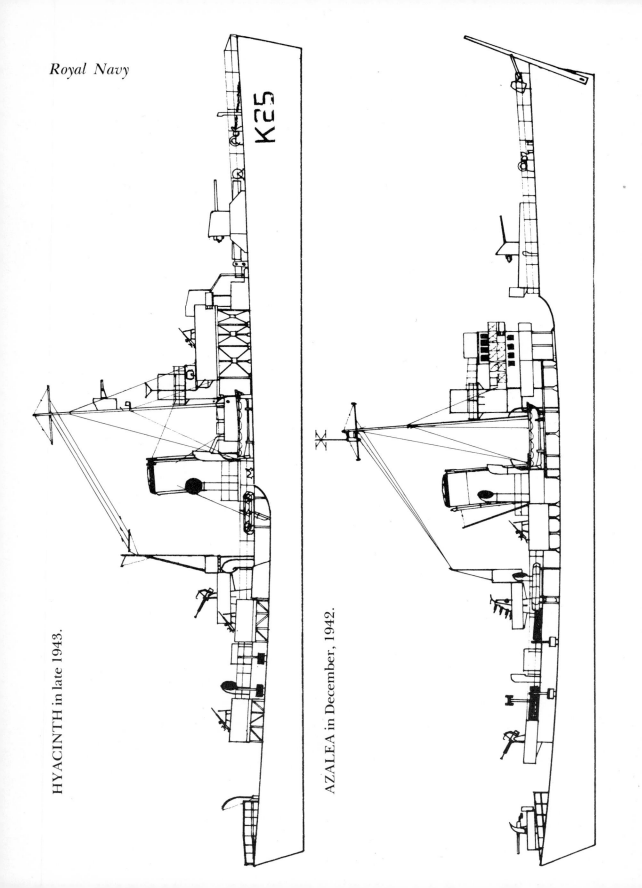

Royal Navy

K25

HYACINTH in late 1943.

AZALEA in December, 1942.

▲ *Betony* in December 1943. She had eighteen
months' RN service before transfer to the RIN.
No funnel cap fitted here, and she has only
three single Oerlikons in all.
*(Ministry of Defence)*

*Arbutus* shows the full Modified after
arrangement. She has her full outfit of
close-range weapons, and the increased sheer
and flare forward stand out.
▼ *(Ministry of Defence)*

## MODIFIED 'FLOWER' CLASS CORVETTES
### 10 ships completed in UK

So many alterations and additions were made to the 'Flower' class, based on progressive North Atlantic experience, that a point came when it was sensible to combine all these changes in any further new building. Thus a separate class, called the Modified class, appeared.

It was inevitable, in this period of evolution, that some of the ships completed before this new class was defined, already incorporated most of the changes and are hard to distinguish from the proper Modified class.

Additionally, almost as soon as the new class was defined, building switched to the bigger and better 'Castle' class; this is explained in the shipbuilding chapter, and resulted in the number of units of the Modified class built for the RN being relatively few. Before this policy switch was made, in April 1943, no less than 57 ships of this Modified class were projected for the RN in the UK alone; but no job numbers, yards or names had apparently been allocated before they were cancelled.

Actual numbers appear to have been as follows:

| | | |
|---|---|---|
| Total ordered in UK | 11 | ships |
| of which | 1 | was cancelled |
| Total completed in UK | 10 | |
| of which transferred to RNZN on completion | 2 | |
| and transferred to RCN on completion | 4 | |
| TOTAL commissioned by RN | 4 | |
| Built in Canada for RN on USN Lend-Lease | 7 | |
| TOTAL OPERATED BY RN | 11 | |

NOTE
The 4 UK-built ships commissioned by the RN were transferred in 1945 from the RN to the RIN.

*Bugloss* in September 1944. She was transferred to the RIN a year later. She has a tall mainmast with gaff, a mark of the Modified class. (*Ministry of Defence*)

The main distinguishing features of the Modified class were:

a) Increased sheer and flare forward.
b) Longer forecastle deck.
c) Higher bridge, with naval appearance.
d) Large funnel cap (but not in all).
e) Upright funnel and mast.
f) Twin power-mounted 20mm Oerlikon aft, and extra Oerlikons fitted aft of funnel.
g) Rocket flare projectors on 4″ gunshield.
h) Old 4″ guns still fitted in the UK-built ships, newer type (as in 'River' class frigates) fitted to Canadian-built ships.
i) Mainmast with gaff added.
j) Admiralty water-tube boilers in at least some of the class.
k) Higher complement—109.

Larger numbers of units of this class were built in Canada for the RCN, and further photographs will be found with that chapter.

## MODIFIED 'FLOWER' CLASS SPECIFICATION

| | |
|---|---|
| Displacement | 1,015 tons |
| Dimensions | |
| length pp | 193′0″ |
| length oa | 208′4″ |
| breadth | 33′1″ |
| draught fwd | 11′10″ |
| aft | 15′7″ |
| Machinery | Triple expansion steam reciprocating |
| Boilers | 1 watertube |
| Shafts | 1 |
| IHP | 2,850 |
| DSpeed | 16 kn |
| Complement | 109 |
| Oil Fuel | 300 tons |
| Endurance | 7,400×10 kn |
| Armament | |
| Main | 1 4″ Mk IX, XIX |
| close-range | 1 2pdr, or twin 20mm Oerlikon |
| | 6 single 20mm Oerlikons |
| | 2 2″ rocket flare projectors |
| Anti-submarine | |
| depth charge rails | 2 |
| throwers | 4 |
| depth charges | 100 |
| Hedgehog | Yes |
| Minesweeping gear | No |
| Radar | Types 271Q, 242, 253 |
| M/F D/F | Yes |
| Foxer gear | Yes |

## MODIFIED 'FLOWER' CLASS—CLASS LIST
### 1941 Supplementary Programme

| Name | Pendant No | Job No | | Builder | Building Time | Completion Date |
|---|---|---|---|---|---|---|
| **UK BUILT** | | | | | | |
| *Betony* | K 274 | J | 1240 | Hall | 11m5d | 31.8.43 |
| *Buddleia* | K 275 | J | 11840 | Hall | 11m18d | 17.11.43 |
| *Bugloss* | K 306 | J | 4640 | Crown | 11m13d | 8.11.43 |
| *Bullrush* | K 307 | J | 4644 | Crown | 11m24d | 15.2.44 |
| *Burnet* | K 348 | J | 1530 | Ferguson | 10m21d | 23.9.43 |
| *Ceanothus* | K 360 | J | 1531 | Ferguson | 10m5d | 10.12.43 |
| *Charlock* | K 395 | J | 1535 | Ferguson | 11m4d | 10.3.44 |

### 1942 Programme

| Name | Pendant No | Job No | | Builder | Building Time | Completion Date |
|---|---|---|---|---|---|---|
| *Arabis* | K 385 | J | 1528 | Brown | 12m18d | 16.3.44 |
| *Arbutus* | K 403 | J | 1529 | Brown | 14m0d | 3.7.44 |
| *Candytuft* | K 382 | J | 1534 | Inglis | 10m19d | 15.1.44 |

NOTES
These ships were all transferred out of RN service, as follows:

*Charlock* on builder's trials in the Clyde, 1944. The full Modified hull form is clear here, with the more naval style of the bridge. (*Ministry of Defence*)

## TO CANADA

| *Buddleia* | became *Giffard* |
| *Bullrush* | became *Mimico* |
| *Candytuft* | became *Long Branch* |
| *Ceanothus* | became *Forest Hill* |

All were transferred on completion; note that pendant numbers were different in RCN service.

## TO NEW ZEALAND

*Arabis, Arbutus*
Both retained their RN names, and were transferred on completion.

## TO INDIA

*Betony, Bugloss, Burnet, Charlock*
Dates of transfer are not available, but three of the four ships had been transferred, and were in RIN service, with the East Indies Fleet before VJ-Day, 1945.

## Canadian Built

### 1941 Programme

| *Dittany* | K 279 | CN 306 | Collingwood |
| ex USN *Beacon* | | | |
| *Honesty* | K 285 | CN 308 | Kingston |
| ex USN *Caprice* | | | |
| *Linaria* | K 282 | CN 309 | Midland |
| ex USN *Clash* | | | |
| *Rosebay* | K 286 | CN 315 | Kingston |
| ex USN *Splendor* | | | |
| *Smilax* | K 280 | CN 316 | Collingwood |
| ex USN *Tact* | | | |
| *Statice* | K 455 | CN 317 | Collingwood |
| ex USN *Vim* | | | |
| *Willowherb* | K 283 | CN 318 | Midland |
| ex USN *Vitality* | | | |

All the above were ordered by the USN, and transferred on completion, under Lease-Lend commitments. Building details are included under the RCN section.

## Cancelled Ships

### 1942 PROGRAMME

| *Amaryllis* | | Fleming & Ferguson | Cancelled 9.12.42 |
| *Balm* | J 11841 | Hall | Cancelled 12.12.42 |

## War Losses

| *Alysse* (France) | 8.2.42 | Torpedoed by *U654*, North Atlantic |
| *Arbutus* (i) | 5.2.42 | Torpedoed by *U136*, North Atlantic |

| | | |
|---|---|---|
| *Asphodel* | 9.3.44 | Torpedoed by *U575*, North Atlantic |
| *Auricula* | 6.5.42 | Mined at Madagascar |
| *Bluebell* | 17.2.45 | Torpedoed by *U711*, Barents Sea |
| *Vervain* | 20.2.45 | Torpedoed by *U1208*, North Atlantic |
| *Erica* | 9.2.43 | Mined off Benghazi |
| *Gardenia* | 9.11.42 | Sunk in collision off Oran |
| *Gladiolus* | 16.10.41 | Torpedoed by *U558*, North Atlantic |
| *Godetia* | 6.9.40 | Sunk in collision off Ireland |
| *Hollyhock* | 9.4.42 | Sunk by aircraft off Ceylon |
| *Marigold* | 9.12.42 | Sunk by aircraft off Algiers |
| *Mimosa* (France) | 9.6.42 | Torpedoed by *U124*, North Atlantic |
| *Montbretia* (Norway) | 18.11.42 | Torpedoed by *U624*, North Atlantic |
| *Orchis* | 21.8.44 | Constructive total loss after torpedo |
| *Picotee* | 12.8.41 | Torpedoed by *U568* off Iceland |
| *Pink* | 27.6.44 | Constructive total loss after torpedo |
| *Polyanthus* | 21.9.43 | Torpedoed by U-boat, North Atlantic |
| *Rose* (Norway) | 26.10.44 | Sunk in collision, North Atlantic |
| *Salvia* | 24.12.41 | Torpedoed by *U568* in Mediterranean |
| *Samphire* | 30.1.43 | Torpedoed by Italian submarine off Bougie |
| *Snapdragon* | 19.12.42 | Sunk by aircraft in Mediterranean |
| *Zinnia* | 23.8.41 | Torpedoed by U-boat, North Atlantic |
| *La Bastiaise* (France) | 22.6.40 | Mined on trials, North Sea |
| *Fleur De Lys* | 14.10.41 | Torpedoed by *U206*, North Atlantic |

## RCN SHIPS

| | | |
|---|---|---|
| *Alberni* | 21.8.44 | Torpedoed by *U480*, English Channel |
| *Charlottetown* | 11.9.42 | Torpedoed by *U517*, E Coast Canada |
| *Levis* | 20.9.41 | Torpedoed by *U74*, North Atlantic |
| *Louisburg* | 6.2.43 | Sunk by aircraft off Oran |
| *Regina* | 8.8.44 | Torpedoed by *U667* in English Channel |
| *Shawinigan* | 24.11.44 | Torpedoed by *U1228* off E coast Canada |
| *Spikenard* | 11.2.42 | Torpedoed by *U136*, North Atlantic |
| *Weyburn* | 22.2.43 | Mined off Gibraltar |
| *Windflower* | 7.12.41 | Sunk in collision off Newfoundland |

## MODIFIED CLASS

| | | |
|---|---|---|
| *Trentonian* | 22.2.45 | Torpedoed by *U1004* in English Channel |

**CHARLOCK in December, 1943.**

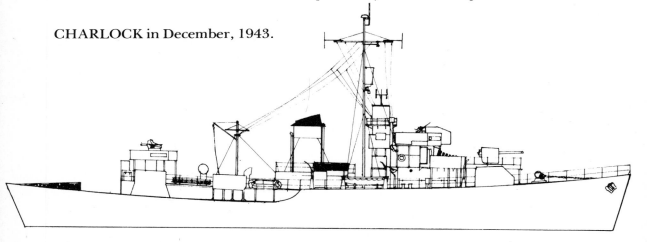

*Bamborough Castle* in seawater so cold it is steaming. She has Type 272 radar atop her lattice mast, with Type 244 on a spur below it. The clear position of the H/F D/F aerial stands out here. *(Ministry of Defence)*

*Hadleigh Castle*, the lead ship of the class, in 1943. She has the newer 4″ gun, but Type 272 radar. *(Ministry of Defence)*

## 'CASTLE' CLASS CORVETTES
## 44 ships completed

This class was the final version of the RN corvette in World War II. It reflected all the lessons learned, and the improvements made in the 'Flower' class, during the early years of the Battle of the Atlantic, and it is interesting to compare the 'Castle' class with the pre-war 'Grimsby' class sloops, which reflected escort vessel thinking of only some five years before. Whereas the 'Algerine' class, the ultimate RN design of fleet minesweeper, confirmed and updated the pre-war 'Halcyon' class design, the 'Flower' class, and the 'Castle' succeeding it, followed a very different course.

The 'Castle' class, like the 'Flower' class, were designed by Smith's Dock Company Ltd, on the Tees, and that company was the lead shipyard for drawings and improvements throughout.

The staff requirement was primarily for A/S escort of ocean convoys: ships capable of operating in any weather, and of operating their Asdic sets in heavy weather to the same capacity as a destroyer; good manoeuvrability, fitted for tropical service (and some for Arctic), a design endurance of 6,500 miles at 15 knots, and a range of equipment, starting with a half Squid ATW mortar, Type B (3 bombs), considerable radiotelephone lines, for talking with fighters as well as ships, provision for an RDF beacon later, and a complement of 99, including 6 officers (less than the Modified 'Flower' class, be it noted).

In general, 'Castle' class corvettes were built by yards which did not have slips long enough to accommodate the longer 'River', and later 'Loch' class, frigates. They were, therefore, a support class to the growing number of frigates, rather than being seen as an ideal design in their own right. They did, however, show very real improvements on the 'Flower' class.

The most obvious difference was in the hull design; a study of the photographs will show significant increases in sheer, flare and tumble home, and the hull is 50 feet longer than that of the 'Flower' class. The midships section, as in the 'Loch' class, looks rectangular compared with the bow and stern sections, but the covered upperdeck is carried right aft to the quarterdeck, and the whole hull design looks strong and sturdy, and specifically designed for North Atlantic work—which, as we have seen, was not the case with the 'Flower' class. The extent of welding was much increased in the units built by Robb, Smith's Dock, Swan Hunter (Neptune Yard) and Harland & Wolff; the others were mainly riveted.

It is an interesting thought that the 'Castle' class may arguably represent the most pleasing and attractive class of all the escort classes of the RN, RCN and USN; the cutaway stem was especially attractive.

Next, it will be seen that the earlier bridge designs of the 'Flower' class have been replaced by a full naval-type bridge, with the wings having steel supports down to the upper deck—following the 'River' class lead. The radar aerial has been lifted aloft by a full lattice mast, giving a much more regular naval appearance. The funnel is larger, with an Admiralty cap, and full naval boats, a motor boat and whaler were fitted in gravity-type davits, as supply of equipment permitted.

The 4″ gun forward was fitted on a bandstand well clear of the forecastle deck, for dryness in heavy weather, and the gun was of a new, wartime design, compared with the old guns fitted in the 'Flower' class. Wartime gun production was beginning to catch up by the time the 'Castle' class appeared.

Similarly, the close-range armament was increased, and power-mounted twin Oerikons appeared on the gundeck aft in most cases. Some plans of this class confirm that it was planned to fit 4 further single Oerlikons on the after decks, where mountings were fitted in preparation.

The new single Squid ATW mortar had pride of place, on the deck forward of the bridge. Details of this weapon are included under the 'Loch' class; the fire-power of this class of corvette was increased enormously by its addition.

Aft, the depth-charge armament was cut right down, amounting to only 2 throwers, 1 set of rails, and 15 depth charges. This dramatic change emphasised the RN's confidence in its new ahead-throwing weapon. The result was a remarkably clear quarterdeck, which was helpful later when Foxer gear was added.

The one surprising feature of this class was the number of small deckhouses, tanks and gear fitted on the upper deck and on the house above and forward of the quarterdeck. Probably, with close-range armament concentrating on fewer, twin mountings, this space could be used more profitably in this way.

This class retained, for reasons of speed and economy in shipbuilding, the basic main machinery fitted in the 'Flower' class, though with watertube boilers. They had an extra $\frac{1}{2}$ knot in speed over the 'Flower' class, and by the end of the war were operating in Support Groups composed entirely of 'Castle' class ships.

During the period when the maximum number of new escorts was being ordered the Admiralty had seen great advantages in having numbers of 'Castle' class corvettes built in Canada, in yards, like those in the UK, where the slips were too small to build frigates. Some 43 were ordered in this way, and are included in the class list; but in December 1943, when the escort orders were being cut back, all were cancelled before they had been laid down.

At the same time, it was decided to complete 5 units of the class as ocean rescue vessels, manned by the Merchant Navy and fitted with merchant ship type lifeboats, and one 24 foot specially equipped rescue motor boat. They were armed, as they could not claim Red Cross protection.

The 'Castle' class corvettes commissioned by the RCN were all built in the UK, the reasons being outlined in the shipbuilding chapter.

This class, with the 'Loch' class frigates, was the first to have progressively fitted the new Type 277 radar set, for which the North Atlantic escorts had been waiting for some years. Until these sets were available these corvettes were fitted with Type 272, either set being fitted at the foremasthead.

No units of this class were allocated to the East Indies or British Pacific Fleets in 1945. All escort units in these fleets were taken from the sloop 'Hunt' and frigate classes, the only corvettes being the air sea rescue vessels of the 'Flower' class with the East Indies Fleet.

In 1948 a proposed modernisation replaced the single 4″ gun forward with a twin 4″ Mark XIX, and Type 293Q radar replaced the Type 277, while A/S homing torpedoes were also added.

### GERMAN U-BOATS SUNK BY 'CASTLE' CLASS

| | | |
|---|---|---|
| U714 | 6.3.44 | *Kenilworth Castle* and others |
| U743 | 9.9.44 | *Portchester Castle* and others |
| U1200 | 11.11.44 | *Pevensey Castle, Portchester Castle, Launceston Castle* and *Kenilworth Castle* |
| U387 | 9.12.44 | *Bamborough Castle* |
| U 425 | 17.2.44 | *Alnwick Castle* and others |
| U878 | 10.4.45 | *Tintagel Castle* and others |

### CASTLE CLASS—COMMAND ALLOCATION
#### (As at 1st January)

| | 1943 | 1944 | 1945 | 7.5.45 |
|---|---|---|---|---|
| Londonderry | 0 | 2 | 6 | 6 |
| Liverpool | 0 | 0 | 8 | 8 |
| Greenock | 0 | 0 | 10 | 9 |
| Totals | 0 | 2 | 24 | 23 |

*Tintagel Castle,* showing the after section and the solid steel bulwark round the stern. Note the single depth charge rail. *(Ministry of Defence)*

*Carisbrooke Castle* in 1954. This shows the deck lay-out, and the single Squid mortar in its pride of place forward. The clear quarterdeck is also conspicuous, and single Bofors have been fitted aft. *(Ministry of Defence)*

A magnificent view of *Tintagel Castle* in June 1953. She has single Bofors aft, and is flying her battle ensign, with the jack on its staff at the stem while under way, as she was attending a naval review at Spithead. *(Wright & Logan)*

## 'CASTLE' CLASS SPECIFICATION

| | |
|---|---|
| Displacement | 1,060-1,100 tons |
| Dimensions | |
| length pp | 225' |
| oa | 252' |
| breadth | 36' 9" |
| draught | 14' |
| Machinery | 4 cylinder triple expansion |
| Boilers | 2 Admiralty 3-drum type |
| Shafts | 1 |
| IHP | 2,980 |
| Speed | 16·5 kn |
| Oil Fuel | 480 tons |
| Endurance | 6,200×15 kn |
| Complement | 99, later 120 |
| Armament | |
| main | 1 4" Mk XIX on Mk XXIV mtg |
| close-range | 2 twin 20mm Oerlikons |
| | 2 single 20mm Oerlikons |
| | 4 further single Oerlikons if required |
| A/S | 1 single Squid ATW mortar |
| | 12 Shark A/S missiles |
| | 15 depth charges |
| | 2 throwers, 1 rail |
| Radar | Type 272, later 277 |
| | Types 242, 253 |
| H/F D/F | Yes |
| M/F D/F | Yes |
| Boats | 1 27' whaler |
| | 1 16' trawler boat |
| | (25' motor boat later replaced trawler boat) |

## 'CASTLE' CLASS—CLASS LIST

| Name | Pendant No. | Job No. | Builder | Building Time | Completion Date |
|---|---|---|---|---|---|
| **1942 Programme** | | | | | |
| *Allington Castle* | K 689 | J 1508 | Fleming & Ferguson | 10m18d | 9.6.44 |
| *Bamborough Castle* | K 386 | J 4799 | Lewis | 10m30d | 30.5.44 |
| *Caistor Castle* | K 690 | J 11852 | ,, | 13m3d | 29.9.44 |
| *Denbigh Castle* | K 696 | J 11853 | ,, | 9m20d | 28.12.44 |
| *Farnham Castle* | K 413 | J 4704 | Crown | 19m5d | 31.1.45 |
| *Hadleigh Castle* | K 355 | J 4702 | Smith's Dock | 5m12d | 18.9.43 |
| *Hedingham Castle* | K 529 | J 4718 | Crown | | 12.2.45 |

| Name | Pendant No. | Job No. | Builder | Building Time | Completion Date |
|------|-------------|---------|---------|---------------|-----------------|
| *Hurst Castle* | K 416 | J 11819 | Caledon | 9m16d | 20.6.44 |
| *Kenilworth Castle* | K 420 | J 4710 | Smith's Dock | 7m15d | 22.11.43 |
| *Lancaster Castle* | K 691 | J 1546 | Fleming & Ferguson | 12m4d | 15.9.44 |
| *Oakham Castle* | K 530 | J 1551 | Inglis | 12m12d | 12.12.44 |
| **1943 Programme** | | | | | |
| *Alnwick Castle* | K 405 | J 1801 | Brown | 16m29d | 11.11.44 |
| *Amberley Castle* | K 386 | J 4799 | Austin | 17m24d | 24.11.44 |
| *Berkeley Castle* | K 387 | J 1812 | Barclay Curle | 7m25d | 18.11.43 |
| *Carisbrooke Castle* | K 379 | J 11805 | Caledon | 9m5d | 17.11.43 |
| *Dumbarton Castle* | K 388 | J 11818 | ,, | 9m22d | 25.2.44 |
| *Flint Castle* | K 383 | J 11812 | Robb | 8m10d | 31.12.43 |
| *Knaresborough Castle* | K 389 | J 4776 | Blyth | 11m13d | 5.4.44 |
| *Launceston Castle* | K 397 | J 4780 | ,, | 12m27d | 20.6.44 |
| *Leeds Castle* | K 384 | J 4779 | Pickersgill | 9m23d | 15.2.44 |
| *Morpeth Castle* | K 693 | J 4877 | ,, | 12m20d | 13.7.44 |
| *Oxford Castle* | K 692 | J 3319 | Harland & Wolff | 8m19d | 10.3.44 |
| *Pevensey Castle* | K 449 | J 3335 | ,, | 11m19d | 10.6.44 |
| *Portchester Castle* | K 362 | J 4778 | Swan Hunter | 8m22d | 8.11.43 |
| *Rushen Castle* | K 372 | J 4782 | ,, | 10m18d | 24.2.44 |
| *Tintagel Castle* | K 399 | J 1804 | Ailsa | 11m8d | 7.4.44 |

## TRANSFERRED TO RCN ON COMMISSIONING

| | | | |
|---|---|---|---|
| *Hespeler* ex *Guildford Castle* | K 378 | J 11813 | Robb |
| *Orangeville* ex *Hedingham Castle* | K 396 | J 11814 | ,, |
| *Coppercliff* ex *Hever Castle* | K 521 | J 4784 | Blyth |
| *Humberstone* ex *Norham Castle* | K 447 | J 1550 | Inglis |
| *Bowmanville* ex *Nunnery Castle* | K 446 | J 4789 | Pickersgill |
| *Tillsonburg* ex *Pembroke Castle* | K 450 | J 1548 | Ferguson |
| *Arnprior* ex *Rising Castle* | K 398 | J 3327 | Harland & Wolff |
| *St. Thomas* ex *Sandgate Castle* | K 373 | J 4706 | Smith's Dock |
| *Petrolia* ex *Sherborne Castle* | K 453 | J 3351 | Harland & Wolff |
| *Kincardine* ex *Tamworth Castle* | K 393 | J 4712 | Smith's dock |

| | | | | |
|---|---|---|---|---|
| *Leaside* | K 460 | J 4714 | ,, | |
| ex *Walmer Castle* | | | | |
| *Huntsville* | K 461 | J 1805 | Ailsa | |
| ex *Wolvesey Castle* | | | | |

Further details of these ships will be found under the RCN section.

## TRANSFERRED TO NORWAY ON COMPLETION

| | | | | |
|---|---|---|---|---|
| *Tunsberg Castle* | K 374 | J 4785 | Swan Hunter | L 16.8.43 |
| ex *Shrewsbury Castle* | | | | |

A good bow view of *Caistor Castle.* The extra height and sheer of the bow, and the full frigate-type bridge stand out. *(Ministry of Defence)*

| Name | Pendant No. | Job No. | Builder | Building Time | Completion Date |
|------|-------------|---------|---------|---------------|-----------------|

## COMPLETED AS MERCANTILE RESCUE SHIPS

| Name | Pendant No. | Job No. | Builder | Building Time | Completion Date |
|------|-------------|---------|---------|---------------|-----------------|
| *Empire Shelter* ex *Barnard Castle* | K 694 | J 1802 | Brown | | |
| *Empire Lifeguard* ex *Maiden Castle* | K 443 | J 1547 | Fleming & Ferguson | | |
| *Empire Rest* ex *Rayleigh Castle* | K 695 | J 1549 | Ferguson | | |
| *Empire Peacemaker* ex *Scarborough Castle* | K 536 | J 1807 | Fleming & Ferguson | | |
| *Empire Comfort* ex *York Castle* | K 537 | J 1808 | Ferguson | | |

## CANCELLED SHIPS

### UK orders for RN

| Name | Job No. | Builder |
|------|---------|---------|
| *Alton Castle* | J 1846 | Fleming & Ferguson |
| *Appleby Castle* | J 4841 | Austin |
| *Bere Castle* | J 1803 | Brown |
| *Caldecott Castle* | J 1804 | ,, |
| *Calshot Castle* | J 1555 | Inglis |
| *Dover Castle* | J 1552 | ,, |
| *Dudley Castle* | J 4931 | ,, |
| *Monmouth Castle* | J 11855 | Lewis |
| *Norwich Castle* | J 4932 | Brown |
| *Oswestry Castle* | J 4933 | Crown |
| *Pendennis Castle* | J 4936 | ,, |
| *Rhuddlan Castle* | J 4783 | ,, |
| *Thornbury Castle* | J 1809 | Ferguson |
| *Tonbridge Castle* | J 4838 | Austin |
| *Warkworth Castle* | J 1847 | Fleming & Ferguson |

### Canadian orders for RN

| Name | Job No. | Builder |
|------|---------|---------|
| *Aydon Castle* | CN 706 | Kingston |
| *Barnwell Castle* | CN 707 | ,, |
| *Beeston Castle* | CN 708 | ,, |
| *Bodiam Castle* | CN 505 | Collingwood |
| *Bolton Castle* | CN 506 | ,, |
| *Bowes Castle* | CN 709 | Kingston |
| *Bramber Castle* | CN 507 | Collingwood |
| *Bridgenorth Castle* | CN 508 | ,, |
| *Brough Castle* | CN 509 | ,, |
| *Canterbury Castle* | CN 700 | Midland |
| *Carew Castle* | CN 701 | ,, |
| *Chepstow Castle* | CN 510 | Collingwood |
| *Chester Castle* | CN 511 | ,, |

| | | |
|---|---|---|
| *Christchurch Castle* | CN 702 | Midland |
| *Clare Castle* | CN 689 | Collingwood |
| *Clavering Castle* | CN 690 | ,, |
| *Clitheroe Castle* | CN 691 | ,, |
| *Clun Castle* | CN 703 | Midland |
| *Colchester Castle* | CN 704 | ,, |
| *Corfe Castle* | CN 692 | ,, |
| *Cornet Castle* | CN 693 | Collingwood |
| *Cowes Castle* | CN 694 | ,, |
| *Cowling Castle* | CN 695 | Midland |
| *Criccieth Castle* | CN 717 | Morton |
| *Cromer Castle* | CN 697 | Midland |
| *Devizes Castle* | CN 710 | Kingston |
| *Dunster Castle* | CN 698 | Midland |
| *Egremont Castle* | CN 711 | Kingston |
| *Fotheringay Castle* | CN 718 | Morton |
| *Helmsley Castle* | CN 719 | ,, |
| *Malling Castle* | CN 720 | ,, |
| *Malmesbury Castle* | CN 721 | ,, |
| *Raby Castle* | CN 722 | ,, |
| *Trematon Castle* | CN 723 | ,, |
| *Tutbury Castle* | CN 724 | ,, |
| *Wigmore Castle* | CN 699 | Midland |

Note how, excepting the last few, all names came from the opening letters of the alphabet, leaving plenty of room for large numbers of further ships of this class.

RUSHEN CASTLE.

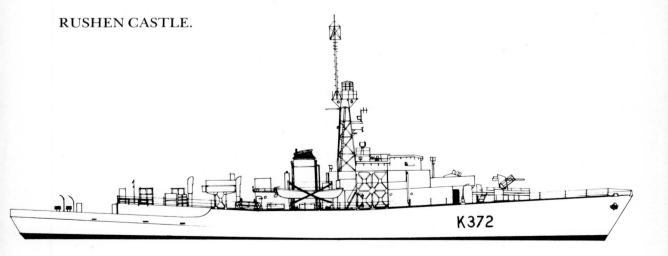

K372

▲ *Lochy* at anchor. The Hedgehog bombs are loaded and her seaboat is turned out. *(Ministry of Defence)*

*Ness* on completion in 1942, on the Forth. She has Western Approaches camouflage, but no H/F D/F aerial. *(Ministry of Defence)* ▼

## 'RIVER' CLASS FRIGATES
### 57 ships completed in UK

Once the demands of the North Atlantic battle took shape, and it also became clear that the 'Flower' class corvettes would not be big or speedy enough for such arduous service, the Admiralty moved fast towards a larger class of escort.

At first referred to as 'twin screw corvettes', orders were quickly placed for construction, as follows:

    1940 Programme 27
    1941 Programme 19
    1942 Programme 11

From that time on, all yards capable of building the 'River' class, and not engaged in specialised warship construction, concentrated on their construction, and the details of their equipment reflected the constantly changing picture of the technical war at sea.

The early 'River' class units were equipped with the full range of minesweeping gear, Mark I Oropesa sweep, LL magnetic sweep, and SA acoustic, and in February 1942 they were being called 'fast corvette mine-sweepers'. Their maximum speed through the water, with Oropesa sweeps out, was 11 knots, but there is no available record of whether they were actually used as sweepers—it seems doubtful.

By mid-1942 the rate of completions of the new fleet minesweepers had reached the point where the 'River' class ships, employed intensively in the North Atlantic, were no longer needed as an additional sweeping force. In June 1942 the Oropesa gear was removed from the long endurance ships, and the LL gear was urgently removed from all ships, for fitting in regular minesweepers. In the frigates this added 85 tons of oil fuel to the ships' range.

During 1942, too, they were first officially described as frigates, and for the rest of World War II this class differentiation by length and speed was maintained, the smaller, slower ships being classed as corvettes.

For speed of construction, the hull structure followed the classification society rules and survey, and merchant ship practice, rather than naval, was in general followed.

The corvette main machinery of triple expansion engines was followed in the frigates, being duplicated for two shafts, but the boilers were changed to water-tube. The first turbine-powered frigate was ordered in May 1941, but the supply of turbine blades restricted the numbers so engined. Rather than redesign the hull, the turbine-engined ships were given increased beam and ballast. They had 6,500 hp, as a design for turbines of that capacity was readily available, and only an extra 0.6 knots was to be gained from every extra 1,000 hp added thereafter.

When we come to the following 'Loch' class frigates, it is interesting to see how much of the basic 'River' class design was retained. The dimensions were closely followed, as were the hull form and upper deck lay-out. The 'River' class was a very successful class of escort, large enough and seaworthy enough to carry any of the weapons as they developed, more comfortable for the crews on the long patrols carried out by the Support Groups, and with the greater speed and endurance required for long-range ocean convoy escort.

*Armament*

*MAIN*   This was specified as two single 4″ guns, Mark XIX , thus doubling the fire-power of the 'Flower' class, but delivery of the new 4″ guns was not as fast as production of the ships, and only the following were expected to have the after 4″ gun at time of completion, the others having a 12 pounder in lieu: *Aire, Ballinderry, Bann, Chelmer, Dart, Derg, Ettrick, Mourne, Ribble, Strule, Tweed.*

*CLOSE-RANGE WEAPONS*   Originally, these comprised 2 single 2 pounder pom poms, on power mountings on the after gundeck, and 2 single 20mm Oerlikons, Mark IIA, in the bridge wings. This varied, however, and in some ships the pom poms were omitted, and 2 further single Oerlikons fitted in lieu.

It seems clear that the originally authorised armament was no less than 10 single Oerlikons, fitted as follows: 1 in the stem of the ship, 2 abreast the Hedgehog, 2 in the bridge wings, 2 on the after gundeck, 1 atop the after 4″ gundeck, and 2 on the quarterdeck. The shortage of guns limited the number of ships to receive the full authorised number, but some ships did, and this can be seen in the photographs.

In 1942 it was recommended that all the single pom pom and single Oerlikon mountings should be replaced with twin power-mounted Oerlikons, as these became available, and this, too, can be followed in the illustrations. This applied, of course, only to the four main close-range positions.

Some ships were fitted, late in 1943, with two 6 pounder Army mountings, aft of the breakwater, for close-range surface actions against U-boats. *Mourne,* which already had two twin power-mounted Oerlikons aft in January 1943, received her 6 pounders in November.

Other close-range armament, fitted mainly in the early days of the class, included PAC projectors, and it was approved that all ships should be fitted with a balloon winch for flying VLA defensive kite balloons on the deckhouse forward of and above the after 4″ gun. This applied especially in the early days of the 'River's, when they were known as the 'Exe' class.

*Minesweeping Gear*

The quarterdeck of the 'River' class was large enough and clear enough for a complete set of sweeping gear to be fitted, as in the specialised 'Algerine' class of fleet minesweeper.

The LL reel was housed under the after 4″ gun platform, the minesweeping winch was immediately abaft of it, and a full set of minesweeping davits, 2 Oropesa floats, and 4 Otters, without restricting the depth-charge equipment which formed the major A/S weapon of the ship. Indeed, some ships (including *Waveney, Tay* and *Wear*) carried 8 depth-charge throwers as well as their full M/S outfit, during the period when the 14 charge pattern was in use.

It was fortunate that the minesweeping gear was removed from the 'River' class before the Foxer gear was needed later in the war, as there could hardly have been room for both.

## A/S Equipment

The Hedgehog was standard, fitted forward of the forward 4″ gun deckhouse. This was a pretty exposed position in heavy seas, and steel weather protection for the operators can be seen in some of the photographs.

In early 1942, when the 14 charge pattern was in vogue, 8 depth-charge throwers, 2 sets of rails, and traps, and over 200 charges were carried.

The normal stowage was 15 in each rail, 8 alongside each thrower, 1 in each thrower, and the rest divided between the depth-charge store and the extra stowage rails sited on the quarterdeck.

In mid 1943, with longer patrols of up to six weeks, made possible through greater built-in endurance and oiling at sea, the depth-charge outfit was increased to its maximum, by enlarging the two-tier storage racks on the quarterdeck. These racks were also prominent in the 'Captain' class frigates, and these two classes probably had the greatest depth-charge armament of their day, in addition to the Hedgehog. This increased stowage was retained, and fully utilised, after the standard pattern had been reduced from 14 charges to 10.

When the Squid A/S mortars came as a great advance on the Hedgehog, it was approved in principle to fit individual ships of the 'River' class as they came in for refit; 44 RN ships, plus 7 RCN ships, were 'eligible' for this alteration, but four to five months were required for the work, and it is thought that no ships were so altered during the war. After the war, *Helmsdale* was fitted with two Squids in place of the forward 4″ gun, to work with the Second Training Flotilla out of Portsmouth; a photograph of her in this configuration is included.

## Boats

The authorised complement was:

1 25 ft motor cutter, carried in destroyer-type davits on the starboard side.

1 27 ft whaler, carried in gooseneck davits on the port side. These davits are prominent, as their feet were housed outside the hull line, and the whaler sat on the deck in its stowed position.

1 16 ft trawler-type motor boat, generous by the supply standards of wartime, and probably seldom fitted.

1 14 ft sailing dinghy, probably also seldom supplied, and the gravity davits specified for it were certainly not.

3 lifefloats (carley rafts).

4 Flotanets (small, square rafts).

## Radar

This was fitted from the outset in this class, and its progress reflected the technical battle itself.

The original set fitted was Type 271, with Type 286. In 1942, this was changed to Type 272, with Type 242 on top. Then, in May 1943, approval was given for Type 277 to be fitted urgently, with a PPI, as it was seen as a possible mastery over the U-boat; it was agreed that, if necessary, up to 20% of the depth charges, and the second radar set, could be landed, in order to fit the Type 277, with its very heavy aerial array.

In 1945, the urgency of fitting Type 277 was still being emphasised, but photographs do not reflect this in numbers so fitted. Type 972, a later design, was then seen to be still experimental, but highly desirable for those ships of the class refitting for the Pacific.

*Proposed conversions*

*A/A ESCORTS*   For the Pacific, the RN decided in July 1944 to leave the 'River' class relatively unconverted, but to convert units of the 'Loch' class on the stocks; the RCN were asked to convert up to 20 of their 'River' class units, depending on the availability of the fire-control gear. This number was later increased to 40.

But before this decision was taken plans had been made for converting some of the RN 'River' class units, within three alternative schemes; these may be compared with the Admiralty proposals to Ottawa for the conversion of RCN 'River' class units for Pacific service, covered under the RCN chapter.

*1. A/A—A/S*   1 twin 4″ Mk XIX forward, with US Type 61 director.
               1 twin 40mm Bofors STAAG mounting, facing aft, on the after deck, in place of the 4″ or 12 pounder gun.
               1 double Squid A/S mortar aft, no Hedgehog forward (probably the first siting aft of an A/S mortar, now standard practice).
               Single power-mounted 40mm Bofors, sited thus: 2 on bridge wings, 2 on after gun platform, 2 on quarterdeck in place of extra depth-charge stowage (depth charges reduced by 44).
               Type 277 radar.

*2. A/A—A/S*   2 twin 4″ Mk XIX, one forward, one aft.
               2 gunnery directors, US Type 61.
               1 single Squid A/S mortar aft.
               Single 40mm Bofors as above.

*3. A/A*   2 twin 4″ Mk XIX, one forward, one aft, on quarterdeck.
               2 gunnery directors, US Type 61.
               1 twin 40mm Bofors on STAAG mtg, facing aft.
               1 single 40 mm Bofors, as above.

*HEDGEHOG*   As the forward position was so untenable in heavy weather, it was approved in 1943 that in some ships a full Hedgehog should be fitted on the port side, at flag deck level, or a split Hedgehog, as in some of the Modified 'Black Swan' class; *Monnow* was the first to be modified in this way, and a photograph of her in this configuration is included.

*LONG-RANGE SUPPLY SHIPS*   In July 1943 some ships were earmarked for this conversion, for Pacific service. It is not clear which ships were to be so refitted, nor whether any of those on station with the British Pacific Fleet by VJ-Day were among this number.

—Hedgehog removed, together with both 4″ guns, and all depth-charge

equipment (4 existing Oerlikons to be retained).
—complement reduced from 126 to 52.
—passengers to be carried in ratio to the reduced complement.
—range to be 2,000 miles at 18 knots, on 360 tons of oil fuel.
—oil fuel tanks holding 280 tons would be available for cargo.
—estimated total weight of cargo—200 tons, at 100 cu ft to 1 ton.
—general cargo, or petrol in containers, to be carried.
—170 tons of cargo to be stowed below, 50 tons on deck aft.
—these ships were seen to be not very suitable for this work, but possible with stripping of topweight, with high speed and fair endurance.

*SMALL MONITORS FOR ASSAULT ON NORMANDY* In 1944, small monitors, mounting heavy guns for shore bombardment, were required for this operation. They would give support fire against enemy batteries in support of beach areas, and would defend ports, once taken. Consideration was, in fact, given to converting units from the 'River', 'Castle' and 'Hunt' classes, but eventually only LCGs were used.

Had units of this class been so converted they would have received:
—2 6″ single guns, 2 twin 40mm Bofors, 6 twin 20mm Oerlikons.
—no A/S equipment, but armour protection instead, after the hull had been stripped bare, and the upperworks re-designed.

It was finally decided that to convert frigates or corvettes would disrupt unduly the new building programme, and their draught was really too great for very close inshore work.

*Chelmer* in September 1943. The steel sidescreens for the wire sweep floats stand out, and her ensign is flown from a gaff on the funnel. *(Ministry of Defence)*

*LANDING SHIPS HEADQUARTERS—LSH(S) Normandy Assault.* *Nith* and *Waveney* were among 6 ships converted to Brigade HQ ships in 1944 for this operation; *Lagan* would have been converted in place of *Waveney*, but she was written off as a constructive total loss a short time before. *Nith* distinguished herself by being painted overall in red lead, for recognition purposes, while lying off the Normandy beachhead.

*Singapore Assault.* Following on previous assault experience, the Admiralty plans in 1944 for the Far East called for six of these small Assault HQ ships.

Of the Normandy HQ ships, the 'Hunt's and 'Captain's had proved too small, or too valuable for other duties. So 4 more 'River's would be required to join *Nith* and *Waveney*. 2 would be required in service by 1st January 1945, and the other 2 by 1st May.

In November 1944 there were only 5 RN 'River's left in the Home Commands, and they were all escort group leaders. It was not possible to withdraw any of these 5, until the German U-boats were finally defeated. All other ships of the class were allocated or on passage to the Far East, or on loan to the Allies.

The 'Loch' class frigates also could not be spared from the European A/S battle, as they had become vital, due to the effectiveness of their new Squid mortars. Those completing as 'Bay' class A/A escorts for the Far East were also too valuable for conversion. 2 of the previous LSH (S) from Normandy, the 'Captain' class *Dacres* and *Kingsmill*, would, in fact, be retained as senior officers' ships of the build-up groups, which did not require such a large staff on board.

So it was decided to ask the RCN if they would release 2 of the 7 'River' class units on loan to them, for these conversions. 2 would be required on station with the East Indies Fleet for October 1945, in the revised plan, and 2 for early January 1946. This meant, in turn, that 2 ships would need to be available in the UK, for conversion, by 30th April and 31st May 1945, the other 2 being left for reconsideration at the end of May 1945.

The RCN agreed to this proposal, and accordingly *Meon* and *Ettrick* were returned by the end of April 1945. The further 2, for conversion later, were never named, since the Far East war moved to its conclusion sufficiently fast to make their conversion later in 1945 not worth while.

*Meon* and *Ettrick* were, however, converted, and a photograph of the result is included. It is possible that *Exe* and *Chelmer* of the RN ships were later converted to make up the numbers required for such an operation.

### HMS *Jed*

This was a 'River' class frigate, built and engined by Charles Hill & Sons Ltd of Bristol. Laid down on 27th September 1941, she was launched on 30th July 1942 and completed on 30th November 1942.

After work-up at Tobermory, *Jed* joined the Western Approaches Command as a unit of the 42nd Escort Group, based on Londonderry, for North Atlantic mid-ocean escort duty. Her first convoy was ONS 163, which sailed from the UK for North America on 26th January 1943. Two days later *Jed* developed rudder defects, and after repairs in Iceland she sailed for St John's. She then joined the eastbound convoy HX 226 on 14th February. On 1st March 1943 she was assigned to one of the new Support Groups, the 1st composed of *Pelican* (SO), *Sennen, Rother, Spey, Wear* and *Jed.*

At the end of April 1943 convoy ONS 5 was attacked in very stormy weather. This story is told elsewhere in this book, and the part played in it by *Jed's* group was very important. Their next convoy was SC 130, eastbound from Halifax on 11th May. Four groups of U-boats were concentrated to attack the convoy, but, in spite of heavy actions, no ships were lost. 5 U-boats were sunk, one by *Jed.*

Further patrols in support of convoys followed, and on 14th June, when with ONS 10, the Group swept along the line of an H/F D/F contact, and *Jed* found the U-boat. An attack was made, and *U 334* broke surface. She was sunk with no survivors. *Jed* hunted another U-boat without success in early July, when with SC 135, and then the Group was diverted to support convoys on the UK-Gibraltar run. Part of these patrols were to back up the RAF attacks on U-boats in the Bay of Biscay, and in August *Jed* gave support to the Canadian destroyer *Athabaskan,* which had been hit by a glider bomb. *Jed* detected a U-boat by radar on the surface with some success at this time.

In early November the Group was withdrawn from the Biscay patrols, and in supporting a convoy, shortly after, *Jed* attacked a U-boat with her sister ship *Tavy.* In November she was allocated to the East Indies Fleet. After refit and work-up she sailed east, and on arrival in April 1944 she was allocated to the 61st Escort Group. She escorted convoys around India and Ceylon while with this group. From November this group was disbanded, and *Jed* operated independently in convoy escort. In December she joined Force 64, after refit at Capetown, and carried out patrols until the end of the war. During these patrols she visited the Andaman Islands and Rangoon.

On 24th November 1945 *Jed* sailed from Colombo for the UK, and reduced to Reserve at Plymouth on arrival. She was scrapped in 1956.

*Rother* in April 1942. One of the original units of the class, wearing the funnel band of a Senior Officer's ship. She has single pom poms aft and eight depth charge throwers, as well as minesweeping gear! *(Ministry of Defence)*

## GERMAN U-BOATS SUNK BY 'RIVER' CLASS

| | | |
|---|---|---|
| U 136 | 11.7.42 | *Spey* and others |
| U 635 | 6.4.43 | *Tay* |
| U 89 | 12.5.43 | *Lagan* and others |
| U 456 | 13.5.43 | *Lagan* and others |
| U 640 | 17.5.43 | *Swale* |
| U 209 | 19.5.43 | *Jed* and others |
| U 436 | 26.5.43 | *Test* and others |
| U 334 | 14.6.43 | *Jed* and others |
| U 536 | 20.11.43 | *Nene* and others |
| U 305 | 17.1.44 | *Glenarm* and others |
| U 406 | 18.2.44 | *Spey* |
| U 386 | 19.2.44 | *Spey* |
| U 302 | 6.4.44 | *Swale* |
| U 390 | 5.7.44 | *Tavy* and others |
| U 198 | 12.8.44 | *Findhorn* and others |
| U 743 | 9.9.44 | *Helmsdale* and others |
| U 1006 | 16.10.44 | *Annan* |

## ITALIAN SUBMARINE SUNK BY 'RIVER' CLASS FRIGATE

| | | |
|---|---|---|
| *Leonardo Da Vinci* | 23.5.43 | *Ness* and others |

## 'RIVER' CLASS—COMMAND ALLOCATION
### (at 1st January, except last two)

| | 1943 | 1944 | 1945 | 7.5.45 | 3.8.45 |
|---|---|---|---|---|---|
| Londonderry | 13 | 5 | 8 | 7 | 1 |
| Liverpool | 0 | 4 | 1 | 2 | 0 |
| Greenock | 1 | 15 | 4 | 2 | 0 |
| Portsmouth | 0 | 0 | 2 | 3 | 0 |
| Plymouth | 0 | 0 | 3 | 7 | 0 |
| Nore | 0 | 0 | 1 | 0 | 0 |
| | | | | | |
| Mediterranean | 0 | 11 | 1 | 2 | 0 |
| South Atlantic | 0 | 9 | 10 | 0 | 0 |
| West Africa | 0 | 0 | 8 | 5 | 0 |
| | | | | | |
| Eastern Fleet | 1 | 1 | 22 | 26 | |
| East Indies Fleet | | | | | 20 |
| British Pacific Fleet | | | | | 9 |
| Totals | 15 | 46 | 60 | 54 | 30 |

NOTE
Above figures do not show allocation to English
Channel commands for the Normandy invasion in
June 1944, nor are RCN ships of this class shown
here.

## 'RIVER' CLASS FOR THE FAR EAST, 1945

|  |  | East Indies Fleet | British Pacific Fleet |
|---|---|---|---|
| Planned | RN | 12 | 5 |
|  | RCN |  | 40 |
| On station 3rd August, 1945 | RN | 20 | 9 |
|  | RCN |  | 0 |

**East Indies Fleet 3.8.45**

*Awe, Dart, Evenlode, Inver, Jed, Kale, Lochy, Lossie, Rother, Taff, Teviot, Deveron, Nadder, Halladale, Ness, Tay, Test, Bann, Shiel, Trent.*

**British Pacific Fleet 3.8.45**

*Avon, Findhorn, Parret, Helford, Barle, Derg, Odzani, Plym, Usk.*
As Command Ship, Logistic Supply Group—*Aire.*

*Wear,* October 1942. Note the Oerlikon right in the eyes of the ship, two more by the Hedgehog, and the others on the bridge and the after gun deck. *(Ministry of Defence)*

## 'RIVER' CLASS PRODUCTION FOR RN

| | | UK | CANADA | TOTAL SHIPS BUILT IN UK | 57 |
|---|---|---|---|---|---|
| 1941 | 1st half | 1 | | Retained by RN | 51 |
| | 2nd half | 2 | | | |
| 1942 | 1st half | 7 | | Built in Canada | 8 |
| | 2nd half | 15 | 5 | Total commissioned by RN | 59 |
| 1943 | 1st half | 16 | 3 | Transferred to France | 5 |
| | 2nd half | 15 | | Transferred to the Netherlands | 1 |
| 1944 | 1st half | 1 | | Transferred to Canada | 8 |
| | | | | Cancelled ships | 0 |

*Tay* leaving for the Far East in 1945, after refit. She has received Type 277 radar on a short lattice at the back of the bridge, and two single Bofors on the after gundeck. She retains the single Oerlikons right forward, and it will be noted that her close-range outfit does not conform with the specified list, probably due to shortage of guns. *(Ministry of Defence)*

## 'RIVER' CLASS SPECIFICATION

| | *1940/41/42* | *1943/44* |
|---|---|---|
| Displacement | 1,370 | 1,445 |
| Dimensions | | |
| length pp | 283' 0" | |
| oa | 301' 6" | |
| breadth | 36' 6" | |
| draught | 11' 6" fwd | |
| | 14' 4" aft | |
| Machinery | steam triple expansion reciprocating (turbines *Cam, Chelmer, Ettrick, Halladale, Helmsdale*) | |
| Boilers | 2 Admiralty water tube | |
| Shafts | 2 | |
| IHP | 5,550 (turbines, SHP 6,500) | |
| Speed | 20 | |
| Endurance | 7,200×12 kn | 7,500×15 kn |
| | 4,500×20 kn | |
| Oil Fuel | 560 | 646 |
| Complement | 107 | 140 |
| Armament | | |
| main | 2 single 4" Mk XIX on Mk XXIII mtgs | |
| close-range | 2 2 pdr | 10 Oerlikons |
| | 2 single Oerlikons | |
| | 2 PAC projectors | |
| A/S Armament | 1 Hedgehog | 1 Hedgehog |
| | 8 dc throwers | 4 dc throwers |
| | 2 rails | 2 rails |
| | 100 depth charges | 200 depth charges |
| Radar | Types 271, 286, 242 | |
| H/F D/F | Yes | |
| M/S Equipment | Mk I Oropesa, LL, SA Mk IV | |

(Later ships same as earlier, except where marked)
*Nith* and *Waveney,* as LSH(S), carried 5 twin Oerlikons and 6 single.

## 'RIVER' CLASS – CLASS LIST

| Name | Pendant No | Job No | Builder | Building Time | Completion Date |
|---|---|---|---|---|---|
| **1940 Programme** | | | | | |
| *Balinderry* | K 255 | J 4432 | Blyth | 21m27d | 2.9.43 |
| *Bann* | K 256 | J 553 | Hill | 11m19d | 7.6.43 |

| Name | Pendant No. | Job No. | Builder | Building Time | Compl Date |
|------|-------------|---------|---------|---------------|-------------|
| Chelmer | K 221 | J 1453 | Brown | 21m1d | 29.9. |
| Dart | K 21 | J 4372 | Blyth | 19m7d | 15.5. |
| Derg | K 257 | J 1225 | Robb | 14m1d | 18.6. |
| Ettrick | K 254 | J 4377 | Crown | 18m11d | 11.7. |
| Exe | K 92 | J 1418 | Fleming & Ferguson | 14m24d | 6.8.4 |
| Itchen | K 227 | J 1419 | ,, | 11m12d | 1.8.4 |
| Jed | K 235 | J 538 | Hill | 14m3d | 30.11 |
| Kale | K 241 | J 1420 | Inglis | 14m12d | 4.12. |
| Lagan | K 259 | J 4375 | Smith's Dock | 16m21d | 23.11 |
| Ness | K 219 | J 1215 | Robb | 15m0d | 27.12 |
| Nith | K 215 | J 1215 | ,, | 17m10d | 16.2. |
| Rother | K 224 | J 4388 | Smith's Dock | 9m7d | 3.4.4 |
| Spey | K 246 | J 4340 | ,, | 10m6d | 19.5. |
| Swale | K 217 | J 4342 | ,, | 10m13d | 24.6. |
| Tay | K 232 | J 4344 | ,, | 10m28d | 5.8.4 |
| Test | K 239 | J 1220 | Hall, Russell | 13m28d | 12.1( |
| Teviot | K 222 | J 1222 | ,, | 15m3d | 30.1. |
| Trent | K 243 | J 543 | Hill | 24m27d | 27.2. |
| Tweed | K 250 | J 1450 | Inglis | 22m17d | 5.4.4 |
| Waveney | K 248 | J 4369 | Smith's Dock | 11m8d | 16.9. |
| Wear | K 230 | J 4371 | ,, | 12m8d | 24.1( |

### 1941 Programme

| Name | Pendant No. | Job No. | Builder | Building Time | Compl Date |
|------|-------------|---------|---------|---------------|-------------|
| Aire | K 262 | J 1507 | Fleming & Ferguson | 13m0d | 13.7. |
| Cam | K 264 | J 1513 | Brown | 18m21d | 21.1. |
| Deveron | K 265 | J 4469 | Smith's Dock | 10m18d | 2.3.4 |
| Dovey | K 523 | J 1520 | Fleming & Ferguson | 11m2d | 25.2. |
| Fal | K 266 | J 4471 | Smith's Dock | 13m20d | 30.6. |
| Helford | K 252 | J 11824 | Hall, Russell | 11m29d | 26.6. |
| Helmsdale | K 253 | J 1514 | Inglis | 14m2d | 15.1( |
| Nene | K 270 | J 4534 | Smith's Dock | 9m18d | 8.4.4 |
| Plym | K 271 | J 4636 | ,, | 9m16d | 16.5. |
| Tavy | K 272 | J 560 | Hill | 8m17d | 3.7.4 |
| Tees | K 293 | J 11826 | Hall, Russell | 10m18d | 28.8. |
| Towy | K 294 | J 4636 | Smith's Dock | 8m7d | 10.6. |
| Usk | K 295 | J 4638 | ,, | 9m8d | 14.7. |
| Wye | K 371 | J 11816 | Robb | 15m9d | 9.2.4 |

### 1942 Programme

| Name | Pendant No. | Job No. | Builder | Building Time | Compl Date |
|------|-------------|---------|---------|---------------|-------------|
| Avon | K 97 | J 392 | Hill | 8m26d | 18.9. |
| Awe | K 526 | J 1539 | Fleming & Ferguson | 10m25d | 21.4. |
| Halladale | K 417 | J 1538 | Inglis | 10m16d | 11.5. |

| *Lochy* | K 365 | J 11820 | Hall, Russell | 12m0d | 8.2.44 |
|---------|-------|---------|---------------|-------|--------|
| *Mourne* | K 261 | J 4434 | Smith's Dock | 14m10d | 30.4.43 |
| *Nadder* | K 382 | J 11817 | ,, | 10m10d | 20.1.44 |
| *Odzani* | K 356 | J 4647 | ,, | 10m4d | 16.9.43 |
| *Taff* | K 367 | J 407 | Hill | 8m23d | 7.1.44 |

## BUILT IN CANADA, TRANSFERRED TO RN ON COMPLETION
### (from US Lend-Lease commitments)

### 1941 Programme

| *Barle* | K 289 | CN 336 | Can Vickers | 10m20d | 30.4.43 |
|---------|-------|--------|-------------|--------|---------|
| *Cuckmere* | K 299 | CN 337 | ,, | 12m10d | 14.5.43 |
| *Evenlode* | K 300 | CN 338 | ,, | 11m6d | 4.6.43 |
| *Findhorn* | K 301 | CN 339 | ,, | 10m2d | 25.6.43 |
| *Inver* | K 302 | CN 340 | ,, | 10m2d | 19.7.43 |
| *Lossie* | K 303 | CN 341 | ,, | 10m13d | 14.8.43 |
| *Parret* | K 304 | CN 342 | ,, | 10m0d | 31.8.43 |
| *Shiel* | K 305 | CN 343 | ,, | 10m12d | 30.9.43 |

## BUILT IN UK AND TRANSFERRED TO FRANCE

### 1940 Programme

| *Moyola* | K 260 | J 4430 | Smith's Dock | 7m5d | 15.1.43 |
|----------|-------|--------|--------------|------|---------|
| became *Tonkinois* | | | | | |
| *Strule* | K 258 | J 1226 | ,, | 7m24d | 30.7.43 |
| became *Croix de Lorraine* | | | | | |

### 1941 Programme

| *Braid* | K 263 | | Simons | 13m21d | 21.1.44 |
|---------|-------|--|--------|--------|---------|
| became *L'Aventure* | | | | | |
| *Frome* | K 267 | J 4530 | Blyth | 22m4d | 3.4.44 |
| became *L'Escarmouche* | | | | | |
| *Torridge* | K 292 | J 4581 | ,, | 17m20d | 6.4.44 |
| became *La Surprise* | | | | | |
| *Windrush* | K 270 | | Robb | 11m15d | 3.11.43 |
| became *La Découverte* | | | | | |

## BUILT IN UK AND TRANSFERRED TO THE NETHERLANDS

| *Ribble* | K 251 | J 1417 | Simons | | 4.8.44 |
|----------|-------|--------|--------|--|--------|

## BUILT IN UK AND TRANSFERRED TO RCN

### 1940 Programme

| *Ettrick* | K 254 | | Crown | 9m10d | 11.7.43 |
|-----------|-------|--|-------|-------|---------|
| (transferred to RCN 29.1.44) | | | | | |

### 1941 Programme

| *Meon* | K 269 | J 1519 | Inglis | 11m24d | 24.12.43 |
|--------|-------|--------|--------|--------|----------|
| (transferred to RCN 7.2.44) | | | | | |
| *Nene* | K 270 | J 4534 | Smith's Dock | 9m18d | 8.4.43 |
| (transferred to RCN 6.4.44) | | | | | |

**1942 Programme**

| | | | | |
|---|---|---|---|---|
| *Annan* | K 404 | Hall, Russell | 9m 0d | 11.3.44 |
| (transferred to RCN 13.6.44) | | | | |
| *Monnow* | K 441 | Hill | 8m 10d | 8.3.44 |
| (transferred to RCN on completion) | | | | |
| *Ribble ex Duddon* | K 251  J 1417 | Blyth | 8m 12d | 12.8.43 |
| (transferred to RCN 24.7.44) | | | | |
| *Teme* | K 458 | Smith's Dock | 9m 25d | 28.2.44 |
| (transferred to RCN on completion) | | | | |

## WAR LOSSES

**Sunk**

| | | |
|---|---|---|
| *Itchen* | 22.9.43 | North Atlantic, torpedoed by *U 260* |
| *Mourne* | 15.6.44 | English Channel, torpedoed by *U 767* |
| *Tweed* | 7.1.44 | South west of Ireland, torpedoed by *U 305* |

**Constructive Total Losses**

| | | |
|---|---|---|
| *Lagan* | 20.9.43 | North Atlantic, torpedoed by *U 260* |
| *Teme* (on loan to RCN) | 29.3.45 | Off Falmouth, English Channel, torpedoed by *U 246* |

*Wye* on the last day of 1944. A good view of the quarterdeck arrangements, and the triangular stern. *(Ministry of Defence)*

*Meon,* in 1953, but showing here in her wartime role as an assault HQ ship. Extended accommodation aft, a tall mainmast for more communications, more boats, and single Bofors as the main armament. *(Wright & Logan)*

*Helmsdale* in 1952. She has been fitted with double Squid A/S mortars on B gun deck forward, and has Type 277 radar, and a partially covered bridge. This refers to the 'River' class chapter. *(Wright & Logan)* ▼

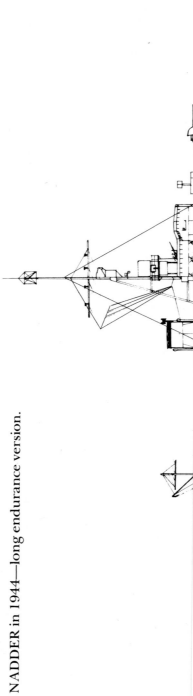

WAVENEY in 1942—M/S version.

NADDER in 1944—long endurance version.

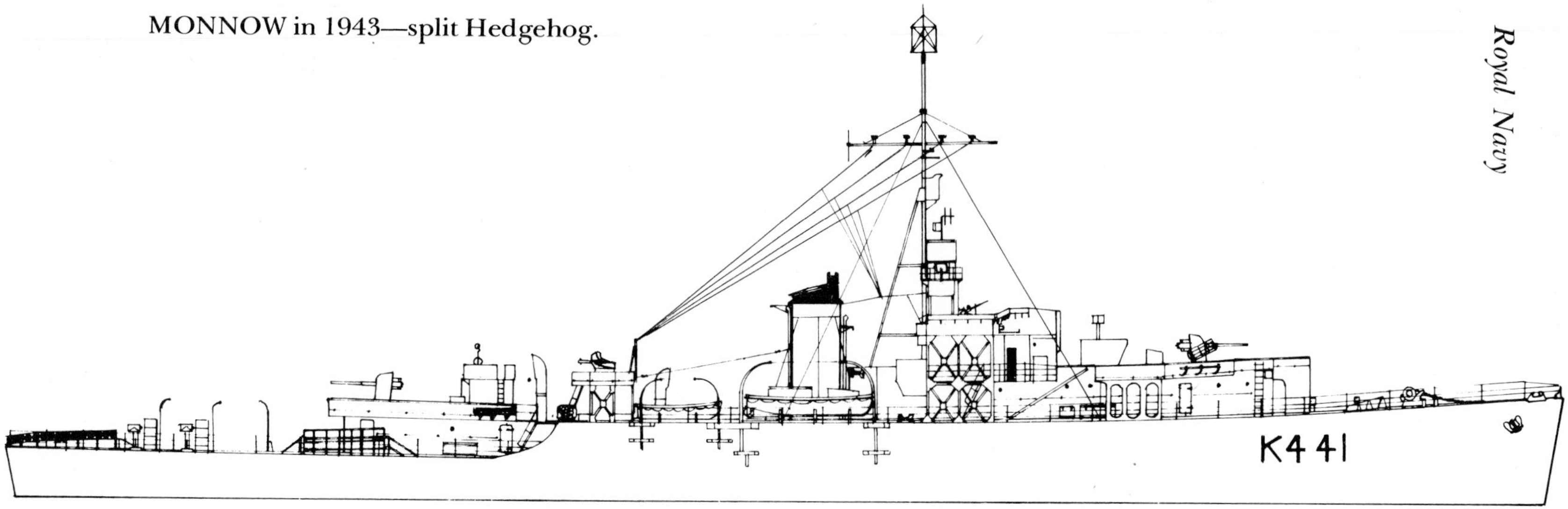

*Royal Navy*

MONNOW in 1943—split Hedgehog.

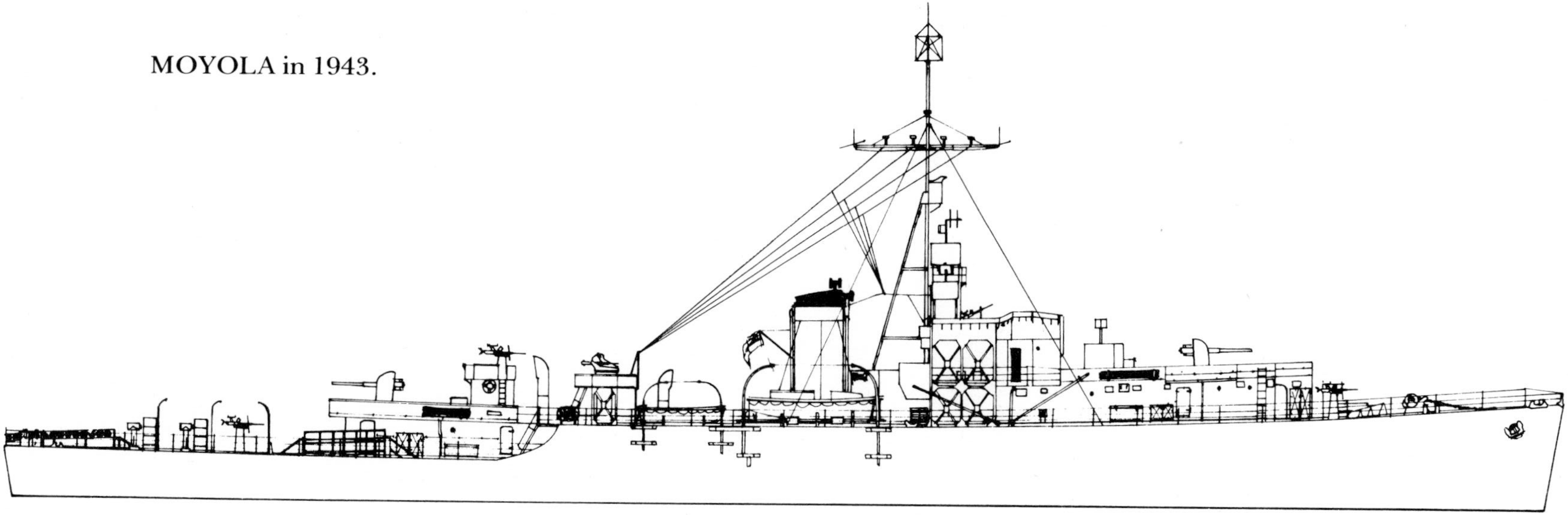

MOYOLA in 1943.

K441

*Loch Achray* in January 1945. This shows the clear quarterdeck with two throwers and one rail, and the clear space for the Foxer equipment. The quadruple pom pom has a clear field of fire. *(Ministry of Defence)*

*Loch Gorm* in February 1945. She is lying at a buoy in a rough sea, perhaps at Tobermory, the West Scotland working-up base. The bulge forward for oiling at sea is prominent, and the motor boat is lying astern. *(Ministry of Defence)*

## 'LOCH' CLASS FRIGATES
### 36 ships completed

This class represented the ultimate in Admiralty design and North Atlantic war experience, in producing the most efficient escort vessel for mid-ocean escort work possible under wartime conditions. The class was specifically designed for the mass-production programme.

The first frigates, the 'River' class, had established the optimum dimensions for an escort, compared with the earlier and smaller corvettes. The hull design and upper deck lay-out lent itself to the installation of new and heavier ahead-throwing A/S weapons, as they were developed, and to the addition of more numerous close-range weapons and radar aerials, as supply and design permitted, together with a larger crew.

The 'Loch' class hull did, in fact, show improvements on the 'River' design. Greater sheer and flare were built into the forward sections, for increased seaworthiness, and to some extent in the after sections as well; the stern was modified, probably for production simplicity. They demonstrated good sea-keeping qualities in service, in spite of their considerable topweight.

The bridge structure took a step forward, too, in becoming a full naval design; comparison with the early 'Flower' units shows the progress made, bearing in mind the need still to use largely non-naval shipbuilders.

The mast changed at this point, from the tripod pole to a full lattice, similar to that concurrently being introduced into the new fleet destroyers; more and heavier radar aerials and radiotelephone aerials dictated the need for the new structure.

In studying this in the photographs we must remember that the Type 277 radar, with its heavy dish aerial, was already at that time regarded as the ideal for escort vessels, and no doubt the lattice mast was designed with this in mind, as soon as supply of the new radar sets permitted.

The boats also left the 'River' class practice, and a full naval 25 foot motor boat and a 27 foot whaler in destroyer-type davits were standard; it is interesting to remember that Canadian-built RCN 'River' class units had already made this change.

But the two most significant changes were in gunnery and anti-submarine armament.

The well-proven Hedgehog ahead-throwing weapon was discarded in the 'Loch' class, for the first production fitting of the new double Squid mortars. These threw, not 24 light bombs exploding on contact (as in the Hedgehog), but 6 much heavier bombs, fused to explode at a set depth, like a depth charge. The range was greater than that of the earlier weapon, and so great was the RN's confidence in the Squid that the depth-charge outfit was reduced from the 'River' class maximum capacity of up to 200 charges, to 2 throwers, one set of rails, and only 15 charges.

The heavy Squids were fitted on the superstructure deck, forward of the bridge, and the single 4″ gun forward was shifted onto a new bandstand just aft of the breakwater. Concurrently, improved Asdic (sonar) equipment was fitted in the control room hung on the forward side of the bridge.

The gun armament also improved. The main gun was still a single 4", and still an obsolete type by 1944 standards; but production was beginning to catch up, and had construction of this class continued a new design of 4", the Mark XXI, would have been fitted in the later ships. Indeed, the first mounting of this type was fitted in *Loch Veyatie*, the last ship of the class to be completed, in 1946.

The class was especially designed for mass-production; indeed, their original type classification was as 'Frigates-Rapid Production'. Production scheduling required large sections of each ship to be pre-fabricated by engineering firms far removed from the shipyard itself, and each ship would only occupy a berth on the building slip for three or four months. *Loch Fada*, built by John Brown on the Clyde, was the prototype ship of the class, to test this prefabrication system, and she ran first-of-class trials on 10th April 1944. During her construction at the yard a maximum of 60 men, and a minimum of 30, were employed on her; photographs of this ship on the slip are included.

The mass-production of this class called for new methods of pre-fabrication by firms unfamiliar with shipyard practice. The hull structure was subdivided into sections of a maximum weight of about 3 tons, with maximum dimensions of 30 feet long, and 9 feet in each of the other dimensions; this enabled existing cranes to handle the loads, and the sections to be transported by road or by rail without disruption. Firms were allowed to use welding or riveting, according to their equipment and experience, and up to four-fifths of the entire hull structure was pre-fabricated in this way. The waterlines forward were re-drawn to straight lines, and curves were avoided wherever possible in the forward transverse sections, to assist the structural engineers as far as possible, and, as can be seen from the photographs, the deck sheer was run in three sections, in place of the usual continuous curve.

Similar considerations of speed in building affected other aspects of the mass-production design—a large drawing office, for the quickest production of greater numbers of plans than usual, the optimum size of the propellers, and so on.

Further than this, to achieve maximum throughput, fitting-out bases were opened at four points—Alloa, Dunmuir, Pickersgill's and Smith's Dock Quay, and possibly elsewhere as well—to which ships building at different yards were to be taken for completion. This was a parallel with the fitting-out base for 'River' class frigates opened at Levis, in Quebec, Canada, during this period. The early units of the class were said to have an austerity wartime finish, but later units were finished more normally.

We have seen that the escort building programmes were drastically cut back in December 1943, as the A/S war was going well. The list of cancelled ships of the 'Loch' class shows that the building programme had already got well under way by that time, and had the welcome cut-back not come large numbers of further 'Loch' class frigates would almost certainly have been ordered from UK yards, and from Canadian yards as well. Orders for an unknown number of

'Loch' class units were being placed in Canada for the RN late in 1943, but due to the cut-back were quickly cancelled, and details are not available of these ships. An estimate of this proposed expansion is included in the shipbuilding chapter.

The class list shows that 'Loch' class ships were entering service in significant numbers in 1944/45, and indeed ships of the class were involved in the sinking of no fewer than 16 U-boats in that period. Their new Squid mortars were quickly proving impressive in service, and had the German Type XXI fast U-boats appeared in any numbers the 'Loch' class ships would have had an increasingly important part to play in the anti-submarine war in the North Atlantic and in UK Home waters.

In studying the 'Flower' class, we saw how the design gradually evolved, from the original version to the full Modified class. With the 'Loch' class there was a definite breakpoint from the 'River' class; but under the RCN 'River' class chapter an interesting photographic comparison is available between a modified 'River' class ship and an RN 'Bay' class ship. Both are developments of the original A/S frigate design, and the 'Loch' class represented the final standard A/S version.

The improvement of the close-range armament is an illustration of the parallel progress in alterations and additions. In the 'Loch' class the after single 4″ gun gave way to a quadruple 2 pounder pom pom. A US-built twin 40mm Bofors mounting had been specified for this position, but USN needs absorbed the available production; a similar situation affected the RCN 'River' class units being refitted in 1945 to join the British Pacific Fleet.

Supply of the excellent hydraulic-operated twin 20mm Oerlikon mountings was increasing, and these were specified fitted on the raised after gundeck; single Oerlikons were usually still fitted in the bridge wings, with twin mountings being substituted as they became available. Note that all RCN 'River' class frigates had by this time been supplied with the twin mountings. Provision was made in the 'Loch' class for a further 6 single Oerlikons, if required—4 on the quarterdeck, and 2 each abreast and below the bridge, but there is no evidence of these extra mountings actually being fitted.

The fitting of mechanical hammers (the SA gear) against acoustic mines was a sign of the times. 'Loch' class frigates were certainly not fitted for minesweeping, but the U-boat war was moving increasingly into UK coastal waters, and protection against magnetic and acoustic mines was all the more essential.

*Loch More*, a fine beam shot showing two-tone green camouflage, the prominent position of the 4″ gun on its bandstand, and the solid bridge superstructure. *(Ministry of Defence)*

### HMS *Loch Fyne*

This ship was built by the Burntisland Shipbuilding Co Ltd, in Fife, and engined by David Rowan & Co Ltd, Glasgow. Laid down on 8th December 1943, she was launched on 24th May 1944, and completed on 9th November 1944.

After working up at Tobermory *Loch Fyne* was allocated to the 18th Escort Group, attached to the Western Approaches Command and based at Greenock. On 5th January 1945 she left the UK, temporarily attached to EG 20 to escort convoy KMF 38 to Gibraltar, arriving there on 10th January. She was then transferred again to assist EG 1 to cover the passage of convoy KMS 77 for the last part of its voyage. On 21st January she left Gibraltar as part of the escort for convoy MKF 38 to the UK, arriving at the Clyde on 27th January.

A quick turn-around was made, and on 29th January she left escorting a further convoy to Gibraltar. En route an Asdic contact was made and she searched and attacked, but without success. She returned to the UK with yet a further convoy.

She was next allocated on loan to the Portsmouth Patrol, giving A/S cover to shipping in the Channel. On 29th April she went to the Clyde for boiler cleaning. On completion, she sailed to Scapa. From there she sailed on 20th May in company with *Keats* and *Kempthorne* to Trondheim, and from there escorted 10 surrendered U-boats to Scapa, arriving on 31st May. On 2nd June, with *Keats* and *Bombardier*, she sailed to Loch Ryan, escorting 9 U-boats.

She was then allocated to the East Indies Fleet escort force. After refit she sailed on 11th August for the East Indies, arriving at Colombo on 25th September. The war had finished while she was en route, and in December she went to Karachi, on patrol duties. She sailed for the UK from Colombo on 13th March 1946, and reduced to Reserve at Portsmouth on arrival. After several subsequent periods of service, she was sold for breaking up on 15th July 1970.

*Loch Fyne* at speed. Type 277 radar, quadruple pom pom aft, and H/F D/F at the masthead. *(Ministry of Defence)*

## GERMAN U-BOATS SUNK BY 'LOCH' CLASS

| U 333 | 31.7.44 | *Loch Killin* and others |
| U 736 | 6.8.44 | *Loch Killin* and others |
| U 354 | 24.8.44 | *Loch Dunvegan* and others |
| U 297 | 6.12.44 | *Loch Insh* and others |
| U 482 | 16.1.45 | *Loch Craggie* and others |
| U 1279 | 3.2.45 | *Loch Eck* and others |
| U 1014 | 4.2.45 | *Loch Scavaig, Loch Shin* and others |
| U 989 | 14.2.45 | *Loch Eck, Loch Dunvegan* and others |
| U 1278 | 17.2.45 | *Loch Eck* and others |
| U 1018 | 27.2.45 | *Loch Fada* |
| U 327 | 27.2.45 | *Loch Fada* and others |
| U 683 | 12.3.45 | *Loch Ruthven* and others |
| U 1024 | 12.4.45 | *Loch Glendhu* |
| U 1063 | 15.4.45 | *Loch Killin* |
| U 307 | 29.4.45 | *Loch Insh* |
| U 286 | 29.4.45 | *Loch Shin* and others |

## 'LOCH' CLASS COMMAND ALLOCATION
### (all at 1st January, except the last two)

|  | 1944 | 1945 | 7.5.45 | 3.8.45 |
|---|---|---|---|---|
| Rosyth | 0 | 0 | 0 | 4 |
| Londonderry | 0 | 4 | 6 | 1 |
| Liverpool | 0 | 2 | 6 | 0 |
| Greenock | 0 | 10 | 7 | 0 |
| East Indies | 0 | 0 | 0 | 16 |
| Totals | 0 | 16 | 19 | 21 |

*Loch Killin,* a killer of U-boats in the last year of the European war. Type 272 radar atop the lattice mast, Type 244 below it, and the clear quarterdeck again. *(Ministry of Defence)*

## 'LOCH' CLASS PRODUCTION

| 1943 | 1st half | 0 | *TOTAL COMPLETED* | 36 |
|------|----------|---|-------------------|----|
|      | 2nd half | 2 | Retained by RN as escorts | 25 |
| 1944 | 1st half | 13 | Completed in other roles | 8 |
|      | 2nd half | 11 | Transferred to South Africa | 3 |
| 1945 | 1st half | 3 | Transferred to Canada | 3 |
|      | 2nd half | 1 | Cancelled | 55 |

## 'LOCH' CLASS SPECIFICATION

Displacement             1,430 tons
(*Derby Haven, Woodbridge Haven,* 1,652 *Loch Fada,*
2,450 (1969))

Dimensions
  length pp        286' 0"
       oa       307' 0"
  breadth          38' 6"
  draught          9' 0"
Machinery                4-cylinder triple expansion
Boilers                  2 Admiralty 3-drum type
Shafts                   2
IHP                      5,500
Speed                    19·5 (clear bottom, 20·25)
Oil Fuel                 730 tons
Endurance                9,500×12 kn
                    7,000×15 kn
NOTE. *Loch Arkaig* and *Loch Tralaig* had double reduction
geared turbines with SHP 6,500=20 kn.
Complement
  war              114
  peace            124/140
                  (*Derby Haven/Woodbridge Haven,* 120)
Armament
  main             1 4" QF Mk V on Mk XXIV mtg
                  (*Loch Veyatie,* 1 4" Mk XXI on
                  Mk XXIV mtg)
  close-range      1 quadruple 2 pdr pom pom
                  2 twin 20mm Oerlikon Mk V
                  2 single 20mm Oerlikon Mk VIIA
                  6 additional single 20mm Oerlikons,
                  if required
                  (*Loch Fada,* 1969, 1 twin 4" Mk XVI,
                  6 40mm Bofors)
  A/S armament     2 Squid ATW mortars
                  1 DCT, 1 rail, 15' depth charges
                  Shark anti-submarine missiles

| Radar | Types 273, 253, 242, 251M |
|---|---|
| H/F D/F | FH3 or FH4 |
| M/F D/F | FM12 |
| SA Gear | Type A Mk III |

## ALERT AND SURPRISE AS DESPATCH VESSELS

| Armament | |
|---|---|
| main | 1 twin 4″ Mk XVI |
| close-range | 2 single 40mm Bofors |
| | 2 single 20mm Oerlikons |
| | 1 3 pdr saluting gun |
| | 2″ rocket flare projectors |

*Loch Glendhu* in February 1945. A fine shot of one of this class at sea, with the double Squids showing clearly. *(Ministry of Defence)*

## 'LOCH' CLASS – CLASS LIST

| Name | Pendant No | Job No. | Builder | Building Time | Completion Date |
|---|---|---|---|---|---|
| **1942 Programme** | | | | | |
| *Loch Achanalt* | K 424 | J 11817 | Robb | 10m28d | 11.8.4 |
| *Loch Dunvegan* | K 425 | J 453 | Hill | 9m1d | 30.6.4 |
| *Loch Eck* | K 422 | J 4777 | Smith's Dock | 12m13d | 7.11.4 |
| *Loch Fada* | K 390 | J 1614 | J.Brown | 10m1d | 14.12 |
| **1943 Programme** | | | | | |
| *Loch Achray* | K 426 | J 4781 | Smith's Dock | 13m19d | 1.2.4 |
| *Loch Alvie* | K 428 | J 1813 | Barclay Curle | 7m25d | 21.8.4 |
| *Loch Arkaig* | K 603 | J 11849 | Caledon | | 17.11 |
| *Loch Craggie* | K 609 | J 3353 | Harland & Wolff | 9m26d | 23.10 |
| *Loch Fyne* | K 429 | J 11832 | Burntisland | 11m1d | 9.11.4 |
| *Loch Glendhu* | K 619 | J 11839 | ,, | 8m25d | 23.2.4 |
| *Loch Gorm* | K 620 | J 3373 | Harland & Wolff | 11m21d | 18.12 |
| *Loch Insh* | K 433 | J 11859 | Robb | 10m2d | 20.10 |
| *Loch Katrine* | K 625 | J 11860 | ,, | 11m29d | 29.12 |
| *Loch Killin* | K 391 | J 11830 | Burntisland | 9m20d | 12.4.4 |
| *Loch Killisport* | K 628 | J 3391 | Harland & Wolff | 17m10d | 9.7.4 |
| *Loch Lomond* | K 437 | J 11845 | Caledon | 11m9d | 16.11 |
| *Loch More* | K 639 | J 11846 | ,, | 10m27d | 12.2. |
| *Loch Morlich* | K 517 | J 4806 | Swan Hunter | 12m18d | 2.8.4 |
| *Loch Quoich* | K 434 | J 4793 | Blyth | 13m8d | 11.1. |
| *Loch Ruthven* | K 645 | J 494 | Hill | 8m2d | 6.10. |
| *Loch Scavaig* | K 648 | J 530 | ,, | 8m22d | 22.12 |
| *Loch Shin* | K 421 | J 4808 | Swan Hunter | 13m2d | 10.10 |
| *Loch Tarbert* | K 431 | J 1826 | Ailsa | 14m22d | 22.2. |
| *Loch Tralaig* | K 655 | J 11848 | Caledon | 12m20d | 4.7.4 |
| *Loch Veyatie* | K 658 | J 1827 | Ailsa | 15m1d | 13.7. |

## TRANSFERRED TO CANADA

| Name | Pendant No | Job No. | Builder | Building Time | Completion Date |
|---|---|---|---|---|---|
| *Loch Achanalt* | K 424 | J 11817 | Robb | | 11.8 |
| *Loch Alvie* | K 428 | J 1813 | Barclay Curle | | 21.8 |
| *Loch Morlich* | K 517 | J 4806 | Swan Hunter | | 2.8.4 |

## TRANSFERRED TO SOUTH AFRICA

| Name | Pendant No | Job No. | Builder | Building Time | Completion Date |
|---|---|---|---|---|---|
| *Transvaal* ex *Loch Ard* | K 602 | | Harland & Wolff | | 21.5 |
| *Good Hope* ex *Loch Boisdale* | K 432 | J 4791 | Blyth | | 9.12 |
| *Natal* ex *Loch Cree* | K 430 | | Swan Hunter | | 8.3.4 |

## COMPLETED AS COASTAL FORCES DEPOT SHIPS

| | | | | |
|---|---|---|---|---|
| *Derby Haven* ex *Loch Assynt* | K 438 | J 4837 | Swan Hunter | 2.8.45 |
| *Woodbridge Haven* ex *Loch Torridon* | K 654 | J 4840 | ,, | L.13.1.45 |

## COMPLETED AS SURVEYING SHIPS

| | | | | |
|---|---|---|---|---|
| *Dampier* ex *Herne Bay*, ex *Loch Eil* | K 611 | J 4790 | Smith's Dock | 6.6.48 |
| *Dalrymple* ex *Luce Bay*, ex *Loch Glass* | K 427 | J 4791 | Pickersgill | 10.2.49 |
| *Cook* ex *Pegwell Bay*, ex *Loch Mochrum* | K 638 | J 4813 | ,, | 20.7.50 |
| *Owen* ex *Thurso Bay*, ex *Loch Muick* | K 640 | J 11844 | Hall Russell | 23.9.49 |

*Dampier* and *Owen* completed by Chatham Dockyard,
*Dalrymple* and *Cook* completed by Devonport Dockyard

## COMPLETED AS DESPATCH VESSELS

| | | | | |
|---|---|---|---|---|
| *Surprise* ex *Gerrans Bay*, ex *Loch Carron* | K 436 | J 4788 | Smith's Dock | 9.9.46 |
| *Alert* ex *Dundrum Bay*, ex *Loch Scamadale* | K 647 | J 4801 | Hill | 24.10.46 |

These two ships became yachts for the Commanders-in-Chief on the Mediterranean and Far East Stations after the war—hence the appropriate names!

## 'LOCH' CLASS CANCELLED SHIPS – UK ORDERS

| | | | |
|---|---|---|---|
| *Loch Affric* | K 601 | J 1828 | Ailsa |
| *Loch Awe* | | | Harland & Wolff |
| *Loch Badcall* | | J 4924 | Pickersgill |
| *Loch Caroy* | | J 4930 | ,, |
| *Loch Clunie* | K 607 | J 1829 | Ailsa |
| *Loch Doine* | | J 4940 | Smith's Dock |
| *Loch Creran* | | J 4935 | ,, |
| *Loch Earn* | | J 601 | Hill |
| *Loch Enoch* | | J 3900 | Harland & Wolff |
| *Loch Ericht* | K 612 | J 1830 | Ailsa |
| *Loch Erisort* | K 613 | J 1815 | Barclay Curle |
| *Loch Eye* | | | Harland & Wolff |
| *Loch Eyenort* | | J 3910 | ,, |
| *Loch Garve* | K 617 | J 11825 | Hall Russell |
| *Loch Glashan* | | J 4798 | Smith's Dock |
| *Loch Goil* | | | Harland & Wolff |
| *Loch Griam* | K 621 | J 4844 | Swan Hunter |
| *Loch Harray* | K 623 | J 4800 | Smith's Dock |
| *Loch Hourn* | | | Harland & Wolff |

| Name | Pendant No. | Job No. | Builder | Building Time | Completion Date |
|------|-------------|---------|---------|---------------|-----------------|
| *Loch Inchard* | | J 3924 | ,, | | |
| *Loch Ken* | K 626 | J 4823 | Smith's Dock | | |
| *Loch Kirbister* | K 629 | J 4842 | Swan Hunter | | |
| *Loch Kirkaig* | | | Harland & Wolff | | |
| *Loch Kishorn* | | J 11850 | Robb | | |
| *Loch Knockie* | | J 4927 | Pickersgill | | |
| *Loch Laro* | | J 3927 | Harland & Wolff | | |
| *Loch Linfern* | K 631 | J 4807 | Smith's Dock | | |
| *Loch Linnhe* | K 632 | J 4810 | Pickersgill | | |
| *Loch Lurgan* | | | Harland & Wolff | | |
| *Loch Lyon* | K 635 | J 4846 | Swan Hunter | | |
| *Loch Maberry* | | J 11865 | Hall Russell | | |
| *Loch Minnick* | K 637 | J 4811 | Smith's Dock | | |
| *Loch Nell* | K 641 | J 11863 | Robb | | |
| *Loch Odairn* | K 642 | J 11864 | ,, | | |
| *Loch Ossian* | K 643 | J 4815 | Smith's Dock | | |
| *Loch Roan* | | J 4796 | Blyth | | |
| *Loch Ronald* | | | Harland & Wolff | | |
| *Loch Ryan* | K 646 | J 4834 | Pickersgill | | |
| *Loch Scrivain* | K 649 | J 4836 | ,, | | |
| *Loch Sheallag* | | J 3933 | Harland & Wolff | | |
| *Loch Shell* | | | ,, | | |
| *Loch Skaig* | | J 4932 | Smith's Dock | | |
| *Loch Skerrow* | | J 602 | Hill | | |
| *Loch Stemster* | | | Harland & Wolff | | |
| *Loch Stenness* | | J 4938 | Smith's Dock | | |
| *Loch Striven* | | | Harland & Wolff | | |
| *Loch Sunart* | | J 3922 | ,, | | |
| *Loch Swin* | | J 3909 | ,, | | |
| *Loch Tanna* | K.652 | J 4865 | Blyth | | |
| *Loch Tilt* | K 653 | J 4839 | Pickersgill | | |
| *Loch Tummell* | | | Harland & Wolff | | |
| *Loch Urgill* | K 656 | J 4809 | Blyth | | |
| *Loch Vanavie* | | J 3918 | Harland & Wolff | | |
| *Loch Vennacher* | K 657 | J 4812 | Blyth | | |
| *Loch Watten* | K 659 | J 4814 | ,, | | |

LOCH GORM in February, 1945.

## 'BAY' CLASS FRIGATES
**19 ships completed**

This class was an offshoot of the 'Loch' class. The requirement arose in 1944 for large numbers of A/A frigates to join the British Pacific Fleet in 1945, and the RN's most rapid and convenient answer was to plan the conversion of 26 of the 'Loch' class frigates while still under construction; on average, this would take an extra three months in the overall construction time, but was seen to be better than taking 'River' class frigates out of service for conversion, at a time when the A/S war in Europe was still going full blast. The RCN was asked to convert similar numbers of 'River' class frigates from those already in service; but in Canada the 'River' class construction programme had moved into high gear, and there it was thought preferable not to interrupt the fast flow of new ships coming from the shipyards.

In the 'Bay' class conversion the hull and bridge structure, the lattice mast and funnel remained the same. But A/S capability gave way to the need for greater numbers of A/A weapons (with the Japanese Kamikaze suicide planes in mind), and so the double Squid ATW mortar disappeared and the Hedgehog made a comeback, in its original position right forward, as in the 'River' class.

Two twin 4″ guns, with a director on the bridge, appeared in B and X positions, and two twin 40mm Bofors replaced the after gundeck, reflecting exactly the USN PF class lay-out. Twin and single Oerlikons were added, and the depth-charge outfit on the quarterdeck, which had been drastically reduced when the Squid mortars were fitted, was not partly reinstated.

The urgent requirement for 52 twin 4″ gun mountings in 1944 for the 'Bay' class caused some difficulty, as new production could not take care of this need, either from UK or from Canadian manufacturing resources; a proportion of these mountings were, therefore, acquired by stripping them from the 'V and W' class 'Wair' conversions, by then being phased out of service, and from the few 'Hunt' class destroyers so equipped, but laid up as constructive total losses after battle damage.

Further, shortage of control equipment dictated that only the following ships could receive twin RPC (remote power controlled) 4″ mountings, with rangefinder director; the others on completion would have to make do with the three-man rangefinder director: *Burghead Bay, Cawsand Bay, Dundrum Bay, Enard Bay, Gerrans Bay, Herne Bay, Hollesley Bay, Largo Bay, Luce Bay, Morecambe Bay, Mounts Bay, Pegwell Bay, Porlock Bay, Veryan Bay.* As some of these units were eventually completed in other configurations, there was probably some re-assignment of the after twin mountings.

This class was eventually limited to 19 ships completed, as opposed to the Admiralty planning for 26 ships of the class, all for the British Pacific Fleet. Progress of the war in the Far East permitted this cutback, though in part this was to provide further specialised maintenance ships, as will be seen from the final form of the class list.

There are three interesting contemporary comparisons which we can make with the 'Bay' class.

The first is with the 'Hunt' class escort destroyer, especially the later Type III. The 'Hunt' class were, of course, well out of production before the first 'Bay' class unit appeared, but the armament was a close parallel. The hull form and machinery gave a very different speed, and the torpedo capability of the 'Hunt' was replaced by the stronger A/S armament of the 'Bay'. Endurance, too, was significantly different, but the 'Bay' does in some ways seem to be a logical development from the 'Hunt', built on a mass-production basis, as opposed to the specialised warship design of the 'Hunt'.

The second comparison is with the RCN's 'River' class frigates, as modified with a twin 4″ mounting forward, and with full naval boats in destroyer-type davits. The comparative photographs of *Outremont* and *Burghead Bay* need close attention to detail, to spot the differences. The planned 'River' class conversions in 1945, for Pacific service, brought the two classes even closer together.

The third comparison is with the Modified 'Black Swan' class sloops. The big difference was not so much in performance (the sloops had a third twin 4″ mounting), as in the naval construction of the sloops, as opposed to the mass-production planning of the frigates. Otherwise, in speed, radar, and close-range and anti-submarine armaments, they were very similar. Note that all the 'Black Swan' class, as well as all the 'Bay' class, were earmarked for the British Pacific Fleet in 1945—as were a significant proportion of the survivors of the 'Hunt' class (the latter for the Indian Ocean, also); thus, in all three classes the twin 4″ high-angle gun mounting became as important to the RN in the Pacific as did the single 3″/50 calibre and the single 5″/38 calibre to the USN in the same period.

It is worth noting, in making these class comparisons, that the American-built PF/'Colony' class did not appear to be regarded as comparable. By 1945 a large proportion of the USN units of this class had been transferred to Russia, and the 21 units transferred to the RN, though very comparable in appearance, as can be seen from the photo-comparisons included, were returned to the USN in 1945 and not sent to the Pacific—although they had been earmarked as Fighter Direction Ships, and some units were actually converted, before return to the USN.

*Alert*, 1950. Two ships of the class were completed as despatch vessels, or private yachts, for the Commanders-in-Chief, Mediterranean and Far East Stations, after the war. The names were appropriate! Large open deck aft, tall mainmast with gaff and derrick, otherwise standard outfit. (*Ministry of Defence*)

*Largo Bay,* showing the after section in close-up. The Foxer equipment and smoke floats occupy much of the quarterdeck, and the twin Bofors show their gunshields.
*(Ministry of Defence)*

*Mounts Bay* at speed, showing the deck lay-out of this class. The twin Bofors aft are visible, and the pole mainmast carries the H/F D/F.
*(Ministry of Defence)*

## 'BAY' CLASS—SPECIFICATION

| | |
|---|---|
| Displacement | 1,600 tons |
| Dimensions | |
| length pp | 286' 0" |
| oa | 301' 0" |
| breadth | 38' 9" |
| draught | 10' 0" |
| Machinery | 4 cylinder triple expansion |
| Boilers | 2 Admiralty 3-drum type |
| Shafts | 2 |
| IHP | 5,500 |
| Speed | 19.5 kn |
| Oil Fuel | 720 tons |
| Complement | 157 |
| Armament | 2 twin 4" Mk XVI |
| main | |
| | Rangefinder Director Mk V++ |
| close-range | 2 twin 40mm Bofors |
| | 4 20mm Oerlikon |
| A/S Armament | Hedgehog |
| | 4 depth charge throwers, 2 rails |
| Radar | Types 276 (in lieu 277) 291, 285, 242 |
| H/F D/F | FH 4 |
| M/F D/F | FM 12 |

## 'BAY' CLASS PRODUCTION

| | | | | |
|---|---|---|---|---|
| 1944 | 2nd half | 7 | Total completed | 19 |
| 1945 | 1st half | 10 | Retained by RN | 19 |
| | 2nd half | 4 | Cancelled Ships | 1 |

CARDIGAN BAY in June, 1945.

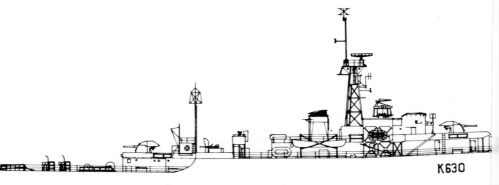

K630

## 'BAY' CLASS—CLASS LIST

| Name | Pendant No. | Job. No. | Builder | Completion Date |
|---|---|---|---|---|
| **1943 Programme** | | | | |
| Bigbury Bay<br>ex *Loch Carloway* | K 606 | J 11822 | Hall Russell | 10.7.45 |
| Burghead Bay<br>ex *Loch Harport* | K 622 | J.11823 | Hill | 20.9.45 |
| Cardigan Bay<br>ex *Loch Laxford* | K 630 | J 11861 | Robb | 15.6.45 |
| Carnarvon Bay<br>ex *Loch Maddy* | K 636 | J 11862 | ,, | 20.9.45 |
| Cawsand Bay<br>ex *Loch Roan* | K 644 | J 4785 | Blyth | 13.11.45 |
| Enard Bay<br>ex *Loch Bracadale* | K 435 | J.4786 | Smith's Dock | 4.1.46 |
| Largo Bay<br>ex *Loch Fionn* | K 423 | J 4792 | Pickersgill | 26.1.46 |
| Morecambe Bay<br>ex *Loch Heilen* | K 624 | J 4802 | ,, | 22.2.46 |
| Mounts Bay<br>ex *Loch Kilbernie* | K 627 | J 4804 | ,, | 11.8.49 |
| Padstow Bay<br>ex *Loch Coulside* | K 608 | J 1814 | Robb | 11.8.46 |
| Porlock Bay<br>ex *Loch Seaforth* | K 650 | J 11847 | Hill | 8.3.46 |
| St Brides Bay<br>ex *Loch Achillty* | K 600 | J 11848 | Harland & Wolff | 15.6.45 |
| St Austell Bay<br>ex *Loch Lydoch* | K 634 | J 3397 | ,, | 29.5.45 |
| Start Bay<br>ex *Loch Arklet* | K 604 | J 3398 | ,, | 6.9.45 |
| Tremadoc Bay<br>ex *Loch Arnish* | K 605 | J 3399 | ,, | 11.10.45 |
| Veryan Bay<br>ex *Loch Swannay* | K 651 | | Hill | 13.5.45 |
| Whitesand Bay<br>ex *Loch Lubnaig* | K 633 | | Harland & Wolff | 30.7.45 |
| Widemouth Bay<br>ex *Loch Frisa* | K 615 | | ,, | 13.4.45 |
| Wigtown Bay<br>ex *Loch Garasdale* | K 616 | | ,, | 19.1.46 |

## CANCELLED SHIP

| Hollesley Bay<br>ex *Loch Fannich* | K 614 | J 4794 | Smith's Dock | |

## 'CAPTAIN' CLASS FRIGATES (EX USN DEs)
## 78 ships built in USA, and transferred on completion

The design, developments, and achievements of this class make one of the most fascinating stories to be covered in this book.

Attached to this chapter, and probably published for the first time, are the statistics of their construction. From these it will be seen that, at the peak of the escort building programme in the UK, the Admiralty in fact asked for 520 ships of this class to be built in the USA for the RN under Lend-Lease terms. Unfortunately, official records do not show the equivalent numbers of 'Loch' class frigates and 'Castle' class corvettes which were to have been ordered in the same period from UK and Canadian shipyards; but it is clear that, had that tremendous shipbuilding programme gone through, the RN's escort forces would have received a terrific boost in numbers, and the pre-war built destroyers and the 'Flower' class corvettes would have been retired to less onerous duties, or placed in reserve.

But by the time the RN's request for 520 DEs had gone through, the USN's own escort requirements were building up fast; the actual orders placed by the RN were, accordingly, cut to 300, and these DE numbers, and the shipyards from which they were ordered, are also shown after this chapter. It is believed that RN names and pennant numbers had not been allocated to all of these ships before USN requirements cut the actual numbers to be built for the RN to a total of 78. In a number of cases, to be seen in the class lists of USN DEs, ships were switched from RN to USN and vice versa while under construction.

If the reader will turn back to the overall RN escort numbers, the effect the larger numbers of DEs would have had, together with the full rapid-construction programme of 'Loch' class and 'Castle' class units, makes a fascinating study. The planned addition of 150 US-built PCEs should also not be overlooked.

The ships of the 'Captain' class were sub-divided into two types—32 ships of the 'Evarts' short-hulled diesel-electric type, and 46 ships of the 'Buckley' long-hulled turbo-electric type.

The design development of the US-built destroyer escorts has been covered in greater detail under the USN section. But we will recall here that the first requirement for such ships to be built in the USA was raised by the RN in 1940, before the USA entered the war; it was only later that the USN defined its own requirement for large numbers of such ships, and placed orders for the rapid construction of over 1,000 units.

So it was that the RN specified the basic length, speed and range of this new US class, but the designs were otherwise entirely American, based on the latest USN design practice of the time. So the long-hulled 'Buckley' class were almost exactly the same length as the RN's 'Loch' class, and the speed of the US-built ships met specified Admiralty staff requirements, due to the better supply of main propulsion units in America, while, as we have seen in the other RN

*Kingsmill*—the view from the forecastlehead. Note two 3″ guns, three Oerlikons, two searchlights, and the Hedgehog behind A gun—an impressive array. (*Lt-Cdr R.P. Hall*, RANR)

chapters, UK-built ships were restricted further in speed, due to the need to use the type of propulsion unit most easily mass-produced in wartime in the UK. The Admiralty asked for ships suitable for service on the North Atlantic convoy routes, and also for tropical service, but said that Arctic service would not be necessary (note, however, that some ships of the class did go to North Russia). Torpedo tubes were not seen to be necessary; air and surface warring RDF, similar to the RN's Types 271 and 290, were required.

So, too, the US-built ships had the USN destroyer hull form, with a continuous main deck, with high sheer forward, and no break, either abreast the bridge, or further aft, as in the RN ships. The superstructure, too, was different, following the centre line, as in RN destroyers, but continuous (in the 'Buckley' class units), giving shelter as far aft as the beginning of the depth-charge equipment.

It was outstanding that the USN design included two single 3"/50 calibre guns forward of the bridge, in A and B positions, with a full Hedgehog fitted just aft of A gun. This made an impressive contrast with the RN's 'River' class, and while it did result in A gun in the US-built ships being very far forward, and so difficult to fight in heavy North Atlantic weather, the fire power of these ships was thus notably increased. A third 3" gun was fitted in its own tub, superimposed over the quarterdeck, paralleling the 'River' class's after weapon.

The DE's mast was a single tall steel pole, well raked, and with a steel platform connecting it with the upper bridge, as support in place of a tripod. This mast was well able to carry all the radar, D/F and radio-telephone equipment required of it (and the 'Captain' class carried a very comprehensive outfit), including the heavy American Types SL and SA aerial arrays; it was only later in the war, with the much heavier Type 277 array, that the Admiralty considered replacing the pole mast with a lattice. This was not, in fact, done in any ship, but some of the 'Captain' class were earmarked for conversion in 1945 to Fighter Direction Ships, as were the 'Colony' class, and one result can be seen in the photograph of *Caicos*, in the latter class, where it was decided to fit the Type 277 on deck aft, rather than replace the pole mast.

The DE's yard followed USN practice, in being fitted aft of the mast and not forward. A large and attractive gaff, for the ensign, was fitted high, at yard level.

Some of the RN ships carried US Type SA aerial warning radar at the masthead, others carried the RN H/F D/F instead. It will be noted that, unlike the USN ships, no RN ship of this class carried H/F D/F on a pole mast, if SA was fitted at the masthead. This was an Admiralty compromise to save topweight. A typical RN Support Group of 'Captain' class frigates would include two ships fitted with Type SA, and four with H/F D/F, so that the group was well covered both for air warning and for U-boat radio transmissions. Some units did not, in fact, carry either aerial, presumably due to shortage of sets when first commissioned.

The short-hulled ships had a break in the deck superstructure, presenting a different profile from the long-hulled ships, and did not have room to carry torpedo tubes. It is noteworthy that all the 5 long-hulled versions of the DEs were designed to carry one set of 3 torpedo tubes, carried on top of the superstructure amidships; but in USN service the later ships often omitted these tubes in favour of a heavier A/A armament, for Pacific service. None of the 46 RN 'Buckley' class ships carried torpedo tubes, and the open space thus created was often used to fit further sided single Oerlikons, either 2 or 4 mountings.

The funnels of both types were distinctive. The short-hulled diesel-electric ships had short funnels, with diesel exhaust pipes inside; the noise of the diesel-powered generators from these exhausts made these ships distinctive in harbour. The long-hulled turbo-electric ships had a tall funnel with a divided trunk at superstructure deck level, as there were separate twinned boiler rooms and engine rooms. Both types carried a steam siren, and the USN-type shrill steam whistle, which also distinguished them when manoeuvring among UK-built ships.

These ships all had a good beam, and while it was a little less than that of the RN 'Loch' class, there were wide side-decks at main deck level, where the RN added two long two-tier depth-charge racks on each side, thus giving these ships, with the RN 'River' class, the highest outfit of depth charges of any escort class.

The USN ships carried one seaboat, a 26 foot motor whaleboat, handled by tall goose-neck davits by the funnel and stowed on chocks on the superstructure deck. Handling this boat called for good seamanship. The RN usually added a 27 foot whaler, in gravity davits, on the port side, as these were found to be useful in North Atlantic service. Life rafts were carried on 4 skids aft, modified by the RN and clearly visible in the photographs, and 2 forward, on skids on the tall vertical sides of the bridge structure.

The quarterdeck was wide and clear, and the depth-charge equipment was well spaced for efficient handling. Four throwers only were fitted, following the 10-charge practice of the time, though the USN ships carried 8 throwers, as had many RN ships a little earlier.

Special comment should be made regarding the close-range weapons. The original outfit closely paralleled the RN 'River' class in number, which is not surprising. Four single Oerlikons were fitted round the bridge structure in the 'Buckley' class ships, and the other 4 in superimposed tubs, 2 each side just aft of the funnel. The RN ships did not follow the USN practice of fitting 2 further single Oerlikons in a large tub on the quarterdeck; this probably proved useful when the requirement to fit Foxer gear aft later became urgent.

*Bayntun*, the first US-built destroyer escort of them all. This was taken in May 1944, with a North Atlantic convoy. (*Ministry of Defence*)

The short-hulled ships, due to their lack of torpedo tubes, actually carried more single Oerlikon than the above, but only 3 around the bridge structure, the rest sided aft of the funnel.

Both classes were specified to carry a twin 40mm Bofors with director, aft, superimposed over the after 3″ gun. Some of the RN ships carried this, some did not, depending on the gun supply position at the time of their completion. These were most useful weapons, and both the RN and the USN increased the emphasis on them later.

Where the RN ships did not carry this mounting, it was either left vacant or two additional single Oerlikons were mounted, one in place of the gun and one in place of the director. In one or two RN ships, engaged in anti-E-boat duties in the English Channel, a second Oerlikon was fitted, sided, in the gun tub, and these guns were in some cases twin manual Oerlikons mounted on the same single mounting.

In the RN long-hulled ships used in anti-E-boat operations in the English Channel and North Sea in 1944/45, a bowchaser 2 pounder pom pom was usually fitted right in the eyes of the ship, with its own spray shield, following 'Hunt' class destroyer practice. In some cases the gun was fitted with no spray shields, or the shields were fitted but no gun, due to rapid change of duties.

Approval was given to fit spray shields, of a distinctive design, to all the 3″ guns in RN ships of this class. But lack of time in port and supply difficulties limited the number so fitted; some had a shield on B gun only, so allowing full 2″ rocket flare projectors to be fitted, others had the full 3 shields. All ships refitted for the Pacific were so fitted. Where no shield was fitted to B gun in the ships employed in the English Channel and North Sea, where surface actions were frequent, 2″ rocket flare projectors of the type designed for motor torpedo boats were fitted in lieu, in most cases to B gun, and in some cases to X gun also.

The details attached to this chapter show the alterations, especially in armament, specified to be made to those long-hulled ships to be refitted for Pacific service in 1945. The Admiralty asked the USN if 5″/38 calibre guns, as in the later USN ships, could be fitted in lieu of the 3″/50 calibre guns, but shortage of time, when the ships were badly needed in operational service, precluded this. Consideration was also given to fitting Squid ATW mortars forward, but this was not carried out, as the 'Loch' class ships were coming forward in some numbers.

The main alterations were in close-range armament, as the 40mm Bofors was seen clearly to be a more effective A/A weapon than the 20mm Oerlikon. Eventually, the ending of the Pacific war finished the requirement for large numbers of RN escorts to be sent east, and most of the planned refits were cancelled; but some of the Coastal Forces Control Frigates were so far advanced that they were completed, and the photograph of *Essington* and *Calder*, the first two DEs to be returned to the USN, shows the 7 single Army-type Bofors fitted, in lieu of Oerlikons, in addition to the twin mounting aft. It is notable that these two ships were converted from North Atlantic duty, and were not among the previous Coastal Forces Control Frigates from the Southern North Sea.

When *Bayntun,* the first ship of the class (and the first DE ever built), arrived in the UK in April 1943, the Admiralty were very pleased with her. They commented that she was in general excellently designed and fitted out, the quarterdeck very well arranged. A large beam to draught ratio, with a relatively light armament, gave a comparatively large initial GM for this size of vessel, and it was thought that this would give a tendency to excessive rolling. Experience with this ship during first-of-class trials, in a beam sea and a Force 5 wind, gave a 48 degree roll in 7 seconds.

*Duckworth,* a long-hull version, in a North Atlantic gale in December 1943, recorded the following movements:

| | | |
|---|---|---|
| Beam sea | Speed 8 knots | Roll 60 degrees in 8 seconds |
| Head sea | Speed 8 knots | Lifted well, better than a destroyer |
| Sea on bow | Speed 8 knots | Roll of 60 degrees in 5 seconds |
| Sea on quarter | Speed 12 knots | Roll of 55 degrees in 7 seconds, corkscrew motion, occasional roll of 60 degrees in $2\frac{1}{2}$ seconds! |
| Following sea | Speed 16 knots | Comfortable motion |

The 'Captain' class frigates made an effective and impressive contribution to the RN's escort forces, both in forming some of the best of the North Atlantic Support Groups, and in providing the original and only Coastal Forces Control Frigates in the English Channel and North Sea (and planned to do the same in the assault on Singapore); their good speed, radar and armament put them in the forefront of these battles, and their war losses, the highest of any RN escort class (other than the 'Hunt' class, on different duties) in a relatively short period, speak for themselves. It is worth ending this chapter by considering again the contribution this class would have made, had it numbered the 520 ships originally requested, rather than the 78 actually transferred!

The whole story of this class is a magnificent example of international co-operation, with the resulting ships carrying the best design and practice of the USN, and supplemented by the RN alterations and additions, founded on different but wide war experience.

*Mounsey,* an 'Evarts' type ship, in August 1944. She has the pale North Atlantic camouflage, and standard configuration. (*Ministry of Defence*)

## LEND-LEASE ORDERS

The original total of Destroyer Escorts asked for by the Admiralty was no less than 520. Of these, 300 were firmly ordered, as shown below, and in the end, only 78 were actually delivered to the RN. It is probable that the 21 PF class patrol frigates, also transferred, were in part restitution for the DEs not made available, due to the USN's own growing escort requirements in 1942/43.

*300 DESTROYER ESCORTS ORDERED BY THE RN*
(they were originally classed by the RN as Convoy Escort Vessels, US Type)

| DE nos | Order placed | From shipyard | For delivery |
|---|---|---|---|
| BDE   1-12 | 1.11.41 | Boston | Jan 1943-July 1943 |
| 13-36 | 1.11.41 | Mare Island | Dec 1942-March 1944 |
| 37-44 | 1.11.41 | Puget | Jan 1944-Oct 1944 |
| 45-50 | 1.11.41 | Philadelphia | Nov 1942-May 1943 |
| DE   51-98 | 10.1.42 | Bethlehem-Hingham | June 1943-June 1944 |
| 99-128 | 10.1.42 | Dravo, Wilmington | June 1943-June 1944 |
| 129-152 | 10.1.42 | Consolidated, Orange | Dec 1942-July 1944 |
| 153-161 | 10.1.42 | Norfolk | Mar 1943-Aug 1943 |
| 162-197 | 18.1.42 | Federal, Newark | Apr 1943-Jan 1944 |
| 198-237 | 18.1.42 | Brown | Sept 1943-Dec 1944 |
| 238-255 | 18.1.42 | Brown | Feb 1943-Sept 1943 |
| 256-280 | 25.1.42 | Boston | Aug 1943-Feb 1944 |
| 281-300 | 25.1.42 | Charleston | Oct 1943-June 1944 |

## 'CAPTAIN' CLASS CONVERSIONS

### A. to Assault Group Headquarters Ships (LSH(S))

February 1944, for Normandy Invasion:
*Dacres, Kingsmill, Lawford.*
Armament revised to:
  2 single 3"/50 cal, mounted forward
  13 single 20mm Oerlikons
Extra deckhouses built aft and round bridge for accommodation.
At least 10 extra R/T and W/T lines installed.
Radar revised to: Types 271, SL, 242, 253, 291.
H/F D/F removed, M/F D/F retained.
Endurance revised to 4,500 miles at 12 knots.
Complement: 141, plus 64 for Combined Operations.
Lost: *Lawford.*

### B. To Coastal Forces Control Ships

*1. JUNE-SEPTEMBER 1944*
English Channel, for Normandy assault operations. Based at Portsmouth:
*Duff, Retalick, Stayner, Thornborough, Torrington, Trollope, Kingsmill* (part-time)
Lost (CTL): *Trollope.*

## 2. OCTOBER 1944-MAY 1945

North Sea, for Walcheren/Antwerp assault, and defence of UK-Antwerp convoy route.

Based at Harwich:

*Curzon, Dakins, Duff, Ekins, Retalick, Riou, Seymour, Stayner, Thornborough, Torrington.*

In last months: *Cubitt, Rutherford.*

Lost (CTL): *Dakins, Ekins.*

Damaged: *Duff.*

Armament revised to:

  3 single 3"/50 cal

  10-12 single 20mm Oerlikons (2-4 extra)

  (In one or two ships, two mountings were twin manual)

 6 2" rocket flare projectors

   (fitted to B gun—in some ships, further projectors were fitted to X gun, as in some hectic night actions, both guns were needed for illuminations)

   1 3" gunnery director

   (this was a standard approved 'Captain' class alteration, but was mainly fitted to ships converted for this duty)

   2 extra R/T lines, Type 86.

*Essington* in March 1944. This shows the stern section of these ships, for comparison with the RN 'Loch' and 'Bay' classes. Note three rubbing strakes on each quarter, extra double-tier depth charge racks on each side forward of the throwers. Type SA radar at masthead, extra liferafts on skids amidships. (*Ministry of Defence*)

*Curzon* had a long refit in March 1945 (but was not earmarked for the Far East). Her armament was revised to:

   3  3"/50 cal
   1  twin 40mm Bofors, with director
   2  single 40mm Bofors (forward of bridge)
   9  single 20mm Oerlikons
   (3 added in triangle, on torpedo tube position).

### 3. *1945*

For East Indies Fleet, for assault on Singapore. The first four ships were actually converted, but never sailed for the Far East, and were returned to the USN in their new configuration:
*Byard, Calder, Duckworth, Essington.*
*Bentinck* was scheduled, but later cancelled.
Armament was revised to:

   3  3"/50 cal (with spray shields)
   1  twin 40mm Bofors, with director
   12-15  single 20mm Oerlikons
   (4-7 extra, all aft of the funnel, including 4 on quarterdeck in superimposed tubs)

During refit, all Oerlikons were removed, and in their place, 7 single 40mm Bofors were fitted, resulting from USN experience in the Pacific. These guns were fitted 4 forward of the bridge, in the original Oerlikon positions, and 3 in a triangle aft of the funnel, the 4 original Oerlikon guntubs being completely removed.

The RN enquired of the USN whether single 5"/38 calibre guns could be fitted in these ships in lieu of the 3"/50 calibre originally fitted, but this plan was abandoned, due to the refitting time required, when the ships were still badly needed in the European war right up to VE-Day.

Depth charges were reduced to 100, for topweight compensation; 10 tons of ballast were also added.

Radar—Types SA, SL, 253P, BL, BN.

A photograph of *Calder* and *Essington* is included, to illustrate this interesting conversion.

---

## C. To Fighter Direction Ships

---

1945, for the British Pacific Fleet.

None sailed for the Far East; it is not known how far the conversions actually proceeded:
*Bentley, Braithwaite, Cotton, Fitzroy, Rutherford.*

   Armament was revised to:
   1  3"/50 calibre gun (forward)
   2  twin 40mm Bofors, with directors
   (1 forward, 1 aft)
   2  single 40mm Bofors, forward
   8  single 20mm Oerlikons

The close-range armament was revised, before refits were commenced, in line with

the Coastal Forces Control Frigate conversions for the Far East, as follows:
2 twin 40mm Bofors, with directors
7 single 40mm Bofors
60 depth charges and all Asdic equipment were to be landed as topweight compensation. 20 tons of ballast were to be added.
Radar—Types 277, SL, SA, 244, BN, B1
H/F D/F, M/F D/F were retained
R/T—TBS retained, several extra lines installed

---

## MOBILE GENERATING STATIONS

---

*1945*—for East Indies Fleet, to provide extra electrical power for liberated ports: *Hotham, Rowley, Spragge, Stockham, Tyler.*
All armament to be removed.
Large distribution and cable points to be installed on superstructure deck, aft of funnel.
Ports to add to hull, in way of accommodation.
Ship to be fitted for tropical service.
Only one of above ships apparently so converted was *Hotham*, see photographs.

*Bentinck* oiling at Norfolk before leaving for Bermuda. The camouflage was the original, but painted out on arrival in the UK in favour of the standard North Atlantic pattern. Note H/F D/F and crow's nest already fitted. (*Ministry of Defence*)

## TORPEDO RECOVERY VESSEL

September 1945
*Riou*
Trials only carried out.
Ship was not thought suitable, and no further action was taken.
Torpedo recovery davits and winches were fitted.
10 tons of extra ballast fitted.

### HMS *Ekins*

This was one of the US-built 'Captain' class frigates, of the long-hu   lled turbo-
electric 'Buckley' type. She was launched on 11th September 1     at the
Bethlehem-Hingham yard at Hingham, near Boston, Massachuse   ts—a yard
renowned for a consistently fast production rate for DEs. She was co   pleted on
29th November 1943—a building time from laying down the keel to    ompletion
of 4 months and 25 days—a very fast time, but only average for    this yard.

She was commissioned at the yard by her Royal Navy crew, and    er trials
proceeded first to Casco Bay, in Maine, for initial working-up, then    to the RN
working-up base at Ireland Island, Bermuda. Here, at the old B    ish naval
dockyard, all the US-built RN escorts went through intensive    orking-up
exercises.

On completion of this period she proceeded through storms    Norfolk,
Virginia, where she picked up a British escort carrier and escorted    to New
York. Thence, she proceeded north again, to the USN base at A   gentia in
Newfoundland, to fuel and rest before joining an eastbound Halifax-   K convoy
as part of the close escort.

This convoy's route ran south of another large convoy, round wh   h Captain
Walker's famous Second Escort group sank 6 U-boats in a few days.    In an effort
to divert the U-boat pack, two Support Groups joined the southern    onvoy, and
R/T traffic was unrestricted. The RCN frigate *Waskesiu* sank a U-bo   t astern of
the convoy, and some contacts were picked up, but no attacks were m   ade on the
convoy.

On arrival, *Ekins* went to the 'Captain' class base at Pollock Do   k, Belfast,
where a number of RN additions were made to her equipment—ex   ra two-tier
depth-charge racks and life rafts for North Atlantic duty, Western A   pproaches
camouflage paint of two tones of light green, etc.

She was then attached to the crack Third Escort Group, *Duckwor   (SO), and
carried out several six-week patrols with them. It so happened that in    his period
the Group did not make any kills, but the patrols took the group    all over the
North Atlantic, supporting convoys and following up leads, and als   almost as
far north as Iceland.

Next, she was allocated to the escort forces for the Norman   dy assault;
painted in gay Channel camouflage, she received the *Philante* assault   raining off
Larne, which turned out to be much more fierce than the real thin   g; then she
escorted two merchant ships north about round Scotland to th    Thames,

arriving at her new base at Sheerness. Here, she received a bowchaser pom pom, extra Oerlikons, as well as the 3″ gun director tower.

She was a member there of the 21st Destroyer Flotilla, normally composed of 'Hunt' and 'V and W' class destroyers, but reinforced for the invasion by North Atlantic sloops, corvettes and frigates. She sailed on the morning of D-Day, with the first convoy of merchant ships to pass through the Straits of Dover for some years; for their pains, they were shelled by the German 15″ guns on the French coast, and *Ekins* laid smoke screens as great water spouts rose close to the ships, but none was damaged.

The convoy ran on down to the beaches, arriving close offshore at dawn. The great scene presented an awesome spectacle, but starting the routine she was to follow for several months, *Ekins* turned straight round and led a convoy of empty ships back to the Thames.

This routine, from the Thames to the beaches and back in a week, continued until September. During that period *Ekins* operated in areas where (at the beaches) magnetic mines had been laid by the Germans in large numbers, and where (in the Channel) one-third of the flying-bombs launched against the UK were landing in the sea, with many near misses on the ships, and with further German shellings through the Straits of Dover. U-boats were also operating intermittently on the convoy routes, and in July *Ekins* and *Curzon,* escorting a convoy off Brighton, sank *U 212* on a dark and stormy night. Three frigates of the class were lost in this area during this period.

In September, as the battle moved up-Channel after the retreating Germans, *Ekins* left this duty and was transferred to Harwich as one of the 8 Coastal Forces Control Ships, attached to the 16th Destroyer flotilla of 'Hunt's, 'V and W's, and 'Guillemot' class corvettes. Three fleet sweeping flotillas and numerous motor minesweepers were also based there, and the big Coastal Forces base was also in the harbour at Felixstowe. For this duty she received extra R/T lines, and Headache equipment.

From September to the end of the war the Coastal Forces Control Frigates patrolled the convoy route from the Thames to Antwerp and up the Dutch coast for some 25 miles; in company they usually had 6 MTBs, and a 'Hunt' class destroyer, with her twin 4″ guns. With her superior radar and R/T, the frigate detected German E-boats coming, first from Ostend and Flushing, then from Holland, to attack shipping and to lay mines.

The fighting was almost continuous at night, with the E-boats out several times a week; in addition, the German small battle units, explosive motor boats and two types of midget submarine operated intensively, especially off Holland. *Ekins* was in the forefront of this battle, as one of the crack control frigates; she was attacked by explosive motor boats, too, and sank several midget submarines, also intercepting a German blockade runner trying to get through to Dunkirk, still in German hands. Flying bombs were frequent visitors, too, and the V2s were plainly visible at night, being launched from Holland against the UK.

The E-boats laid many ground mines around Ostend and the convoy route, and after a pitched battle with E-boats on 14th April 1945, in which two were seriously damaged, *Ekins* ran over not one but two of them, on the night of 16th April, off Ostend. She was holed in the forward engine room by the first, and in the Asdic dome compartment by the second; for a while she seemed to be sinking, but great efforts by her crew at damage control (and the good compartment design) kept her afloat, and she struggled under tow into Sheerness the following afternoon, down to her pendant numbers forward and aft, with no power and with her back broken. She was written off as a constructive total loss, and was scrapped in Holland in 1946.

## 'CAPTAIN' CLASS COMMAND ALLOCATION

|  | Jan 1944 | June 1944 | Dec 1944 | April 194 |
|---|---|---|---|---|
| **BELFAST** | | | | |
| Escort Groups (no) | 2 | 4 | 6 | |
| Ships included | 12 | 25 | 36 | |
| Refitting | 9 | 0 | 4 | |
| Unallocated | 2 | 4 | 1 | |
| In transit from USA | 28 | | | |
| Beyond repair (CTL) | | | 2 | |
| **BELFAST TOTAL** | 51(23) | 29 | 43 | |
| **LONDONDERRY** | | | | |
| Attached to EGs | 2 | 8 | 0 | |
| Unallocated | | 1 | | |
| **LIVERPOOL** | | | | |
| Attached to EGs | 2 | 2 | 5 | |
| Unallocated | | 2 | | |
| **CLYDE** | | | | |
| Attached to EGs | | 5 | 5 | |
| Milford Haven | | 1 | | |
| **OTHER WA PORTS TOTAL** | 4 | 19 | 10 | |
| **WESTERN APPROACHES TOTAL** | 55 | 48 | 53 | |
| **SOUTH AND SE COAST** | | | | |
| Harwich | | 6 | 9 | |
| Sheerness | | 8 | 3 | |
| Portsmouth | | 7 | 3 | |
| Plymouth | | 2 | | |
| Assault HQ ships | | 3 | 2 | |
| Unallocated | | 3 | | |
| Beyond Repair (CTL) | | | 2 | |
| **SOUTH AND SE COAST TOTAL** | | 29 | 19 | |

## GERMAN U-BOATS SUNK BY 'CAPTAIN' CLASS

| U 841 | 17.10.43 | *Byard* |
|---|---|---|
| U 538 | 21.11.43 | *Foley* and others |
| U 648 | 23.11.43 | *Bazely, Blackwood* and *Drury* |
| U 600 | 25.11.43 | *Bazely* and *Blackwood* |
| U 757 | 8.1.44 | *Bayntun* and others |
| U 91 | 25.2.44 | *Affleck, Gore* and *Gould* |
| U 358 | 1.3.44 | *Affleck, Gore, Gould* and *Garlies* |
| U 392 | 16.3.44 | *Affleck* and others |
| U 765 | 6.5.44 | *Bickerton, Bligh, Aylmer* and others |
| U 1191 | 25.6.44 | *Affleck* and *Balfour* |
| U 269 | 25.6.44 | *Bickerton* |
| U 988 | 29.6.44 | *Essington, Duckworth, Domett, Cooke* and others |
| U 672 | 18.7.44 | *Balfour* |
| U 212 | 21.7.44 | *Curzon* and *Ekins* |
| U 214 | 26.7.44 | *Cooke* |
| U 671 | 4.8.44 | *Stayner* and others |
| U 618 | 14.8.44 | *Duckworth, Essington* and others |
| U 445 | 24.8.44 | *Louis* |
| U 297 | 6.12.44 | *Goodall* and others |
| U 1172 | 26.1.45 | *Aylmer, Calder, Bentinck* and *Manners* |
| U 1051 | 27.1.45 | *Tyler, Keats* and *Bligh* |
| U 1279 | 3.2.45 | *Bayntun, Braithwaite* and others |
| U 989 | 14.2.45 | *Bayntun, Braithwaite* and others |
| U 1278 | 17.2.45 | *Bayntun* and others |
| U 480 | 24.2.45 | *Duckworth* and *Rowley* |
| U 399 | 26.3.45 | *Duckworth* |
| U 965 | 27.3.45 | *Conn* |
| U 722 | 27.3.45 | *Fitzroy, Redmill* and *Byron* |
| U 246 | 29.3.45 | *Duckworth* |
| U 1021 | 30.3.45 | *Rupert* and *Conn* |
| U 1001 | 8.4.45 | *Fitzroy* and *Byron* |
| U 774 | 8.4.45 | *Calder* and *Bentinck* |
| U 285 | 15.4.45 | *Grindall* and *Keats* |
| U 636 | 21.4.45 | *Bazely, Drury* and *Bentinck* |
| U 286 | 29.4.45 | *Cotton* and others |

*Balfour*, August 1944, at speed off the Devon coast. She has the Channel two-tone grey camouflage, extra depth charge racks, but no Bofors aft. (*Ministry of Defence*)

## 'CAPTAIN' CLASS—PRODUCTION

|  | 'Evarts' class | 'Buckley' class |
|---|---|---|
| 1943 1st quarter | 4 | 0 |
| 2nd quarter | 2 | 2 |
| 3rd quarter | 9 | 6 |
| 4th quarter | 15 | 28 |
| 1944 1st quarter | 2 | 10 |
| Total ships built in USA and transferred | 78 | |
| Ordered, and cancelled | 222 | |
| Original request from RN | 520 | |

## WAR LOSSES

**'BUCKLEY' CLASS**

| *Affleck* | 27.12.44 | U-boat torpedo, CTL |
|---|---|---|
| *Bickerton* | 22.8.44 | Torpedoed and sunk by U-boat |
| *Bullen* | 16.12.44 | Torpedoed and sunk by U-boat |
| *Dakins* | 16.1.45 | E-boat laid ground mine, CTL |
| *Ekins* | 16.4.45 | E-boat laid ground mine, CTL |
| *Halsted* | 10.6.44 | German torpedo boat, CTL |
| *Trollope* | 6.7.44 | U-boat torpedo, CTL |
| *Whitaker* | 1.11.44 | U-boat torpedo, CTL |

**'EVARTS' CLASS**

| *Blackwood* | 15.6.44 | Torpedoed and sunk by U-boat |
|---|---|---|
| *Capel* | 26.12.44 | Torpedoed and sunk by U-boat |
| *Gould* | 1.3.44 | Torpedoed and sunk by U-boat |
| *Goodall* | 29.4.45 | Torpedoed and sunk by U-boat |
| *Lawford* | 8.6.44 | Bombed and sunk by German aircraft |

*Curzon* in April 1945 after refit for the Far East. She has three extra single Oerlikons aft of the funnel, and two single Bofors in place of Oerlikons forward of the bridge. The gunnery control tower has been added to the bridge, and she has her original twin Bofors. (*Ministry of Defence*)

## 'CAPTAIN' CLASS SPECIFICATION

|  | 'Evarts' class | 'Buckley' class |
|---|---|---|
| Displacement | 1,085 tons | 1,300 tons |
| Dimensions |  |  |
| length oa | 289½ ft | 306 ft |
| breadth | 35 ft | 36¾ ft |
| depth | 10¾ ft | 10¾ ft |
| Machinery | diesel-electric | turbo-electric |
|  | BHP 6,000 | SHP 12,000 |
| Machinery builder | GM | GE |
| Shafts | 2 | 2 |
| Speed | 21 kn | 24 kn |
| Armament |  |  |
| main | 3 3″/50 cal | 3 3″/50 cal |
| close-range | 2 40mm (some) | 2 40mm (some) |
|  | 9 20mm | 8, 10, or 12 20mm |
|  |  | 1 2pdr pom pom (some) |
| Anti-submarine |  |  |
| Armament | 1 Hedgehog | 1 Hedgehog |
|  | 2 sets rails | 2 sets rails |
|  | 4 throwers | 4 throwers |
|  | 200 d/cs | 200+ d/cs |
| Radar | Type SL | Type SL |
|  | Type SA (some) | Type SA (some) |
|  | Type 244, 253 | Type 244, 253 |
| H/F D/F | Some (not with SA) | Some (not with SA) |
| M/F D/F | All | All |
| Navigational D/F | Loran | Loran |
|  |  | QH3 (some) |
| Foxer Gear | All on North | |
|  | Atlantic | |
| Complement | 175 | 200 |

*Calder* in November 1943. Note she has her torpedo davit on the upper deck, though no tubes were fitted. A good beam shot of a 'Buckley' type destroyer escort. (*Ministry of Defence*)

## 'CAPTAIN' CLASS – CLASS LIST

| Name | Pendant No | Builder | Building Time | Completion Date |
|------|-----------|---------|---------------|-----------------|

### A. 'EVARTS' DIESEL-ELECTRIC TYPE

| Name | Pendant No | Builder | Building Time | Completion Date |
|------|-----------|---------|---------------|-----------------|
| Bayntun<br>ex *DE 1* | K 310 | Boston | 9m14d | 20.1.43 |
| Bazely<br>ex *DE 2* | K 311 | ,, | 10m12d | 18.2.43 |
| Berry<br>ex *DE 3* | K 312 | ,, | 5m23d | 18.2.43 |
| Blackwood<br>ex *DE 4* | K 313 | ,, | 6m4d | 27.3.43 |
| Burges<br>ex *DE 12* | K 347 | ,, | 5m25d | 2.6.43 |
| Drury<br>ex *DE 46* | K 316 | Philadelphia | 21m20d | 4.12.43 |
| Capel<br>ex *DE 266* | K 470 | Boston | 5m5d | 16.8.43 |
| Cooke<br>ex *DE 267* | K 471 | ,, | 5m5d | 16.8.43 |
| Dacres<br>ex *DE 268* | K 472 | ,, | 4m20d | 28.8.43 |
| Domett<br>ex *DE 269* | K 473 | ,, | 4m26d | 3.9.43 |
| Foley<br>ex *DE 270* | K 474 | ,, | 5m0d | 8.9.43 |
| Garlies<br>ex *DE 271* | K 271 | ,, | 5m5d | 13.9.43 |
| Gould<br>ex *DE 272* | K 476 | ,, | 4m25d | 18.9.43 |
| Grindall<br>ex *DE 273* | K 477 | ,, | 4m30d | 23.9.43 |
| Gardiner<br>ex *DE 274* | K 478 | ,, | 4m8d | 28.9.43 |
| Goodall<br>ex *DE 275* | K 479 | ,, | 4m15d | 4.10.43 |
| Goodson<br>ex *DE 276* | K 480 | ,, | 4m20d | 9.10.43 |
| Gore<br>ex *DE 277* | K 481 | ,, | 4m25d | 14.10.43 |
| Keats<br>ex *DE 278* | K 482 | ,, | 4m13d | 19.10.43 |
| Kempthorne<br>ex *DE 279* | K 483 | ,, | 4m17d | 23.10.43 |
| Kingsmill<br>ex *DE 280* | K 484 | ,, | 3m21d | 29.10.43 |

| | | | | |
|---|---|---|---|---|
| *Lawford*<br>ex *DE 516* | K 514 | ,, | 3m25d | 3.11.43 |
| *Louis*<br>ex *DE 517* | K 515 | ,, | 4m0d | 8.11.43 |
| *Lawson*<br>ex *DE 518* | K 516 | ,, | 4m6d | 15.11.43 |
| *Pasley*<br>ex *DE 519*<br>ex *Lindsay* | K 564 | ,, | 4m0d | 20.11.43 |
| *Loring*<br>ex *DE 520* | K 565 | ,, | 4m7d | 27.11.43 |
| *Hoste*<br>ex *DE 521*<br>ex *Mitchell* | K 566 | ,, | 3m20d | 3.12.43 |
| *Moorsom*<br>ex *DE 522* | K 567 | ,, | 4m2d | 16.12.43 |
| *Manners*<br>ex *DE 523* | K 568 | ,, | 3m23d | 6.12.43 |
| *Mounsey*<br>ex *DE 524* | K 569 | ,, | 4m9d | 23.12.43 |
| *Inglis*<br>ex *DE 525* | K 570 | ,, | 3m3d | 29.12.43 |
| *Inman*<br>ex *DE 526* | K 571 | ,, | 3m18d | 13.1.44 |

*Ekins* at Harwich, December 1944. She was one of the Coastal Forces Control Frigates; she has a bowchaser, Headache below the Type SL aerial, and the bridge gunnery control tower added to a number of this class. (*Imperial War Museum*)

## 'BUCKLEY' TURBO-ELECTRIC TYPE

| | | | | |
|---|---|---|---|---|
| Bentinck<br>ex DE 52 | K 314 | Bethlehem-<br>Hingham | 10m20d | 19.5.43 |
| Byard<br>ex DE 55 | K 315 | ,, | 8m4d | 18.6.43 |
| Calder<br>ex DE 58 | K 349 | ,, | 7m4d | 15.7.43 |
| Duckworth<br>ex DE 61 | K 351 | ,, | 6m19d | 4.8.43 |
| Duff<br>ex DE 64 | K 352 | ,, | 5m29d | 23.8.43 |
| Essington<br>ex DE 67 | K 353 | ,, | 5m30d | 7.9.43 |
| Affleck<br>ex DE 71 | K 462 | ,, | 5m24d | 29.9.43 |
| Aylmer<br>ex DE 72 | K 463 | ,, | 5m18d | 30.9.43 |
| Balfour<br>ex DE 73 | K 464 | ,, | 5m18d | 30.9.43 |
| Bentley<br>ex DE 74 | K 465 | ,, | 5m17d | 14.10.43 |
| Bickerton<br>ex DE 75 | K 466 | ,, | 5m14d | 17.10.43 |
| Bligh<br>ex DE 76 | K 467 | ,, | 5m19d | 22.10.43 |
| Braithwaite<br>ex DE 77 | K 468 | ,, | 6m8d | 13.11.43 |
| Bullen<br>ex DE 78 | K 460 | ,, | 5m8d | 25.10.43 |
| Byron<br>ex DE 79 | K 508 | ,, | 5m6d | 30.10.43 |
| Conn<br>ex DE 80 | K 509 | ,, | 4m28d | 31.10.43 |
| Cotton<br>ex DE 81 | K 501 | ,, | 5m4d | 8.11.43 |
| Cranstoun<br>ex DE 82 | K 511 | ,, | 5m7d | 13.11.43 |
| Cubitt<br>ex DE 83 | K 512 | Bethlehem-<br>Hingham | 5m11d | 17.11.43 |
| Curzon<br>ex DE 84 | K 513 | ,, | 4m30d | 20.11.43 |
| Dakins<br>ex DE 85 | K 550 | ,, | 5m2d | 23.11.43 |
| Deane<br>ex DE 86 | K 551 | ,, | 4m27d | 26.11.43 |
| Ekins<br>ex DE 87 | K 552 | ,, | 4m25d | 29.11.43 |

The forecastle of *Ekins*, looking down from the bridge. The bowchaser detail is plain, and the Coastal Forces type rocket flare projectors can be seen on B gun. The anchors were stowed level with the upper deck, and not in hawse pipes. (*P.W. Hayward*)

*Calder* and *Essington*, the first 'Captain' class frigates to be returned to the US Navy after the war, at Brooklyn Navy Yard, 20th October 1945. Both had completed refits as Coastal Forces Control Ships for service with the East Indies Fleet before return. Note all Oerlikons aft of the funnel removed, replaced by three single 40mm Bofors; four single Bofors also replaced the four Oerlikons forward of the bridge. All 3″ guns on *Essington*, at left, have spray shields, and Foxer gear is prominent on sterns of both ships. Type SA radar at mastheads of both, and extra depth charge racks can be seen forward of throwers.

*Spragge* in June 1945. This shows the deck
lay-out of this class, especially the quarterdeck.
Note the extra liferafts and depth charge racks.
(*Ministry of Defence*)

*Opposite: Kingsmill* at Spithead, March 1945. She still has her tall mainmast and extra yard at the fore, from her role as assault HQ ship for the Normandy invasion. Note Type 271 radar at back of the bridge, in addition to Type SL high on the mast. 1945 camouflage pattern. (*Lt-Cdr R.P. Hall,* RANR)

| | | | | |
|---|---|---|---|---|
| *Fitzroy* ex *DE 88* | K 553 | ,, | 1m23d | 16.10.43 |
| *Redmill* ex *DE 89* | K 554 | ,, | 4m17d | 30.11.43 |
| *Retalick* ex *DE 90* | K 555 | ,, | 4m18d | 8.12.43 |
| *Halsted* ex *DE 91* | K 556 | ,, | 3m24d | 3.11.43 |
| *Riou* ex *DE 92* | K 557 | ,, | 4m10d | 14.12.43 |
| *Rutherford* ex *DE 93* | K 558 | ,, | 4m12d | 16.12.43 |
| *Cosby* ex *DE 94* | K 559 | ,, | 4m9d | 20.12.43 |
| *Rowley* ex *DE 95* | K 560 | ,, | 4m4d | 22.12.43 |
| *Rupert* ex *DE 96* | K 561 | ,, | 3m30d | 24.12.43 |
| *Stockham* ex *DE 97* | K 562 | ,, | 4m3d | 28.12.43 |
| *Seymour* ex *DE 98* | K 563 | ,, | 3m24d | 23.12.43 |
| *Spragge* ex *DE 563* | K 572 | ,, | 3m29d | 14.1.44 |
| *Stayner* ex *DE 564* | K 573 | Bethlehem-Hingham | 3m7d | 30.12.43 |
| *Thornborough* ex *DE 565* | K 574 | ,, | 3m8d | 31.12.43 |
| *Trollope* ex *DE 566* | K 575 | ,, | 3m11d | 10.1.44 |
| *Tyler* ex *DE 567* | K 576 | ,, | 3m8d | 14.1.44 |
| *Torrington* ex *DE 568* | K 577 | ,, | 3m26d | 18.1.44 |
| *Narborough* ex *DE 569* | K 578 | ,, | 3m15d | 21.1.44 |
| *Waldegrave* ex *DE 570* | K 579 | ,, | 3m9d | 25.1.44 |
| *Whittaker* ex *DE 571* | K 580 | ,, | 3m8d | 28.1.44 |
| *Holmes* ex *DE 572* | K 581 | ,, | 3m4d | 31.1.44 |
| *Hargood* ex *DE 573* | K 582 | ,, | 3m11d | 7.2.44 |
| *Hotham* ex *DE 574* | K 583 | ,, | 3m2d | 8.2.44 |

Above class is listed in order of original DE numbers, for easy reference.

Builders were: Boston Navy Yard
Philadelphia Navy Yard
Bethlethem-Hingham, Hingham, Mass

K310

BAYNTUN in March, 1943.

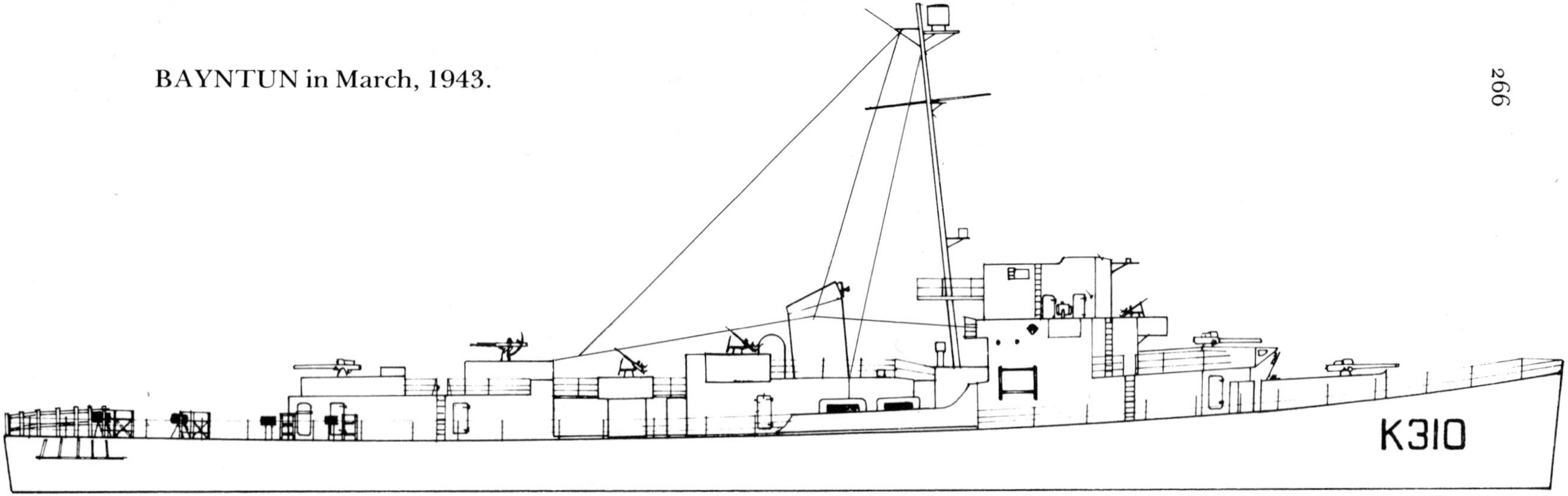

RIOU in early 1944.

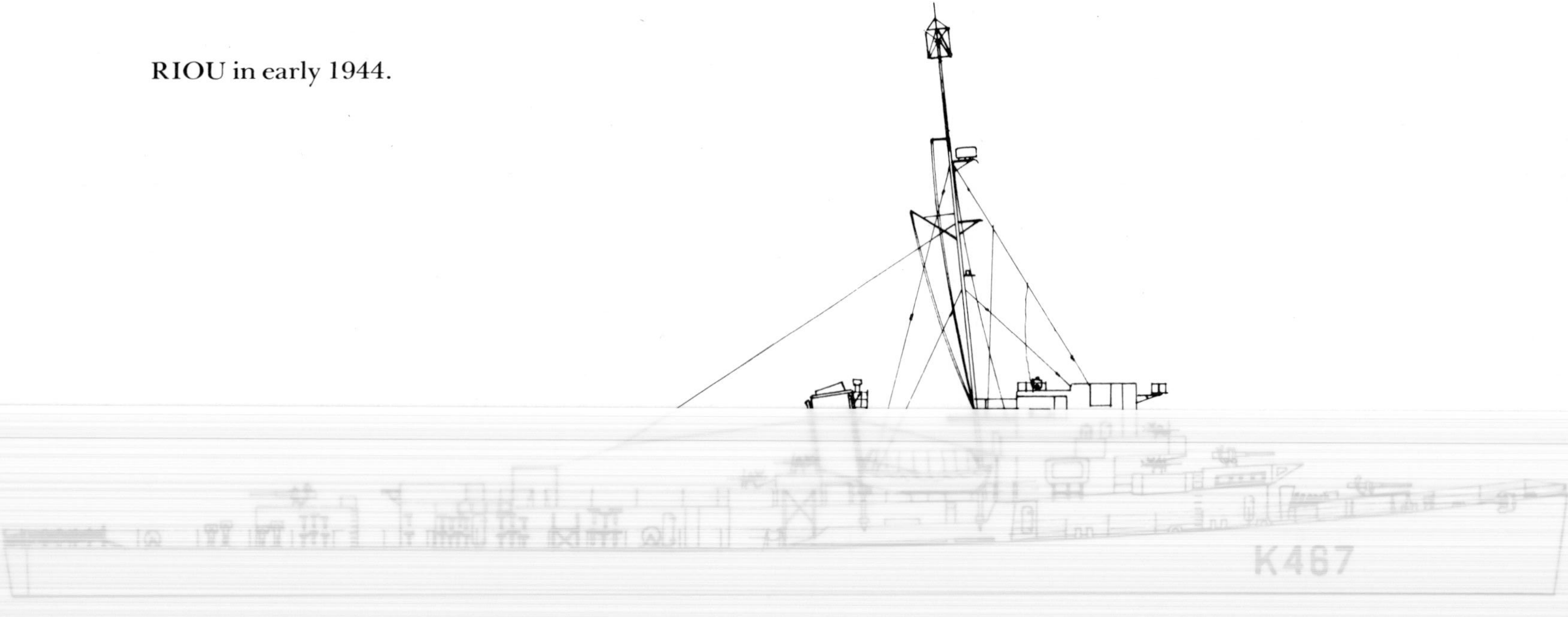

K467

Royal Navy

K557

BLIGH in late 1943.

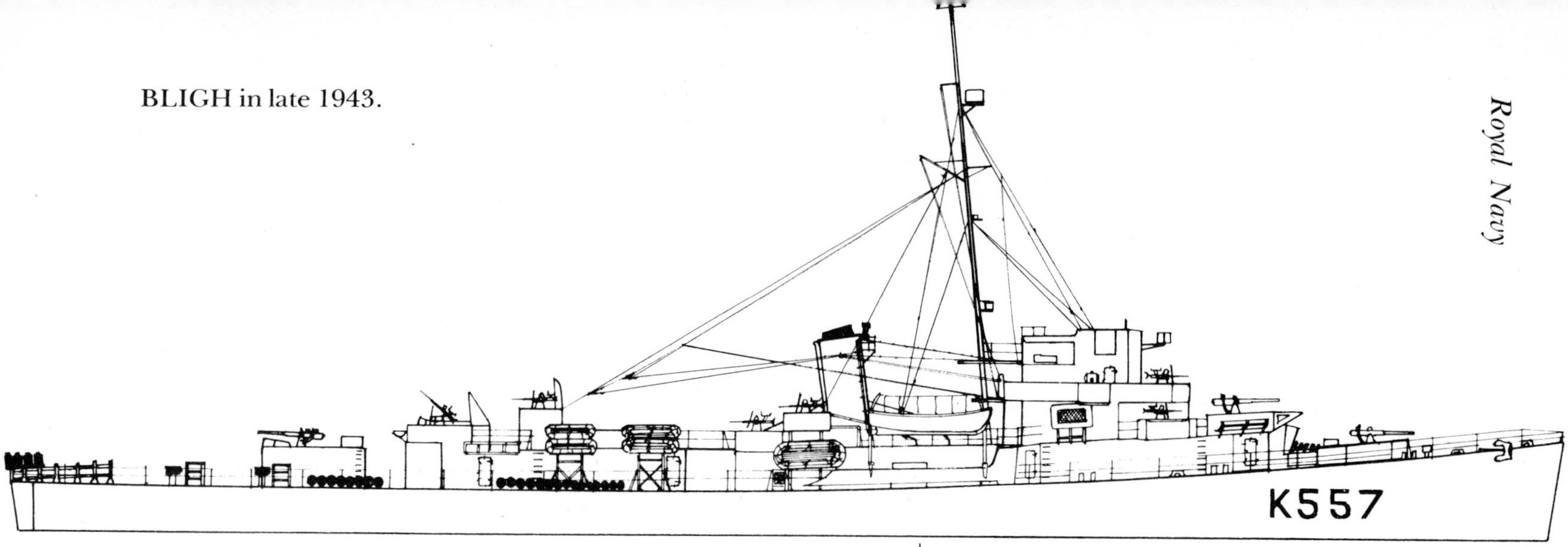

LAWFORD in mid-1944, as HQ ship.

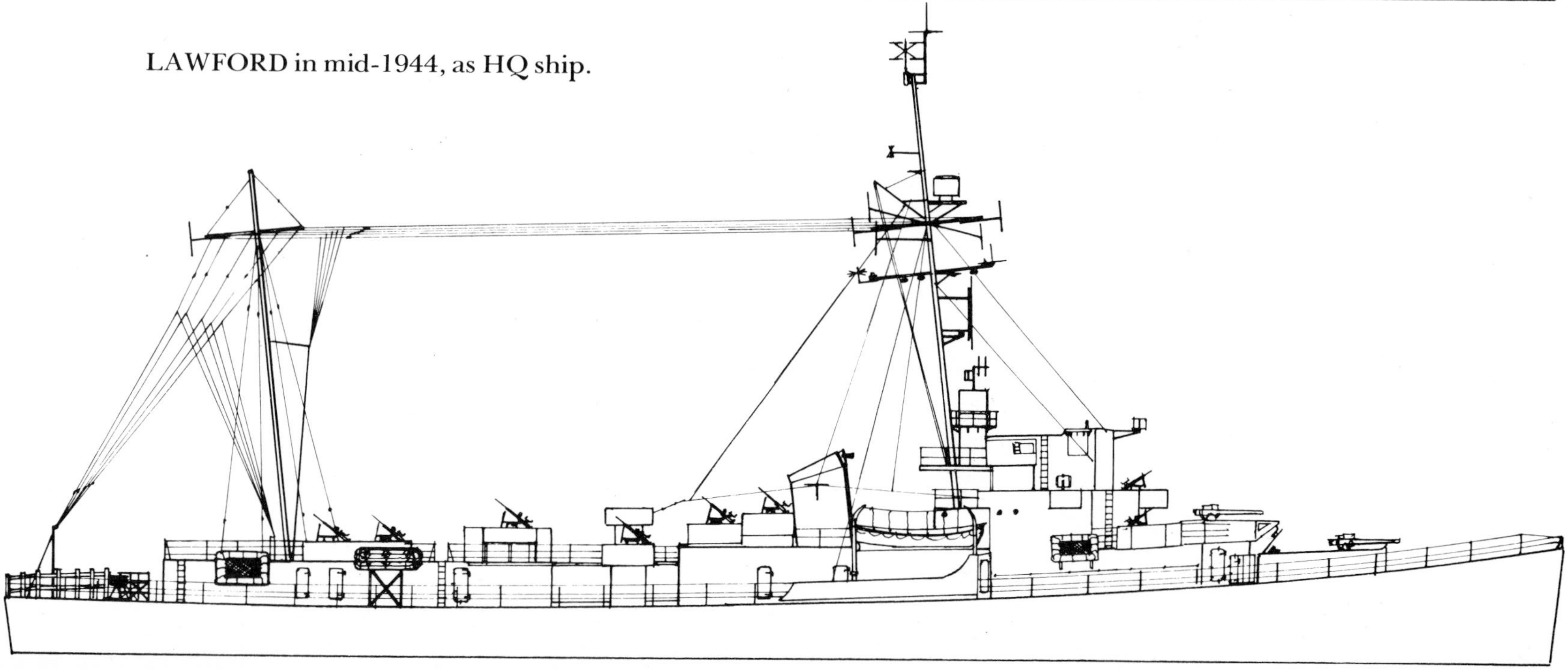

*Sarawak* and another 'Colony', probably taken at Bermuda en route to be returned to the USN, 1946. All 3″ guns have spray shields and the twin Bofors have been removed, probably for transfer to ships earmarked for the Far East in 1945. *(P.A. Vicary)*

*Anguilla* in North Atlantic camouf[...]ge and with the two twin 40mm Bofors mounti[...]ps at the break of the shelter deck clear. No[...] that no whaler is carried on the port side. *(Imperial War Museum)*

## 'COLONY' CLASS FRIGATES
### 21 ships built in USA

In the USN section will be found details of the Patrol Frigate (PF) class. These were based on the RN 'River' class frigate design, two ships of that class, built in Canada, having been transferred to the USN on completion.

Under Lend-Lease, 21 ships of the PF class, built in the United States by the Kaiser organisation, were delivered to the RN on completion, picked up by RN crews at the builder's yard, and brought back to the UK, where they joined the Western Approaches escort forces.

These ships were mass-produced, and were almost entirely welded throughout. The RN batch were all built at the Walsh-Kaiser shipyard at Providence, Rhode Island. The rate of building was phenomenal, launches being as follows:

| | |
|---|---|
| July 1943 | 2 |
| August | 6 |
| September | 3 |
| October | 5 |
| November | 4 |

There were some mechanical troubles on completion, which was not surprising, in view of this tremendous effort by this yard.

The 'Colony' class had the benefit of some of the improvements made to the basic RN 'River' class design by the USN. This is covered in more detail in the USN PF class chapter. The standard USN DE type equipment, such as the excellent surface warning radar, Type SL, and in some ships the equally good air warning set, Type SA, with the bedstead aerial at the masthead, were fitted. In addition, two twin 40mm Bofors mountings, with directors, were fitted aft, in the same position as that in the 'Bay' class, and this, with a full outfit of 20mm Oerlikons (in some cases, more than an RN 'River' class unit usually enjoyed), gave them a formidable close-range armament.

The anti-submarine armament was as impressive as in the 'Captain' class, with a full Hedgehog fitted abaft the forward 3″ gun, and a well-laid-out quarterdeck, but the extra depth-charge stowage racks fitted in the 'Captain' and 'River' classes by the RN were not always fitted.

The Admiralty approved that most of the standard Western Approaches alterations and additions should be fitted progressively as time permitted, but this class did not receive priority for this work, and in a number of units by no means all the improvements were carried out. Although some units of the class were involved in U-boat kills, they did not become engaged in the North Atlantic or UK inshore battles to any extent, as did the 'Captain' class, and no ships of the class were lost, while the war losses of the 'Captain' class speak for themselves. RN improvements approved included the fitting of spray-shields to the 3″/50 calibre guns, 2″ rocket flare projectors to the spray-shields on 'B' gun, and Foxer gear in late 1944.

*Conversions for the Far East*

Late in 1944, when plans were under way for the transfer of a large number of RN escorts to the Far East for the closing stages of the war against Japan, it was approved that most, if not all, of the ships of this class should be converted to Fighter Direction Ships, to give some measure of aircraft protection to convoys not covered by aircraft carriers or cruisers.

This refit included the following alterations:

A Type 277 radar was to be fitted aft, just forward of the after 3" gun. This radar set had an aerial which was too heavy for the 'Colony' class pole mast; consideration was given to fitting a new lattice mast, as in the 'Loch' class, but this would have meant mounting the air warning Type SA aerial on a pole topmast, superior to the lattice mast, and the after position was considered to be more practical. This excellent combination of up-to-date radar sets gave high (Type SA) cover as well as low cover (Types 277 and SL). The new VH/F D/F set, Type FV4, was also to be fitted aft, on a pole, directly on top of the Type 277 radar office.

An aircraft direction room was to be built at the foot of the foremast, and a good number of extra radiotelephone sets were added. An additional yard, 16 feet long, was added to the foremast in a fore and aft direction, in way of the existing yard, to take the extra R/T aerial arrays; an alternative to this yard was two spurs, each 8 feet long.

A standard Admiralty pattern 27 foot whaler was fitted in gravity davits on the port side.

While it was approved in principle that all ships of the class should be so converted, the first 10 units which came in for refit were to take priority; among these, in the event, were *Ascension, Cayman, Caicos* and *Dominica.* But it was finally decided that the inadequate ventilation below decks made these ships less than ideal for Pacific or East Indies service, and the rapid progress of the war dictated the cancellation of most of these conversions. The official position lists as at VJ-Day do not show any of them as being on station or on passage for either of the two commands by that time.

*Caicos,* the first to be taken in hand for long refit, was, however, completed in the early months of 1945. In the closing months of the European war she was employed as a floating radar and fighter direction station, anchored in the North Sea east of Harwich. Her job was to detect and report V1 flying bombs, and possibly V2 rockets, which were at that time being fired against the UK from Holland. For this purpose she had shore-based fighters under her control. A photograph of *Caicos,* in this configuration, showing the results of the refit, is included. It is not known if any of the other ships were similarly converted, but if they were they were probably not employed operationally before their return to the USN.

## Fitting of Squid mortars

In early 1944, in line with other escort classes of the RN, consideration was given to the fitting of 2 Squid mortars in each ship of the 'Colony' class. The early operational results of these new A/S mortars had been so encouraging that such a drastic alteration was well worth examination.

The mortars were to be sited on the superstructure deck forward, as in the 'Loch' class, and would displace the second 3″/50 calibre gun, in B position, as well as the Hedgehog. It is believed that no ship was so converted, but that the USN was interested in this planned alteration to the PF class.

### Return to the USN

Kept in reserve after the end of the European war, the entire 'Colony' class was returned to the USN in 1946.

### HMS Ascension

This was the third unit in the 'Colony' class of frigates. PF 74, then with the RN name *Hargood,* she was completed under her final name of *Ascension.* She was laid down on 30th April 1943, launched on 6th August, and completed for trials on 25th November—a remarkable achievement by the American builders, Walsh-Kaiser of Providence, Rhode Island. An RN crew commissioned her, and after acceptance trials she worked-up at Casco Bay, in US waters, then in March went to the RN working-up base in Bermuda for intensive exercises.

Later that month she left Bermuda for UK waters, and on arrival went to Ardrossan for the fitting of additional RN equipment. On 23rd May 1944, joining the 5th Escort Group, she left Londonderry for the first of three uneventful round voyages to Gibraltar, escorting convoys. She returned from the third on 7th September 1944, to find that she had been designated Senior Officer's ship of the 17th Escort Group, based on Greenock.

The Group was employed on patrols in the north-west approaches in the Irish Sea, and in the western English Channel until the end of the European war. On 10th November 1944 her Group, composed of *Ascension, Burges, Cranstoun, Loch Killin* and *Moorsom,* left Scapa Flow for an anti-submarine patrol between the Shetland and Faeroe Islands, to keep the U-boats' heads down while a convoy returned from Russia. Early on 25th November a Sunderland of No 330 Squadron, Royal Norwegian Air Force, reported a radar contact about 120 miles west of the Shetlands, and 17th Escort Group went to the area to investigate. Shortly after arrival, *Ascension* gained Asdic contact with *U 322,* and she and *Moorsom* attacked with their Hedgehogs, scoring an almost immediate success and sinking the U-boat with all hands.

A month later, in the Channel, the Group had less success in their hunt for *U 772,* which had sunk HMS *Capel* and damaged HMS *Affleck,* both of the 1st Escort Group, off Cherbourg on Boxing Day. On 16th April 1945 *Loch Killin* sank *U 1063* off the coast of Devon, and at the end of the month the Group was involved in a long but unsuccessful hunt off the Eddystone Light.

With the end of the war in Europe, consideration was given to sending *Ascension* to the Far East. The 'River' and 'Colony' class ships were not particularly well suited for hot-weather deployment, being designed for operation in the North Atlantic, and as considerable modification would be required it was decided that she would be retained in European waters. In practice, this meant reduction to reserve, for after the surrendering U-boats had been shepherded to Allied ports the escorts available far exceeded the number required.

After spending much of May 1945 in the south-west approaches, *Ascension* was laid up at Dartmouth in mid-June. In April 1946 she was brought out of reserve and commissioned for the return passage to the United States. Calling at the Azores and Bermuda en route, *Ascension* arrived at the New York Navy Yard on 17th May and was returned to the US Navy. The latter had no use for these ships in peacetime, so after a period in reserve *PF 74*, ex *Ascension*, ex *Hargood*, ex *PF 74*, ex *PG 182*, was sold on 16th October 1947 to the Hudson Valley Shipwrecking Corporation of Newburg, NY.

Battle Honours awarded to ships of this name in the Royal Navy had progressed; to Armada, 1588, were now added Atlantic, 1944, and North Sea, 1944!

### GERMAN U-BOATS SUNK BY 'COLONY' CLASS

| | | |
|---|---|---|
| *U 322* | 25.11.44 | *Ascension* and others |
| *U 400* | 17.12.44 | *Nyasaland* |
| *U 1014* | 4.2.45 | *Nyasaland*, *Papua* and others |
| *U 327* | 27.2.45 | *Labuan* and others |
| *U 714* | 14.3.45 | *Natal* |
| *U 286* | 29.4.45 | *Anguilla* and others |

*Somaliland*, showing USN variations on the RN 'River' class theme; rounded bridge front, three 3"/50 guns, two forward of the bridge, pole mast carrying Types SA and SL radar, and Oerlikons on the quarterdeck and forward of the Bofors position. *(Imperial War Museum)*

## 'COLONY' CLASS SPECIFICATION

| | |
|---|---|
| Displacement | 1,318 tons standard |
| | 1,430 tons full load |
| Dimensions | |
| length pp | 285' 6" |
| oa | 304' 0" |
| breadth | 37' 6" |
| draught | 12' 0" mean |
| Machinery | 4 cylinder triple expansion |
| Shafts | 2 |
| IHP | 5,500 |
| Speed | 20 kn |
| Complement | 120 |
| Armament | |
| main | 3 3"/50 cal |
| close-range | 2 twin 40 mm Bofors |
| | 8 single 20 mm Oerlikon |
| A/S Armament | 1 Hedgehog |
| | 4 depth charge throwers, 2 rails |
| Radar | Types, SL, SA, 242, IFF |

*Caicos* at Harwich in April 1945 as a Fighter Direction Ship. She was converted for the Far East, but was employed against flying bombs launched in Holland against the UK in the spring of 1945. Note Type 277 radar on hut aft, with VH/F D/F on pole mast immediately forward, extra aerials on spurs on foremast, and extra deckhouse aft of bridge. *(Imperial War Museum)*

## 'COLONY' CLASS COMMAND ALLOCATION (All at 1st January)

|              | 1944 | 1945 | 7.5.45 |
|--------------|------|------|--------|
| Londonderry  | 1    | 6    | 6      |
| Liverpool    | 0    | 5    | 7      |
| Greenock     | 0    | 8    | 6      |
| Harwich      | 0    | 1    | 1      |
| Totals       | 1    | 20   | 20     |

## 'COLONY' CLASS—CLASS LIST

| Name | Pendant No. | Builder | Building Time | Comp Date |
|------|-------------|---------|---------------|-----------|
| Anguilla<br>ex *Hallowell*<br>ex USN *PF 72* | K 500 | Walsh-Kaiser Providence | 9m21d | 21.10 |
| Antigua<br>ex *Hammond*<br>ex USN *PF 73* | K 501 | ,, | 7m1d | 4.11. |
| Ascension<br>ex *Hargood*<br>ex USN *PF 74* | K 502 | ,, | 6m8d | 8.11. |
| Bahamas<br>ex *Hotham*<br>ex USN *PF 75* | K 503 | ,, | 7m13d | 20.11 |
| Barbados<br>ex *Halsted*<br>ex USN *PF 76* | K 504 | ,, | 6m20d | 30.11 |
| Caicos<br>ex *Hannam*<br>ex USN *PF 77* | K 505 | ,, | 8m0d | 8.12. |
| Cayman<br>ex *Harland*<br>ex USN *PF 78* | K 506 | ,, | 5m1d | 16.12 |
| Dominica<br>ex *Harnam*<br>ex USN *PF 79* | K 507 | ,, | 4m27d | 23.12 |
| Labuan<br>ex *Harvey*<br>ex USN *PF 80* | K 584 | ,, | 5m6d | 30.12 |
| Montserrat<br>ex *Hornby*<br>ex USN *PF 82* | K 586 | ,, | 10m2d | 11.1. |
| Nyasaland<br>ex *Hoste*<br>ex USN *PF 83* | K 587 | ,, | 10m10d | 19.1. |
| Papua<br>ex *Howett*<br>ex USN *PF 84* | K 588 | ,, | 4m30d | 23.1. |

| | | | | |
|---|---|---|---|---|
| *Pitcairn*<br>ex *Pilford*<br>ex USN *PF 85* | K 589 | ,, | 5m11d | 28.1.44 |
| *St Helena*<br>ex *Pasley*<br>ex USN *PF 86* | K 590 | ,, | 4m10d | 2.2.44 |
| *Sarawak*<br>ex *Patton*<br>ex USN *PF 87* | K 591 | ,, | 4m9d | 7.2.44 |
| *Seychelles*<br>ex *Pearl*<br>ex USN *PF 88* | K 592 | ,, | 4m14d | 12.2.44 |
| *Perim*<br>ex *Phillimore*<br>ex USN *PF 89* | K 593 | ,, | 4m10d | 17.2.44 |
| *Somaliland*<br>ex *Popham*<br>ex USN *PF 90* | K 594 | ,, | 4m11d | 22.2.44 |
| *Tobago*<br>ex *Hong Kong*<br>ex *Holmes*<br>ex USN *PF 81* | K 585 | ,, | 10m6d | 15.1.44 |
| *Tortola*<br>ex *Peyton*<br>ex USN *PF 91* | K 595 | ,, | 4m11d | 27.2.44 |
| *Zanzibar*<br>ex *Prowse*<br>ex USN *PF 92* | K 596 | ,, | 4m13d | 2.3.44 |

RN 'Captain' class frigate *Gore* operating inshore off the Devon coast in August 1944. The U-boat war moved inshore in the last year of the war, and the crack support groups often found themselves in unfamiliar waters. *(Ministry of Defence)*

*Kilbride*, 18th May 1944, proba[bly off Gibraltar]. This gives a good picture of the [deck lay-out of] the USN PCE class; note two si[ngle 40mm] Bofors in tubs aft, good quarte[rdeck] arrangement, single whaleboat [on starboard] side, worked by derrick, and H[edgehog aft of] 3"/50 gun on forecastle. *(Minis[try of Defence)*

*Kilbride*, May 1944. A good qu[arter view,] showing the depth charge rails [dominating the] quarterdeck, the Type SL rada[r carried right on] top of the pole mast, and the d[iesel exhaust] stains on the hull, in ships not f[itted with the] short funnel. *(Ministry of Defen[ce)*

## 'KIL' CLASS AUXILIARY A/S VESSELS
### 15 ships completed

The 'Kil' class were built in the United States, and transferred on completion to the RN under Lend-Lease.

Originally, some 150 ships of this class (at first known as A/S Vessels, 180 ft type) were to be allocated to the RN under the 1941 Lend-Lease Plan, and 94 were actually ordered. However, only 15 were in the end delivered to the RN, due to the re-allocation of new escorts agreed between the RN, USN and RCN, after the original allocation had been made.

Of the USN PCE (Patrol Craft Escort) type, they were at first classified by the RN as BEC (British Escort Craft), and indeed about the first half of the class commissioned under their BEC numbers (see the photograph of *Kilchrenan*) and operated thus until the Admiralty approved the 'Kil' names being substituted. It seems probable that these names, like the 'Flower' class, were a happy reflection of a similarly-named class of escort in World War I (in this case, the 'Kil' class whalers, from Smith's Dock designs).

All the 'Kil' class were built by one yard, the Pullman Standard Car Co, Inc, of Chicago, Illinois. They were commissioned by RN crews in Chicago and had a unique voyage, of some 1,000 miles, to make before they reached the sea. Their first contact with operational forces was at the RCN bases at Quebec and Halifax.

They proceeded to Bermuda for working-up, but some ships were a little delayed during this period by mechanical troubles. They served in two locations during the war, at Freetown, Sierra Leone, and at Gibraltar, where they reinforced the anti-submarine forces, and released other ships for ocean work. The 'Kil' class did not operate in the north Atlantic, in the main convoy areas, probably due to their build. It is interesting to note that the RN designated groups of these ships as 'A/S Groups', rather than as 'Escort Groups', as was the case with corvettes.

They were of the standard USN PCE design of that time; reference to the USN section of this book will show variations in armament in later ships of the class. The RN ships did not have the short funnel, which was added in later ships.

Their design had many distinctive features, by RN comparison. The Hedgehog, sited on the centre-line immediately abaft the 3″ gun on the foredeck, was a neat arrangement, reflecting the USN DE design. The two single 40mm Bofors mounted aft compared very well with the 'Flower' class close-range armament, and were supplemented by the two single 20mm Oerlikons on the flag deck—note that the USN added further Oerlikons forward of the bridge in later versions.

The quarterdeck had a full range of depth-charge equipment, compactly fitted in, and the USN-type motor cutter was stowed on chocks on the upper deck, and handled by a boom or derrick.

On the pole mast it will be noted that this class had the benefit of the excellent Type SL radar, with PPI, and TBS was also fitted. The class had one unique feature—the gaff fitted on the forward, as well as the after side of the mast. The yard was fitted on the after side of the mast, following USN practice.

The open bridge was particularly clear and roomy; note that there were no ports in the ship's side.

The class was allocated pennant number 5, rather than flag K, and this will be seen in the photographs of *Kilbride*. The result was rather more complicated than the standard RN pennant number practice.

The comparison of the specifications of this class and the 'Flower' class is interesting. The 'Kil' class upper deck, covered right aft to the quarterdeck, compares well for rough weather work.

### HMS Kilbride

*Kilbride* was a US-built PCE class ship, which served with the RN on Lend-Lease. She was built by the Pullman-Standard Car Company of Chicago, Illinois, and engined by General Motors. Laid down on 17th November 1942, she was launched on 15th May 1943 and completed on 2nd August 1943.

Like her 14 sister ships, all built at the same yard, *Kilbride* had to sail 1,000 miles of inland waterway before reaching the sea and joining the RN and RCN forces. She proceeded right through the Great Lakes, meeting the first RCN 'Flower' class operational corvettes at Quebec, and then going down the St Lawrence to Halifax. From there she went to Bermuda for full working-up, and then went on again to European waters, where she joined the 51st Auxiliary A/S Group, based at Gibraltar. This group, which was attached to the Mediterranean Fleet, was made up of ships of this class, with a second group based at Freetown.

In August 1944 *Kilbride* briefly worked with the 41st Escort Group, also operating from Gibraltar, but the following month she left Gibraltar on loan to the Western Approaches Command, arriving at Plymouth on 1st September. She was then based at Milford Haven until March 1945. Her attachment was an indication of the growing commitment at that time of large numbers of A/S vessels in UK Home waters, when as many ships as could be spared were needed to go for refit before joining the two Far East fleets. She returned to Gibraltar to rejoin her original group, arriving on 16th March 1945.

With the cessation of European hostilities, *Kilbride* was nominated for the reserve Fleet and went to Sheerness, where she was laid up with all other units of her class before being returned to the US Navy at the end of 1945.

---

### GERMAN U-BOAT SUNK BY 'KIL' CLASS

*U 731*   15.5.44   *Kilmarnock* and others

---

### PCE CLASS—LEND-LEASE ALLOCATIONS

Originally, the RN asked for 150 ships of this class, under Lend-Lease arrangements, 94 only were firmly ordered, and in the end, only 15 were delivered. Apart from increasing USN escort requirements, it is probable that this class, superior as it was to the

RN's Flower class for coastal escort and patrol work (but not for mid-ocean work), fell short of the capabilities of the later RN frigate designs and the USN destroyer escort designs, and the RN would probably not have taken up its full request of 150 ships, even had they been available in good time. But, as the USN commissioning records for this class show, they appeared too late for the 1942/43 escort crisis, and were cancelled or largely completed in other configurations for the USN.

Orders for the 94 ships for the RN were placed as follows; it will be noted that the 15 finally delivered, all from the Pullman-Standard yard in Chicago, carried different PCE numbers from those originally allocated:

PCE 827-876   Charleston Navy Yard   Ordered 7th May 1942, for delivery between March 1943 and April 1944

PCE 877-890   Pullman-Standard Car Co   Ordered 7th May 1942, for delivery between January 1943 and March 1944

PCE 891-920   Albina Engineering and Machinery Works, Portland, Oregon   Ordered 7th May 1942, for delivery between July 1943 and May 1944

Orders for the remaining 56 units were suspended in September 1942. It is not known if hull numbers, yards or delivery dates were allocated before suspension.

## 'KIL' CLASS SPECIFICATION

| | | | |
|---|---|---|---|
| Displacement | 795 tons | Complement | 100 |
| Dimensions | | Armament | |
| length pp | 176' 6" | main | 1 3"/50 cal |
| oa | 184' 6" | close-range | 2 single 40mm Bofors |
| beam | 33' 0" | | 2 single 20 mm Oerlikon |
| draught | 9' 6" | A/S | 1 Hedgehog ATW mortar |
| Machinery | Diesel | | 2 depth charge rails |
| Shafts | 2 | | 4 throwers |
| BHP | 1,800 | Radar | Type SL, IFF |
| Speed | 16 kn | M/F D/F | Yes |

## 'KIL' CLASS—CLASS LIST

| Name | Pendant No | Builder | Building Time | Completion Date |
|---|---|---|---|---|
| Kilbirnie ex *BEC 1*, ex USN *PCE 827* | 5-01 | Pullman-Standard | 9m2d | 16.7.43 |
| Kilbride ex *BEC 2*, ex USN *PCE 828* | 5-02 | ,, | 8m15d | 2.8.43 |
| Kilchattan ex *BEC 3*, ex USN *PCE 829* | 5-03 | ,, | 8m30d | 18.8.43 |
| Kilchrenan ex *BEC 4*, ex USN *PCE 830* | 5-04 | ,, | 8m8d | 1.9.43. |
| Kildary ex *BEC 5*, ex USN *PCE 831* | 5-05 | ,, | 7m28d | 14.9.43 |

| | | | | |
|---|---|---|---|---|
| *Kildwick* | 5-06 | ,, | 7m21d | 28.9.4 |
| ex *BEC 6*, ex USN *PCE 832* | | | | |
| *Kilham* | 5-07 | ,, | 8m10d | 10.10. |
| ex *BEC 7*, ex USN *PCE 833* | | | | |
| *Kilkenzie* | 5-08 | ,, | 8m8d | 20.10. |
| ex *BEC 8*, ex USN *PCE 834* | | | | |
| *Kilhampton* | 5-09 | ,, | 7m2d | 1.11.4 |
| ex *BEC 9*, ex USN *PCE 835* | | | | |
| *Kilmacolm* | 5-10 | ,, | 8m9d | 8.11.4 |
| ex *BEC 10*, ex USN *PCE 836* | | | | |
| *Kilmarnock* | 5-11 | ,, | 7m5d | 28.11. |
| ex *BEC 11*, ex USN *PCE 837* | | | | |
| *Kilmartin* | 5-12 | ,, | 7m8d | 12.12. |
| ex *BEC 12*, ex USN *PCE 838* | | | | |
| *Kilmelford* | 5-13 | ,, | 7m7d | 20.12 |
| ex *BEC 13*, ex USN *PCE 839* | | | | |
| *Kilmington* | 5-14 | ,, | 7m4d | 28.12 |
| ex *BEC 14*, ex USN *PCE 840* | | | | |
| *Kilmore* | 5-15 | ,, | 7m12d | 15.1.4 |
| ex *BEC 15*, ex USN *PCE 841* | | | | |

*Kilchrenan* in the St Lawrence River, en route from Chicago to Bermuda, October 194 Note the two gaffs forward and aft of the mast, the boat derrick, and the two Bofors aft.

## 'KINGFISHER' CLASS CORVETTES
### 3 completed during war years

This was a small class of patrol vessel, classified later in the war as a corvette, designed and built largely before mass-production methods had become imperative.

They are mentioned in greater detail in the policy chapter; here, we are concerned only with the 3 ships (out of a total of 9) which were completed after (just after) the outbreak of war in 1939.

Further ships of this class were not built during the war, partly due to shortage of turbine blades, and partly due to their being outclassed by later designs. In the last year of the European war, from the Normandy invasion onwards, when some of the more sophisticated of the Western Approaches frigates came round to the south-east coast of England for the first time, and berthed near the 'Kingfisher' class, the design progress made during the war years seemed particularly noticeable and impressive. These little ships were, however, smart-looking, and followed pre-war naval practice, thus being quite distinctive from the 'Flower' class.

The 'Kingfisher' class were employed exclusively on the east coast of England, and were based at Harwich, where their main adversaries were the E-boats. Their speed—relatively high for an escort vessel before frigates appeared on the scene—made them useful on this duty.

Points to notice in the design detail of this class are the destroyer-type hull, the funnel similarly, the 4″ gun forward with only a half-shield, covered by mattress padding, the relatively light A/A and A/S equipment, and the covered bridge.

One of the three ships became a war loss.

### 'KINGFISHER' CLASS SPECIFICATION

| | | | |
|---|---|---|---|
| Displacement | 580 tons | Shafts | 2 |
| Dimensions | | SHP | 3,600 |
| length pp | 224′0″ | Speed | 20 kn |
| oa | 233′6″ | Oil fuel, tons | 160 |
| breadth | 26′6″ | Armament | 1 4″ BL Mk IX |
| draught | 7′3″ | | 3 single 20mm Oerlikons |
| Machinery | Parsons geared turbines | Complement | 60 |
| Boilers | 2 Admiralty 3-drum type | | |

### 'KINGFISHER' CLASS PRODUCTION

| **Built Pre-War** | 1935—1 | **Built during War** | 1939—3 |
|---|---|---|---|
| | 1936—3 | | |
| | 1937—1 | | |
| | 1938—1 | | |

## 'KINGFISHER' CLASS—CLASS LIST

| 1937 Programme | Pennant No | | Builder | Building Time | Completion Date |
|---|---|---|---|---|---|
| Guillemot | L 89 (later K 89) | | Denny | 14m6d | 28.10.39 |
| Pintail | L 21 | | Denny | 13m20d | 10.11.39 |
| Shearwater | L 39 | K 39 | White | 12m23d | 7.9.39 |

**War Loss**

| Pintail | 10.6.41 | Mined in River Humber |
|---|---|---|

*Shearwater,* showing early radar Type 286 at masthead, 4″ gun with only half shield, and light A/A armament. This is a 1941 photograph, and as she is wearing North Atlantic camouflage she was probably attached to Western Approaches at the time. *(Ministry of Defence)*

*Guillemot* in May 1942. In spite of the camouflage, this is probably a UK east coast photograph. She has an early Type 271 radar on the bridge, and now has two single Oerlikons aft, in addition to the quadruple 0.5″ machine gun. *(Ministry of Defence)*

## HMS *Mallard*

This was a patrol vessel, specially built for coastal convoy service, and later in the war re-classified as a corvette. She was built and engined by Stephen & Sons, of Glasgow, launched on 26th March 1936, and completed on 15th July 1936. Three ships of the class were completed after the outbreak of war, and thus come within the scope of this book.

In September 1939 the ship was allocated to Western Approaches Command, but a fortnight later was transferred to the Nore Command and based at Dover. In November 1939 she was a part of the Northern Patrol, Humber Force, still based at Dover, but in mid-month was allocated to the First A/S Striking Force, Western Approaches, based at Belfast. On 4th December 1939 she attacked an enemy submarine in Liverpool Bay, but without result.

The base of the First A/S Striking Force was transferred to Harwich in January 1940, under Nore Command, and *Mallard* took part in searches for enemy submarines in the southern North Sea and off Zeebrugge. On 6th March an enemy aircraft attacked her off Lowestoft, but was driven off, with smoke coming from its tail, by two of the *Mallard*'s guns. The *Mallard* was on anti-submarine patrol off Dunkirk on 28th May, during the evacuation of Allied troops. A few days later she was patrolling with the A/A cruiser *Calcutta* when the latter was bombed, but fortunately only slightly damaged. On the same day she stood by the hospital ship *Worthing,* which had been attacked on her way to the French coast.

In August 1940 *Mallard* sailed as escort to convoy FS 39 (Firth of Forth to Thames), the first of a long series of operations in the dangerous East Coast waters that continued without respite to the end of the war. Besides her primary duty of defending shipping against U-boat attacks, she had also to meet the challenge of enemy aircraft and high-speed E-boats. She was frequently called out to assist damaged merchant ships making their way to port, and to search for survivors from sunken ships. For example, in August 1940 she took off the entire crew of HMS *Wychwood,* which had been sunk by a mine off the Shipwash lightvessel; in September 1941, after SS *Pontfield* had been mined and had broken in two, she stood by with the armed trawler *Turquoise,* and escorted the stern portion of the ship to Yarmouth, in tow of tugs; in December, when SS *Welsh Prince* was mined, she landed the crew of 49 on the Humber. Similar operations took place in October 1942; on 7th, when a convoy had suffered considerable damage from E-boats, she located SS *Shearwater* north-east of Cromer and escorted the ship to Yarmouth; on 14th she stood by after a convoy was attacked off Cromer and two ships had been torpedoed.

She also sailed with minelayers, to cover them against enemy attacks. An operation to lay mines at the entrance to Ooste Gat, to hinder shipping at Flushing, planned for the night of 22nd/23rd September 1940, had to be abandoned at the first attempt, owing to repeated attacks by E-boats on *Mallard* and her sister escort *Sheldrake.* It was completed successfully at the second attempt later that night.

At the end of September 1940, *Mallard* was hit and seriously damaged by an enemy aircraft in the Thames Approaches and went to Sheerness for repairs. Determined air attacks continued to be made on the East Coast convoys, and in July 1941 *Mallard* reported that she had hit an aircraft with her 4" shells, but this could not be confirmed. While on patrol in August 1942 *Mallard* and *Hambledon* sighted some E-boats near Smith's Knoll; *Hambledon* engaged and attacked, causing them to scatter, and *Mallard* joined in a second engagement. On 12th May 1943 she shot down a Dornier off the Nore. A further incident occurred off Southwold in February 1944, when *Mallard* and *Shearwater* engaged 6 E-boats, and by their prompt action the two corvettes undoubtedly prevented the enemy from laying their mines.

After the Normandy landings in June 1944, *Mallard* was first transferred to the Nore Patrol, then to the North Sea Patrol, and back again to the Nore. She remained on patrols until June 1945, when she reduced to Reserve. She was in Reserve at Harwich until May 1947, when she was sold for scrapping.

*Blackthorn*, of the 'Tree' class, in July 1946. Note the depth charge rail ports at the stern and the tripod mast with radar on the bridge. She has been converted for danlaying. *(Ministry of Defence).*

## ADMIRALTY TRAWLERS
### 239 ships completed

To readers in North America it may seem surprising that we include Admiralty trawlers in this book. But our aim is to cover all significant, steel-hulled escort vessels designed and built during the war years.

To this end, we have arrived at a lower threshold of 150 feet overall length, plus steel hull, to merit inclusion. This covers, as it needs to do, the great PC class of the USN; equally, and happily, it covers no less than 9 out of the 11 classes of Admiralty trawlers.

Of the other two classes, the RNZN 'Castle' class falls just below the limit, and the RN 'Round Table' class likewise, though the latter class was probably only used for minesweeping. The two Portuguese-built classes also fall outside our scope, and the RN's 'Basset' class vessels were completed before the war.

*Maximum completions*

Again, it may seem surprising that with the 'Military' class, for instance, nearly as long as a 'Flower' class corvette, the trawlers were not shelved and more corvettes built in their place—limiting the overall number of classes, for simplicity, as was done in the United States.

The answer is, in fact, clear. In the UK, with its big distant-water fishing industry, a small number of shipyards specialised in trawlers, and indeed built little else except tugs. The best way of utilising their resources, and producing as many new escorts and minesweepers as possible, was seen to be to allow them to continue with a small number of approved commercial trawler types, which could be readily modified as escorts or minesweepers.

A rare shot of one of the first wartime class, *Ellesmere*, of the 'Lake' class. A 1942 shot, this shows the original whaler configuration, with the high bow, deckhouse built right up to the stern, and Oerlikon on top of it. The bridge has been built up for visibility, and Type 290 radar is, surprisingly, at the masthead. *(Tom Molland)*.

This was done, and the following totals show the results (in rough time sequence of construction by classes):

| Class | No. built | No. yards involved |
|-------|-----------|--------------------|
| 'Lake' | 6 | 1 |
| 'Tree' | 20 | 4 |
| 'Dance' | 20 | 4 |
| 'Shakespeare' | 12 | 4 |
| 'Hill' | 8 | 1 |
| 'Fish' | 10 | 1 |
| 'Military' | 9 | 1 |
| 'Isles' | 130 | 9 |

Apart from the 'Isles' class (at first known as the 'Western Isles' class), each was based on an existing commercial design; if few differences can be seen between them in some cases, this reflected the commercial types of trawlers being produced in 1939.

The 'Isles' class was the one real Admiralty design, evolved from the experimental pre-war 'Basset' class, and the large numbers built of this class speak for themselves.

Trawler production from these yards was carefully planned, so that when cutbacks came in the escort building programme late in 1943 there were very few cancellations of trawlers. The last 20 'Isles' class units were, however, completed as danlayers, in attendance on fleet minesweeping flotillas.

It has not proved reasonably possible to divide these trawlers in all cases into those employed wholly on A/S duties, and thus to exclude from this book those wholly employed on M/S duties. The following classes were probably only used on A/S work:

| | Commercial type equivalent |
|---|---|
| 'Lake' class | Smith's Dock Norwegian whaler |
| 'Hill' class | 'Barnett' class |
| 'Fish' class | 'Gulfoss' class |
| 'Military' class | 'Lady Madeleine' class |

But the others, and especially the 'Isles' class, which was described as an A/S-M/S class, were fitted for both duties, and were undoubtedly employed from time to time on both. In December 1940 the priority was to fit all Admiralty-sponsored trawlers for both A/S and M/S work, with trawlers having priority over corvettes for Oropesa equipment if this was short. In May 1945 we find that no less than 23 trawlers of these classes were operating in A/S Groups in the Mediterranean, and a further 17 from Freetown.

Of the 'Isles' class, 4 ships were transferred to the RNZN, 6 were lent to Portugal, and others after the war to Italy. 3 similar ships, named the 'Kiwi' class, were built to direct order for the RNZN, and are described under that section.

16 'Isles' class ships were ordered for the RN from Canadian shipyards, but 8 were retained by the RCN on loan on completion; these are described under the RCN section. Two of the units built in Canada and delivered to the RN were

frozen in at Quebec for the winter of 1942-43, showing another hazard in the shipbuilding programme! A significant number of this class were also programmed to be built in India; the results of this can be found under the RIN chapter.

All these trawler classes followed commercial fishing company practice of the time in their hull form, their scantlings, and their coal-fired boilers. They were very largely manned by ex-fishing trawler crews, engaged on a special form of agreement called T124X.

While they were not as fast as the corvettes or the sloops, their design fitted them well not only for coastal patrol and escort, but also for long-distance ocean convoy work. They could not chase submarines on the surface, and their Asdic (sonar) was of a simplified design, but they could keep going in all weathers, and so performed valuable service, not least in keeping the ships in a convoy closed up in station, and in carrying out rescue work—for which service some of them were specifically attached to ocean convoys.

For up-to-date equipment they inevitably found themselves at the back of the escort queue. Radar was non-existent in most of them until the later years of the war, when several types were fitted, as supply allowed. These included Types 286, 290, and 271. 4″ guns were usually only fitted in the 'Dance' class, and twin Lewis 0.303″ machine guns were the usual close-range weapons, until single manual Oerlikons were in more plentiful supply. Individual initiatives resulted in some improvements on this situation; close examination of the photograph of *Texada* will reveal a manual twin Oerlikon mounted aft! It should, however, be noted that the A/S trawlers carried a more impressive depth-charge lay-out than the 'Bangor' class fleet minesweepers.

Exceptionally, the 'Military' class can be seen in the photographs to present a very naval appearance, with a more solid, naval-type bridge than most of the 'Flower' class corvettes possessed; many of the later 'Isles' class units followed suit. The crew complement was only one-third that of a corvette.

A chart of comparative specifications of the war-built trawler classes is included, in rough chronological order; detailed comments are also included in the photograph captions, to illustrate the different trawler classes.

*Macbeth*, of the 'Shakespeare' class, in December 1942. She has full depth charge rails and three Oerlikons. Note the short bow. *(Ministry of Defence)*

*Inkpen,* of the 'Hill' class, in July 1942 on
commissioning. The sheer and tumble home
stand out clearly, and she has a 12 pounder
forward and three Oerlikons.
*(Ministry of Defence)*

*Guardsman* in August 1944. The largest trawler
class, she has a naval type bridge, two tripod
masts, and five Oerlikons. *(Ministry of Defence)*

## GERMAN U-BOATS SUNK BY WAR-BUILT TRAWLERS

| | | |
|---|---|---|
| *U 732* | 31.10.43 | *Imperialist* and others |
| *U 343* | 10.3.44 | *Mull* |

## ITALIAN SUBMARINE SUNK BY WAR-BUILT TRAWLERS

| | | |
|---|---|---|
| *Scira* | 10.8.42 | *Islay* |

## ADMIRALTY TRAWLER PRODUCTION

| | UK | CANADA | INDIA | UK for RNZN |
|---|---|---|---|---|
| 1939 1st half | | | | |
| 2nd half | 11 | | | |
| 1940 1st half | 16 | | | |
| 2nd half | 26 | | | |
| 1941 1st half | 29 | | | 1 |
| 2nd half | 30 | 6 | 2 | |
| 1942 1st half | 27 | 6 | 4 | |
| 2nd half | 16 | 10 | 4 | |
| 1943 1st half | 16 | | 1 | |
| 2nd half | 20 | | 3 | |
| 1944 1st half | 8 | | 2 | |
| 2nd half | 12 | | | |
| 1945 1st half | 7 | | | |
| TOTALS | 218 | 16 | 20 | 3 |

*CANCELLED SHIPS*     24

| | | | |
|---|---|---|---|
| TOTAL BUILT | UK | 228 | Transferred to RNZN (in addition) 4 |
| | Canada for RN | 16 | Transferred to Norway 4 |
| | India for RIN | 20 | Transferred to RCN 8 |
| | UK for RNZN | 3 | Transferred to Portugal 1 |
| | | | Cancelled ships (all in India) 24 |
| Retained by RN 217 | | | War Losses 27 |

## SHIPYARDS PRODUCING ADMIRALTY TRAWLERS

| | | | |
|---|---|---|---|
| Cook, Welton & Gemmell | 68 ships | Lewis | 9 |
| Cochrane | 56 | Ferguson | 7 |
| Goole | 15 | Hall, Russell | 6 |
| Smith's Dock | 15 | Fleming & Ferguson | 4 |
| Ardrossan | 11 | Crown | 2 |
| Robb | 10 | Hall | 2 |
| Inglis | 9 | Brown | 1 |

## ADMIRALTY TRAWLERS COMPARATIVE SPECIFICATIONS

|  | *Lake* | *Tree* | *Dance* | *Shakespeare* | *Isles* | *Kiwi* | *Hill* | *Fish* | *Military* |
|---|---|---|---|---|---|---|---|---|---|
| Displacement | 560 | 530 | 530 | 545 | 545 | 600 | 750 | 670 | 750 |
| Dimensions |  |  |  |  |  |  |  |  |  |
| length pp | 138½ | 150 | 150 | 150 | 150 | 150 | 166¼ | 146 | 175 |
| length oa | 147½ | 164 | 160½ | 164 | 164 | 156 | 181½ | 162 | 193 |
| breadth | 26½ | 27½ | 27½ | 27¾ | 27½ | 30 | 28 | 25½ | 30 |
| draught | 14¾ | 10½ | 10½ | 11 | 10½ | 13 | 12 | 12½ | 13 |

All main machinery was reciprocating, triple expansion
Shafts—all were single

|  | *Lake* | *Tree* | *Dance* | *Shakespeare* | *Isles* | *Kiwi* | *Hill* | *Fish* | *Military* |
|---|---|---|---|---|---|---|---|---|---|
| IHP | 1,400 | 850 | 850 | 950 | 850 | 1,000 | 970 | 700 | 1,000 |
| Speed knots | 13¾ | 11½ | 11½ | 12 | 12½ | 14 | 11 | 11 | 11 |
| Armament |  |  |  |  |  |  |  |  |  |
| main | 12pdr | 12pdr | 4″ | 12pdr | 12pdr | 4″ | 12pdr | 12pdr | 4″ |
| close-range |  |  |  |  |  |  |  |  |  |
| 20mm | 1 | 0 | 3 | 3 | 3 | 1 | 3 | 3 | 4 (2 twin, 2 single) |
| MG | 2 | 2 |  |  |  |  |  |  |  |
| Complement | 35 | 35 | 35 | 35 | 40 | 35 | 35 | 35 | 40 |

NOTE:
All the above are approximate, especially the armament, which varied between ships and at various periods of the war.

*Cotillion*, of the 'Dance' class, in June 1943. Note the 4″ gun forward, the only class to carry this, and the tripod mast stepped aft of the bridge with Type 290 radar atop. She gives a good solid-looking escort appearance. (*Ministry of Defence*)

## ADMIRALTY TRAWLERS—CLASS LISTS

| Name | Pendant No. | Job No. | Builder | Building Time | Completion Date |
|------|-------------|---------|---------|---------------|-----------------|
| **'LAKE' CLASS** | | | | | |
| **All 1939 Programme—Commercial Whalers Building for Norway** | | | | | |
| *Buttermere* ex *KOS XXV* | FY 205 | | Smith's Dock | 5m20d | 18.10.39 |
| *Ellesmere* ex *KOS XXIV* | FY 204 | | ,, | 5m10d | 9.10.39 |
| *Thirlmere* ex *KOS XXVI* | FY 206 | | ,, | 5m7d | 27.10.39 |
| *Ullswater* ex *KOS XXIX* | FY 252 | | ,, | 4m10d | 17.11.39 |
| *Wastwater* ex *Grasmere* ex *KOS XXVIII* | FY 239 | | ,, | 4m0d | 7.11.39 |
| *Windermere* ex *KOS XXVII* | FY 207 | | ,, | 5m19d | 8.11.39 |
| **'TREE' CLASS** | | | | | |
| **All 1939 Programme** | | | | | |
| *Acacia* | T 02 | | Ardrossan | 10m4d | 20.6.40 |
| *Almond* | T 14 | | ,, | | L22.5.40 |
| *Ash* | T 39 | | Cochrane | | L13.12.39 |
| *Bay* | T 77 | | ,, | 9m26d | 10.6.40 |
| *Birch* | T 93 | | Cook, Welton & Gemmell | 7m27d | 17.4.40 |
| *Blackthorn* | T 100 | | ,, | 9m6d | 31.5.40 |
| *Chestnut* | T 110 | | Goole | | L24.2.40 |
| *Deodar* | T 124 | | ,, | 10m13d | 1.7.40 |
| *Elm* | T 105 | | Inglis | 7m28d | 10.3.40 |
| *Fir* | T 129 | | ,, | 8m20d | 30.4.40 |
| *Hazel* | T 108 | | Robb | 6m24d | 9.3.40 |
| *Hickory* | T 116 | | ,, | | L24.2.40 |
| *Juniper* | T 113 | | Ferguson | | L15.12.39 |
| *Mangrove* | T 112 | | ,, | | L15.2.40 |
| *Olive* | T 126 | | Hall, Russell | 7m21d | 20.5.40 |
| *Pine* | T 101 | | ,, | | L25.3.40 |
| *Rowan* | T 119 | | Smith's Dock | 6m17d | 14.12.39 |
| *Walnut* | T 103 | | ,, | 6m15d | 31.12.39 |
| *Whitehorn* | T 127 | | ,, | 7m16d | 28.2.40 |
| *Wisteria* | T 111 | | ,, | 6m28d | 16.2.40 |

| Name | Pendant No. | Job No. | Builder | Building Time | Completion Date |
|------|-------------|---------|---------|---------------|-----------------|

**'DANCE' CLASS**

**All War Emergency Programme**

| Name | Pendant No. | Job No. | Builder | Building Time | Completion Date |
|------|-------------|---------|---------|---------------|-----------------|
| *Cotillion* | T 104 | J 1010 | Ardrossan | 15m14d | 8.8.41 |
| *Coverley* | T 106 | J 1011 | ,, | 13m17d | 8.8.41 |
| *Fandango* | T 107 | | Cochrane | 8m18d | 11.7.40 |
| *Foxtrot* | T 109 | | ,, | 10m6d | 30.8.40 |
| *Gavotte* | T 115 | | Cook, Welton & Gemmell | 8m16d | 24.8.40 |
| *Hornpipe* | T 120 | | ,, | 9m8d | 14.9.40 |
| *Mazurka* | T 30 | J 1016 | Ferguson | 9m18d | 8.1.41 |
| *Minuet* | T 131 | J 1017 | ,, | 13m11d | 10.6.41 |
| *Morris Dance* | T 117 | J 5005 | Goole | 9m20d | 7.10.40 |
| *Pirouette* | T 39 | | ,, | 8m12d | 30.8.40 |
| *Polka* | T 139 | J 1018 | Hall, Russell | 11m28d | 17.6.41 |
| *Quadrille* | T 133 | J 1019 | ,, | 12m25d | 14.7.41 |
| *Rumba* | T 122 | J 1014 | Inglis | 8m4d | 2.10.40 |
| *Sarabande* | T 125 | J 1015 | ,, | 9m12d | 17.12.40 |
| *Saltarello* | T 128 | J 1012 | Robb | 9m7d | 19.10.40 |
| *Sword Dance* | T 132 | J 1013 | ,, | | 16.1.41 |
| *Tango* | T 146 | J 4118 | Smith's Dock | 7m29d | 21.4.41 |
| *Two Step* ex *Tarantella* | T 142 | J 4122 | ,, | 8m2d | 9.5.41 |
| *Valse* | T 151 | J 4127 | ,, | 7m16d | 23.5.41 |
| *Valeta* | T 130 | J 4133 | ,, | 7m16d | 6.6.41 |

**'SHAKESPEARE' CLASS**

**All War Emergency Programme**

| Name | Pendant No. | Job No. | Builder | Building Time | Completion Date |
|------|-------------|---------|---------|---------------|-----------------|
| *Celia* | T 134 | J 2612 | Cochrane | 7m5d | 30.12.40 |
| *Coriolanus* | T 140 | J 2617 | ,, | | 20.5.41 |
| *Fluellen* | T 157 | J 2619 | ,, | | 21.5.41 |
| *Hamlet* | T 167 | J 2609 | Cook, Welton . & Gemmell | 9m5d | 28.11.40 |
| *Horatio* | T 153 | J 2611 | ,, | | 14.2.41 |
| *Juliet* | T 136 | J 2613 | ,, | 9m27d | 19.3.41 |
| *Laertes* | T 137 | J 2615 | ,, | | 10.4.41 |
| *Macbeth* | T 138 | J 2616 | Goole | 9m16d | 13.1.41 |
| *Ophelia* | T 05 | J 2618 | ,, | 7m25d | 25.11.40 |
| *Othello* | T 76 | J 1158 | Hall, Russell | 10m23d | 22.12.41 |

**'ISLES' CLASS. Previously 'WESTERN ISLES' Class**

**1940 Programme**

| Name | Pendant No. | Job No. | Builder | Building Time | Completion Date |
|------|-------------|---------|---------|---------------|-----------------|
| *Arran* | T 06 | | Cook, Welton & Gemmell | 9m7d | 1.5.40 |

| Name | Pendant No. | Job No. | Builder | Building Time | Completion Date |
|------|-------------|---------|---------|---------------|-----------------|
| *Balta* | T 50 | | ,, | 9m9d | 19.5.41 |
| *Bern* | T 294 | J 2671 | ,, | 9m16d | 9.10.42 |
| *Bressay* | T 214 | J 2661 | ,, | 7m13d | 10.5.42 |
| *Brora* | T 99 | J 2662 | ,, | | 11.6.41 |
| *Bruray* | T 236 | J 2673 | ,, | | 1.12.42 |
| *Burra* | T 158 | | Goole | 9m18d | 18.7.41 |
| *Bute* | T 168 | | ,, | 11m1d | 15.9.41 |
| *Canna* | T 161 | | Cochrane | | 3.3.41 |
| *Cava* | T 161 | | Cochrane | | 3.3.41 |
| *Coll* | T 207 | J 1412 | Ardrossan | 14m1d | 21.9.42 |
| *Copinsay* | T 147 | | Cochrane | 8m19d | 25.4.41 |
| *Cumbrae* | T 154 | | ,, | 8m15d | 17.5.41 |
| *Earraid* | T 297 | J 4292 | Crown | 11m21d | 11.5.42 |
| *Eday* | T 201 | J 2644 | Cochrane | 7m22d | 22.11.41 |
| *Egilsay* | T 215 | J 2663 | Cook, Welton & Gemmell | 19m28d | 28.5.43 |
| *Ensay* | T 216 | J 2665 | ,, | 7m21d | 15.6.42 |
| *Eriskay* | T 217 | J 1449 | Fleming & Ferguson | 11m8d | 28.10.42 |
| *Fara* | T 162 | | Cochrane | 9m23d | 28.6.41 |
| *Fetlar* | T 202 | J 2646 | ,, | 8m14d | 13.12.41 |
| *Fiaray* | T 238 | J 2666 | Goole | 7m21d | 27.9.42 |
| *Filla* | T 212 | J 4355 | Crown | 10m21d | 20.8.42 |
| *Flotta* | T 171 | | Cochrane | | 7.6.41 |
| *Foula* | T 203 | J 2648 | ,, | 8m18d | 3.1.42 |
| *Graemesay* | T 291 | J 1457 | Ardrossan | 17m15d | 15.6.43 |
| *Gruinard* | T 239 | J 4440 | Crown | 10m1d | 1.3.43 |
| *Hildasay* | T 173 | | Cook, Welton & Gemmell | 9m5d | 30. 9.41 |
| *Hoxa* | T 16 | | ,, | 9m28d | 18.7.41 |
| *Hoy* | T 114 | | ,, | 8m21d | 10.7.41 |
| *Hunda* | T 298 | J 1411 | Ferguson | 9m14d | 31.3.42 |
| *Inchcolm* | T 18 | | Cook, Welton & Gemmell | 9m5d | 25.7.41 |
| *Inchkeith* | T 155 | | Lewis | 10m8d | 24.10.41 |
| *Inchmarnock* | T 166 | | ,, | 9m0d | 28.11.41 |
| *Islay* | T 172 | | Smith's Dock | 6m29d | 17.6.41 |
| *Jura* | T 169 | J 1196 | Ardrossan | | L.22.11.41 |
| *Kerrera* | T 200 | J 1403 | Fleming & Ferguson | 7m17d | 31.10.41 |
| *Killegray* | T 174 | | Cook, Welton & Gemmell | 8m21d | 14.10.41 |
| *Kintyre* | T 165 | J 1197 | Ardrossan | 12m10d | 24.4.42 |
| *Mousa* | T 295 | J 2664 | Goole | 6m21d | 30.8.42 |
| *Mull* | T 110 | | Cook, Welton & Gemmell | 8m30d | 19.8.41 |

| Name | Pendant No. | Job No. | Builder | Building Time | Completion Date |
|------|-------------|---------|---------|---------------|-----------------|
| *Oxna* | T 296 | J 1455 | Inglis | 14m26d | 18.7. |
| *Pladda* | T 144 | | Cook, Welton & Gemmell | 7m21d | 19.8. |
| *Ronaldsay* | T 149 | | Cochrane | 9m7d | 14.7. |
| *Rousay* | T 210 | J 2650 | Goole | 8m4d | 17.4. |
| *Ruskholm* | T 211 | J 2652 | ,, | 8m27d | 10.5. |
| *Rysa* | T 164 | | Cochrane | | 9.8.4 |
| *St Kilda* | T 209 | J 1214 | Hall | 21m28d | 30.9. |
| *Sanda* | T 160 | | Goole | 10m11d | 3.11. |
| *Scalpay* | T 237 | J 2675 | Cook, Welton & Gemmell | 8m3d | 20.1 |
| *Scarba* | T 175 | | ,, | 8m20d | 25.1 |
| *Shapinsay* | T 176 | | Cochrane | 9m16d | 5.9.4 |
| *Sheppey* | T 292 | J 2697 | Cook, Welton & Gemmell | 9m10d | 18.9 |
| *Shiant* | T 170 | | Goole | 8m28d | 24.1 |
| *Skye* | T 163 | J 1201 | Robb | 11m30d | 22.7 |
| *Sluna* | T 177 | | Cochrane | 10m7d | 10.1 |
| *Staffa* | T 159 | J 1202 | Robb | 12m9d | 31.8 |
| *Stroma* | T 150 | | Hall, Russell | 9m18d | 22.1 |
| *Switha* | T 179 | J 1402 | Inglis | 12m15d | 15.6 |
| *Tiree* | T 180 | | Goole | 8m26d | 12.1 |
| *Trondra* | T 181 | | Lewis | 8m30d | 16.1 |
| *Unst* | T 213 | J 1437 | Ferguson | 9m15d | 31.7 |
| *Westray* | T 182 | J 1207 | Lewis | 8m25d | 2.3. |

**1941 Programme**

| Name | Pendant No. | Job No. | Builder | Building Time | Completion Date |
|------|-------------|---------|---------|---------------|-----------------|
| *Bardsey* | T 273 | J 1515 | Fleming & Ferguson | 8m16d | 15.9 |
| *Damsay* | T 208 | J 1410 | Brown | 12m14d | 3.9. |
| *Gweal* | T 246 | J 2662 | Cook, Welton & Gemmell | 7m22d | 3.11 |
| *Lundy* | T 272 | J 2683 | ,, | 7m8d | 15.1 |
| *Neave* | T 247 | J 2677 | ,, | 7m15d | 25.1 |
| *Orfasy* | T 204 | J 1209 | Hall | | L.1 |
| *Stronsay* | T 178 | J 1401 | Inglis | | L.4. |
| *Ulva* | T 248 | J 2679 | Cook, Welton & Gemmell | 8m0d | 15.1 |
| *Whalsay* | T 293 | J 2669 | ,, | | 28.8 |

**1942 Programme**

| Name | Pendant No. | Job No. | Builder | Building Time | Completion Date |
|------|-------------|---------|---------|---------------|-----------------|
| *Ailsa Craig* | T 377 | J 2725 | ,, | 5m4d | 24.1 |
| *Annet* | T 341 | J 2701 | ,, | 5m29d | 19.6 |
| *Benbecula* | T 379 | J 2727 | ,, | 5m23d | 13.1 |
| *Bryher* | T 350 | J 2703 | ,, | 6m23d | 20.7 |
| *Caldy* | T 359 | J 11811 | Lewis | 7m8d | 14.1 |

| Name | Pendant No. | Job No. | Builder | Building Time | Completion Date |
|------|-------------|---------|---------|---------------|-----------------|
| *Crowline* | T 380 | J 2729 | Cook, Welton & Gemmell | 5m12d | 28.1.44 |
| *Farne* | T 353 | J 2765 | ,, | 7m21d | 31.8.43 |
| *Flatholm* | T 354 | J 2707 | ,, | 5m25d | 20.8.43 |
| *Foulness* | T 342 | J 11806 | Lewis | 8m15d | 30.6.43 |
| *Gairsay* | T 290 | J 1456 | Ardrossan | | 2.9.43 |
| *Gilstone* | T 355 | J 2680 | Cochrane | 6m20d | 13.11.43 |
| *Gorregan* | T 387 | J 1532 | Ardrossan | 13m7d | 16.6.44 |
| *Grain* | T 360 | J 2682 | Cochrane | 6m23d | 16.11.43 |
| *Grassholm* | T 344 | J 11807 | Lewis | 8m24d | 17.8.43 |
| *Gulland* | T 365 | J 2717 | Cook, Welton & Gemmell | 5m30d | 30.10.43 |
| *Hayling* | T 271 | J 2681 | ,, | | L17.8.42 |
| *Kittern* | T 382 | J 2719 | ,, | 5m17d | 13.11.43 |
| *Lindisfarne* | T 361 | J 2711 | ,, | 6m6d | 17.9.43 |
| *Longa* | T 366 | J 2684 | Cochrane | 7m11d | 13.2.44 |
| *Mewstone* | T 374 | J 2721 | Cook, Welton & Gemmell | 5m18d | 26.11.43 |
| *Minalto* | T 362 | J 2713 | ,, | 5m16d | 30.9.43 |
| *Mincarlo* | T 388 | J 1533 | Ardrossan | 17m0d | 24.10.44 |
| *Oronsay* | T 375 | J 2686 | Cochrane | 6m2d | 16.2.44 |
| *Rosevean* | T 363 | J 2715 | Cook, Welton & Gemmell | 6m0d | 16.10.43 |
| *St Agnes* | T 352 | J 11808 | Lewis | 7m26d | 21.9.43 |
| *Skokholm* | T 376 | J 2723 | Cook, Welton & Gemmell | 5m19d | 10.12.43 |
| *Skomer* | T 381 | J 11809 | Lewis | 7m24d | 4.11.43 |
| *Steepholm* | T 356 | J 11810 | ,, | 7m24d | 1.12.43 |
| *Vatersay* | T 378 | J 2688 | Cochrane | 6m13d | 9.3.44 |
| **1943 Programme** | | | | | |
| *Biggal* | T 404 | J 1537 | Ferguson | | L4.12.44 |
| *Calvay* | T 383 | J 2731 | Cook, Welton & Gemmell | 4m26d | 16. 2.44 |
| *Colsay* | T 384 | J 2733 | ,, | | L15.12.43 |
| *Fuday* | T 385 | J 2735 | ,, | 5m24d | 24.3.44 |
| *Ganilly* | T 376 | J 2709 | ,, | | L.22.5.43 |
| *Hannaray* | T 389 | J 2739 | ,, | 6m0d | 3.5.44 |
| *Harris* ex *Gilsay* | T 386 | | ,, | 5m12d | 12.4.44 |
| *Hascosay* | T 390 | J 2741 | ,, | 6m6d | 26.5.44 |
| *Hellisay* | T 391 | J 2690 | Cochrane | 7m30d | 17.7.44 |
| *Hermetray* | T 392 | J 2692 | ,, | 9m4d | 22.8.44 |
| *Imersay* | T 422 | J.2694 | ,, | 7m26d | 8.12.44 |
| *Lingay* | T 423 | J 2696 | ,, | 8m24d | 6.1.45 |

| Name | Pendant No. | Job No. | Builder | Building Time | Completion Date |
|------|-------------|---------|---------|---------------|-----------------|
| *Orsay* | T 450 | J 2698 | ,, | | L1.1.45 |
| *Ronay* | T 429 | J 2700 | ,, | | L15.2.45 |
| *Sandray* | T 424 | J 2753 | Cook, Welton & Gemmell | 6m16d | 27.12.44 |
| *Scaravay* | T 425 | J 2755 | ,, | 6m27d | 14.1.45 |
| *Shillay* | T 426 | J 2757 | ,, | 6m4d | 30.1.45 |
| *Sursay* | T 427 | J 2759 | ,, | 6m4d | 26.2.45 |
| *Tahay* | T 452 | J 2761 | ,, | 6m30d | 23.3.45 |
| *Tocogay* | T 451 | J 2763 | Cook, Welton & Gemmell | | L7.2.45 |
| *Trodday* | T 431 | J 2765 | ,, | | L3.3.45 |
| *Vaceasay* | T 432 | J 2767 | ,, | | L17.3.45 |
| *Vallay* | T 434 | J 2769 | ,, | | L10.4.45 |
| *Wallasea* | T 345 | J 11803 | Robb | | 26. 7.43 |
| *Wiay* | T 441 | J 2771 | Cook, Welton & Gemmell | | L26.4.45 |

*Foulness* in September 1943. A good stern view of an 'Isles' class unit with full A/S capabilities. The size of depth charge pattern was limited, but she could pack a punch. *(Ministry of Defence)*

## BUILT IN CANADA FOR THE RN

| Name | Pendant No. | Job No. | Builder | Building Time | Completion Date |
|---|---|---|---|---|---|
| **1941 Programme** | | | | | |
| *Campobello* | T 278 | CN 292 | Collingwood | | L19.6.42 |
| *Dochet* | T 286 | CN 300 | G.T.Davie | 12m15d | 13.11.42 |
| *Flint* | T 287 | CN 301 | ,, | 13m13d | 11.12.42 |
| *Gateshead* | T 288 | CN 302 | ,, | 16m30d | 11.5.43 |
| *Herschell* | T 289 | CN 303 | ,, | 16m15d | 29.5.43 |
| *Porcher* | T 281 | CN 295 | Midland | 10m16d | 27.10.42 |
| *Prospect* | T 296 | CN 296 | ,, | 7m22d | 4.11.42 |
| *Texada* | T 283 | CN 297 | ,, | 6m20d | 17.11.42 |

## 'ISLES' CLASS completed as DANLAYERS

*Imersay Lingay Sandray Shillay Sursay Tahay Orsay Tocogay Ronay Troddday Vaceasay Vallay Wiay Hermetray Hellisay Hascosay Hannaray Fuday Gilsay*

| Name | Pendant No. | Job No. | Builder | Building Time | Completion Date |
|---|---|---|---|---|---|
| **'HILL' CLASS** | | | | | |
| **1940 Programme** | | | | | |
| *Birdlip* | T 218 | J 2645 | Cook, Welton & Gemmell | | 11.12.41 |
| *Butser* | T 219 | J 2647 | ,, | 9m8d | 8.1.42 |
| *Bredon* | T 223 | J 2655 | ,, | | 2.4.42 |
| *Duncton* | T 220 | J 2649 | ,, | 8m29d | 27.1.42 |
| *Dunkery* | T 224 | J 2657 | ,, | 9m13d | 23.4.42 |
| *Inkpen* | T 225 | J 2659 | ,, | 9m0d | 23.5.42 |
| *Portsdown* | T 221 | J 2658 | ,, | 9m15d | 19.2.42 |
| *Yestor* | T 222 | J 2653 | ,, | 9m5d | 12.3.42 |
| **'FISH' CLASS** | | | | | |
| **1940 Programme** | | | | | |
| *Bonito* | T 231 | J 2654 | Cochrane | 7m8d | 16.2.42 |
| *Grayling* | T 243 | J 2658 | ,, | 8m12d | 4.7.42 |
| *Mullet* | T 311 | J 2668 | ,, | 7m1d | 14.11.42 |
| *Whiting* | T 232 | J 2656 | ,, | 7m14d | 9.3.42 |
| **1942 Programme** | | | | | |
| *Bream* | T 306 | J 2672 | ,, | 6m30d | 30.3.43 |
| *Grilse* | T 368 | J 2776 | ,, | 6m6d | 29.6.43 |
| *Herring* | T 307 | J 2674 | ,, | | 10.4.43 |
| *Pollock* | T 347 | J 2678 | ,, | 6m23d | 20.7.43 |

## 'MILITARY' CLASS

### 1941 Programme

| | | | | | |
|---|---|---|---|---|---|
| *Grenadier* | T 334 | J 2685 | Cook, Welton & Gemmell | 7m27d | 10. 2.43 |
| *Lancer* | T 335 | J 2687 | ,, | 7m25d | 25.2.43 |
| *Sapper* | T 336 | J 2689 | ,, | 7m9d | 19.3.43 |

### 1942 Programme

| | | | | | |
|---|---|---|---|---|---|
| *Bombardier* | T 304 | | ,, | 7m6d | 19.5.43 |
| *Coldstreamer* | T 337 | J 2691 | ,, | 7m29d | 10.4.43 |
| *Fusilier* | T 305 | J 2693 | ,, | 7m19d | 30.4.43 |

### 1943 Programme

| | | | | | |
|---|---|---|---|---|---|
| *Guardsman* | T 393 | J 2743 | ,, | 7m25d | 22.8.44 |
| *Home Guard* | T 394 | J 2745 | ,, | 7m30d | 19.9.44 |
| *Royal Marine* | T 395 | J 2747 | ,, | 7m31d | 30.10.44 |

## WAR LOSSES

| | | | |
|---|---|---|---|
| *Ellesmere* | 'Lake' class | 24.2.45 | Torpedoed, U-boat, English Channel |
| *Ullswater* | ,, | 9.11.42 | Torpedoed, E-boat, English Channel |
| *Almond* | 'Tree' class | 2.2.41 | Mined off Falmouth |
| *Ash* | ,, | 5.6.41 | Mined, Thames Estuary |
| *Chestnut* | ,, | 22.4.41 | Mined, Thames Estuary |
| *Hickory* | ,, | 22.10.40 | Mined, English Channel |
| *Juniper* | ,, | 8.6.41 | Surface gunfire, Norway |
| *Pine* | ,, | 31.1.44 | Torpedoed, E-boat, English Channel |
| *Sword Dance* | 'Dance' class | 5.7.42 | Collision, Scotland |
| *Coriolanus* | 'Shakespeare' class | 5.5.45 | Mined, Adriatic |
| *Horatio* | ,, | 7.1.43 | Torpedoed, Mediterranean |
| *Laertes* | ,, | 25.7.42 | Torpedoed, U-boat, W Africa |
| *Brora* | 'Isles' class | 6.9.41 | N Scotland |
| *Campobello* | ,, | 16.6.43 | Foundered, N Atlantic |
| *Canna* | ,, | 5.12.42 | Lost by fire, W Africa |
| *Colsay* | ,, | 2.11.44 | Torpedoed, small battle unit, North Sea |
| *Flotta* | ,, | 6.11.41 | Shipwrecked, N Scotland |
| *Gairsay* | ,, | 3.8.44 | Hit by small battle unit, off Normandy |
| *Ganilly* | ,, | 5.7.44 | Mined, English Channel |
| *Hildasay* | ,, | 21.6.45 | Shipwrecked, Indian Ocean |
| *Jura* | ,, | 7.1.43 | Torpedoed, Mediterranean |
| *Orfasy* | ,, | 22.10.43 | Torpedoed, W Africa |
| *Rysa* | ,, | 8.12.43 | Mined, Mediterranean |
| *Stronsay* | ,, | 5.2.43 | Torpedoed, Mediterranean |
| *Wallasea* | ,, | 6.1.44 | Torpedoed, E-boat, English Channel |
| *Birdlip* | 'Hill' class | 13. 6.44 | Torpedoed, W Africa |
| *Bredon* | ,, | 8.2.43 | Torpedoed, N Atlantic |
| *Herring* | 'Fish' class | 22.4.43 | Collision, North Sea |

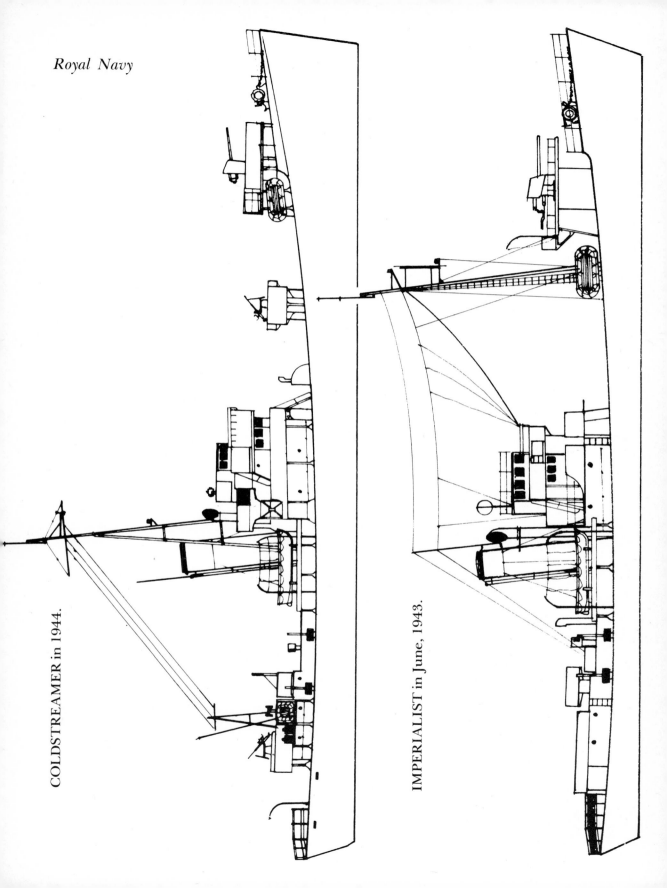

Royal Navy

COLDSTREAMER in 1944.

IMPERIALIST in June, 1943.

## FLEET MINESWEEPERS

Under this section are described the three classes of fleet minesweepers built during the war, and appearing in the RN lists.

In varying degrees, they carried at least a part of the same Asdic and depth-charge equipment as the corvettes, and they are therefore worthy of inclusion here. But while they have often been described as 'frequently used as escort vessels' there is no reliable record available of how far this actually happened.

It is probable that in the early years of the war fleet minesweepers were so used, though they do not appear to have been attached to the regular Western Approaches escort groups. On the other hand, we have seen how 'Flower' class corvettes, and then 'River' class frigates, were fitted with full minesweeping equipment, and it must be assumed that, if some interchange of duties did not actually take place, it was at least envisaged; certainly, 'Flower' class corvettes were employed as fleet minesweepers in the Mediterranean, as we have seen.

We can be sure that the increasing complexity and specialisation of both anti-submarine and minesweeping vessels as the war progressed meant that the ships in the later years were kept to the roles for which they had primarily been designed, and their crews trained, as the increasing flow of newly-completed escort vessels and minesweepers gave flexibility to the naval authorities.

Under the 'Flower' and 'River' classes we saw how the minesweeping equipment was actually removed from the ships by 1944; yet 'Algerine' class minesweepers were used occasionally as escorts right through to VJ-Day. The 18th Minesweeping Flotilla (*Ready*, SO) was so used in European waters in April 1945. We should remember, too, the gallant contribution made in June/July 1944 by the 'Catherine' class to the defence of the Normandy assault area by night, while minesweeping by day. No less than 3 ships of the class were lost in a period of a few days while in defence against German E-boats and small battle units. Further examples may be found in the 'Algerine' class flotillas used widely as inshore escorts and bombardment ships during the closing operations of the East Indies Fleet.

Two of the three fleet minesweeper classes at work—*Bramble* of the 'Algerine' class in the background, *Foam* of the US-built 'Catherine' class in foreground, with US-built escort carrier in the background. Note 3″ gunshield on *Foam*, and high-hung whaler amidships. *(Imperial War Museum)*

## 'BANGOR' CLASS FLEET MINESWEEPERS
### 54 built in UK, and 6 in Canada, for RN

This class of fleet minesweeper also warrants inclusion, though it could not rank with the 'Algerine' class as an anti-submarine vessel. Their respective qualities are more fully dealt with under the Canadian chapter, since many RCN units of this class were used only as escorts. They should be compared also with the anti-submarine versions of the RAN 'Bathurst' class A/S-M/S vessels.

The UK-built ships, and the 6 Canadian-built ships, followed a standard anti-submarine pattern. It will be seen from the photographs that their sweep deck, so much smaller than that of the 'Algerine' class, could not accommodate standard depth-charge rails as well as sweep gear, and there were 2 throwers, rather than 4. Charges were stowed singly in traps around the deck edge of the stern, and in small ready-use racks of 2 or 3 charges, and a 5-charge pattern was probably the most that they could produce.

This is an interesting comparison with the Admiralty trawlers, whose A/S capability was greater than that of the 'Bangor' class, though with less speed. The 'Bangor' class could not mount a Hedgehog forward, and their Asdic (sonar) equipment was usually of the simpler trawler type.

It is not known how far they were used as escort vessels, but as they date to the early years of the war, it is probable that they were often so used at that time. There is no record of their having been attached to the regular escort groups, except in the Mediterranean.

It will be noted that the builders of this class included experienced naval builders, not least in the turbine-engined ships. Four units were built in India for the RIN and are described under the RIN section.

Four more were ordered from Hong Kong, as shown in the class list. These orders were placed in September 1940: 2 were laid down in January 1941, and 2 in February, 1941. Their estimated completion dates were in September and October 1941 respectively; this was put back to May 1942, and they were lost on the stocks when Hong Kong fell.

*Eastbourne* in 1942. 12 pounder forward, quadruple 0.5″ aft, no radar, and a high mainmast.
*(Ministry of Defence)*

## 'BANGOR' CLASS SPECIFICATION

|                  | *Reciprocating* | *Turbine* | *Diesel* |
|------------------|-----------------|-----------|----------|
| Displacement     | 672             | 650       | 605      |
| Dimensions       |                 |           |          |
| length pp        | 171'6"          | 162'0"    | 153'6"   |
| oa               | 180'0"          | 174'0"    | 162'0"   |
| breadth          | 28'6"           | 28'6"     | 28'0"    |
| draught          | 9'6"            | 9'6"      | 9'0"     |
| Machinery        | Triple expansion Geared turbines 2 sets H&W | | |
| Boilers          | 2 Admiralty 3-drum type | |       |
| Shafts           | 2               | 2         | 2        |
| HP               | 2,400           | 2,400     | 2,000    |
| Speed            | 16 kn           | 16 kn     | 16 kn    |
| Oil Fuel         | 183 tons        |           |          |
| Complement       | 60              | 60        | 60       |

| Armament        | 1 12pdr 12 cwt |
|-----------------|----------------|
|                 | 2/3 single 20mm Oerlikons |
| A/S Armament    | 15-40 depth charges |
|                 | 2 or 4 double chutes |
|                 | 2 throwers |

## 'BANGOR' CLASS PRODUCTION

|                  | UK | CANADA (FOR UK) |
|------------------|----|-----------------|
| 1940 1st half    | 4  |                 |
| 2nd half         | 11 |                 |
| 1941 1st half    | 11 | 1               |
| 2nd half         | 10 | 5               |
| 1942 1st half    | 6  |                 |
| 2nd half         | 3  |                 |

TOTAL SHIPS BUILT IN UK ... 54

BUILT IN CANADA FOR RN ... 6

COMMISSIONED BY RN   5...

TRANSFERRED TO INDIA ... 9

CANCELLED SHIPS   0

*Lyme Regis* in August 1942, showing the crowded sweep deck and balloon fitting on main.
*(Ministry of Defence)*

## 'BANGOR' CLASS—CLASS LIST

| Name | Pendant No | Job No | Builder | Building Time | Completion Date |
|------|-----------|--------|---------|---------------|-----------------|
| **DIESEL-ENGINED** | | | | | |
| **1939 Programme** | | | | | |
| *Bangor* | J 00 | J 1020 | Harland & Wolff | 10m22d | 7.11.40 |
| *Blackpool* | J 27 | J 1021 | ,, | 16m14d | 3.2.41 |
| *Bridlington* | J 65 | J 1249 | Denny | 14m17d | 28.9.40 |
| *Bridport* | J 50 | J 1250 | ,, | 14m17d | 28.11.40 |
| **RECIPROCATING-ENGINED** | | | | | |
| **1939 Programme** | | | | | |
| *Blyth* | J 15 | J 4041 | Blyth | 14m18d | 29.3.41 |
| *Peterhead* | J 59 | J 4046 | ,, | 18m18d | 5.9.41 |
| *Rhyl* | J 36 | J 1032 | Lobnitz | 10m18d | 11.10.40 |
| *Romney* | J 77 | J 1033 | ,, | 9m13d | 12.12.40 |
| *Sidmouth* | J 47 | J 1030 | Robb | 13m23d | 4.8.41 |
| *Stornoway* | J 31 | J 1031 | ,, | 16m1d | 17.11.41 |
| **1939 War Emergency Programme** | | | | | |
| *Bude* | J 116 | J 1087 | Lobnitz | 10m9d | 12.2.41 |
| *Clydebank* | J 200 | J 1199 | ,, | | L20.11.41 |
| *Cromer* | J 128 | J 1088 | ,, | | 25.3.41 |
| *Eastbourne* | J 127 | J 1089 | ,, | 9m18d | 17.4.41 |
| *Felixstowe* | J 126 | J 1090 | ,, | | L15.1.41 |
| *Fraserburgh* | J 124 | J 1091 | ,, | 12m13d | 23.9.41 |
| *Lyme Regis* | J 197 | J 1200 | ,, | 7m21d | 30.4.42 |
| *Seaham* | J 123 | J 1092 | ,, | 14m5d | 19.12.41 |
| *Tilbury* | J 228 | | ,, | | 12.6.42 |
| **TURBINE-ENGINED** | | | | | |
| **1939 Programme** | | | | | |
| *Beaumaris* | J 07 | J 1024 | Ailsa | 20m7d | 28.8.41 |
| *Boston* | J 14 | J 1025 | ,, | 24m17d | 14.1.42 |
| *Dunbar* | J 53 | J 4060 | Blyth | 20m11d | 2.3.42 |
| *Ilfracombe* | J 95 | J 1028 | Hamilton | 12m7d | 18.10.40 |
| *Llandudno* | J 67 | J 1024 | ,, | 29m18d | 28.3.42 |
| *Polruan* | J 97 | J 1022 | Ailsa | 18m2d | 9.5.41 |
| *Rothesay* | J 19 | J 1026 | Hamilton | 20m20d | 19.6.41 |
| *Rye* | J 76 | J 1023 | Ailsa | 22m29d | 20.10.41 |
| *Tenby* | J 34 | J 1027 | Hamilton | 25m27d | 26.11.41 |
| **1939 War Emergency Programme** | | | | | |
| *Ardrossan* | J 131 | J 4126 | Blyth | 18m24d | 1.4.42 |
| *Bootle* | J 143 | J 1181 | Ailsa | 10m19d | 15.11.41 |

| Name | Pendant No. | Job No. | Builder | Building Time | Completion Date |
|------|-------------|---------|---------|---------------|-----------------|
| *Brixham* | J 105 | J 4132 | Blyth | | L21.10.41 |
| *Clacton* | J 151 | J 1182 | Ailsa | | 4.6.42 |
| *Cromarty* | J 09 | J 4053 | Blyth | | L24.2.41 |
| *Dornoch* | J 173 | J 1183 | Ailsa | | L4.2.42 |
| *Greenock* | J 182 | J 4227 | Blyth | | 20.10.42 |
| *Hartlepool* | J 155 | J 4231 | ,, | | 23.12.42 |
| *Harwich* | J 190 | J 1176 | Hamilton | | L17.2.42 |
| *Hythe* | J 194 | J 1180 | Ailsa | | 15.10.41 |
| *Middlesbrough* | J 164 | J 1177 | Hamilton | | L2.5.42 |
| *Newhaven* | J 199 | J 1178 | ,, | | L29.7.42 |
| *Padstow* | J 180 | J 1179 | ,, | | 5.2.42 |
| *Poole* | J 147 | J 1481 | Stephen | 14m14d | 8.10.4 |
| *Sunderland* later *Lyme Regis* | J 319 | J 1482 | ,, | | 5.6.42 |
| *Whitehaven* | J 121 | J 6004 | Philip | 15m21d | 14.11.41 |
| *Worthing* | J 72 | J 6063 | ,, | 16m4d | 20.3.4 |

## TRANSFERRED TO INDIA

| *Clydebank* | became | *Orissa* | 1942 |
|-------------|--------|----------|------|
| *Lyme Regis* | became | *Rajputana* | 1942 |
| *Tilbury* | became | *Konkan* | 1942 |
| *Greenock* | became | *Baluchistan* | 1942 |
| *Hartlepool* | became | *Kathiawar* | 1942 |
| *Harwich* | became | *Khyber* | 1942 |
| *Middlesbrough* | became | *Kumaon* | 1942 |
| *Newhaven* | became | *Carnatic* | 1942 |
| *Padstow* | became | *Rohilkand* | 1942 |

*Seaham*, showing few depth charges stowed in traps on sweep deck, single pom pom aft, conning position on the upper bridge. Probably a late 1943 photo. *(Ministry of Defence)*

## BUILT IN CANADA FOR THE RN
### RECIPROCATING-ENGINED

| Name | Pendant No | Job No | Builder | Building Time | Completion Date |
|------|-----------|--------|---------|---------------|-----------------|
| **1940 Programme** | | | | | |
| Fort York | J 119 | | Dufferin | 12m1d | 27.2.42 |
| Parrsborough | J 117 | | ,, | 14m8d | 27.5.42 |
| Qualicum | J 138 | | ,, | 13m5d | 13.5.42 |
| Shippigan | J 212 | | ,, | 13m29d | 17.6.42 |
| Tadoussac | J 220 | | ,, | 11m11d | 28.3.42 |
| Wedgeport | J 139 | | ,, | 11m25d | 21. 4.42 |

## BUILT IN CANADA FOR THE RN, LOANED TO RCN ON COMPLETION

Bayfield, Canso, Caraquet, Guysborough, Ingonish
Details are included in the RCN section.

## BUILT IN INDIA FOR THE RIN

Bihar, Deccan, Malwa, Oudh
Details are included under the RIN section.

## WAR LOSSES

| | |
|---|---|
| Cromer | 9.11.42 |
| Felixstowe | 18.12.43 |
| Peterhead | 8.6.44 |
| Clacton | 31.12.43 |
| Cromarty | 23.10.43 |
| Hythe | 11.10.43 |

POOLE in 1944.

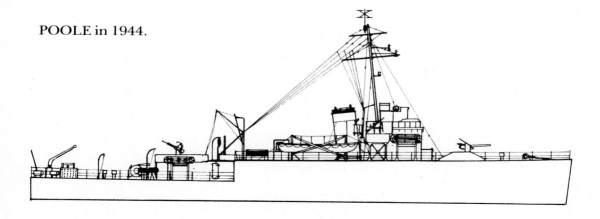

▲ *Rowena* on commissioning, September 1944.
She shows the excellent sweep deck lay-out, the
clear after gundeck, with two twin Oerlikons,
and the large upper deck, easily
accommodating the 27 foot whaler.
*(Ministry of Defence)*

*Stormcloud* in March 1944. The 4″ has rocket
flare rails attached, the Type SA derrick is on
the foredeck forward of the bridge, main
Oerlikons in the bridge wings, and the big
rangefinder, for minesweeping, aft.
*(Ministry of Defence)* ▼

## 'ALGERINE' CLASS FLEET MINESWEEPERS
### 48 ships built in UK, 49 ships built in Canada

This class of fleet minesweeper can clearly be seen to have evolved from the pre-war sloops. When these diverged into the anti-submarine 'Black Swan' class and the minesweeping 'Halcyon' class, the specialised equipment for each purpose changed their silhouettes. But the resemblance of the 'Algerine' class to the pre-war ships is very striking.

Their covered main deck, running right aft as far as the beginning of the sweep deck, gave good accommodation to their crews, and good shelter to the standby minesweeping parties; even in wartime, part both of the forecastle and of the sweep deck were planked in wood, and a 16 foot sailing dinghy was provided, in gravity davits of its own.

The bridge was fully a naval design, and the tripod mast equally so. The Type 271 radar fitted happily onto the roomy after section of the bridge, and the Admiralty-capped funnel gave these ships a touch of class.

The sweep deck aft was roomy, and the flat triangular-shaped stern, good for handling heavy sweep gear, also gave ample space for full depth-charge rails, and 4 throwers and racks forward of them. The big minesweeping winch, and the equally bulky LL cable reel forward of it, obviated any further on-deck stowage of depth charges, but otherwise the 'Algerine' class units could rank with the corvettes and frigates for depth-charge equipment.

Forward, no Hedgehog was ever fitted in these ships, but they had a vintage single 4″ gun, and either 2 single Oerlikons or 2 power-mounted twins, forward, and usually 2 twin mountings on the cleanly-designed gundeck over the LL cable reel. It is worth noting that the 'Algerine' class ships seemed to obtain their supply of these excellent twin Oerlikons ahead of other escort classes!

A number of ships were fitted with 2, or even 4, single 40mm Bofors, in place of the Oerlikon mountings, in 1944/45, before joining the East Indies or British Pacific Fleets. In the East Indies Fleet, in particular, although active minesweeping was required ahead of the assault forces, the ships of this class were employed regularly as convoy or landing craft escorts.

The Asdic equipment, in a full frigate-type compartment, was slung on the forward edge of the bridge, and ranked in every way with that of the regular convoy escort vessels.

These ships had twin screws and rudders for manoeuvrability while minesweeping in restricted waters, which made them very handy ships, and their wartime complement was higher than that of the 'Flower' class corvettes.

In the Canadian section it will be found that the 'Algerine' class units built in that country and retained by the RCN were completed as escorts, without minesweeping equipment, and they were used only as senior officers' ships of close escort groups in the western part of the Atlantic, operating from Halifax.

After the war, but perhaps with the requirements of the British Pacific Fleet in mind, *Fierce* and *Niger,* were completed respectively as Senior Officer's Ship of M/S Flotillas, and M/S Headquarters Ship. *Pluto,* as tender to *Vernon,* the torpedo school, also worked as an A/S experimental ship at one stage, and her 4″ gun forward was replaced with a single Squid mortar; if this is compared with the proposals to fit Squid mortars in other escort classes in 1944/45, as described elsewhere, it will be seen how drastic and bulky a conversion would have been entailed to accommodate the weight and thrust of the big mortar, together with its supply of heavy missiles.

*Cheerful,* showing the deck lay-out of the class. The 4″ is prominent, but there is no Hedgehog; the bridge compares well with the corvettes, as does the tripod mast with its two yards. *(Ministry of Defence)*

## 'ALGERINE' CLASS PRODUCTION

| | UK | CANADA | |
|---|---|---|---|
| 1941 2nd half | 1 | | TOTAL BUILT |
| 1942 1st half | 6 | | UK   48 |
| 2nd half | 9 | 8 | CANADA-DIRECT RN ORDER   24 |
| 1943 1st half | 10 | 5 | EX USN ORDERS   9 |
| 2nd half | 8 | 10 | EX RCN ORDERS   16 |
| 1944 1st half | 7 | 11 | GRAND TOTAL   97 |
| 2nd half | 4 | 14 | TOTAL RETAINED |
| 1945 1st half | 2 | 1 | OR COMMISSIONED BY RN   97 |
| 2nd half | 1 | | TRANSFERRED TO OTHER NAVIES   0 |
| | | | CANCELLED SHIPS UK   6 |
| | | | CANADA   6 |
| | | | TOTAL   12 |

## 'ALGERINE' CLASS SPECIFICATION

| | |
|---|---|
| Displacement | 950/990 tons |
| Dimensions | |
|    length pp | 212' 6" |
|        oa | 235' 0" |
|    breadth | 35' 6" |
|    draught | 10' 6" |
| Machinery | geared turbines or reciprocating |
| Shafts | 2 |
| IHP | 2,000 |
| Speed | 16.5 kn |
| Complement | 104/138 |
| Armament | |
|    main | 1 single 4" Mark Vc |
|    close-range | 2 twin 20mm Oerlikons Mk XII |
| | 2 single 20mm Oerlikons |
| | (4 ships in 1945 had 4 twins, no singles, and 13 ships had 4 singles only. Ships for Far East in 1945 received 4 single 40mm Bofors in lieu of all Oerlikons) |
| A/S Armament | 4 depth charge throwers, 2 rails 92 depth charges |
| Radar | Type 271 (later Type 268), 242, 253 |
| Boats | 1 25' motor boat |
| | 1 27' whaler |
| | 1 16' sailing dinghy |

## 'ALGERINE' CLASS—CLASS LIST

| Name | Pendant No | Job No | Builder | Building Time | Completion Date |
|---|---|---|---|---|---|
| **UK-BUILT—RECIPROCATING-ENGINED** | | | | | |
| **1940 Programme** | | | | | |
| *Cockatrice* | J 229 | J 1448 | Fleming & Ferguson | 15m12d | 10.4.43 |
| *Rattlesnake* | J 297 | J 1516 | Lobnitz | 12m17d | 23.2.43 |
| *Waterwitch* | J 304 | J 1517 | ,, | 11m12d | 6.8.42 |
| **1941 Programme** | | | | | |
| *Fly* | J 306 | J 1451 | Lobnitz | 12m14d | 20.10.43 |
| *Hound* | J 307 | J 1452 | ,, | 12m9d | 11.12.42 |
| *Hydra* | J 275 | J 1458 | ,, | | 12.2.43 |
| *Larne* | J 274 | J 1523 | ,, | 10m14d | 22.11.43 |
| *Lennox* | J 276 | J 1524 | ,, | 10m15d | 18.1.44 |
| *Orestes* | J 277 | J 1459 | ,, | 12m14d | 10.4.43 |
| *Pelorus* | J 291 | J 1518 | ,, | 11m30d | 7.10.43 |
| **1942 Programme** | | | | | |
| *Bramble* | J 11 | J 1840 | Lobnitz | | 28.6.45 |
| *Disdain* | J 442 | J 1841 | ,, | | 5.9.45 |
| *Fierce* | J 453 | J 1842 | | | 28.11.45 |
| *Rowena* | J 384 | J 1543 | ,, | 10m8d | 6.9.44 |
| *Stormcloud* | J 367 | J 1540 | ,, | 10m24d | 28.4.44 |
| *Sylvia* | J 382 | J 1541 | ,, | 10m12d | 17.5.44 |
| *Tanganyika* | J 383 | J 1542 | ,, | 9m16d | 7.7.44 |
| *Wave* | J 385 | J 1544 | ,, | 8m28d | 14.11.44 |
| *Welcome* | J 386 | J 1545 | ,, | 8m17d | 20.1.45 |
| **UK-BUILT—TURBINE-ENGINED** | | | | | |
| **1940 Programme** | | | | | |
| *Alarm* | J 140 | J 3312 | Harland & Wolff | | L5.2.42 |
| *Albacore* | J 101 | J 3324 | ,, | 10m23d | 16.6.42 |
| *Acute* | J 106 | J 3330 | ,, | 12m16d | 30.7.42 |
| *Algerine* | J 213 | J 3304 | ,, | | 12.9.42 |
| *Cadmus* | J 230 | J 3352 | ,, | 13m19d | 9.9.42 |
| *Circe* | J 214 | J 3374 | ,, | 14m26d | 16.10.42 |
| *Espiègle* | J 216 | J 3398 | ,, | 9m24d | 1.12.42 |
| *Fantome* | J 224 | J 3306 | ,, | 10m3d | 19.11.42 |
| *Loyalty*<br>  ex *Rattler* | J 217 | J 3332 | ,, | | 1.4.43 |
| *Mutine* | J 227 | J 3310 | ,, | 15m1d | 26.2.43 |
| *Onyx* | J 221 | J 3326 | ,, | 16m2d | 26.2.43 |
| *Ready* | J 223 | J 3358 | ,, | 13m6d | 21.5.43 |
| *Rinaldo* | J 225 | J 3376 | ,, | 20m26d | 18.6.44 |

| *Rosario* | J 219 | J 3392 | ,, | 9m17d | 9.7.43 |
|---|---|---|---|---|---|
| *Spanker* | J 226 | J 3308 | ,, | 10m28d | 20.8.43 |
| *Vestal* | J 215 | J 3354 | ,, | 7m3d | 24.8.43 |

**1941 Programme**

| *Brave* | J 305 | J 4374 | Blyth | 15m10d | 3.8.43 |
|---|---|---|---|---|---|
| *Fancy* | J 308 | J 4428 | ,, | 15m30d | 21.11.43 |
| *Pickle* | J 293 | J 3301 | Harland & Wolff | 10m4d | 15.10.43 |
| *Pincher* | J 294 | J 3359 | ,, | 11m1d | 12.11.43 |
| *Plucky* | J 295 | J 3313 | ,, | 9m20d | 10.12.43 |

**1942 Programme**

| *Chameleon* | J 387 | J 3371 | Harland & Wolff | 12m25d | 14. 9.44 |
|---|---|---|---|---|---|
| *Cheerful* | J 388 | J 3365 | ,, | 13m24d | 13.10.44 |
| *Hare* | J 389 | J 3357 | ,, | 11m13d | 10.11.44 |
| *Jewel* | J 390 | J 3339 | ,, | 15m5d | 20. 7.44 |
| *Liberty* | J 391 | J 3321 | ,, | 13m21d | 18. 1.45 |

## CANADIAN-BUILT—RECIPROCATING-ENGINED

## DIRECT ORDERS BY RN

**1943 Programme**

| *Jaseur* | J 428 | CN 664 | Redfern | 10m0d | 27.10.44 |
|---|---|---|---|---|---|
| *Laertes* | J 335 | CN 666 | ,, | 11m20d | 9.12.44 |
| *Maenad* | J 335 | CN 665 | ,, | 8m15d | 16.11.44 |
| *Magicienne* | J 436 | CN 667 | ,, | | L24.6.44 |
| *Mameluke* | J 437 | CN 668 | ,, | 12m3d | 19.3.45 |
| *Mandate* | J 438 | CN 669 | ,, | 11m21d | 22.3.45 |
| *Marvel* | J 443 | CN 670 | ,, | | L30.8.44 |
| *Michael* | J 444 | CN 671 | ,, | | L20.9.44 |
| *Minstrel* | J 445 | CN 672 | ,, | | L5.10.44 |
| *Myrmidon* | J 454 | CN 673 | ,, | | L21.10.44 |
| *Mystic* | J 455 | CN 674 | ,, | | L11.11.44 |
| *Nerissa* | J 456 | CN 675 | ,, | 10m20d | 18.1.45 |
| *Orcadia* | J 462 | CN 681 | Port Arthur | | L8. 8.44 |
| *Ossory* | J 463 | CN 682 | ,, | | L3.10.44 |
| *Pluto* | J 446 | CN 683 | ,, | | L21.10.44 |
| *Polaris* | J 447 | CN 664 | ,, | | L3.12.45 |
| *Pyrrhus* | J 448 | CN 685 | ,, | | L19.5.45 |
| *Romola* | J 449 | CN 686 | ,, | | L.19.5.45 |
| *Rosamund* | J 439 | CN 687 | ,, | | L20.12.44 |

## ORDERED FOR RCN, TRANSFERRED TO RN BEFORE COMPLETION.

| *Courier* <br> ex RCN *Arnprior* | J 349 | CN 544 | Redfern | 11m23d | 22.12.43 |
|---|---|---|---|---|---|
| *Coquette* <br> ex RCN *Bowmanville* | J 350 | CN 543 | ,, | 11m4d | 13.7.44 |
| *Felicity* <br> ex RCN *Coppercliff* | J 369 | CN 545 | ,, | 10m18d | 10.8.44 |

| Name | Pendant No. | Job No. | Builder | Building Time | Completion Date |
|------|-------------|---------|---------|---------------|-----------------|
| Providence<br>ex RCN *Forest Hill* | J 325 | CN 500 | ,, | 12m28d | 15.5.44 |
| Lysander<br>ex RCN *Hespeler* | J 379 | CN 552 | ·Port Arthur | 17m18d | 21.1.44 |
| Golden Fleece<br>ex RCN *Humberstone* | J 376 | CN 547 | Redfern | 10m4d | 29.8.44 |
| Prompt<br>ex RCN *Huntsville* | J 378 | CN 549 | ,, | 10m2d | 27.9.44 |
| Mariner<br>ex RCN *Kincardine* | J 380 | CN 553 | Port Arthur | 24m20d | 16.9.44 |
| Serene<br>ex RCN *Leaside* | J 354 | CN 553 | Redfern | 13m26d | 14.9.44 |
| Regulus<br>ex RCN *Longbranch* | J 327 | CN 501 | Toronto | | L18.?.45 |
| Marmion<br>ex RCN *Orangeville* | J 381 | CN 554 | Port Arthur | | L15.6.44 |
| Lioness<br>ex RCN *Petrolia* | J 377 | CN 548 | Redfern | 13m0d | 11.12.44 |
| Seabear<br>ex RCN *St Thomas* | J 333 | CN 502 | Redfern | 11m10d | 22.6.44 |
| Skipjack<br>ex RN *Scorpion*, ex RCN *Solebay* | J 300 | CN 330 | ,, | 17m10d | 29.4.44 |
| Flying Fish<br>ex RCN *Tillsonburg* | J 370 | CN 546 | ,, | 11m15d | 14.10.44 |
| Mary Rose<br>ex RCN *Toronto* | J 360 | CN 498 | ,, | 13m27d | 24.4.44 |
| Moon<br>ex RCN *Mimico* | J 329 | CN 547 | ,, | 15m10d | 6.7.44 |

NOTE

These ships were transferred to the RN in exchange for the same number of UK-built 'Castle' class corvettes. The RCN names above were in most cases used for the equivalent UK-built ships, but the RN equivalent names will be found in more than this one section of the Canadian-built 'Algerine' class.

## BUILT IN CANADA FOR THE USN, TRANSFERRED TO THE RN UNDER LEND-LEASE

### 1941 Programme

| Name | Pendant No. | Job No. | Builder | Building Time | Completion Date |
|------|-------------|---------|---------|---------------|-----------------|
| Antares<br>ex USN *AM 325* | J 282 | CN 319 | Toronto | 18m28d | 23.8.44 |
| Arcturus<br>ex USN *AM 326* | J 283 | CN 320 | ,, | 19m30d | 23.10.44 |
| Aries<br>ex USN *AM 327* | J 284 | CN 321 | ,, | 12m1d | 17.7.44 |
| Clinton<br>ex USN *AM 328* | J 286 | CN 322 | ,, | 16m15d | 25.8.44 |

| Name | Pendant No. | Job No. | Builder | Building Time | Completion Date |
|---|---|---|---|---|---|
| *Friendship*<br>ex USN *AM 329* | J 398 | CN 323 | ,, | 16m23d | 15.9.43 |
| *Gozo*<br>ex USN *AM 330* | J 287 | CN 324 | ,, | 13m23d | 9.9.43 |
| *Lightfoot*<br>ex USN *AM 331* | J 288 | CN 325 | ,, | 13m30d | 19.10.43 |
| *Melita*<br>ex USN *AM 332* | J 289 | CN 326 | ,, | 15m18d | 20.12.43 |
| *Octavia*<br>ex USN *AM 333* | J 290 | CN 327 | Toronto | 17m4d | 24.2.44 |
| *Persian*<br>ex USN *AM 334* | J 347 | CN 328 | Redfern | 13m4d | 12.11.43 |
| *Postillion*<br>ex USN *AM 335* | J 286 | CN 329 | ,, | 12m7d | 25.11.43 |
| *Thisbe*<br>ex USN *AM 337* | J 302 | CN 351 | ,, | 17m25d | 8.6.44 |
| *Truelove*<br>ex USN *AM 338* | J 303 | CN 332 | ,, | 14m27d | 3.4.44 |
| *Welfare*<br>ex USN *AM 339* | J 356 | CN 333 | ,, | 13m24d | 4.4.44 |

## CANCELLED SHIPS

| Name | Pendant No. | Job No. | Builder | Cancelled |
|---|---|---|---|---|
| *Fireball* | J 464 | J 1843 | Lobnitz | 10.44 |
| *Gabriel* | J 465 | J 1844 | ,, | 10.44 |
| *Happy Return* | J 466 | J 1845 | ,, | 10.44 |
| *Larne* | | | Simons | 3.42 |
| *Lennox* | | | ,, | 3.42 |
| *Lysander* | | J 3307 | Harland &<br>Wolff | 5.43 |
| *Mariner* | | J 3315 | ,, | 5.43 |
| *Marmion* | | J 3323 | ,, | 5.43 |
| *Mary Rose* | | J 3331' | ,, | 5.43 |
| *Moon* | | J 3355 | ,, | 5.43 |
| *Providence* | | J 3377 | ,, | 5.43 |
| *Regulus* | | J 3309 | ,, | 5.43 |
| *Rowena* | | J 1525 | ,, | 5.43 |
| *Seabear* | | J 5647 | ,, | 5.43 |
| *Serene* | | J 4658 | ,, | 5.43 |

NOTE

The Harland & Wolff ships were cancelled, in order to build a greater number of
'Loch' class frigates in the time available. Some of the cancelled names were later
re-used for other ships of the class.

| Name | Pendant No. | Job No. |
|------|-------------|---------|
| **Canadian Orders** | | |
| *Niger* | J 442 | CN 676 |
| *Nicator* | J 457 | CN 677 |
| *Nonpareil* | J 459 | CN 678 |
| *Nox* | J 460 | CN 679 |
| *Odin* | J 461 | CN 680 |
| *Styx* | J 440 | CN 688 |

## WAR LOSSES

**Sunk**

| | | |
|------|------|------|
| *Algerine* | 15.11.42 | Torpedoed by Italian submarine *Asciaglia* off Bougie |
| *Loyalty* | 22.8.44 | Torpedoed by *U480* in English Channel |
| *Regulus* | 12.1.45 | Mined in Corfu Channel |
| *Squirrel* | 24.7.45 | Mined off Siam |
| *Vestal* | 26.7.45 | Bombed by Japanese aircraft off Siam |

**CTL**

| | | |
|------|------|------|
| *Alarm* | 2.1.43 | Bombed by German aircraft at Bone |
| *Fantome* | 20.5,43 | Mined in Mediterranean |
| *Hydra* | 10.11.44 | Mined off Ostend |
| *Prompt* | 9.5.45 | Mined off Ostend |

*Laertes* in 1952. This was the final war configuration for this class, as for the Far East in 1945: four single 40mm Bofors, no Oerlikons, Type 268 radar, with Type 291 still at the masthead. *(Ministry of Defence)*

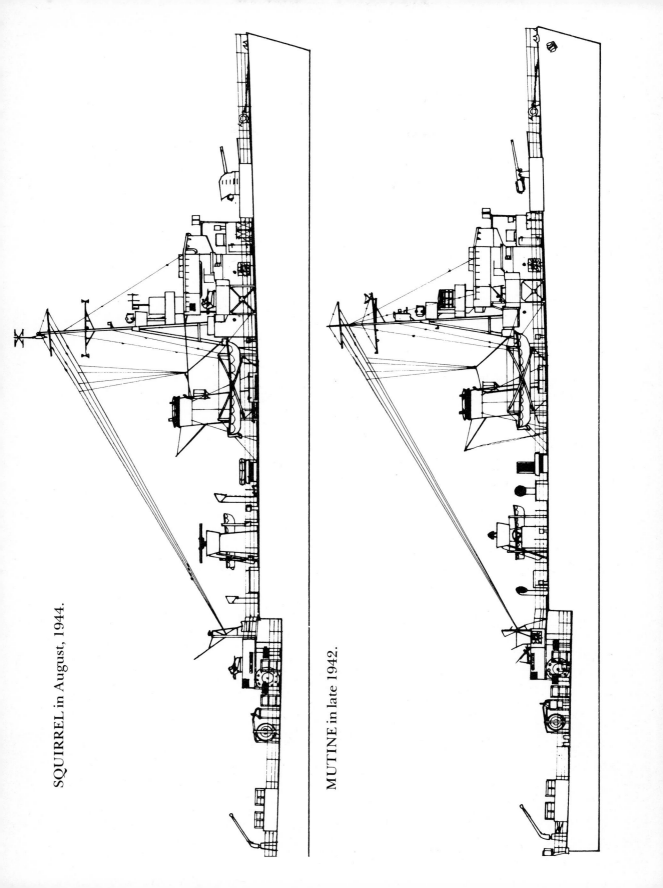

SQUIRREL in August, 1944.

MUTINE in late 1942.

*Gazelle* in March 1944. On the mast is the Type SL radar aerial, and on the yard the TBS aerial to starboard, and the IFF transpondor Type ABK to port. The Asdic compartment slung on the bridgefront is prominent, with the large searchlight above. There is a Hedgehog aft of the forward 3″ gun. *(Ministry of Defence)*

*Steadfast* in 1944. The 3″ gun forward has a light, 12 pounder-type gunshield; there are only depth charge traps on the sweep deck, no rails. The boat was handled in the ordinary ships by the large boom or derrick, seen behind the forefunnel. *(Ministry of Defence)*

## 'CATHERINE' CLASS FLEET MINESWEEPERS
### 22 ships built in USA

These were US designed and built, of the USN 'Raven' class, and transferred on completion in 1943/44 to the RN, being first classed as British American Minesweepers, and then BAM.

Their design was very different from the RN's 'Algerine' class, their nearest equivalent. The forecastle deck stopped abreast the foremast, compared with the built-up deck carried aft to the sweep deck in the 'Algerine' class, and it is interesting to see how the US design used platforms and guntubs aft of that point to provide the necessary positions for the motor whaleboat and the close-range armament. The after funnel also gives these ships a distinctive appearance, together with the solidly-plated forecastle-head and turtleback forecastle deck—a unique feature among all the war-built classes.

RN alterations, approved for all ships, and carried out to some, included a spray shield on the 3"/50 calibre gun forward, as in the 'Captain' class frigates, and a standard RN 27 foot whaler, rigged high in gravity davits on the port side. The pennant numbers did not follow standard RN practice in their painting application, probably due to the shipbuilders being so far from RN operating areas.

These ships did sterling work in RN service. Their employment on real escort duty was probably limited to their being attached to the close escort of aneastbound transatlantic convoy, on completion of working-up in Bermuda; but during the Normandy assault they were employed not only as sweepers but as part of the outer defence ring round the invasion beaches at night. In a period of three days no less than 3 ships of the class were lost on this duty, a fourth becoming a constructive total loss through similar causes two weeks later. German small battle units were the cause of these losses.

The original number of ships of this class requested by the RN in 1942 was 80. This was cut to 48, and then to 34; but the USN retained 212 of these latter ships, and turned over to the RN instead 9 'Algerine' class ships it had ordered in Canada—a sensible rationalisation of the position. The class list shows that there was some switching of ships between the USN and the RN while they were under construction, and also the interesting RN names allocated to the units retained by the USN. The 22 RN ships of the class were ordered on 6th December 1941, and it should particularly be noted in the USN chapter on this class how many units were ordered before the USA entered the war.

The photographs show that there were two different depth-charge lay-outs on the sweep decks of this class. Early units were restricted to individual charges, stowed in traps round the edge of the stern, as in the RN's 'Bangor' class fleet minesweepers; but later units carried 2 full depth-charge rails, and throwers, though the room for manoeuvre of the sweep deck and depth-charge crews must have been severely restricted, compared with the RN's 'Algerine' class. Variations in radar types, and in the number of single 20mm Oerlikons carried, may also be noted. Equipment throughout in these ships, at the time of delivery to the RN, was, of course, entirely American.

## 'CATHERINE' CLASS - CLASS LIST

| Name | Pendant No | Builder | Building Time | Completion Date |
|------|-----------|---------|---------------|-----------------|
| Catherine<br>ex BAM 9 | J 12 | Associated | 14m28d | 8.7.43 |
| Cato<br>ex BAM 10 | J 16 | ,, | | 28.7.43 |
| Pique<br>ex RN *Celebrity,*<br>ex BAM 11 | J 23 | ,, | 14m28d | 30.8.43 |
| Chamois<br>ex BAM 12 | J 28 | ,, | 16m19d | 22.10.43 |
| Chance<br>ex BAM 13 | J 340 | ,, | 16m2d | 22.10.43 |
| Combatant<br>ex BAM 14 | J 341 | ,, | 16m11d | 22.10.43 |
| Cynthia<br>ex BAM 15 | J 345 | ,, | 14m2d | 7.12.43 |
| Elfreda<br>ex BAM 16,<br>ex USN *Overseer* | J 402 | ,, | 15m15d | 22.12.43 |
| Gazelle<br>ex BAM 17 | J 342 | Savannah | 12m25d | 27.7.43 |
| Gorgon<br>ex BAM 18 | J 346 | ,, | 12m23d | 28.8.43 |
| Grecian<br>ex BAM 19 | J 352 | ,, | 12m21d | 22.9.43 |
| Magic<br>ex BAM 20 | J 400 | ,, | | 25.10.43 |
| Pylades<br>ex BAM 21 | J 401 | ,, | | 24.11.43 |
| Fairy<br>ex BAM 25 | J 403 | Lake Washington | 15m26d | 24.3.44 |
| Florizel<br>ex BAM 26 | J 404 | ,, | 14m18d | 14.4.44 |
| Foam<br>ex BAM 27 | J 405 | ,, | 15m2d | 28.4.44 |
| Frolic<br>ex BAM 28 | J 406 | ,, | 14m13d | 18.5.44 |
| Jasper<br>ex BAM 29 | J 407 | ,, | 17m6d | 12.8.44 |
| Steadfast<br>ex BAM 31 | J 375 | Gulf | 15m23d | 29.9.43 |
| Tattoo<br>ex BAM 32 | J 374 | ,, | 16m20d | 26.10.43 |
| Strenuous<br>ex USN *Vital,* AM 129 | J 338 | ,, | 16m18d | 18.5.43 |

| *Tourmaline* | J 339 | ,, | | 17m7d | 6.7.43 |
|---|---|---|---|---|---|
| ex USN *Usage* AM 130 | | | | | |

## SHIPS OF THE CLASS ALLOCATED TO RN, BUT RETAINED BY USN

| USN | *Champion* | AM 314 | ex RN | *Akbar* | BAM 1 |
|---|---|---|---|---|---|
| USN | *Chief* | AM 315 | ex RN | *Alice* | BAM 2 |
| USN | *Competent* | AM 316 | ex RN | *Amelia* | BAM 3 |
| USN | *Defense* | AM 317 | ex RN | *Amity* | BAM 4 |
| USN | *Devastator* | AM 318 | ex RN | *Augusta* | BAM 5 |
| USN | *Gladiator* | AM 319 | ex RN | *Blaze* | BAM 6 |
| USN | *Impeccable* | AM 320 | ex RN | *Brutus* | BAM 7 |
| USN | *Speer* | AM 322 | ex RN | *Errant* | BAM 22 |
| USN | *Triumph* | AM 323 | ex RN | *Espoir* | BAM 23 |
| USN | *Vigilance* | AM 324 | ex RN | *Exploit* | BAM 24 |
| USN | *Ardent* | AM 340 | ex RN | *Buffalo* | BAM 8 |
| USN | *Dextrous* | AM 341 | ex RN | *Sepoy* | BAM 30 |

*Grecian* in February 1946. Note the marked contrast in this quarter view with the 'Algerine' class; the whaleboat is slung high, the after funnel takes up some room, and the sweep deck appears more crowded. *(Ministry of Defence)*

## 'CATHERINE' CLASS SPECIFICATION

| | | | |
|---|---|---|---|
| Displacement | 890 tons | BHP | 2,400 |
| Dimensions | | Speed | 18 kn |
| length pp | 215' 0" | Complement | 109 |
| oa | 220' 6" | Armament | |
| breadth | 32' 0" | main | 1 3"/50 cal |
| draught | 9' 6" | close-range | 6 single 20 mm Oerlikons |
| Machinery | 2 sets diesels | Radar | Type SL, 242, IFF |
| Shafts | 2 | | |

## 'CATHERINE' CLASS PRODUCTION

1942 2nd half   8          1943 1st half   14

*Bramble* on trials in the Clyde, early in 1945. She has the standard end-of-the-war camouflage pattern, full naval motor boat, and the four depth charge throwers on the sweep deck are clear. *(Ministry of Defence)*

## UK ESCORT SHIPBUILDERS

Ailsa Shipbuilding Co Ltd, Troon.
Ardrossan Dockyard Co Ltd, Ardrossan.
Barclay, Curle & Co. Ltd, Glasgow.
Blyth Shipbuilding & Drydock Co Ltd, Blyth.
John Brown & Co Ltd, Clydebank.
Burntisland Shipbuilding Co Ltd, Forth.
Caledon Shipbuilding & Engineering Co Ltd, Dundee.
Cammell Laird & Co Ltd, Birkenhead.
Chatham Dockyard, Chatham.
Cochrane & Sons Ltd, Selby.
Cook, Welton & Gemmell Ltd, Beverley.
John Crown & Sons Ltd, Sunderland.
William Denny & Brothers Ltd, Dumbarton.
Fairfield Shipbuilding & Engineering Co Ltd, Govan.
Ferguson Brothers Ltd, Port Glasgow.
Fleming & Ferguson Ltd, Paisley.
Furness Shipbuilding Co Ltd, Haverton Hill.
Goole Shipbuilding & Repair Co Ltd, Goole.
Grangemouth Dockyard Co Ltd, Grangemouth.
Hall & Co Ltd, Aberdeen.
Hall, Russell & Co Ltd, Aberdeen.
William Hamilton & Co Ltd, Port Glasgow.
Harland & Wolff Ltd, Belfast.
Hawthorn Leslie & Co Ltd, Hepburn-on-Tyne.
Charles Hill & Sons Ltd, Bristol.
A.&J. Inglis Ltd, Glasgow.
John Lewis & Sons Ltd, Aberdeen.
Lobnitz & Co Ltd, Renfrew.
Philip & Son Ltd, Dartmouth.
William Pickersgill & Sons Ltd, Sunderland.
Portsmouth Dockyard, Portsmouth.
Henry Robb Ltd, Leith
Scott's Shipbuilding & Engineering Co Ltd, Greenock.
William Simons & Co Ltd, Renfrew.
Smith's Dock Co Ltd, South Bank on Tees.
Alexander Stephen & Sons Ltd, Govan.
Swan Hunter & Wigham Richardson Ltd, Wallsend-on-Tyne.
John I. Thornycroft Ltd, Woolston.
Vickers Armstrongs Ltd, Barrow in Furness.
Vickers Armstrongs Ltd, Newcastle.
J. Samuel White & Co Ltd, Cowes.
Yarrow & Co Ltd, Scotstoun.

*Arvida* coming alongside the RCN destroyer
*Ottawa*, November 1943. The forefoot is lifting
clear of the swell, early radar at the masthead,
even at this date. Short forecastle, trawler boats,
and minesweeping gear aft.
*(Public Archives of Canada)*

*Woodstock,* of the Revised 'Flower' class, off
Halifax in December 1943. Note the increased
flare and sheer, the rather better bridge
structure, and the four extra Oerlikon
platforms aft. *(Public Archives of Canada)*

## ROYAL CANADIAN NAVY

### PROPOSED DISTRIBUTION OF RCN SHIPS, ON COMPLETION OF 1940/41 BUILDING PROGRAMME

|  | 'Flower' | 'Bangor' |
|---|---|---|
| **Atlantic Coast Command** | | |
| Western Local Escort Force | 26 | 4 |
| Halifax Force | 0 | 11 |
| Halifax A/S Training | 1 | 5 |
| Sydney | 0 | 8 |
| Shelburne | 0 | 4 |
| Gaspe | 0 | 2 |
| | | |
| **Newfoundland Command** | | |
| **Mid-Ocean Escort Force** | | |
| American Groups   A1-A5 | 20 | |
| Canadian Groups   C1-C4 | 20 | 0 |
| Newfoundland Force | 0 | 4 |
| St Johns Defence Force | 0 | 4 |
| | | |
| **Pacific Coast Command** | 7 | 6 |
| **Under Training in UK** | 3 | |
| Totals | 77 | 48 |

*Shediac* off the British Columbian coast, December 1944. The Hedgehog is clear, to starboard and aft of the 4″ gun. The depth charge thrower stalks are stowed against the after deckhouse, and she has two-tone camouflage. *(Public Archives of Canada)*

## RCN SHIPS IN COMMISSION, WITH COMMAND ALLOCATION

**1.1.40**                         Nil (war-built)

**1.1.41**
11 'Flower'

**1.1.42**
                       69 'Flower', 27 'Bangor'

**1.1.43**
                       80 'Flower', 54 'Bangor', 8 'Isles'

**1.1.44**
                       87 'Flower, 16 'River', 53 'Bangor', 5 'Algerine', 7 'Isles'

| | | |
|---|---|---|
| Londonderry | 6th EG | 3 'River', 7 'Flower' |
| | C1 | 1 'River', 6 'Flower' |
| | C2 | 1 'River', 7 'Flower' |
| | C3 | 1 'River', 7 'Flower' |
| | C4 | 7 'Flower' |
| | C5 | 1 'River', 8 'Flower' |
| WLEF | | 40 'Flower', 15 'Bangor' |
| Halifax Force | | 12 'Bangor', 7 'Isles' |
| Sydney Force | | 6 'Bangor' |
| Quebec Force | | 3 'Flower' |
| Newfoundland Force | | 13 'Bangor' |
| Training Duties (working-up) | | 9 'River', 5 'Algerine' |
| Esquimalt (Pacific) | | 2 'Flower', 5 'Bangor' |

*Chilliwack* at Halifax, June 1942. Type 286 radar at masthead, merchant-type bridge, heavily padded, and single Oerlikon aft in the bandstand. *(Public Archives of Canada)*

**1.1.45**

|  | Londonderry | 6th EG | 2 'Loch', 7 'River' |
|---|---|---|---|
|  |  | 9th | 1 'Loch', 6 'River' |
|  |  | 16th | 6 'River' |
|  |  | 25th | 5 'River' |
|  |  | 27th | 5 'River' |
|  |  | C1 | 2 'River', 6 'Flower' |
|  |  | C2 | 2 'River', 4 'Flower' |
|  |  | C3 | 2 'River', 5 'Flower' |
|  |  | C4 | 2 'River', 6 'Flower' |
|  |  | C5 | 2 'River', 5 'Flower' |
|  |  | C6 | 2 'River', 4 'Flower' |
|  |  | C7 | 2 'River', 5 'Flower' |
|  |  | C8 | 2 'River', 4 'Flower' |
|  | Sheerness |  | 5 'Flower' |
|  | Plymouth |  | 8 'Flower' |
|  | UK WATERS, Minesweeping |  | 14 'Bangor' |
| CANADA | WLEF | W1 Group | 1 'Algerine', 4 'Bangor' |
|  |  | W2 | 1 'Algerine', 4 'Bangor' |
|  |  | W3 | 2 'Algerine', 3 'Bangor' |
|  |  | W4 | 1 'Algerine', 5 'Bangor' |
|  |  | W5 | 1 'Algerine', 4 'Bangor' |
|  |  | W6 | 1 'Algerine', 4 'Bangor' |
|  |  | W7 | 1 'Algerine', 4 'Bangor' |
|  |  | W8 | 1 'Algerine', 4 'Bangor' |
|  | Halifax Force |  | 6 'Flower', 8 'Bangor' |
|  | Sydney Force |  | 11 'Bangor' |
|  | Quebec Force |  | 1 'Bangor' |
|  | Newfoundland Force |  | 8 'Bangor' |
|  | Training (working-up) |  | 3 'Flower' |
|  | Unallocated |  | 2 'Algerine', 15 'Flower' |
|  |  |  | 16 'River', 3 'Bangor' |
|  | Esquimalt |  | 4 'Flower', 4 'Bangor' |
|  | Prince Rupert |  | 3 'Bangor' |

**7.5.45**

|  | Londonderry | 6th EG | 2 'Loch', 5 'River' |
|---|---|---|---|
|  |  | 9th | 1 'Loch', 5 'River' |
|  |  | 16th | 5 'River' |
|  |  | 25th | 5 'River' |
|  |  | 26th | 4 'River' |
|  |  | 27th | 6 'River' |
|  |  | 28th | 5 'River' |
|  |  | C1 | 2 'River', 5 'Flower', 1 'Castle' |
|  |  | C2 | 2 'River', 5 'Flower' |

|                              |                  |                                |
|------------------------------|------------------|--------------------------------|
|                              | C3               | 2 'River', 4 'Flower'          |
|                              | C4               | 2 'River', 5 'Flower',         |
|                              |                  | 2 'Castle'                     |
|                              | C5               | 2 'River'                      |
|                              | C6               | 2 'River', 4 'Flower'          |
|                              | C7               | 1 'River', 6 'Flower'          |
|                              | C8               | 2 'River', 4 'Flower',         |
|                              |                  | 2 'Castle'                     |
|                              | C9               | 2 'River', 4 'Flower'          |

| UK WATERS, Minesweeping Escorts |                  | 14 'Bangor'                  |
|                              |                  | 13 'Flower'                    |

*CANADA*

| WLEF                         | W1 Group         | 1 'Algerine', 4 'Flower'       |
|                              | W2               | 2 'Algerine', 3 'Flower'       |
|                              | W3               | 2 'Algerine', 3 'Flower'       |
|                              | W4               | 1 'Algerine', 6 'Flower'       |
|                              | W5               | 1 'Algerine', 4 'Flower'       |
|                              | W6               | 2 'Algerine', 3 'Flower'       |
|                              | W7               | 1 'Algerine', 5 'Flower'       |
|                              | W8               | 3 'Algerine', 3 'Flower'       |

| Halifax Force                |                  | 10 'Flower', 12 'Bangor', 7 'Isles' |
| Sydney Force                 |                  | 3 'Flower', 5 'Bangor'         |
| Newfoundland Force           |                  | 9 'Bangor'                     |
| Training                     |                  | 3 'Flower'                     |
| Unallocated                  |                  | 5 'Flower', 5 'Bangor', 8 'River' |
| Esquimalt                    |                  | 4 'Flower', 4 'Bangor'         |
| Prince Rupert                |                  | 3 'Bangor'                     |
| Pacific Coast Unallocated    |                  | 1 'River', 1 'Bangor'          |

|            | 1.1.41 | 1.1.42 | 1.1.43 | 1.1.44 | 1.1.45 | 7.5.45 |
|------------|--------|--------|--------|--------|--------|--------|
| 'Bangor'   |        | 27     | 54     | 53     | 52     | 52     |
| 'Flower'   | 11     | 69     | 80     | 87     | 112    | 109    |
| 'Algerine' |        |        |        | 5      | 11     | 12     |
| 'River'    |        |        |        | 16     | 61     | 61     |
| 'Loch'     |        |        |        |        | 3      | 3      |
| 'Castle'   |        |        |        |        |        | 5      |
| 'Isles'    |        |        | 8      | 7      | 7      | 7      |

## GROWTH OF RCN OPERATIONAL ESCORTS

|                 | 30.6.42 | 1.1.44 | 1.1.45 | 7.5.45 |
|-----------------|---------|--------|--------|--------|
| **Mid-Ocean Escort** |         |        |        |        |
| 'Flower'        | 34      | 42     | 39     | 50     |
| 'River'         |         | 7      | 45     | 52     |
| 'Loch'          |         |        | 3      | 3      |
| 'Castle'        |         |        |        | 5      |

## CANADA

**Western Local Escort Force**

| | | | | |
|---|---|---|---|---|
| 'Flower | 27 | 38 | 32 | 32 |
| 'Bangor' | | 15 | | |
| 'Algerine' | | | 8 | 12 |

**Other East Coastal Local Forces**

| | | | | |
|---|---|---|---|---|
| 'Flower' | 4 | 3 | 6 | 13 |
| 'Bangor' | 18 | 31 | 28 | 26 |

*Trillium* and others in the stream at Halifax in 1942. Note the tall mainmast with gaff, short forecastle, no radar but crow's nest, and minesweeping davits aft. *(Public Archives of Canada)*

**Pacific Coast**

| | | | | |
|---|---|---|---|---|
| 'Flower' | | 2 | 4 | 4 |
| 'Bangor' | 6 | 5 | 7 | 8 |

**TRAINING** (including working-up)

| | | | | |
|---|---|---|---|---|
| 'River' | | 9 | | |
| 'Flower' | 5 | | 3 | 3 |
| 'Bangor' | 5 | | | |
| 'Algerine' | | 5 | | |

**UNALLOCATED**

| | | | | |
|---|---|---|---|---|
| 'River' | | | 18 | 9 |
| 'Flower' | | | 15 | 8 |
| 'Algerine' | | | 2 | |
| 'Bangor' | | | | |

**UK WATERS** (M/S)

| | | | | |
|---|---|---|---|---|
| 'Bangor' | | | 14 | 14 |
| Totals | 99 | 157 | 223 | 239 |

## RCN TOTAL OF ESCORTS BUILT, 1939-45

| | 'Flower' Class | Modified 'Flower' Class | 'Castle' Class | 'Algerine' Class | 'Bangor' Class | 'River' Class | 'Isles' Class | Totals |
|---|---|---|---|---|---|---|---|---|
| TOTAL BUILT IN CANADA | 79 | 42 | 0 | 53 | 60 | 70 | 16 | 320 |
| Retained by RCN | 79+ | 27 | 0 | 12 | 54 | 60 | 8 | 240 |
| Received from UK | 0 | 4 | 12 | 0 | 0 | 7 | 0 | 26 |
| TOTAL RCN SHIPS OF CLASS | 79 | 31 | 12 | 12 | 54 | 67 | 8 | 266 |
| Built for USN | 0 | 8 | 0 | 0 | 0 | 2 | 0 | 10 |
| Built for RN | 0 | 7 | 0 | 41 | 6 | 8 | 8 | 70 |
| Cancelled | 0 | 6 | 36 | 6 | 0 | 52 | 0 | 102+? |

NOTES:
1. 'Flower' class—includes 11 ships building in Canada on Admiralty account, and transferred to the RCN on completion.
2. 'Algerine' class—see breakdown of transfers of orders in class chapter.
3. 'Castle' class—ships cancelled were on RN account.
4. 'Bangor' class—includes 6 ships building in Canada on Admiralty account, and transferred to the RCN on completion.
5. 'Isles' class—all 16 were originally for Admiralty account, but 8 were loaned by the RN to the RCN on completion.

*Kamsack* in March 1944. She has by now both Types 271 and 291 radar, a full whaler, but few Oerlikons aft. Note the cartoon on the 4" gunshield. *(Ministry of Defence)*

## NOTES ON RCN OPERATIONAL GROWTH

5.41  RCN took over Newfoundland Station from RN for Mid-Ocean Escort. By end year, 11 destroyers and 43 corvettes operating from St John's.

9.41  First 'Bangor' arrived at Halifax.

6.42  St Lawrence Escort Groups now made up of 1 corvette, 2 'Bangor' class, and 1 armed yacht. 17 'Flower' class lent to RN for Mediterranean operations, 6 to USN for the Carribean, and 2 to USN for Alaska.

1.43  4 Canadian escort groups detached from mid-ocean escort work for North African operations.

3.43  6 'Flower' class, *Oakville, Fredericton, Halifax, Lethbridge, Snowberry* and *Sudbury,* running tanker convoys from New York to Trinidad for USN. New construction frigates on West Coast manned entirely from East Coast resources, to retain North Atlantic experience.

4.43  First Canadian Support Group ready—4 'Flower' class corvettes, *Algoma, Kitchener, Port Arthur* and *Woodstock,* plus two 'River' class frigates, at first *Nene* and *Tweed* on loan from RN, then RCN ships later.
6 'Bangor' units transferred from Pacific to Atlantic (Halifax).

5.43  Mid-ocean escort force grows to 5 groups, each of 2 or 3 frigates, plus 5 or 6 corvettes. 2 'Flower' class ships, *Dawson* and *Drumheller,* participated in heavy fighting during US investment of Attu Island, in the Outer Aleutians.

7.43  Mines laid in a 6-7 mile radius off Halifax by German U-boats. Pacific Coast escort maintenance requirements stepped up, presumably with a view to the Far East war.

4.44  'Bangor' class units take lion's share of escort work in Canadian coastal waters.

5.45  Of 42 escort groups based on UK Western Approaches ports, 16 were RCN, numbering 97 ships.

7.51  18 'Bangor' class units refitted as escorts, with Hedgehog, and 40mm and 20mm A/A guns.

*Midland* off No 3 Jetty, Halifax, April 1944. The full Asdic compartment has been buil[t]
to the front of the bridge, and the extended hull is clear. She was a unit of the local W [2]
escort group. *(Public Archives of Canada)*

## RCN 'FLOWER' CLASS CORVETTES
### 79 ships built in Canada

We have seen the evolution of this class described in the RN section in some detail. All the Canadian ships of the class followed very closely, in basic design, and in alterations and additions, on the RN ships, so that we will not repeat this detail here.

But the number of ships built in Canada, and operated by the RCN, were so impressive that they receive full photographic coverage in this chapter.

|  | Original 'Flower' | Modified 'Flower' |
|---|---|---|
| Built in Canada | 79 | 42 |
| Built in UK | 135 | 10 |
| Operated by RCN | 79 | 31 |
| Operated by RN | 102 | 11 |

This shipbuilding effort by Canada was one of the most remarkable aspects of the escort building programmes of the Allies during the war years. Indeed, starting with the two 'Flower' classes, and continuing through the later classes, Canada established herself as by far the leading builder and operator of escort vessels in the Commonwealth, other than the RN itself.

The same major improvements, to fit the 'Flower' class for mid-ocean escort work, were carried out to RCN ships as in the RN—lengthened forecastle deck, improved bridges, added Hedgehog, and, in some, increased sheer and flare built in forward. Smith's Dock sent over the drawings for the latter to Canada in June 1941.

In fact, the forecastle was lengthened in all Canadian ships of the class, except *Alberni, Chicoutimi, Levis, Louisburg, Nanaimo, Rosthern, Shawinigan, The Pas, Spikenard, Weyburn* and *Windflower*. The ships on loan from the RN were also altered in this way, except the two mentioned above.

The first 54 ships had Scotch marine boilers, built to Smith's Dock drawings, while the last 25 had water-tube boilers.

The first 54 ships, too, were fitted with full wire minesweeping gear, including Mark II Oropesa sweeps, winches, and davits. The last 25 vessels were not so fitted, but were strengthened in way of the sweeping positions, in case this were required later. Depth-charge outfits were: with M/S gear, 60; without, 70.

There were some major differences visible in some of the Canadian ships:
a) some had 27 foot whalers fitted in gravity davits (the RN ships did not have this).
b) some early vessels had merchant navy-type wooden slatted life rafts fitted aft—*Mayflower* still had some as late as June 1944.
c) the pom pom bandstand was moved to the after end of the superstructure.
d) the boats were moved aft, to a position abreast the funnel.
e) *Calgary,* in January 1943, had as her foremast a steel tube bracketed to the side of the funnel.

The Canadian maple leaf happily started appearing on the funnels of RCN ships later in the war, and some 'Flower' class ships carried cartoon-type paintings on the sides of their 4″ gunshields, which can clearly be seen in the photographs. *Calgary*, predictably, sported a cowboy sitting astride a bucking corvette, brandishing his 6-shooter over a kneeling U-boat!

The original 'Flower' class ships, as in the RN, had by the end of the war been largely outdated by later-designed classes, and nearly all the ships of the class were declared surplus to the RCN's requirements in July 1945.

## RCN 'FLOWER' CLASS PRODUCTION

| | | Original | Modified | | | |
|---|---|---|---|---|---|---|
| 1940 | 1st half | 3 | | **TOTAL BUILT IN** | | |
| | 2nd half | 42 | | **CANADA** | 79 | 42 |
| 19541 | 1st half | 17 | | **Commissioned by RCN** | 79 | 27 |
| | 2nd half | 17 | | **Transferred from UK** | 0 | 4 |
| 1942 | 1st half | | | **Transferred to UK** | 0 | 7 |
| | 2nd half | | | **Cancelled ships** | 0 | 6 |
| 1943 | 1st half | | 5 | | | |
| | 2nd half | | 14 | | | |
| 1944 | 1st half | | 8 | | | |
| | 2nd half | | 4 | | | |

NOTE.
a. Above figures are for ships commissioned by the RCN only.
b. Note the 12 month gap between the two classes.

*Kitchener* in October 1943. A unit of the Revised class, the changed bow form stands out in this shot at full speed, and the extra Oerlikons have been grouped together in pairs aft. *(Public Archives of Canada)*

## GERMAN U-BOATS SUNK BY CANADIAN 'FLOWER' CLASS

| | | |
|---|---|---|
| *U 501* | 10.9.41 | *Chambly* and *Moosejaw* |
| *U 94* | 28.8.42 | *Oakville* and others. |
| *U 356* | 27.12.42 | *Chilliwack, Battleford* and *Napanee* |
| *U 224* | 13.1.43 | *Ville de Quebec* |
| *U 87* | 4.3.43 | *Shediac* and others |
| *U 456* | 13.5.43 | *Drumheller* and others |
| *U 536* | 20.11.43 | *Snowberry, Calgary* and others |
| *U 757* | 8.1.44 | *Camrose* and others |
| *U 744* | 6.3.44 | *Chilliwack, Chaudière, Fennel* and others |

## ITALIAN SUBMARINES SUNK BY CANADIAN 'FLOWER' CLASS

| | | |
|---|---|---|
| *Tritone* | 19.1.43 | *Port Arthur* |
| *Avorio* | 8.2.43 | *Regina* |

## RCN 'FLOWER' CLASS SPECIFICATION (as in 1945)

| | |
|---|---|
| Displacement | 1,085 tons standard |
| Dimensions | |
|    length pp | 190′0″ |
|          oa | 205′1″ |
|    breadth | 33′1″ |
|    draught | 8′3″ forward |
| | 13′5″ aft |
| Machinery | 4 cylinder triple expansion |
| Boiler | 1 Admiralty single-ended |
| Shafts | 1 |
| IHP | 2,750 |
| Speed | 16 kn |
| Oil Fuel | 230 tons |
| Endurance | 3,450×12 kn |
| | 2,630×full speed |
| Complement | 6 officers, 87 men |
| Armament | |
|    main | 1 4″ BL Mk IX on Mk CP1 mtg |
|    close-range | 1 2pdr pom pom Mk VIII on Mk VIII mtg |
| | 2, 4, or 6 single 20mm Oerlikons Mk IIIA, V, or VIIA |
| | 2 rocket flare projectors |
| | 2 6pdr Hotchkiss (in some) |
| A/S Armament | 1 Hedgehog |
| | 70 depth charges |
| | 4 throwers, 2 rails |
| Radar | Types 271Q, 242, 253 |
| M/F D/F | FM7 (MDF5 or FM12 in some) |
| Foxer Gear | CAT Mk II |
| M/S Gear (where | |
|    fitted) | Oropesa Mk I or II |
| | LL Mk IV |

## RCN 'FLOWER' CLASS REVISED SPECIFICATION (as in 1945)

| | |
|---|---|
| Displacement | 1,015 tons standard |
| Dimensions | |
|    length pp | 190'0" |
|       oa | 208'4" |
|    breadth | 33'1" |
|    draught | 11'10" forward |
| | 15'7" aft |
| Machinery | 4 cylinder triple expansion |
| Boiler | 1 Admiralty water tube |
| Shafts | 1 |
| IHP | 2,750 |
| Speed | 16 kn |
| Oil Fuel | 230 tons |
| Endurance | 3,450×23 kn |
| | 2,369×full sped |
| Complement | 7 officers, 89 men |
| Armament | |
|    main | 1 4" BL Mk IX+ on CP1 mtg |
|    close-range | 1 2pdr pom pom Mk VIII on Mk VIII Canadian mtg |
| | 4 or 6 single 20mm Oerlikons, Mk III or IV |
| | 2 2" rocket flare projectors |
| A/S Armament | 1 Hedgehog |
| | 70 depth charges |
| | 4 throwers, 2 rails |
| Radar | Type 271P, SW2CP, 242, 253 |
| M/F D/F | MDF 5 |
| Foxer Gear | CAT Mk II |

*Arvida* in May 1944, showing improvements since the earlier photo. She now has Type 291 radar, a full whaler, and rocket flare projectors. *(Public Archives of Canada)*

## RCN 'FLOWER' CLASS – CLASS LIST

| Name | Pendant No | Job No | Builder | Building Time | Completion Date |
|------|------------|--------|---------|---------------|-----------------|
| **1939-40 Programme** | | | | | |
| *Agassiz* | K 129 | P/V 4 | Burrard | 8m24d | 23.1.41 |
| *Alberni* | K 103 | P/V 5 | Yarrow | 9m10d | 4.2.41 |
| *Algoma* | K 127 | P/V 49 | Port Arthur | 12m23d | 11.7.41 |
| *Amherst* | K 148 | P/V 1 | St John | 14m13d | 5.8.41 |
| *Arrowhead* | K 145 | P/V 8 | Marine | 8m11d | 21.11.40 |
| *Arvida* | K 113 | P/V 5 | Morton | 13m17d | 22.5.41 |
| *Baddeck* | K 147 | P/V 14 | Davie | 9m4d | 18.5.41 |
| *Barrie* | K 138 | P/V 41 | Collingwood | 12m28d | 12.5.41 |
| *Battleford* | K 165 | P/V 44 | ,, | 10m0d | 31.7.41 |
| *Brandon* | K 149 | P/V 17 | Davie | 9m12d | 22.7.41 |
| *Buctouche* | K 179 | P/V 15 | ,, | 9m22d | 5.6.41 |
| *Camrose* | K 154 | P/V 27 | Marine | 9m13d | 30.6.41 |
| *Chambly* | K 116 | P/V 31 | Vickers | 9m26d | 18.12.40 |
| *Chicoutimi* | K 156 | P/V 32 | ,, | 10m7d | 12.5.41 |
| *Chilliwack* | K 131 | P/V 57 | Burrard | 9m5d | 8.4.41 |
| *Cobalt* | K 124 | P/V 47 | Port Arthur | 7m26d | 25.11.40 |
| *Collingwood* | K 180 | P/V 39 | Collingwood | 9m8d | 9.11.40 |
| *Dauphin* | K 157 | P/V 33 | Vickers | 10m11d | 17.5.41 |
| *Dawson* | K 104 | P/V 61 | Victoria | 12m29d | 6.10.41 |
| *Drumheller* | K 167 | P/V 45 | Collingwood | 9m10d | 13.9.41 |
| *Dunvegan* | K 177 | P/V 25 | Marine | 12m19d | 9.9.41 |
| *Edmundston* | K 106 | P/V 64 | Yarrow | 13m28d | 21.10.41 |
| *Galt* | K 163 | P/V 42 | Collingwood | 11m19d | 15.5.41 |
| *Kamloops* | K 176 | P/V 10 | Victoria | 10m29d | 17.3.41 |
| *Kamsack* | K 171 | P/V 11 | Port Arthur | 10m14d | 4.10.41 |
| *Kenogami* | K 125 | P/V 48 | ,, | 14m0d | 29.6.41 |
| *Lethbridge* | K 160 | P/V 35 | Vickers | 10m21d | 26.6.41 |
| *Levis* | K 115 | P/V 18 | Davie | 12m10d | 16.5.41 |
| *Louisburg* | K 143 | P/V 7 | Morton | 9m16d | 29.9.41 |
| *Lunenburg* | K 151 | P/V 20 | Davie | 14m6d | 4.12.41 |
| *Matapedia* | K 112 | P/V 4 | Morton | 13m4d | 9.5.41 |
| *Moncton* | K 139 | P/V 3 | St John | 16m7d | 24.4.42 |
| *Moosejaw* | K 164 | P/V 43 | Collingwood | 10m8d | 19.6.41 |
| *Morden* | K 170 | P/V 51 | Port Arthur | 10m8d | 6.9.41 |
| *Nanaimo* | K 101 | P/V 63 | Yarrow | 11m29d | 26.4.41 |
| *Napanee* | K 118 | P/V 36 | Kingston | 13m23d | 12.5.41 |
| *Oakville* | K 178 | P/V 53 | Port Arthur | 10m28d | 18.11.41 |
| *Orillia* | K 119 | P/V 40 | Collingwood | 13m26d | 29.4.41 |
| *Pictou* | K 146 | P/V 13 | Davie | 9m18d | 29.4.41 |
| *Prescott* | K 161 | P/V 37 | Kingston | 9m26d | 26.6.41 |
| *Quesnel* | K 133 | P/V 60 | Victoria | 12m14d | 23.5.41 |
| *Rimouski* | K 121 | P/V 12 | Davie | 9m15d | 26.4.41 |
| *Rosthern* | K 169 | P/V 50 | Port Arthur | 11m29d | 17.6.41 |

| Sackville | K 181 | P/V 2 | St John | 19m3d | 30.12.41 |
| Saskatoon | K 158 | P/V 34 | Vickers | 10m5d | 9.6.41 |
| Shawinigan | K 136 | P/V 19 | Davie | 10m7d | 19.9.41 |
| Shediac | K 110 | P/V 16 | ,, | 8m29d | 8.7.41 |
| Sherbrooke | K 152 | P/V 24 | Marine | 10m0d | 5.6.41 |
| Sorel | K 153 | P/V 26 | ,, | 11m26d | 19.8.41 |
| Sudbury | K 162 | P/V 38 | Kingston | 8m21d | 15.10.41 |
| Summerside | K 141 | P/V 6 | Morton | 11m9d | 11.9.41 |
| The Pas | K 168 | P/V 46 | Collingwood | 9m14d | 21.10.41 |
| Trail | K 174 | P/V 58 | Burrard | 9m11d | 30.4.41 |
| Wetaskiwin | K 175 | P/V 55 | ,, | 8m4d | 16.12.40 |
| Weyburn | K 173 | P/V 54 | Port Arthur | 9m16d | 26.11.41 |

### 1940-41 Programme

| Brantford | K 218 | CN 120 | Midland | 16m19d | 15.5.42 |
| Midland | K 220 | CN 121 | ,, | 9m17d | 8.11.41 |
| New Westminster | K 228 | CN 124 | Victoria | 11m24d | 31.1.42 |
| Timmins | K 223 | CN 122 | Yarrow | 13m17d | 10.2.42 |
| Vancouver | K 240 | P/V 272 | ,, | 12m20d | 20.3.42 |

## REVISED 'FLOWER' CLASS (increased sheer and flare)

| Name | Pendant No | Job No | Builder | Building Time | Comp Date |
| --- | --- | --- | --- | --- | --- |

### 1940-41 Programme

| Calgary | K 231 | P/V 266 | Marine | 8m27d | 16.12 |
| Charlottetown | K 244 | P/V 274 | Kingston | 8m16d | 13.12 |
| Dundas | K ??? | CN 125 | Victoria | 12m13d | 1.4.42 |
| Fredericton | K 245 | P/V 275 | Marine | 8m17d | 8.12.4 |
| Halifax | K 237 | P/V 270 | Collingwood | 7m30d | 26.11 |
| Kitchener | K 225 | CN 123 | Davie | 12m12d | 28.6.4 |
| La Malbaie | K 273 | CN 124 | Marine | 13m7d | 28.4.4 |
| Port Arthur | K 233 | P/V 267 | Port Arthur | 12m28d | 26.5.4 |
| Regina | K 234 | P/V 268 | Marine | 10m6d | 22.1.4 |
| Ville de Quebec | K 242 | P/V 273 | Morton | 11m16d | 24.5.4 |
| Woodstock | K 238 | P/V 271 | Collingwood | 11m9d | 1.5.42 |

## BUILT FOR RN, TRANSFERRED TO RCN ON COMPLETION

### 1939-40 Programme

| Arrowhead | K 145 | P/V 8 | Marine | 8m11d | 21.11.40 |
| Bittersweet | K 182 | ,, | ,, | 9m4d | 23.1.41 |
| Eyebright | K 150 | ,, | Vickers | 9m4d | 26.11.40 |
| Fennel | K 194 | ,, | Marine | 9m3d | 15.1.41 |
| Hepatica | K 159 | ,, | Davie | 7m20d | 12.11.40 |
| Mayflower | K 191 | ,, | Vickers | 9m29d | 9.11.41 |
| Snowberry | K 166 | ,, | Davie | 9m2d | 30.11.40 |
| Spikenard | K 198 | ,, | ,, | 9m12d | 8.12.4 |
| Trillium | K 172 | ,, | Vickers | 9m17d | 22.10.40 |
| Windflower | K 155 | ,, | Davie | 9m16d | 26.10.40 |

## WAR LOSSES

| | | |
|---|---|---|
| *Alberni* | 21.8.44 | Mined or torpedoed, 25m SE of St Catherines |
| *Charlottetown* | 11.9.42 | Torpedoed, Gulf of St Lawrence |
| *Levis* | 20.9.41 | Torpedoed, North Atlantic |
| *Louisburg* | 6.2.43 | Sunk by aircraft off Oran |
| *Regina* | 8.8.44 | Torpedoed off Trevose Head, Cornwall |
| *Shawinigan* | 24.11.44 | Torpedoed, Gulf of St Lawrence |
| *Spikenard* | 11.2.42 | Torpedoed, North Atlantic |
| *Weyburn* | 22.2.43 | Mined, off Gibraltar |
| *Windflower* | 7.12.41 | Collision, off Newfoundland |

▲ *Fennel,* in September 1943. Built for the RN, she was retained by the RCN on loan. Here, she has an Admiralty camouflage pattern, and the colourful Canadian cartoon on the 4″ gunshield. *(Ministry of Defence)*

*Snowberry* in January 1942, lying alongside a carrier with a Swordfish aircraft on deck. She has an early radar lantern, and the mast still stepped forward of the bridge. *(Ministry of Defence)* ▼

*Longbranch* in UK waters, December 1944. She was built as the RN *Candytuft,* and was transferred on completion with a different pennant number. Note the extra height above water of the 4″ gun, compared with the earlier class. *(Public Archives of Canada)*

*Rivière Du Loup* at Halifax, the great RCN east coast naval base, in April 1944. She is just in from sea, with well-worn paintwork on the hull, and she shows the improved tumblehome aft of her class. *(Public Archives of Canada)*

## RCN MODIFIED 'FLOWER' CLASS CORVETTES
### 42 ships built in Canada

With this class, a significant difference arose between the RN and RCN escort building programmes.

When the RN switched orders from the original 'Flower' class, the shorter building slips were then used for only a few of the Modified class, and orders were then placed for large numbers of the bigger 'Castle' class corvettes. In Canada, larger numbers of Modified class ships were laid down, and 'Castle' class units were not ordered until a little later.

The result was that 42 Modified class ships were built in Canada, as opposed to only 10 built in the UK. We have a good photographic coverage of these fine ships, which formed nearly one-third of all the corvettes operated by the RCN.

It will be seen that 10 units were built in the UK, but the RN operated 11! Study of the transfer lists for this class will disclose that some units originally ordered in Canada by the USN for itself were eventually transferred on completion to the RN, under Lend-Lease, at the same time as the RN was building ships of the class in the UK, and transferring 4 of them to the RCN on completion. These 4 were part of the agreement, covered in more detail in the 'Castle' class chapter, to exchange UK-built corvettes for Canadian-built 'Algerine' class fleet minesweepers.

It will be noted that Admiralty-type funnel caps were by no means generally fitted in this class of ship, but mainmasts usually were. Other comments under the RN Modified class chapter also apply to these Canadian-built ships.

The Modified class had specified single 4″ guns, QF, Mark XIX, a new gun, as opposed to the vintage 4″ guns fitted in the earlier ships. These new guns had a maximum elevation of 60 degrees, and in June 1942 no less than 74 guns of this type were ordered in Canada, for fitting to Canadian-built vessels.

The other major change was that RN-type 27 foot whalers carried in gravity davits were fitted in all ships of this class, on the starboard side, while Carley life rafts only were usually carried on the port side, abreast the funnel. The motor dinghy originally specified was either landed or not fitted while building.

*Smiths Falls* at Halifax, February 1945. The hull lines come out well in this beam shot, which has a wintry backdrop. *(Public Archives of Canada)*

## RCN MODIFIED 'FLOWER' CLASS—SPECIFICATION

| | |
|---|---|
| Displacement | 980 tons standard |
| Dimensions | |
|    length pp | 193'0" |
|          oa | 208'4" |
|    breadth | 33'1" |
|    draught | 11'5" forward |
| | 16'0" aft |
| Machinery | 4 cylinder triple expansion |
| Boilers | 2 Admiralty water tube |
| Shafts | 1 |
| IHP | 2,880 |
| Speed | 16 kn |
| Endurance | 7,400×10 kn |
| Complement | 7 officers, 102 men |
| Armament | |
|    main | 1 single 4" QF Mk XIX on Mk XXIII HA/LA mtg |
|    close range | 1 single 2pdr pom pom, Mk VIII on Mk VIII mtg |
| | 6 single 20mm Oerlikons |
| | 2 2" rocket flare projectors |
| A/S Armament | 1 Hedgehog |
| | 100 depth charges |
| | 4 throwers, 2 rails |
| Radar | Types 271Q, 242, 253, 251M |
| M/F D/F | FM 7 |
| Foxer Gear | CAT Mk II |

*Hawkesbury* passing Wolfe's Cove, Quebec, after commissioning, July 1944. A splendid bow shot, with the newer type of 4" gun supplied to this class in Canada. *(Public Archives of Canada)*

## RCN MODIFIED 'FLOWER' CLASS—CLASS LIST
### (or Revised 'FLOWER' class, increased endurance)

| Name | Pendant No | Job No | Builder | Building Time | Completion Date |
|---|---|---|---|---|---|
| **1942-43 Programme** | | | | | |
| Athol | K 15 | P/V 400 | Morton | 14m0d | 14.10.43 |
| Coburg | K 333 | P/V 441 | Midland | 17m17d | 11.5.44 |
| Fergus | K 686 | P/V 439 | Collingwood | 11m9d | 18.11.44 |
| Frontenac | K 335 | P/V 399 | Kingston | 8m4d | 26.10.43 |
| Guelph | K 687 | P/V 507 | Collingwood | 11m14d | 9.5.44 |
| Hawkesbury | K 415 | P/V 445 | Morton | 10m25d | 14. 6.44 |
| Lindsay | K 338 | P/V 398 | Midland | 13m15d | 15.11.43 |
| Louisburg | K 401 | P/V 402 | Morton | 11m27d | 13.12.43 |
| Norsyd | K 520 | P/V 403 | ,, | 11m8d | 22.12.43 |
| North Bay | K 339 | P/V 396 | Collingwood | 12m30d | 25.10.43 |
| Owen Sound | K 340 | CN 397 | ,, | 12m6d | 17.11.43 |
| Rivière Du Loup | K 357 | P/V 401 | Morton | 10m26d | 21.11.43 |
| St Lambert | K 343 | P/V 444 | ,, | 10m17d | 27.5.44 |
| Trentonian | K 368 | P/V 443 | Kingston | 9m14d | 1.12.43 |
| Whitby | K 346 | P/V 442 | Midland | 14m6d | 6.6.44 |
| **1943-44 Programme** | | | | | |
| Asbestos | K 358 | P/V 521 | Morton | 10m27d | 16.6.44 |
| Beauharnois | K 540 | P/V 581 | ,, | 10m17d | 25.9.44 |
| Belleville | K 332 | P/V 518 | Kingston | 9m28d | 19.10.44 |
| Lachute | K 440 | P/V 524 | Morton | 11m2d | 26.10.44 |
| Merrittonia | K 688 | P/V 663 | ,, | 11m17d | 10.11.44 |
| Parry Sound | K 341 | P/V 512 | Midland | 14m18d | 30.8.44 |
| Peterborough | K 342 | P/V 517 | Kingston | 8m16d | 1.6.44 |
| Smiths Falls | K 345 | P/V 519 | ,, | 11m19d | 28.11.44 |
| Stellarton | K 457 | P/V 523 | Morton | 10m13d | 29.9.44 |
| Strathroy | K 455 | P/V 515 | Midland | | 20.11.44 |
| Thorlock | K 394 | P/V 514 | ,, | 13m18d | 6.10.44 |
| West York | K 369 | P/V 513 | ,, | 14m14d | 6.10.44 |

## BUILT IN UK, TRANSFERRED TO RCN ON COMPLETION

### 1942-43 Programme

| Name | Pendant No | Job No | Builder | Building Time | Completion Date |
|---|---|---|---|---|---|
| Forest Hill<br>ex RN *Ceanothus* | K 486 | J 1531 | Ferguson | 10m5d | 10.12.43 |
| Giffard<br>ex RN *Buddleia* | K 485 | J 11840 | A.Hall | 11m18d | 17.11.43 |

## 1943-44 Programme

| | | | | | |
|---|---|---|---|---|---|
| *Longbranch*<br>ex RN *Candytuft* | K 487 | J 1534 | Brown | 10m19d | 15.1.44 |
| *Mimico*<br>ex RN *Bullrush* | K 307 | J 4644 | ,, | 11m24d | 15.2.44 |

## BUILT IN CANADA, FOR USN

| | | | | | |
|---|---|---|---|---|---|
| USS *Action*<br>ex RN *Comfrey* | PG 86<br>K277 | CN 304 | Collingwood | 15m1d | 22.11.42 |
| USS *Alacrity*<br>ex RN *Cornel* | PG 87<br>K278 | CN 305 | ,, | 11m16d | 10.12.42 |
| USS *Brisk*<br>ex RN *Flax* | PG 89<br>K 284 | CN 307 | Kingston | | 6.12.42 |
| USS *Haste*<br>ex RN *Mandrake* | PG 92<br>K 285 | CN 310 | Morton | 14m26d | 6.4.43 |
| USS *Intensity*<br>ex RN *Milfoil* | PG 93<br>K 288 | CN 311 | ,, | 14m20d | 31.3.43 |
| USS *Might*<br>ex RN *Musk* | PG 94<br>K 289 | CN 312 | ,, | | 22.12.42 |
| USS *Pert*<br>ex RN *Nepeta* | PG 95<br>K 290 | CN 313 | ,, | 12m0d | 23.7.43 |
| USS *Prudent*<br>ex RN *Privet* | PG 96<br>K 291 | CN 314 | ,, | 12m2d | 16.8.43 |

## BUILT IN CANADA FOR USN, AND TRANSFERRED TO RN ON COMPLETION

| Name | Pendant No | Job No | Builder | Completion Date |
|---|---|---|---|---|
| *Dittany*<br>ex USN *Beacon* | K 279<br>PG 88 | CN 306 | Collingwood | L31.10.42 |
| *Honesty*<br>ex USN *Caprice* | K 285<br>PG 90 | CN 308 | Kingston | L28.9.42 |
| *Linaria*<br>ex USN *Clash* | K 282<br>PG 91 | CN 309 | Midland | L28.11.42 |
| *Rosebay*<br>ex USN *Splendor* | K 286<br>PG 97 | CN 315 | Kingston | L11.5.43 |
| *Smilax*<br>ex USN *Tact* | K 280<br>PG 98 | CN 316 | Collingwood | L24.12.42 |
| *Statice*<br>ex USN *Vim* | K 455<br>PG 99 | CN 317 | ,, | L10.4.43 |
| *Willowherb*<br>ex USN *Vitality* | K 283<br>PG 100 | CN 318 | Midland | L24.3.43 |

## CANCELLED SHIPS

| | | |
|---|---|---|
| *Brampton* | | Morton |
| *Carleton* | CN 52 | Port Arthur |

| *Ingersoll* | K 336 | Morton |
| *Listowel* | K 439 | Kingston |
| *Meaford* |  | Midland |
| *Renfrew* | K 452 | Kingston |
| *Simcoe* |  | Morton |

All cancelled in December, 1943

## WAR LOSSES

| *Merrittonia* | 30.11.45 | Wrecked on Nova Scotian coast |
| *Trentonian* | 22.2.45 | Torpedoed, North Atlantic |

▲ *Beauharnois* off Quebec City, September 1944. She has the new 4″ gun, Types 271 and 291 radar, a pom pom aft, and the upright funnel of her type. *(Public Archives of Canada)*

*Belleville* celebrating in October 1944. She has the North Atlantic camouflage and the cleaner silhouette of the Modified class; but she has no boat on the port side. *(Public Archives of Canada)* ▼

*Guysborough* at Halifax, March 1944. 12
pounder forward, full whaler slung outboard,
covered bridge (unique among wartime
escort/M/S classes), Type 290 radar. *(Public
Archives of Canada)*

*Granby* at Halifax. She was one of the few
diesel-engined ships of the class; note the clear
forecastle without Hedgehog, few depth
charges aft, with two throwers and some traps.
*(Public Archives of Canada)* ▼

## RCN 'BANGOR' CLASS FLEET MINESWEEPERS
### 54 ships completed

These, too, followed the RN specification, and few alterations and additions seem to have been made to them.

The interesting point about the RCN 'Bangor' class is that they were very largely used for coastal escort (the original role of the 'Flower' class), and not for minesweeping. As they switched from one duty to another, it is not clear how they were divided, but a number were certainly used as minesweepers both in Canadian waters and as part of the Allied minesweeping forces for the Normandy invasion. Indeed, the 31st RCN Minesweeping Flotilla was still in European waters in July 1945, and participated in the clearance of Bordeaux.

Some were fitted with wire sweeping gear (Mark II Oropesa, sweeps, winches and davits), but they were apparently too small efficiently to take an LL sweep as well, as it had to be stowed below decks (only 12 were so fitted). Their full speed without sweeps streamed was: diesel, $15\frac{1}{2}$ knots; steam, $16\frac{1}{2}$ knots. With a single Oropesa sweep out, the figures were $10\frac{3}{4}$ and 12 knots respectively, and with double wire sweeps out, 9 and $10\frac{1}{2}$ knots.

While they were based at Halifax, Sydney and St John's, units of this class operated chiefly as local escort ships, the lion's share of which duty they cheerfully carried out. They had limited oil fuel endurance, and, while they could make direct transatlantic passages via the Azores, they could not act effectively as mid-ocean escorts, where innumerable variations from course would burn up more fuel than they could carry. By the time oiling at sea had become routine, other newly completed escorts had taken on the mid-ocean task. Captain (D) Halifax reported on 19th December 1942: 'Approximately one-third of the combined Western Local Escort Force and the Halifax Force is composed of 'Bangor' sweepers.'

To make these ships more efficient escorts it was recommended that the topweight be reduced and the firepower increased, by removing the mine-sweeping gear. It was recommended that suitable buildings be constructed for the storage of both 'Bangor' and 'Algerine' minesweeping gear, so that it could be re-embarked at short notice if required. In 1944 it was so refitted in the 'Bangor' class units which crossed the Atlantic to take part in the Normandy invasion. In August 1944 it was agreed that the RCN 'Bangor' class ships should be fitted with extra ballast to enable more close-range weapons to be fitted.

The forward guns were usually single 12 pounders in RCN ships, and the depth-charge stowage can be seen in the photographs; there was not room on the sweep deck for full-size depth-charge rails, so 5 charges were stowed in individual traps along the ship's side, and 2 ready-use racks, each containing 3 charges, alongside them. 2 depth-charge throwers only could be fitted at the forward end of the sweep deck.

Six Canadian-built units on order for the RCN were transferred to the RCN on completion. As with the 'Isles' class, it would appear that the RN had allottedthese ships some Canadian names before they were transferred to the RCN. In the RN section the other 6 Canadian-built units, delivered to the RN, can be found, also with Canadian names.

## 'Bangor' Class—production

| 1940 1st half | 1  | 2nd half | 9  |
|---------------|----|----------|----|
| 1941 1st half | 22 | 2nd half | 12 |
| 1942 1st half | 7  | 2nd half | 3  |

## RCN 'BANGOR' CLASS SPECIFICATION

| | |
|---|---|
| Displacement | 672 tons standard |
| Dimensions | |
| length oa | 180'0" |
| breadth | 28'6" |
| draught | 9'10" forward |
| | 10'2" aft |
| Machinery | a) 3 cylinder steam triple expansion |
| | Boilers 2 Admiralty 3-drum type |
| | IHP 2,400   Speed 16.5 kn |
| | b) twin Sulzer diesels |
| | SHP 1,000   Speed 16 kn |
| Shafts | 2 |
| Oil fuel | 143 tons (steam) |
| Endurance | |
| steam type | 2,950×11½ kn |
| | 1,440×full speed |
| diesel type | 2,700×13 kn |
| Complement | 6 officers and 77 men |
| Armament | |
| main | 1 12 pdr 12 cwt Mk V on Mk IX mtg |
| close-range | 1 2 pdr pom pom Mk VIII on Mk VIIIA HA mtg |
| alternatives | 1 3" 20cwt Mk IV on Mk IVx mtg |
| | (in place of 12 pdr) |
| | 1 twin 20mm Oerlikon Mk Vc on power mtg |
| | 2 single 20mm Oerlikon Mk V |
| Anti-submarine | 2 throwers, 4 chutes |
| | 40 depth charges |
| Radar (when fitted | Types SW2CP, 252, ABK |
| H/F D/F | Not fitted |
| M/F D/F | FM 7 or MDF 5 |
| Foxer Gear | CAT Mk II |

## RCN 'BANGOR' CLASS

TOTAL BUILT IN CANADA  60
Retained by RCN  54
Ordered by and delivered to, RN   6
Cancelled   0

## RCN 'BANGOR' CLASS—CLASS LIST

| Name | Pendant No | Job No | Builder | Building Time | Completion Date |
|------|-----------|--------|---------|---------------|-----------------|

### A. STEAM RECIPROCATING-ENGINED

**1939-40 Programme**

| Name | Pendant No | Job No | Builder | Building Time | Completion Date |
|------|-----------|--------|---------|---------------|-----------------|
| *Bellechasse* | J 170 | M/S 12 | N Vancouver | 7m27d | 26.2.42 |
| *Burlington* | J 250 | M/S 16 | Dufferin | 14m3d | 6.9.41 |
| *Chedabucto* | J 168 | M/S 10 | Burrard | 14m1d | 27.9.41 |
| *Chignecto* | J 160 | M/S 5 | N Vancouver | 14m19d | 31.10.41 |
| *Clayoquot* | J 174 | M/S 13 | Prince Rupert | 14m19d | 22.8.41 |
| *Cowichan* | J 146 | M/S 1 | N Vancouver | 14m10d | 4.7.41 |
| *Georgian* | J 144 | M/S 17 | Dufferin | 11m12d | 23.9.41 |
| *Mahone* | J 159 | M/S 4 | N Vancouver | 13m17d | 29.9.41 |
| *Malpeque* | J 148 | M/S 2 | ,, | 15m10d | 4.8.41 |
| *Minas* | J 165 | M/S 8 | Burrard | 9m15d | 2.8.41 |
| *Miramichi* | J 169 | M/S 11 | ,, | 9m15d | 26.11.41 |
| *Nipigon* | J 154 | M/S 15 | Dufferin | 13m7d | 11.8.41 |
| *Outarde* | J 161 | M/S 6 | N Vancouver | 13m20d | 4.12.41 |
| *Quatsino* | J 152 | M/S 14 | Prince Rupert | 16m13d | 3.11.41 |
| *Quinte* | J 166 | M/S 9 | Burrard | 8m16d | 30.8.41 |
| *Thunder* | J 156 | M/S 18 | Dufferin | 10m10d | 14.10.41 |
| *Ungava* | J 149 | M/S 3 | N Vancouver | 16m11d | 5.9.41 |
| *Wasaga* | J 162 | M/S 7 | Burrard | 10m9d | 1.7.41 |

**1940 Programme**

| Name | Pendant No | Job No | Builder | Building Time | Completion Date |
|------|-----------|--------|---------|---------------|-----------------|
| *Bayfield* | J 08 | | N Vancouver | 13m27d | 26.2.42 |

*Ingonish* at Halifax, March 1944. The ship is encrusted with ice, and the guns and sweep winch are covered. *(Public Archives of Canada)*

| | | | | | |
|---|---|---|---|---|---|
| Canso | J 21 | | N Vancouvre | 14m6d | 5.3.42 |
| Caraquet | J 38 | | ,, | 14m0d | 31.3.42 |
| Guysborough | J 52 | | ,, | 10m25d | 22.4.42 |
| Ingonish | J 69 | | ,, | 11m1d | 8.5.42 |
| Lockeport | J 100 | | ,, | 11m9d | 29.9.41 |

**1940-41 Programme**

| | | | | | |
|---|---|---|---|---|---|
| Courtenay | J 262 | CN 117 | Prince Rupert | 13m24d | 21.3.42 |
| Drummondville | J 253 | CN 96 | Vickers | 9m22d | 30.10.41 |
| Gananoque | J 259 | CN 114 | Dufferin | 10m24d | 8.11.41 |
| Goderich | J 260 | CN 115 | ,, | 10m9d | 23.11.41 |
| Grandmère | J 258 | CN 101 | Vickers | 6m9d | 1.1.12.41 |
| Kelowna | J 261 | CN 116 | Prince Rupert | 13m9d | 5.2.42 |
| Medicine Hat | J 256 | CN 99 | Vickers | 10m25d | 4.12.41 |
| Red Deer | J 255 | CN 98 | Vickers | 11m15d | 24.11.41 |
| Swift Current | J 254 | CN 97 | ,, | 11m1d | 11.11.41 |
| Vegreville | J 257 | CN 100 | ,, | 6m7d | 10.12.41 |

**1941-42 Programme**

| | | | | | |
|---|---|---|---|---|---|
| Blairmore | J 314 | CN 181 | Port Arthur | 11m16d | 17.11.42 |
| Fort William | J 311 | CN 177 | ,, | 12m7d | 25.8.42 |
| Kenora | J 281 | CN 176 | ,, | 11m19d | 6.12.42 |
| Kentville | J 312 | CN 176 | ,, | 9m26d | 10.10.42 |
| Milltown | J 317 | CN 178 | ,, | 13m0d | 18.9.42 |
| Mulgrave | J 313 | CN 180 | ,, | 10m20d | 4.11.42 |
| Port Hope | J 280 | CN 172 | Dufferin | 10m20d | 30.7.42 |
| Sarnia | J 309 | CN 173 | ,, | 10m25d | 13.8.42 |
| Stratford | J 310 | CN 174 | ,, | 10m0d | 29.8.42 |
| Westmount | J 318 | CN 175 | ,, | 10m18d | 10.12.42 |

## B. DIESEL-ENGINED

**1940-41 Programme**

| | | | | | |
|---|---|---|---|---|---|
| Brockville | J 270 | CN 93 | Marine Ind | 21m2d | 19.9.42 |
| Digby | J 267 | CN 90 | Davie | 16m23d | 26.7.42 |
| Esquimalt | J 272 | CN 95 | Marine Ind | 21m5d | 26.10.42 |
| Granby | J 264 | CN 87 | Davie | 16m16d | 20.6.42 |
| Lachine | J 266 | CN 89 | ,, | 17m25d | 20.6.42 |
| Melville | J 263 | CN 86 | ,, | 17m25d | 4.12.41 |
| Noranda | J 265 | CN 88 | ,, | 16m19d | 15.5.42 |
| Transcona | J 271 | CN 94 | Marine Ind | 23m7d | 1.12.42 |
| Trois Rivières | J 269 | CN 92 | ,, | 19m27d | 12.8.42 |
| Truro | J 268 | CN 91 | Davie | 17m24d | 27.8.42 |

## BUILT IN CANADA FOR THE RN

| | | | |
|---|---|---|---|
| Fort York | J 119 | | Dufferin |
| Parrsborough | J 117 | | ,, |
| Qualicum | J 138 | | ,, |
| Shippigan | J 212 | | ,, |
| Tadoussac | J 220 | | ,, |

Wedgeport          J 139                   ,,
Details of these ships will be found under the RN section.

## WAR LOSSES

| | | |
|---|---|---|
| *Chedabucto* | 21.10.43 | Grounded after collision |
| *Clayoquot* | 24.12.44 | Torpedoed by U-boat off Halifax |
| *Esquimalt* | 16.4.45 | Torpedoed by U-boat off Halifax |
| *Guysborough* | 17.3.45 | Torpedoed by U-boat off Ushant |
| *Mulgrave* | 8.10.44 | Constructive total loss by mine in English Channel |

*Swift Current* at Halifax, August 1944, giving an excellent view of the depth charge trap lay-out.
The big fairleads were for the large LL sweep, the davits for the wire sweep.
*(Public Archives of Canada)*

## RCN 'ISLES' CLASS TRAWLERS
## 8 ships built in Canada

In 1940, when the Admiralty were expanding the RN's escort building programme as quickly as possible, orders were being placed in Commonwealth countries to the limits of their shipbuilding capacity.

One of the escort classes thus expanded with the 'Isles' class of A/S-M/S trawlers, at that time designated the 'Western Isles' class. Orders were placed for 16 units in Canada, for delivery in 1942, with the design being identical with the UK-built ships.

This was an interesting departure, for the Canadian units were to be built by shipyards which were at the same time building 'Flower' class corvettes, and it may seem surprising that the equivalent number of extra corvettes were not ordered instead. Just before the war, when both the RN and RCN were experimenting with escort vessel types, the RCN had built 4 units of the RN-designed 'Basset' class trawlers in Canada (these were the predecessors of the 'Isles' class); but when the 'Flower' and 'Bangor' class plans became available in Ottawa no further trawlers were ordered by the RCN.

The 16 ships now ordered in Canada were to bear Canadian names, as did the Canadian-built 'Bangor' class units for the RN. This was a pleasant and colourful departure from normal RN naming procedures.

When the RCN, too, was looking for every available escort vessel, all of these 16 ships were retained on loan by the RCN, on commissioning, with RCN crews. One was lost during the war years, and the rest were returned to the RN in 1945. They were used on coastal escort work in Canadian waters.

The photograph of one of the Canadian-built units of this class in the RN section shows that some of these ships were armed with manually-operated twin 20mm Oerlikons—a fairly rare fitting.

## RCN 'ISLES' CLASS PRODUCTION

1942 1st half 8

*Miscou*, of the 'Isles' class, built in Canada for the RN but retained by the RCN on loan. She has both A/S and M/S outfits. *(Canadian Forces Photo Unit)*

## RCN 'ISLES' CLASS

| | |
|---|---|
| Displacement | 530 tons stand |
| Dimensions | |
|   length oa | 164'0" |
|   breadth | 27'8" |
|   draught | 8'7" mean |
| Machinery | steam reciprocating triple expansion |
| Boiler | 1 Admiralty single-hended |
| Shafts | 1 |
| IHP | 850 |
| Speed | 12.5 kn |
| Complement | 40 |
| Armament | 1- 12 pdr 12 cwt |
|   main | 2/4 single 20mm Oerlikons |
|   close range | (some twin manual Oerlikons in some) |
| A/S armament | 2 throwers |
| | 2 rails |

## RCN 'ISLES' CLASS BUILT IN CANADA—CLASS LIST

| Name | Pendant No | Job No | Builder | Building Time | Completion Date |
|---|---|---|---|---|---|
| **BUILT FOR RN, BUT TRANSFERRED TO RCN ON COMPLETION** | | | | | |
| **1941-42 Programme** | | | | | |
| *Anticòsti* | T 274 | CN 288 | Collingwood | 9m30d | 8.8.42 |
| *Baffin* | T 275 | CN 289 | ,, | 10m6d | 20.8.42 |
| *Cailiff* | T 276 | CN 290 | ,, | 9m16d | 16.9.42 |
| *Ironbound* | T 284 | CN 298 | Kingston | 11m29d | 5.10.42 |
| *Liscomb* | T 285 | CN 299 | ,, | 7m27d | 3.9.42 |
| *Magdalen* | T 279 | CN 293 | Midland | 10m10d | 19.8.42 |
| *Manitoulin* | T 280 | CN 294 | ,, | 9m13d | 8.9.42 |
| *Miscou* | T 277 | CN 291 | Collingwood | 10m19d | 20.10.42 |
|   ex *Carpenia* | | | | | |
| **BUILT IN CANADA FOR THE RN** | | | | | |
| **1941-42 Programme** | | | | | |
| *Campobello* | T 278 | CN 292 | Collingwood | 10m23d | 9.11.42 |
| *Dochet* | T 286 | CN 300 | GT Davie | 12m15d | 13.11.42 |
| *Flint* | T 287 | CN 301 | ,, | 13m13d | 11.12.42 |
| *Gateshead* | T 288 | CN 302 | ,, | 16m30d | 11.5.43 |
| *Herschell* | T 289 | CN 303 | ,, | 17m12d | 29.5.43 |
| *Porcher* | T 281 | CN 295 | Midland | 10m16d | 27.10.42 |
| *Prospect* | T 282 | CN 296 | ,, | 7m22d | 4.11.42 |
| *Texada* | T 283 | CN 297 | ,, | 6m20d | 17.11.42 |

## RCN 'ALGERINE' CLASS A/S ESCORT VESSELS
### 53 ships built in Canada

We have seen elsewhere that, of the 53 fleet minesweepers of this class built in Canada during the war, only 12 were retained by the RCN.

Sufficient 'Bangor' class units had been built to cover RCN minesweeping requirements, and the 'Algerine' class were thought to be inferior in design as escorts to the Modified 'Flower' class, let alone the frigates; but the 12 retained were, in fact, completed as escorts, not being fitted with minesweeping gear at all. They were all fitted for Arctic service.

This gave them a clear quarterdeck, for full depth-charge equipment, while a Hedgehog was fitted forward. The Type 291 radar and the rangefinder were omitted, and some further single 20mm Oerlikons were fitted. 90 depth charges were carried, and some ships were fitted with H/F D/F. They acted largely as the senior officers' ships of the Western Local Escort Force and the Halifax Force.

Of the ships built in Canada for the RN, the first 6 were fitted with LL magnetic sweeps on arrival in the UK, the rest being fitted in Canada. The RN found it very helpful to be able to order so many ships of this class in Canada, thus freeing UK building capacity for other warship types.

The RCN ships retained their 'J' pennant numbers, following RN class practice, although they were only used as escorts. They were named after towns, following RCN practice.

*Sault Ste Marie* in August 1943. Her 4″ gun has no shield, as in the early RN units; she has no M/S gear, being classed as an escort vessel, and she has a searchlight in the rangefinder position. Other units of the class carried H/F D/F at the masthead. *(Public Archives of Canada)*

## RCN 'ALGERINE' CLASS PRODUCTION

| | | | | | |
|---|---|---|---|---|---|
| 1942 | 1st | half | 0 | TOTAL BUILT IN CANADA 58 | |
| | 2nd | half | 5 | Retained by RCN 12 | |
| 1943 | 1st | half | 2 | Ordered by USN, transferred to RN | 12 |
| | 2nd | half | 4 | Ordered by RCN, transferred to RN | 15 |
| 1944 | 1st | half | 1 | Ordered direct by RN 19 | |
| | | | | Cancelled ships (? RN) 6 | |

## RCN 'ALGERINE' CLASS SPECIFICATION

| | |
|---|---|
| Displacement | 990 tons |
| Dimensions | |
|    length pp | 2,2'6" |
|       oa | 225'0" |
|    breadth | 35'6" |
|    draught | 10'5" |
| Machinery | triple expansion reciprocating |
| Boilers | 2 Admiralty 3-drum type |
| IHP | 2000 |
| Speed | 16·5/17 kn |
| Shafts | 2 |
| Endurance | 4,500×11½ kn |
| Complement | 104 to 138 |
| Armament | |
|    main | 1 single 4" BL Mk Vc |
|    close-range | 2 twin 20mm Oerlikon Mk Vc on power mtg |
| | 2 single 20mm Oerlikon Mk V |
| | 2 2" rocket flare projectors |
| A/S Armament | 1 Hedgehog ATW mortar |
| | 4 throwers, 2 rails |
| | 90 depth charges |
| Radar | Types 271P, 253, 251, 242 |
| H/F D/F | FH 3 |
| M/F D/F | FM 7 |
| Foxer Gear | CAT Mk II |

*Border Cities* at Halifax, July 1944. Note she has no M/S gear aft, and four twin Oerlikons. Her clear sweep deck gave a splendid depth charge handling area, and she made a good Senior Officer's ship in the Halifax Local escort force. *(Public Archives of Canada)*

## RCN 'ALGERINE' CLASS—CLASS LIST

| Name | Pendant No | Job No | Builder | Building Time | Completion Date |
|------|-----------|--------|---------|---------------|-----------------|
| **1942/43 Programme** | | | | | |
| *Border Cities* | J 344 | CN 366 | Port Arthur | 8m23d | 18.5.44 |
| *Kapuskasing* | J 326 | CN 369 | ,, | 19m29d | 17.8.44 |
| *Middlesex* | J 328 | CN 367 | ,, | 8m9d | 8.6.44 |
| *Oshawa* | J 330 | CN 368 | ,, | 19m18d | 6.7.44 |
| *Portage* | J 331 | CN 364 | ,, | 16m30d | 22.10.43 |
| *Rockcliffe* | J 355 | CN 370 | ,, | 21m8d | 30.9.44 |
| *Sault Ste Marie* | J 334 | CN 361 | ,, | 16m28d | 24.6.44 |
| *St Boniface* | J 332 | CN 363 | ,, | 15m20d | 10.9.43 |
| *Wallaceburg* | J 336 | CN 365 | ,, | 16m12d | 18.11.43 |
| *Winnipeg* | J 337 | CN 362 | ,, | 17m29d | 29.7.43 |
| **1943/44 Programme** | | | | | |
| *Fort Frances* | J 396 | CN 350 | ,, | 17m17d | 28.10.44 |
| *New Liskeard* | J 397 | CN 551 | ,, | 16m14d | 22.11.44 |

### Ordered in Canada by USN, but transferred on completion to RN

| Name | Pendant No | | Name | Pendant No |
|------|-----------|---|------|-----------|
| *Antares* ex USN AM 325 | J 282 | | *Persian* ex USN AM 334 | J 347 |
| *Arcturus* ex USN AM 326 | J 283 | | *Postillion* ex USN AM 335 | J 296 |
| *Aries* ex USN AM 327 | J 284 | | *Skipjack* ex *Scorpion*, ex USN AM 336 | J 300 |
| *Clinton* ex USN AM 328 | J 286 | | *Thisbe* ex USN AM 337 | J 302 |
| *Friendship* ex USN AM 329 | J 398 | | *Truelove* ex USN AM 338 | J 303 |
| *Gozo* ex USN AM 330 | J 287 | | *Welfare* ex USN AM 339 | J 356 |
| *Lightfoot* ex USN AM 331 | J 288 | | | |
| *Melita* ex USN AM 332 | J 289 | | | |
| *Octavia* ex USN AM 333 | J 290 | | | |

**NOTES:**
a) Details of the above will be found under the RN section.
b) There is some doubt in official records as to the true history of some of the above; 6 ships are listed in USN records as 'completed on an unspecified basis for the Royal Navy'.

### Built in Canada for the RCN, transferred to the RN on completion

| Name | Pendant No. | | Name | Pendant No. |
|------|-----------|---|------|-----------|
| *Coquette* ex RCN *Bowmanville* | J 350 | | *Courier* ex RCN *Arnprior* | J 349 |

| | | | | |
|---|---|---|---|---|
| *Felicity* | J 369 | | *Moon* | J 329 |
| ex RCN *Coppercliff* | | | ex RCN *Mimico* | |
| *Providence* | J 325 | | *Marmion* | J 381 |
| ex RCN *Forest Hill* | | | ex RCN *Orangeville* | |
| *Lysander* | J 379 | | *Lioness* | J 377 |
| ex RCN *Hespeler* | | | ex RCN *Petrolia* | |
| *Golden Fleece* | J 376 | | *Seabear* | J 333 |
| ex RCN *Humberstone* | | | ex RCN *St Thomas* | |
| *Prompt* | J 378 | | *Flying Fish* | J 370 |
| ex RCN *Huntsville* | | | ex RCN *Tillsonburg* | |
| *Mariner* | J 380 | | | |
| ex RCN *Kincardine* | | | | |
| *Serene* | J 354 | | | |
| ex RCN *Leaside* | | | | |
| *Regulus* | J 327 | | | |
| ex RCN *Longbranch* | | | | |

**NOTE.**

All the above were transferred to the RN in exchange for the same number of 'Castle' class corvettes built in the UK. The latter carry the same RCN names as the above; they are listed above in RCN name order, and full details will be found under the RN section.

## Built in Canada direct for the RN

| Name | Pendant No. | | Name | Pendant No. |
|---|---|---|---|---|
| *Jaseur* | J 428 | | *Nerissa* | J 456 |
| *Laertes* | J 433 | | *Orcadia* | J 462 |
| *Maenad* | J 335 | | *Ossory* | J 463 |
| *Magicienne* | J 436 | | *Pluto* | J 446 |
| *Mameluke* | J 437 | | *Polaris* | J 447 |
| *Mandate* | J 438 | | *Pyrrhus* | J 448 |
| *Marvel* | J 443 | | *Romola* | J 449 |
| *Michael* | J 444 | | *Rosamund* | J 439 |
| *Minstrel* | J 445 | | | |
| *Myrmidon* | J 454 | | Details of these ships will be | |
| *Mystic* | J 455 | | found under the RN section. | |

## Cancelled Ships

| Name | Pendant No | Builder |
|---|---|---|
| *Nicator* | J 457 | Toronto |
| *Niger* | J 442 | Toronto |
| *Nonpareil* | J 459 | Toronto |
| *Nox* | J 460 | Toronto |
| *Odin* | J 461 | Toronto |
| *Styx* | J 440 | Toronto |

## War Losses

## RCN—nil.

▲ *Ettrick* in December 1944, after transfer from the RN. She retains her RN gooseneck whaler davits, and as she accelerates at speed away from a consort she gives a good view of her depth charge outfit aft.
*(Public Archives of Canada)*

*Dunver* in October 1943, with two s...gle...guns, revealing her as one of the fir...ships of the Canadian class. Four single C...tions only, no H/F D/F, but an impressive... quarterdeck. *(Public Archives of Can...)* ▼

## RCN 'RIVER' CLASS FRIGATES
### 70 ships completed in Canada

The planning and production of this large class is one of the more fascinating stories of the escort building programmes.

On the face of it, this was simply a carry-on from the RN 'River' class building programme in the UK. But it was a magnificent achievement for the Canadian yards to switch from the much simpler 'Flower' class corvette programme to these more sophisticated frigates, and if the Canadian ships are examined closely a number of significant improvements can be found over the UK-built ships.

This stems partly from the fact that in general the Canadian-built 'River' class units were completed later than their UK-built counterparts, so that later equipment could be added, and advantage taken of previous sea experience with ships of the class. More frigates of this class were built in Canada than in the UK, and in addition there was a long cancellation list from the Canadian programme; if these ships had all been built, there would have been about three Canadian-built ships of the class to every one which was UK-built. In part, this was due to the RN switching to the mass-production 'Loch' class, while the Canadian 'River' class was still in production, and it is probable that, had the escort building momentum been maintained in 1943/45, we should have seen a number of the 'Loch' class being built in Canada as well as the UK.

The class was originally known in Canada, as in the UK, as Lengthened Twin Screw Corvettes. The specification closely followed that of the UK-built ships, the plans and building schedules being produced in the UK and sent to Canada.

Alterations and additions followed RN lists throughout the war, but the RCN made a number of impressive improvements to their ships.

In February 1942 the Admiralty asked that all 'River' class frigates building in Canada should be completed as long endurance ships, with no Oropesa or LL minesweeping gear. Similarly, when *Ettrick* was transferred from the RN to the RCN, she was fitted with this gear; it was removed by the RCN, due to the difficulty in maintaining it in working order while the ship was on North Atlantic escort duty.

The RCN took an interesting direction in the fitting of main and close-range armament. Apart from the first 15 units of the class, all others received a twin 4″ mounting forward, and a single 12 pounder aft. The first 15 ships also received the twin forward mounting on coming in for their first major refit.

The RCN went all out for the excellent twin power-mounted Oerlikons, and ordered 643 mountings in Canada in March 1943. At that time these guns were in short supply, and being delivered from the USA. As the Canadian mountings came into full production the following year, a severe shortage of them appeared in the UK for larger ships, and some of the Canadian-produced mountings were diverted to the RN for a time.

It is interesting to find that a quadruple power-operated Oerlikon mounting was under trial by the John Inglis company in Canada in June 1943; it could be adapted for naval use if required, but none is apparent in photographs.

Hedgehog mountings, standard fittings in all these ships, were obtained from the UK, where they were in quantity production.

The Canadian-built ships showed a significant improvement ove... the UK-built ships in the provision and handling of boats. The Canadian shi... were all fitted with 25 foot naval motor cutters and 27 foot whalers, all slung in gravity davits, a great improvement over the UK-built ships. The 7 RN ships tr...sferred to the RCN came with their UK boat outfits; some were altered whi...e serving with the RCN.

Some 'River' class units, ordered in Canada by the USN, were de...ered on completion to the RN, as described elsewhere. *Barle,* the first unit so ...elivered, impressed the RN authorities on her arrival in the UK; she had ...her full complement of 10 Oerlikon mountings, and some of them were twin... and her boats were in the Schat welded davits. There was more welding used i...her hull than was at that time usual in the UK-built units.

When the RCN 'River' class ships were coming into service, t...e North Atlantic policy was to have the close escort groups composed of 2 frigat...s and 4-6 corvettes. This required the 'River' class units to act as Senior Officer'... ship of a group more often than units of other classes; as a result, no less than 3...of the 60 RCN ships of this class were fitted as Senior Officer's ships.

The detailed specification attached shows the equipment authorise... for each ship; but due to temporary shortages of some items not all ships rece...ed their full quota on first commissioning, and the missing guns and sets w...re fitted either during lay-over periods or in the first long refit.

One result was that ships stationed on the Pacific coast of Canada u... to 1945, not having the same level of submarine opposition, were not usually f...ted with H/F D/F, and indeed, in some photographs, their depth-charge equ...ment is under canvas covers while at sea. Their camouflage may have followe... a USN Pacific pattern, rather than the North Atlantic patterns to be seen ...other photographs.

## Refit for Pacific service, 1945

In late 1944, plans were made by the Admiralty for the provision ...f large numbers of escorts for the British Pacific and East Indies Fleets. For th... British Pacific Fleet there was a joint requirement for large numbers of both ...A and A/S frigates and sloops. For the latter, the Admiralty converted up to ...0 'Loch' class frigates on the stocks, and renamed them the 'Bay' class of A/A fri...tes; the RCN was also invited to convert 20 'River' class units, and this number ...s later increased to 40 units, out of the original RCN total of 60 ships of th... class.

The Admiralty proposed three alternative schemes to Ottawa, but ...he latter did not consider that any of the schemes produced a sufficiently improv...d escort to justify the work involved in the conversion. It was estimated that fou... months' work would be involved in producing the detailed drawings, followed b... four to six months' conversion work in a yard, and it looked as if no ships ...uld be completed much before the end of 1945.

The conversion mainly involved the addition of Bofors as close-range weapons—but at that time the total substitution of Bofors for Oerlikons, even the twin mountings, had not been approved.

It would appear from all official records that no RCN 'River' class units were refitted in time to join the British Pacific Fleet before VJ-Day. Certainly none are shown as being on station at that time, though some ships must have been completing refitting, working-up, or on passage by then. The photographs included of ships of this class after refit, at the end of 1945, show some of the variations made by the RCN, notably in the purchase of Type SU radar sets from the USA, and the fitting of more advanced H/F D/F sets. But equally it would appear that some of the delays foreseen in the provision of new equipment actually occurred; the photographs of *Swansea* and *Outremont* after refit show empty gun platforms aft, where the new twin Bofors should have been. A comparison is with *Tay,* refitted in the UK for the Far East, where the single 4″ guns originally fitted have been left in place, but 2 single Bofors have been fitted on the after gun platform; the Canadian ships probably would have retained their twin power-mounted Oerlikons.

We will list here, first, the Admiralty proposals for these refits, and then the revised plans from Ottawa.

## ADMIRALTY PROPOSALS

| Schemes | A | B | C |
|---|---|---|---|
| Armament | | | |
| 4″ twin | 1 twin | 1 twin | |
| 4″ single | 2 singles | 1 single | |
| Twin 40mm Mk V with austerity director | 2 twin | 2 twin | |
| Twin 20mm Mk V | 2 twin | 2 twin | |
| Single 20mm Mk VIIA | 5 | 5 | 4 |
| Rangefinder director for 4″ guns | Yes | Yes | Yes |
| Depth charges reduced to | 60 | 60 | 60 |

Radar, Types 285, 291, 293, 242, 258, for all three schemes. Bridge to be reconstructed, no deckhouse forward of it. Mast to be strengthened, or new lattice mast to be fitted. New deckhouse to be fitted amidships, for extra officers. Permanent extra ballast to be supplied, A-70 tons, B-110 tons, C-85 tons. An inclining experiment to be carried out on the first ship to be completed.

*RCN REVISED PROPOSALS* Main Armament The first 15 ships completed were the only RCN ones with two single 4″ guns; these would have a twin 4″ mounting substituted forward, and the single 4″ aft retained. All other RCN ships were already fitted with a twin 4″ mounting forward, thus being ahead of the Admiralty proposals.

*Close-range Armament*   The RCN planned to replace the 12 pounder gun fitted aft with a twin 40mm Bofors. These were to be produced in the USA, where production of these weapons had been stepped up so fast for the Pacific war; it was hoped that 6 complete equipments would be delivered to the RCN each month, commencing in April 1945, but actual deliveries are not clear.

All frigates were already fitted throughout with 4 twin power-mounted Oerlikons, and no plan was apparent to replace these with single 40mm Bofors, or with single pom poms.

*Radar*   The RCN ordered 25 sets of Type SU from the USA, and 20 sets of Type 277 from the UK. These were all for delivery during 1945, but apart from the photographic details actual fitting by individual ships is not available. Certainly it was planned that all ships joining the British Pacific Fleet should be fitted with one of these two advanced sets.

*Direction Finding*   The existing H/F D/F sets were to be replaced by Type DAU, and the delivery situation was fairly easy, as again the photographs demonstrate. Where Type SU radar was fitted, it was put at the foremasthead, necessitating the H/F D/F aerial being moved to a new pole mast aft, which was kept separate from the small mainmast which carried the main wireless aerials. The existing types of navigational equipment were to be replaced by the new Loran Type DAS3. It was not expected that VH/F D/F equipment would be available in time for these ships' departure for the Far East.

*St Stephen* off Esquimalt, BC, August 1944. The twin 4″ forward, and 12 pounder aft, are clear. She has four power-operated twin Oerlikon mountings. *(Public Archives of Canada)*

*RADIO EQUIPMENT* Fighter Direction radio-telephone equipment, Type TDQ-RCK, was to be fitted in the main W/T Office.

*ASDIC* All ships were to be fitted with the complete Type 144 set. 'Q' attachments would be completed at refit, and the depth-finding set, Type 147B, would also be added to each ship.

*TROPICALISATION* Naturally, this was to be carried out to each ship, mainly involving the fitting of extra fans to all living and fighting compartments, and the insulation against heat of deckheads, wherever exposed to direct sunlight.

*REFITTING FACILITIES* Clearly, this was a major factor in the arrival of these ships in the Pacific. No firm plans could be made to step up the capability of Canadian yards to accept frigates for these special refits while the war against Germany was still demanding the operational presence of these ships in the North Atlantic and UK inshore waters. So it was May 1945 before the full programme could commence, and then the relatively very short interval to VJ-Day precluded the possibility of many of these ships being refitted and on station with the British Pacific Fleet.

The main Canadian refitting yards were Halifax, Sydney and Shelburne naval bases, and it was expected that the total number of frigates which could be refitted by these and five smaller yards, once the programme was going full blast, and assuming that all new equipment was readily available, appeared to be 10 per month.

In order to achieve this it would be necessary to defer the refits of 'Algerine' and 'Flower' class ships, and the de-storing of ships not required for the Pacific war would need to be deferred. In parallel, we may see here the need to de-commission a large proportion of the corvettes and fleet minesweepers as soon as possible after the end of the European war, not only to conserve the refitting facilities for the Pacific frigates, but also to release the necessary manpower for the remanning of these frigates, at a time when demobilisation of men had already become a requirement in its own right.

### Headquarters Ships for the East Indies

During the same period the Admiralty asked for the return of 4 out of the 7 ships of this class, on loan to the RCN. These 4 ships were needed back in the UK for conversion to Landing Ships Headquarters (Small), and this is fully described under the RN 'River' class frigate chapter.

### Postwar Conversions

Briefly, we should touch on the interesting post-war conversions made to some of the RCN 'River' class ships. These may be compared with the RN's conversion of war-built fleet destroyers to fast frigates, and also with the staff requirements for improved A/S weapons and tactics, originating in 1944, for fighting the new fast German U-boats.

By 1949 *Swansea* had had a further refit from the intermediate one illustrated and had received remote power control training for her 4" guns, Type 277 radar as well as the USN Type SU, a lattice mast to carry the heavier Type 277 aerial, and yet she was still only in a fast-moving interim phase.

At the same time *St Stephen* had part of her upper bridge enclosed, and later all ships remaining in commission had new enclosed bridges, with open bridges constructed above, and new tripod masts. The upper deck was built up right through to the stern, to enable double Squid or Limbo mortars to be fitted aft, and *Buckingham*, among others, had a helicopter flight deck fitted aft—a precursor of the later postwar frigates. We have located an interesting set of comparative photographs to illustrate these changes.

## GERMAN U-BOATS SUNK BY CANADIAN 'RIVER' CLASS

| U 257 | 24.2.44 | *Waskesiu* |
|-------|---------|-----------|
| U 744 | 6.3.44 | *St Catherines* and others |
| U 845 | 10.3.44 | *Owen Sound, Swansea* and others |
| U 448 | 14.4.44 | *Swansea* and others |
| U 247 | 1.9.44 | *St John, Swansea* and others |
| U 484 | 9.9.44 | *Dunver* and others |
| U 877 | 27.12.44 | *St Thomas* |
| U 309 | 16.2.45 | *St John* |
| U 1302 | 7.3.45 | *La Hulloise, Strathadam* and *Thetford Mines* |
| U 1003 | 20.3.45 | *New Glasgow* |

*Swansea* after refit for the Far East in 1945. She now has a twin 4" mounting forward, but her after position is empty, presumably due to delays in the specified twin Bofors mounting. She has Type 271 radar, not Type SU or 277, but she has the newer H/F D/F aerial aft. She has four twin Oerlikons. *(Ministry of Defence)*

## RCN 'RIVER' CLASS SPECIFICATIONS

For this class, more detailed breakdowns are given than usual; this results from much information becoming available in London and Ottawa, which gives in this case a particularly clear picture of the progressive fitting of new equipment.

| | |
|---|---|
| Displacement | 1,445 tons standard |
| Dimensions | |
|     length pp | 283' 0" |
|         oa | 301' 6" |
|     breadth | 36' 7" |
|     draught | 11' 6" forward |
| | 14' 4" aft |
| Machinery | 4 cylinder triple expansion |
| Boilers | 2 Admiralty 3-drum type |
| Shafts | 2 |
| IHP | 5,500 |
| Speed | 20 kn designed |
| | 19 kn full speed at deep draught |
| Oil Fuel | 646 tons |
| Endurance | 7,200×12 kn |
| | 4,500×full speed |
| Complement | 13 officers, 144 men |
| Armament | |
|     main | |

1) 2 single 4" QF HA/LA Mk XI on Mk XXIII mtgs. 200 rounds per gun (This was carried by the first 15 ships of the class to be completed in Canada—
   *Waskesiu, St Catherines, Prince Rupert, Dunver, Swansea, Matane, Cape Breton, Montreal, Port Colborne, Outremont, Stormont, Grou, Wentworth, St John, New Glasgow*)

2) This was revised, during the first refits in 1945, to the following, for all the above 15 ships, except *Matane*, which refitted in the UK due to battle damage; *Matane* retained her original 2 single 4" guns:
   1 twin 4" Mk XVI on Mk XXIII HA/LA mtg forward
   1 single 4" as above, aft

3) All other Canadian-built ships of this class (45 in number) were fitted on completion with:
   1 twin 4" Mk XIX on Mk XXIII mtg HA/LA forward.
   252 rounds per gun
   1 single 12-pdr Mk V on Mk XX HA/LA mtg aft

4) The 7 units transferred on loan from the RN retained their original armament of:
   2 single 4" Mk XIX on Mk XXIII HA/LA mtgs, with 220 rounds per gun

5) All ships received on completion, or at refit:
   2 2" rocket flare projectors, fitted to the forward gun
   2 Snowflake rocket projectors on the bridge
   2 PAC projectors in some units

| | |
|---|---|
| Close-Range | All Canadian-built ships of the class were fitted on completion, or during 1944, with the following:<br>4 twin 20mm Oerlikon Mk Vc on power-operated mtgs<br>2 Bren machine-guns<br>The 7 units on loan from the RN were fitted as follows:<br>2 twin 20mm Oerlikons, Mk Vc<br>2 single 20mm Oerlikons, Mk IIIA or VIIA<br>2 Bren Machine-guns |
| A/S Armament | 1 Hedgehog<br>4 depth charge throwers<br>2 depth charge rails<br>150-200 depth charges |
| Radar | The main warning set, on completion, was as follows:<br>21 ships Type RXC (similar to Type 271, and with the same lantern)<br>9 ships Type 271P<br>30 ships Type 271Q<br>All ships in addition received Types 242, 253, and 251M. But 20 ships received the American Type ABK interrogator in place of the RN-type equipment |
| H/F D/F | All ships were designated to receive an H/F D/F set, but it is clear from the photographs that not all ships were so fitted on completion. Sets supplied were Type FH3 for 10 ships, Type DAQ to 1 *(Wentworth)*, and Type FH4 for the remainder |
| M/F D/F | All ships were designated to receive a set.<br>13 received Type MDF5, 2 Type FM7, and the remainder Type FM12 |
| Navigational D/F | This was not so widely fitted, though most useful in the North Atlantic. 12 ships were not fitted on completion, the remainder received Loran Type IA (12 ships), Type II *(St Stephen,* and Type III *Buckingham, Incharran* and *Victoriaville)*, while 6 ships received the more advanced Type DAS1 |
| Foxer Gear | 19 ships were not fitted on completion (no doubt only due to shortage of equipment), the rest received CAT Mk II |
| Asdic Equipment | Only the lead ship, *Waskesiu,* received Type 128DV. The others all received variants of the more advanced Type 144, mostly with the 'Q' attachment. 4 ships received the depth-finding set, Type 147B *(Beacon Hill, Thetford Mines, La Hulloise* and *Seacliff)* |
| Units on loan from RN | These generally followed the same pattern, the RN ships being fitted very similarly in the UK. 2 ships, *Ettrick* and *Annan,* had the RN Foxer Gear, and not CAT Mk II, and 4 ships, *Meon, Teme, Monnow* and *Annan* had SA Gear, Type A, Mk II, as also fitted to the 3 'Loch' class transferred from the RN to the RCN on completion in the UK. |

## RCN 'RIVER' CLASS PRODUCTION

| | | | | |
|---|---|---|---|---|
| 1942 | 2nd half | 5 | TOTAL SHIPS BUILT IN CANADA | 70 |
| 1943 | 1st half | 7 | Retained by RCN | 60 |
| | 2nd half | 27 | Transferred from UK | 7 |
| 1944 | 1st half | 17 | TOTAL RCN SHIPS OF CLASS | 67 |
| | 2nd half | 4 | Built for USN | 2 |
| | | | Built for USN, and transferred to RN | 8 |
| | | | Cancelled ships | 97 |

*Ste Thérèse* at Halifax, August 1944. A good view of the 'River' class bow section, compared with the bluffer 'Flower' class. She has the twin 4″ forward, H/F D/F at the masthead, and twin Oerlikons in the bridge wings, as well as aft. *(Public Archives of Canada)*

## RCN 'RIVER' CLASS—CLASS LIST

| Name | Pendant No | Job No | Builder | Building Time | Completion Date |
|------|-----------|--------|---------|---------------|-----------------|
| **BUILT IN CANADA** | | | | | |
| **1942-43 Programme** | | | | | |
| Beacon Hill | K 407 | CN 377 | Yarrow | 10m1d | 16.5.4 |
| Cap de la Madeleine | K 663 | CN 350 | Morton | 10m26d | 30.9.4 |
| Cape Breton | K 350 | CN 345 | ,, | 17m20d | 25.10. |
| Charlottetown | K 244 | CN 492 | Davie | 15m3d | 28.4.4 |
| Chebogue | K 317 | CN 387 | Yarrow | 11m6d | 22.2.4 |
| Dunver ex Verdun | K 388 | CN 344 | Morton | 16m6d | 11.9.4 |
| Eastview | K 665 | CN 376 | Vickers | 9m8d | 23.6.4 |
| Grou | K 518 | CN 354 | ,, | 7m4d | 5.12.4 |
| Joliette | K 418 | CN 349 | Morton | 10m26d | 14.6.4 |
| Jonquière | K 318 | CN 493 | Davie | 15m21d | 10.5.4 |
| Kirkland Lake ex St Jérôme | K 337 | CN 491 | Morton | 9m4d | 21.8.4 |
| Kokaneé | K 419 | CN 378 | Yarrow | 9m12d | 6.6.44 |
| La Hulloise | K 668 | CN 375 | Vickers | 9m10d | 20.5.4 |
| Longueuil | K 672 | CN 374 | ,, | 10m1d | 18.5.4 |
| Magog | K 673 | CN 373 | ,, | 10m21d | 7.5.44 |
| Matane | K 444 | CN 353 | ,, | 5m21d | 23.10. |
| Montreal ex Stormont | K 319 | CN 352 | ,, | 11m20d | 12.11. |
| New Glasgow | K 320 | CN 385 | Yarrow | 11m19d | 23.12. |
| New Waterford | K 321 | CN 386 | ,, | 11m0d | 21.1.4 |
| Orkney | K 448 | CN 389 | ,, | 11m30d | 18.4.4 |
| Outremont | K 322 | CN 346 | Morton | 12m9d | 27.11. |
| Port Colborne | K 326 | CN 383 | Yarrow | 11m30d | 15.11. |
| Prince Rupert | K 324 | CN 381 | ,, | 13m0d | 30.8.4 |
| St Catherines | K 325 | CN 379 | ,, | 14m2d | 31.7.4 |
| St John | K 456 | CN 371 | Vickers | 7m15d | 14.12. |
| Springhill | K 323 | CN 388 | Yarrow | 10m16d | 21.3.4 |
| Stettler | K 681 | CN 372 | Vickers | 11m7d | 7.5.44 |
| Stormont | K 327 | CN 351 | ,, | 6m26d | 28.11. |
| Swansea | K 328 | CN 382 | Yarrow | 14m20d | 24.10. |
| Thetford Mines | K 459 | CN 348 | Morton | 10m17d | 24.5.4 |
| Valleyfield | K 329 | CN 347 | ,, | 10m5d | 7.12.4 |
| Waskesiu | K 330 | CN 380 | Yarrow | 12m18d | 17.6.4 |
| Wentworth | K 331 | CN 384 | ,, | 12m27d | 7.12.4 |
| **1943-44 Programme** | | | | | |
| Antigonish | K 661 | CN 557 | ,, | 5m3d | 4.7.44 |
| Buckingham ex Royal Mount | K 685 | | Davie | 12m22d | 2.11.4 |

| | | | | | |
|---|---|---|---|---|---|
| *Capilano* | K 409 | CN 559 | Yarrow | 9m6d | 25.8.44 |
| *Carlplace* | K 664 | CN 587 | Davie | 12m13d | 13.12.44 |
| *Coaticook* | K 410 | CN 579 | ,, | 13m10d | 25.7.44 |
| *Fort Erie* | K 670 | CN 479 | G. T. Davie | 11m23d | 27.10.44 |
| ex *La Tuque* | | | | | |
| *Glace Bay* | K 414 | CN 495 | ,, | 11m9d | 2.9.44 |
| ex *Lauzon* | | | | | |
| *Hallowell* | K 666 | CN 566 | Vickers | 8m16d | 8.8.44 |
| *Inch Arran* | K 667 | | Davie | 12m20d | 18.11.44 |
| *Lanark* | K 669 | CN 556 | Vickers | 9m11d | 6.7.44 |
| *Lasalle* | K 519 | CN 578 | Davie | 12m24d | 29.6.44 |
| *Lauzon* | K 671 | CN 496 | G. T. Davie | 13m27d | 30. 8.44 |
| ex *Glace Bay* | | | | | |
| *Levis* | K 400 | CN 494 | ,, | 16m24d | 21.7.44 |
| *Penetang* | K 676 | CN 516 | Davie | 12m27d | 19.10.44 |
| *Poundmaker* | K 675 | CN 568 | Vickers | 8m19d | 17.9.44 |
| *Prestonian* | K 662 | | Davie | 13m24d | 13.9.44 |
| ex *Beauharnois* | | | | | |
| *Royal Mount* | K 677 | CN 584 | Vickers | 8m18d | 25.8.44 |
| ex *Alvington* | | | | | |
| *Runnymede* | K 678 | CN 555 | ,, | 9m3d | 14.6.44 |
| *St Pierre* | K 680 | CN 580 | Davie | 13m22d | 22.8.44 |
| *St Stephen* | K 454 | CN 558 | Yarrow | 9m23d | 28.7.44 |
| *Ste Thérèse* | K 366 | CN 577 | Davie | 12m9d | 28.5.44 |
| *Seacliff* | K 394 | CN 712 | ,, | 14m6d | 26.9.44 |
| ex *Megantic* | | | | | |
| *Stonetown* | K 531 | CN 565 | Vickers | 8m3d | 21.7.44 |

*Lévis* off Lévis, Quebec. Ocean escorts were not only built here, but came here operationally as well. *(Ministry of Defence)*

| Name | Pendant No | Job No | Builder | Building Time | Completion Date |
|------|-----------|--------|---------|---------------|-----------------|
| *Strathadam* | K 682 | CN 560 | Yarrow | 9m23d | 29.9.44 |
| *Sussexvale* | K 683 | CN 661 | Davie | 12m14d | 29.11.44 |
| ex *Valdorien* | | | | | |
| *Toronto* | K 538 | CN 576 | ,, | 11m27d | 6.5.44 |
| ex *Giffard* | | | | | |
| *Victoriaville* | K 684 | CN 573 | G.T.Davie | 11m9d | 11.11.44 |

## UK-BUILT, TRANSFERRED TO RCN        TRANSFER DATE

| Name | Pendant No | Builder | Transfer Date |
|------|-----------|---------|---------------|
| *Annan* | K 404 | Hall Russell | 13.6.44 |
| *Ettrick* | K 254 | Crown | 29.1.44 |
| *Meon* | K 269 | Inglis | 7.2.44 |
| *Monnow* | K 441 | Hill | 8.3.44 |
| *Nene* | K 270 | Smith's Dock | 6.4.44 |
| *Ribble* | K 251 | Blyth | 24.7.44 |
| *Teme* | K 458 | Smith's Dock | 28.2.44 |

Further building details of these ships will be found under RN section.

## BUILT IN CANADA FOR USN

| Name | Pendant No | Job No | Builder | |
|------|-----------|--------|---------|---|
| USS *Asheville* | PF 1 | CN 334 | Vickers | L22.8.42 |
| ex RN *Adur* | | | | |
| ex RCN *Nadur* | | | | |
| USS *Natchez* | PF 2 | CN 335 | ,, | L12.9.42 |
| ex RCN *Annan* | | | | |

## BUILT IN CANADA FOR USN, DELIVERED TO RN ON COMPLETION

| Name | Pendant No | Builder |
|------|-----------|---------|
| *Barle* | K 289 | Vickers |
| ex *PG 103* | | |
| *Cuckmere* | K 299 | ,, |
| ex *PG 104* | | |
| *Evenlode* | K 300 | ,, |
| ex USS *Danville,* | PG 105 | |
| *Findhorn* | K 301 | ,, |
| ex *PG 106* | | |
| *Inver* | K 301 | ,, |
| ex *PG 107* | | |
| *Lossie* | K 303 | ,, |
| ex *PG 108* | | |
| *Parret* | K 304 | ,, |
| ex *PG 109* | | |
| *Shiel* | K 305 | ,, |
| ex *PG 110* | | |

Further details of these ships are under the RN section.

## CANCELLED SHIPS

|  | Job No | Building Yard Location |  |  |  |
|---|---|---|---|---|---|
| *Alexandria* | CN 643 | Montreal | *Rouyn* | CN 583 | ,, |
| *Alwington* | CN 567 | ,, | *Ste Agathe* | CN 571 | ,, |
| *Fort Erie* | CN 644 | Quebec | *St Edouard* | CN 659 | ,, |
| *Fort Etic* | | ,, | *St Romuauld* | CN 575 | ,, |
| *Foster* | CN 660 | Lauzon | *Shipton* | CN 572 | ,, |
| *Hardrock* | CN 570 | Montreal | *Tisdale* | CN 569 | Montreal |
| *Henryville* | CN 657 | ,, | *Valdorien* | CN 586 | Lauzon |
| *La Tuque* | CN 479 | Lauzon | *Westbury* | CN 574 | Montreal |
| *Le Havre* | CN 563 | Montreal | *Wulastock* | CN 564 | Victoria |
| *Lingabar* | CN 658 | Lauzon | 9 unnamed ships | CN 635-643 | Montreal |
| *Megantic* | CN 562 | ,, | 10 unnamed ships | CN 654-663 | Lauzon |
| *Northumberland* | CN 562 | Victoria | 8 unnamed ships | CN 646-653 | Victoria |
| *Pesaquid* | CN 561 | ,, | 2 unnamed ships | CN 644-645 | Quebec |
| *Plessiville* | CN 589 | Lauzon | 44 further projected ships | | |
| *Ranney Falls* | CN 662 | ,, | TOTAL | | 97 ships |

## WAR LOSSES

| | | |
|---|---|---|
| *Chebogue* | 4.10.44 | CTL, Gnat torpedo |
| *Magog* | 14.10.44 | ,, |
| *Teme* | 29.3.45 | ,, |
| *Valleyfield* | 7.5.44 | ,, |

NEW WATERFORD in early 1944.

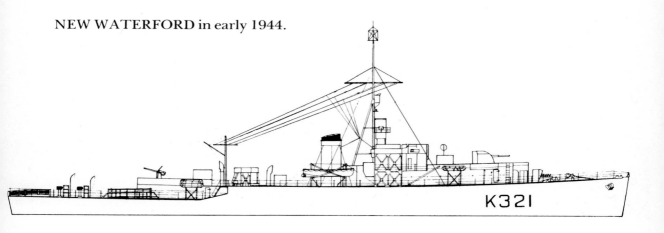

▲ *Tillsonburg* in September 1944. She has Type 272 atop the lattice mast, with H/F D/F at the topmasthead; the new 4″ gun, with single Squid in B position, and a trawler-type boat. *(Ministry of Defence)*

*Petrolia,* July 1944. A good view of the stern, with the squared-off, solid bulwark, and lack of depth charge outfit due to the Squid forward. Twin Oerlikons on the after gundeck. *(Ministry of Defence)* ▼

## RCN 'CASTLE' CLASS CORVETTES
### 12 ships transferred from UK

These ships were built in the UK and transferred on completion to the RCN. They were in part exchange for some of the 'Algerine' class fleet minesweepers being built in Canada for the RN.

These ships, with the three 'Loch' class frigates, were the only ones operated by the RCN during the war to be fitted with the new Squid ahead-throwing mortar against submarines. Stocks of the heavy missiles had been built up at Halifax and St. John's, and these 'Castle' class units were fitted exactly as their counterparts in the RN, with a single Squid.

They were also the first escorts built for the RCN to have the new lattice masts, supporting either the originally specified Type 272 radar aerial, or the later elliptical Type 277. Both types can be seen in the RCN photographs.

Some of these ships carried the Canadian maple leaf emblem on their funnels on commissioning in the UK, the others probably added it on arrival in Canada.

The new RN escorts were now carrying, when available, the full 25 foot motor boat and 27 foot whaler, as the Canadian 'River' class units had already been carrying for some time. The Canadian 'Castle' class ships came so fitted, though it will be seen that *Orangeville* on commissioning had only a small motor dinghy, in older-type gooseneck davits on the port side.

As with the RN, these ships were for some time referred to during the construction period as Lengthened Single Screw Corvettes, before they received the 'Castle' class name in the RN. The RCN ships continued their escort tradition by carrying names of Canadian towns.

*Kincardine* on commissioning at Middlesbrough in July 1944. Type 272 radar, with Type 244 below it on a spur, and H/F D/F at the topmasthead—not fitted in the 'Flower' class. *(Ministry of Defence)*

## RCN 'CASTLE' CLASS SPECIFICATION

| | |
|---|---|
| Displacement | 1,010 tons standard |
| Dimensions | |
|   length pp | 225' 0" |
|       oa | 251' 9" |
|   breadth | 36' 8" |
|   draught | 19' 0" mean |
| Machinery | 4 cylinder triple expansion |
| Boilers | 1 Admiralty water tube |
| Shafts | L |
| IHP | 2,750 |
| Speed | 16.5 kn |
| Oil Fuel | 480 tons |
| Endurance | 6,200×15 kn |
| Complement | 7 officers, 112 men |
| Armament | |
|   main | 1 4" QF Mk XIX on Mk XXXII mtg. |
|   close range | 2 twin 20mm Oerlikons Mk V on power mtg |
| | 2 single 20mm Oerlikons Mk VIIA or VIIIA |
| | 2 2" rocket flare projectors |
| A/S Armament | 1 single Squid ATW mortar |
| | 15 depth charges |
| | 2 throwers, 1 rail |
| Radar | Types 272Q, 242, 253, 251M (277 later) |
| H/F D/F | FH 3 |
| M/F D/F | FM 12 |
| Navigational D/F | Loran |
| Foxer Gear | CAT Mk II |

## RCN 'CASTLE' CLASS PRODUCTION

| 1943 | 2nd half | 2 | | 1944 | 1st half | 6 |
|---|---|---|---|---|---|---|
| | | | | | 2nd half | 4 |

## RCN 'CASTLE' CLASS—CLASS LIST

**Built in the UK, and transferred to the RCN on completion**

| Name | Pendant No | Builder | Building Time | Completion Date |
|---|---|---|---|---|
| **1943-44 Programme** | | | | |
| *Arnprior* | K 494 | Harland & Wolff | 11m17d | 8.6.44 |
|   ex RN *Rising Castle* | K 398 | | | |
| *Hespeler* | K 489 | Robb | 10m17d | 28.2.44 |
|   ex RN *Guildford Castle* | K 378 | | | |
| *Huntsville* | K 499 | Fleming & | 12m6d | 6.6.44 |
|   ex RN *Wolvesey Castle* | K 461 |   Ferguson | | |

| | | | | |
|---|---|---|---|---|
| *Orangeville* | K 491 | Robb | 9m1d | 24.4.44 |
| ex RN *Hedingham Castle* | K 396 | | | |
| *St Thomas* | K 488 | Smith's Dock | 10m12d | 24.4.44 |
| ex RN *Sandgate Castle* | K 373 | | | |

**1944-45 Programme**

| | | | | |
|---|---|---|---|---|
| *Bowmanville* | K 493 | Pickersgill | 13m17d | 28.9.44 |
| ex RN *Nunnery Castle* | K 446 | | | |
| *Coppercliff* | K 495 | Blyth | 12m26d | 25.7.44 |
| ex RN *Hever Castle* | K 521 | | | |
| *Humberstone* | K 497 | Inglis | 12m16d | 6.9.44 |
| ex RN *Norham Castle* | K 447 | | | |
| *Kincardine* | K 490 | Smith's Dock | 9m25d | 10.6.44 |
| ex RN *Tamworth Castle* | K 393 | | | |
| *Leaside* | K 492 | ,, | 10m28d | 21.8.44 |
| ex RN *Walmer Castle* | K 460 | | | |
| *Petrolia* | K 498 | Harland & Wolff | 12m8d | 29.6.44 |
| ex RN *Sherborne Castle* | K 453 | | | |
| *Tillsonburg* | K 496 | Ferguson | 12m26d | 29.6.44 |

## CANCELLED

RCN Name unknown
    ex RN *Tonbridge Castle*

## WAR LOSSES

Nil

*Bowmanville*, October 1944. She shows the handsome bow lines of her class, and Type 277 radar at the top of the lattice mast. North Atlantic blue and white camouflage. *(Ministry of Defence)*

*Loch Alvie,* Canadian-manned but retaining her RN name. Type 277 radar atop the lattice mast, with Type 244 on a spur below it; H/F D/F at the topmasthead a quadruple pom pom mounting aft, and twin Squid mortars forward. Note the single 4″ gun raised on a bandstand, but fairly exposed forward in a rough sea. *(Ministry of Defence)*

*Loch Morlich,* showing the differences in the after sections compared with the 'River' class, for mass production purposes. The quarterdeck seems clear, too, with only two throwers and one rail, but the Foxer davits and gear have plenty of space. *(Ministry of Defence)*

## RCN 'LOCH' CLASS FRIGATES
### 3 ships built in the UK

Three ships of this class, completed to the standard class specification, were transferred to the RCN on completion, and picked up by Canadian crews at the UK builders' yards. These three were a part of the 10 frigates built in the UK for the RN, and transferred to the RCN late in 1943, while still building, at the time when the joint building programmes were being cut back. A fourth ship of this class, *Loch Fionn,* was earmarked for final transfer, but she was retained by the RN as a 'Bay' class unit, in view of the need for great numbers of A/A escorts in the Far East in 1945.

They were the only RCN ships to carry the new Squid double ahead-throwing A/S mortar, though the 'Castle' class units in the RCN had the single mortar of this type. These three ships retained their RN names. They were returned to the RN after the war, and were all further transferred to new Zealand in 1948.

During the war they served in the 6th Escort Group (2 'Loch' and 7 'River', and the 9th Escort Group (1, 'Loch' and 6 'River'), both all-Canadian groups based on Londonderry.

*Loch Alvie* was the unit in the 9th Escort Group, and in October 1944 she took part in a search for a U-boat north-east of Madeira; she also attacked *U 1195* with the Free French 'River' class frigate *L'Escarmouche,* after the torpedoing of the merchant ship *Cuba* off the Nab Tower in the approaches to Portsmouth Harbour in April 1945. She was also a member of the escort of two convoys on the Russian run in November 1944 and in May 1945.

Note the fast building times recorded for these three ships.

## RCN 'LOCH' CLASS CLASS LIST

| Name | Pendant No. | Builder | Building Time | Completion Date |
|------|-------------|---------|---------------|-----------------|
| *Loch Achanalt* | K 424 | Robb | 11m0d | 31.7.44 |
| *Loch Alvie* | K 428 | Barclay Curle | 11m0d | 10.8.44 |
| *Loch Morlich* | K 517 | Swan Hunter | 1m0d | 17.7.44 |

### Cancelled

*Loch Fionn*  Completed as RN 'Bay' class unit—see RN class list.

## RCN 'LOCH' CLASS SPECIFICATION

| | |
|--|--|
| Displacement | 1,435 tons standard |
| Dimensions | |
| length pp | 286' 0" |
| oa | 307' 0" |
| breadth | 38' 6" |
| draught | 10' 6" mean |

| | |
|---|---|
| Machinery | 4-cylinder triple expansion |
| Boilers | 2 Admiralty water tube |
| Shafts | 2 |
| IHP | 5,500 |
| Speed | 19·5 kn |
| Endurance | 7,200×15 kn |
| Complement | 9 officers and 130 men |
| Armament | |
|   main | 1 single 4″ Mk V or Vc on Mk IIIxx HA/LA mtg |
|   close-range | 1 quadruple 2 pdr pom pom Mk VIII on VIIP mtg (the only ones in RCN escorts) |
| | 2 twin 20mm Oerlikon Mk V |
| | 2 single 20mm Oerlikon Mk VIIA |
| | 2 2″ rocket flare projectors |
| A/S Armament | 1 double Squid ATW mortar |
| | 2 depth charge throwers, 1 rail |
| | 15 depth charges |
| Radar | Types 277, 251M, 253, 242 |
| H/F D/F | FH3 or FH4 |
| M/F D/F | FM12 |
| Foxer Gear | CAT Mk II |
| SA Gear | Type A Mk III |

## CANADIAN ESCORT SHIPBUILDERS

Burrard Drydock Co Ltd, Vancouver, BC.
Canadian Vickers Ltd, Montreal, Que.
Collingwood Shipyards Ltd, Collingwood, Ont.
Davie Shipbuilding Co Ltd, Quebec, Que.
Dufferin Shipbuilding Co Ltd, Vancouver, BC.
G. T. Davie & Sons Ltd, Lauzon, Que.
Kingston Shipbuilding Co Ltd, Kingston, Ont.
Marine Industries Ltd, Sorel, Que.
Midland Shipbuilding Co Ltd, Midland, Ont.
Morton Engineering & Drydock Co Ltd, Morton, Ont.
North Vancouver Ship Repairs Co Ltd, Vancouver, BC.
Port Arthur Shipbuilding Co Ltd, Port Arthur, Ont.
Prince Rupert Drydock Co Ltd, Prince Rupert, BC.
Redfern Shipbuilding & Engineering Co Ltd, Toronto, Ont.
  (later renamed Toronto Shipbuilding Co Ltd).
St John Drydock & Shipbuilding Co Ltd, St John, NB.
Victoria Machinery Depot Ltd, Victoria, BC.
Yarrows Ltd, Montreal, Que.

# ROYAL AUSTRALIAN NAVY

## RAN ESCORT BUILDING POLICY

Australia, far removed from the fierce North Atlantic battle, followed a different policy during the war years.

Apart from one sloop of the RN 'Grimsby' class, ordered before the war but completed in 1940, the RAN concentrated on two escort classes. Of these, by far the most important was the 'Bathurst' class of A/S-M/S vessels, a large and effective class, numbering 60, resembling the RN 'Bangor' class in appearance but largely used on escort work. This was the only war-built class among the Commonwealth navies which was original in its own right, and the ships of the class ranged far and wide in service. As it deserves to be better known outside Australia, we have covered this class in some detail.

The second class was the Modified 'River'/'Bay' class of frigates. These were completed later than their RN counterparts, and so show some interesting variations. They, with the 'Bathurst' class, formed an effective part of the British Pacific Fleet when the emphasis switched to the Far East in 1945.

The building of these two classes represented a remarkable shipbuilding effort by Australia—this is enlarged upon in the chapter on the 'Bathurst' class. In addition to ships, however, a big programme for the manufacture of guns was started; 600 4″ QF Mark XIX on HA/LA Mark XXIII mountings were ordered in 1942, of which no less than 500 were on Admiralty account. Some appear in later photographs of ships of the 'Bathurst' class, and by February 1945 177 had been delivered. The programme was subsequently reduced to 300 units, as the war finished, and of these 200 were for Admiralty account.

*Barcoo* in her original configuration. Note the two single 4″ guns in HA mountings and with twin 4″ type shields. There are four single Oerlikons, two a side, on the main deck, in place of the RN type after gun deck, and two more on the quarterdeck. Type 271 radar on the bridge and the Australian air warning set at the masthead. *(Royal Australian Navy)*

*Diamantina* in a different post-refit configuration. The forward 4″ has been moved right forward onto a bandstand, as in the RN 'Loch' class, and Squid mortars have probably been added on B deck. The mast has been strengthened, and has an unusual lattice yard. *(P.A. Webb)*

*Warrego,* a sloop of pre-war design, completed after the war started. She has the pre-war tall masts and wide yards, two twin 4″ mountings with a bridge director, and a quadruple 0.5″ gun in B position. She is also fitted for minesweeping. *(Royal Australian Navy)*

After the Pacific war finished, a great surveying operation was needed to rechart the waters over which the battles had been fought. A surveying force was formed to cover NW and NE Australian waters, New Guinea and the Philippines, and was composed as follows, each unit comprising roughly 1 frigate, 1 RN vessel, on loan, and some 6 AMS.

Task Unit 70.5.1. *Warrego, Lachlan* and USN ships
Task Unit 70.5.2. *Challenger, Polaris, Goolgwai* and 2 ships
Task Unit 70.5.3. *Moresby, Benalla, Horsham, Shepperton, Castlemaine, Echuca* and 2 ships

## RAN CUMULATIVE TOTAL OF NEW ESCORTS BUILT

|      |          | 'Grimsby' | 'Bathurst' | 'River' | TOTALS |
|------|----------|-----------|------------|---------|--------|
| 1939 | 1st half | 1         |            |         | 1      |
|      | 2nd half |           |            |         |        |
| 1940 | 1st half |           |            |         |        |
|      | 2nd half |           | 2          |         | 2      |
| 1941 | 1st half |           | 6          |         | 6      |
|      | 2nd half |           | 7          |         | 7      |
|      | 2nd half |           | 18         |         | 18     |
| 1942 | 1st half |           | 18         |         | 18     |
| 1943 | 1st half |           | 7          | 1       | 8      |
|      | 2nd half |           | 2          | 3       | 5      |
| 1944 | 1st half |           | 4          | 2       | 6      |
|      | 2nd half |           |            | 5       | 5      |
| 1945 | 1st half |           |            | 1       | 1      |
|      | 2nd half |           |            |         |        |
|      | Totals   | 1         | 64         | 12      | 77     |

## RAN 'GRIMSBY' CLASS SLOOPS
### 4 ships built, 1 completed during war

In 1934 the RAN decided to build 4 ships to the RN's latest sloop design of the day, the 'Grimsby' class. The Cockatoo Yard was given the orders, and 3 of the 4 ships, *Yarra, Swan* and *Parramatta*, were built and had been delivered before war broke out.

The fourth unit, *Warrego*, was delivered late in 1940, and therefore comes within the scope of this book. These were good-looking ships, well proportioned, with fine lines and attractive rigging. But the wartime designs superseded them, and the RAN did not build further units of this class.

*Warrego* was reported to have been armed at first with 2 single 4″ guns, one forward and one aft, with probably a quadruple 0.5″ machine-gun in B position. Her armament was undoubtedly increased during the war years, as our photograph shows, but its date is uncertain.

*Warrego* was employed latterly as a surveying ship, was paid off into reserve in August 1963, and sold in April 1965.

## RAN MODIFIED 'RIVER'/'BAY' CLASS FRIGATES
**12 ships completed**

The RAN ordered 22 ships of this class, which followed the basic RN 'River' design closely in hull, deckhouses and main machinery, but differed considerably in main and close-range armament, and in radar.

This was largely because, as with the later RCN 'River' class units, the completed ships appeared later than any of their RN equivalents. 12 ships only were completed, the remaining 10 being cancelled in April 1944.

These 12 ships seem to fall into three main groups, divided by the progress of modifications authorised by their completion dates. It is hoped that the details which follow are correct, though some points are not entirely clear.

*1. Modified 'River' Class—early completions. 5 ships*

*Barcoo, Burdekin, Gascoyne, Hawkesbury, Lachlan*

These ships differed from the RN 'River' class units in having 2 single 4" mountings, 1 forward and 1 aft, in the 'River' positions, but without 2" rocket flare projectors forward, when first completed. They also omitted the after gun deckhouse and substituted 4 single Oerlikons, 2 on each side, facing outboard. Some units had air-warning radar Type 286, but otherwise they followed the RN 'River' design, including Type 271 radar at the back of the bridge. The bridge front was flatter in the beam section than in the RN ships.

They were refitted October 1944–early 1945 (*Gascoyne*, May 1945). *Gascoyne* received the 3 single 40mm Mark III, as in *Barwon/Macquarie*. Type 276 radar was fitted in place of Type 271. Bridge Oerlikons were dropped one deck, also following the *Barwon* modification; the 4 single Oerlikons amidships were retained, and the 2 quarterdeck guns resited on the forecastle, abreast the Hedgehog, in RN 'River' fashion.

*Barcoo* and *Burdekin* were refitted to match the *Barwon* type. *Hawkesbury* retained her Type 271 radar, and her bridge Oerlikons were not lowered by one deck. She received the 2 twin power-mounted Oerlikons amidships, but 2 single Bofors, sided, were fitted on the quarterdeck, rather than 1. The other 2 single Bofors, forward of the bridge and at the after end of the forecastle deck, were added as in *Barwon*.

*POST-WAR REFITS*  After the war, *Barcoo*, *Diamantina* and *Gascoyne* were heavily modified, to the equivalent of the RN's 'Loch' class frigates. The forward twin 4" mounting was moved forward and down, to a new bandstand on the forecastle, and the Hedgehog was removed and 2 triple Squid ATW mortars were fitted in the superstructure forward of the bridge.

A single power-mounted Bofors was fitted forward of the bridge, high above a deckhouse, and a large helicopter platform was fitted on the quarterdeck, with a hangar forward of it. The other two Bofors were not, therefore, fitted. A heavier yard was fitted to the mast, and the whaler was fitted in destroyer-type gravity davits. A torpedo recovery davit appears to have been fitted on the port quarter.

Diamantina and *Gascoyne* had their Squid removed in 1959, and were then used for oceanographical research and survey work. Their pennant numbers were changed to A266 and A276 respectively.

*Lachlan* was converted to a survey ship in 1949 and then transferred to the RNZN. A photograph of her in that configuration appears under that section.

All ships of the class were fitted for tropical service, with awnings and elaborate natural and mechanical ventilation. In addition, 2″ thick slagwood insulating board was applied to the deckheads throughout the accommodation.

As with the 'Bathurst' class which follows, we have received details of the geographical war service of these ships by courtesy of the RAN, and these are included as they may be of especial interest. It will be seen that all of the first 5 ships, completed in wartime, were engaged in bombardment of shore positions; the twin 4″ guns must have been very handy for this work, as in the RN's 'Hunt' class at the Normandy invasion.

10 ships were cancelled in April 1944; they would all have been of the later 'Bay' type. *Balmain* and *Williamstown* were named after the places where they would have been built, and not after rivers.

*2. Modified 'River' Class—later completions. 3 ships*

*Barwon, Diamantina, Macquarie*

Some further modifications were incorporated. The twin 4″ mountings were in the same positions, but 2″ rocket flare projectors were added forward. The bridge wings were reduced by one deck level, and the single Oerlikons were fitted at the sides of the flag deck, in RN destroyer fashion.

The 4 single Oerlikons aft on the forecastle deck were replaced by 2 twin power-mounted Oerlikons, and 3 single power-mounted 40mm Bofors added, 1 on top of the guncrew shelter forward of the bridge, 1 on a new deckhouse just forward of the after 4″ mounting, and 1 on the quarterdeck. Radar was changed to Type 276, and Type 286 in *Macquarie* only. Oiling at sea fittings were added to the bows, and a cap was fitted to the funnel.

*Barwon after refit. Three single, power-operated Bofors have been added, but single Oerlikons are retained in the bridge wings. Surface warning aerial on a spur on the mast, and a gun director without radar is on the bridge. (Royal Australian Navy)*

### 3. 'Bay' Class—post-war completions. 4 ships

*Condamine, Culgoa, Murchison, Shoalhaven*

These ships to a large extent did parallel the RN's 'Bay' class of the same period, designed for Pacific service. The 2 twin 4″ mountings were lowered, 1 to a bandstand on the forecastle, 1 to a similar bandstand on the quarterdeck, and a gunnery director with Type 285 radar was added at the back of the bridge. The Hedgehog was retained in its original position right forward.

3 single Bofors were mounted at the after end of the forecastle deck, in a triangular pattern, with a clear field of fire. 2 twin power-mounted Oerlikons were fitted at flag deck level in the bridgewings, replacing the single mountings fitted in the earlier ships. All the other modifications seen in the second group were also made to these ships.

They were fitted with lattice masts to match the RN 'Bay' class, in post-war refits, but *Shoalhaven* shows modifications to the topmast and aerial arrangements. Their original Bofors and Oerlikons were all removed in later refits and replaced by 5 Bofors Mark VII.

*Murchison,* as completed. She has two twin 4″ guns, with gunnery director with Type 285 radar. There is a main surface warning array on a spur on the mast, and the air warning set at the masthead. There are twin Oerlikon mountings in the bridge wings. Oiling at sea bulges are at each side of the forecastle by the big bollards. *(Evans, Deakin, Brisbane)*

## RAN MODIFIED 'RIVER'/'BAY' CLASS SPECIFICATION

| | Mod 'River' (early) | Mod 'River' (later) | 'Bay' (postwar) | A/S conversion (postwar) |
|---|---|---|---|---|
| | *Barcoo* *Burdekin* *Gascoyne* *Hawkesbury* *Lachlan* | *Barwon* *Diamantina* *Macquarie* | *Condamine* *Culgoa* *Murchison* *Shoalhaven* | *Barcoo* *Diamantina* *Gascoyne* |
| **Displacement** | | | | |
| standard | 1,420 | 1,420 | 1,544 | 1,340 |
| full load | 2,220 | 2,220 | 2,187 | 2,127 |
| **Dimensions** | | | | |
| length pp | 283'0" | 283'0" | 283'0" | 283'0" |
| oa | 301'6" | 301'6" | 301'6" | 301'6" |
| breadth | 36'6" | 36'6" | 36'6" | 36'6" |
| draught | 12'0" | 12'0" | 12'0" | 12'0" |
| **Machinery** | 4-cylinder triple expansion reciprocating | | | |
| **Boilers** | 2 Yarrow Admiralty 3-drum type | | | |
| **Shafts** | 2 | 2 | 2 | 2 |
| **IHP** | 5,500 | 5,500 | 5,500 | 5,500 |
| **Speed** | 20 kn | 20 kn | 20 kn | 20 kn |
| **Oil Fuel** | | | 500 | |
| **Endurance** | | | 5180×12 kn | |
| **Complement** | 140 | 140 | 177 | 125 |
| **Armament** | | | | |
| main | 2 4" Mk V on Mk XX HA mtgs | 4 4" Mk XVI T | 4 4" Mk XVI | 2 4" Mk XVI |
| close-range | 8 single Oerlikons *later* 3 single Bofors Mk III 8 single Oerlikons | 3 single Bofors Mk III 2 twin power-mounted Oerlikons Mk V 2 single Oerlikons | 3 single Bofors Mk III 2 twin power-mounted Oerlikons Mk V *later* 5 single Bofors Mk VII | 1/2 single Bofors |
| **A/S Armament** | 1 Hedgehog 150 d/cs* | 1 Hedgehog 150 d/cs | 1 Hedgehog 150 d/cs | 2 Squids ? 15 d/cs |
| **Radar** | Type 271 Type 286 (some) | Type 276 | Type 276 Type 285 Type 286 or 291 | Type 276 |

\* *Hawkesbury* and *Gascoyne* 116 only.

## RAN MODIFIED 'RIVER/BAY' CLASS WARTIME SERVICE

| | |
|---|---|
| *Barcoo* | New Guinea, New Britain, Borneo escort, A/S patrols, bombardment Japanese shore positions |
| *Burdekin* | New Guinea, Halmaheras, Philippines, Borneo, escort, A/S patrols, bombardments Japanese shore positions |
| *Diamantina* | Solomon Islands, bombardments |
| *Gascoyne* | New Guinea escort, survey, Philippines, Borneo, bombardments and escort |
| *Hawkesbury* | New Guinea—Pacific escort, New Guinea—Philippines escort, Borneo escort, bombardments, Moluccas—Timor surveillance |
| *Lachlan* | survey duty, Philippines, Borneo, Morotai |

TOTAL BUILT IN AUSTRALIA  12    Retained by RAN  12    War Losses  0
Cancelled Ships  10

*Macquarie*, with the single Bofors before and abaft the after single 4″ gun. A clear view of the RAN-type air warning array at the masthead. *(Royal Australian Navy)*

## RAN MODIFIED 'RIVER'/'BAY' CLASS—CLASS LIST

| Name | Pendant No | Builder | Building Time | Completion Date |
|------|-----------|---------|---------------|-----------------|
| **'River' Class: early completions** | | | | |
| *Barcoo* | K 375 | Cockatoo | 21m27d | 17.8.44 |
| *Burdekin* | K 376 | Walkers | 20m20d | 27.6.44 |
| *Gascoyne* | K 354 | Morts | 16m8d | 18.11.43 |
| *Hawkesbury* | K 363 | ,, | 22m7d | 5.7.44 |
| *Lachlan* | K 364 | ,, | 22m23d | 14.2.45 |
| **Later Completions** | | | | |
| *Barwon* | K 406 | Cockatoo | | L12.1.46 |
| *Diamantina* | K 377 | Walkers | 24m15d | 27.4.45 |
| *Macquarie* | K 532 | Morts | | 21.12.45 |
| **'Bay' Class** | | | | |
| *Condamine* | K 698 | Newcastle | | L20.10.44 |
| *Culgoa* | K 408 | Williamstown | | L22.9.44 |
| *Murchison* | K 442 | Evans, Deakin | | 17.12.46 |
| *Shoalhaven* | K 535 | Walkers | | 1.5.45 |
| **Cancelled Ships** | | | | |
| *Balmain* | K 467 | Sydney | | |
| *Bogam* | K 09 | Newcastle | | |
| *Campaspe* | K 24 | Sydney | | |
| *Murrumbidgee* | K 534 | Melbourne | | |
| *Naomi* | K 55 | Sydney | | |
| *Nepean* | | ,, | | |
| *Warburton* | K 533 | Evans, Deakin | | |
| *Williamstown* | | Melbourne | | |
| *Wimmera* | K 86 | Sydney | | |
| *Wollondilly* | | ,, | | |

*Shoalhaven* after refit, with lattice mast, a large spur on the forward edge, and probably Type 293 radar just aft of it, an unusual arrangement. She has three single Bofors, two in the bridge wings, one aft, and the 4″ mountings have been lowered onto new bandstands. *(P.A. Webb)*

▲ *Bathurst,* the name ship of her class, flying the red ensign on builder's trials. She has the tall main and mizzen masts and full minesweeping gear aft, but no depth charges. A 4" gun forward without shield, and there are no close-range weapons visible. *(Royal Australian Navy)*

*Geraldton,* an RN unit with upper conning position above the covered wheelhouse and Type 290 radar at the masthead. The 4" gun barrel is being changed. The ship alongside has Type 271 radar and an Australian air warning array at the masthead. *(Royal Australian Navy)* ▼

## RAN 'BATHURST' A/S-M/S VESSELS
## 60 ships completed

We have commented in the RAN policy chapter on the particular interest of this class; we will now cover it in some detail, as much of this will not be at all well known outside Australia.

The class was in the design stage during 1939. The ships were first rated as AMS (Australian Minesweepers), but they were also widely referred to as corvettes. In the early years it was estimated that U-boats would not operate in Australian waters, and that mine warfare would be the greatest threat; early ships of the class reflect this emphasis heavily, while in some later ships a full A/S version can be seen.

This was a unique class in its own right, not following closely on any RN class, as did other Commonwealth countries, though there are resemblances to both the RN 'Bangor' and, to some extent, to 'Flower' designs. Indeed, the 'Bathurst' class combined many of the best qualities of both classes, and though they also had restrictions on their range they must have made very handy little A/S vessels, with their roomy quarterdeck and twin screws.

In August 1939 the Admiralty commented that they resembled the 'Bangor' class to some degree, though the 'Bathurst' horsepower was seen to be lower, and indeed this was increased at a later stage. Their full speed, free of sweeps, was originally 15 knots, and later 16, while their sweeping speed was 10 knots. They had a separate bridge and wheelhouse, one above the other, whereas in the 'Bangor' design, with a closed bridge too, they were combined. The overall Admiralty comment was that they were a bit larger than the 'Bangor' class, and better fitted, though initially with a lower speed. One report from Australia suggested that they were in some respects a 'Flower' class corvette with the midships section taken out.

In late 1939 4 ships of the class were laid down for the RAN, while in January 1940 the Admiralty ordered 10, for delivery 1 per month in 1941. Further orders were placed: up to a total of 36 by the RAN, 10 more by the RN, and 4 by the RIN.

*Townsville,* completed a year after *Bathurst* but apparently still no depth charge equipment or close range weapons. No radar yet, but the 4″ gun has a shield. *(Evans, Deakin, Brisbane)*

At that time it was planned that there would be 15 slips in Australi capable of building AMS, and a remarkable shipbuilding effort followed. At Evans, Deakin in Brisbane alone, 11 ships of the class were built, and a fitting-out berth was constructed where 3 ships could be fitted out at the same time Of the 20 ships ordered by the RN,

| the first 10 were: | | The second 10 were: | |
|---|---|---|---|
| *Bathurst* | *Kalgoorlie* | *Broome* | *Ipswich* |
| *Ballarat* | *Lismore* | *Cairns* | *Launceston* |
| *Bendigo* | *Maryborough* | *Cessnock* | *Pirie* |
| *Burnie* | *Toowoomba* | *Gawler* | *Tamworth* |
| *Goulburn* | *Whyalla* | *Geraldton* | *Wollongong* |

It is not clear whether all ships were originally fitted with Mark I Oropesa sweeps against moored mines; all 20 RN-ordered ships were fitted with LL sweeps Mark Vx against magnetic mines, the reels being stowed below the sweep deck, as in the 'Bangor' class. The RN ships were also fitted with the SA sweep against acoustic mines. Among the RAN ships it is not clear how many were fitted with LL sweeps, but certainly *Colac* and *Armidale* appear to have been.

The 4 ships built for the RIN were fitted with all 3 sweeps (photographs are included in the RIN section). 4 ships of the class were also built in India.

A single 4″ gun was fitted forward in most ships, but, as the photographs show, the mark of a gun varied as the war progressed and some ships only received a 12 pounder. A table of probable guns actually fitted is included. The supply position naturally governed this situation. *Bathurst* and *Ballarat* had no gunshield on their forward guns on commissioning; these were probably added later. 2″ rocket flares were not fitted in these ships.

Close-range weapons also varied considerably. *Bathurst* on commissioning appears to have had none; then rifle-calibre machine-guns were added; later ships show 3 single Oerlikons, 2 in the bridge wings, 1 on the centreline aft of the mainmast. 2 twin 0.303″ machine-guns appear in shields on either side of the sweep deck in some ships. Some (as *Benalla, Cessnock)* had the bridge single Oerlikons replaced by manual twin Oerlikons, while others (*Horsham, Ipswich, Lismore)* carried a single 2 pounder pom pom aft. By the end of the war most had the after single Oerlikon replaced by a single Bofors Mark I on a Mark III mounting.

*Bathurst* had a high open bridge on commissioning, but the covered bridge became standard for most of the class. An open upper conning position appears in a later photograph of *Geraldton.*

2 high, vertical masts were shipped, with 2 yards on the foremast and 1 on the main. A crow's nest was fitted. A 27 foot whaler was carried in gravity davits on the starboard side, and a 16 foot trawler boat, also is gravity davits, on the port side. This followed 'Bangor' class practice quite closely.

Most ships of this class were not fitted with radar during the war years, but a Type 271 Mark II set appears above the 20″ searchlight on the after end of the bridge in later ships, especially the A/S version. A Type 286 'bedstead' air warning aerial appears at the foremasthead in some ships.

In these latter ships the minesweeping gear aft was removed, 2 full depth-charge rails installed, and the number of depth charges carried stepped up from 20 to 40 or 50. Among ships altered to full A/S versions were *Cowra, Glenelg, Gympie, Kiama, Rockhampton* and others. Ships completed in late 1943/44 were fitted with radar on completion—*Cowra, Junee, Kiama, Parkes, Strahan, Stawell,* and possibly *Ararat, Cootamundra* and *Fremantle*.

## Operational Service

Of the 20 ships ordered by the RN all were eventually manned on commissioning by the RAN, and only 13 were finally under the operational control of the Admiralty, due to the changing geographical stresses of the war. These 12 served in the Eastern Fleet, the Red Sea Force, the British Pacific Fleet and the Levant Force; some went as far afield as Sicily. They were: *Bathurst, Burnie, Cairns, Cessnock, Gawler, Geraldton, Ipswich, Launceston, Lismore, Maryborough, Tamworth, Toowoomba, Wollogong.*

*Bathurst* and *Lismore,* the first 2, joined the Mediterranean Fleet in Alexandria on 4th August 1941, but were shortly afterwards returned to the Red Sea, as they were thought to be unsuitable for operations in waters subject to daylight air attack, owing to insufficiency of armament.

By 1st February 1942, 20 'Bathurst' class ships were in commission, of which 9 were being operated for the Admiralty. 2 ships were with the Far East Fleet, 7 in the ABDA area, 4 in the Darwin area, 2 escorting convoys on the Australian coast, and 5 were working-up.

All 'Bathurst' class ships had been completed and were in service by mid-1944, with most having been completed a year earlier than that.

The RAN Historical Section has been of great assistance in providing information on the areas of operation of each ship of this class, and in view of its special interest the class list is more detailed here than elsewhere in the book.

As a further item of interest, Messrs Evans, Deakin of Brisbane have kindly supplied a full war history of *Kiama,* 1 of the units of the class built by them, and again this is reproduced in full so that the exploits of this class may become better known.

After the war 8 of the RN-ordered ships were sold to the Netherlands, in 1945, and 4 ships were transferred to the RNZN in 1952; photographs are included under that section.

In September 1973, 1 ship, *Castlemaine,* was given to the museum being set up in Melbourne by the Maritime Trust of Australia. This ship saw four years of war service around the Pacific, and was used as a training ship after the war until 1971.

War losses were:

| | | |
|---|---|---|
| *Armidale* | 1.12.42 | Sunk by Japanese air attack, Timor Sea |
| *Geelong* | 18.10.44 | Sunk following collision with US tanker *York* in New Guinea area |
| *Wallaroo* | 11.6.43 | Sunk off West Australian coast after collision with merchant ship *Henry Gilbert Costin* |
| *Warrnambool* | 13.9.47 | Sunk by mine off Queensland coast |

*HMAS 'Kiama'—War history*

This ship, of the 'Bathurst' class A/S-M/S vessels, was built by Evans, Deakin Ltd, and was commissioned on 26th January 1944.

She carried out the usual trials and working-up, and passed into operational service in March 1944, when she went to Milne Bay, New Guinea. She spent her next three months escorting New Guinea coastal convoys. In June she carried out patrols in the Solomon Sea, and in July returned to convoy duties, based again on New Guinea.

In September she acted as a troop transport between the main island of New Guinea and New Britain, and along the New Guinea coast. For the next three months she again operated as a convoy escort. By the end of 1944 the ships had spent eight months in New Guinea waters, except for a brief visit to Cairns, and had steamed some 30,000 miles. On December 21st 1944 she returned to Sydney.

On Christmas Day the ship's company was recalled from leave to go to the aid of an American merchant ship, the *Robert J. Walker*, which had been torpedoed and sunk by a Japanese submarine off the New South Wales coast. She then carried out anti-submarine patrols until 3rd January 1945, when she left for a routine refit at Adelaide.

She resumed service in February, and carried out exercises with US submarines from Fremantle for two months. On 2nd May she returned to New Guinea for a further tour of duty, and for two months bombarded the Japanese along the north-east coast of Bougainville and in the Buka Islands. In July she went to Torokina in the Solomons to embark the Duke of Gloucester for his passage to Mutupina Point in those islands. She returned to Brisbane on 5th August. On 24th August she returned to New Guinea, and spent five months in troop and stores transportation, in minesweeping, and in general duties. On 29th January 1946 she returned to Sydney, and on 3rd April paid off into the Reserve. She had steamed 60,882 miles in twenty-six months, with 6,869 hours under way. In 1952 she was transferred to the New Zealand Navy.

*Kiama,* an A/S version of this class. There are four depth charge throwers and two full rails on the quarterdeck, without M/S gear; a newer-type 4″ gun on the forecastle, but no Hedgehog; and three single Oerlikons have been added. *(Royal Australian Navy)*

*Kalgoorlie*—a good view of the hull form, good-looking, with the shelter deck ending by the funnel, but solid bulwarks running well aft. (*Royal Australian Navy*)

*Warrnambool,* also on builder's trials, and with two high masts, a covered bridge, but no radar. (*Royal Australian Navy*)

## RAN 'BATHURST' CLASS SPECIFICATION

| | RAN 'BATHURST' | RN 'BANGOR' | RN 'Flower' |
|---|---|---|---|
| Displacement | 650 | 650 | 92 |
| *(Ballarat, Bathurst,* | | | |
| *Bendigo, Goulburn,* | 733 | | |
| *Maryborough, Whyalla)* | | | |
| *(Cootamundra, Cowra,* | | | |
| *Junee)* | 790 | | |
| Dimensions | | | |
| length pp | 162 | 162 | 19 |
| oa | 186 | 174 | 20 |
| breadth | 31 | 28.5 | 3 |
| draught | 10 | 8.25 | 1 |
| Machinery | Triple expansion, 230 rpm | | |
| Boilers | 2 Yarrow Admiralty 3-drum type | | |
| Shafts | 2 | 2 | |
| IHP | 1,750 | 2,400 | 2,7 |
| | (2,000 later) | | |
| Speed | 15 kn | 16 kn | 16 |
| | (16 kn later) | | |
| Oil Fuel | 180 | | |
| Complement | 80/90 | 60 | 85 |
| Armament | | | |
| main | 1 4" BL Mk IX | | |
| | on CP1 mtg | | |
| | or 1 12 pdr | | |
| *Stawell, Bathurst, Cessnock* | 1 3" | | |
| close-range | 4 0·303" MG | | |
| | 1 2 pdr pom pom | | |
| | *later* | | |
| | 3 20mm Oerlikon | | |
| | *later* | | |
| | 1 single Bofors, | | |
| | or three | | |
| A/A Armament | 2 DCT, 2 rails | | |
| Depth charges | *originally* | | |
| | As M/S 2 | | |
| | As A/S 25 | | |
| | *later* | | |
| | 40/50 | | |
| Radar *(later)* | Type 271 Mk II | | |
| | Type 286M | | |

## RAN 'BATHURST' CLASS MAIN ARMAMENT AND HORSEPOWER

| | 4″ gun | 12 pdr gun | 1,750 IHP | 2,000 IHP |
|---|---|---|---|---|
| *Ararat* | ● | | | ● |
| *Armidale* | ● | | | ● |
| *Ballarat* | ● | | ● | |
| *Bathurst* | ● | | ● | |
| *Benalla* | | ● | | ● |
| *Bendigo* | ● | | ● | |
| *Bowen* | | ● | | ● |
| *Broome* | | ● | | ● |
| *Bunbury* | ● | | | ● |
| *Bundaberg* | ● | | | ● |
| *Burnie* | ● | | ● | |
| *Cairns* | ● | | ● | |
| *Castlemaine* | ● | | | ● |
| *Cessnock* | | ● | | ● |
| *Colac* | | ● | | ● |
| *Cootamundra* | ● | | | ● |
| *Cowra* | ● | | | ● |
| *Deloraine* | | ● | | ● |
| *Dubbo* | ● | | | ● |
| *Echuca* | | ● | | ● |
| *Fremantle* | ● | | | ● |
| *Gawler* | ● | | ● | |
| *Geelong* | ● | | ● | |
| *Geraldton* | ● | | | ● |
| *Gladstone* | ● | | | ● |
| *Glenelg* | | ● | | ● |
| *Goulburn* | ● | | ● | |
| *Gympie* | | ● | | ● |
| *Horsham* | ● | | | ● |
| *Inverell* | ● | | | ● |
| *Ipswich* | | ● | | ● |
| *Junee* | ● | | | ● |
| *Kalgoorlie* | ● | | ● | |
| *Kapunda* | ● | | | ● |
| *Katoomba* | | ● | ● | |
| *Kiama* | ● | | | ● |
| *Latrobe* | ● | | | ● |
| *Launceston* | | ● | | ● |
| *Lismore* | ● | | ● | |
| *Lithgow* | ● | | ● | |
| *Maryborough* | ● | | ● | |
| *Mildura* | ● | | ● | |
| *Parkes* | ● | | | ● |
| *Pirie* | | ● | | ● |

| | | | |
|---|:---:|:---:|:---:|
| *Rockhampton* | ● | ● | |
| *Shepparton* | ● | ● | |
| *Stawell* | ● | | ● |
| *Strahan* | ● | | ● |
| *Tamworth* | | ● | ● |
| *Toowoomba* | ● | ● | |
| *Townsville* | ● | ● | |
| *Wagga* | ● | | ● |
| *Warrnambool* | ● | ● | |
| *Whyalla* | ● | ● | |
| *Wollongong* | | ● | ● |

## RIN Ships

| | | | |
|---|:---:|:---:|:---:|
| *Bengal* | | ● | ● |
| *Bombay* | | ● | ● |
| *Madras* | | ● | ● |
| *Punjab* | | ● | ● |

*Note* These records by courtesy Mr Paul Webb of Williamstown.

## RAN 'BATHURST' CLASS COMPLETIONS

| | | | | | |
|---|---|---|---|---|---|
| 1940 | 2nd half | 2 | 1943 | 1st half | |
| 1941 | 1st half | 6 | | 2nd half | |
| | 2nd half | 7 | 1944 | 1st half | |
| 1942 | 1st half | 18 | | | |
| | 2nd half | 18 | | | |

*Echuca,* with a Pacific-type camouflage including anti-wave reflection areas under the bow flare and the stern. Two depth charge throwers and traps, as in the RN 'Bangor' class. *(P.A. Webb)*

## RAN 'BATHURST' CLASS—CLASS LIST

| Name | Pendant No | Builder | Engined by | Ordered | Building Time | Completed |
|------|-----------|---------|-----------|---------|---------------|-----------|
| *Ararat* | K 34 | Evans, Deakin | Sergeant | 7.8.41 | 7m14d | 16.6.43 |
| *Armidale* | J 240 | Morts | Morts | 24.1.41 | 9m11d | 11.6.42 |
| *Ballarat* | J 184 | Melbourne | Walkers | 4.12.39 | 16m10d | 30.8.41 |
| *Bathurst* | J 158 | Cockatoo | Cockatoo | 9.12.39 | 9m24d | 6.12.40 |
| *Benalla* | J 323 | Melbourne | WA Govt | 2.8.41 | 13m5d | 28.4.43 |
| *Bendigo* | J 187 | Cockatoo | Cockatoo | 16.4.40 | 9m3d | 10.5.41 |
| *Bowen* | J 285 | Walkers | Walkers | 7.8.41 | 9m0d | 9.11.42 |
| *Broome* | J 191 | Evans, Deakin | WA Govt | 24.9.40 | 14m26d | 29.7.42 |
| *Bunbury* | J 241 | ,, | Sergeant | 16.5.41 | 14m3d | 3.1.43 |
| *Bundaberg* | J 231 | ,, | ,, | 24.9.40 | 15m5d | 12.9.42 |
| *Burnie* | J 198 | Morts | Morts | 16.4.40 | 10m9d | 15.4.41 |
| *Cairns* | J 183 | Walkers | Walkers | 24.9.40 | 13m12d | 12.5.42 |
| *Castlemaine* | J 244 | Melbourne | Thompson | 24.9.40 | 16m17d | 17.6.42 |
| *Cessnock* | J 175 | Cockatoo | Cockatoo | 29.7.40 | 9m9d | 26.1.42 |
| *Colac* | J 242 | Morts | Morts | 24.9.40 | 8m14d | 6.1.42 |
| *Cootamundra* | J 316 | Poole & Steele | Perry | 7.8.41 | 13m5d | 3.4.43 |
| *Cowra* | J 351 | ,, | Hoskins | 7.8.41 | 13m27d | 8.10.43 |
| *Deloraine* | J 232 | Morts | Morts | 24.9.40 | 8m3d | 22.11.41 |
| *Dubbo* | J 251 | ,, | ,, | 24.1.41 | 9m18d | 31.7.42 |
| *Echuca* | J 252 | Melbourne | WA Govt | 24.9.40 | 6m15d | 7.9.42 |
| *Fremantle* | J 246 | Evans, Deakin | Walkers | 16.5.41 | 13m10d | 24.3.43 |
| *Gawler* ex *Gambier* | J 188 | BHP Whyalla | Perry | 31.7.40 | 18m15d | 14.8.42 |
| *Geelong* | J 201 | Melbourne | Thompsons | 5.6.40 | 15m1d | 16.1.42 |
| *Geraldton* | J 178 | Poole & Steele | WA Govt | 31.7.40 | 16m16d | 6.4.42 |
| *Gladstone* | J 324 | Walkers | Walkers | 7.8.41 | 7m18d | 22.3.43 |
| *Glenelg* | J 236 | Cockatoo | Cockatoo | 24.9.40 | 9m14d | 16.11.42 |
| *Goulburn* | J 167 | ,, | ,, | 16.4.40 | 7m21d | 28. 2.41 |
| *Gympie* | J 283 | Evans, Deakin | Sergeant | 24.9.40 | 17m8d | 4.11.42 |
| *Horsham* | J 235 | Melbourne | WA Govt | 5.3.41 | 16m24d | 18.11.42 |
| *Inverell* | J 233 | Morts | Thompsons | 16.5.41 | 9m10d | 17. 9.42 |
| *Ipswich* | J 186 | Evans, Deakin | Walkers | 31.7.40 | 15m8d | 13.6.42 |
| *Junee* | J 362 | Poole & Steele | Hoskins | 7.8.41 | 13m22d | 11.4.44 |
| *Kalgoorlie* | J 192 | BHP Whyalla | Walkers | 5.6.40 | 8m11d | 7.4.42 |
| *Kapunda* | J 218 | Poole & Steele | ,, | 24.9.40 | 13m25d | 21.10.42 |
| *Katoomba* | J 204 | ,, | WA Govt | 2.7.40 | 15m7d | 17.12.41 |
| *Kiama* | J 353 | Evans, Deakin | Walkers | 7.8.41 | 14m23d | 26.1.44 |
| *Latrobe* | J 234 | Morts | Morts | 16.5.41 | 9m10d | 6.11.42 |
| *Launceston* | J 179 | Evans, Deakin | Walkers | 31.7.40 | 15m17d | 9.4.42 |
| *Lismore* | J 145 | Morts | Morts | 4.12.39 | 10m26d | 24.1.41 |
| *Lithgow* | J 206 | ,, | ,, | 12.6.40 | 9m25d | 14.6.41 |
| *Maryborough* ex *Cairns* | J 195 | Walkers | Walkers | 8.12.39 | 13m26d | 12.6.41 |
| *Mildura* | J 207 | Morts | Thompsons | 31.7.40 | 10m12d | 22.7.41 |

| | | | | | | |
|---|---|---|---|---|---|---|
| *Parkes* | J 361 | Evans, Deakin | WA Govt | 7.8.41 | 14m9d | 25.5.4 |
| *Pirie* | J 189 | BHP Whyalla | Perry | 31.7.40 | 16m22d | 10.10.42 |
| *Rockhampton* | J 203 | Walkers | Walkers | 12.6.40 | 14m19d | 26.1.4 |
| *Shepparton* | J 248 | Melbourne | Perry | 5.3.41 | 14m17d | 1.2.43 |
| *Stawell* | J 348 | ,, | ,, | 2.8.41 | 13m19d | 7.8.43 |
| *Strahan* | J 363 | NSW State | WA Govt | 7.8.41 | 6m5d | 14.3.4 |
| *Tamworth* | J 181 | Walkers | Walkers | 24.9.40 | 11m14d | 8.8.42 |
| *Toowoomba* | J 157 | ,, | ,, | 5.6.40 | 14m4d | 9.10.41 |
| *Townsville* | J 205 | Evans, Deakin | WA Govt | 10.7.40 | 13m3d | 19.12.41 |
| *Wagga* | J 315 | Morts | Morts | 7.8.41 | 9m12d | 18.12.42 |
| *Wallaroo* | J 222 | Poole & Steele | Walkers | 24.9.40 | 15m21d | 15.7.42 |
| *Warrnambool* | J 202 | Morts | Thompsons | 31.7.40 | 10m9d | 23.9.4 |
| *Whyalla*<br>  ex *Glenelg* | J 153 | BHP Whyalla | Walkers | 5.6.40 | 5m15d | 8.1.42 |
| *Wollongong* | J 172 | Cockatoo | Cockatoo | 29.7.40 | 8m25d | 23.10.41 |

## RIN SHIPS

| | | | | | | |
|---|---|---|---|---|---|---|
| *Bengal* | J 243 | Cockatoo | Cockatoo | 24.9.40 | 9m11d | 14.8.4 |
| *Bombay* | J 249 | ,, | Thompsons | 24.1.41 | 8m27d | 25.4.4 |
| *Madras* | J 237 | ,, | Cockatoo | 24.9.40 | 9m15d | 19.5.4 |
| *Punjab* | J 239 | Morts | Morts | 24.1.41 | 9m 10d | 5.3.42 |

*Wollongong,* one of the RN units, with full M/S gear but apparently no depth charges. She carries a single 40mm Bofors aft of the mizzen mast, and two single Oerlikons in the bridge wings
*(Royal Australian Navy)*

## RAN 'BATHURST' CLASS – WAR SERVICE AREAS

| | |
|---|---|
| *Arara* | New Guinea, Borneo |
| *Armidale* | North Australia, New Guinea |
| *Ballarat* | North Australia, Malaya, New Guinea, Philippines, Japan |
| *Bathurst* | Singapore, Colombo, Red Sea, New Guinea, Philippines |
| *Benalla* | New Guinea convoys, Philippines, North Australia |
| *Bendigo* | North Australia, Singapore, New Guinea, Philippines |
| *Bowen* | New Guinea convoys, North Australia |
| *Broome* | New Guinea convoys, North Australia, Philippines |
| *Bunbury* | New Guinea, North Australia, coastal convoys |
| *Bundaberg* | New Guinea, Borneo, coastal convoys |
| *Burnie* | Singapore, Bombay, Aden, Philippines, Hong Kong |
| *Cairns* | Indian Ocean, Mediterranean, Philippines, Hong Kong |
| *Castlemaine* | New Guinea, North Australia, Philippines, Hong Kong |
| *Cessnock* | Indian Ocean, Aden, Persian Gulf, Sicily, Colombo, New Guinea |
| *Colac* | New Guinea |
| *Cootamundra* | New Guinea, Ambon, North Australia, coastal convoys |
| *Cowra* | New Guinea coastal convoys |
| *Deloraine* | Indonesia, North Australia, New Guinea |
| *Dubbo* | West Australia, New Guinea |
| *Echuca* | New Guinea, North Australia, coastal convoys |
| *Fremantle* | North Australia, New Guinea, Hong Kong, coastal convoys |
| *Gawler* | Indian Ocean, Sicily, Aden, West Australia, Hong Kong |
| *Geelong* | Noumea, New Guinea, coastal convoys |
| *Geraldton* | Indian Ocean, Persian Gulf, Aden, Bombay, Philippines |
| *Gladstone* | Indonesia, New Guinea, North Australia, coastal convoys |
| *Glenelg* | New Guinea, Ambon, Philippines, coastal convoys |
| *Goulburn* | Singapore, North Australia, New Guinea, Hong Kong, convoys |
| *Gympie* | North Australia, Timor, New Guinea, coastal convoys |
| *Horsham* | North and West Australia, Timor |
| *Inverell* | North Australia, New Guinea, coastal convoys |
| *Ipswich* | Persian Gulf, Sicily, Colombo, Indian Ocean, Japan |
| *Junee* | Ambon, Borneo, Indonesia, New Guinea, North Australia |
| *Kalgoorlie* | Timor, Philippines, New Guinea, North Australia, coastal convoys |
| *Kapunda* | New Guinea, Borneo, coastal convoys |
| *Katoomba* | Timor, New Guinea, North Australia |
| *Kiama* | West Australia, New Guinea, coastal convoys |
| *Latrobe* | Indonesia, Borneo, North Australia, New Guinea |
| *Launceston* | Burma, Persian Gulf, Hong Kong, Aden, Indian Ocean, New Guinea |
| *Lismore* | Indian Ocean, Sicily, Red Sea, Timor, Philippines |
| *Lithgow* | New Guinea, North Australia, coastal convoys |
| *Maryborough* | Indian Ocean, Persian Gulf, Sicily, Singapore, New Guinea |
| *Mildura* | West Australia, Borneo, Philippines, coastal convoys |
| *Parkes* | Timor, West Australia, New Guinea, North Australia |
| *Pirie* | New Guinea, North Australia, Japan, Philippines, Hong Kong |
| *Rockhampton* | Noumea, Indonesia, New Guinea, coastal convoys |
| *Shepparton* | New Guinea, North Australia |
| *Stawell* | New Guinea, Borneo, Hong Kong, convoys |

| | |
|---|---|
| *Strahan* | New Guinea, Borneo, Hong Kong |
| *Tamworth* | Indian Ocean, Persian Gulf, Philippines, Hong Kong |
| *Toowoomba* | Indonesia, Indian Ocean, Hong Kong, New Guinea, convoys |
| *Townsville* | New Guinea, North Australia, convoys |
| *Wagga* | New Guinea, Hong Kong, convoys |
| *Wallaroo* | West Australia, coastal convoys |
| *Warrnambool* | Timor, North and West Australia, convoys |
| *Whyalla* | New Guinea, Philippines, coastal convoys |
| *Wollongong* | Singapore, Indian Ocean, Persian Gulf, New Guinea, coastal convoys |

## AUSTRALIAN ESCORT SHIPBUILDERS

Broken Hill Proprietary Ltd, Whalla.
Cockatoo Shipbuilding Co Ltd, Sydney.
Evans, Deakin Ltd, Brisbane.
Melbourne Harbour Trust, Williamstown.
Morts Dock Co Ltd, Sydney.
New South Wales State Dock Co Ltd, Newcastle.
Poole & Steele Ltd, Sydney.
Walkers Drydock Co Ltd, Maryborough.

## Engine Builders

Hoskins Foundry Ltd, Perth, WA.
Perry Engineering, Co Pty Ltd, Adelaide, SA.
Sargeant & Co Ltd, Brisbane, Queensland.
Thompsons Engineering & Pipe Co, Castlemaine, Vic.
WA Government Railways, Midland Junction, WA.

*Benalla* on completion, one of the last units of the class. She has extended accommodation aft, with reduced depth charge outfit, and may have been used as an inshore headquarters ship in the New Guinea area. *(P.A. Webb)*

# ROYAL INDIAN NAVY

## ESCORT BUILDING POLICY

Shipbuilding capacity, and especially engine building capacity, were rather limited in India during the war years. Some 'Bangor' class fleet minesweepers, and an impressive programme of 'Isles' class trawlers, were, however, tackled, with good results, though quite a number of the trawlers were cancelled in the end, as the class list will show.

Otherwise, ships were transferred from the United Kingdom; and it is noteworthy that India was the only Commonwealth country to receive units of the excellent 'Black Swan' class sloops; and these were ordered direct from the U.K. builders.

### RIN OVERALL NUMBERS BUILT

|  | 'Black Swan' | 'Bangor' | 'Bathurst' | 'Isles' | Modified 'Flower' |
|---|---|---|---|---|---|
| Built in India |  | 4 |  | 22 |  |
| Built in UK | 6 | 9 |  |  | 4 |
| Built in Australia |  |  | 4 |  |  |
| Retained by RIN | 6 | 13 | 4 | 22 | 4 |
| Cancelled | 0 | 4 | 3 | 25 | 0 |

*Gondwana,* ex RN *Burnet,* a Modified 'Flower' class unit built in the UK and transferred to India in 1945. She has only three single Oerlikons, despite her relatively late completion, and no funnel cap. *(Ministry of Defence)*

## RIN 'BLACK SWAN' CLASS SLOOPS

*6 ships built in UK*

6 ships of this class were ordered direct for the RIN, from UK shipyards involved in the building of this class. 4 were built under the 1940 Programme of the original class, and 2 under the 1940 Supplementary Programme, of the Modified class. All 6 were unchanged versions of the RN class, with the exception that the close-range armament was rather less than in the RN ships, which were improved at a later stage of the war; details of the close-range armament of these 6 ships in 1945 is included under the special section on this point, in the RN class.

## RIN 'BLACK SWAN' CLASS—CLASS LIST

| Name | Pennant No | Builder | Launching Date |
|------|-----------|---------|----------------|
| *Jumna* | U 21 | Denny | 13.5.41 |
| *Sutlej* | U 95 | Denny | 23.4.41 |
| *Godavari* | U 52 | Thornycroft | 28.6.43 |
| *Narbada* | U 40 | Thornycroft | 29.4.43 |
| *Cauvery* | U 10 | Yarrow | 21.10.43 |
| *Kistna* | U 46 | Yarrow | 26.8.43 |

## RIN 'BLACK SWAN' CLASS SPECIFICATION

| | |
|---|---|
| Displacement | 1,350 tons |
| Dimensions | |
|   length pp | 283' 0" |
|       oa | 299' 6" |
|   breadth | 38' 0" |
|   draught | 8' 9" |
| Machinery | Geared turbines |
| SHP | 4,500 |
| Shafts | 2 |
| Speed | 20 kn |
| Complement | 220 |
| Armament | 6 4" Ha/La |
|   close-range | As in RN section |
| A/S Armament | 1 Hedgehog ATW mortar |
| | 4 depth charge throwers |
| | 2 rails |

NARBADA in 1943.

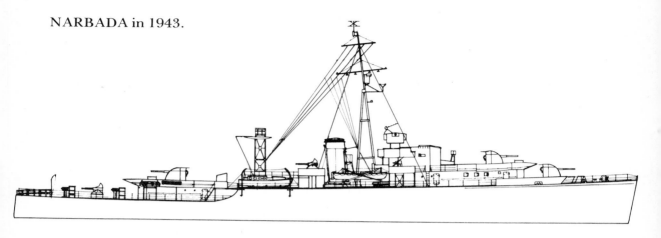

*Narbada,* a standard UK-built 'Black Swan' class sloop. Only the RIN received ships of this class, by direct order. One of six, this ship had the standard armament and radar of her class at time of completion, but probably not the subsequent modifications. *(Imperial War Museum)*

## RIN 'BANGOR' CLASS FLEET MINESWEEPERS

*9 ships built in the UK, plus 4 ships built in India*

The 9 UK-built ships were standard units of their class, and were transferred after some RN service. The 4 units built in India were ordered on 7th June 1941. 4 further units of the class were under construction in Hong Kong, but were lost on the stocks when the colony was invaded.

## RIN 'BANGOR' CLASS—CLASS LIST

| Name | Pennant No | Job No | Builder | Building Time | Compl. Date |
|------|-----------|--------|---------|---------------|-------------|
| **Reciprocating-Engined Type** | | | | | |
| *Rajputana* | J 197 | J 1200 | Lobnitz | 10m5d | 30. 4.42 |
| ex RN *Lyme Regis* | | | | | |
| *Orissa* | J 200 | J 1199 | ,, | 9m30d | 14. 3.42 |
| ex RN *Clydebank* | | | | | |
| *Konkan* | J 228 | J 1180 | ,, | 9m28d | 12. 6.42 |
| ex RN *Tilbury* | | | | | |
| **Turbine-Engined Type** | | | | | |
| *Baluchistan* | J 182 | J 4227 | Blyth | 14m23d | 20.10.42 |
| ex RN *Greenock* | | | | | |
| *Kathiawar* | J 155 | J 4231 | ,, | 13m26d | 23.12.42 |
| ex RN *Hartlepool* | | | | | |
| *Khyber* | J 190 | J 1176 | Hamilton | 20m3d | 12. 8.42 |
| ex RN *Harwich* | | | | | |
| *Kumaon* | J 164 | J 1177 | ,, | 23m19d | 30.11.42 |
| ex RN *Middlesbrough* | | | | | |
| *Carnatic* | J 199 | J 1178 | ,, | 19m0d | 27.10.42 |
| ex RN *Newhaven* | | | | | |
| *Rohilkand* | J 180 | J 1179 | ,, | 15m7d | 5. 2.43 |
| ex RN *Padstow* | | | | | |
| **BUILT IN INDIA** | | | | | |
| **Reciprocating-Engined Type** | | | | | |
| *Bihar* | J 247 | NCP 12 | Garden Reach | 32m23d | 29. 2.44 |
| *Deccan* | J 129 | NCP 93 | ,, | 22m28d | 1. 3.45 |
| *Malwa* | J 55 | NCP 92 | ,, | | L2 . 6.44 |
| *Oudh* | J 245 | NCP 11 | ,, | 28m13d | 21.10.43 |

## RIN 'BANGOR' CLASS SPECIFICATION

| | |
|---|---|
| Displacement | 670 tons |
| Dimensions | |
|   length pp | 171'6" |
|         oa | 180'0" |
|   breadth | 28'6" |
|   draught | 8'6" |
| Machinery | Vertical reciprocating or geared turbines |
| Shafts | 2 |
| Speed | 16 kn |
| Complement | 85 |
| Armament | 1 3" or 1 12 pdr |
| | 3 20mm Oerlikons |
| | or 1 2 pdr pom pom and 4 0.5" |
| A/S Armament | 4 double depth charge chutes |
| | 2 depth charge throwers |
| | 40 depth charges |

## RIN 'BATHURST' CLASS A/S—M/S VESSELS

### 4 ships built in Australia

These were standard units of the Australian class, ordered direct by India. They were delivered direct on completion. 6 were originally earmarked, but this was reduced to 4 at an early stage. These ships were used in a dual purpose A/S—M/S role, and the fight of *Bengal* against a raider in the Indian Ocean is touched on in the Far East chapter.

Three further ships of this class were ordered in Calcutta on 22nd January 1942, but were cancelled in March 1945; their main machinery would originally have come from Singapore, and the estimated completion date was first June 1943, then 1944, before cancellation. Their names would have been: *Assam, Gondhwana* and *Sind*

## RIN 'BATHURST' CLASS—CLASS LIST

| Name | Pennant No | Builder | Launching Date |
|---|---|---|---|
| *Bengal* | J 243 | Cockatoo | 28.5.42 |
| *Bombay* | J 249 | Morts | 17.6.42 |
| *Madras* | J 237 | Cockatoo | 17.2.42 |
| *Punjab* | J 239 | Morts | 11.10.41 |

## RIN 'BATHURST' CLASS SPECIFICATION

| | |
|---|---|
| Displacement | 650 tons |
| Dimensions | |
|   length pp | 162'0" |
|        oa | 186'0" |
|   breadth | 31'6" |
|   draught | 8'6" |
| Machinery | Vertical steam reciprocating |
| Shafts | 2 |
| Speed | 16 kn |
| Complement | 85 |
| Armament | 1 3" |
| | 3 single 20mm Oerlikons |

## RIN 'ISLES' CLASS TRAWLERS

### *22 ships built in India*

This was part of the big building programme for this class, which also included the 16 ships built in Canada. The units built in India were apparently engined by UK firms, and this must have presented logistical difficulties. A large proportion of the units ordered were cancelled, more than those among the UK orders.

### RIN 'ISLES' CLASS—CLASS LIST

| Name | Pennant No | Job No | Builder | Launching Date |
|---|---|---|---|---|
| *Agra* | T 254 | NCP 2 | Hooghlie | 18.3.42 |
| *Ahmedabad* | T 264 | NCP 17 | Burns | 28.10.43 |
| *Amritsar* | T 261 | NCP 19 | Garden Reach | 19.12.41 |
| *Baroda* | T 249 | NCP 4 | Shalimar | 22.10.41 |
| *Berar* | T 256 | NCP 3 | Hooghlie | 31.7.42 |
| *Calcutta* | T 339 | NCP 6 | ,, | 8.3.43 |
| *Cochin* | T 315 | NCP 57 | Burns | 29.12.43 |
|   ex *Multan* | | | | |
| *Cuttack* | T 251 | NCP 23 | ,, | 16.6.43 |
| *Karachi* | T 262 | NCP 8 | Alcock | 1.12.41 |
| *Lahore* | T 253 | NCP 7 | Shalimar | 21.12.41 |
| *Lucknow* | T 267 | NCP 9 | Alcock | 3.4.42 |
| *Madura* | T 268 | NCP 21 | Garden Reach | 21.12.42 |
| *Multan* | T 322 | NCP 74 | Scindia | 23.5.44 |
|   ex *Cochin* | | | | |
| *Nagpur* | T 269 | NCP 18 | Burns | 11.4.44 |
| *Nasik* | T 258 | NCP | Shalimar | 23.5.44 |
| *Patna* | T 255 | NCP 5 | Hooghlie | 1.9.42 |
| *Peshawar* | T 263 | NCP 10 | Alcock | 2.5.42 |
| *Poona* | T 260 | NCP 20 | Garden Reach | 5.4.42 |

| | | | | | |
|---|---|---|---|---|---|
| *Quetta* <br> ex *Jubbalpore* | T 332 | NCP 75 | Scindia | | 7.2.44 |
| *Rampur* <br> ex *Barisal* | T 212 | NCP | Burns | | 18.7.42 |
| *Shillong* | T 250 | NCP 22 | ,, | | 22.8.42 |
| *Travancore* | T 312 | NCP 1 | Garden Reach | | 7.7.41 |

## Cancelled Ships

| Name | Pennant No | Job No | Builder | Cancelled |
|---|---|---|---|---|
| *Allahabad* | T 317 | NCP 59 | Hooghlie | March 1943 |
| *Ambala* | T 320 | NCP 62 | Alcock | March 1943 |
| *Bannu* | T 331 | NCP 119 | Shalimar | February 1944 |
| *Barreily* | T 319 | NCP 63 | ,, | March 1943 |
| *Barisal* <br> ex *Sholapore* | T 270 | NCP 34 | Burns | March 1945 <br> (Ordered 23rd September 1941) |
| *Benares* | T 318 | NCP 60 | Hooghlie | January 1945 |
| *Cawnpore* | T 346 | NCP 58 | Burns | January 1945 |
| *Chittagong* | T 265 | NCP 33 | ,, | March 1945 <br> 0Ordered 23 September 1941) |
| *Dacca* | T 252 | NCP 32 | ,, | March 1945 <br> (Ordered 23rd September 1941) |
| *Dinapore* | T 326 | NCP 209 | Garden Reach | January 1945 |
| *Gaya* | T 325 | NCP 208 | ,, | January 1945 |
| *Jubbalpore* <br> ex *Quetta* | T 323 | NCP 120 | Scindia | January 1945 |
| *Kiamari* | T 330 | NCP 118 | ,, | January 1945 |
| *Kolaba* <br> ex *Cochin* | T 266 | NCP 57 | Alcock | January 1945 <br> (Ordered 14th November 1941) |
| *Monghyr* | T 327 | NCP 115 | ,, | January 1945 |
| *Nasik* | T 326 | NCP 36 | Shalimar | January 1945 <br> (Ordered 14th November 1941) |
| *Pachmari* | T 324 | NCP 207 | Calcutta | January 1945 |
| *Puri* | T 328 | NCP 116 | Alcock | January 1945 |
| *Sholapore* | T 259 | NCP 35 | Burns | January 1945 <br> (Ordered 23rd September 1941) |
| *Sialkot* | T 321 | NCP 63 | Alcock | January 1945 |
| *Sylhet* <br> ex *Sholapore* | T 329 | NCP 117 | Scindia | January 1945 |
| *Trichinopoly* | T 314 | NCP 56 | Burns | January 1945 |
| *Vizagapatam* | T 313 | NCP 55 | ,, | January 1945 |

4 further ships were ordered in Burma, but were lost on the stocks, when Rangoon was invaded:

| Name | Job No | Builder | Launched | Est Completion |
|---|---|---|---|---|
| *Bay Innaung* | J 9982 | Irrawadi | 8.41 | 7.42 |
| *Cochrane* | J 9981 | ,, | 8.41 | 10.42 |
| *Elare* | | ,, | for Ceylon | |
| *Gemmu* | | ,, | for Ceylon | |

## RIN 'ISLES' CLASS SPECIFICATION

| | | | |
|---|---|---|---|
| Displacement | 545 tons | Machinery | Vertical reciprocating |
| Dimensions | | Shaft | 1 |
|    length pp | 150'0" | Speed | 12 kn |
|       oa | 164'0" | Complement | 45 |
|    breadth | 27'6" | Armament | 1 12 pdr |
|    draught | 10'0" | | |

## RIN Modified 'FLOWER' CLASS CORVETTES

### 4 ships built in the UK

These were standard units of this class, and were transferred to India after a period of RN service. The names were the same as those planned for the cancelled 'Bathurst' class units which were to have been built in India. The first 3 of the ships were transferred and on station with the East Indies Fleet *before* VJ-Day.

## RIN Mod. 'FLOWER CLASS LIST

| | | | | | |
|---|---|---|---|---|---|
| *Assam* | K 306 ex RN *Bugloss* | *Mahratta* | K 395 ex RN *Charlock* |
| *Gondhwana* | K 348 ex RN *Burnet* | *Sind* | K 274 ex RN *Betony* |

Further details will be found under the RN section.

## RIN Mod. 'FLOWER' CLASS SPECIFICATION

| | | | |
|---|---|---|---|
| Displacement | 970 tons | Armament | 1 4" |
| Dimensions | | | 6 20mm Oerlikons |
|    length pp | 194'0" | A/S Armament | 1 Hedgehog ATW mortar |
|       oa | 208'6" | | 4 depth charge throwers |
|    breadth | 33'6" | | 2 rails |
|    draught | 13'0" | | |
| Machinery | Vertical steam reciprocating, 4 cylinder | | |
| Shafts | 1 | | |
| Speed | 16 kn | | |
| Complement | 110 | | |

## INDIAN ESCORT SHIPBUILDERS

It is regretted that full details of these firms are not available.
Alcock. Burns. Garden Reach, Calcutta. Hooghlie. Scindia. Shalimar.

*Cowra*, with English Channel type camouflage, and in the A/S configuration. She has Type 271 radar on the back of the bridge and an air warning aerial at the masthead. *(Royal Australian Navy)*

*Arbutus*, a Modified 'Flower' class ship built in the UK and transferred to the RNZN on completion, here seen in Pacific waters. She was used as a radar stores and repair ship with the British Pacific Fleet in 1945. *(Royal New Zealand Navy)*

*Lachlan*, completed as an RAN 'River' class frigate, converted to a surveying ship to meet the Pacific war needs in 1945, and transferred to the RNZN in this configuration in 1949. She closely resembles the similarly converted RN 'Loch' class ships. *(Royal New Zealand Navy)* ▼

## ROYAL NEW ZEALAND NAVY

### RNZN—ESCORT BUILDING POLICY

Strictly speaking, 3 out of the 6 RNZN classes we include are outside the scope of this book, on one count only—the ships themselves were not acquired until the war years were over. But as all 3 classes are war-built escorts, and as their acquisition no doubt represented the extension of an existing escort policy, they are included here. They are also interesting ships, since they all show alterations to the original design of their class.

The RNZN also built a class of some 17 trawlers during the war, the 'Castle' class. But these ships fall below our length yardstick, as they were 134 feet overall, and it is believed that they were primarily used for minesweeping duties. They are not, therefore, included in this book; but they were the one class which was constructed during this period in New Zealand.

### RNZN WARTIME STATISTICS

|  | *'Kiwi'* Class | *'Isles'* Class | Mod *'Flower'* Class |
|---|---|---|---|
| Built in UK | 3 | 4 | 2 |
| Cancelled ships | 0 | 0 | 0 |
| War losses | 1 | 0 | 0 |

*Kiwi,* one of three ships ordered from the UK and closely resembling the RN 'Isles' class trawlers. She mounts a 4″ gun forward, with rocket flare projectors, a single Bofors aft, and, unusually, has a radar aerial on a spur on her mast and has retained her two high masts. *(Royal New Zealand Navy)*

## RNZN 'KIWI' CLASS A/S TRAWLERS

### *3 ships built in UK by direct order*

This little class of 3 ships makes an interesting comparison with the RN 'Isles' class trawlers. They were some 8 feet shorter overall, but the same length between perpendiculars; they had 2 ft 6 ins greater beam, and 2 ft 6 ins greater depth. Their speed was 2 knots greater, and, as the photographs demonstrate they carried a full 4″ gun.

Indeed, their appearance is impressive—especially in the postwar shot of *Kiwi.*

They were all built for New Zealand by Henry Robb Ltd of Leith, and engined by Plenty & Son Ltd of Newbury. *Moa* was sunk by Japanese bombers at Tulugai on 7th April 1943; *Kiwi* was sold in 1962 and scrapped in 1965, and *Tui* was sold for scrap in 1969.

## RNZN 'KIWI' CLASS SPECIFICATION

| | |
|---|---|
| Displacement | 600 tons standard, 825 tons full load |
| Dimensions | |
| length pp | 150′ 0″ |
| oa | 156′ 0″ |
| breadth | 30′ 0″ |
| draught | 14′ 0″ |
| Machinery | Triple expansion |
| Boiler | 1 cylindrical |
| IHP | 1,000 |
| Speed | 13 kn |
| Complement | 54 |
| Armament | |
| main | 1 4″ |
| close-range | 5 light guns |
| A/S Armament | Depth charges |

### RNZN 'KIWI' CLASS—CLASS LIST

| Name | Pennant No | Builder | Completion Date |
|---|---|---|---|
| *Kiwi* | T 102 | Henry Robb | 20.10.41 |
| *Moa* | T | ,, | 12.8.41 |
| *Tui* | T 234 | ,, | 26.11.41 |

## RNZN 'ISLES' CLASS A/S-M/S TRAWLERS

### *4 ships built in UK, and transferred*

4 ships of this class, built in the UK, were transferred to the RNZN on completion. They were standard ships of the class, and no doubt supplemented well the 3 rather similar ships of the 'Kiwi' class.

## RNZN 'ISLES' CLASS SPECIFICATION

| | |
|---|---|
| Displacement | 545 tons standard, 770 tons full load |
| Dimensions | |
|   length pp | 150' |
|       oa | 164' |
|   breadth | 27' 6" |
|   draught | 10' 6" |
| Machinery | Triple expansion steam reciprocating |
| Boiler | 1 cylindrical |
| IHP | 800 |
| Shafts | 1 |
| Speed | 10.5 kn |
| Armament | |
|   main | 1 12 pdr |
|   close-range | 3 20mm Oerlikon |
| A/S armament | depth charges |

## RNZN 'ISLES' CLASS – CLASS LIST

| Name | Pendant No | Builder | Completion Date |
|---|---|---|---|
| *Inchkeith* | T 155 | Lewis | 24.10.41 |
| *Killegray* | T 174 | Cook, Welton & Gemmell | 7.11.41 |
| *Sanda* | T 160 | Goole | 4.11.41 |
| *Scarba* | T 175 | Cook, Welton & Gemmell | 25.11.41 |

## RNZN MODIFIED 'FLOWER' CLASS CORVETTES

### *2 ships built in UK, and transferred*

2 ships of this class were turned over to the RNZN on commissioning in the UK shipyards. They were 2 of the only 10 ships of this class built in the UK, and they were specially transferred to New Zealand as a token of appreciation by the Admiralty of the co-operation received in escort allocation from the RNZN; the latter had originally sought some ships of the RN 'Castle' class, but it was eventually not thought to be practicable, in view of the supply problems with Squid missiles and probable maintenance requirements for the new ATW mortars then entering service. It was even considered whether it would be possible to complete units of the 'Castle' class for the RNZN, armed with Hedgehog in place of Squids; but this was eventually ruled out, as it would have thrown out the production schedule in the UK shipyards.

These ships followed the standard lay-out and armament of the Modified 'Flower' class; they were returned to the RN in 1948, and scrapped in 1951.

## RNZN MODIFIED 'FLOWER' CLASS SPECIFICATION

| | |
|---|---|
| Displacement | 980 tons |
| Dimensions | |
|   length pp | 193' 0" |
|      oa | 208' 6" |
|   breadth | 33' 6" |
|   draught | 12' 6" |
| Machinery | 4-cylinder triple expansion |
| Boiler | 2 Admiralty water tube |
| IHP | 2,800 |
| Speed | 16 kn |
| Complement | 85 |
| Armament | |
|   main | 1 4" |
|   close-range | 6 single 20mm Oerlikon |
| A/S armament | 1 Hedgehog |
| | 4 DCT, 2 rails |
| Radar | Types 271, 242 |

## RNZN 'FLOWER' CLASS – CLASS LIST

| Name | Pendant No | Builder | Completion Date |
|---|---|---|---|
| *Arabis* | K 385 | Brown | 22.2.44 |
| *Arbutus* | K 403 | ,, | 16.6.44 |

## RNZN 'BATHURST' A/S-M/S VESSELS

### *4 ships built in Australia, and transferred postwar*

These 4 ships were transferred from the RAN to the RNZN in April 1952. They were presented to New Zealand by the Australian Government, and on arrival in New Zealand, refitted and placed temporarily in reserve.

They were recommissioned in 1955 and 1956, their minesweeping gear removed, and 2 ships, *Kiama* and *Inverell,* are now used as training/fishery protection vessels.

It will be seen that during refit their deckhouse was extended aft on to the quarterdeck, their 4" guns removed, and 2 single 40mm Bofors substituted, 1 forward and 1 aft, and 4 tall whip aerials made their appearance, together with (probably) a Type 268 radar, and updated IFF equipment.

They make an interesting comparison with the wartime configuration of the RAN ships of this class.

## RNZN 'BATHURST' CLASS SPECIFICATION

| | |
|---|---|
| Displacement | 1,025 tons |
| Dimensions | |
|    length oa | 186' |
|    breadth | 31' |
| Machinery | Triple expansion |
| Boilers | 2 Admiralty 3-drum type |
| Shafts | 2 |
| IHP | 1,800 |
| Speed | 15 kn |
| Complement | 85 |
| Armament | 2 single 40mm Bofors |

## RNZN 'BATHURST' CLASS – CLASS LIST

| Name | Pendant No | Builder | Completed | Transferred |
|---|---|---|---|---|
| *Echuca* | M 252 | Williamstown | 17.1.42 | 4.52 |
| *Inverell* | M 233 | Morts Dock | 2.5.42 | 4.52 |
| *Kiama* | M 353 | Evans, Deakin | 3.7.43 | 4.52 |
| *Stawell* | M 348 | Williamstown | 3.4.43 | 4.52 |

*Inchkeith,* one of three RN 'Isles' class trawlers transferred to the RNZN, retaining their RN names. *(Ministry of Defence)*

## RNZN 'RIVER' CLASS FRIGATE

### *1 ship built in Australia, and transferred*

This ship was transferred from the RAN to the RNZN on 5th October 1949, on loan. She was purchased outright by New Zealand in 1962, and is still in service.

She was converted to a Hydrographic Survey ship by the RAN before transfer. The photograph makes an interesting comparison with the 'Loch' class ships similarly converted by the RN, and it shows the attractive RNZN ensign quite clearly.

The forecastle deck was extended aft, giving a helicopter platform 50 feet by 30 feet, standing 7 feet above the quarterdeck.

## RNZN 'RIVER' CLASS SPECIFICATION

| | |
|---|---|
| Displacement | 2,220 tons |
| Dimensions | |
|     length oa | 301' 4" |
|     breadth | 36' 8" |
| Machinery | 4 cylinder triple expansion |
| Boilers | 2 Admiralty 3-drum |
| Shafts | 2 |
| IHP | 5,500 |
| Speed | 20 kn |
| Armament | Removed 1949 |
| Complement | 140 |

| Name | Pendant No | Builder | Completed | Transferred |
|---|---|---|---|---|
| *Lachlan* | K 364 | Morts | 25.3.44 | 5.10.49 |

## RNZN 'LOCH' CLASS FRIGATES
## 6 ships built in UK, transferred in 1948/49

6 frigates of this class were transferred from the RN, after RN service, to the RNZN in 1948/49. 2 ships, *Pukaki* ex *Loch Achanalt* and *Tutira* ex *Loch Morlich*, had also previously served in the RCN, as described under that navy's section. They were renamed after New Zealand lakes, and formed the 11th Frigate Flotilla. *Hawea* and *Taupo* served in the Mediterranean Fleet on an exchange basis in 1950.

The photographs show some modernisation, either in refit before transfer to the RNZN or later while in that service. The bridge wings were built out solid to ship's side width, giving extra cabin and plot accommodation; the quadruple pom pom was removed, and the close-range armament became 6 single 40mm Bofors, sited—2 in the bridge wings, 2 on the after deckhouse, and 2 on the old pom pom platform. All 20mm Oerlikons were landed, and in some cases the depth-charge throwers and rails from the quarterdeck as well.

Up-to-date R/T and IFF equipment was added, and extra radar scanners were mounted below the Type 277 at yard level. The ships were fitted with awnings, giving these 'Loch' units an unaccustomed appearance. They carried the postwar Flag F pennant numbers abreast the bridge and were painted light grey.

*Hawea* and *Tutira* have not had the alterations and additions outlined above; it is not known if they were added in these 2 ships at a later date.

## RNZN 'LOCH' CLASS SPECIFICATION

| | |
|---|---|
| Displacement | 2,260 tons full load, 1,435 tons standard. |
| Dimensions | length pp 286' |
| | oa 307' 6" |
| | breadth 38' 9" |
| | draught 12' |
| Machinery | 4 cylinder triple expansion |
| Boilers | 2 Admiralty 3-drum type |
| Shafts | 2 |
| IHP | 5,500 |
| Speed | 19.5 km |
| Oil Fuel | 724 tons |
| Complement | 114 |
| Armament | main 1 4" |
| | close-range 6 40mm Bofors |
| A/S armament | 2 Squid ATW mortars |
| | 2 dct, 1 rail |
| Radar | Type 277 |

## RNZN 'LOCH' CLASS—CLASS LIST

| Name | | Completed | Transferred |
|---|---|---|---|
| Hawea | ex *Loch Eck* | 25.4.44 | 1.10.48 |
| Kaniere | ex *Loch Achray* | 7.7.44 | 7.7.48 |
| Pukaki | ex *Loch Achanalt* | 23.3.4 | 3.9.48 |
| Rotoiti | ex *Loch Katrine* | 21.8.44 | 7.7.49 |
| Taupo | ex *Loch Shin* | 23.2.44 | 3.9.48 |
| Tutira | ex *Loch Morlich* | 25.1.44 | 11.4.49 |

## SOUTH AFRICAN NAVAL FORCES

### SANF ESCORT BUILDING

No major new escort vessels were built in South Africa during the war years. The following vessels fall into the period of this book, others being transferred after the cessation of hostilities.

### SANF 'LOCH' CLASS FRIGATES

These 3 ships were standard units of the UK-built class, and were transferred to South Africa on completion. Further details will be found under the RN chapter; the RN names were not retained.

*Good Hope*    K 432   ex *Loch Boisdale*
*Natal*          K 430   ex *Loch Cree*
*Transvaal*   K 602   ex *Loch Ard*

   *Natal* was involved in the killing of the German U-boat U 714 off Berwick on the UK east coast, in February 1945. The 'V and W' class destroyer *Wivern* detected the submarine and called up *Natal*, which was passing north on her way to work up at Scapa. Both ships attacked, and *Natal* was credited with the kill, but there seems to be some doubt in official records as to which of the two ships actually delivered the fatal blow.

### SANF 'LOCH' CLASS SPECIFICATION

| | |
|---|---|
| Displacement | 1,435 tons |
| Dimensions | |
|    length pp | 286' 0" |
|          oa | 307' 9" |
|    breadth | 38' 6" |
|    draught | 8' 9" |
| Machinery | Vertical reciprocating, 4 cylinder |
| Shafts | 2 |
| Speed | 20 kn |
| Complement | 115 |
| Armament | 1 single 4" Mk Vc |
| | 1 quadruple 2 pdr pom pom |
| | 6 20mm Oerlikons |
| A/S Armament | 1 double Squid mortar |
| | 2 depth charge throwers, 1 set rail |
| | 15 depth charges |

### SANF 'RIVER' CLASS FRIGATES
### 2 ships built in UK, manned by SANF 1945

In November 1944 the RN was faced with an acute shortage of manpower, while the SANF had 60 officers and 500 men surplus to requirements, due to the lessened need for minesweepers in South African waters.

It was therefore made a condition of the transfer of the 3 'Loch' class frigates to the SANF that this surplus manpower should be made available for manning RN escort vessels in the Indian Ocean. At first corvettes were proposed for this purpose, as the ratings would have been used to minesweepers, but the new 'Castle' class were seen as being too sophisticated for this purpose.

'River' class frigates were then proposed; but only 5 RN ships of this class were still available in Home waters at that time, and they were valuable as escort group leaders, while all other 'River' class units had already been allocated to the East Indies or British Pacific Fleets.

The discussions continued through to February 1945, when it was decided to allocate 4 'River' class frigates, already in the Indian Ocean, to the SANF for manning. Ships which had already served two years or more in the East were preferred, as their crews would be due for return to the UK; *Bann, Helford, Plym* and *Teviot* were identified at that time as probables for transfer in July or August 1945. Their crews could be changed over at the Cape, and they could be worked up on the East Indies Station. An additional advantage was that they could still be used as fleet minesweepers, with crews experienced in that work. *Kale* and *Swale* were added to the list of probables.

In April 1945 the SANF agreed to man 3 or 4 'River' class units with volunteers. *Teviot* and *Swale* arrived at the Cape for refit and transfer in early May. *Teviot* commissioned under the South African flag on 10th June, and *Swale* on 26th July. Due to the rapid progress of the war in the Far East no further ships were then transferred.

*Natal*, a 'Loch' class frigate built in the UK and transferred to South Africa on completion. She was a standard ship of her class, with Type 277 radar atop the lattice mast, two twin Oerlikons aft, and a quadruple pom pom. *(Imperial War Museum)*

*Tenacity,* ex RN *Candytuft,* in March 1944. A clear view of the Hedgehog to starboard of the US 4" gun, and a steel wheelhouse has been added to the bridge. *(US Bureau of Ships)*

*Surprise,* ex RN *Heliotrope,* in May 1944. She has Type SG radar at the masthead, a US 4" gun forward and aft, and four single Oerlikons. A good view of the corvette stern lay-out. *(US Bureau of Ships)*

# UNITED STATES NAVY

## USN OVERALL NUMBERS OF ESCORTS BUILT

|  | *PG* *Class* | *PC* *Class* | *PCE* *Class* | *PF* *Class* | *DE* *Classes* | *AM* *Classes* |
|---|---|---|---|---|---|---|
| Built in USA |  | 354 | 63 | 96 | 565 | 234 |
| Retained by USN in original role |  | 284 | 35 | 75 | 381 | 194 |
| Retained by USN in another role |  | 62 | 13 |  | 94 |  |
| Transferred to RN |  |  | 15 | 21 | 78 | 22 |
| Transferred to other navies |  | 44 |  | 28 | 12 | 38 |
| Built in UK and transferred | 10 |  |  |  |  |  |
| Built in Canada and transferred | 8 |  |  | 2 |  | 15 |
| Cancelled |  | 45 | 205 | 4 | 450 | 61 |

## USN CUMULATIVE COMPLETIONS OF NEW ESCORT VESSELS

|  |  | *PC* | *PCE* | *PF* | *DE* | *AM* | *Totals* |
|---|---|---|---|---|---|---|---|
| 1942 | 1st half | 32 |  |  | 2 | 2 | 36 |
|  | 2nd half | 60 |  |  | 29 | 14 | 103 |
| 1943 | 1st half | 54 | 1 |  | 142 | 14 | 211 |
| 1940 | 2nd half | 66 | 7 | 12 | 236 | 22 | 343 |
| 1944 | 1st half | 36 | 15 | 28 | 126 | 49 | 254 |
|  | 2nd half | 21 | 15 | 27 | 29 | 41 | 129 |
| 1945 | 1st half | 12 | 17 | 8 | 9 | 12 | 58 |
|  | 2nd half |  |  |  | 1 | 1 | 2 |
|  | Totals | 281 | 55 | 75 | 570 | 155 | 1,136 |

*Ready*, ex RN *Calendula*, in February 1944. The old Merchant Navy-type liferafts have been retained aft on their skids, but larger depth charge rails have been added to the stern. *(US Bureau of Ships)*

## USN PATROL GUNBOAT (PG) CLASS
### 10 built in UK and transferred, 8 built in Canada

This was a small class of ex-RN and Canadian-built 'Flower' and Modified 'Flower' class corvettes, asked for by the USN in the early days of the war, when they were critically short of A/S vessels, and transferred under reverse Lend-Lease.

There were 2 groups of ships under this class.

The first group, 10 ships of the original 'Flower' class design, were built in the UK for the RN, serving first under their flower names, and then transferred to the USN. Alterations effected by the USN, as opportunity permitted, were to replace the RN's single 4″ gun forward, and the 2 pounder pom pom aft (where fitted), with 2 single 4″ guns, without gunshields, which in the photographs appear to be old US models (the flow of new 3″/50 calibre guns not having started to flow at that time). The RN Type 271 radar was also replaced or supplemented by a USN type, probably SG.

A USN type motor whaleboat was installed in gravity davits, usually on the port side, extra life rafts added, and in some cases some additional Oerlikons also. These can be spotted by the rectangular gunshields where fitted in the USA, whereas UK-fitted guns had circular pieces cut out of the top inner corner of the shield, to widen the gunner's field of vision.

The second group, of 8 ships, were of the Modified 'Flower' class, and built in Canada. The USN made similar modifications to these ships, though not all were made in every case. For example, the Type 271 radar was left for a while in *Intensity*, after the guns were altered.

All ships were returned to the UK after the war.

A further 7 ships, ordered in Canada for the USN, were finally turned over to the RN on completion, under Lend-Lease numerical commitments. This explains why the RN was taking new Modified 'Flower' class corvettes from Canada, while transferring new UK-built ships of the same class in the same period to the RCN!

## USN PG CLASS PRODUCTION

| | | | |
|---|---|---|---|
| 1942 1st half | 10 | 2nd half | 4 |
| 1943 1st half | 3 | 2nd half | 1 |

## USN PG CLASS SPECIFICATION
### (For fuller details, see under RN 'Flower' class corvettes).

| | |
|---|---|
| Displacement | 925 |
| Dimensions | |
|    length pp | 190′0″ |
|    oa | 205′4″ |
|    breadth | 33′1″ |

| | |
|---|---|
| draught | 14′6″ |
| Machinery | triple expansion reciprocating |
| Boilers | 1 Admiralty single-ended |
| Shafts | 1 |
| IHP | 2,750 |
| Speed | 16 km |
| Complement | 85 |
| Armament | |
| main | 2 3″ or 4″ |
| close-range | 4/6 single 20mm Oerlikons |
| Anti-submarine armament | 1 Hedgehog |
| | 4 throwers, 2 rails |
| Radar | Types 271, SL |

## USN PG CLASS—CLASS LIST

### 'FLOWER' CLASS

The following corvettes were transferred from the RN to the USN after some RN service. The last dates shown for each are the dates of transfer to the USN, and building details of these ships can be found in the RN 'Flower' class chapter.

| Name | No | Builder | Transfer Date |
|---|---|---|---|
| Temptress | PG 62 | Smith's Dock | 21.3.42 |
| ex RN *Veronica* | | | |
| Surprise | PG 63 | Crown | 24.3.42 |
| ex RN *Heliotrope* | | | |
| Spry | PG 64 | Harland & Wolff | 2.5.42 |
| ex RN *Hibiscus* | | | |
| Saucy | PG 65 | ,, | 30.4.42 |
| ex RN *Arabis* | | | |
| Restless | PG 66 | ,, | 30.4.42 |
| ex RN *Periwinkle* | | | |
| Ready | PG 67 | ,, | 12.3.42 |
| ex RN *Calendula* | | | |
| Impulse | PG 68 | Cook, Welton & Gemmell | 16.3.42 |
| ex RN *Begonia* | | | |
| Fury | PG 69 | Fleming & Ferguson | 17.3.42 |
| ex RN *Larkspur* | | | |
| Courage | PG 70 | Harland & Wolff | 18.3.42 |
| ex RN *Heartsease* | | | |
| Tenacity | PG 71 | Grangemouth | 11.6.42 |
| ex RN *Candytuft* | | | |

### MODIFIED 'FLOWER' CLASS

The following ships were ordered from Canadian shipyards taking over ships originally ordered by the RN. While still under construction, some were re-allocated to the RN to fulfil US Lend-Lease commitments. In the latter cases, building details will be found under the RN class chapter; these ships retained the RN class names originally allocated to them under the original order.

| Name | No | Job No | Builder | Building Time | Completion Date |
|------|-----|--------|---------|---------------|-----------------|
| *Action*<br>ex RN *Comfrey* | PG 86 | CN 304 | Collingwood | 6m3d | 22.11.42 |
| *Alacrity*<br>ex RN *Cornel* | PG 87 | CN 305 | ,, | 11m4d | 10.12.42 |
| *Beacon*<br>ex RN *Dittany* | PG 88 | CN 306 | ,, | Transferred to RN | |
| *Brisk*<br>ex RN *Flax* | PG 89 | CN 307 | Kingston | | 6.12.42 |
| *Caprice*<br>ex RN *Honesty* | PG 90 | CN 308 | ,, | Transferred to RN | |
| *Clash*<br>ex RN *Linaria* | PG 91 | CN 309 | Midland | Transferred to RN | |
| *Haste*<br>ex RN *Mandrake* | PG 92 | CN 310 | Morton | 15m26d | 6.4.43 |
| *Intensity*<br>ex RN *Milfoil* | PG 93 | CN 311 | ,, | 15m12d | 31. 3.43 |
| *Might*<br>ex RN *Musk* | PG 94 | CN 312 | ,, | | 22.12.42 |
| *Pert*<br>ex RN *Nepeta* | PG 95 | CN 313 | ,, | 12m0d | 22.12.42 |
| *Prudent*<br>ex RN *Privet* | PG 96 | CN 314 | ,, | 12m2d | 16. 8.43 |
| *Splendor*<br>ex RN *Rosebay* | PG 97 | CN 315 | Collingwood | Transferred to RN | |
| *Tact*<br>ex RN *Smilax* | PG 98 | CN 316 | ,, | Transferred to RN | |
| *Vim*<br>ex RN *Statice* | PG 99 | CN 317 | ,, | Transferred to RN | |
| *Vitality* | PG 100 | CN 318 | Midland | Transferred to RN | |

**WAR LOSSES**

Nil

**SAUCY in May, 1942.**

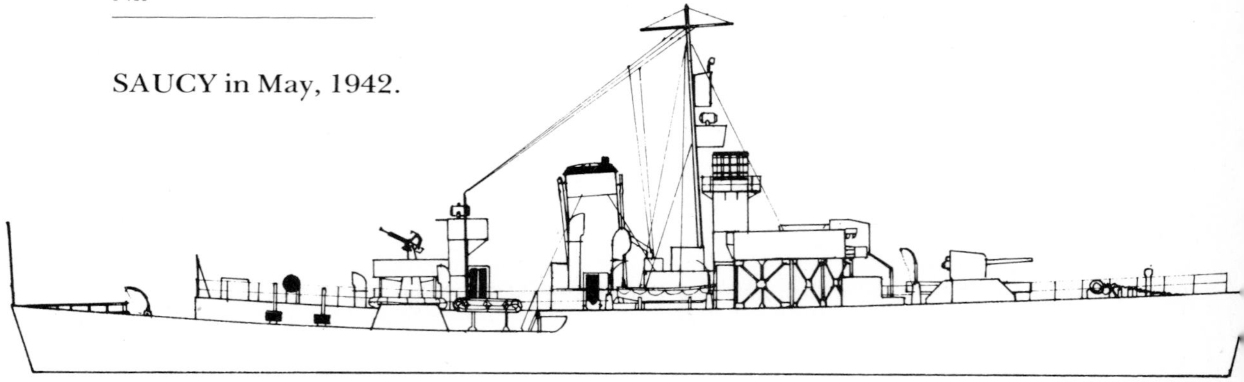

## USN PATROL CRAFT (PC) CLASS
**354 built**

From the combined production chart it will be seen that this class appeared in large numbers in 1942, a remarkable achievement in the first year of the war, and ahead of the main production period of the Destroyer Escorts.

From the PC production chart we see that the first ship, a prototype, was in fact commissioned in the third quarter of 1941, before America joined in the war; so that this foresight, as with the RN's 'Flower' class corvettes, enabled the US shipyards concerned to swing quickly into an accelerated production programme.

There were in fact 3 ships in the prototype class, PC 451, PC 452 and PC 457. They bore a resemblance to the pre-war Coastguard cutters, and had a break in the forecastle, a large funnel, and a bridge similar to that of the main PC class which followed, with a mast rising from it, fitted with a crow's nest. A large boat sat on the after deck in gooseneck davits, and the armament seems to have varied.

The main PC design makes an interesting comparison with the RN's 'Flower' class corvettes. Designed as a warship from the start, the PC shows a displacement nearly one-quarter that of the corvette; the length of the PC was only 30 feet shorter, but her beam was no less than 10 feet, or one-third less. The PC's armament was impressive, 2 3″/50 calibre guns, and up to 5 20mm Oerlikons, with variations, and the depth-charge equipment was also outstanding for its size.

The PC class was designed as a coastal escort and submarine chaser. They look smaller in their photographs than they really were, and it is understandable that we do not find them appearing in mid-ocean escort duties. For the latter, the larger PFs and DEs were used, as soon as they started coming off the slips in numbers; and for inshore work the larger PCE design was laid down. But the PCs were a very large class of coastal escort and must have made a very significant contribution to the USN's war effort, both on the Atlantic seaboard and in the Caribbean (where we find them hunting in groups), and in the wider Pacific.

By the end of 1943 production of PCs was already tailing off as the larger escorts made their appearance; but some 354 ships of the class were constructed in a period of something over 2 years. As the PCE design took precedence, so some 45 PCs were cancelled, and 44 were transferred during the war to other Allied navies (it is interesting, however, that the RN placed orders for PCEs but not for PCs).

17 US shipyards contributed to the PC building programme, spread on both seaboards of the continent, and in the Great Lakes.

A number of PCs were converted to other duties. Reflecting the RN's original thinking on the 'Flower' class corvettes, some 18 PCs were first completed as minesweepers but later reconverted as escorts when the supply of purpose-built fleet minesweepers started flowing. Some 36 were converted to the role of PCC, or landing craft control ships. 24 were completed as PGM, motor gunboats, and 2 others became naval auxiliaries.

The PC class was seen to be so successful as an inshore patrol boat that after the war a number of very similar vessels were built, usually outside the United States, under US offshore aid programmes.

Thus we may find these similar but post-war classes in the navies of France, Greece, Italy, Japan, Portugal, Turkey and Yugoslavia.

## USN PC CLASS PRODUCTION FIGURES

| | |
|---|---|
| Total Built  354 | **NOTE** |
| Commissioned by USN as PCs  284 | PGM figure does not include 36 converted to Landing Craft Control Ships (PCC) later, after commissioning. |
| To PGM, etc (see note)  26 | |
| To other navies in wartime  44 | |
| Cancelled after launch  3 | |
| Cancelled before launch  42 | |
| Total ordered  399 | |

## USN PC CLASS LAUNCHING FIGURES

| | | | | | |
|---|---|---|---|---|---|
| 1940 | 2nd half | 3 | 1944 | 1st half | 36 |
| 1941 | 1st half | | | 2nd half | 21 |
| | 2nd half | | 1945 | 1st half | 12 |
| 1942 | 1st half | 32 | | 2nd half | 1 |
| | 2nd half | 60 | | | |
| 1943 | 1st half | 54 | | | |
| | 2nd half | 66 | | | |

*PC 576, showing how two single 3″ guns were mounted on this slim hull. The small boat was handled by the boom, and the funnel usually had this large cap in the later units.*
*(US Bureau of Ships)*

## USN PC CLASS—CLASS LIST

| Name | Builder | Building Time | Completion Date |
|------|---------|---------------|-----------------|
| PC 451 | Defoe | 10m18d | 12.8.40 |
| PC 452 | ,, | | L 1941 |
| PC 457 | ,, | | L 1941 |
| PC 461 | Lawley | 8m30d | 19.3.42 |
| PC 462 | ,, | 8m24d | 15.4.42 |
| PC 463 | ,, | 8m27d | 28.4.42 |
| PC 464 | ,, | 9m7d | 15.5.42 |
| PC 465 | ,, | 9m15d | 25.5.42 |
| PC 466 | ,, | 8m18d | 3.6.42 |
| PC 469 | ,, | 5m14d | 13.7.42 |
| PC 470 | ,, | 5m14d | 31.7.42 |
| PC 476 | Defoe | 5m16d | |
| PC 477 | ,, | 4m8d | 30.3.42 |
| PC 478 | ,, | 3m15d | 1.4.42 |
| PC 479 | ,, | 3m16d | 30.4.42 |
| PC 483 | Consolidated, NY | 14m12d | 12.3.42 |
| PC 484 | ,, | 11m26d | 3.4.42 |
| PC 485 | ,, | 11m8d | 23.4.42 |
| PC 486 | ,, | 5m20d | 14.5.42 |
| PC 487 | ,, | 5m26d | 2.6.42 |
| PC 488 | Sullivan | 17m5d | 12.8.42 |
| PC 489 | ,, | 15m28d | 14.7.42 |
| PC 490 | Dravo, Pittsburgh | 12m3d | 12.5.42 |
| PC 491 | ,, | 11m4d | 13.4.42 |
| PC 492 | ,, | 9m10d | 5.4.42 |
| PC 493 | ,, | 9m19d | 28.5.42 |
| PC 494 | ,, | 9m14d | 23.5.42 |
| PC 495 | ,, | 10m12d | 23.4.42 |
| PC 548 | Defoe | 3m8d | 2.8.42 |
| PC 549 | ,, | 3m1d | 2.8.42 |
| PC 552 | Sullivan | 14m9d | 29.7.42 |
| PC 553 | ,, | 12m21d | 12.10.42 |
| PC 555 | ,, | 11m21d | 6.2.43 |
| PC 560 | Jeffersonville | 7m23d | 17.6.42 |
| PC 563 | Consolidated, NY | 5m28d | 17.6.42 |
| PC 564 | ,, | 5m8d | 2.7.42 |
| PC 565 | Brown | 10m1d | 25.5.42 |
| PC 566 | ,, | 11m1d | 15.6.42 |
| PC 567 | ,, | 10m12d | 27.6.42 |
| PC 568 | ,, | 11m2d | 13.7.42 |
| PC 569 | Albina | 7m28d | 9.5.42 |
| PC 570 | ,, | 7m6d | 18.4.42 |
| PC 571 | ,, | 8m22d | 19.6.42 |
| PC 572 | ,, | 7m30d | 26.5.42 |

| PC 573 | Dravo, Pittsburgh | 7m30d | 13.6.42 |
| PC 574 | ,, | 6m3d | 2.7.42 |
| PC 575 | ,, | 5m12d | 8.8.42 |
| PC 576 | ,, | 5m7d | 10.9.42 |
| PC 577 | ,, | 5m8d | 15.10.42 |
| PC 578 | Albina | 6m26d | 15.7.42 |
| PC 579 | ,, | 7m20d | 25.8.42 |
| PC 580 | ,, | 8m4d | 26.9.42 |
| PC 581 | ,, | 7m27d | 9.10.42 |
| PC 582 | ,, | 8m1d | 22.10.42 |
| PC 583 | Defoe | 3m26d | 2.9.42 |
| PC 584 | ,, | 3m8d | 22.8.42 |
| PC 585 | ,, | 3m15d | 6.9.42 |
| PC 586 | ,, | 4m13d | 5.10.42 |
| PC 587 | ,, | 3m14d | 19.9.42 |
| PC 588 | Leathem | 7m29d | 22.6.42 |
| PC 589 | ,, | 4m14d | 23.7.42 |
| PC 590 | ,, | 5m21d | 5.10.42 |
| PC 592 | Dravo, Pittsburgh | 7m29d | 28.11.42 |
| PC 593 | ,, | 8m5d | 26.12.42 |
| PC 594 | ,, | 10m8d | 9.3.43 |
| PC 595 | ,, | 11m12d | 30.4.43 |
| PC 596 | Commercial | 9m4d | 23.1.43 |
| PC 597 | ,, | 9m6d | 15.2.43 |
| PC 598 | ,, | 9m13d | 5.3.43 |
| PC 599 | ,, | 9m13d | 15.5.43 |
| PC 600 | Consolidated, NY | 5m18d | 18.8.42 |
| PC 601 | ,, | 5m15d | 1.9.42 |
| PC 602 | ,, | 5m4d | 16.9.42 |
| PC 603 | ,, | 4m23d | 1.10.42 |
| PC 606 | Luders | 3m23d | 7.8.43 |
| PC 608 | Brown | 7m30d | 7. 9.42 |
| PC 609 | ,, | 7m10d | 18.8.42 |
| PC 610 | ,, | 7m4d | 28.9.42 |
| PC 611 | ,, | 8m4d | 26.10.42 |
| PC 612 | Gibbs | 10m1d | 1.5.43 |
| PC 613 | ,, | 10m23d | 2.6.43 |
| PC 614 | ,, | 12m2d | 9.7.43 |
| PC 615 | ,, | 12m9d | 16.7.43 |
| PC 616 | Lawley | 5m20d | 19.8.42 |
| PC 617 | ,, | 4m30d | 28.8.42 |
| PC 618 | ,, | 4m9d | 7.9.42 |
| PC 619 | ,, | 4m17d | 16.9.42 |
| PC 620 | Nashville | 10m9d | 8.1.43 |
| PC 623 | ,, | 9m17d | 10.4.43 |
| PC 776 | Commercial | 7m17d | 28.3.43 |
| PC 777 | ,, | 6m31d | 8.4.43 |
| PC 778 | ,, | 7m23d | 30.4.43 |
| PC 779 | ,, | 8m4d | 31.5.43 |

| | | | |
|---|---|---|---|
| PC 780 | ,, | 7m23d | 19.6.43 |
| PC 781 | ,, | 7m28d | 9.7.43 |
| PC 782 | ,, | 7m23d | 19.7.43 |
| PC 783 | ,, | 8m7d | 14.8.43 |
| PC 784 | ,, | 9m1d | 17.9.43 |
| PC 785 | ,, | 9m16d | 9.10.43 |
| PC 786 | ,, | 9m30d | 30.10.43 |
| PC 787 | ,, | 10m0d | 13.11.43 |
| PC 788 | ,, | 13m28d | 15.2.44 |
| PC 789 | ,, | 14m14d | 6.3.44 |
| PC 790 | ,, | 11m14d | 23.3.44 |
| PC 791 | ,, | 12m15d | 28.3.44 |
| PC 792 | ,, | 13m19d | 10.4.44 |
| PC 793 | ,, | 13m7d | 10.5.44 |
| PC 794 | ,, | 13m1d | 25.5.44 |
| PC 795 | ,, | 12m12d | 10.6.44 |
| PC 796 | ,, | 12m10d | 19.6.44 |
| PC 797 | ,, | 12m12d | 5.7.44 |
| PC 798 | ,, | 12m16d | 19.7.44 |
| PC 799 | ,, | 12m10d | 3.8.44 |
| PC 800 | ,, | 13m23d | 23.9.44 |
| PC 801 | ,, | 16m0d | 20.12.44 |
| PC 802 | ,, | 16m23d | 6.1.45 |
| PC 803 | ,, | 17m5d | 23.1.45 |
| PC 804 | ,, | 17m11d | 6.2.45 |
| PC 807 | ,, | 16m18d | 7.11.45 |
| PC 808 | ,, | 25m22d | 7.11.45 |
| PC 809 | ,, | 16m24d | 20.3.45 |
| PC 810 | ,, | 17m4d | 3.4.45 |
| PC 811 | ,, | 17m11d | 17.4.45 |
| PC 814 | ,, | 3m2d | 19.4.45 |
| PC 815 | Albina | 6m11d | 20.4.43 |
| PC 816 | ,, | 6m5d | 9.6.43 |
| PC 817 | ,, | 6m5d | 13.7.43 |
| PC 818 | ,, | 4m30d | 3.8.43 |
| PC 819 | ,, | 4m28d | 28.8.43 |
| PC 820 | ,, | 4m11d | 30.9.43 |
| PC 821 | Leathem | 9m23d | 23.6.44 |
| PC 822 | ,, | 7m7d | 2.6.44 |
| PC 823 | ,, | 8m16d | 24.7.44 |
| PC 824 | | *5m22d* | *28.8.44* |
| PC 825 | ,, | 5m24d | 20.9.44 |
| PC 1077 | Albina | 9m27d | 14.12.42 |
| PC 1078 | ,, | 9m6d | 5.2.43 |
| PC 1079 | ,, | 10m8d | 7.3.43 |
| PC 1080 | ,, | 10m30d | 29.3.43 |
| PC 1081 | ,, | 8m20d | 16.4.43 |
| PC 1082 | ,, | 8m 12d | 8.5.43 |
| PC 1083 | Lawley | 12m1d | 16.8.43 |

| PC 1084 | Lawley | 11m23d | 31.8.43 |
|---|---|---|---|
| PC 1085 | ,, | 9m13d | 19.10.43 |
| PC 1086 | ,, | 11m14d | 19.1.44 |
| PC 1087 | ,, | 13m10d | 22.5.44 |
| PC 1119 | Defoe | 8m6d | 18.12.42 |
| PC 1120 | ,, | 6m29d | 18.1.43 |
| PC 1121 | ,, | 17m20d | 10.12.43 |
| PC 1122 | ,, | 5m21d | 1.1.43 |
| PC 1123 | ,, | 6m14d | 5.2.43 |
| PC 1125 | ,, | 9m7d | 26.5.43 |
| PC 1126 | ,, | 8m29d | 27.5.43 |
| PC 1127 | ,, | 8m12d | 29.5.43 |
| PC 1128 | ,, | 8m16d | 31.5.43 |
| PC 1130 | ,, | 8m12d | 19.6.43 |
| PC 1131 | ,, | 9m7d | 28.7.43 |
| PC 1132 | ,, | 9m4d | 10.8.43 |
| PC 1133 | ,, | 8m29d | 24.8.43 |
| PC 1134 | ,, | 9m8d | 11.9.43 |
| PC 1135 | ,, | 9m26d | 7.10.43 |
| PC 1136 | ,, | 10m30d | 16.11.43 |
| PC 1137 | ,, | 9m25d | 23.10.43 |
| PC 1138 | ,, | 8m8d | 17.9.43 |
| PC 1139 | ,, | 9m24d | 18.11.43 |
| PC 1140 | ,, | 11m10d | 22.1.44 |
| PC 1141 | ,, | 9m16d | 28.12.43 |
| PC 1142 | ,, | 13m4d | 3.6.44 |
| PC 1143 | ,, | 13m0d | 16.6.44 |
| PC 1144 | ,, | 12m13d | 20.5.44 |
| PC 1145 | ,, | 11m0d | 1.6.44 |
| PC 1146 | ,, | 9m22d | 13.7.44 |
| PC 1147 | ,, | 10m1d | 12.8.44 |
| PC 1149 | ,, | 7m16d | 22.6.44 |
| PC 1167 | Sullivan | 8m0d | 3.12.43 |
| PC 1168 | ,, | 8m28d | 31.12.43 |
| PC 1169 | ,, | 6m23d | 26.1.44 |
| PC 1170 | ,, | 7m18d | 21.2.44 |
| PC 1171 | Leathem | 6m12d | 24.9.43 |
| PC 1172 | ,, | 6m7d | 6.10.43 |
| PC 1173 | ,, | 6m10d | 1.11.43 |
| PC 1174 | ,, | 5m18d | 5.11.43 |
| PC 1175 | ,, | 5m23d | 1.12.43 |
| PC 1176 | ,, | 5m22d | 20.11.43 |
| PC 1177 | , | 4m27d | 20.12.43 |
| PC 1178 | ,, | 4m26d | 6.1.44 |
| PC 1179 | ,, | 4m1d | 22.1.44 |
| PC 1180 | ,, | 4m5d | 10.2.44 |
| PC 1181 | Gibbs | 10m12d | 17.9.43 |
| PC 1182 | ,, | 12m18d | 27.10.43 |
| PC 1183 | ,, | 13m11d | 7.12.43 |

▲ *PC 1590* with an upper conning position on top of the bridge. A single Bofors has displaced the after 3″ gun, and she has some strange aerials on a cross structure at the masthead. *(US Bureau of Ships)*

*PC 545* in 1943. Her dazzle camouflage has been well worn by heavy weather, and she has no radar. The forward 3″ gun looks very exposed compared with the RN Corvettes. *(US Bureau of Ships).* ▼

| | | | |
|---|---|---|---|
| PC 1184 | ,, | 12m16d | 24.1.44 |
| PC 1185 | ,, | 12m27d | 24.4.44 |
| PC 1186 | ,, | 13m19d | 9.6.44 |
| PC 1187 | ,, | 13m0d | 18.7.44 |
| PC 1188 | ,, | 13m24d | 5.9.44 |
| PC 1190 | ,, | 17m6d | 6.2.45 |
| PC 1191 | Consolidated, Morris Heights | 5m10d | 2.11.42 |
| PC 1192 | ,, | 5m13d | 26.11.42 |
| PC 1193 | ,, | 6m21d | 21.1.43 |
| PC 1194 | ,, | 6m14d | 8.2.43 |
| PC 1195 | ,, | 7m15d | 23.3.43 |
| PC 1196 | ,, | 5m9d | 7.4.43 |
| PC 1197 | ,, | 7m2d | 22.4.43 |
| PC 1198 | ,, | 6m31d | 3.5.43 |
| PC 1199 | ,, | 6m24d | 17.5.43 |
| PC 1200 | ,, | 7m13d | 29.5.43 |
| PC 1201 | ,, | 6m30d | 11.6.43 |
| PC 1202 | ,, | 5m21d | 23.6.43 |
| PC 1203 | Consolidated, | 5m25d | 17.7.43 |
| PC 1204 | Morris Heights | 5m7d | 6.8.43 |
| PC 1205 | ,, | 5m14d | 26.8.43 |
| PC 1206 | ,, | 4m18d | 27.10.43 |
| PC 1207 | ,, | 4m16d | 12.11.43 |
| PC 1208 | ,, | 4m4d | 24.11.43 |
| PC 1209 | ,, | 8m14d | 1.5.44 |
| PC 1210 | ,, | 7m20d | 5.5.44 |
| PC 1211 | Luders | 12m4d | 16.8.43 |
| PC 1212 | ,, | 12m22d | 18.9.43 |
| PC 1213 | ,, | 10m29d | 6.10.43 |
| PC 1214 | ,, | 8m6d | 28.10.43 |
| PC 1215 | ,, | 8m4d | 26.11.43 |
| PC 1216 | ,, | 8m3d | 31.12.43 |
| PC 1217 | ,, | 11m1d | 27.4.44 |
| PC 1218 | ,, | 10m14d | 29.5.44 |
| PC 1219 | ,, | 10m27d | 1.7.44 |
| PC 1220 | ,, | 10m21d | 29.7.44 |
| PC 1221 | ,, | 10m21d | 19.4.44 |
| PC 1122 | Penn-Jersey | 8m12d | 7.7.44 |
| PC 1223 | ,, | 13m17d | 13.11.44 |
| PC 1224 | ,, | 16m8d | 8.1.45 |
| PC 1225 | Leathem | 6m31d | 12.1.43 |
| PC 1228 | ,, | 8m13d | 21.5.43 |
| PC 1229 | ,, | 9m3d | 11.6.43 |
| PC 1230 | ,, | 6m26d | 15.7.43 |
| PC 1231 | Sullivan | 10m13d | 13.7.43 |
| PC 1232 | ,, | 11m10d | 18.8.43 |
| PC 1233 | ,, | 12m3d | 24.9.44 |
| PC 1237 | Consolidated, | 5m12d | 26.7.43 |
| PC 1238 | Morris Heights | 5m3d | 6.9.43 |

PC 1170 in 1944. She has the Mousetrap, the
modified Hedgehog for this class, right forward
on the forecastle, a single Bofors aft and three
single Oerlikons atop the bridge.
(US Bureau of Ships)

PC 597 in Pacific dark blue camouflage, with
three single Oerlikons on top of her bridge.
(US Bureau of Ships)

| | | | |
|---|---|---|---|
| PC 1239 | ,, | 5m13d | 27.9.43 |
| PC 1240 | ,, | 4m29d | 13.10.43 |
| PC 1241 | Nashville | 8m23d | 28.5.43 |
| PC 1242 | ,, | 9m20d | 12.7.43 |
| PC 1243 | ,, | 9m3d | 12.9.43 |
| PC 1244 | ,, | 8m16d | 5.10.43 |
| PC 1245 | ,, | 7m21d | 30.10.43 |
| PC 1246 | ,, | 7m25d | 29.11.43 |
| PC 1247 | ,, | 6m24d | 20.12.43 |
| PC 1251 | Brown | 9m7d | 27.2.43 |
| PC 1252 | ,, | 8m18d | 27.3.43 |
| PC 1253 | ,, | 9m15d | 1.4.43 |
| PC 1254 | ,, | 9m21d | 13.4.43 |
| PC 1256 | Luders | 11m30d | 27.10.44 |
| PC 1257 | ,, | 13m9d | 21.2.44 |
| PC 1258 | ,, | 12m27d | 24.1.45 |
| PC 1259 | ,, | 13m9d | 6.3.45 |
| PC 1260 | Leathem | 6m4d | 24.4.43 |
| PC 1262 | ,, | 5m8d | 29.6.43 |
| PC 1263 | ,, | 4m26d | 28.7.43 |
| PC 1264 | Consolidated, | 6m1d | 25.4.44 |
| PC 1265 | Morris Heights | 6m13d | 12.5.44 |
| PC 1546 | ,, | 6m7d | 5.6.44 |
| PC 1547 | ,, | 7m13d | 7.7.44 |
| PC 1549 | ,, | 5m26d | 25.7.44 |
| PC 1563 | Leathem | 4m25d | 29.6.44 |
| PC 1564 | ,, | 5m8d | 4.8.44 |
| PC 1569 | ,, | 17m18d | 14.3.45 |
| PC 1586 | Commercial | 11m3d | 28.7.42 |
| ex AM 82 | | | |
| PC 1587 | ,, | 11m3d | 15.8.43 |
| ex AM 83 | | | |
| PC 1588 | ,, | 8m30d | 2.9.42 |
| ex AM 84 | | | |
| PC 1589 | ,, | 7m8d | 5.9.42 |
| ex AM 85 | | | |
| PC 1590 | ,, | 7m0d | 21.9.42 |
| ex AM 86 | | | |
| PC 1591 | Leathem | 6m29d | 10.10.42 |
| ex AM 87 | | | |
| PC 1592 | ,, | 6m21d | 27.10.42 |
| ex AM 88 | | | |
| PC 1593 | Dravo, Neville Island | 9m6d | 31.8.42 |
| ex AM 89 | | | |
| PC 1594 | ,, | 8m5d | 31.8.42 |
| ex AM 90 | | | |
| PC 1595 | ,, | 7m30d | 15.9.42 |
| ex AM 91 | | | |
| PC 1596 | ,, | 7m2d | 1.10.42 |
| ex AM 92 | | | |

| | | | |
|---|---|---|---|
| *PC 1597* | ,, | 7m27d | 22.10.42 |
| ex *AM 93* | | | |
| *PC 1598* | Jacobson | 11m23d | 11.12.42 |
| ex *AM 94* | | | |
| *PC 1599* | ,, | 8m24d | 5.2.43 |
| ex *AM 95* | | | |
| *PC 1600* | Nashville | 10m12d | 6.9.42 |
| ex *AM 96* | | | |
| *PC 1601* | ,, | 11m24d | 12.10.42 |
| ex *AM 97* | | | |
| *PC 1602* | Penn-Jersey | 18m21d | 10.4.43 |
| ex *AM 98* | | | |
| *PC 1603* | ,, | 18m27d | 16.6.43 |
| ex *AM 99* | | | |

## CANCELLED SHIPS

*PC 1092-1118, PC 1570-1585*
Numbers not included above, and not in list of ships transferred to Allied navies during the war, were not used.

**PC 597 in 1942.**

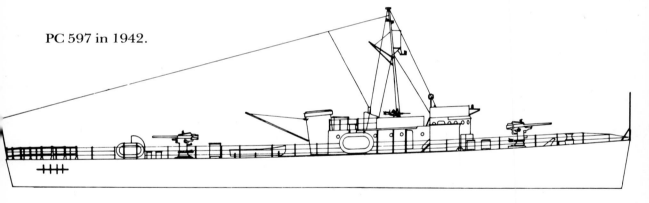

*PC 1593*, one of the last units to be completed. She has a 3″ gun forward, a single Bofors right aft, and good A/S equipment. Type SG radar at the masthead, dwarfed by the crow's nest.
(*US Bureau of Ships*)

## USN PC CLASS AND RN 'FLOWER' CLASS SPECIFICATION

|  | USN PC CLASS | RN 'FLOWER' CLASS |
|---|---|---|
| (Figures shown are typical for class during service) | | |
| Displacement | 280/330/375 | 950 |
| Dimensions | | |
|   length oa | 174' 9" | 205' 1" |
|   breadth | 23' 0" | 33' 1" |
|   draught | 7' 6" | 8' 3"/13' 5" |
| Machinery | 2 GM 2-stroke diesels | Vertical reciprocating |
| Speed | 19/20 kn | 16 |
| Endurance | 3,450 m×12 kn | |
| Oil Fuel | 60 | |
| Complement | 80 | 50-80 |
| Armament | | |
|   main | 1/2 3"/50 cal | 1 4" |
|   close-range | 1 40mm Bofors (if 1 3") | 1 2 pdr |
| | 2/3 20mm Oerlikons | 2/6 20mm Oerlikons |
| Anti-submarine | $\frac{1}{2}$ Hedgehog? | 1 Hedgehog |
| | 2 dct | 4 dct |
| | 2 rails | 2 rails |

### PC 451/452/457

| Length oa | | 170/174' |
|---|---|---|
| Machinery | PC 451 | 2 sets GM diesels |
| | PC 452 | geared turbines |

*PC 797* with two extra single Oerlikons added in the boat position, making a total of five with the single 3" forward, and single Bofors aft. A Pacific picture. (*US Bureau of Ships*)

## TRANSFERRED TO ALLIED NAVIES DURING THE WAR YEARS

**To Brazil**
*PC 544, PC 547, PC 554, PC 561, PC 604-605, PC 607, PC 1236*

**To Greece**
*PC 622*

**To other configurations in USN**
*PC 805-606* to PGM  *PC 1088-1091* to PGM  *PC 1124* to auxiliary vessel  *PC 1148* to PGM  *PC 1189* to PGM  *PC 1255* to PGM  *PC 1548* to PGM  *PC 1550-1559* to PGM

**To Norway**
*PC 467*

**To the Netherlands**
*PC 468*

**To France**
*PC 471-475, PC 480-482, PC 542-543, PC 545-546, PC 550-551, PC 556-557, PC 559, PC 562, PC 591, PC 621, PC 625, 627, PC 1226-1227, PC 1235, PC 1248-1250, PC 1560-1562*

## WAR LOSSES

| | | |
|---|---|---|
| *PC 457* | | |
| *PC 496* | 4.6.43 | Mine, 37.23N,9.52W |
| *PC 558* | 9.5.44 | Torpedo, 38.41N,13.43E |
| *PC 815* | | |
| *PC 1129* | 31.5.45 | Surface warship off Luzon, Philippines |
| *PC 1261* | 6.6.44 | Shore gunfire, off France |
| *PC 1603* | 21.5.45 | Air attack, 26.25N,127.56E |

*PC 1191* with two single 3"/50 calibre guns, the large bridge structure with two single Oerlikons on top, and little other equipment. *(US Bureau of Ships)*

*PCE 867* in 1945. The bridge structure looks too large for the hull, but gave a very roomy bridge and Asdic lay-out. Note the gaffs forward and aft of the mast, the supporting struts to the mast from the bridge, and the short funnel added in later units to take the diesel fumes clear of the air intakes in the hull. *(US Bureau of Ships)*

*PCE 899* in 1945. She has been used as a PCE(C), for inshore control on landing beaches, as the extra radio room has been added on the starboard side by the short funnel. A good view of the deck lay-out of this class (but see *Kilbride* in the RN section also). Three single Bofors aft, in large tubs, Type SL radar moved to a spur below the masthead, and Type SA added above. *(US Bureau of Ships)*

## USN PATROL CRAFT ESCORT (PCE) CLASS
**63 ships built**

This was the successor to the PC class, with 10 feet extra length, but also no less than 10 feet extra beam. The bridge structure was built up, and a break in the main deck aft to provide a quarterdeck was introduced, similar to the RN 'River' class design.

This class was fairly flat-bottomed, and with the increased topweight had a tendency to roll. They were much better suited to open sea work than their predecessors; but by the time they appeared the Atlantic war was going well and 64 were cancelled, plus some 135 originally asked for by the RN but not laid down.

Their armament was particularly impressive for their size. Their basic outfit was a single 3"/50 calibre gun forward, with a full Hedgehog immediately aft of it, as in the DEs.

The single Oerlikons round the bridge structure largely paralleled RN practice, though some ships had either 1 or 2 extra guns forward of the wheelhouse. But aft there was a dramatic difference from the RN corvettes. The original PCEs, fitted for ocean escort work, had two single 40mm Bofors in large guntubs on the fantail (quarterdeck), and the other superimposed forward of it. Later ships, fitted as landing craft control ships (PCEC), had 2 twin Bofors, with directors, side by side on the after end of the main deck.

In either case the after close-range weapons did not inhibit a full range of depth-charge throwers and rails on the fantail, excellently placed for clear and efficient handling of charges by the crew.

The bridge was open and large, and the steel pole mast carried a Type SL (or later SG) radar on top, rather than on a spur. This mast was distinctive for having a gaff, with signal halliards, fitted on the forward as well as the after side. There were variations in radar outfit, of course, towards the end of the war and later.

Some later units were completed as rescue ships (PCE(R)), and the main deck was carried further aft, almost to the stern. The armament was retained during the war period.

The main propelling machinery was diesel, with twin screws, making the ships very handy in manoeuvring. The earlier ships did not have a funnel, and the diesel exhausts, low down near the waterline, could be sucked into the air intakes, when the ships were lying alongside each other in harbour. Stove pipe vents were fitted on the upper deck in some units, and in many later ones a short conventional funnel was substituted, giving the ships a much more attractive appearance.

3 US shipyards built those units which were completed. One was situated at Chicago, the Pullman Standard Car Co, demonstrating the energy and imagination of the American warship construction programme. The other two yards were both in Portland, Oregon.

The boat arrangements were unusual, though similar to those in the smaller PC class. A standard USN motor whaleboat was stowed on chocks on the upper deck, and handled by a long boom (derrick) attached to the mast.

15 units, all from the Chicago yard, were transferred to the RN on completion under Lend-Lease. After the war the Netherlands built a later version of the PCE, under US offshore aid programmes.

| USN PCE CLASS NUMBERS | |
| --- | --- |
| Total ships built | 63 |
| Commissioned by USN as escorts | 35 |
| To PCE(R) (see note) | 13 |
| To RN | 15 |
| Cancelled | 64 |
| PCE(R) | 6 |
| RN | 135 |
| | 205 |

NOTE
Later to PCEC, included in escort nos.  10
Later to WPG, similarly  2
Later to other types of auxiliary  5
  17

| USN PCE CLASS PRODUCTION SCHEDULE | | |
| --- | --- | --- |
| 1943 | 2nd half | 8 |
| 1944 | 1st half | 15 |
| | 2nd half | 8 |
| 1945 | 1st half | 17 |

*PCE(R) 851* in 1952. The main deck has been carried almost to the stern, and many extra R/T aerials added at the masthead. The bridge front carries what are probably massive wind deflection vanes, and the Hedgehog is still carried immediately aft of the forward single 3″/50 gun. *(US Bureau of Ships)*

## USN PCE CLASS SPECIFICATION

| | |
|---|---|
| Displacement | 850 standard, 903 full load |
| Dimensions | |
| length wl | 180' 0" |
| oa | 184' 6" |
| breadth | 33' 1" |
| draught | 9' 5" |
| Machinery | GM Diesel 12-278A single reduction gear |
| SHP | 2,000 |
| Shafts | 2 |
| Speed | 15·7 kn |
| Complement | 9 officers, 90 men |
| | (PCE(R), 107,+57 patients) |
| Armament | |
| main | 1 3"/50 calibre |
| close-range | 2 single 40mm Bofors (3 in some) |
| | 2, 4 or 5 single 20mm Oerlikons |
| | (PCE(R) 1 3"/50, 2 single Bofors, 6 Oerlikons, |
| | PCEC 1 3"/50, 3 twin Bofors, 4 Oerlikons) |
| A/S Armament | 1 Hedgehog |
| | 4 throwers |
| | 2 rails |
| | (PCE(R) 2 throwers, 2 rails) |
| Radar | Type SL, IFF |

*PCE(R) 856* in 1944. Many of the later units of this class were completed in the rescue configuration and played an important role in the Kamikaze phase of the Pacific war. The main deck was extended aft to give extra accommodation, and extra Bofors added above the extension. A second whaleboat is carried on the starboard side. *(US Bureau of Ships).*

## USN PCE CLASS—CLASS LIST

| Name | Builder | Building Time | Completion Date |
|------|---------|---------------|-----------------|
| *PCE 842* | Pullman-Standard | 7m16d | 29.1.44 |
| ex *PCE(R) 842* | | | |
| *PCE 843* | ,, | 7m4d | 30.1.44 |
| ex *PCE (R) 843* | | | |
| *PCE 844* | ,, | 7m10d | 18.2.44 |
| ex *PCE(R) 844* | | | |
| *PCE 845* | ,, | 7m8d | 1.3.44 |
| ex *PCE(R) 845* | | | |
| *PCE 846* | ,, | 6m25d | 4.3.44 |
| ex *PCE (R) 846* | | | |
| *PCE 847* | ,, | 6m25d | 18.3.44 |
| ex *PCE(R) 847* | | | |
| *PCE 867* | Albina | 11m12d | 20.6.43 |
| *PCE 868* | ,, | 12m20d | 31.8.43 |
| *PCE 869* | ,, | 12m16d | 19.9.43 |
| *PCE 870* | ,, | 10m5d | 5.10.43 |
| *PCE 871* | ,, | 10m27d | 29.10.43 |
| *PCE 872* | ,, | 10m0d | 29.11.43 |
| *PCE 873* | ,, | 10m9d | 15.12.43 |
| *PCE 874* | ,, | 9m30d | 31.12.43 |
| *PCE 875* | ,, | 9m9d | 19.1.44 |
| *PCE 877* | ,, | 9m8d | 14.2.44 |
| *PCE 880* | ,, | 8m18d | 29.4.44 |
| *PCE 881* | ,, | 11m20d | 31.7.43 |
| *PCE 882* | ,, | 17m23d | 23.2.45 |
| *PCE 884* | ,, | 17m3d | 30.3.45 |
| *PCE 885* | ,, | 26m3d | 30.4.45 |
| *PCE 886* | ,, | 26m2d | 31.5.45 |
| *PCE 891* | Willamette | 19m19d | 15.6.44 |
| *PCE 892* | ,, | 20m11d | 8.7.44 |
| *PCE 893* | ,, | 20m24d | 25.7.44 |
| *PCE 894* | ,, | 20m3d | 10.8.44 |
| *PCE 895* | ,, | 22m28d | 30.10.44 |
| *PCE 896* | Willamette | 23m26d | 27.11.44 |
| *PCE 897* | ,, | 24m11d | 6.1.45 |
| *PCE 898* | ,, | 25m8d | 24.1.45 |
| *PCE 899* | ,, | 26m6d | 17.3.45 |
| *PCE 900* | ,, | 27m1d | 12.4.45 |
| *PCE 902* | ,, | 27m2d | 30.4.45 |
| *PCE 903* | ,, | 27m5d | 16.5.45 |
| *PCE 904* | ,, | 27m10d | 31.5.45 |

## COMPLETED AS PCE(R)

| | | | |
|---|---|---|---|
| *PCE(R) 848* | Pullman-Standard | 18m22d | 30.3.45 |
| *PCE(R) 849* | ,, | 6m17d | 11.4.44 |
| *PCE(R) 850* | ,, | 6m11d | 17.4.44 |
| *PCE(R) 851* | ,, | 6m28d | 15.5.44 |
| *PCE(R) 852* | ,, | 6m29d | 26.5.44 |
| *PCE(R) 853* | ,, | 6m30d | 16.6.44 |
| *PCE(R) 854* | ,, | 13m10d | 4.1.45 |
| *PCE(R) 855* | ,, | 10m24d | 1.11.44 |
| *PCE(R) 856* | ,, | 10m25d | 11.11.44 |
| *PCE(R) 857* | ,, | 16m5d | 26.4.45 |
| *PCE(R) 858* | ,, | 16m17d | 16.5.45 |
| *PCE(R) 859* | ,, | 13m27d | 10.3.45 |
| *PCE(R) 860* | ,, | 14m6d | 31.3.45 |

*PCE 861-866* cancelled—would have been completed as PCE(R)

## COMPLETED IN OTHER CONFIGURATIONS

*PCE 876,`879, 883* to de-gaussing ships (YDG)
*PCE 901* to small auxiliary transport (ACM)
*PCE 873, 882, 896, 898* to PCE(C)

## CANCELLED SHIPS

*PCE 887-890, 905-960*

PCE 899 in 1945.

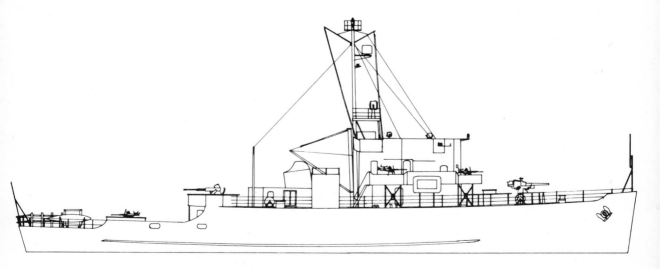

*Asheville*, PF 1, in February 1944. One of the two units of this class built in Canada, she has both Type 271 radar on the bridge and Type SL at the masthead, while she has been refitted with three 3″/50 USN guns, and two twin Bofors mountings aft, thus presenting a fascinating combination of RN/RCN and USN equipment. *(US National Archives)*

*Allentown*, PF 52, in August 1944. A fine quarter shot at speed, and showing an extra deckhouse built between the feet of the tripod foremast. There is Type SA radar at the masthead, Type SL below it, and Type TBS on the port yard. H/F D/F on a pole mast aft, and two extra single Oerlikons fitted forward of the twin Bofors. *(US National Archives)*

## USN PATROL FRIGATE (PF) CLASS
## 77 ships built in the USA and commissioned by the USN

This was a large class of ocean escort, built in the United States, in parallel with the 6 types of destroyer escort. The class was, in fact, included in the Patrol Gunboat (PG) class, until the PF class was established in 1943, and ships prior to that time were designated PG 101-102, 111-179, 201-202, 207-210. The class was technically designated US Maritime Commission, Modified 'River' version, type S2-S2-AQ1.

The class originated from the RN's first frigate design, the 'River' class. This itself was a result of the RN's earlier North Atlantic war experience, and no doubt the USN felt that on entering the war it would be helpful to gain from the RN's experience.

So the first 2 units of the 'River' class built in Canada were transferred to the USN on completion, on reverse Lend-Lease, and became the first 2 units of the PF class. The USN ordered a further 8 units of the class in Canada, but as the US escort production swung into full gear, and the USN requirements for the Pacific rapidly rose, the USN turned these 8 units over to the RN as part of its Lend-Lease commitments. This explains why these 8 ships were delivered to the RN in Canada, when at the same time a similar number of UK-built 'River' class units were being turned over to the RCN!

9 US shipyards participated in the PF building programme, and the ships were built largely on mercantile lines, as were the frigates in the UK and Canada.

The USN improved on the 'River' class design in some respects, with the Admiralty's co-operation. The hull length was increased by 2 feet 6 inches, and the beam by 1 foot, the hull was almost entirely welded, and there were no side scuttles in the hull. A ram bow was added.

But many features followed USN design. Thus the funnel followed the RN pattern, but the rounded bridge, with large portholes, was entirely American. A cap was not, however, fitted to the funnel in all cases. A Danforth-type anchor was substituted for the more usual stockless type, and a windlass was fitted to work it—following RN practice, and probably the only instance of a windlass, rather than a capstan, being fitted in a US-built escort during the war.

There was a USN-type steel pole foremast, in place of the RN tripod. This foremast carried an American Type SL radar aerial on a spur, for the main surface warning set, and in some units a Type SA aerial at the masthead for the aerial warning set. The yard was mounted aft of the mast, following USN practice, and Types TBS and ABK (IFF) aerials were carried on it. In the RN 'Colony' class chapter we recalled that, later in the war, this pole foremast was found to be too light to carry the heavier RN Type 277 radar aerials.

A USN motor whaleboat was fitted in gravity davits on the starboard side, compared with the large gooseneck davits for the same type of boat in the DEs. No boat was fitted on the port side, again following current USN practice.

Where the Type SA radar aerial was fitted at the masthead, the H/F D/F aerial was usually fitted on a shorter pole mast, further aft, and raked. There was a prominent galley exhaust pipe carried up the side of the foremast, which is clear in some of the photographs.

The gun armament was entirely American, and the after gun deckhouse seen in the RN 'River' class units did not appear in the USN ships.

The main armament was 3 single 3″/50 calibre guns, disposed as in the DEs. A Hedgehog was fitted aft of A gun, following DE practice also—an interesting comparison with the forward arrangements in the RN ships. A gunnery control range-finder was fitted at the after end of the bridge, where the main radar aerial was fitted in the RN and RCN units.

The close-range armament also differed. Two twin 40mm Bofors, sided, were fitted, with directors, aft at the break of the forecastle deck. 4 single Oerlikons were fitted on and below the bridge, which did follow RN practice; and further single Oerlikons were fitted on the quarterdeck, and in some ships on the upper deck, aft of the funnel.

The depth-charge outfit followed RN practice, except that 8 throwers were fitted in some ships, and the heavy extra stowage racks fitted in most of the RN units for North Atlantic service were omitted. The USN ships largely used their camouflage measures 14, 22 and 31 in this class.

The PF class served widely in the Atlantic and Pacific theatres, and must have provided much of the escort for Pacific fleet train convoys and forces. They disappeared rapidly from active USN lists when the war ended, and many units were then transferred to Allied navies, and some can still be found in service with them.

75 ships, out of the 77 commissioned by the USN, were manned by the US Coastguard during the war years.

*San Pedro* in San Pedro Harbour, late in 1943. All-blue camouflage, she has Type SA radar at the masthead, with Type SL on the short spur below it. Three single Oerlikons have been added on the quarterdeck, and there are possibly single Bofors in place of Oerlikons in the upper bridge wings. *(US Bureau of Ships)*

## USN PF CLASS PRODUCTION

(by quarterly periods)

| | | | | | | | |
|---|---|---|---|---|---|---|---|
| 1942 | 4th quarter | 2 | | 1944 | 1st quarter | 16 |
| | (Canadian prototypes) | | | | 2nd quarter | 12 |
| 1943 | 1st quarter | 0 | | | 3rd quarter | 17 |
| | 2nd quarter | 0 | | | 4th quarter | 10 |
| | 3rd quarter | 1 | | 1945 | 1st quarter | 8 |
| | 4th quarter | 11 | | | | |

TOTAL BUILT Canada 2

USA 75

TOTAL 77

Cancelled 4

## USN PF CLASS SPECIFICATION

| | |
|---|---|
| Displacement | 1,430 tons |
| Dimensions | |
| length w.l | 285'0" |
| oa | 304'0" |
| breadth | 37'6" |
| draught | 12'6" |
| Machinery | Triple expansion steam reciprocating |
| Shafts | 2 |
| SHP | 5,500 |
| Speed | 20 kn |
| Complement | 180 |
| Armament | |
| main | 3 single 3"/50 calibre |
| close-range | 2 twin 40mm Bofors |
| | 8 single 2mm Oerlikons |
| A/S Armament | 1 Hedgehog ATW mortar |
| | 8 depth charge throwers |
| | 2 rails |
| Radar | Types SL, SA (some), IFF |
| | (PF 1 and 2 only—RN Type 271 also) |
| Boat | 1 25ft motor whaleboat |
| Average Cost | $2,530,000 |

## USN PF CLASS—CLASS LIST

| Name | Number | Builder | Building Time | Completion Date |
|---|---|---|---|---|
| *Asheville* | PF 1 | Can Vickers | 8m21d | 1.12.42 |
| *Natchez* | PF 2 | ,, | 9m0d | 16.12.42 |

| | | | | |
|---|---|---|---|---|
| *Tacoma* | PF 3 | Kaiser | 7m27d | 6.11.43 |
| *Sausalito* | PF 4 | ,, | 10m27d | 4.3.44 |
| *Hoquiam* | PF 5 | ,, | 12m28d | 8.5.44 |
| *Pasco* | PF 6 | ,, | 9m8d | 15.4.44 |
| *Albuquerque* | PF 7 | ,, | 5m0d | 20.12.43 |
| *Everett* | PF 8 | ,, | 5m22d | 22.1.44 |
| *Pocatello* | PF 9 | ,, | 7m1d | 18.2.44 |
| *Brownsville* | PF 10 | ,, | 7m22d | 6.5.44 |
| *Grand Forks* | PF 11 | ,, | 5m19d | 18.3.44 |
| *Casper* | PF 12 | ,, | 5m14d | 31.3.44 |
| *Pueblo* | PF 13 | ,, | 6m12d | 27.5.44 |
| *Grand Island* | PF 14 | ,, | 5m30d | 27.5.44 |
| *Annapolis* | PF 15 | American, Cleveland | 13m15d | 4.7.44 |
| *Bangor* | PF 16 | ,, | 15m2d | 22.8.44 |
| *Key West* | PF 17 | ,, | 13m14d | 7.8.45 |
| *Alexandria* | PF 18 | ,, | 20m18d | 11.3.45 |
| *Huron* | PF 19 | American, Lorain | 18m15d | 7.9.44 |
| *Gulfport* | PF 20 | ,, | 16m1d | 16.9.44 |
| *Bayonne* | PF 21 | ,, | 21m8d | 14.2.45 |
| *Gloucester* | PF 22 | Walter Butler | 7m6d | 10.12.43 |
| *Shreveport* | PF 23 | ,, | 13m16d | 24.4.44 |
| *Muskegon* | PF 24 | ,, | 7m4d | 16.12.43 |
| *Charlottesville* | PF 25 | ,, | 10m29d | 10.4.44 |
| *Poughkeepsie* | PF 26 | ,, | 15m3d | 6.9.44 |
| *Newport* | PF 27 | ,, | 15m30d | 8.9.44 |
| *Emporia* | PF 28 | ,, | 10m29d | 12.6.44 |
| *Groton* | PF 29 | ,, | 13m21d | 5.9.44 |
| *Hingham* | PF 30 | ,, | 15m9d | 3.11.44 |
| *Grand Rapids* | PF 31 | ,, | 14m27d | 26.10.44 |
| *Woonsocket* | PF 32 | ,, | 11m16d | 27.7.44 |
| *Dearborn* | PF 33 | ,, | 11m2d | 17.7.44 |
| *Long Beach* | PF 34 | Consolidated, San Pedro | 5m20d | 8.9.43 |
| *Belfast* | PF 35 | ,, | 7m29d | 24.11.43 |
| *Glendale* | PF 36 | ,, | 5m25d | 1.10.43 |
| *San Pedro* | PF 37 | ,, | 6m6d | 23.10.43 |
| *Coronado* | PF 38 | ,, | 6m11d | 17.11.43 |
| *Ogden* | PF 39 | ,, | 6m30d | 20.12.43 |
| *Eugene* | PF 40 | ,, | 7m2d | 15.1.44 |
| *El Paso* | PF 41 | ,, | 5m13d | 1.12.43 |
| *Van Buren* | PF 42 | ,, | 5m23d | 17.12.43 |
| *Orange* | PF 43 | ,, | 5m25d | 1.1.44 |
| *Corpus Christi* | PF 44 | ,, | 6m12d | 29.1.44 |
| *Hutchinson* | PF 45 | ,, | 6m6d | 3.2.44 |
| *Bisbee* | PF 46 | ,, | 6m8d | 15.2.44 |
| *Gallup* | PF 47 | ,, | 6m18d | 26.2.44 |
| *Rockford* | PF 48 | ,, | 6m9d | 6.3.44 |
| *Muskogee* | PF 49 | ,, | 5m28d | 16.3.44 |
| *Carson City* | PF 50 | ,, | 5m26d | 24.3.44 |
| *Burlington* | PF 51 | ,, | 5m15d | 3.4.44 |

| | | | | |
|---|---|---|---|---|
| *Allentown* | PF 52 | Froemming | 12m1d | 24.3.44 |
| *Machias* | PF 53 | ,, | 10m21d | 29.3.44 |
| *Sandusky* | PF 54 | ,, | 9m10d | 18.4.44 |
| *Bath* | PF 55 | ,, | 12m9d | 1.9.44 |
| *Covington* | PF 56 | Globe | 16m8d | 7.8.44 |
| *Sheboygan* | PF 57 | ,, | 17m28d | 14.10.44 |
| *Abilene* | PF 58 | ,, | 17m22d | 28.10.44 |
| *Beaufort* | PF 59 | ,, | 13m7d | 28.8.44 |
| *Charlotte* | PF 60 | ,, | 14m1d | 9.10.44 |
| *Manitowoc* | PF 61 | ,, | 15m10d | 5.12.44 |
| *Gladwyne* | PF 62 | ,, | 10m4d | 18.8.44 |
| *Moberly* | PF 63 | ,, | 9m22d | 30.8.44 |
| *Knoxville* | PF 64 | Leathem | 12m13d | 29.4.44 |
| *Uniontown* | PF 65 | ,, | 16m24d | 15.9.44 |
| *Reading* | PF 66 | ,, | 14m25d | 19.8.44 |
| *Peoria* | PF 67 | ,, | 16m8d | 15.10.44 |
| *Brunswick* | PF 68 | ,, | 14m18d | 3.10.44 |
| *Davenport* | PF 69 | ,, | 18m8d | 15.2.45 |
| *Evansville* | PF 70 | ,, | 15m7d | 4.12.44 |
| *New Bedford* | PF 71 | ,, | 9m15d | 17.7.44 |
| *Lorain* | PF 93 | American, Cleveland | 14m21d | 15.1.45 |
| *Milledgeville* | PF 94 | ,, | 14m8d | 18.1.45 |
| *Orlando* | PF 99 | American, Lorain | 15m9d | 11.11.44 |
| *Racine* | PF 100 | ,, | 16m7d | 22.1.45 |
| *Greensboro* | PF 101 | ,, | 16m7d | 29.1.45 |
| *Forsyth* | PF 102 | ,, | 14m5d | 11.2.45 |

USN PF as in 1944

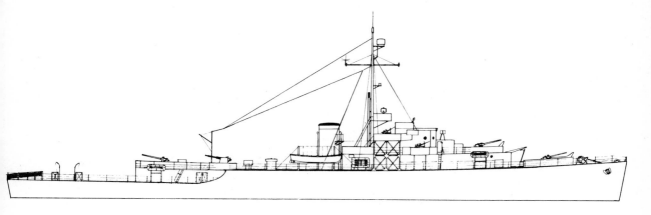

## CANCELLED SHIPS

| | |
|---|---|
| *Stamford* | PF 95 |
| *Macon* | PF 96 |
| *Lorain* | PF 97 |
| *Vallejo* | PF 98 |

All cancelled December 1943, from American SBCo

## TRANSFERRED TO RN ON COMPLETION, UNDER LEND-LEASE

PF 72-92 (21 ships)
Details will be found under the RN section

## TRANSFERRED TO RUSSIA, 1945

*Tacoma, Sausalito, Hoquiam, Pasco, Albuquerque, Everett, Bayonne, Gloucester, Charlottesville, Poughkeepsie, Newport, Long Beach, Belfast, Glendale, San Pedro, Coronado, Ogden, Bisbee, Gallup, Rockford, Muskogee, Carson City, Burlington, Allentown, Machias, Sandusky, Bath, Evansville.*

*Burlington* in January 1945. She is in all-blue paint, and the windlass on the forecastle, following RN 'River' class practice but unusual for the USN, is clearly visible. *(US National Archives)*

*Greensboro,* the last PF but one, probably on commissioning in 1944. Even the fantastic American shipbuilding effort could not always keep pace with the rate of completions. Here, she is short of both her radar aerials, her twin Bofors aft, and there is no H/F D/F; but note the three extra Oerlikons on the quarterdeck in raised tubs, and the dazzle camouflage pattern. *(US National Archives)*

*Gloucester* in 1944. She has two-tone grey camouflage, eight depth charge throwers, and standard gunnery and radar outfit. *(US National Archives)*

## USN DESTROYER ESCORTS (DE) CLASS
### 565 ships completed, 381 as DES

Numerically, this was by far the most important class of new escort built during the war. But there were only 3 large classes of USN escorts in this category, the others being the Patrol Frigates (PF) and Patrol Craft/Patrol Craft Escort (PC/PCE); and the DEs were broken down into 6 types within the class. It is, therefore, difficult to compare them in general with the RN's more numerous escort classes.

There is a further aspect of interest in such a comparison. The USN took one basically excellent escort design, made arrangements to build ships to that design on a very large scale indeed, and made minor alterations only to that design. These ships were built on naval lines, and the scale and quality of equipment were excellent; the comparative difficulties of producing large numbers of naval-designed escorts in wartime in the UK stand out very clearly.

The chart showing the rate of production by launches shows how the programme built rapidly up to a remarkable climax of results in 1943. Ships were being launched several on the same day from the same yard, and the mammoth problems of supply logistics in armament and equipment stagger the imagination.

Yet only in main propulsion units does there seem to have been any compromise with production difficulties. The differences in main propulsion will be outlined in the notes on each type, and it is impressive that in main and close-range armament the designed outfit was nearly always fitted on completion, whereas the new RN escorts were, for some years, 'making do' with old 4″ guns and often half the specified close-range outfit of Oerlikons or Bofors.

The table of completions shows the *very* large numbers ordered (up to 1,015), and the cancellation of 450 of that number, not including the large number of RN cancellations in this class. The 3 original types were completed almost in their entirety, but cancellations in the last 2 classes were very high, and, of those completed, 54 out of 81 of the last class were as high-speed transports.

The list of transfers and conversions is also outstanding. During the war years, apart from the 78 ships transferred to the RN, 12 were transferred to Brazil and France, and 94 were completed or converted as APD (high-speed transports). The rest were completed in their DE configuration.

But after the war a large-scale programme was undertaken. 79 more ships were transferred to other navies, and 81 were converted to other roles. Thus 348 of the 565 ships completed left their original DE role.

At this point it must be mentioned that it has been difficult to arrive at accurate breakdown figures for the chart of completions and conversions. Individual ships often served in more than one role, and the reader's understanding is sought, if he disagrees with any of the figures quoted.

*Burden R. Hastings*, of the 'Evarts' type. A good bow view, showing the anchor stowage in this class; in the long-hull ships, the casting on which it lay was flush with the upper deck. The two radar aerials have a clear field at the masthead, and the camouflage pattern is different on each side. *(US Navy)*

All the DE types follow one excellent, basic design, which shows close similarities to the USN destroyer designs of the same period; the flush-deck hull, with high sheer forward and little flare to the bows, the guntub layout, and the masts are quite distinctive.

In considering the 6 different types, we shall see a gradual progression, in main and close-range armament, with very little change in the anti-submarine armament, the radar or the boats. It is notable that while the RN's Hedgehog was quickly adopted by the USN, and carried in every escort from PCEs upwards, the RN's later development, the Squid, was not so adopted; so that, had the escort building programme of each of the two navies continued as planned, the USN DEs, and those transferred to the RN, would have continued to rely on the Hedgehog, while the RN would have increasingly relied on the Squid, in ships of the 'Loch' and 'Castle' classes. Both weapons were effective, and both would have been vital in combating the new German high-speed U-boats.

As with the RN, the pressures of the war were such that it was difficult to effect major alterations to escorts once they had entered service. So the later types of DE differed from the earlier types in their armament, reflecting the changing emphasis of Pacific war requirements.

The full USN specifications in armament for each of the 6 DE types, including some sub-types, are included, and the photographs illustrate these differences. The USN did not adopt the RN's twin power-mounted Oerlikons, and in DEs the latter were in almost every case on single mountings. The quadruple 1.1″ machine-gun was soon replaced by the much more effective 40mm twin Bofors, and in the later ships single 5″/38 calibre guns were replacing the 3″/50 calibre. It is a significant indicator of the USN's fast rate of progress in close-range armament that soon after the war the main close-range weapons were changed to twin power-mounted 3″ guns, with Bofors and Oerlikons practically eliminated.

One of the first 'Evarts' type DEs, possibly *Evarts* herself. In the early versions some of the equipment was missing—here, there is no twin Bofors or quadruple 1.1″ mounting aft, only one Oerlikon forward of the bridge, and no radar. The welded hull sides show the usual ripples between the frames. *(US Bureau of Ships)*

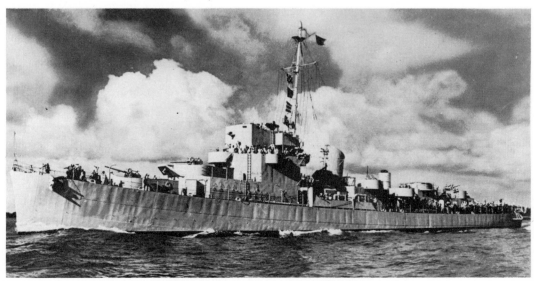

*Wartime DE types*

*1. 'EVARTS' (GMT)*   This was the original, short-hulled type. It did not carry torpedo tubes, though it had one more single Oerlikon than the original 'Buckley' type. It quickly disappeared from the USN active lists when the war ended. The profile is distinctive, in comparison with any of the long-hull types, with a break in the superstructure aft, and a shorter diesel funnel (stack).

*2. 'BUCKLEY' (TE)*   By far the largest number of actual completions. The first of the long-hull types; all subsequent types retained the long hull, intended to allow the installation of main propulsion units giving the high speed of 24 knots.

One set of triple torpedo tubes was carried high on the after superstructure deck, in the original configuration, and the trunked stack for the twinned turbine engine rooms and boiler rooms was distinctive. Quadruple 1.1″ machine-guns were fitted aft in the earlier units, and the photographs show a fascinating progression in armament during the production period of this type.

*3. 'EDSALL' (FMR)*   Difficulties were beginning to be experienced in the production of main propulsion units (the LSTs were taking priority), and the designed horsepower was cut in half, giving a speed of only 21 knots in place of the designed 24. A higher diesel-type stack was fitted, but otherwise this type in general followed the previous one.

*4. 'BOSTWICK' (DET)*   A diesel-electric type, hard to distinguish from the previous one, and again giving a speed of 21 knots due to production difficulties. Note the increase in 40mm armament now specified.

*Evarts,* the first USN DE and lead ship of the short-hull type. Although taken in August 1944, she still has her quadruple 1.1″ gun aft in place of the Bofors. There are two single Oerlikons on the quarterdeck, in a tub, and four of the eight depth charge throwers are angled 135 degrees aft from the ship's course to enlarge the pattern. *(US Navy)*

*5. 'JOHN C. BUTLER' (WGT)*   The first of the 2 final designs, with very large numbers planned for production but comparatively few actually completed. 5"/38 calibre guns were now specified to replace the 3"/50s, with no less than 10 40 mm, plus 6 20 mm. The heavy close-range armament had arrived. The turbo-electric drive of the 'Buckley' type was back in business, and the speed of 24 knots, and the distinctive type of stack returned though reduced in height.

To help combat the fast-growing topweight, a problem which was plaguing the RN also, the bridge also was reduced in height; the torpedo tubes were often omitted in favour of the heavier close-range armament.

*6. 'RUDDEROW' (TEV)*   Very similar to the previous type, and again very large numbers were planned but only few actually completed. The cutback in production of these last two types, in late 1943, illustrates clearly the massive programme which was by then under way, and this is worth comparing with the RN's similar action with the 'Loch' class frigates and 'Castle' class corvettes.

*Postwar conversions*

A total of some 81 DEs were modified after the war, and although this is, strictly speaking, outside the scope of this book, a short description of these conversions is included. They were carried out on existing hulls, whereas the RN moved more quickly into new post-war designs, and so the USN conversions may complete this interesting wartime picture.

*APD (High Speed Transports)*   The conversions consisted of installing 4 LCVP (landing craft, vehicles and personnel), 2 on each side, under heavy luffing booms. These APDs carried 162 troops and were internally laid out with troop

Inboard view of *Engstrom*, of the 'Evarts' type, showing detail aft of the bridge. Note the 3" training loader forward of the funnel. *(US National Archives)*

decks. A lattice mainmast was fitted, for handling twin cargo booms. The 'Buckley' class ships retained their high bridge but were given 1 5″/38 calibre gun forward in some cases. Some of these ships later underwent the FRAM modernisation. Their bridge structures were built up, and forward to no 2 gun position a new covered bridge was fitted, and a new tripod mast, with updated radar aerials, installed. ASW torpedoes were also added. 8 ships were later fitted as transport flagships, with increased quarters for staff. Some APDs were later redesignated as LPR (amphibious transport, small).

*DER (Radar Picket Ship)*   45 DEs were so converted, 7 'Buckley' type, 36 'Edsall' type, and 2 'John C. Butler' type. This was mainly carried out in the period 1950-58. The latter 2 were the only steam-driven DERs. 11 of these ships were on loan to the US Coastguard in 1951-54, and were then designated WDE (coastguard destroyer escort).

The conversion to DER was as follows:
a) A new, aluminium-sided mess compartment on the maindeck level.
b) 2 new and heavy tripod masts to support the new radar and navigation antennae. The CIC was also expanded for this duty.
c) Spray shield fitted to the forward 3″ gun, and in some cases to the after 3″ also. These were apparently the only 3″ spray shields fitted to USN DEs, and make an interesting comparison with those fitted in the RN's 'Captain' class.
d) A traversing Hedgehog fitted in place of the second 3″ forward.
e) Two ASW torpedo tube racks.
f) 6 Oerlikons were retained, but no Bofors or torpedo tubes.

*DEC (Amphibious Control Ships)*   3 'Buckley' type—*Cronin, Raby* and *Frybarger* —were so modified soon after the war, to enable them to control boat waves during assault landings.

*FLOATING POWER STATIONS*   7 ships were converted to supply electric power to shore stations. They carried large cable reels amidships, together with heavy duty contact points. See similar RN conversions in this class.

*EDE (Experimental Destroyer Escort)*   3 ships were fitted with heavy experimental gear at the stern, probably an early form of what is now known as variable depth sonar.

*DE (A/S)*   4 ships—*Lewis, Tweedy, Peterson* and *Vammen*—underwent extensive alterations in 1951-52, to give them specialised A/S capability.

Two traversing Hedgehogs were fitted forward of the bridge, in the no 2 gun position. Enlarged bridges with better A/S control rooms and CICs were added. Close-range armament was reduced. A mainmast and further aerials appeared. *Tweedy* had 2 traversing Hedgehogs fitted on top of a very large new bridge structure, and her fantail depth-charge equipment was removed. ASW torpedo tubes were fitted, though actual positions seem to have varied. Note how this differed from RN post-war conversions, reflecting the diverging views of the 2 naval staffs on the best weapons with which to fight the new fast German U-boats.

## USN DE CLASS PRODUCTION

This chart shows how the types succeeded one another, with the final 2 running in parallel. The cancellation figures show that these 2 would have shown high production figures in 1944, and through into 1945.

| Type/Designation | 1942 | | | | 1943 | | | | 1944 | | | | 1945 | | | | Totals |
|---|---|---|---|---|---|---|---|---|---|---|---|---|---|---|---|---|---|
| | 1 | 2 | 3 | 4 | 1 | 2 | 3 | 4 | 1 | 2 | 3 | 4 | 1 | 2 | 3 | 4 | |
| 'Evarts' (GMT) | 0 | 2 | 10 | 10 | 16 | 24 | 26 | 6 | 4 | 2 | 0 | 0 | 0 | 0 | 0 | 0 | 97 |
| 'Edsall' (FMR) | 0 | 0 | 0 | 8 | 21 | 24 | 17 | 15 | 0 | 0 | 0 | 0 | 0 | 0 | 0 | 0 | 85 |
| 'Buckley' (TE) | 0 | 0 | 1 | 0 | 11 | 32 | 47 | 52 | 7 | 3 | 0 | 0 | 0 | 0 | 0 | 0 | 152 |
| 'Bostwick' (DET) | 0 | 0 | 0 | 0 | 2 | 12 | 21 | 24 | 10 | 4 | 4 | 0 | 0 | 0 | 0 | 0 | 76 |
| 'John C. Butler' (WGT) | 0 | 0 | 0 | 0 | 0 | 0 | 0 | 18 | 32 | 13 | 11 | 0 | 0 | 0 | 0 | 0 | 74 |
| 'Rudderow' (TEV) | 0 | 0 | 0 | 0 | 0 | 0 | 0 | 10 | 43 | 8 | 8 | 2 | 3 | 6 | 0 | 1 | 81 |
| Total Ships Launched Each Quarter | 0 | 2 | 11 | 18 | 50 | 92 | 111 | 125 | 96 | 30 | 23 | 2 | 3 | 6 | 0 | 1 | 565 |

## USN DE CLASS BUILDING STATISTICS

| Class | 'Evarts' | 'Edsall' | 'Buckley' | 'Bostwick' | 'John C. Butler' | 'Rudderow' | Total |
|---|---|---|---|---|---|---|---|
| **TOTAL ORDERED** | 105 | 85 | 152 | 120 | 285 | 268 | 1015 |
| Cancelled before launch | 5 | 0 | 0 | 38 | 211 | 187 | 441 |
| Cancelled after launch | 3 | 0 | 0 | 6 | 0 | 0 | 9 |
| TOTAL COMPLETED | 97 | 85 | 152 | 76 | 74 | 81 | 565 |
| **ALLOCATIONS OF SHIPS** | | | | | | | |
| Completed as USN DE | 65 | 85 | 66 | 64 | 74 | 27 | 381 |
| Completed as USN APD | 0 | 0 | 40 | 0 | 0 | 54 | 94 |
| To Royal Navy | 32 | 0 | 46 | 0 | 0 | 0 | 78 |
| To Brazil and France | 0 | 0 | 0 | 12 | 0 | 0 | 12 |

*NOTE* All armament is as originally specified; many changes took place in individual ships, and in some cases while in service.

**WAR LOSSES (USN & RN)**

| | 'Evarts' | 'Edsall' | 'Buckley' | 'Bostwick' | 'John C. Butler' | 'Rudderow' | Total |
|---|---|---|---|---|---|---|---|
| Sunk | 5 | 3 | 6 | 0 | 3 | 0 | 17 |
| Constructive Total Losses | 0 | 2 | 8 | 0 | 1 | 0 | 11 |
| Totals | 5 | 5 | 14 | 0 | 4 | 0 | 28 |
| To Allied Navies after 1945 | 2 | 2 | 15 | 38 | 2 | 20 | 79 |

## USN DE CLASS SPECIFICATION

| Class | 'Evarts' | 'Edsall' | 'Buckley' | 'Bostwick' | 'John C. Butler' | 'Rudderow' |
|---|---|---|---|---|---|---|
| **Dimensions** | | | | | | |
| length, feet oa | 289½ | 306 | 306 | 306 | 306 | 306 |
| breadth | 35 | 37 | 35 | 35 | 35 | 35 |
| **Displacement, tons** | | | | | | |
| standard | 1,140 | 1,200 | 1,400 | 1,240 | 1,350 | 1,450 |
| full load | 1,360 | 1,490 | 1,720 | 1,520 | 1,660 | 1,780 |
| **Machinery** | | | | | | |
| type | diesel electric | geared diesel | turbo electric | diesel electric | turbo electric | turbo electric |
| makers | General Motors | Fairbanks Morse | General Electric | General Motors | Westinghouse or Gen Electric | General Electric |
| horsepower | BHP6,000 | BHP6,000 | SHP12,000 | BHP6,000 | SHP12,000 | SHP12,000 |
| speed, knots | 21 | 21 | 24 | 21 | 24 | 24 |
| **Armament** | | | | | | |
| main | 3 3"/50 | 3 3"/50 | 3 3"/50 | 3 3"/50 | 2 5"/38 | 2 5"/38 |
| close-range | 4 1.1" or 2 40mm 9 20mm | 2 40mm 8 20mm | 4 1.1" or 2 40mm 8 20mm | 6 40mm 8 20mm | 10 40mm 6 20mm | 10 40mm 6 20mm |
| **A/S Armament** | | | | | | |
| Hedgehog | Yes | Yes | Yes | Yes | Yes | Yes |
| depth charge throwers (K guns) | 8 | 8 | 8 | 8 | 8 | 8 |
| depth charge rails | 2 | 2 | 2 | 2 | 2 | 2 |
| Torpedo Tubes (21") | 0 | 3 | 3 | 3 | 0 | 0 |
| Complement | 198 | 220 | 220 | 220 | 220 | 220 |

## USN DE CLASS—CLASS LIST

| Name | No | Builder | Building Time | Completion Date |
|------|----|---------|---------------|-----------------|

### 1. 'EVARTS' TYPE (GMT)

**Diesel-electric, short hull**

| Name | No | Builder | Building Time | Completion Date |
|------|----|---------|---------------|-----------------|
| *Evarts* ex *BDE 5* | DE 5 | Boston | 5m29d | 15.4.43 |
| *Wyffels* ex *BDE 6* | DE 6 | ,, | 6m4d | 28.4.43 |
| *Griswold* ex *BDE 7* | DE 7 | ,, | 5m0d | 28.4.43 |
| *Steele* ex *BDE 8* | DE 8 | ,, | 5m7d | 4.5.43 |
| *Carlson* ex *BDE 9* | DE 9 | ,, | 5m13d | 10.5.43 |
| *Bebas* ex *BDE 10* | DE 10 | ,, | 5m18d | 15.5.43 |
| *Crouter* ex *BDE 11* | DE 11 | ,, | 5m13d | 25.5.43 |
| *Brennan* ex RN *Bentinck* | DE 13 / BDE 13 | Mare Island | 10m20d | 20.1.43 |
| *Doherty* ex RN *Berry* | DE 14 / BDE 14 | ,, | 11m0d | 6.2.43 |
| *Austin* ex RN *Blackwood* | DE 15 / BDE 15 | ,, | 10m30d | 13.2.43 |
| *Edgar T. Chase* ex RN *Burges* | DE 16 / BDE 16 | ,, | 12m6d | 20.3.42 |
| *Edward C. Daly* ex RN *Byard* | DE 17 / BDE 17 | ,, | 11m29d | 3.4.43 |
| *Gilmore* ex RN *Calder* | DE 18 / BDE 18 | ,, | 12m16d | 17.4.43 |
| *Burden R. Hastings* ex RN *Duckworth* | DE 19 / BDE 19 | ,, | 12m16d | 1.5.43 |
| *Lehardy* ex RN *Duff* | DE 20 / BDE 20 | ,, | 12m30d | 15.5.43 |
| *Harold C. Thomas* ex RN *Essington* | DE 21 / BDE 21 | ,, | 13m0d | 31.5.43 |
| *Wileman* ex RN *Foley* | DE 22 / BDE 22 | Mare Island | 13m11d | 11.6.43 |
| *Charles R. Greer* ex *BDE 23* | DE 23 | ,, | 9m18d | 26.6.43 |
| *Whitman* ex *BDE 24* | DE 24 | ,, | 9m26d | 3.7.43 |
| *Wintle* ex *BDE 25* | DE 25 | ,, | 9m10d | 10.7.43 |
| *Dempsey* ex *BDE 26* | DE 26 | ,, | 9m29d | 24.7.43 |

| | | | | |
|---|---|---|---|---|
| *Duffy* | DE 27 | ,, | 9m7d | 5.8.43 |
| ex *BDE 27* | | | | |
| *Emery* | DE 28 | ,, | 8m15d | 14.8.43 |
| ex *BDE 28* | | | | |
| *Stadtfeld* | DE 29 | ,, | 8m24d | 26.8.43 |
| ex *BDE 29* | | | | |
| *Martin* | DE 30 | ,, | 9m8d | 4.9.43 |
| ex *BDE 30* | | | | |
| *Sederstrom* | DE 31 | ,, | 8m18d | 1.9.43 |
| ex *BDE 31* | | | | |
| *Fleming* | DE 32 | ,, | 8m25d | 18.9.43 |
| ex *BDE 32* | | | | |
| *Tisdale* | DE 33 | ,, | 8m19d | 11.10.43 |
| ex *BDE 33* | | | | |
| *Eisele* | DE 34 | ,, | 8m26d | 18.10.43 |
| ex *BDE 34* | | | | |
| *Fair* | DE 35 | ,, | 7m27d | 23.10.43 |
| ex *BDE 35* | | | | |
| *Manlove* | DE 36 | ,, | 8m12d | 8.11.43 |
| ex *BDE 36* | | | | |
| *Greiner* | DE 37 | Puget | 11m10d | 18.8.43 |
| ex *BDE 37* | | | | |
| *Wyman* | DE 38 | ,, | 11m24d | 1.9.43 |
| ex *BDE 38* | | | | |
| *Lovering* | DE 39 | Puget | 12m12d | 19.9.43 |
| ex *BDE 39* | | | | |
| *Sanders* | DE 40 | ,, | 12m24d | 1.10.43 |
| ex *BDE 40* | | | | |
| *Brackett* | DE 41 | ,, | 9m6d | 18.10.43 |
| ex *BDE 41* | | | | |
| *Reynolds* | DE 42 | ,, | 9m19d | 1.11.43 |
| ex *BDE 42* | | | | |
| *Mitchell* | DE 43 | ,, | 10m5d | 17.11.43 |
| ex *BDE 43* | | | | |
| *Donaldson* | DE 44 | ,, | 10m20d | 1.12.43 |
| ex *BDE 44* | | | | |
| *Andres* | DE 45 | Philadelphia | 13m0d | 15.3.43 |
| ex RN *Capel* | BDE 45 | | | |
| *Decker* | DE 47 | ,, | 13m2d | 3.5.43 |
| ex *BDE 47* | | | | |
| *Dobler* | DE 48 | ,, | 13m16d | 17.5.43 |
| ex *BDE 48* | | | | |
| *Doneff* | DE 49 | ,, | 14m9d | 10.96.43 |
| ex *BDE 49* | | | | |
| *Engstrom* | DE 50 | ,, | 14m20d | 21.6.43 |
| ex *BDE 50* | | | | |
| *Seid* | DE 256 | Boston | 5m1d | 12.6.43 |
| *Smartt* | DE 257 | ,, | 5m8d | 15.6.43 |
| *Walter S. Brown* | DE 258 | ,, | 5m15d | 25.6.43 |
| *William C. Miller* | DE 259 | ,, | 5m23d | 21.7.43 |

| | | | | |
|---|---|---|---|---|
| *Cabana* | DE 260 | ,, | 5m 13d | 7.7.43 |
| *Dionne* | DE 261 | ,, | 5m 20d | 16.7.43 |
| *Canfield* | DE 262 | ,, | 4m 7d | 22.7.43 |
| *Deede* | DE 263 | ,, | 5m 4d | 29.7.43 |
| *Elden* | DE 264 | ,, | 5m 11d | 5.8.43 |
| *Cloues* | DE 265 | ,, | 5m 15d | 10.8.43 |
| *Lake* | DE 301 | Mare Island | 9m 13d | 5.2.44 |
| *Lyman* | DE 302 | ,, | 9m 27d | 19.2.44 |
| *Crowley* | DE 303 | ,, | 11m 1d | 25.3.44 |
| *Rall* | DE 304 | ,, | 11m 15d | 8.4.44 |
| *Halloran* | DE 305 | ,, | 11m 5d | 27.5.44 |
| *Connolly* | DE 306 | ,, | 12m 17d | 8.7.44 |
| *Finnegan* | DE 307 | ,, | 13m 14d | 19.8.44 |
| *O'Toole* | DE 527 | Boston | 3m 27d | 22.1.44 |
| *John J. Powers* | DE 528 | ,, | 5m 5d | 29.2.44 |
| *Mason* | DE 529 | ,, | 5m 6d | 20.3.44 |
| *John M. Birmingham* | DE 530 | ,, | 5m 26d | 8.4.44 |

*William T. Powell*, DE 213—a fine speed shot at 24 knots. The hull gave a greater impression of speed than the RN frigate types; note the smaller breadth on the forecastle, but still the most effective use of space. The H/F D/F mast aft is raked, and has a tripod support. *(US Navy)*

## CANCELLED SHIPS

| | | | Cancelled |
|---|---|---|---|
| *Creamer* | DE 308 | Mare Island | 9.5.44 |
| *Ely* | DE 309 | ,, | 9.5.44 |
| *Delbert W. Halsey* | DE 310 | ,, | 9.5.44 |
| *Keppler* | DE 311 | ,, | 13.3.44 |
| *Lloyd Thomas* | DE 312 | ,, | 13.3.44 |
| *William C. Lawe* | DE 313 | ,, | 13.3.44 |
| *Willard Keith* | DE 314 | ,, | 13.3.44 |
| | DE 315 | ,, | 13.3.44 |

## 2. 'BUCKLEY' TYPE (TE)

### Turbo-electric, long hull

| | | | | |
|---|---|---|---|---|
| *Buckley* | DE 51 | Bethlehem-Hingham | 9m10d | 30.4.43 |
| *Charles Lawrence* | DE 53 | ,, | 10m0d | 31.5.43 |
| *Daniel T. Griffin* | DE 54 | ,, | 9m1d | 31.5.43 |
| *Donnell* | DE 56 | ,, | 6m29d | 26.6.43 |
| *Fogg* | DE 57 | ,, | 7m4d | 7.7.43 |
| *Foss* | DE 59 | ,, | 6m23d | 23.7.43 |
| *Gantner* | DE 60 | ,, | 6m23d | 23.7.43 |
| *George W. Ingram* | DE 62 | ,, | 6m2d | 11.8.43 |
| *Ira Jeffery* | DE 63 | ,, | 5m30d | 15.8.43 |
| *Lee Fox* | DE 65 | ,, | 7m27d | 30.8.43 |
| *Amesbury* | DE 66 | ,, | 5m23d | 31.8.43 |
| *Bates* | DE 68 | ,, | 6m14d | 12.9.43 |
| *Blessman* | DE 69 | ,, | 5m28d | 19.9.43 |
| *Joseph E. Campbell* | DE 70 | ,, | 5m21d | 23.9.43 |
| *Reuben James* | DE 153 | Norfolk | 5m24d | 1.4.43 |
| *Sims* | DE 154 | ,, | 6m13d | 24.4.43 |
| *Hopping* | DE 155 | ,, | 5m8d | 24.5.43 |
| *Reeves* | DE 156 | ,, | 3m30d | 9.6.43 |
| *Fechteler* | DE 157 | ,, | 4m22d | 1.7.43 |
| *Chase* | DE 158 | ,, | 4m2d | 18.7.43 |
| *Laning* | DE 159 | ,, | 3m9d | 1.8.43 |
| *Loy* | DE 160 | ,, | 4m19d | 12.9.43 |
| *Barber* | DE 161 | ,, | 5m14d | 10.10.43 |
| *Lovelace* | DE 198 | ,, | 5m16d | 7.11.43 |
| *Manning* | DE 199 | Charleston | 7m14d | 1.10.43 |
| *Neuendorf* | DE 200 | ,, | 8m0d | 18.10.43 |
| *James E. Craig* | DE 201 | ,, | 6m16d | 1.11.43 |
| *Eichenberger* | DE 202 | ,, | 7m2d | 17.11.43 |
| *Thomason* | DE 203 | ,, | 6m4d | 10.12.43 |
| *Jordan* | DE 204 | ,, | 6m11d | 17.12.43 |
| *Newman* | DE 205 | ,, | 5m17d | 26.11.43 |
| *Liddle* | DE 206 | ,, | 5.28d | 6.12.43 |
| *Kephart* | DE 207 | ,, | 7m26d | 7.1.44 |
| *Kafer* | DE 208 | ,, | 8m7d | 19.1.44 |
| *Lloyd* | DE 209 | Charleston | 6m16d | 11.2.44 |

| | | | | |
|---|---|---|---|---|
| Otter | DE 210 | ,, | 6m26d | 21.2.44 |
| Hubbard | DE 211 | ,, | 6m26d | 6.3.44 |
| Hayter | DE 212 | ,, | 7m5d | 16.3.44 |
| William T. Powell | DE 213 | ,, | 7m2d | 28.3.44 |
| Scott | DE 214 | Philadelphia | 6m20d | 20.7.43 |
| Burke | DE 215 | ,, | 7m20d | 20.8.43 |
| Enright | DE 216 | ,, | 7m21d | 21.9.43 |
| Coolbaugh | DE 216 | ,, | 7m21d | 15.10.43 |
| Darby | DE 218 | ,, | 8m21d | 15.1.43 |
| J. Douglas Blackwood | DE 219 | ,, | 9m21d | 15.1.44 |
| Francis M. Robinson | DE 220 | ,, | 10m21d | 15.1.44 |
| Solar | DE 221 | ,, | 11m21d | 15.2.44 |
| Fowler | DE 222 | ,, | 12m21d | 15.3.44 |
| Spangenburg | DE 223 | ,, | 13m21d | 15.4.44 |
| Ahrens | DE 575 | Bethlehem-Hingham | 3m5d | 12.2.44 |
| Barr | DE 576 | ,, | 3m9d | 15.2.44 |
| Alexander J. Luke | DE 577 | ,, | 3m13d | 19.2.44 |
| Robert I. Paine | DE 578 | ,, | 3m23d | 28.2.44 |
| Foreman | DE 633 | Bethlehem Steel | 7m15d | 22.10.43 |
| Whitehurst | DE 634 | ,, | 7m29d | 19.11.43 |
| England | DE 635 | ,, | 8m5d | 10.12.43 |
| Witter | DE 636 | ,, | 8m0d | 29.12.43 |
| Bowers | DE 637 | ,, | 7m30d | 27.1.44 |
| Willmarth | DE 638 | ,, | 8m18d | 13.3.44 |
| Gendreau | DE 639 | ,, | 7m18d | 7.3.44 |
| Fieberling | DE 640 | ,, | 7m2d | 11.4.44 |
| William C. Cole | DE 641 | ,, | 8m0d | 12.5.44 |
| Paul G. Baker | DE 642 | ,, | 7m29d | 25.5.44 |
| Damon M. Cummings | DE 643 | ,, | 8m12d | 29.6.44 |
| Vammen | DE 644 | ,, | 11m27d | 27.7.44 |
| Jenks | DE 665 | Dravo, Pittsburgh | 8m7d | 19.1.44 |
| Durik | DE 666 | ,, | 14m2d | 24.3.44 |
| Wiseman | DE 667 | ,, | 8m9d | 4.4.44 |

*Osmus*, DE 701, of the 'Buckley' type, showing dazzle camouflage. (*US National Archives*)

| Name | No | Builder | Building Time | Completion Date |
|------|-----|---------|---------------|-----------------|
| *Weber* | DE 675 | Bethlehem Steel | 4m6d | 30.6.43 |
| *Schmitt* | DE 676 | ,, | 4m30d | 24.7.43 |
| *Frament* | DE 677 | ,, | 3m16d | 15.8.43 |
| *Harmon* | DE 678 | ,, | 3m1d | 31.8.43 |
| *Greenwood* | DE 679 | ,, | 2m26d | 25.9.43 |
| *Loeser* | DE 680 | ,, | 2m14d | 10.10.43 |
| *Gillette* | DE 681 | ,, | 2m4d | 22.10.43 |
| *Underhill* | DE 682 | ,, | 1m29d | 15.11.43 |
| *Henry R. Kenyon* | DE 683 | ,, | 2m1d | 30.11.43 |
| *Bull* | DE 693 | Defoe | 7m28d | 12.8.43 |
| *Bunch* | DE 694 | ,, | 5m30d | 24.8.43 |
| *Rich* | DE 695 | ,, | 6m5d | 1.10.43 |
| *Spangler* | DE 696 | ,, | 6m2d | 31.10.43 |
| *George* | DE 697 | ,, | 5m29d | 20.8.43 |
| *Raby* | DE 698 | ,, | 5m30d | 7.12.43 |
| *Marsh* | DE 699 | ,, | 6m19d | 12.1.44 |
| *Currier* | DE 700 | ,, | 6m14d | 1.2.44 |
| *Osmus* | DE 701 | ,, | 6m6d | 23.2.44 |
| *Earl V. Johnson* | DE 702 | ,, | 6m5d | 18.3.44 |
| *Holton* | DE 703 | ,, | 7m3d | 1.5.44 |
| *Cronin* | DE 704 | ,, | 6m17d | 15.5.44 |
| *Frybarger* | DE 705 | ,, | 6m9d | 18.5.44 |
| *Tatum* | DE 789 | Consolidated, Orange | 6m30d | 22.11.43 |
| *Borum* | DE 790 | ,, | 7m2d | 30.11.43 |
| *Maloy* | DE 791 | ,, | 7m5d | 13.12.43 |
| *Haines* | DE 792 | ,, | 7m10d | 27.12.43 |
| *Runels* | DE 793 | ,, | 6m26d | 3.1.44 |
| *Hollis* | DE 794 | ,, | 6m17d | 24.1.44 |
| *Gunason* | DE 795 | ,, | 5m23d | 1.2.44 |
| *Major* | DE 796 | ,, | 5m27d | 12.2.44 |
| *Weeden* | DE 797 | ,, | 6m1d | 19.2.44 |
| *Varian* | DE 798 | ,, | 6m4d | 29.2.44 |
| *Scroggins* | DE 799 | ,, | 6m25d | 30.3.44 |
| *Jack W. Wilke* | DE 800 | ,, | 4m20d | 7.3.44 |

## 3. 'EDSALL' TYPE (FMR)

### Geared diesels, long hull

| Name | No | Builder | Building Time | Completion Date |
|------|-----|---------|---------------|-----------------|
| *Eadsall* | DE 129 | Consolidated, Orange | 9m8d | 10.4.43 |
| *Jacob Jones* | DE 130 | ,, | 10m3d | 29.4.43 |
| *Hammann* | DE 131 | ,, | 10m7d | 17.5.43 |
| *Robert E. Peary* | DE 132 | ,, | 11m3d | 31.5.43 |
| *Pillsbury* | DE 133 | ,, | 10m20d | 7.6.43 |
| *Pope* | DE 134 | ,, | 11m11d | 26.6.43 |
| *Flaherty* | DE 135 | ,, | 6m18d | 26.6.43 |
| *Frederick C. Davis* | DE 136 | ,, | 8m3d | 14.7.43 |
| *Herbert C. Jones* | DE 137 | ,, | 7m21d | 21.7.43 |

| | | | | |
|---|---|---|---|---|
| Douglas L. Howard | DE 138 | ,, | 6m21d | 29.7.43 |
| Farquhar | DE 139 | ,, | 7m22d | 6.8.43 |
| J.R.Y. Blakely | DE 140 | ,, | 8m0d | 10.8.43 |
| Hill | DE 141 | ,, | 7m26d | 16.8.43 |
| Fessenden | DE 142 | ,, | 7m21d | 25.8.43 |
| Fiske | DE 143 | ,, | 7m21d | 25.8.43 |
| Frost | DE 144 | ,, | 7m0d | 30.8.43 |
| Huse | DE 145 | ,, | 7m19d | 30.8.43 |
| Inch | DE 146 | ,, | 7m20d | 8.9.43 |
| Blair | DE 147 | ,, | 7m25d | 13.9.43 |
| Brough | DE 148 | ,, | 7m27d | 18.9.43 |
| Chatelain | DE 149 | ,, | 7m28d | 22.9.43 |
| Neunzer | DE 150 | ,, | 7m29d | 27.9.43 |
| Poole | DE 151 | ,, | 7m13d | 27.9.43 |
| Peterson | DE 152 | ,, | 7m29d | 29.9.43 |
| Stewart | DE 238 | Brown | 10m16d | 31.5.43 |
| Sturtevant | DE 239 | ,, | 11m1d | 31.5.43 |
| Moore | DE 240 | ,, | 11m11d | 1.7.43 |
| Keith | DE 241 | ,, | 11m18d | 19.7.43 |
| Tomich | DE 242 | ,, | 10m11d | 26.7.43 |
| J. Richard Ward | DE 243 | ,, | 9m5d | 5.7.43 |
| Otterstetter | DE 244 | ,, | 8m27d | 6.8.43 |
| Sloat | DE 245 | ,, | 8m25d | 16.8.43 |
| Snowden | DE 246 | ,, | 8m16d | 25.8.43 |
| Stanton | DE 247 | ,, | 8m0d | 7.8.43 |
| Swasey | DE 248 | Brown | 8m1d | 31.8.43 |
| Marchand | DE 249 | ,, | 8m9d | 8.9.43 |
| Hurst | DE 250 | ,, | 7m3d | 30.8.43 |
| Camp | DE 251 | ,, | 7m20d | 16.9.43 |
| Howard D. Crow | DE 252 | ,, | 7m18d | 27.9.43 |
| Pettit | DE 253 | ,, | 7m14d | 23.9.43 |
| Ricketts | DE 254 | ,, | 6m20d | 5.10.43 |
| Sellstrom | DE 255 | ,, | 6m27d | 16.10.43 |
| Harveson | DE 316 | Consolidated, Orange | 7m3d | 12.10.43 |
| Joyce | DE 317 | ,, | 6m23d | 30.9.43 |
| Kirkpatrick | DE 318 | ,, | 7m8d | 23.10.43 |
| Leopold | DE 319 | ,, | 6m25d | 18.10.43 |
| Menges | DE 320 | ,, | 7m5d | 26.10.43 |
| Mosley | DE 321 | ,, | 6m23d | 30.10.43 |
| Newell | DE 322 | ,, | 6m24d | 30.10.43 |
| Pride | DE 323 | ,, | 7m1d | 13.11.43 |
| Falgout | DE 324 | ,, | 5m20d | 15.11.43 |
| Lowe | DE 325 | ,, | 5m29d | 22.11.43 |
| Thomas J. Gray | DE 326 | ,, | 5m11d | 27.11.43 |
| Brister | DE 327 | ,, | 5m16d | 30.11.43 |
| Finch | DE 328 | ,, | 5m14d | 13.12.43 |
| Kretschmer | DE 329 | ,, | 5m15d | 13.12.43 |
| O'Reilly | DE 330 | ,, | 4m30d | 28.12.43 |
| Koiner | DE 331 | ,, | 5m1d | 27.12.43 |
| Price | DE 332 | ,, | 4m19d | 12.1.44 |

| | | | | |
|---|---|---|---|---|
| *Strickland* | DE 333 | ,, | 4m18d | 10.1.44 |
| *Forster* | DE 334 | ,, | 4m25d | 23.1.44 |
| *Daniel* | DE 335 | ,, | 4m23d | 24.1.44 |
| *Roy O. Hale* | DE 336 | ,, | 4m20d | 3.2.44 |
| *Dale W. Peterson* | DE 337 | ,, | 3m23d | 17.2.44 |
| *Martin H. Ray* | DE 338 | ,, | 4m1d | 28.2.44 |
| *Ramsden* | DE 382 | Brown | 6m24d | 19.10.43 |
| *Mills* | DE 383 | ,, | 6m17d | 12.10.43 |
| *Rhodes* | DE 384 | ,, | 6m5d | 25.10.43 |
| *Richey* | DE 385 | ,, | 6m10d | 30.10.43 |
| *Savage* | DE 386 | ,, | 5m29d | 29.10.43 |
| *Vance* | DE 387 | ,, | 6m0d | 1.11.43 |
| *Lansing* | DE 388 | ,, | 5m26d | 10.11.43 |
| *Durant* | DE 389 | ,, | 6m1d | 16.11.43 |
| *Calcaterra* | DE 390 | ,, | 5m20d | 17.11.43 |
| *Chambers* | DE 391 | ,, | 5m25d | 22.11.43 |
| *Merrill* | DE 392 | ,, | 4m28d | 27.11.43 |
| *Haverfield* | DE 393 | ,, | 4m30d | 29.11.43 |
| *Swenning* | DE 394 | ,, | 4m15d | 1.12.43 |
| *Willis* | DE 395 | ,, | 4m24d | 10.12.43 |
| *Janssen* | DE 396 | ,, | 4m14d | 18.12.43 |
| *Wilhoite* | DE 397 | ,, | 4m12d | 16.12.43 |
| *Cockrill* | DE 398 | ,, | 3m25d | 24.12.43 |
| *Stockdale* | DE 399 | ,, | 3m31d | 31.12.43 |
| *Hissem* | DE 400 | ,, | 3m7d | 13.1.44 |
| *Holder* | DE 401 | ,, | 3m12d | 18.1.44 |

The famous DE *England*, which sank 6 Japanese submarines in just a few days in the Pacific. Note the large rangefinder on the bridge. *(US National Archives)*

## 4. 'BOSTWICK' TYPE (DET)

**Diesel-electric, long hull**

| | | | | |
|---|---|---|---|---|
| Cannon | DE 99 | Dravo, Wilmington | 10m11d | 26.9.43 |
| Christopher | DE 100 | ,, | 10m16d | 23.9.43 |
| Alger | DE 101 | ,, | 10m10d | 12.11.43 |
| Thomas | DE 102 | Norfolk | 10m5d | 21.11.43 |
| Bostwick | DE 103 | ,, | 11m5d | 1.12.43 |
| Breeman | DE 104 | ,, | 8m23d | 12.12.43 |
| Burrows | DE 105 | ,, | 8m26d | 19.12.43 |
| Corbesier | DE 106 | ,, | 9m6d | 2.1.44 |
| Cronin | DE 107 | ,, | 8m11d | 23.1.44 |
| Crosley | DE 108 | ,, | 7m18d | 11.2.44 |
| | DE 109 | ,, | 5m23d | 29.2.44 |
| | DE 110 | ,, | 5m23d | 18.3.44 |
| | DE 111 | ,, | 5m17d | 9.4.44 |
| Carter | DE 112 | ,, | 5m13d | 2.5.44 |
| Clarence Evens | DE 113 | ,, | 6m1d | 25.6.44 |
| Levy | DE 162 | Federal, Newark | 6m25d | 13.5.43 |
| McConnell | DE 163 | ,, | 7m9d | 28.5.43 |
| Osterhaus | DE 164 | ,, | 7m0d | 12.6.43 |
| Parks | DE 165 | ,, | 7m11d | 22.6.43 |
| Baron | DE 166 | ,, | 7m5d | 5.7.43 |
| Acree | DE 167 | ,, | 7m19d | 19.7.43 |
| Amick. | DE 168 | ,, | 7m26d | 26.7.43 |
| Atherton | DE 169 | Norfolk | 7m15d | 29.8.43 |
| Booth | DE 170 | ,, | 7m20d | 19.9.43 |
| Carroll | DE 171 | ,, | 8m25d | 24.10.43 |
| Cooner | DE 172 | Federal, Newark | 5m29d | 21.8.43 |
| Eldridge | DE 173 | ,, | 6m1d | 27.8.43 |
| Marts | DE 174 | ,, | 4m13d | 3.9.43 |
| Penniwill | DE 175 | ,, | 4m25d | 15.9.43 |
| Micka | DE 176 | ,, | 4m10d | 23.9.43 |
| Reybold | DE 177 | ,, | 4m16d | 29.9.43 |
| Herzog | DE 178 | ,, | 4m20d | 6.10.43 |
| McAnn | DE 179 | ,, | 4m25d | 11.10.43 |
| Trumpeter | De 180 | ,, | 4m8d | 16.10.43 |
| Straub | DE 181 | Federal, Newark | 4m17d | 25.10.43 |
| Gustafson | DE 182 | ,, | 3m27d | 1.11.43 |
| Samuel S. Miles | DE 183 | ,, | 3m30d | 4.11.43 |
| Wesson | DE 184 | ,, | 3m13d | 11.11.43 |
| Riddle | DE 185 | ,, | 3m19d | 17.11.43 |
| Swearer | DE 186 | ,, | 3m12d | 24.11.43 |
| Stern | DE 187 | ,, | 3m20d | 1.12.43 |
| O'Neill | DE 188 | ,, | 3m11d | 6.12.43 |
| Bronstein | DE 189 | ,, | 3m16d | 13.12.43 |
| Baker | DE 190 | ,, | 3m15d | 23.12.43 |
| Coffman | DE 191 | ,, | 3m19d | 27.12.43 |
| Eisner | DE 192 | ,, | 3m8d | 1.1.44 |

| Name | No | Builder | Building Time | Completion Date |
|------|-----|---------|---------------|-----------------|
| Garfield Thomas | DE 193 | ,, | 4m0d | 29.1.44 |
| Wingfield | DE 144 | ,, | 3m21d | 28.1.44 |
| Thornhill | DE 195 | ,, | 3m25d | 1.2.44 |
| Rhinehart | DE 196 | ,, | 4m0d | 12.2.44 |
| Roche | DE 197 | ,, | 4m9d | 21.2.44 |
| Bangust | DE 739 | Western Pipe & Steel | 8m15d | 30.10.43 |
| Waterman | DE 740 | ,, | 9m4d | 30.11.43 |
| Weaver | DE 741 | ,, | 9m18d | 31.12.43 |
| Nilbert | DE 742 | ,, | 10m12d | 4.2.44 |
| Lamons | DE 743 | ,, | 10m20d | 29.2.44 |
| Kyne | DE 744 | ,, | 11m24d | 4.9.43 |
| Snyder | DE 745 | ,, | 12m7d | 5.5.44 |
| Hemminger | DE 746 | ,, | 12m22d | 30.5.44 |
| Bright | DE 747 | ,, | 12m21d | 30.6.44 |
| Tills | DE 748 | ,, | 13m15d | 5.8.44 |
| Roberts | DE 749 | ,, | 13m26d | 2.9.44 |
| McClelland | DE 750 | ,, | 13m29d | 19.9.44 |
| Cates | DE 763 | Tampa | 8m16d | 15.12.43 |
| Gandy | DE 764 | ,, | 10m8d | 7.2.44 |
| Earl K. Olsen | DE 765 | ,, | 13m1d | 10.4.44 |
| Slater | DE 766 | ,, | 13m23d | 1.5.44 |
| Oswald | DE 767 | ,, | 13m13d | 12.6.44 |
| Ebert | DE 768 | ,, | 14m13d | 12.7.44 |
| Neal A. Scott | DE 769 | ,, | 13m0d | 31.7.44 |
| Muir | DE 770 | ,, | 13m30d | 30.8.44 |
| Sutton | DE 771 | ,, | 15m30d | 22.12.44 |

Two destroyer escorts laying a smokescreen near the escort carrier *Gambier Bay*, during the battle off Samar, 25th October 1944. (*US National Archives*)

## CANCELLED SHIPS

| Name | Pendant No. | Builder | Cancelled |
|---|---|---|---|
| | DE 114-128 | Dravo, Wilmington | 10.2.43 |
| *Gaynier* | DE 751 | Western Pipe & Steel | 1.9.44 |
| *Curtis W. Howard* | DE 752 | ,, | 1.9.44 |
| *John J. Vanburen* | DE 753 | ,, | 1.9.44 |
| | DE 754 | ,, | 2.10.43 |
| | DE 755 | ,, | 2.10.43 |
| | DE 756-762 | ,, | 2.10.43 |
| *Milton Lewis* | DE 772 | Tampa | 1.9.44 |
| *George M. Campbell* | DE 773 | ,, | 1.9.44 |
| *Russell M. Cox* | DE 774 | ,, | 1.9.44 |
| | DE 775-788 | ,, | 2.10.43 |

*Eldridge* of the 'Bostwick' type doing her full speed. These ships retained the long hull form of the 'Buckley' type, but are distinguished by their funnel form, taller than that of the 'Evarts' type. *(US Navy)*

| Transferred to Brazil | | | Transferred to France | | |
|---|---|---|---|---|---|
| *Baependi* | ex | *Cannon* | *Arago* | ex | *DE 111* |
| *Bauru* | ex | *Reybold* | *Hova* | ex | *DE 110* |
| *Benevente* | ex | *Christopher* | *Marocain* | ex | *DE 109* |
| *Bertioga* | ex | *Pennewill* | *Oise* | ex | *Cronin* |
| *Bocaina* | ex | *Marts* | *Tunisien* | ex | *Crosley* |
| *Bracui* | ex | *McAnn* | *Yser* | ex | *Corbesier* |

## 5. 'RUDDEROW' TYPE (TEV)

### Turbo-electric, long hull, 5″ guns

| | | | | |
|---|---|---|---|---|
| *Rudderow* | DE 224 | Philadelphia | 10m0d | 15.5.44 |
| *Day* | DE 225 | ,, | 10m26d | 10.6.44 |
| *Chafflee* | DE 230 | Charleston | 8m14d | 7.5.44 |
| *Hodges* | DE 231 | ,, | 8m17d | 21.5.44 |
| *Riley* | DE 579 | Bethlehem-Hingham | 4m24d | 13.3.44 |
| *Leslie L.B. Knox* | DE 580 | ,, | 4m16d | 22.3.44 |
| *McNulty* | DE 581 | ,, | 4m13d | 31.3.44 |
| *Metivier* | DE 582 | ,, | 4m13d | 7.4.44 |
| *George A. Johnson* | DE 583 | ,, | 4m21d | 15.4.44 |
| *Charles J. Kimmel* | DE 584 | ,, | 4m19d | 20.4.44 |
| *Daniel A. Joy* | DE 585 | ,, | 4m27d | 28.4.44 |
| *Lough* | DE 586 | ,, | 4m25d | 2.5.44 |
| *Thomas F. Nickel* | DE 587 | ,, | 5m25d | 9.6.44 |
| *Peiffer* | DE 588 | ,, | 5m25d | 15.6.44 |
| *Tinsman* | DE 589 | ,, | 6m5d | 26.6.64 |
| *Delong* | DE 684 | Bethlehem, Quincy | 2m12d | 31.12.43 |
| *Coates* | DE 685 | ,, | 2m16d | 24.1.44 |
| *Eugene M. Elmore* | DE 686 | ,, | 2m7d | 4.3.44 |
| *Holt* | DE 706 | Defoe | 6m11d | 9.6.44 |
| *Jobb* | DE 707 | ,, | 6m15d | 4.7.44 |
| *Parle* | DE 708 | ,, | 7m7d | 29.7.44 |
| *Bray* | DE 709 | ,, | 8m1d | 4.9.44 |

## CANCELLED SHIPS

| Name | Pendant No. | Builder | Cancelled |
|---|---|---|---|
| *Vogelgesang* | DE 284 | Charleston | 10.6.44 |
| *Weeks* | DE 285 | ,, | 10.6.64 |
| *Sutton* | DE 286 | Bethlehem-Hingham | 12.3.44 |
| *William M. Woods* | DE 287 | ,, | 12.3.44 |
| *William R. Rush* | DE 288 | ,, | 12.3.44 |
| | DE 289 | ,, | 12.3.44 |
| *Williams* | DE 290 | ,, | 12.3.44 |
| | DE 291-300 | ,, | 12.3.44 |

| Name | Number | Builder | Completed |
|------|--------|---------|-----------|
| | DE 607-616 | Bethlehem-Hingham | 10.6.44 |
| | DE 617-632 | ,, | 12.8.44 |
| | DE 645-646 | ,, | 12.3.44 |
| | DE 647-664 | ,, | 2.10.43 |
| | DE 723-724 | Bravo, Pittsburgh | 12.3.44 |
| | DE 647-664 | ,, | 2.10.43 |
| | DE 723-724 | Dravo, Pittsburgh | 12.3.44 |
| | DE 725-738 | ,, | 2.10.43 |
| | DE 905-959 | Bethlehem-Hingham | 15.9.43 |
| | DE 960-995 | Charleston | 15.9.43 |
| | DE 996-1005 | Defoe | 15.9.43 |

Launch sideways of US DE *Swasey* at the Brown Shipbuilding Yard at Houston, Texas, March 18, 1943. *(US National Archives)*

## 6. 'JOHN C. BUTLER' TYPE (WGT)

### Geared turbines, long hull, 5″ guns

| | | | | |
|---|---|---|---|---|
| *John C. Butler* | DE 339 | Consolidated, Orange | 5m26d | 31.3.44 |
| *O'Flaherty* | DE 340 | ,, | 6m5d | 8.4.44 |
| *Raymond* | DE 341 | ,, | 5m12d | 15.4.44 |
| *Richard W. Suesens* | DE 342 | ,, | 5m20d | 26.4.44 |
| *Abercrombie* | DE 343 | ,, | 5m22d | 1.5.44 |
| *Oberrender* | DE 344 | ,, | 5m31d | 11.5.44 |
| *Robert Brazier* | DE 345 | ,, | 6m1d | 8.5.44 |
| *Edwin A. Howard* | DE 346 | ,, | 6m9d | 26.5.44 |
| *Jesse Rutherford* | DE 347 | ,, | 6m8d | 31.5.44 |
| *Key* | DE 348 | ,, | 5m22d | 5.6.44 |
| *Gentry* | DE 349 | ,, | 6m1d | 14.6.44 |
| *Traw* | DE 350 | ,, | 6m1d | 30.6.44 |
| *Maurice J. Manuel* | DE 351 | ,, | 6m9d | 30.6.44 |
| *Naifeh* | DE 352 | ,, | 6m0d | 4.7.44 |
| *Doyle C. Barnes* | DE 353 | ,, | 6m2d | 13.7.44 |
| *Kenneth M. Willett* | DE 354 | ,, | 6m9d | 19.7.44 |
| *Jaccard* | DE 355 | ,, | 6m2d | 26.7.44 |
| *Lloyd E. Acree* | DE 356 | ,, | 6m7d | 1.8.44 |
| *George E. Davis* | DE 357 | ,, | 5m26d | 11.8.44 |
| *Mack* | DE 358 | ,, | 5m30d | 16.8.44 |
| *Woodson* | DE 359 | ,, | 5m17d | 24.8.44 |
| *Johnnie Hutchins* | DE 360 | ,, | 5m22d | 28.8.44 |
| *Walton* | DE 361 | ,, | 5m14d | 4.9.44 |
| *Rolf* | DE 362 | ,, | 5m18d | 7.9.44 |
| *Pratt* | DE 363 | ,, | 5m4d | 18.9.44 |
| *Rombach* | DE 364 | ,, | 5m9d | 20.9.44 |
| *McGinty* | DE 365 | ,, | 4m22d | 25.9.44 |
| *Alvin C. Cockrell* | DE 366 | ,, | 5m8d | 7.10.44 |
| *French* | DE 367 | ,, | 5m10d | 9.10.44 |
| *Cecil J. Doyle* | DE 368 | ,, | 5m4d | 16.10.44 |
| *Thaddeus Parker* | DE 369 | ,, | 5m2d | 25.10.44 |
| *John L. Williamson* | DE 370 | ,, | 5m9d | 31.10.44 |
| *Presley* | DE 371 | ,, | 5m0d | 7.11.44 |
| *Williams* | DE 372 | ,, | 5m5d | 11.11.44 |
| *Richard S. Bull* | DE 402 | Brown | 6m8d | 26.2.44 |
| *Richard M. Rowell* | DE 403 | ,, | 6m22d | 9.3.44 |
| *Eversole* | DE 404 | ,, | 6m5d | 21.3.44 |
| *Dennis* | DE 405 | ,, | 6m4d | 20.3.44 |
| *Edmonds* | DE 406 | ,, | 5m4d | 3.4.44 |
| *Shelton* | DE 407 | ,, | 5m5d | 11.4.44 |
| *Strauss* | DE 408 | ,, | 4m18d | 6.4.44 |
| *Laprade* | DE 409 | ,, | 5m2d | 20.4.44 |
| *Jack Miller* | DE 410 | ,, | 4m14d | 13.4.44 |
| *Stafford* | DE 411 | ,, | 4m20d | 19.4.44 |
| *Walter C. Wann* | DE 412 | ,, | 4m27d | 2.5.44 |
| *Samuel B. Roberts* | DE 413 | ,, | 4m23d | 28.4.44 |
| *Leray Wilson* | DE 414 | ,, | 4m27d | 10.5.44 |

| | | | | |
|---|---|---|---|---|
| *Lawrence C. Taylor* | DE 415 | ,, | 4m24d | 13.5.44 |
| *Melvin R. Nawman* | DE 416 | ,, | 4m19d | 16.5.44 |
| *Oliver Mitchell* | DE 417 | ,, | 5m17d | 14.6.44 |
| *Tabberer* | DE 418 | ,, | 5m25d | 23.5.44 |
| *Robert F. Keller* | DE 419 | ,, | 6m17d | 17.6.44 |
| *Leland E. Thomas* | DE 420 | ,, | 6m0d | 19.6.44 |
| *Chester T. O'Brien* | DE 421 | ,, | 5m24d | 13.7.44 |
| *Douglas A. Monro* | DE 422 | ,, | 5m12d | 11.7.44 |
| *Dufilho* | DE 423 | ,, | 5m22d | 21.7.44 |
| *Haas* | DE 424 | ,, | 5m7d | 2.8.44 |
| *Corbesier* | DE 438 | Federal, Newark | 4m26d | 13.3.44 |
| *Conklin* | DE 439 | ,, | 5m14d | 21.4.44 |
| *McCoy Reynolds* | DE 440 | ,, | 5m14d | 2.5.44 |
| *William Sieverling* | DE 441 | ,, | 5m30d | 1.6.44 |
| *Ulvert M. Moore* | DE 442 | ,, | 7m16d | 18.7.44 |
| *Kendall C. Campbell* | DE 443 | ,, | 7m15d | 31.7.44 |
| *Goss* | DE 444 | ,, | 8m10d | 26.8.44 |
| *Grady* | DE 445 | ,, | 8m9d | 11.9.44 |
| *Charles E. Brannon* | DE 446 | ,, | 9m18d | 1.11.44 |
| *Albert T. Harris* | DE 447 | ,, | 10m17d | 29.11.44 |
| *Cross* | DE 448 | ,, | 9m20d | 8.11.44 |
| *Hanna* | DE 449 | ,, | 10m6d | 27.1.45 |
| *Joseph E. Connolly* | DE 450 | ,, | 10m24d | 28.2.45 |
| *Gilligan* | DE 508 | Federal, Newark | 5m24d | 12.5.44 |
| *Formoe* | DE 509 | ,, | 9m8d | 5.10.44 |
| *Heyliger* | DE 510 | ,, | 10m27d | 24.3.45 |
| *Edward H. Allen* | DE 531 | Boston | 3m17d | 10.12.43 |
| *Tweedy* | DE 532 | ,, | 5m12d | 12.2.44 |
| *Howard F. Clark* | DE 533 | ,, | 5m18d | 25.5.44 |
| *Silverstein* | DE 534 | ,, | 9m6d | 14.7.44 |

*Harmon*, DE 678, of the 'Buckley' type, but with 5″ guns in place of 3″, and 8 Bofors aft in three mounts. *(US National Archives)*

| Lewis | DE 535 | ,, | 10m1d | 5.9.44 |
| Bivin | DE 536 | ,, | 11m27d | 31.10.44 |
| Rizzi | DE 537 | ,, | 19m23d | 26.6.45 |
| Osberg | DE 538 | ,, | 25m6d | 17.2.45 |
| Wagner | DE 539 | ,, | 24m17d | 31.12.55 |
| Vandivier | DE 540 | ,, | 23m0d | 11.2.55 |

## CANCELLED SHIPS

| Name | Number | Builder | Cancelled |
| --- | --- | --- | --- |
| William C. Lawe | DE 373 | Consolidated, Orange | 6.6.44 |
| Lloyd Thomas | DE 374 | ,, | 6.6.44 |
| Keppler | DE 375 | ,, | 6.6.44 |
| Kleinsmith | DE 376 | ,, | 6.6.44 |
| Henry W. Tucker | DE 377 | ,, | 6.6.44 |
| Weiss | DE 378 | ,, | 6.6.44 |
| Francovich | DE 379 | ,, | 6.6.44 |
| | DE 380-381 | ,, | 6.6.44 |
| | DE 425-437 | Boston | 13.3.44 |
| Woodrow H. Thompson | DE 451 | Federal, Newark | 6.6.44 |
| Steinaker | DE 452 | ,, | 6.6.44 |
| | DE 453-456 | ,, | 6.6.44 |
| | DE 457-477 | ,, | 12.3.44 |
| | DE 478-507 | ,, | 2.10.43 |
| | DE 511 | ,, | 6.6.44 |
| | DE 512-515 | ,, | 12.3.44 |
| Sheehan | DE 541 | Boston | 7.1.44 |
| Oswald A. Powers | DE 542 | ,, | 7.1.44 |
| Groves | DE 543 | ,, | 5.9.44 |
| Alfred Wolf | DE 544 | ,, | 5.9.44 |
| Harold J. Ellison | DE 545 | ,, | 10.6.44 |
| Myles C. Fox | DE 546 | ,, | 10.6.44 |
| Charles R. Ware | DE 547 | ,, | 10.6.44 |
| Carpellotti | DE 548 | ,, | 10.6.44 |
| Eugene A. Greene | DE 549 | ,, | 10.6.44 |
| Gyatt | DE 550 | ,, | 10.6.44 |
| Benner | DE 551 | ,, | 10.6.44 |
| Kenneth D. Bailey | DE 552 | ,, | 10.6.44 |
| Dennis J. Buckley | DE 553 | ,, | 10.6.44 |
| Everett F. Larson | DE 554 | ,, | 10.6.44 |
| | DE 555-562 | ,, | 10.6.44 |
| | DE 801-832 | ,, | 15.9.43 |
| | DE 833-840 | Mare Island | 15.9.43 |
| | DE 841-872 | Brown | 15.9.43 |
| | DE 873-886 | Dravo, Wilmington | 15.9.43 |
| | DE 887-898 | Western Pipe & Steel | 15.9.43 |
| | DE 899-904 | Federal, Newark | 15.9.43 |

## 7. DEs Converted to APDs (Fast Destroyer Transports)

| Name | APD No | Commissioning/ Launching Dates |
|---|---|---|
| Charles Lawrence ex DE 53 | APD 37 | C31.5.43 |
| Daniel T. Griffin ex DE 54 | APD 38 | C9.6.43 |
| Barr ex DE 576 | APD 39 | C15.2.44 |
| Bowers ex DE 637 | APD 40 | C22.1.44 |
| Gantner ex DE 60 | APD 42 | C29.7.43 |
| George W. Ingram ex DE 62 | APD 43 | C11.8.43 |
| Ira Jeffery ex DE 63 | APD 44 | C15.8.43 |
| Lee Fox ex DE 65 | APD 45 | C30.8.43 |
| Amesbury ex DE 66 | APD 46 | C31.8.43 |
| Bates ex DE 68 | APD 47 | C12.9.43 |
| Blessman ex DE 69 | APD 48 | C19.9.43 |
| Joseph E. Campbell ex DE 70 | APD 49 | C23.9.43 |
| Sims ex DE 154 | APD 50 | C24.4.43 |
| Hopping ex DE 155 | APD 51 | C21.5.43 |
| Reeves ex DE 156 | APD 52 | C9.6.43 |
| Joseph C. Hubbard DE 211 | APD 53 | C6.3.44 |
| Chase ex DE 158 | APD 54 | C18.7.43 |
| Laning ex DE 159 | APD 55 | C1.8.43 |
| Loy ex DE 160 | APD 56 | C12.9.43 |
| Barber ex DE 161 | APD 57 | C10.10.43 |
| Witter ex DE 636 | APD 58 | C29.12.43 |
| Newman ex DE 205 | APD 59 | C26.11.43 |
| Liddle ex DE 206 | APD 60 | C6.12.43 |
| Kephart ex DE 207 | APD 61 | C7.1.44 |
| Cofer ex DE 208 | APD 62 | C19.1.44 |
| Lloyd ex DE 209 | APD 63 | C11.2.44 |
| Scott ex DE 214 | APD 64 | C20.7.43 |
| Burke ex DE 215 | APD 65 | C20.8.43 |
| Enright ex DE 216 | APD 66 | C21.9.43 |
| Jenks ex DE 665 | APD 67 | C19.1.44 |
| Durik ex DE 666 | APD 68 | C24.3.44 |
| Yokes ex DE 668 | APD 69 | L27.11.43 |
| Pavlic ex DE 669 | APD 71 | L18.12.43 |
| Odum ex DE 670 | APD 72 | L19.1.44 |
| Jack C. Robinson ex DE 671 | APD 72 | C8.1.44 |
| Bassett ex DE 672 | APD 73 | C15.1.44 |
| John B. Gray ex DE 673 | APD 74 | C18.3.44 |
| Weber ex DE 675 | APD 75 | C30.6.43 |
| Schmitt ex DE 676 | APD 76 | C24.7.43 |
| Frament ex DE 677 | APD 77 | C15.8.43 |
| Bull ex DE 693 | APD 78 | C12.8.43 |
| Bunch ex DE 694 | APD 79 | C21.8.43 |
| Hayter ex DE 212 | APD 80 | C16.3.44 |
| Tatum ex DE 789 | APD 81 | C22.11.43 |

| | | |
|---|---|---|
| Borum ex *DE 790* | APD 82 | C30.11.43 |
| Maloy ex *DE 791* | APD 83 | C12.12.43 |
| Haines ex *DE 792* | APD 84 | C27.12.43 |
| Runnels ex *DE 793* | APD 85 | C3.1.44 |
| Hollis ex *DE 794* | APD 86 | C24.1.44 |
| Crosley ex *DE 226* | APD 87 | L12.2.44 |
| Cread ex *DE 227* | APD 88 | L12.2.44 |
| Ruchamkin ex *DE 228* | APD 89 | L14.6.44 |
| Kirwin ex *DE 229* | APD 90 | L15.6.44 |
| Kinzer ex *DE 232* | APD 91 | L9.12.43 |
| Register ex *DE 233* | APD 92 | L20.1.44 |
| Brock ex *DE 234* | APD 93 | L20.1.44 |
| John Q. Roberts *DE 235* | APD 94 | L11.2.44 |
| William M. Hobby *DE 236* | APD 95 | L11.2.44 |
| Ray K. Edwards *DE 237* | APD 96 | L19.2.44 |
| Arthur L. Bristol *DE 281* | APD 97 | L19.2.44 |
| Truxtun ex *DE 282* | APD 98 | L9.3.44 |
| Upham ex *DE 283* | APD 99 | L9.3.44 |
| Tinsman ex *DE 590* | APD 100 | C26.4.44 |
| Knudson ex *DE 591* | APD 101 | C26.6.44 |
| Rednour ex *DE 592* | APD 102 | L12.2.44 |
| Tollberg ex *DE 593* | APD 103 | L12.2.44 |
| William T. Pattisson *DE 594* | APD 104 | L15.2.44 |
| Myers *DE 595* | APD 105 | L15.2.44 |
| Walter B. Cobb ex *DE 596* | APD 106 | L23.3.44 |
| Earle B. Hall ex *DE 597* | APD 107 | L1.3.44 |
| Harry L. Corl ex *DE 598* | APD 108 | L1.3.44 |
| Belet ex *DE 599* | APD 109 | L3.3.44 |
| Julius A. Raven ex *DE 600* | APD 110 | L3.3.44 |
| Walsh ex *DE 601* | APD 111 | L28.4.45 |
| Hunter Marshall ex *DE 602* | APD 112 | L5.5.45 |
| Earheart ex *DE 603* | APD 113 | L12.2.45 |
| Walter S. Gorka ex *DE 604* | APD 114 | L26.5.45 |
| Rogers Blood ex *DE 605* | APD 115 | L2.6.45 |
| Francovich ex *DE 606* | APD 116 | L5.6.45 |
| Joseph M. Auman ex *DE 674* | APD 117 | C25.12.43 |
| Don O. Woods ex *DE 721* | APD 118 | L19.2.44 |
| Beverly W. Reid ex *DE 722* | APD 119 | L.14.3.44 |
| Kline ex *DE 687* | APD 120 | L26.6.44 |
| Raymond W. Berndon ex *DE 668* | APD 121 | L15.7.44 |
| Scribner ex *DE 689* | APD 122 | L1.8.44 |
| Diachenko ex *DE 690* | APD 123 | L15.8.44 |
| Horace A. Bass ex *DE 691* | APD 124 | L12.9.44 |
| Wantuck ex *DE 692* | APD 125 | L25.9.44 |
| Gosselin ex *DE 710* | APD 126 | L4.5.44 |
| Begor ex *DE 711* | APD 127 | L25.4.44 |
| Cavallaro ex *DE 712* | APD 128 | L15.6.44 |
| Donald W. Wolf ex *DE 713* | APD 129 | L22.7.44 |
| Cook ex *DE 714* | APD 130 | L26.8.44 |

| | | |
|---|---|---|
| *Walter W. Young* ex *DE 715* | APD 131 | L30.9.44 |
| *Balduck* ex *DE 716* | APD 132 | L27.10.44 |
| *Brudoo* ex *DE 717* | APD 133 | L25.11.44 |
| *Kleinsmith* ex *DE 718* | APD 134 | L27.1.45 |
| *Weiss* ex *DE 719* | APD 135 | L27.1.45 |
| *Carpellotti* ex *DE 720* | APD 136 | L10.3.45 |
| *De Long* ex *DE 684* | APD 137 | C31.12.43 |
| *Coates* ex *DE 685* | APD 138 | C24.1.44 |
| *Bray* ex *DE 709* | APD 139 | C4.9.44 |

Dates marked 'L' are launching dates, 'C' are commissioning dates as APD. Some ships were converted after completion, and transfer dates are not in all cases clear.

A later bow view of *Marsh*, which illustrates the divergence of naval staff views between the RN and USN at war's end, in dealing with the fast U-boats. While the RN went in for the Squid mortars, the USN relied on the Hedgehog, and here two are fitted side by side in the B position. *(US Navy)*

A 'John C. Butler' type ship, *Woodson,* after the war. This was the final wartime version of the DE, and very large numbers of this type were cancelled, as were many of the RN's 'Loch' class frigates. This photo shows the three twin Bofors aft, and postwar radar aerials at the masthead. *(US Navy)*

*Jack C. Wilke* of the 'Buckley' type. She had her torpedo tubes replaced by four single hand-worked Bofors, for Pacific service. This gave her a close-range armament of six Bofors and ten Oerlikons. *(US Navy)*

*Seer* in March 1945. A single Oerlikon is fitted
on the crowded sweep deck, there are two
single Bofors aft, and a tall signal pole on the
after stack. *(US National Archives)*

*Raven*, name ship of her class, in August 1942.
Note no radar is fitted, and there is a twin
40mm aft. *(US National Archives)*

## USN FLEET MINESWEEPER (AM) CLASSES

As with the RN section, we include here brief details of the two main classes of fleet minesweeper built for the USN during the war years.

It will be seen that each was fitted out with anti-submarine gear, in much the same way as the RN's 'Algerine' and 'Bangor' classes. We assume that, again in parallel, some of these USN fleet minesweepers were used on anti-submarine escort duties from time to time during the war, especially in the Pacific. They merit a place in this book for that reason.

But no precise information is readily available on this point, and as these two classes were produced largely during the same period as the numerous DEs, PCs and PCEs, it may be that the USN fleet minesweepers could keep to their specialised role more than was the case in the RN in the early years of the war; there, the main flow of new escorts came after 1942, and before that time fleet minesweepers were undoubtedly pressed into service as escorts quite often.

## USN 'RAVEN' CLASS FLEET MINESWEEPERS (AM)
### 95 ships completed

This was one of the two classes of fleet minesweeper designed and built for the USN during the war. It was an original class design, and ships of the class were not, as a rule, converted for other duties.

The silhouette of this class was quite distinct from any other. The hull had little sheer, the stern was not greatly cut away, and the forecastle had rounded deck edges and a steel forecastlehead, a feature only found elsewhere in the PCE/'Admirable' class hull. There was a break in the forecastle deck by the bridge, and there were 2 large stacks, widely separated, with boat decks, Oerlikon platforms, and life-raft skids being built up above the main deck. There was a solid steel bulwark along the main deck, broken only at the fantail for handling sweeps. There were continuous drainage slots at the foot of this bulwark, where it met the deck.

There was no doubt about the efficiency of the equipment built into this hull. There was a large steel bridge forward, a steel pole mast with Type SL surface warning radar, and the usual IFF and R/T aerials.

The armament was composed of 2 3″/50 calibre guns, 1 forward and 1 aft, or 1 such gun forward (in a large bandstand on the forecastle), and between 4 and 7 single Oerlikons, with single Bofors sometimes added aft.

The anti-submarine equipment included a Hedgehog, fitted just aft of the forward 3″ gun (note that neither of the RN's two fleet minesweeper classes carried this weapon), and 4 depth-charge throwers, and either rails or individual chutes on the fantail. Some of the earlier ships carried chutes, as in the RN's 'Bangor' class, but some of the later ships show 2 full sets of rails.

The fantail, needless to say, showed a full range of minesweeping equipment. It is not known how many of this class were employed in the Pacific, but it is assumed it was the majority.

11 US shipyards participated in the building of this class.

9 ships of the class were lost by enemy action.

22 ships were transferred to the RN under Lend-Lease; 4 were lost, the remainder returned after the war.

It will be seen that the production of this class really fell into three parts (not including the ships built for the RN). In the first were 2 ships only, built in 1940. In the second were 51 ships, launched between the beginning of 1942 and the end of 1943. In the third were 20 ships, launched in late 1944 and early 1945, after a gap of a year, in which there was only 1 ship of the class launched.

### USN 'Raven' class production schedule

| 1940 | 2nd half | 2  | 1943 | 1st half | 12 |
|------|----------|----|------|----------|----|
| 1941 | 1st half | 0  |      | 2nd half | 0  |
|      | 2nd half | 1  | 1944 | 1st half | 1  |
| 1942 | 1st half | 18 |      | 2nd half | 14 |
|      | 2nd half | 20 | 1945 | 1st half | 5  |

### USN 'Raven' class statistics

| Ships completed      | 95 | Transferred to RN | 22 |
|----------------------|----|-------------------|----|
| Commissioned by USN  | 73 | Cancelled         | 10 |

*Threat* in March 1944. The sweep winch and LL cable reel aft stand out clearly.
*(US National Archives)*

## USN 'RAVEN' CLASS SPECIFICATION

|  | RAVEN/OSPREY | ALL OTHERS |
|---|---|---|
| Displacement | 810 | 890 |
| Dimensions | | |
|   length oa | 220'6" | 221'2" |
|   breadth | 32'2" | 32'2" |
|   draught | 9'4" | 10'9" |
| Engines | FM Diesel | Diesel-electric |
|   SHP | 1,800 | see below |
| Speed | 18.1 km | 18.1 km |
| Fuel | | 1640bbls |
| Complement | 9+96 | 9/10+96/107 |
| Armament | | |
|   main | 1/2 3"/50 | 1 3"/50 |
|   close-range | 2 single 40mm | 1/2 40mm |
| | 4/7 20mm | 4/7 20mm |

### Diesel electric engine builders

| Alco | AM 57-65 |
|---|---|
| BS | AM 100-111 |
| GM | AM 112-131, 321-324, 341, 371-390 |
| Baldwin | AM 314-320, 340 |

**Designed SHP**

| 3118 | AM 57-65, 100-111 |
|---|---|
| 3532 | AM 113-131, 322-324, 341, 371-390 |
| 2976 | AM 314-320, 340 |

### FOLLOWING SHIPS ORIGINALLY ALLOCATED TO RN

Full details appear under the 'CATHERINE' class in RN section. *Champion, Chief, Competent, Defense, Devastator, Gladiator, Impeccable, Overseer, Spear, Triumph, Vigilance, Ardent, Dextrous.*

### WAR LOSSES

| *Osprey* | AM 56 | Lost 5th June 1944 |
|---|---|---|
| *Portent* | AM 106 | Lost 23rd January 1944 |
| *Sentinel* | AM 113 | Lost 10th July 1943 |
| *Skill* | AM 115 | Lost 16th September 1943 |
| *Swerve* | AM 121 | Lost 9th July 1944 |
| *Tide* | AM 125 | Lost 7th July 1944 |
| *Minivet* | AM 371 | Lost 29th December 1944 |

### HULL NUMBERS NOT USED

AM 342-350

## USN 'RAVEN' CLASS—CLASS LIST

| Name | Pendant No | Builder | Building Time | Completion Date |
|------|------------|---------|---------------|-----------------|
| Raven | AM 55 | Norfolk | 16m13d | 11.11.40 |
| Osprey | AM 56 | ,, | 17m18d | 16.12.40 |
| Auk | AM 57 | ,, | 8m30d | 15.1.42 |
| Broadbill | AM 58 | Defoe | 14m21d | 13.10.42 |
| Chickadee | AM 59 | ,, | 14m19d | 9.11.42 |
| Nuthatch | AM 60 | ,, | 5m28d | 19.11.42 |
| Pheasant | AM 61 | ,, | 4m21d | 12.12.42 |
| Sheldrake | AM 62 | General | 15m20d | 14.10.42 |
| Skylark | AM 63 | ,, | 4m16d | 25.11.42 |
| Starling | AM 64 | ,, | 5m7d | 21.12.42 |
| Swallow | AM 65 | ,, | 5m26d | 14.1.43 |
| Heed | AM 100 | ,, | 12m14d | 27.2.43 |
| Herald | AM 101 | ,, | 12m9d | 23.3.43 |
| Motive | AM 102 | ,, | 12m0d | 17.4.43 |
| Oracle | AM 103 | ,, | 12m7d | 14.5.43 |
| Pilot | AM 104 | Penn | 15m7d | 3.2.43 |
| Pioneer | AM 105 | ,, | 16m1d | 27.2.43 |
| Portent | AM 106 | ,, | 16m18d | 3.4.43 |
| Prevail | AM 107 | ,, | 17m1d | 17.4.43 |
| Pursuit | AM 108 | Winslow | 17m18d | 30.4.43 |
| Requisite | AM 109 | ,, | 18m25d | 7.6.43 |
| Revenge ex *Right* | AM 110 | ,, | 13m1d | 21.7.43 |
| Sage | AM 111 | ,, | 12m21d | 23.8.43 |
| Seer | AM 112 | American | 10m23d | 21.10.42 |
| Sentinel | AM 113 | ,, | 12m5d | 3.11.42 |
| Staff | AM 114 | ,, | 11m19d | 17.11.42 |
| Skill | AM 115 | ,, | 11m19d | 17.11.42 |
| Speed | AM 116 | ,, | 10m28d | 15.10.42 |
| Strive | AM 117 | ,, | 11m9d | 27.10.42 |
| Steady | AM 118 | ,, | 11m29d | 16.11.42 |
| Sustain | AM 119 | ,, | 11m22d | 16.11.42 |
| Sway | AM 120 | Mathis | 20m1d | 20.7.43 |
| Swerve | AM 121 | ,, | 20m0d | 23.1.43 |
| Swift | AM 122 | ,, | 18m2d | 29.12.42 |
| Symbol | AM 123 | Savannah | 12m22d | 10.12.42 |
| Threat | AM 124 | ,, | 14m30d | 14.3.43 |
| Tide | AM 125 | ,, | 13m24d | 9.5.43 |
| Token | AM 126 | Gulf | 17m10d | 28.3.42 |
| Tumult | AM 127 | ,, | 19m10d | 27.2.43 |
| Velocity | AM 128 | ,, | 20m13d | 3.4.43 |
| Vital | AM 129 | ,, | 16m18d | 18.5.43 |
| Usage | AM 130 | ,, | 17m7d | 7.6.43 |
| Zeal | AM 131 | ,, | 17m28d | 9.7.43 |
| Champion | AM 314 | General | 14m2d | 8.9.43 |

| | | | | |
|---|---|---|---|---|
| *Chief* | AM 315 | ,, | 14m15d | 9.10.43 |
| *Competent* | AM 316 | ,, | 14m22d | 10.11.43 |
| *Defense* | AM 317 | ,, | 15m8d | 10.1.44 |
| *Devastator* | AM 318 | ,, | 12m28d | 12.1.44 |
| *Gladiator* | AM 319 | ,, | 13m21d | 25.2.44 |
| *Impeccable* | AM 320 | ,, | 14m24d | 24.4.44 |
| *Overseer* | AM 321 | ,, | 15m14d | 22.12.43 |
| *Spear* | AM 322 | Associated | 14m3d | 31.12.43 |
| *Triumph* | AM 323 | ,, | 15m7d | 3.2.44 |
| *Vigilance* | AM 324 | ,, | 15m2d | 28.2.44 |
| *Ardent* | AM 340 | General | 15m2d | 25.2.44 |
| *Dextrous* | AM 341 | Gulf | 13m30d | 8.9.43 |
| *Minivet* | AM 371 | Savannah | 10m10d | 29.5.45 |
| *Murrelet* | AM 372 | ,, | 11m28d | 21.8.45 |
| *Peregrine* | AM 373 | ,, | 11m3d | 27.9.45 |
| *Pigeon* | AM 374 | ,, | 11m19d | 30.10.45 |
| *Pochard* | AM 375 | ,, | 9m17d | 27.11.44 |
| *Ptarmigan* | AM 376 | ,, | 10m5d | 15.1.45 |
| *Quail* | AM 377 | ,, | 10m23d | 5.3.45 |
| *Redstart* | AM 378 | ,, | 9m20d | 4.4.45 |
| *Roselle* | AM 379 | Gulf | 11m10d | 6.2.45 |
| *Ruddy* | AM 380 | ,, | 12m1d | 28.4.45 |
| *Scoter* | AM 381 | ,, | 11m12d | 17.3.45 |
| *Shoveler* | AM 382 | ,, | 12m22d | 22.5.45 |
| *Surfbird* | AM 383 | American | 9m5d | 25.11.44 |
| *Sprig* | AM 384 | ,, | 13m17d | 4.4.45 |
| *Tanager* | AM 385 | ,, | 16m1d | 28.7.45 |
| *Tercel* | AM 386 | ,, | 15m5d | 21.8.45 |
| *Toucan* | AM 387 | ,, | 9m5d | 25.11.44 |
| *Towhee* | AM 388 | ,, | 11m28d | 18.3.45 |
| *Waxwing* | AM 389 | ,, | 14m13d | 26.9.45 |
| *Wheatear* | AM 390 | ,, | 9m5d | 3.10.45 |

*Steady* off the Sicilian coast in July 1943. She has no normal funnel casings, and only a small exhaust over the after funnel position. The SA gear is mounted on the stem. *(US National Archives)*

## USN 'ADMIRABLE' CLASS FLEET MINESWEEPERS (AM)
### 124 ships completed

This was the second class of fleet minesweeper built for the US Navy during the war years.

They used the same hull, engine and upperworks design as the PCE class escorts; the details under that chapter therefore apply equally to this class.

The fantail was redesigned as a sweep deck, with minesweeping davits, winch, floats, etc. The depth-charge gear was retained, though probably on a rather more restricted basis than in the PCEs. The Hedgehog was still carried forward, fitted just aft of the single 3"/50 calibre gun.

The close-range armament was reorganised, in that the guntub on the fantail had to be eliminated to make way for the minesweeping winch. Two guntubs were therefore fitted on the after end of the main deck, side by side, looking over the fantail, and each contained a twin 40mm Bofors mounting. The 20mm Oerlikon outfit around the bridge structure remained as before.

The exhaust problem outlined under the PCE class was similarly solved in the 'Admirable' class, first by a tall stovepipe exhaust, and later by a small raked stack with cap, mounted on the centreline.

A large number of this class were transferred to Russia, as is noted below. The RN did not order or take any units of this class.

As with the 'Raven' class, it is not clear how far units of this class may have been used in an A/S role from time to time.

### USN 'ADMIRABLE' CLASS PRODUCTION CHART

| | | | |
|---|---|---|---|
| Ships completed | 124 | Cancelled | 44 |
| Commissioned by USN as AM | 121 | Cancelled after launch | 7 |
| Commissioned by USN as YDG | 1 | To Russia in wartime, after USN service | 34 |
| Completed as merchant ships | 2 | To China, similarly | 4 |
| War loss | 1 | | |

### USN 'ADMIRABLE' CLASS PRODUCTION SCHEDULE

| | | | | | | |
|---|---|---|---|---|---|---|
| 1942 | 2nd half | 21 | 1944 | 1st half | | 32 |
| 1943 | 1st half | 26 | | 2nd half | | 8 |
| | 2nd half | 34 | | | | |

*Ruddy* in 1945, in dark blue camouflage. This gives a good view of the deck lay-out. The Hedgehog is prominent aft of the 3" gun, in contrast to the RN 'Algerine' class. *(US National Archives)*

## USN 'ADMIRABLE' CLASS SPECIFICATION

| | |
|---|---|
| Displacement | 650 |
| Dimensions | |
|    length oa | 184'6" |
|    breadth | 33' |
|    draught | 9'9" |
| Engines | diesel, 2 shafts |
|    SHP | 1,710 |
| Speed | 14.8 km |
| Fuel | 1,050 bbls |
| Complement | 11+93 |
| Armament | |
|    main | 1 3"/50 |
|    close-range | 2 twin 40mm |
| | (1 twin 40mm, |
| | AM 214 and 215 only) |

## USN 'ADMIRABLE' CLASS

| Name | Pendant No | Builder | Building Time | Completion Date |
|---|---|---|---|---|
| Admirable ex *AMC 113* | AM 136 | Tampa | 12m11d | 20.4.43 |
| Adopt ex *AMC 114* | AM 137 | ,, | 13m22d | 31.5.43 |
| Advocate ex *AMC 115* | AM 138 | ,, | 14m6d | 25.6.43 |
| Agent ex *AMC 116* | AM 139 | ,, | 16m1d | 10.7.43 |
| Alarm ex *AMC 117* | AM 140 | ,, | 13m27d | 5.8.43 |
| Alchemy ex *AMC 118* | AM 141 | ,, | 14m2d | 11.8.43 |
| Apex ex *AMC 119* | AM 142 | ,, | 14m19d | 17.8.43 |
| Arcade ex *AMC 120* | AM 143 | ,, | 14m17d | 26.8.43 |
| Arch ex *AMC 121* | AM 144 | ,, | 10m19d | 9.9.43 |
| Armada ex *AMC 122* | AM 145 | ,, | 10m29d | 16.9.43 |
| Aspire ex *AMC 123* | AM 146 | ,, | 10m29d | 29.9.43 |
| Assail ex *AMC 124* | AM 147 | ,, | 11m5d | 5.10.43 |
| Astute ex *AMC 125* | AM 148 | ,, | 13m11d | 17.1.44 |

| | | | | |
|---|---|---|---|---|
| *Augury* | AM 149 | ,, | 15m11d | 17.3.44 |
| ex *AMC 126* | | | | |
| *Barrier* | AM 150 | ,, | 17m3d | 10.5.44 |
| ex *AMC 127* | | | | |
| *Bombard* | AM 151 | ,, | 17m24d | 31.5.44 |
| ex *AMC 128* | | | | |
| *Bond* | AM 152 | Willamette | 16m19d | 30.8.43 |
| ex *AMC 129* | | | | |
| *Buoyant* | AM 153 | ,, | 17m15d | 30.9.43 |
| ex *AMC 130* | | | | |
| *Candid* | AM 154 | ,, | 18m3d | 31.10.43 |
| ex *AMC 131* | | | | |
| *Capable* | AM 155 | ,, | 19m7d | 5.12.43 |
| ex *AMC 132* | | | | |
| *Captivate* | AM 156 | ,, | 19m19d | 30.12.43 |
| ex *AMC 133* | | | | |
| *Caravan* | AM 157 | ,, | 20m16d | 21.1.44 |
| ex *AMC 134* | | | | |
| *Caution* | AM 158 | ,, | 20m17d | 10.2.44 |
| ex *AMC 135* | | | | |
| *Change* | AM 159 | ,, | 21m8d | 28.2.44 |
| ex *AMC 136* | | | | |
| *Clamour* | AM 160 | ,, | 21m19d | 14.3.44 |
| ex *AMC 137* | | | | |
| *Climax* | AM 161 | ,, | 21m29d | 24.3.44 |
| ex *AMC 138* | | | | |
| *Compel* | AM 162 | ,, | 21m23d | 8.4.44 |
| ex *AMC 139* | | | | |
| *Concise* | AM 163 | ,, | 22m5d | 25.4.44 |
| ex *AMC 140* | | | | |
| *Control* | AM 164 | ,, | 22m28d | 11.5.44 |
| ex *AMC 141* | | | | |
| *Counsel* | AM 165 | ,, | 23m10d | 27.5.44 |
| ex *AMC 142* | | | | |
| *Crag* | AM 214 | Tampa | 31m24d | 1.8.45 |
| ex *Craig* | | | | |
| *Cruise* | AM 215 | ,, | 33m14d | 21.9.45 |
| *Deft* | AM 216 | ,, | 27m20d | 16.4.45 |
| *Delegate* | AM 217 | ,, | 28m4d | 30.4.45 |
| *Density* | AM 218 | ,, | 14m25d | 15.6.44 |
| *Design* | AM 219 | ,, | 15m18d | 29.6.44 |
| *Device* | AM 220 | ,, | 12m7d | 7.7.44 |
| *Diploma* | AM 221 | ,, | 12m22d | 15.7.44 |
| *Disdain* | AM 222 | American | 14m3d | 26.12.44 |
| *Dour* | AM 223 | ,, | 12m11d | 4.11.44 |
| *Eager* | AM 224 | ,, | 10m25d | 23.11.44 |
| *Elusive* | AM 225 | ,, | 13m21d | 19.2.45 |
| *Embattle* | AM 226 | ,, | 12m19d | 25.4.45 |
| *Execute* | AM 232 | Puget | 8m17d | 15.11.44 |
| *Facility* | AM 233 | ,, | 8m1d | 29.11.44 |

| Fancy | AM 234 | ,, | 7m12d | 13.12.44 |
|-------|--------|----|-------|----------|
| Fixity | AM 235 | ,, | 6m17d | 29.1.44 |
| Garland | AM 238 | Winslow | 10m13d | 26.8.44 |
| Gayety | AM 239 | ,, | 10m8d | 23.9.44 |
| Hazard | AM 240 | ,, | 8m8d | 31.10.44 |
| Hilarity | AM 241 | ,, | 8m8d | 27.11.44 |
| Inaugral | AM 242 | ,, | 7m8d | 30.12.44 |
| Implicit | AM 246 | Savannah | 10m4d | 20.1.44 |
| Improve | AM 247 | ,, | 8m0d | 29.2.44 |
| Incessant | AM 248 | ,, | 8m22d | 25.3.44 |
| Incredible | AM 249 | ,, | 7m7d | 17.4.44 |
| Indicative | AM 250 | ,, | 8m27d | 26.6.44 |
| Inflict | AM 251 | ,, | 10m2d | 28.8.44 |
| Instill | AM 252 | ,, | 5m28d | 22.5.44 |
| Intrigue | AM 253 | ,, | 7m14d | 31.7.44 |
| Invade | AM 254 | ,, | 7m30d | 18.9.44 |
| Jubilant | AM 255 | American | 10m5d | 27.8.43 |
| Knave | AM 256 | ,, | 11m22d | 14.10.43 |
| Lance | AM 257 | ,, | 10m9d | 4.11.43 |
| Logic | AM 258 | ,, | 12m25d | 21.11.43 |
| Lucid | AM 259 | ,, | 9m8d | 1.12.43 |
| Magnet | AM 260 | ,, | 11m25d | 10.3.44 |
| Mainstay | AM 261 | ,, | 12m13d | 24.4.44 |
| Marvel | AM 262 | ,, | 13m27d | 9.6.44 |
| Measure | AM 263 | ,, | 8m28d | 13.5.44 |
| Method | AM 264 | ,, | 13m2d | 10.7.44 |
| Mirth | AM 265 | ,, | 12m12d | 12.8.44 |
| Nimble | AM 266 | ,, | 13m17d | 15.9.44 |
| Notable | AM 267 | Gulf | 15m16d | 23.12.43 |
| Nucleus | AM 268 | ,, | 16m11d | 19.1.44 |
| Opponent | AM 269 | ,, | 16m27d | 18.2.44 |
| Palisade | AM 270 | ,, | 17m16d | 9.3.44 |
| Penetrate | AM 271 | ,, | 11m0d | 31.3.44 |
| Peril | AM 272 | ,, | 12m2d | 2.4.44 |
| Phantom | AM 273 | ,, | 15m17d | 17.5.44 |
| Pinnacle | AM 274 | ,, | 15m24d | 24.5.44 |
| Pirate | AM 275 | ,, | 11m16d | 16.6.44 |
| Pivot | AM 276 | ,, | 12m12d | 12.7.44 |
| Pledge | AM 277 | ,, | 12m29d | 29.7.44 |
| Project | AM 278 | ,, | 13m22d | 22.8.44 |
| Prime | AM 279 | ,, | 11m27d | 12.9.44 |
| Prowess | AM 280 | ,, | 12m11d | 27.9.44 |
| Quest | AM 281 | ,, | 11m0d | 25.10.44 |
| Rampart | AM 282 | ,, | 11m24d | 18.11.44 |
| Ransom | AM 283 | General | 13m0d | 5.8.44 |
| Rebel | AM 284 | ,, | 15m31d | 12.9.44 |
| Recruit | AM 285 | ,, | 17m15d | 8.11.44 |
| Reform | AM 286 | ,, | 20m16d | 28.2.45 |
| Refresh | AM 287 | ,, | 18m10d | 10.4.45 |
| Reign | AM 288 | ,, | 30m11d | 10.5.46 |

| | | | | |
|---|---|---|---|---|
| *Report* | AM 289 | ,, | 31m1d | 12.7.46 |
| *Salute* | AM 294 | Winslow | 12m23d | 4.12.43 |
| *Saunter* | AM 295 | ,, | 13m29d | 22.1.44 |
| *Scout* | AM 296 | ,, | 12m23d | 3.3.44 |
| *Scrimmage* | AM 297 | ,, | 13m12d | 4.4.44 |
| *Scuffle* | AM 298 | ,, | 11m29d | 2.5.44 |
| *Sentry* | AM 299 | ,, | 12m14d | 30.5.44 |
| *Serene* | AM 300 | ,, | 10m13d | 24.6.44 |
| *Shelter* | AM 301 | ,, | 10m24d | 9.7.44 |
| *Signet* | AM 302 | ,, | 14m13d | 20.6.44 |
| *Skirmish* | AM 303 | ,, | 14m22d | 30.6.44 |
| *Skurry* | AM 304 | Associated | 14m5d | 29.7.44 |
| *Spectacle* | AM 305 | ,, | 12m18d | 11.8.44 |
| *Specter* | AM 306 | ,, | 11m24d | 30.8.44 |
| *Staunch* | AM 307 | ,, | 12m3d | 9.9.44 |
| *Strategy* | AM 308 | ,, | 11m18d | 22.9.44 |
| *Strength* | AM 309 | ,, | 11m27d | 30.9.44 |
| *Success* | AM 310 | ,, | 7m28d | 18.10.44 |
| *Superior* | AM 311 | ,, | 10m21d | 1.11.44 |
| *Creddock* | AM 356 | Willamette | 25m7d | 18.12.45 |
| *Dipper* | AM 357 | ,, | 25m6d | 26.12.45 |
| *Dunlin* | AM 361 | ,, | 24m18d | 16.2.45 |
| *Gadwell* | AM 362 | ,, | 24m23d | 23.6.45 |
| *Gavia* | AM 363 | ,, | 24m15d | 23.7.45 |
| *Graylag* | AM 364 | ,, | 25m16d | 31.8.45 |
| *Harlequin* | AM 365 | ,, | 25m26d | 28.9.45 |
| *Harrier* | AM 366 | ,, | 26m20d | 31.10.45 |

*Tide* in June 1943. Note the sweep deck lay-out, and the single 3"/50 calibre gun aft. The spare Oropesa float is stowed by the funnel. *(US National Archives)*

## CANCELLED SHIPS

| Name | Pendant No | Builder | Cancelled |
|------|-----------|---------|-----------|
| AM 166-AM 208 | | | 9.4.42 |
| AM 209-AM 213 | | | 10.4.42 |
| *Embroil* | AM 227 | American | 6.6.44 |
| *Enhance* | AM 228 | ,, | 6.6.44 |
| *Equity* | AM 229 | ,, | 6.6.44 |
| *Esteem* | AM 230 | ,, | 6.6.44 |
| *Event* | AM 231 | ,, | 6.6.44 |
| *Flame* | AM 236 | Puget | 6.6.44 |
| *Fortify* | AM 237 | ,, | 6.6.44 |
| *Illusive* | AM 243 | Winslow | 6.6.44 |
| *Imbue* | AM 244 | ,, | 6.6.44 |
| *Impervious* | AM 245 | ,, | 6.6.44 |
| *Reproof* | AM 290 | General | 1.11.45 |
| *Risk* | AM 291 | ,, | 1.11.45 |
| *Rival* | AM 292 | ,, | 6.6.44 |
| *Sagacity* | AM 293 | ,, | 6.6.44 |
| | AM 312 | Associated | 7.5.42 |
| | AM 313 | ,, | 7.5.42 |
| *Adjutant* | AM 351 | Willamette | 1.11.45 |
| *Bittern* | AM 352 | ,, | 1.11.45 |
| *Breakhorn* | AM 353 | ,, | 1.11.45 |
| *Cariama* | AM 354 | ,, | 1.11.45 |
| *Chukor* | AM 355 | ,, | 1.11.45 |
| *Dotterel* | AM 358 | ,, | 1.11.45 |
| *Driver* | AM 360 | ,, | 1.11.45 |
| *Hummer* | AM 367 | Puget | 6.6.44 |
| *Jackaw* | AM 368 | ,, | 6.6.44 |
| *Medrick* | AM 369 | ,, | 6.6.44 |
| *Minah* | AM 370 | ,, | 6.6.44 |
| *Albatross* | AM 391 | Defoe | 1.11.45 |
| *Bullfinch* | AM 392 | ,, | 1.11.45 |
| *Cardinal* | AM 393 | ,, | 1.11.45 |
| *Firecrest* | AM 394 | ,, | 1.11.45 |
| *Goldfinch* | AM 395 | ,, | 1.11.45 |
| *Grackle* | AM 396 | ,, | 11.8.45 |
| *Grosbeak* | AM 367 | ,, | 11.8.45 |
| *Grouse* | AM 398 | ,, | 11.8.45 |
| *Gull* | AM 399 | ,, | 11.8.45 |
| *Hawk* | AM 400 | ,, | 11.8.45 |
| *Hummer* | AM 401 | ,, | 11.8.45 |
| *Jackdaw* | AM 402 | ,, | 11.8.45 |
| *Kite* | AM 403 | ,, | 11.8.45 |
| *Longspur* | AM 404 | ,, | 11.8.45 |
| *Merganser* | AM 405 | ,, | 11.8.45 |
| *Osprey* | AM 406 | ,, | 11.8.45 |
| *Partridge* | AM 407 | ,, | 11.8.45 |

| Plover | AM 408 | ,, | 11.8.45 |
| Redhead | AM 409 | ,, | 11.8.45 |
| Sanderling | AM 410 | ,, | 11.8.45 |
| Scaup | AM 411 | ,, | 11.8.45 |
| Sentinel | AM 412 | ,, | 11.8.45 |
| Shearwater | AM 413 | ,, | 11.8.45 |
| Waxbill | AM 414 | ,, | 11.8.45 |
| Bluebird | AM 415 | ,, | 11.8.45 |
| Flicker | AM 416 | ,, | 11.8.45 |
| Linnet | AM 417 | ,, | 11.8.45 |
| Magpie | AM 418 | ,, | 11.8.45 |
| Parrakeet | AM 419 | ,, | 11.8.45 |
| Pipit | AM 420 | ,, | 11.8.45 |

## WAR LOSSES

| Portent | AM 106 | Lost 23rd January 1944 |
| Tide | AM 125 | Lost 7th June 1944 |

## TRANSFERRED TO RUSSIA

**1943**
*Advocate, Agent, Alarm, Alchemy, Apex, Arcade, Arch, Armada, Aspire, Assail*
**1945**
*Admirable, Adopt, Astute, Augury, Barrier, Bombard, Bond, Candid, Capable, Captivate, Caravan, Caution, Disdain, Fancy, Indicative, Marvel, Measure, Method, Mirth, Nucleus, Palisade, Penetrate, Peril, Rampart*

## TRANSFERRED TO CHINA

**1945**
*Lance, Logic, Lucid, Magnet*

*Swerve* in 1944. Two single Oerlikons atop the covered bridge, two amidships and two single Bofors aft. Type SL radar at the masthead. Some units omitted the wire sweep gear aft, in favour of two more single Oerlikons. *(US National Archives)*

## USN 'ALGERINE' CLASS FLEET MINESWEEPERS (AM)

### 15 SHIPS COMPLETED IN CANADA

Fifteen ships of the RN's 'Algerine' class were ordered by the USN, all from the same Canadian shipbuilding company, Redfern Construction, in Toronto, Ontario.

Before completion, they were all transferred to the RN under numerical Lend-Lease commitments, as the USN was retaining some of the BAM class, originally ordered by the RN in the USA.

For the sake of clarity, these ships are listed here; details will be found under the RN's 'Algerine' class.

*became* RN

| | | | |
|---|---|---|---|
| AM 325 Antares | J 282 | AM 333 Octavia | J 290 |
| AM 326 Arcturus | J 283 | AM 334 Persian | J 347 |
| AM 327 Aries | J 284 | AM 335 Postillion | J 296 |
| AM 328 Clinton | J 286 | AM 336 Skipjack | J 300 |
| AM 329 Friendship | J 398 | AM 337 Thisbe | J 302 |
| AM 330 Gozo | J 287 | AM 338 Truelove | J 303 |
| AM 331 Lightfoot | J 288 | AM 339 Welfare | J 356 |
| AM 332 Melita | J 289 | | |

### AMERICAN ESCORT SHIPBUILDERS

Albina Engineering & Machinery Works, Portland, Ore
American Shipbuilding Corp, Cleveland, Ohio
American Shipbuilding Corp, Lorain, Ohio
Associated Shipbuilders Inc, Seattle, Wash
Bethlehem-Hingham Shipyard, Hingham, Mass
Bethlehem Steel Corp Inc, Quincy, Mass
Bethlehem Steel Corp Inc, San Francisco, Calif
Boston Navy Yard, Boston, Mass
Brown Shipbuilding Corp Inc, Houston, Texas
Charleston Navy Yard, Charleston, S Car
Commercial Iron Works Inc, Portland, Ore
Consolidated Shipbuilding Corp Inc, Morris Heights, NY
Consolidated Shipbuilding Corp Inc, New York, NY
Consolidated Steel Corp Inc, Orange, Texas
Consolidated Steel Corp Inc, San Pedro, Calif
Defoe Shipbuilding Corp Inc, Bay City, Mich
Dravo Corp Inc, Neville Island, Pa
Dravo Corp Inc, Pittsburgh, Pa
Dravo Corp Inc, Wilmington, Del
Federal Shipbuilding Corp Inc, Newark, NJ
Froemming Brothers Inc, Milwaukee, Wis
General Engineering & Drydock Corp Inc, Alameda, Calif
Gibbs Gas Engine Corp Inc, Jacksonville, Fla
Globe Shipbuilding Corp Inc, Superior, Wis

Gulf Shipbuilding Corp Inc, Chickasaw, Ala
Jacobson Shipyard Inc, Oyster Bay, LI
Jeffersonville Boat & Machine Corp Inc, Jeffersonville, Ind
John H. Mathis Corp Inc, Camden, NJ
Kaiser Cargo Corp Inc, Richmond, Calif
G. Lawley & Sons Inc, Neponset, Mass
Leathem Smith Coal & Shipbuilding Corp Inc, Sturgeon Bay, Wis
Mare Island Navy Yard, Mare Island, NY
Nashville Bridge Corp Inc, Nashville, Tenn
Norfolk Navy Yard, Norfolk, Va
Penn-Jersey Shipbuilding Corp Inc, Camden, NJ
Pennsylvania Shipyards Inc, Beaumont, Texas
Philadelphia Navy Yard, Philadelphia, Pa
Puget Sound Bridge & Dredging Corp Inc, Seattle, Wash
Puget Sound Navy Yard, Seattle, Wash
Pullman-Standard Manufacturing Corp Inc, Chicago, Ill
Savannah Machine & Foundry Corp Inc, Savannah, Ga
Sullivan Drydock & Repair Corp Inc, Brooklyn, NY
Tampa Shipbuilding Corp Inc, Tampa, Fla
Walter Butler Shipbuilding Corp Inc, Superior, Wis
Walsh-Kaiser Shipbuilding Corp Inc, Rhode Island
Western Pipe & Steel Corp Inc, San Pedro, Calif
Willamette Iron & Steel Corp Inc, Portland, Ore
Winslow Marine Railway & Shipbuilding Corp Inc, Seattle, Wash

*Lorain* in 1945, on the north-east coast of the USA. She has two-tone grey camouflage painted very carefully aft. She has H/F D/F at the topmasthead and standard armament, except that the after 3″ gun has been replaced by a deckhouse for duty as a weather ship. *(US Bureau of Ships)*

After end of a DE with the final wartime armament pattern—single 5″/38, one quadruple, and two twin 40mm Bofors, all with directors, and two single 20mm Oerlikons right aft.
*(US National Archives)*

Type 277 radar aerial array at Halifax 1946. Note the heavy-looking support and motors, requiring a lattice mast to carry them, and the large circular network aerial.
*(Public Archives of Canada)*

# CHAPTER FIVE

# Armaments and Electronics

THROUGHOUT this book, and especially in the class chapters, a great amount of descriptive detail will be found regarding the individual gun outfits, radar sets fitted, and anti-submarine weapons and outfits.

This chapter sets out to supplement that detail, by explaining in each of these categories the types employed, the classes they covered, and the progression during the war years from one type to the next. It is hoped that this will be of equal interest to the specialised reader as to the more general.

In addition, operating and specification details are given for each type; in almost all cases these have come from official sources and are published in this form for the first time. As with the other statistics in this book, the passage of time since the war has produced some gaps, and also some conflicting figures; but in this chapter the reader will be able to compare together not only the differing types of weapon and electronics in one navy, but also between the navies. Only in the close-range weapons was there much uniformity between the United Kingdom and the United States, and even in this category there are some significant differences. Efforts were being made by the naval staffs during the war to introduce some uniformity, especially in these outfits, which needed maintenance wherever the ships went; but this chapter will also demonstrate how difficult a task they were tackling!

A shot of *Monnow*, with the first split Hedgehog fitted. The heavy sponsons under the mountings at the sides of the 4″ gundeck are clear. She was later transferred to the RCN. *(Imperial War Museum)*

A "LOCH" class frigate, showing the typical guns and radar sets for a ship of this class, in 1945. Forward there is a 4″ Mk.V gun, with the Double Squid mortar aft and above it. On the mast, there are radar aerials for Types 293 and FH4 (the latter is the H/F D/F aerial). Inset is the rig for a "BAY" class frigate, showing radar Types 277 and 290/291. Aft, twin 20mm. Oerlikons are on the after gundeck, with the Quadruple 2 pdr. Pom Pom overlooking the quarterdeck, where the Depth Charge rails complete the picture.

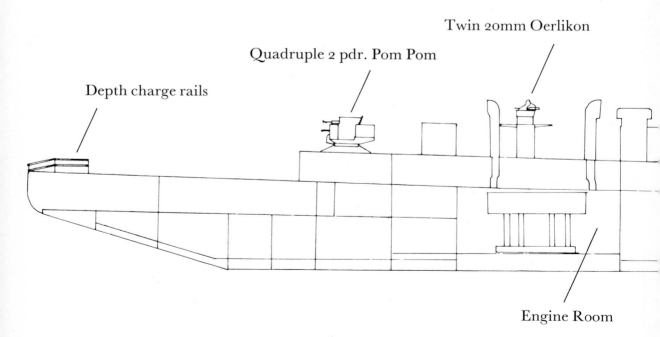

Twin 20mm Oerlikon

Quadruple 2 pdr. Pom Pom

Depth charge rails

Engine Room

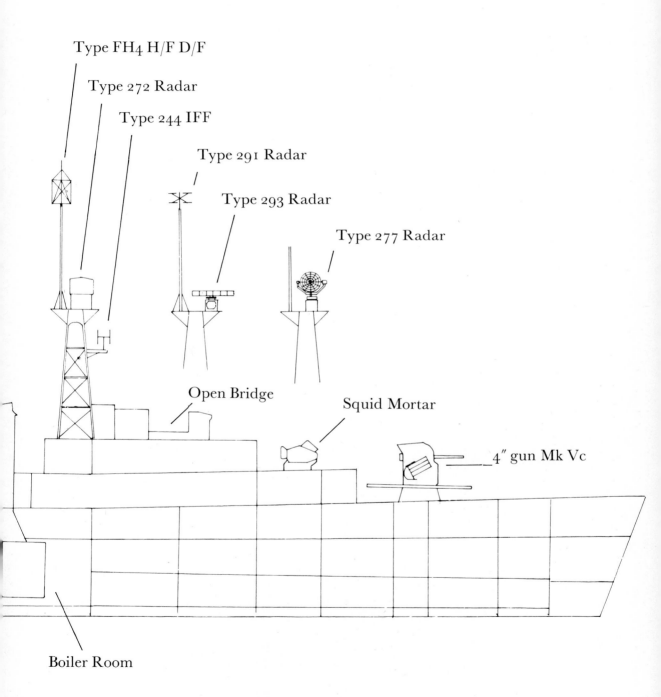

Type FH4 H/F D/F

Type 272 Radar

Type 244 IFF

Type 291 Radar

Type 293 Radar

Type 277 Radar

Open Bridge

Squid Mortar

4″ gun Mk Vc

Boiler Room

## ROYAL AND COMMONWEALTH NAVIES

### A. MAIN ARMAMENT

1. *4" GUN*, single, *Mark IX*, BL

    Mounting: Mark CP1, or Mark XX

Classes fitted: 'Flower, 'Dance', 'Bathurst' (some), 'Guillemot'

Photographs: *Campion, Charlock, Cotillion, Regina, Kamsack, Woodstock*

This was a gun of World War I vintage, still available in quantity at the beginning of World War II. It thus became the standard 4" gun for fitting in the earlier classes of new escorts, where twin 4" or 12 pounders were not fitted instead.

    Full operating details of this gun are no longer readily available; but the placing of orders for large numbers of 4" Mark XIX showed that it was seen as inadequate for the new A/A warfare conditions, even as early as that.

    In World War I these guns in most cases did not have shields, and while these were almost invariably added in World War II (except for some of the early 'Bathurst' class), the shapes of the shields were apt to vary somewhat, as can be seen in the photographs. In World War I it was recorded that this gun was first produced for use in capital ships, against the new torpedo-boat destroyers!

| | |
|---|---|
| Range: | probably 12,000 yds |
| Muzzle velocity: | 2,550 ft/sec |
| Rounds carried per gun: | 220 |
| Weight of projectile: | 31 lbs |
| Weight of gun: | $42\frac{1}{2}$ cwt, with breech mechanism |
| Length of gun: | 184.6 ins. |

The 4" Mark IX gun on the forecastle of the RCN 'Flower' class corvette *Athol* at Halifax, 31st January 1944. *(Public Archives of Canada)*

2. *4″ GUN*, single QF, *Mark V+, V++, or Vc*
    Mounting: HA Mark III+ or IV

Classes fitted: 'Loch, 'Algerine

Photographs: *Loch Arkaig, Loch Alvie, Loch Glendhu, Bramble, Stormcloud, Sault Ste*

*Marie*

This, too, was an older gun, but it could be mounted on an HA mounting, and was thus useful in anti-aircraft actions. It was therefore at first fitted in the 'Algerine' class fleet minesweepers, working in narrow seas, and in many early units no shield was fitted.

Later, 'Loch' class frigates were fitted with it, until the new mark XXI was available in sufficient numbers—which did not happen for this class in time, except for *Loch Veyatie*. The shield fitted was distinctive, and was also fitted to all later 'Algerine' class units.

The gun was semi-automatic, with fixed ammunition.

| | |
|---|---|
| Bore: | 45 cal |
| Maximum range: | 16,200 yds |
| Maximum altitude: | 30,000 ft |
| Rounds per minute: | 15-20 |
| Maximum elevation: | 80 deg |
| Maximum depression: | 5 deg |
| Muzzle velocity: | 2,625 ft/sec |
| Rounds carried per gun: | 350 |
| Weight of gun: | 3 tons |
| Weight of mounting: | 2 tons, 3 cwt, 1 qtr, 18 lbs |
| Length of projectile: | 44 ins |
| Weight of projectile (QF-FA): | 31 lbs |
| Weight of full charge: | 57/8 lbs |
| Weight of complete round: | 56 lbs |

3. *4″ GUN*, twin, *Mark XVI*
    Mounting: Mark XIX, or XXXIII, and RP50/51/52

*Classes fitted:* 'Black Swan', 'Hunt', 'Bay', RCN 'River'

*Photographs: Woodcock, Carnarvon Bay, Shelburne*

This was the very efficient standard twin 4″ mounting for all Commonwealth navies. Numbers produced limited it to what in effect were the A/A escort classes, plus the Canadian 'River' class.

It was first introduced in the 1937 Programme, and was put into quantity production. It had a very significant part to play in the English Channel, North Sea and Mediterranean battles throughout the war, and even in 1945 its presence greatly influenced the choice of escorts for the two fleets in the Far East, and it was the automatic choice for the new 'Bay' class for that theatre.

A spray and blast shield was fitted from the first, but this mounting did produce severe blast for the crew, and so as the war progressed the shield was extended aft on canvas supports or steel, on both the top and sides, until it became a well-protected mounting for the crew.

Later models were fitted with remote power control, and these guns were fitted in the RN classes in conjunction with a rangefinder director, fitted with Type 285 radar. The single forward mounting in the Canadian 'River' class did not have this director.

The guns were semi-automatic, with fixed ammunition.

| | |
|---|---|
| Bore: | 45 cal. |
| Maximum range: | 19,400 yds |
| Maximum altitude: | 38,000 ft |
| Rounds per minute: | 12 |
| Maximum elevation: | 80 deg |
| Maximum depression: | 10 deg |
| Muzzle velocity: | 2,600 ft/sec |
| Rounds carried per gun: | 220 (some RCN 'River' 250) |
| Barrel life: | 2,000 rounds |
| Weight of mounting: | 2 tons, 23 lbs. |
| Crew: | 20 |
| Length of projectile: | $44\frac{1}{2}$ ins |
| Weight of shell—QF(FA): | 35 lbs |
| Weight of complete round: | 66 lbs |
| Fuses used: | T, VT, or DA |

The twin 4″ mounting, Mark XVI. This one was on board the RCN *Prince Robert*, with gun drill in progress in July 1943. The shield has not yet been extended aft, as was usually done in escorts. *(Public Archives of Canada)*

4. *4" GUN*, single, *Mark XIX*
   Mounting: HA/LA Mk. XXIII, or IX, IX*

*Classes fitted:* 'River', 'Castle', RCN Mod 'Flower'

*Photographs: Test, Smiths Falls, Tillsonburg*

This was the first replacement 4" gun produced during the war years for these navies. It was a much neater-looking gun and shield than the old models it replaced. Due to the great need for guns for the numerous new escorts completing, it was only supplied to the new frigates and corvettes. The Canadian-built Modified 'Flower' class received it, whereas the few UK-built ships of that class did not. The 'Flower' class were not rearmed with it, partly due to the need to get the maximum number of guns to sea, and partly because by the time these new guns were coming off the production lines, building programmes of the new mass-production frigates and corvettes indicated that the original corvettes would, in any case, be phased out of service by the end of 1945.

Note the use planned for the succeeding 4" Mark XXI in rearming some of the existing classes of escort.

Orders for the Mark XIX were placed as follows:

| | | |
|---|---|---|
| 30.12.40 | 60 | |
| 27.7.40 | 40 | |
| 27.7.40 | 100 | |
| 8.1.41 | 200 | |
| 27.9.41 | 200 | |
| 27.9.41 | 200 | |
| 27.9.41 | 432 | Canadian order, for 'River' class frigates, and merchant ships |
| 28.5.42 | 200 | |
| 28.5.42 | 362 | Canadian order—138 guns retained by Canada |
| 28.5.42 | 500 | Australian order, reduced to 130. 80 were retained by the RAN |

To elaborate a little on the classes fitted, the Australian programme in fact included 44 of the 'Bathurst' class, though even official records in Australia do not agree on the actual numbers fitted, as the class chapter shows; in addition, the early units of the Australian 'River' class received this gun, though mounted on an HA/LA mounting, with a shield resembling the twin 4" Mark XVI. In addition, the three UK-built units of the 'Kiwi' class of the RNZN were marked for this gun, but from the photographs it is hard to tell whether in fact these were not Mark IX guns.

The gun was semi-automatic, with fixed ammunition.

| | |
|---|---|
| Bore: | 40 cal |
| Maximum range: | 9,500 yds |
| Maximum altitude: | 21,000 ft |

Rounds per minute:        15
Maximum elevation:        60 deg
Maximum depression:       10 deg
Muzzle velocity:          1,275 ft/sec
Rounds carried per gun:   200 (Can 'River' 252; Mod 'Flower' 270)
Weight of gun:            1 ton, 5 cwt, 3 qtrs, 12 lbs
Weight of mounting:       3 tons, 2 cwt, 3 qtrs, 14 lbs
Length of projectile:     44 ins
Weight of projectile:     35 lbs
Barrage sights,
    aim-off speeds:       100 and 200 knots

### 5. *4″ GUN*, single, *Mark XXI*
   Mounting: Mark XXIV

*Class fitted:* 'Loch' (1 ship only)

*Photographs: Loch Veyatie*

This gun was a further development from the Mark XIX, but before it could come off the production lines in large numbers the war was over. It is interesting to compare the production of these two guns with the maximum effort put by the United States into the ubiquitous 3″/50 cal gun, which appeared in all classes in large numbers. In the end it appears that only one of these guns was actually fitted, in the *Loch Veyatie,* the last unit of the 'Loch' class to be completed.

The gun was ordered from 1943 onwards, for fitting as follows:
32 'Loch' class (the 'Bay' class were not included in this);
46 'Castle' class, covering the ships later cancelled in both the UK and Canada;
26 'Algerine' class, planned for completion later than July 1944—note that some of these ships were not cancelled, but completed as before with 4″ Mark V.
108 for rearmament of RN 'River' class frigates;
18 for rearmament of Canadian 'River' class frigates—note that all RCN units of this class received twin 4″ mountings forward; this presumably was to replace the single 4″ Mark XIX fitted aft in a number of units.
50 for rearmament of RN 'Algerine' class;
41 for rearmament of Canadian-built 'Algerine' class;
note that most of the latter were serving with the RN. For the 'Algerine' class rearmament was scheduled to take place during refits in the second half of 1945, before going to the Far East. In the event, no 'River' or 'Algerine' class units

received this gun.

131 of the guns required for this programme would have been manufactured in Canada.

The gun was semi-automatic, with fixed ammunition.

| | |
|---|---|
| Bore: | 45 cal |
| Maximum range: | 19,400 yds |
| Maximum altitude: | 38,000 ft |
| Rounds per minute: | 15 |
| Maximum elevation: | 80 deg |
| Maximum depression: | 10 deg |
| Muzzle velocity; | 2,600 ft/sec |
| Weight of gun: | 1 ton, 10 cwt, 1 qtr, 11 lbs |
| Length of projectile: | 44 ins |
| Weight of projectile: | 35 lbs |
| Weight of full round: | 66 lbs |

6. *12 POUNDER GUN,* single, *Mark V*
   Mounting: Mark VA or IX, or IV or IV+ on HA/LA mounting

*Classes fitted:* Canadian 'River', Admiralty trawlers, 'Bangor' class

*Photographs: Inkpen, Oronsay, Prestonian, Granby*

This was the standard light gun still classed as main armament. It is interesting to see that, while the RN 'River' class carried two single 4″ Mark XIX, the Canadian units with twin 4″ Mark XVI carried this lighter gun aft, perhaps for stability reasons. Otherwise, this gun was only to be found in the trawlers, and in the 'Bangor' class fleet minesweepers.

| | |
|---|---|
| Bore: | 40 cal |
| Maximum range: | 11,500 yds |
| Maximum altitude: | 18,000 ft |
| Rounds per minute: | 15 |
| Maximum elevation: | 70 deg |
| Muzzle velocity: | 2,175 ft/sec |
| Rounds carried per gun: | 262 |
| Weight of gun: | 11 cwt, 2 qtrs |
| Length of projectile: | 11 ins |
| Weight of projectile: | 13 lbs |
| Weight of charge: | 2 lbs |
| Crew: | 5 |

12 pounder gun as main armament on the forecastle of the RCN 'Bangor' class fleet minesweeper *Chignecto,* at Esquimalt in December 1941. *(Public Archives of Canada)*

The frigate *Loch Veyatie,* the last of her class to be completed, with the only Mark XXI 4″ gun ever fitted, on her forecastle. This was the replacement gun for the 4″ Mark V, and for some of the Mark XIX. *(Wright & Logan)*

**4. 40mm BOFORS GUN**, single, hand-worked, *Mark I*
     Mounting: Marks VII, VIII, and IX

*Ships fitted:* Various, especially for Far East duty in 1945.
     No one class had it generally specified.

*Photographs: Tay, Essington, Calder, Laertes, Fierce*

This was essentially an Army type gun, numbers of which were fitted in RN ships later in the war, especially when fitting out for the Far East. The specification was in general the same as for the twin and American mountings, but a few details are included here:
The mounting could be hand-worked, or, in later versions, hydraulic powered, and controlled by radar or tachometric.

| | |
|---|---|
| Bore: | 56.25 cal |
| Maximum range: | 10,750 yds |
| Maximum altitude: | 23,500 ft |
| Maximum elevation: | 90 deg |
| Muzzle velocity: | 2,800 ft/sec |
| Rounds per minute: | 120 |
| Weight of mounting: | 6 cwt, 1 qtr, 3 lbs |
| Length of projectile: | $17\frac{3}{4}$ ins |
| Weight of projectile: | $4\frac{1}{2}$ lbs |

**5. 20mm OERLIKON**, single, *Marks IIA, IV, VIIA, VIIIA*

*Classes fitted:* All.

This became the standard desirable close-range weapon in all classes of escort, in all navies, including that of the United States. The gun was produced in quantity under licence, but despite all production efforts in the main countries the number available was insufficient to give all escorts their specified requirements before the change-over to 40mm Bofors came in 1944/45.
     The gun was mounted on a variety of single, hand-worked mountings, the differences largely being in efforts to lighten the weight of the steel pedestal. In some cases a shield was fitted, in two parts, which stands out clearly in the photographs. There was a clear distinction between those produced in the United States and other countries, in that the former had shields of two rectangular plates, while the latter had small, circular corners taken out at the upper inward corner to widen the gunlayer's view.
     The crew of this gun was two, with the gunlayer standing on the circular steps of a bandstand, which enabled him to swing the gun easily and quickly when tracking a fast aircraft. The second man supplied the spare drums of ammunition from the ready-use lockers. In sites where the bandstand could not easily be fitted, the gun was simply bolted to the deck.
     The gun was a fast firing one, but was subject to a number of stoppages. It was effective against fast-moving surface craft as well as against aircraft, and it replaced the quadruple 0.5″ gun, and, of course, the twin Lewis 0.303″ machine-guns, as it became more readily available.

| Bore: | 70 cal |
|---|---|
| Maximum range: | 6,000 yds |
| Maximum altitude: | 6,000 ft |
| Rounds per minute: | 400-500 |
| Maximum elevation: | 70 or 85 deg |
| Muzzle velocity: | 2,725 ft/sec |
| Rounds carried per gun: | 2,400 |
| Weight of gun: | 10 cwt, 12 lbs, with mtg |
| Crew: | 2 |
| Length of projectile: | 11 ins |
| Weight of round: | 125 grams |

Shell was explosive, self-destructing at maximum range, also tracer. An aim-off ring sight was fitted, which was converted to a gyro sight at a later stage.

### 6. *20mm OERLIKON*, single, *Mark IX*

*Classes fitted:* A few mountings appeared in some RN and RCN ships, but were not specified for particular classes.

This was a twin mounting, with two Oerlikons side by side, mounted on a single gun pedestal. A steel guide rod was fitted between the muzzles to connect with the safety rails mounted around the gun, to avoid hitting the ship's structure when traversing rapidly.

Only a few of these mountings appeared at sea in escorts, notably in Canadian-built 'Isles' class trawlers, and one or two of the 'Captain' class frigates, allocated to the English Channel and southern North Sea.

### 7. *20mm OERLIKON,* twin, *Mark XII and XIIA*

*Classes fitted:* All except US-built Lend-Lease ships and Admiralty trawlers. The number of mountings specified varied.

*Photographs: Kincardine, Bramble*

This was a very effective mounting, developed by the RN and produced in the UK and Canada only. It was not adopted by the USN.

The mounting was quite different from the other marks of Oerlikon. It consisted of a much larger, circular steel base, on which was mounted a wide steel tray with two standard Oerlikons mounted side by side on it. On the left of the guns the gunlayer sat on a fitted seat, with a shield all round it except at the back. The mounting was operated by a hydraulic system, and the gunlayer used an aircraft-type joystick to elevate and train at speed.

This was a very efficient mounting, and of course, as it could be fitted in the same space as a single Oerlikon, it doubled the number of guns wherever it was fitted. The usual sites were on the after gundeck house in frigates and corvettes, in the bridge wings rather later, and in both positions in 'Algerine' class minesweepers.

This mounting was not fitted at all in Lend-Lease ships, either because of the fitting of the hydraulic system required, or because the RN wished to retain the mountings after the war.

In 1945, when ships were being refitted under pressure for the two Far East fleets, and 2 pounders or Bofors were favoured in place of Oerlikons for use against the Japanese suicide planes, some of these mountings were adapted to carry a 2 pounder single pom pom, in place of the two Oerlikons; this is referred to separately in this chapter.

The gun itself was identical with that described above under the single mounting; these notes therefore cover only the twin mounting itself.

| | |
|---|---|
| Weight of mounting: | 2,125 lbs |
| Weight of ready-use ammunition: | 1,464 lbs |
| Weight of RU lockers: | 1,344 lbs |
| Total weight on deck: | 4,478 lbs |
| Additional ammunition: | 1,288 lbs |

8. *0.5″ GUN*, quadruple, *Marks M, I\*\*, II\*, and III.*

*Classes fitted:* Early 'Black Swan', early 'Hunt', 'Bangor', a few 'Flower'

*Photographs: Lowestoft, Primula, Warrego.*

This gun and mounting was available in some numbers at the outbreak of war, and at that time, with the pom poms, constituted the escorts' main anti-aircraft armament. Like the USN's 1.1″ gun, however, it was not sufficiently effective, and while it was retained until Oerlikons were available in some numbers, it was gradually phased out from the newer escort classes by the middle of the war.

The guns were automatic and water-cooled. They were mounted vertically, one above the other, each in separate trunnions. These were linked together, so that all four guns elevated and depressed together. Laying was by handwheel and gearing, with the gunlayer on the left of the mounting. The ammunition was loaded on belts, which were stowed in drums, much as in the later Oerlikons.

The gun was specified to make $2\frac{1}{2}$ hits in 10 seconds on a target at 1,000 yards, if the target remained within the gun's pattern, which was 60 feet wide and 50 feet high at that range.

| | |
|---|---|
| Bore: | 0.5″ |
| Maximum range: | 1,500 yds |
| Rounds per minute: | 700 approx |
| Muzzle velocity: | 2,520 ft/sec |
| Ammunition drums: | 200 rounds each |
| Rate of fire: | 800 rounds in approx 20 secs, reloading in 30 secs |
| Weight of 4 guns complete: | 2,440, 3,128 or 2,932 lbs, depending on the mark |
| Weight of bullet: | 1.32 ozs |
| Weight of complete round: | 2.9 ozs |
| Weight of loaded drum: | 60 lbs |
| Weight of single gun, with waterjacket full: | 62 lbs |
| Length of gun: | 52 ins |

| Length of barrel: | 31.11 ins |
|---|---|
| Length of round: | 4.28 ins |

## 9. 2  *ROCKET FLARES,* RFL *Mark I*

*Classes fitted:* All main classes

This flare was introduced primarily for North Atlantic U-boat warfare, as the starshell used in the main armament of escorts was insufficiently bright in identifying conning towers in bad conditions. It was so efficient that it became a standard fitting for escorts, and was extensively used in the English Channel and southern North Sea, and in the Mediterranean.

It was fired electrically by a hand push, from triple launchers mounted on the outside of the sides of the gunshields of the forward main armament. This gave a spread of six flares, and the rails were angled to provide a pattern when fired together.

Single separate launchers were developed for use by Coastal Forces, and these were also mounted in threes on the single 3″/50 guns in the 'Captain' class frigates on English Channel/North Sea duty, before the 3″ gunshields were fitted to that class. In other classes, the launchers were fitted to the single forward gun, or to B gun where there were two guns forward; in the 'Captain' class frigates mentioned, the sets of three single launchers were fitted both to B gun, and to X gun aft, so that several spreads of rocket flares could be fired at once, when in action with groups of E-boats.

As these flares were classed as fireworks, all had to be stowed on deck, and large steel ready-use lockers were required for this purpose. These show up well in the photographs, around the gun on which the launchers were mounted.

The rocket propellant was solid.

| Length of rocket, excluding fins: | $50\frac{3}{4}$ ins |
|---|---|
| Diameter of rocket: | 2.25 ins |
| Weight of rocket: | 13 lbs |
| Weight of triple launcher: | 4 cwts, 1 qtr the pair |

### *Close-range armament for British Pacific Fleet escorts*

Learning from US Navy experience in the Pacific, the RN decided, early in 1945, to upgrade the close-range weapon armament in all escort vessels allocated to the Far East.

At first, this was seen to mean the maximum number of guns available, including large numbers of 20mm Oerlikons; but US Navy experience gave the following picture, once the suicide bombers started coming in:

a) 1 Bofors barrel=1 pom pom barrel=2 Oerlikon barrels, against Zeke aircraft;

b) 1 Bofors barrel=2 pom pom barrels for torpedo bombers and longer-range defence, the objective being to shoot down all aircraft before they could close to within 500 yards.

c) It was therefore essential to increase the numbers of 40mm Bofors wherever possible, in addition to existing 40mm and 20mm outfits. Where topweight would not permit of both, 40mm should replace 20mm mountings, and single power-operated pom poms, Mark XVI, or single Bofors, even on hand-worked mountings, were to replace even the twin power-operated Oerlikons. It was found that 2 pounder barrels could be mounted on twin Oerlikon power-operated mountings, and these were known as 2 pounder Mark VI*.

But availability of the heavier guns was, of course, the critical path, and the few photographs available of escorts which completed refits for the Far East before VJ-Day show a mixed picture of actual fittings.

Thus, *Magpie* and *Mermaid,* of the Modified 'Black Swan' class, were each to receive two twin Bofors, with radar control, before leaving in May 1945.

All 'Black Swan', 'Hunt', 'Bay' and 'Captain' class ships were to receive the maximum number of Bofors available, and an interesting example was the 'Captain' class ships refitting as Coastal Forces Control Ships for the East Indies Fleet; as described in the class chapter, the close-range outfit was first upgraded to 1 twin Bofors and 15 single Oerlikons, and then changed during the refit to 1 twin Bofors and 7 single Bofors, with all Oerlikons being removed.

Availability in general was seen as being:

4-barrel Pom Poms Mk VIIXP—many were available, but they were too heavy for general mounting.

Single Power Pom Poms Mark XVI—80/100 were available from Coastal Forces boats being reduced to reserve, and gyro gunsights could easily be added.

Twin Utility Bofors—only just becoming available, with gyro gunsights, and these had already been allocated to British Pacific Fleet ships.

Single Power Bofors—none available.

Single Hand-worked Bofors Mark IIICN—an Army adaptation, of which some were available.

*See photographs:* 'River' class— *Tay, Outremont, Swale* 'Captain' class— *Essington/ Calder*

The ubiquitous American 3″/50 calibre gun. This was installed almost universally in US-built escorts throughout the war. It was so light that two mountings could be carried aboard a PC. *(US National Archives)*

## B. CLOSE-RANGE ARMAMENT

1. *6 POUNDER GUN,* single, *Mark IIA*
   Mounting: Mark VII

*Classes fitted:* Some 'Flower' and 'River' on North Atlantic

This was really an Army gun, a Hotchkiss 2.25 ins weapon, some of which were fitted on the upper bridge, or less commonly forward of the bridge, in some of the North Atlantic escorts. It was intended for use during close-range actions with U-boats, when the main armament particularly was unable to depress far or quickly enough to be effective.

A twin version of this gun was fitted in a few of the old 'V and W' class destroyers operating against E-boats on the UK east coast, but these fall outside the scope of this book.

The gun was hydraulically operated, with fixed ammunition.

| | |
|---|---|
| Bore: | 43 cal |
| Maximum range: | 6,200 yds |
| Maximum height: | 1,450 ft |
| Rounds per minute: | 80 max, 72 normal |
| Maximum elevation: | 12 deg |
| Muzzle velocity: | 2,150 ft/sec |
| Crew: | 9 |
| Weight of gun: | 10 cwt |
| Length of projectile: | 21 ins |
| Weight of projectile: | 9 lbs |

Single 2-pounder pom pom, fitted aft in the Canadian corvette *Stratford*, off St John's, November, 1943.

2. *2 POUNDER POM POM,* 1.575 ins, single
     Hand-operated, Mark VIII on Mark VIII mounting
     Power-operated, Mark XVI on Mark XVI mounting

*Classes fitted:* Frigates and corvettes, fleet minesweepers.
     (Not all, a variation on Oerlikon outfits)

*Photographs: frontispiece, Fennel, Holmes, Ekins*

This was a World War I gun available in large quantities during World War II, and very effective it proved in A/A warfare—so much so that in 1945, when escorts were being refitted for service in the Far East, with maximum A/A requirements, this gun in its power-operated version was the next best choice to the 40mm Bofors.

It had a very distinctive thudding sound in operation, and the flame guard fitted on the barrel mouth was also unique, together with the less distinctive guard on the Bofors.

The gun could fire starshell and tracer, and the ammunition was loaded in belts. It was a reliable gun, with few stoppages, and was popular with the escort crews.

| | |
|---|---|
| Bore: | 40 cal |
| Maximum range: | 5,000 yds |
| Maximum altitude: | 10,000 ft |
| Rounds per minute: | 90-120 |
| Maximum elevation: | 80 deg |
| Muzzle velocity: | 2,300 ft/sec |
| Rounds per barrel: | 1,800 |
| Weight of mounting: | 2,464 lbs |
| Weight of RU ammunition: | 840 lbs |
| Weight of RU lockers: | 448 lbs |
| Total weight on deck: | 4,478 lbs |
| Additional ammunition: | 1,288 lbs |
| Crew: | 2 |

3. *2 POUNDER POM POM,* 1.575 ins, quadruple, *Mark VIII or VIIIA*
     Mounting: Mark VII*

*Classes fitted:* Some 'Black Swan', 'Hunt' and 'Loch' classes.

*Photographs: Black Swan, Loch Achray, Loch More, Wilton*

This was an excellent RN mounting, and until the appearance of the twin, and then the quadruple, 40 mm Bofors the most favoured multiple close-range weapon for A/A use during the war years.

Its fitting in escorts was initially limited to the two classes with warship specifications, but it was specified as the main after armament for the A/S 'Loch' class frigates.

The guns themselves were four of the same 2 pounder pom poms used singly. The crew numbered 8. Otherwise, the technical details of this mounting are the same as for the single gun.

## UNITED STATES NAVY, INCLUDING LEND-LEASE SHIPS

### A. MAIN ARMAMENT

1. *3"/50 calibre GUN, Mark 22*

*Classes fitted:* DEs, PFs, PCs, PCEs, AMs

This was the standard main armament for all USN escort classes, until the single 5" was introduced in some of the Destroyer Escort classes in 1944/45.

It was a simple gun, produced in large quantities. It was relatively light, and although there were sometimes difficulties with some of the fixed ammunition, it was highly reliable and much favoured. It produced a very loud bang but relatively little blast. A shield was not fitted in USN ships with this gun until the DERs started appearing in 1945; but the RN added a standard alteration to fit spray shields to all three guns in the 'Captain' class frigates, and this was extended later to the 'Colony' and 'Catherine' classes, but not to the 'Kil' class. This shield was of a distinctive shape, and stands out in the RN class photographs; it was at first fitted only to B gun, the duty gun, until supplies of shields were readily available. By no means all Lend-Lease ships received this modification—see, for example, *Caicos* refitted as a Fighter Direction Ship in 1945.

| | |
|---|---|
| Bore: | 50 cal |
| Maximum range: | 14,600 yds/at 45° elev |
| Maximum altitude: | 29,800ft/at 85° elev |
| Rounds per minute: | 20 |
| Maximum elevation: | 85 deg |
| Maximum depression: | 10 deg |
| Muzzle velocity: | 2,700 ft/sec |
| Weight of gun barrel: | 1,240 lbs |
| Total weight of assembly: | 6,700 to 7,510 lbs |
| Oscillating weight: | 3,180 to 3,780 lbs |
| Recoiling weight: | 1,850 lbs |
| Brake load: | 27,500 lbs |
| Trunnion pressure, horizontal fire: | 27,500 lbs |
| Trunnion pressure, 85° elevation fire: | 31,100 lbs |
| Training limits: | 360 deg maximum |
| Weight of projectiles—AA | 13.05 lbs |
| illuminating | 13.07 lbs |
| cartridge | 11 lbs |

2. *5"/38 calibre GUN, single, Mark 30*

*Classes fitted:* Later DE types, and some refitted DES.

This gun was much heavier than the 3"/50, and was primarily developed as secondary armament for large warships, and as the main armament for the new fleet destroyers. As the Pacific war progressed, however, this gun was seen as being more effective in destroyer escorts which were used in the front line, where suicide planes were attacking the radar pickets. So the last two types of destroyer escort switched to this gun, as did some of the refitted 'Buckley' type. This entailed restructuring the ship forward of the bridge and moving the depth-charge throwers further forward so that they were clear of the larger gun mounting.

This gun had a large, totally enclosed shield, and it will be seen that the total weight of the assembly was greatly in excess of that of the 3″/50; single mountings forward and aft were, therefore, as much as the destroyer escorts could take.

The gun was classed as dual-purpose, enclosed, base ring type. The gun itself was Mark 12, the shield mark 38, and a large number of modifications were made to each.

| | |
|---|---|
| Bore: | 38 cal |
| Maximum range: | 18,200 yds/at 45°10′ elev |
| Maximum altitude: | 37,200 ft/at 85° elev |
| Rounds per minute: | 20 |
| Maximum elevation: | 85 deg |
| Maximum depression: | 10 deg |
| Training limits: | 300 deg |
| Muzzle velocity: | 2,600 ft/sec |
| Shield thickness: | 0.25 ins |
| Total weight of assembly: | 45,000 lbs |
| Total weight of shield: | 8,740 lbs |
| Oscillating weight: | 14,090 lbs |
| Recoiling weight: | 8,150 lbs |
| Brake load: | 77,600 lbs |

US Navy quadruple 40 mm Bofors mounting, in December 1944. This was an excellent mounting, to obtain the maximum close-range firepower in the Pacific, and some were mounted in the main after close-range position of later and refitted destroyer escorts. *(US National Archives)*

Trunnion pressure, horizontal fire:   78,900 lbs
Trunnion pressure, 85° elevation fire: 91,630 lbs
Weight of barrel:   3,990 lbs
Weight of projectile: A/A common   55.2 lbs
Weight of cartridge:   27.5 lbs

## B. CLOSE-RANGE

1. *40 mm BOFORS,* quadruple *Mark 2*

*Classes fitted:* Normally, only the later destroyer escorts

This was the ultimate in close-range weapons in any navy during World War II. It represented the best in the American talent for developing, and then producing in quantities, a reliable and impressive gun mounting.

The Pacific need for ever greater close-range firepower to deal with the Japanese suicide planes produced the requirement for first the maximum number of A/A weapons to throw up a curtain of fire round the fleet and individual ships, and then for the maximum number of Bofors, as the proven best weapon for destruction of aircraft at the longest range, before they could get close enough to make their final dive.

So the Oerlikon, while still in service in great numbers, gave way in new and refitted ships to Bofors in a variety of different forms, and this quadruple mounting was the largest and best.

In escorts it only appeared in the main after close-range position in the later destroyer escorts; but contrast this with the quadruple 1.1″ mounting found in the very same position in the early destroyer escorts only three years earlier!

Indeed, the pace of USN thinking on close-range weapons is well demonstrated by the fact that even this quadruple Bofors mounting was soon seen as inadequate, and the excellent post-war twin and quadruple 3″ mounting was developed to replace it—the gun which, through most of the war, had been the standard main armament of all United States escort classes!

The gun mounting was open or part shielded, of the base ring type.

Bore:   60 cal
Maximum range:   11,000 yds at 42° elev
Maximum altitude:   22,800 ft at 90° elev
Rounds per minute:   160 per barrel
Maximum elevation:   90 deg
Maximum depression:   15 deg
Training limits:   720 deg
Muzzle velocity:   2,890 ft/sec
Total weight of assembly:   24,900 lbs
Weight of shield:   1,700 lbs
Oscillating weight, four guns   5,700 lbs
Recoiling weight, per gun:   490 lbs
Brake load, per gun:   4,800 lbs
Barrel weight:   202 lbs
Ammunition self-destroying at:   4,000-5,000 yds

Weight of projectile A/A:        4.75 lbs
Weight of cartridge:             2.5 lbs
Power-driven mounts had maximum speeds of 24 degrees per second in elevation, 30 degrees per second in training.

## 2. *40mm BOFORS,* twin *Mark I*

*Classes fitted:* All DE types, PFs, later PCEs

This was fitted increasingly in the above classes of escorts, as supplies became available. But the early DEs had to be content with the quadruple 1.1″ mounting, and even in 1945 there were not enough mountings available for fitting RCN and RN 'River' class frigates proceeding to the Pacific.

The mounting was an excellent one, and very popular; it had its own director, usually mounted in a small, superimposed bandstand just forward of the gun mounting itself, or aft of it, in the few cases where this mounting was installed forward of the bridge.

Total weight of assembly:        13,200 lbs
Oscillating weight, two guns:    3,450 lbs
Operating system was manual drive, local control, or automatic.
The fire control system was Mark 63.
No gunshield was fitted.
Training limits were: 360 deg.
All details of the gun itself are identical with those above.

*NOTE.* A very similar twin Bofors mounting was fitted in RN escorts—'Black Swan' and 'Bay' class. The above details are sufficient to cover these mountings also—the RN Hazemeyer mounting did not appear in escorts during the war years.

A single 40mm Bofors gun aboard a USN Patrol Craft near the Anzio beachhead in May 1944 *(US Navy)*

### 3. *40mm BOFORS,* single

*Classes fitted:* Some destroyer escorts, some PCEs, some PCs.
In RN ships, escorts refitting for the Far East received some of these mountings

Full details of these mountings are not to hand, but the gun was a standard Bofors, similar in all respects to those described above. The mounting was during the war years a simple, hand-worked one, and was in many cases ex-Army equipment. The fitting again arose out of the need to fit as many 40mm Bofors as possible in 1944/45, in ships proceeding to the Pacific campaign where the maximum weight of firepower was essential.

### 4. *20mm OERLIKON,* single, various marks

*Classes fitted:* All escort classes

Maximum production of these guns was made during the middle war years, and the specified number of guns per escort was high, as described in the class chapters.
The United States Navy only fitted the standard single mounting, and the twin mountings to be found in the RN/RCN sections did not appear.
All details of this mounting are identical with that described under the RN sections.

### 5. *1.1″ GUN,* quadruple, *Mark 2*

*Classes fitted:* Early destroyer escorts

This gun was available in some quantity when the United States entered the war, and it was fitted in the early destroyer escorts, in the main after close-range position, later occupied by the twin Bofors mountings. This was mainly because, as in other countries, the rate of gun production was slower than that of the new hulls and engines, but the mounting was not found to be very efficient, and in most ships fitted it was replaced by twin Bofors at refit, while no mountings of this type were fitted after the middle of 1943.
The gun had no shield, and the barrels were mounted horizontally, as seen in the photograph. Operating selection was manual drive, local control, or automatic, and drive was hydraulic.

| | |
|---|---|
| Bore: | 75 cal |
| Maximum range: | 7,400 yds at 40°53′ elev |
| Maximum altitude: | 19,000 ft at 90° elev |
| Rounds per minute: | 150 |
| Maximum elevation: | 110 deg |
| Maximum depression: | 15 deg |
| Training limits: | 360 deg |
| Muzzle velocity: | 2,700 ft/sec |
| Total weight of assembly: | 14,000 lbs |
| Oscillating weight, four guns: | 5,000 lbs |
| Recoiling weight, four guns: | 840 lbs |

| Brake load, four guns: | 17,500 lbs |
| Barrel weight, per gun: | 556 lbs |
| Weight of projectile: | 0.917 lbs |
| Weight of cartridge: | 0.720 lbs |

Power-driven mounts had a maximum speed of 24 degrees per second in elevation, 30 degrees per second in training.

US Navy quadruple 1.1″ gun mounting, December 1942. This was fitted in the main after close-range position in the earlier destroyer escorts, until the newer and more effective twin Bofors mountings became available. *(US National Archives)*

# RADAR

*Introduction*

In the design and development of the optimum ocean escort vessel in World War II, nothing was more important than the development and installation of new weapons and detection devices.

Of the latter, radar was by far the most important, in all the major navies. First developed in the UK, it was known in its early years as RDF (radio direction finding), and its name was only changed to Radar in 1943, in line with USN nomenclature.

Basically, the radar system acted above the surface, as Asdic acted below it; a pulse was sent out electrically, and was reflected back by any metallic object —wood did reflect, but not nearly as well. This reflection was returned to the receiver in the sending ship, and was shown visually to the operator on a screen.

At first, this screen was called an 'A' scan, and gave a green horizontal line of light on a cathode ray tube, like a miniature television set. The range was calibrated along this line of light, and when an echo (reflection) was received, a blip, or vertical spike, appeared in the green line at the marked range of the object reflecting the electrical pulse.

Later, by 1942, Plan Position Indicators (PPIs) had been developed, and added to existing sets. Still on a cathode ray tube, the echoes were presented in plan form, with the ship's position in the centre of the circle, and range circles spreading out from that. The pulse was shown as a sweeping green line, and as it revolved round the circle it left a green blip wherever it came across an echo. This blip would last for rather longer than one sweep of the green line.

Skilled operators could interpret these PPIs in increasing detail, giving course and speed of the echo, size, and even probable type of ship. Other developments gave identification and, in the case of air warning sets, the height also.

From the viewpoint of this book, it is the identification of the various radar and allied aerials in the photographs that is important. For this purpose, notes follow, with photographs where available, on the various main types of radar to which reference is made in the captions to the photographs and in the specifications of the individual classes.

Too much emphasis should not be placed on the type numbers, as all types were subject to many modifications, which changed the aerial arrays almost beyond recognition. The Type 286, for example, with a fixed masthead aerial, became the Type 286M with a rotating array; the Type 286P with a higher powered transmitter, and with other lesser modifications, the Type 286PM, PQ, and PQ*. It developed from there, with the same 214Mhz equipment, towards the Types 290 and 291, with their succeeding 'families'.

*RN Radar and H/F D/F policy for escorts in 1945*

In January 1945, with the greater diversity and efficiency of the radar sets becoming available, the RN revised its policy for escort vessels, with an eye also to the operational needs of escorts going out in numbers to the Far East in that year. The following plan emerged, though it was subject, as always, to the right sets being available at the right time, and, as the photographs will show, was not always followed strictly at refit time.

*A/A ESCORTS* were to have Type 293 or Type 272, plus Type 291, and H/F D/F. These were the Modified 'Black Swan' and 'Bay' classes—the 'Hunt' class appear to have stayed with their existing Types 271, 291, and 285.

*A/S ESCORTS* were to have Type 277 (Type 972 if available, which was doubtful), plus H/F D/F. This covered the 'River', 'Loch' and 'Castle' classes, though, in the event, neither RN nor RCN 'Castle' class ships were allocated to the Far East.

*TYPE 291* was still seen as an important set, to give 40-mile range air warning cover. It needed a clear field above all structures, and therefore usually took the topmasthead position. It was approved that 50% of all 'River' class frigates allocated to the Far East should receive Type 291 in this position, in place of H/F D/F.

*H/F D/F* This was seen as essential for A/S escorts, though it was agreed that it was not essential for A/A escorts. Thus, while some 'Black Swan' and 'Hunt' class ships already fitted retained this set, it was not fitted in the 'Bay' class.

As forward policy, it was thought better in further new construction to put Type 291 forward at the topmasthead, and the H/F D/F on a pole mast aft. This also would facilitate the fitting of more advanced H/F D/F sets, VH/F D/F and UH/F D/F, Types RU1 and RU4, with heavier aerials, at a later date.

It was agreed that, if supply of sets permitted, Types RU1 or RU4 should be fitted in one-third of the 'Bay' class ships going to the British Pacific Fleet, thus covering the existing radar frequencies. The RCN was fitting Type DAU in 'River' class ships refitting for the British Pacific Fleet.

*See photographs: Black Swan, Outremont, Loch Arkaig, Burghead Bay.*

*RN/RCN Radar sets*

*SURFACE/AIR WARNING* The sets are listed roughly in chronological order of the years in which they were first introduced; but the earlier types usually continued right through to the end of the war, with many modifications to keep their performance as comparable as possible with the newer sets.

*TYPE 286* An early RDF set, with fixed aerial, of simple bedstead type, so that initially the search had to be carried out by aiming the ship!

Presentation was on a simple 'A' scan; a similar set was fitted in early RCN 'Flower' and 'Bangor' class ships, though the aerial is different, resembling a single long fish-bone type, fixed fore and aft.

*See photographs:* RN—*Garth, Meynell, Lamerton, Shearwater*
RCN—*Chilliwack, Arvida*

*TYPE 271* The mainstay of the anti-submarine escorts, in Western Approaches 'Flower' class corvettes, from its introduction in 1941 to the end of the war.

Type 271 radar lantern on the bridge of an 'Algerine' class escort vessel at Halifax in 1946. The two cheese-shaped transmitter receiver units can be seen through the perspex, and the quadruple egg-timer aerial of the Type 244 interrogator is mounted on top. The M/F D/F aerial is, unusually, mounted aft and above it, rather than in front of the bridge. *(Public Archives of Canada)*

The set had a directional beam and power rotation from the outset, with a broad elevation to compensate for the heavy rolling of small ships in the North Atlantic. The aerial was in two parts, a transmitter and a receiver, mounted one above the other in connecting cheese-shaped reflectors. The set sent out pulses of $1\frac{1}{4}$ microseconds each.

Part of the power output needed was attached to the aerial array, which was, in consequence, covered to protect it in heavy weather. In early installations this cover, known as the lantern, was of a wooden framework with glass panels; but later a cast perspex dome was evolved, which shows up in later illustrations.

A PPI was also added in later versions. The developing stages of this set are marked by letters added as a suffix, ie Type 271P and 271Q. The initial output of this set was only 5 kilowatts, but with the addition of the 'strapped' magnetron this rose to no less than 90 kilowatts in the Q version.

Type 244, the IFF interrogator set, often had its aerial added on the top of the Type 271 lantern, revolving with the aerials inside it.

In the 'Flower' class, Type 271 was always sited on the bridge, but it was moved to various positions, including the bridge wings, to minimise the effects of back echoes from the funnel and masts.

In the 'River' class it was always fitted on the back of the bridge, but in the 'Hunt' class, with a gunnery director in that position, it was sited on the searchlight platform aft, where added in later years.

Note the relatively low position of this aerial, due to overall size and weight, compared with the American Type SL, sited high on the tall pole mast of the DEs and PFs.

In RN ships the height above sea level did not usually exceed 32-48 feet. In calm seas, as improvements were made to the set, there was a gradual rise in the U-boat detections made, from 1,000 yards to 4,000 yards, but even with the Type 271P there was a sharp drop beyond 4,000 yards. In rough seas there was much lower detection at close ranges, due to the rolling of the escort vessel and the U-boat being lost in the sea return from the waves. The reliable maximum range, with the PPI added in the Type 271Q, was 4,500 yards.

A type similar to Type 271, designated Type RXC, was fitted in many RCN 'River' class units—the lantern appeared to be identical with the RN type.

*See photographs:  Shelburne, Arvida, Kamsack, Midland*
*Later versions: Dacres, Bleasdale, Betony, Stormcloud*

*Type 272*  A later version of Type 271. Usually found in the Modified 'Black Swan' class sloops, and in those units of the 'Loch' and 'Castle' classes not fitted at the outset with Type 277.

The aerial lantern was smaller than that of Type 271, but was usually of the wooden slat and glass panel variety. A possible variant is the perspex domes seen in the later units of the 'Isles' class trawlers.
*See photographs:  Chanticleer, Dumbarton Castle, Tillsonburg*

*TYPE 290/291*  This started as an early set, which was improved during the war years and retained in the escort classes with twin 4" main armament. It may, therefore, best be found in photographs of the 'Black Swan', 'Hunt', 'Bay' and RCN Modified 'Flower' classes.

It was primarily an air warning set, but it had surface capability too. It was especially important to the 'Black Swan' and 'Hunt' classes, before Type 271/272 was available to them, and was retained after the latter was added. As the supply of radar sets increased in the later war years, this set was also to be found in the A/S—M/S trawlers.

The aerial was light-weight, and was, therefore, nearly always mounted at the topmasthead, though in a few cases it was mounted on a pole mast aft. At first it was rotated by hand, and then by power, though in the early days of the latter overheating was likely to occur if the set was used continually for long periods.

'A' scan presentation was standard at first, but PPIs were added from 1943 onwards. The aerial resembled four 'X's, with short cross-bars.

*See photographs: Frontispiece, Hunt, Largo Bay, Ingonish, Shippigan, Belleville, Oronsay*

A galaxy of aerials at Halifax! Type 291 aerials at the mainmasthead in the foreground, with the egg-timer Type 253 below; note the rotating motor fitted at the foot of the former. On the 'Algerine' foremast at left, the birdcage of the H/F D/F is at the masthead, Type 86M R/T aerial at the starboard yardarm, and the American respondor, Type ABK at the port side. The Type 271 radar lantern on the bridge has the older-type slatted framework. *(Public Archives of Canada)*

*TYPE 277* The high definition set, seen in the later war years as the radar answer to the A/S escorts' needs—see the plans for installation, outlined in the 'River' class chapter especially.

The heavy dish aerial was about the first of its kind to be fitted in ships as small as escorts, though this type of aerial became a familiar sight in post-war years.

The 'Loch' and 'Castle' classes, for which it was specified, received a sturdy lattice mast, on top of which it could be mounted to obtain maximum range; due to production difficulties, a number of units of both classes were first commissioned with Type 272 in the same position, but Type 277 was usually installed later, as it became available.

Type 277 was also specified for 'River' class frigates fitting out for the Far East in 1945. The photograph of *Tay* shows this installed on a short lattice platform at the back of the bridge, in the old Type 271 position; this avoided the need for replacing the pole mast with a lattice to carry it, but probably reduced the performance of the set. *Swale*, refitted in Cape Town before being manned by South Africa, also received the set in the same way. RCN frigates did not seem to have these sets available in 1945, though specified, and Type SU was fitted in lieu in some cases.

*See photographs: Tay, Loch Alvie, Loch Fyne, Bowmanville*

*TYPE 293* This was a more advanced surface/air warning set, with gunnery control target indication capabilities. It was fitted from 1945 on in fleet destroyers, and appears in 'Bay' class frigates at that time, though not in the other escort classes.

The aerial array was a large cheese-shaped section, of relatively shallow depth, and was always mounted at the top of a lattice mast, not on a pole mast.

*See photograph: Largo Bay*

*TYPE 268* A smaller set, installed in the later war years in escorts. It combined effectiveness with compactness, and gave PPI displays not only at the main set, but also by slaves at the plot and on the bridge.

The aerial array was a small, cheese-shaped one, and can be seen in later photographs of 'Algerine' class fleet minesweepers.

*See photographs: Algerine, Cheerful, Fierce*

*Gunnery direction sets*

*TYPE 285* A gunnery radar set, only fitted in escorts on the gunnery director for twin 4″ guns in 'Hunt' class destroyers, 'Black Swan' class sloops, and later in 'Bay' class frigates.

Of multiple fish-bone type, it is clear in a number of photographs of ships of these classes. It was good on bearing, but not so good in giving an accurate elevation.

*See photographs: Puckeridge, Chanticleer, Padstow Bay*

*TYPE 282* A later set, developed for fitting on power-operated twin 40mm Bofors mountings, such as the Hazemeyer mountings, found in 'Black Swan' class sloops and 'Bay' class frigates. It could also be fitted on pom pom directors, but there was rarely room to fit the latter in escort vessels.

*Interrogation—Friend or foe*

*TYPES 242, 244, 253P.* These were the RN/RCN IFF sets. The transmitter sent out a distinctive pulse, which would be triggered off in the receiving or detected ship, and would activate the receiver, or transpondor. The transmission was controlled by an operator in the sending ship, but the receiver worked entirely automatically, and the ship detected would not know it had sent a friendly reply. The system was especially useful to close fighting at night in inshore waters, or when escorts were rejoining a convoy at night.

Type 244, with four egg-timer aerials disposed like a weather vane on a central pole, was the interrogator. It was mounted either atop a Type 271 lantern or separately, on a spur on the mast, pole, or lattice. It operated on an 'A' scan.

Types 242 and 253P were the transpondors, on the interrogated ship. Of single egg-timer type, they were light, and easily mounted on light spurs on the yards or yardarms of escort vessels.

*See photographs: Alert, Ekins*

*Operating Details of* RN/RCN *Radar sets*

| Type No | Frequency (Mhtz/Mc/s) | Wavelength | Power output | Range |
|---------|-----------------------|------------|--------------|-------|
| 286 | 214 | 1.5 metres | Not known | Not known |
| 271 | 3,000 | 10 cm | 90 | 10/25 miles |
| 272 | 3,000 | 10 cm | 90 | 10/25 miles |
| 290/291 | 214 | 1.5 metres | Not known | Not known |
| 277 | 3,000 | 10 cm | 500 | 25/35 miles |
| 293 | 3,000 | 10 cm | 500 | $12\frac{1}{2}$ miles 200/20,000 ft |
| 285 | 600 | 50 cm | 25/50 | $8\frac{1}{2}$ miles |
| 282 | 600 | 50 cm | 25/50 | $3\frac{1}{2}$ miles |

## AMERICAN RADAR SETS

*SURFACE WARNING* These sets were developed to some extent from the British research results. It is interesting, in examining the results, to see how America received and adapted these ideas (while also carrying out radar research of its own), and put a few standard radar sets of high quality and advanced design into rapid production; this resulted in greater numbers of US-built escorts carrying advanced radar sets in the war years than was possible for RN escorts. It is hoped that the details which follow are accurate.

*Type SG* An early microwave radar, which was being installed in US-built escorts from mid-1942. The small aerial was housed under a fibre dome of deep profile.

*See photographs:* PG conversions, some PCs

*Type SL*   This was the main surface warning set of USN escort classes during the war years. All DEs and PFs carried it (some 700 ships), as well as the earlier PCEs.

It was a very efficient set, operating on a PPI without an 'A' scan. Slave PPIs were not normally fitted, but a viewing device was fitted between the open bridge and the radar set on the deck below.

It had high definition and good ranges, and improvements were being made in the 1944/45 period to increase its sensitivity at very low ranges, so that even planks with nails in them, floating in the water, were easily detected at a mile or two. This was useful against German small battle units, and against submerged German U-boats using Schnorkel in the closing year of the European war. The excellence of the Type SL radar was also one of the reasons for the selection of the 'Captain' class frigates as the first and only Coastal Forces Control Frigates in the English Channel and North Sea in 1944/45.

The aerial array, a horizontal dish shape, was protected by a fibre dome of lower profile than the Types SG and SU, and as it was relatively light, fitted in DEs and PFs on a short spur, high up on the tall pole mast. In PCEs it was fitted right on top of the mast itself.
*See photographs: Ekins, Caicos, Kilbride, Gazelle* and all USN DEs and PFs

*Type SU*   A further advance on the Type SL, appearing in 1945. It can be seen in some of the RCN 'River' class frigates fitted out for service with the British Pacific Fleet, as Canada purchased 25 of these sets at that time from America, due to lack of availability of the British Type 277 at that time.
*See photographs: Outremont, Swansea.*

*Air Warning set Type SA*   The standard USN air warning radar set in the main war years. It was efficient and compact, but was not available in sufficient numbers for universal installation, as was the Type SL.

It was, therefore, fitted in a selected number of DEs and PFs, including those transferred to the RN as 'Captain' and 'Colony' class frigates, under Lend-Lease. Typically, 2 ships in a group of 6 would be fitted with Type SA, and would between them keep a continuous air-warning radar watch, thus resting the set from continuous use.

The aerial was the first of the true bedstead types, mounted always right at the top of the mast, rotating clear of all structures.
*See photographs: DEs, PFs, RN 'Captain' and 'Colony' classes, especially RN Essington* and *Somaliland*

*IFF SETS   Types BN, BY, BK, and ABK*   These were the American IFF interrogators and transpondors; the aerials represented a circle mounted on a small pole, and were light and easily mounted on the yards of escort vessels. The transpondors were usually supplied and monted in duplicate, so that in case of failure of one set identification problems did not occur in night actions.

## DIRECTION FINDING

*H/F D/F* High Frequency Direction Finding, a British invention to detect the radio transmissions of German U-boats at sea, primarily in the North Atlantic battle.

The birdcage aerial was prominent in the ships fitted, and was usually at the topmasthead, clear of all obstructions, but where Type 290/291 radar was fitted in this position the H/F D/F aerial was fitted on a pole mast aft, both in RN and in USN escorts. The many sections of the aerial were very accurate in directional sensitivity, and a skilled operator could greatly influence the results; moreover, if the U-boat's transmissions were found to be in the ground wave of the set, then it would be known that the U-boat was within 20 miles of the escort.

The standard sets fitted in RN and RCN ships during the main war years were the Types FH 3 or 4, but later versions, as Type FV4, were appearing in 1945, and this is referred to above, in the fitting policy comments. The USN set was similar, as was the aerial, and appeared in DEs and in some PFs.

The aerial was not fitted in 'Flower' class corvettes, presumably as their full speed was insufficient to chase and catch a surfaced U-boat, but the set was widely fitted in 'River' and 'Captain' class frigates, some 'Black Swan' and 'Hunt' class ships, and, surprisingly, in view of their speed, in 'Castle' class corvettes. *See photographs: Ledbury, Shelburne, Swansea, Ste Thérèse, Lochy, Loch Fyne, Loch More, Dumbarton Castle*

H/F D/F aerial on board a 'River' class frigate at Halifax in 1946. This was mounted on a pole mast aft, and was the replacement aerial for the earlier birdcage, probably a VH/F D/F. *(Public Archives of Canada)*

*M/F D/F*  Medium Frequency Direction Finding. This was used largely as a navigational set, designated Type FM 4 or FM 12. It was not operative in mid-ocean on an effective basis.

The aerial was usually mounted on the superstructure on the forward side of an escort's bridge, and consisted of two concentric squares or circles, mounted on a small platform.

*QH3*  This was a British navigational direction-finding set. The aerial consisted of a wire, and the results were presented on a small 'A' scan.

It was developed from wartime aircraft navigational systems, relying on shore transmitters, and was very accurate. If a ship was passing close to a navigational buoy, the set could detect which side of the buoy it was passing. The set was fitted mainly in escorts in the English Channel, for the invasion of Normandy, and was also useful in the ensuing North Sea campaign.

*LORAN*  Long Range navigation. This was an American designed and made set for use in the wide open spaces of the Atlantic and Pacific Oceans.

The aerial again consisted of a wire, and the results were shown on dials on a compact set. It was mainly fitted to the long-range mid-ocean escorts, to fix their positions in bad weather, and operated on the same basis as QH3, with triangular fixes from transmitting shore stations. Type descriptions were DAS 1, DAS 2, and DAQ.

## RADIO TELEPHONE

This warrants a place here, as great strides were made during the war in this technology, and it was of great importance to both the close escort and the support groups.

Communication between escorts in the early days of the war was mainly by flag, semaphore or light—with, of course, radio, when out of visual touch, and if radio silence was not being kept. Gradually, medium frequency radio telephones came into use, but their capabilities in bad weather or atmospheric conditions were somewhat limited, with crackling and distortion.

High frequency radio telephones were then quickly developed which could operate without interference of any significance even in the worst weather. The need for escort groups to be very highly trained, and to operate very closely together in well-rehearsed tactics, especially in the presence of the enemy, became very great, both in the A/S war and in operations against, for example , German E-boats in the narrow seas. Fitting of these sets became, therefore, a high priority, and played a major part in the electronic equipment of all front-line escort vessels in the last two years of the war.

The main RN/RCN type was *Type 86M*, with a short pole aerial, mounted vertically at the end of a long horizontal pole, and usually fitted at the yardarms, though sometimes they were to be found on spurs on the mast.

The USN set was called TBS, or Talk Between Ships, and all US-built escorts carried this excellent set. The aerial consisted of five wires, fitted at right angles to each other, with a vertical pole mounted under them on the yards of all escorts.

Examples of both these aerials may be found in numerous photographs of all the later escort classes.

*HEADACHE*   This was a receiving set only, fitted mainly in escorts in action with German E-boats, and, in some cases, in the A/S war also.

It was used to monitor German radio-telephone conversations, and with a German-speaking operator gave quick and vital information during actions to the captains of escort vessels. It was especially useful in the English Channel and North Sea, in fast-moving night actions against German E-boats. The aerial was a long pole, fitted vertically on a long bracket on the foremast, usually high up.
*See photographs: Ekins, Bleasdale*

## ASDIC EQUIPMENT

This was the anti-submarine detection equipment fitted in all escort vessels. It was developed after the First World War (when German U-boats first threatened North Atlantic commerce), and its title was derived from the UK Anti-Submarine Detection Investigation Committee, which sponsored the development of this equipment between the wars. The American equivalent was called *Sonar,* and was similar technically in every way. The British equipment was fairly highly developed by 1939, and improvements during the war years concentrated on refinements rather than any drastic alterations in direction.

*THE OSCILLATOR*   The basic item was a quartz crystal oscillator, which was housed in a streamlined dome beneath the ship. This dome, in a compartment at keel level, a little forward of the bridge, was retractable; this meant that when the Asdic equipment was in use the dome was lowered, and this in calm weather could be done up to about 25 knots; the dome was raised when the Asdic was shut down.

Normally, an escort vessel at sea would always have her dome lowered, and the Asdic equipment carrying out a continuous search. Only in very heavy weather, when the rush of water past the dome drowned the reception of echoes, would the set be switched off and the dome raised. A further hazard was when the ship was coming to anchor, since, if the dome had not been raised in good time, the anchor cable could easily tear it from the ship's hull!

The quartz oscillator transmitted by regular electric impulses, which were converted into underwater sound in a highly directional sense. This would be reflected off any objects encountered, and would travel back to the oscillator, where the echo would be received and relayed to the control equipment.

*THE CONTROL EQUIPMENT*   This was sited on the bridge, close to the Captain. The usual location was in a cabin slung on the forefront of the upper bridge above the wheelhouse. In this narrow compartment would be the one or two Asdic operators, seated at their controls, plus the A/S Control Officer standing behind them. This was known in the RN as the Asdic Control Room.

The equipment consisted of a gyro compass repeater, with a knob in the centre which controlled the direction of the oscillator. The latter was usually rotated in 5 degree steps, in whatever search was ordered by the Captain; a normal search would be, say, 40 degrees on either side of the bow.

An alarm push was located beside the repeater to ring a loud bell on the bridge once an echo was heard, and voicepipe and later loudspeaker communication with the bridge was normal. The ACR also had a bell to the depth-charge crews, and later the Hedgehog crew too, to tell them when to fire their charges in an attack.

There was a bridge slave loudspeaker, giving the 'ping' of the Asdic transmission, and the echoes, when received. There was a great deal of skill in interpreting these sounds, both in calculating the submarine's course and speed, and alterations of these, and in differentiating, in inshore waters especially, between submarines, fish shoals, tide-rips, and wrecks. The Captain, the A/S CO and the operators formed a close-knit little team, and the teams in the crack escorts were very impressive indeed.

The next development in equipment was the range recorder, a typewriter-like set beside the gyro compass repeater, which could record visually on chemically-treated paper the transmission and the range of any echo. It also gave the relative speed of approach, and again there was skill in interpretation.

Later with an improved basic equipment, the Type 144, which gave automatic search and better recording, came the depth-calculating set, the Type 147B, with a separate dome beneath the hull which resembled the sheath of a sword.

## ANTI-SUBMARINE WEAPONS

*1. Depth Charges*

*ROYAL AND COMMONWEALTH NAVIES   Mark VII*

*Classes fitted:* All.

A simple drum, filled with high explosive, with a hollow tube running through the centre, into which was inserted at one end the priming charge, and at the other the pressure fuse and detonator.

The charge was set to detonate at any one of a number of depths, from 50 feet minimum, by hydrostatic pressure; iron weights were bolted to one end of the drum to increase the sinking rate when deep settings were required.

The dropping speed of the firing ship, to escape damaging herself, was usually a minimum of 15 knots (full speed for corvettes and trawlers), especially at the shallow settings where the effect on the firing ship could be quite shattering.

The charges were dropped from traps, or rails, mounted on the stern of the firing ship. In 'Bangor' and 'Catherine' class fleet minesweepers these were usually single traps (see photograph of *Swift Current*); in other ships inclined rails were fitted, usually two sets (in earlier years, occasionally three); the rails held about 12 depth charges each.

Depth-charge throwers were also carried, mounted forward of the rails on the sides of the ship. These each held one charge in a mushroom-shaped stalk holder, and fired the charge and holder together by an explosive charge; once in the air, the charge and stalk separated. These throwers had a range of about 120 feet, and though they were sometimes angled were usually fixed to fire directly outwards at 90 degrees to the firing ship's course. Combined with the charges dropped from the rails or traps, this gave a wider plan or pattern of charges.

Depth-charge throwers were usually mounted two on each side, but in the earlier war years, when the largest possible pattern of charges was the objective, 6 or even 8 throwers were sometimes mounted, with 4 being angled at 135 degrees aft from the ship's course, or all 8 angled directly to the beam. This was especially to be found in the 'Black Swan' and 'River' classes at that time.

Depth charges were handled at the stern by small davits, which can clearly be seen in many of the photographs.

Racks of 4-6 ready-use depth charges were kept by each thrower, with a sliding rack to move the next charge to be used on to the thrower. Ready-use stalks were stowed along the inboard sections of the adjacent deck, or slung in clips along the side of deckhouses.

In RN and RCN ships, employed especially in the North Atlantic, extra depth charges were often stowed in long, single or double tier ready-use racks. A single tier rack can be seen in the RCN 'Flower' class corvette photograph, page 000, while in the 'River' and 'Captain' classes these racks were increased to double tier, 2 or 4 on each side, stowed forward of the throwers. This brought the total depth-charge stowage to record proportions in these two classes, which made them particularly valuable for long-range mid-ocean patrols, due to the difficulty of transferring depth charges at sea from tankers to escort vessels.

The minimum size of pattern was usually 5 charges, the more usual 10, and in the North Atlantic creep attacks up to 26. After firing the pattern the escort would continue to run out, to escape the detonation effects, and would turn at about 1,200 yards from the dropping point, to see the results.
Charge: HE, later Torpex
Dead time: 30 seconds

### USN  Standard Depth Charge

*Classes fitted:* All.

Starting with a design similar to that of the RN, this was in later years revised to a shaped drum with fins, rather like an aircraft bomb, to speed sinking time.

The throwers were of a rather simpler pattern than those of the RN ships, but operated on an exactly similar basis. In the earlier war years the USN used a twin thrower, named a 'Y' gun, but this was soon abandoned in favour of a single thrower with a greater range, the 'K' gun, similar to the standard RN pattern. PCs retained a 'Y' gun, for space reasons.

In all other respects, USN depth-charge stowage and practice was identical to that of the RN.

*Mark X Depth Charge   RN and RCN ships only*  This was, in effect, the first anti-submarine torpedo, and was only used in ships already fitted with full size torpedo tubes. By definition, this meant only pre-war destroyers employed on ocean escort work, and no war-built escort was so fitted. It will be noted that no US-built DE transferred to the RN carried her torpedo tube outfit, so that this restriction applied equally to that class also.

The objective of this torpedo was to attack U-boats at depths where normal depth charges were inoperative. This meant depths of first 600 feet, then 900 feet and later 1,500 feet, as the Asdic equipment improved in parallel.

Only 1 Mark X depth charge was issued to each ship so fitted, and they were rarely used, as the resulting explosion could scare the firing ship as much as the U-boat! It was considered safe to fire it at a speed of 11 knots minimum, but as destroyers usually had speed in hand this minimum effectively was usually not less than 18 knots.

Charge: 1 ton explosive, equivalent to 10 depth charges

Weight of torpedo: $\frac{1}{2}$ ton, exclusive of the explosive

Overall length: 15 ft 2 ins

## HEDGEHOG

*Classes fitted:*

RN— 'Black Swan', 'Flower', 'Kil', 'River', 'Bay', 'Captain', 'Colony', 'Catherine'

RCN—'Flower', 'River'

USN—PG, PCE, PF, DE, AM

The Hedgehog mortar was developed early in the war by the RN. The objective was to cut out the dead time between the firing ship losing contact with the U-boat, as she ran over it, to the firing time of the depth charges dropped from the stern. This dead time on many occasions gave the U-boat time to alter course and escape.

By throwing charges ahead of the ship the Hedgehog cut down this dead time to the period the bombs were in flight, a much reduced period.

The hedgehog was always sited forward of the bridge, to obtain the greatest possible range. In classes such as the 'Black Swan' and 'Flower', which were in commission before the Hedgehog was developed, makeshift siting arrangements had to be made.

In the 'Flower's the Hedgehog was sited aft of the 4″ gun, on the starboard side, on an extended platform. Its weight was counterbalanced by the ready-use lockers, including those for rocket flares, mounted in the equivalent position on the port side.

In the 'Black Swan' class the best site was one deck up, aft of B gun, but due to restricted space the mortar was split into two halves, one half being mounted on each side of the deck.

In later classes, the 'River' and 'Bay', the Hedgehog was specially sited right forward between the anchor capstan and the forward end of the deckhouse. This position was, however, very exposed in bad weather; in some ships, steel protection for the operators was built in round the after sides, and in the 'River' class *Monnow,* and some other units of that class, a split Hedgehog was experimentally fitted on new sponsons on the sides of the forward 4″ gundeck.

These sponsons required heavy undersupports to take the thrust at the moment of firing.

In US designs, PCE, PF and all DE types, the Hedgehog was mounted just aft of the forward 3″ gun. In the latter two classes this gave a very impressive armament forward of the bridge, but again the forward positions were difficult to fight in heavy weather. In the USN 'Sumner' class fleet destroyers two full Hedgehogs were fitted, one on either side of the raised No 2 gundeck.

In all cases the deck beneath the Hedgehog needed to be strengthened, as the downward thrust at the moment of firing was very great. For this reason the bombs were fired in quick succession, controlled by a ripple firing switch behind the blast shield.

It is noteworthy that some RN classes, 'Hunt' class destroyers, and both classes of fleet minesweepers, did not have Hedgehog mortars fitted at all. In the former case, space limitations and largely narrow seas employment away from U-boats were probably the cause, while the fleet sweepers also were rarely employed on A/S work and thus did not justify this fitting.

Hedgehogs were fitted as rapidly as possible to all A/S escort classes, and proved very effective. While it was still difficult to be accurate, training of Asdic crews and technical improvements such as the mortar were making remarkable strides. The major drawback of the Hedgehog bomb was that it only exploded on impact with the U-boat, and therefore if a hit was not obtained there was no morale effect on the U-boat's crew.

The estimated probability of success with this weapon was put by the RN as 60% at normal depths, and by the USN at 30%. Actual RN war experience, however, gave these results:

2nd half 1943—$7\frac{1}{2}$% successful attacks
1st  half 1944—15% successful attacks
2nd half 1944—28% successful attacks

The success rate was, therefore, doubling in each successive six-month period.

USN PCs, due to space restrictions, had a smaller version of the Hedgehog fitted, called the Mousetrap.

| | |
|---|---|
| Bombs: | 24 in number |
| | Fitted on spigots, in 4 rows, rising to the rear. The propellant charge was solid, fitted in the stalk, and firing was electrical through the steel spigots. The bomb was armed while in flight by a propeller-type vane to increase safety in the firing ship |
| Content: | 32 lbs of Torpex |
| Range: | 200 yds |
| Training: | The spigots could be tilted together either side, up to 20 deg, to compensate for ship's roll and last-minute aim adjustments |
| Sinking time: | 22 ft per sec |
| Maximum depth: | 1,300 ft |
| Flight time: | $7\frac{1}{2}$ secs |
| Pattern: | Evenly spread, over the perimeter of an oval, 120 ft long by 140 ft wide. |

*SQUID MORTAR*
*Classes fitted:*
RN/RCN—'Castle', 'Loch'
USN—Nil

The Squid mortar, developed also by the RN, was a natural progression from the Hedgehog. It aimed for greater accuracy, by training and by explosive force; it retrieved the morale effect on the U-boat's crew by a fused explosion of great force, and it added a new dimension, by the new probability of this greatly increased explosion blowing the U-boat to the surface, where it could be dealt with by gunfire.

It was designed to kill a slow-moving U-boat with one salvo, up to 800 feet, and was to operate in conjunction with no less than three new Asdic sets coming into service, including the Type 147B depth-finding set, which could give depths accurately up to 880 feet, later increased to 1,300 feet.

Due to the weight of the equipment, and the space needed for the stowage of the much larger bombs, the Squid was only fitted to new classes designed around this formidable new A/S weapon.

Thus the 'Castle' class corvettes and 'Loch' class frigates had the Squid mounted on B gundeck, with the single 4″ gun mounted on a raised bandstand forward of it. The latter was not in such an exposed position, as the flare and height of the bows were increased in both classes, compared with earlier war-built escort classes.

The decks needed great strengthening, and the bombs were too heavy to be transferred at sea without risk, so that these ships only operated where supplies of Squid bombs were readily available—in the North Atlantic, and, for the 'Loch' class frigates only, in 1945, in the East Indies.

The RN and RCN had great faith from the start in this new weapon, and partly to save weight, partly in fulfilment of this confidence, depth charges in these two classes were reduced to 15 per ship, fired from one rail and two throwers on the quarterdeck, which took on a surprisingly clean appearance, but giving room for the increasingly important Foxer equipment against acoustic torpedoes.

Consideration was seriously given (as outlined in the class chapters) to heavy structural alterations to permit the Squid to be fitted in the 'River', 'Flower' and 'Captain' classes; but the long refit time required, and the urgent operational need for these new escorts to be in service in the closing phase of the A/S war in Europe, ruled out these alterations.

Again, greater reliability of the new equipment, and intensive training of the crews, gave increasingly impressive results with this new weapon. To the end of 1944, actual success rates in attacks by RN Squid-fitted ships were 18% for the 'Castle' class and 33% for the 'Loch' class; but in the first four months of 1945 this rate increased to 60% for all Squid-fitted ships.

As recounted in an earlier chapter, the RN saw the Squid as their main weapon against the new fast German U-boats; they planned to adapt the Squid for use as an A/S gun, with greater training flexibility, and rocket propulsion added to the charge.

The Asdic Control Room of the 'River' class frigate *Nene,* at Halifax in July 1944. The main oscillator control is in the centre, on the gyro compass repeater, while the recorders are on either side probably Types 144 and 147B. The chemically-treated paper used to show echoes visually is clearly seen.
*(Public Archives of Canada)*

The bridge lay-out of the RCN 'River' class frigate *La Salle* at Halifax in March 1945. The main gyro compass repeater is in the centre, with the magnetic compass behind it. The Asdic Control Room is beneath the steel frame forward of the bridge screen; the Captain's position was on the right hand side, with the chart table on the left.
*(Public Archives of Canada)*

Typical corvette depth charge rails at the stern of *Athol* at Halifax in January 1944; a 'Bangor' class fleet minesweeper is berthed astern. Note the extra storage racks on the centreline (with ice on them). *(Public Archives of Canada)*

The Hedgehog ahead-throwing A/S weapon. This one was on board the RCN corvette *North Bay,* undergoing trials at Halifax in October 1943. Note the bombs are angled to obtain a spread, and have aerodynamic fins at the rear end. *(Public Archives of Canada)*

|          |                                                                                  |
|----------|----------------------------------------------------------------------------------|
| Bombs:   | 3 in 'Castle' class, 6 in 'loch' class, in one salvo. Fused to explode at set depth |
| Range:   | 600 yds                                                                          |
| Flight time: | $7\frac{1}{2}$ secs                                                         |
| Sinking rate: | 40-45 ft per sec=30 secs to 1,300 ft                                     |
| Pattern: | *Single mortar*—equilateral triangular pattern of 3 charges, evenly spaced round circumference of circle 140 ft in diameter |
|          | *Double mortar*—2 patterns, superimposed, giving in plan a hexagonal pattern as above. The upper and lower layers of the double pattern were 65 feet apart, and the lethal diameter was 60 yds wide in plan and 35 yds wide in depth |
| Depth:   | First 1,150 ft, then 1,500 ft, later to 2,000 ft against fast U-boats            |

*See photographs: Carisbrooke Castle* and *Helmsdale*

**FOXER GEAR** Devised for the protection of escort vessels against German acoustic torpedoes. A pair of towed noisemakers, handled by davit from the stern of the escort vessel; each consisted of two loosely fitting steel bars, which

*Robert I. Paine* of the 'Buckley' type. Taken in May 1945, she too had four single Bofors added for service in the Pacific. She had H/F D/F on a short tripod mainmast, and both Types SL and SA radar. A good example of a standard escort at its best. *(US Navy)*

clattered together at speeds of 10 knots or more, giving a louder noise than that of the propellers, and so attracting to themselves the acoustic torpedo, which would explode harmlessly in the escort's wake. The difficulty was that this noise also drowned the echo of the U-boat in the ship's Asdic sets, so that the *Unifoxer* was produced, with one clattering bar only, giving an acceptable noise level.

## DEPTH CHARGE AND AHEAD-THROWING WEAPON OUTFITS, 1945

| | D/Cs | Hedgehog | Squid |
|---|---|---|---|
| | | *Projectiles* | |
| **RN** | | | |
| 'Black Swan' class | 110 | 144 | — |
| 'Hunt' class Type I | 70 | — | — |
| Type II | 60 | — | — |
| Type III | 70 | — | — |
| Type IV | 30? | — | — |
| 'Flower' class | 72 | 120 | — |
| Modified 'Flower' class | 100 | 120 | — |
| 'Castle' class | 15 | — | 81 |
| 'Kil' class | 75? | 100? | — |
| 'Guillemot' class | 10 | — | — |
| 'River' class | 150/200 | 240 | — |
| 'Loch' class | 15 | — | 150 |
| 'Bay' class | 50 | 240 | — |
| 'Captain' class | 150/200 | 360 | — |
| 'Colony' class | 64 | 432 | — |
| Admiralty Trawlers | 40? | — | — |
| 'Bangor' class | 40 | — | — |
| 'Algerine' class | 90 | — | — |
| 'Catherine' class | 30 | 100? | — |
| 'Bathurst' class (as A/S vessel) | 40 | — | — |

### RCN/RAN/RIN SHIPS OF ABOVE CLASSES
Generally similar to above figures

| **USN** | | | |
|---|---|---|---|
| PG class | 72 | 120 | — |
| PC class | 15 | 50? | — |
| PCE class | 75? | 100? | — |
| PF class | 64 | 432 | — |
| DE class | 100 | 360 | — |
| AM classes 'Raven' class | 30 | 100? | — |
| 'Admirable' class | 60 | 100? | — |

*Padstow Bay* in April 1946. Compare this view with that of the later USN destroyer escorts, her contemporaries. *(Ministry of Defence)*

*Kenora* at Halifax in 1944. Early radar at masthead, the whaler looks too large for the hull! *(Public Archives of Canada)*

# Ships Transferred during the War

**'Black Swan' class (6)**
6 to India (direct order)
**'Hunt' class (13)**
Type II 2 to Greece
*Braham, Hursley*
3 to Poland
*Bedale, Oakley, Silverton*
Type III 5 to Greece
*Bolebroke, Border, Catterick, Hatherleigh, Modbury*
2 to Norway
*Eskdale, Glaisdale*
1 to France
*Haldon*
**'Flower' class (33)**
10 to USA
*Arabis, Begonia, Calendula, Candytuft, Heliotrope, Hibiscus, Larkspur, Heartsease, Periwinkle, Veronica*
10 to France
*Aconite, Alyssum, Chrysanthemum, Coriander, Lobelia, Lotus, Mimosa, Ranunculus, Sundew, La Bastiaise*
1 to Netherlands
*Carnation*
6 to Norway
*Acanthus, Buttercup, Eglantine, Montbretia, Potentilla, Rose*
4 to Greece
*Coreopsis, Hyacinth, Peony, Tamarisk*
1 to Yugoslavia
*Mallow*

**Modified 'Flower' class (6)**
2 to New Zealand
*Arabis, Arbutus*
4 to Canada
*Buddleia, Bulrush, Candytuft, Ceanothus*
**'Castle' class (13)**
1 to Norway
*Shrewsbury Castle*
12 to Canada
*Guildford Castle, Hedingham Castle, Hever Castle, Norham Castle, Nunnery Castle, Pembroke Castle, Rising Castle, Sandgate Castle, Sherborne Castle, Tamworth Castle, Walmer Castle, Wolvesey Castle*
**'River' class (14)**
6 to France
*Braid, Frome, Moyola, Strule, Torridge, Windrush*
1 to Netherlands
*Ribble*
7 to Canada
*Annan, Ettrick, Meon, Monnow, Nene, Ribble, Teme*
**'Loch' class (3)**
3 to South Africa
*Loch Ard, Loch Boisdale, Loch Cree*
**Admiralty Trawlers (11)**
5 to Portugal
*Mangrove, Burray, Eriskay, Gruinard, Whalsay*
4 to New Zealand
*Inchkeith, Killegray, Sanda, Scarba*
2 to Norway
*Mincarlo, Shiant*

**'Bangor' class (9)**
9 to India
*Clydebank, Lyme Regis, Tilbury, Greenock,*

*Hartlepool, Harwich, Middlesbrough, New-haven, Padstow*

## RCN

**Modified 'Flower' class (15)**
8 to USA
*Comfrey, Cornel, Flax, Mandrake, Milfoil, Musk, Nepeta, Privet*
7 to UK
*Dittany, Honesty, Linaria, Rosebay, Smilax, Statice, Willowherb*
**'Bangor' class (6)**
6 to UK
*Fort York, Parrsborough, Qualicum, Shippi-gan, Tadoussac, Wedgeport*

**'Isles' class (8)**
8 to UK
*Campobello, Dochet, Flint, Gateshead, Herschell, Porcher, Prospect, Texada*
**'Algerine' class (34)**
34 to UK (direct order)
**'River' class (10)**
2 to USA
*Nadur, Annan*
8 to RN
*Barle, Cuckmere, Evenlode, Findhorn, Inver, Lossie, Parret, Shiel*

## RAN

**'Bathurst' class (4)**
4 to India

*Bengal, Bombay, Madras, Punjab*

## USN

**PC class (44)**
8 to Brazil   see class lists
31 to France   see class lists
1 to Greece
*PC 622*
1 to Netherlands
*PC 468*
1 to Nigeria
*PC 469*
1 to Norway
*PC 467*
1 to Uruguay
*PC 1234*
**PCE class (15)**
15 to UK
*PCE 827-841*

**PF class (28)**
28 to Russia   see class lists
**DE classes (90)**
78 to UK   see class lists
6 to France   see class lists
6 to Brazil   see class lists
**AM classes**
  **'Raven' class (22)**
  22 to UK   see class lists
  **'Admirable' class (38)**
  34 to Russia   see class lists
  4 to China   see class lists
**'Algerine' class (15)**
15 to UK
*AM 325-339*

*NOTE*
These lists are as accurate as is reasonably possible; some units were transferred more than once, and some were built on direct order from the navy concerned. Full details in all cases are contained in the navy section of the building country, as in the receiving country also.

*Test* in November 1942. Note the quarterdeck carries wire sweep gear, and two Oerlikons in addition to the depth charge outfit. Three single Oerlikons on the exposed forecastle—specified, but not often fitted. *(Ministry of Defence)*

*Kingsmill* in drydock at Portsmouth, UK, December 1944. She shows the DE sheerline, and the standard 1945 camouflage scheme. She has a tall mainmast as she was fitted as an assault landing ship (headquarters). *(Lt-Cdr R.P. Hall,* RANR *)*

▲ *Oronsay* in April 1944. Note the naval type
bridge, compared with a corvette, tall Type 290
radar aerial at the topmasthead, and capstan
forward. *(Ministry of Defence)*

*Ironbound,* also Canadian-built in 1942. Her
tripod mast is stepped abaft the naval-type
bridge, and she has a short mainmast.
*(Canadian Forces Photo Unit)* ▼

# Combined
# Pendant List

THE following is probably the first complete list of pendant numbers (the distinguishing number of each warship, painted on each side of her bows, and on her stern, and flown as a flag hoist when entering or leaving harbour) ever published, covering all the war-built escorts and fleet minesweepers of the Royal and Commonwealth navies. The United States Navy ships are listed in pendant number order, which is not possible with the numerous RN classes.

Where numbers are missing from this list they were either used by ships built pre-war or the numbers not utilised at all. In a few cases numbers were used twice during the war years, and the names of both ships are then shown. RN ships have no suffix, others are all identified by the letters of their navy.

In most cases where ships were transferred from one Commonwealth navy to another during the building period, two pendant numbers usually appear—the original, under which the ship was ordered, and, separately, the number under which she was commissioned by the other navy. When ships were transferred while actually in commission, the original number was usually retained.

*Hotham* at Malta, July 1948, as floating power station; all guns have been removed and ports cut in hull forward and aft. Power points in Nos 3 & 4 Oerlikon positions and aft of funnel. She is flying paying-off pennant from masthead. *(A. & J. Pavia)*

## FLAG 'J' SUPERIOR

| | | | | | | |
|---|---|---|---|---|---|
| J 00 | *Bangor* | J 139 | *Wedgeport* | J 194 | *Hythe* |
| J 07 | *Beaumaris* | J 140 | *Alarm* | J 195 | *Maryborough* (RAN) |
| J 08 | *Bayfield* (RCN) | J 143 | *Bootle* | J 197 | *Rajputana* (RIN) |
| J 09 | *Cromarty* | J 144 | *Georgian* (RCN) | J 198 | *Burnie* (RAN) |
| J 11 | *Bramble* | J 145 | *Lismore* (RAN) | J 199 | *Carnatic* (RIN) |
| J 12 | *Catherine* | J 146 | *Cowichan* (RCN) | J 200 | *Orissa* (RIN) |
| J 14 | *Boston* | J 147 | *Poole* | J 201 | *Geelong* (RAN) |
| J 15 | *Blyth* | J 148 | *Malpeque* (RCN) | J 202 | *Warrnambool* (RAN) |
| J 16 | *Cato* | J 149 | *Ungava* (RCN) | J 203 | *Rockhampton* (RAN) |
| J 19 | *Rothesay* | J 151 | *Clacton* | J 204 | *Katoomba* (RAN) |
| J 21 | *Canso* (RCN) | J 152 | *Quatsino* (RCN) | J 205 | *Townsville* (RAN) |
| J 23 | *Pique* | J 153 | *Whyalla* (RAN) | J 206 | *Lithgow* (RAN) |
| J 27 | *Blackpool* | J 154 | *Nipigon* (RCN) | J 207 | *Mildura* (RAN) |
| J 28 | *Chamois* | J 155 | *Kathiawar* (RIN) | J 208 | *Lantan* (Ceylon) |
| J 31 | *Stornoway* | J 156 | *Thunder* (RCN) | J 209 | *Lyemun* (Ceylon) |
| J 36 | *Rhyl* | J 157 | *Toowoomba* (RAN) | J 211 | *Waglan* (Burma) |
| J 38 | *Caraquet* (RCN) | J 158 | *Bathurst* (RAN) | J 212 | *Shippigan* |
| J 47 | *Sidmouth* | J 159 | *Mahone* (RCN) | J 213 | *Algerine* |
| J 50 | *Bridport* | J 160 | *Chignecto* (RCN) | J 214 | *Circe* |
| J 52 | *Guysborough* (RCN) | J 161 | *Outarde* (RCN) | J 215 | *Vestal* |
| J 53 | *Dunbar* | J 162 | *Wasaga* (RCN) | J 216 | *Espiègle* |
| J 55 | *Malwa* (RIN) | J 164 | *Kumaon* (RIN) | J 217 | *Rattler/Loyalty* |
| J 59 | *Peterhead* | J 165 | *Minas* (RCN) | J 218 | *Kapunda* (RAN) |
| J 65 | *Bridlington* | J 166 | *Quinte* (RCN) | J 219 | *Rosario* |
| J 67 | *Llandudno* | J 167 | *Goulburn* (RAN) | J 220 | *Tadoussac* |
| J 69 | *Ingonish* (RCN) | J 168 | *Chedabucto* (RCN) | J 221 | *Onyx* |
| J 72 | *Worthing* | J 169 | *Miramichi* (RCN) | J 222 | *Wallaroo* (RAN) |
| J 76 | *Rye* | J 170 | *Bellechasse* (RCN) | J 223 | *Ready* |
| J 77 | *Romney* | J 172 | *Wollongong* (RAN) | J 224 | *Fantôme* |
| J 95 | *Ilfracombe* | J 172 | *Dornoch* | J 225 | *Rinaldo* |
| J 97 | *Polruan* | J 174 | *Clayoquot* (RCN) | J 226 | *Spanker* |
| J 100 | *Lockeport* (RCN) | J 175 | *Cessnock* (RAN) | J 227 | *Mutine* |
| J 105 | *Brixham* | J 178 | *Geraldton* (RAN) | J 228 | *Konkan* (RIN) |
| J 106 | *Acute* | J 179 | *Launceston* (RAN) | J 229 | *Cockatrice* |
| J 116 | *Bude* | J 180 | *Rohilkand* (RIN) | J 230 | *Cadmus* |
| J 117 | *Parrsborough* | J 181 | *Tamworth* (RAN) | J 231 | *Bundaberg* (RAN) |
| J 119 | *Fort York* | J 182 | *Baluchistan* (RIN) | J 232 | *Deloraine* (RAN) |
| J 121 | *Whitehaven* | J 183 | *Cairns* (RAN) | J 233 | *Inverell* (RAN) |
| J 123 | *Seaham* | J 184 | *Ballarat* (RAN) | J 234 | *Latrobe* (RAN) |
| J 124 | *Fraserburgh* | J 186 | *Ipswich* (RAN) | J 235 | *Horsham* (RAN) |
| J 126 | *Felixstowe* | J 187 | *Bendigo* (RAN) | J 236 | *Whyalla* (RAN) |
| J 127 | *Eastbourne* | J 188 | *Gawler* (RAN) | J 237 | *Madras* (RIN) |
| J 128 | *Cromer* | J 189 | *Pirie* (RAN) | J 238 | *Gympie* (RAN) |
| J 129 | *Deccan* (RIN) | J 190 | *Khyber* (RIN) | J 239 | *Punjab* (RIN) |
| J 131 | *Ardrossan* | J 191 | *Broome* (RAN) | J 241 | *Bunbury* (RAN) |
| J 138 | *Qualicum* | J 192 | *Kalgoorlie* (RAN) | J 242 | *Colac* (RAN) |

| | | | | | |
|---|---|---|---|---|---|
| J 243 | *Bengal* (RIN) | J 295 | *Plucky* | J 347 | *Persian* |
| J 244 | *Castlemaine* (RAN) | J 296 | *Postillion* | J 348 | *Stawell* (RAN) |
| J 245 | *Oudh* (RIN) | J 297 | *Rattlesnake* | J 349 | *Courier* |
| J 246 | *Fremantle* (RAN) | J 298 | *Recruit* | J 350 | *Coquette* |
| J 247 | *Bihar* (RIN) | J 299 | *Rifleman* | J 351 | *Cowra* (RAN) |
| J 248 | *Shepparton* (RAN) | J 301 | *Squirrel* | J 353 | *Kiama* (RAN) |
| J 249 | *Bombay* (RIN) | J 302 | *Thisbe* | J 354 | *Serene* |
| J 250 | *Burlington* (RCN) | J 303 | *Truelove* | J 355 | *Rockcliffe* (RCN) |
| J 251 | *Dubbo* (RAN) | J 304 | *Waterwitch* | J 356 | *Welfare* |
| J 252 | *Echuca* (RAN) | J 305 | *Brave* | J 358 | *Rossland* (RCN) |
| J 253 | *Drummondville* (RCN) | J 306 | *Fly* | J 360 | *Mary Rose* |
| J 254 | *Swift Current* (RCN) | J 307 | *Hound* | J 361 | *Parkes* (RAN) |
| J 255 | *Red Deer* (RCN) | J 308 | *Fancy* | J 362 | *Junee* (RAN) |
| J 256 | *Medicine Hat* (RCN) | J 309 | *Sarnia* (RCN) | J 363 | *Strahan* (RAN) |
| J 257 | *Vegreville* (RCN) | J 310 | *Stratford* (RCN) | J 364 | *Coquitlam* (RCN) |
| J 258 | *Grandmère* (RCN) | J 311 | *Fort William* (RCN) | J 367 | *Stormcloud* |
| J 259 | *Gananoque* (RCN) | J 312 | *Kentville* (RCN) | J 369 | *Felicity* |
| J 260 | *Goderich* (RCN) | J 313 | *Mulgrave* (RCN) | J 370 | *Flying Fish* |
| J 261 | *Kelowna* (RCN) | J 314 | *Blairmore* (RCN) | J 374 | *Tattoo* |
| J 262 | *Courtenay* (RCN) | J 315 | *Wagga* (RAN) | J 375 | *Steadfast* |
| J 263 | *Melville* (RCN) | J 316 | *Cootamundra* (RAN) | J 376 | *Golden Fleece* |
| J 264 | *Granby* (RCN) | J 317 | *Milltown* (RCN) | J 377 | *Lioness* |
| J 265 | *Noranda* (RCN) | J 318 | *Westmount* (RCN) | J 378 | *Prompt* |
| J 266 | *Lachine* (RCN) | J 319 | *Lyme Regis* (RCN) | J 379 | *Lysander* |
| J 267 | *Digby* (RCN) | J 320 | *Sind* (RIN) | J 380 | *Mariner* |
| J 268 | *Truro* (RCN) | J 321 | *Gondhwana* (RIN) | J 381 | *Marmion* |
| J 269 | *Trois Rivières* (RCN) | J 322 | *Assam* (RIN) | J 382 | *Sylvia* |
| J 270 | *Brockville* (RCN) | J 323 | *Benalla* (RAN) | J 383 | *Tanganyika* |
| J 271 | *Transcona* (RCN) | J 324 | *Gladstone* (RAN) | J 384 | *Rowena* |
| J 272 | *Esquimalt* (RCN) | J 325 | *Providence* | J 385 | *Wave* |
| J 274 | *Larne* | J 326 | *Kapuskasing* (RCN) | J 386 | *Welcome* |
| J 275 | *Hydra* | J 327 | *Middlesex* (RCN) | J 387 | *Chameleon* |
| J 276 | *Lennox* | J 329 | *Moon* | J 388 | *Cheerful* |
| J 277 | *Orestes* | J 330 | *Oshawa* (RCN) | J 389 | *Hare* |
| J 278 | *Llewellyn* (RCN) | J 331 | *Portage* (RCN) | J 390 | *Jewel* |
| J 280 | *Port Hope* (RCN) | J 332 | *St Boniface* (RCN) | J 391 | *Liberty* |
| J 281 | *Kenora* (RCN) | J 333 | *Seabear* | J 396 | *Fort Francis* (RCN) |
| J 282 | *Antares* | J 334 | *The Soo* (RCN) | J 397 | *New Liskeard* (RCN) |
| J 283 | *Arcturus* | J 335 | *Maenad* | J 398 | *Friendship* |
| J 284 | *Aries* | J 336 | *Wallaceburg* (RCN) | J 400 | *Magic* |
| J 285 | *Bowen* (RAN) | J 337 | *Winnipeg* (RCN) | J 401 | *Pylades* |
| J 286 | *Clinton* | J 338 | *Strenuous* | J 402 | *Elfreda* |
| J 287 | *Berar* (RIN) | J 339 | *Tourmaline* | J 403 | *Fairy* |
| J 288 | *Lightfoot* | J 340 | *Chance* | J 404 | *Florizel* |
| J 289 | *Melita* | J 341 | *Combatant* | J 405 | *Foam* |
| J 290 | *Octavia* | J 342 | *Gazelle* | J 406 | *Frolic* |
| J 291 | *Pelorus* | J 344 | *Border Cities* (RCN) | J 407 | *Garnet* |
| J 293 | *Pickle* | J 345 | *Cynthia* | J 422 | *Imersay* |
| J 294 | *Pincher* | J 346 | *Gorgon* | J 423 | *Lingay* |

| J 424 | Sandray | J 426 | Shillay | J 427 | Sursay |
| J 425 | Scaravay | | | | |

## Flag 'K' Superior

| K 00 | Carnation | K 46 | La Malouine | K 95 | Dianthus |
|------|-----------|------|-------------|------|----------|
| K 01 | Acanthus | K 48 | Anemone | K 96 | Aubrietia |
| K 02 | Shearwater | K 49 | Crocus | K 97 | Salvia/Avon |
| K 03 | Heliotrope | K 50 | Erica | K 98 | Zinnia/ |
| K 04 | Saxifrage | K 51 | Rockrose | | Wollondilly (RAN) |
| K 06 | Sheldrake | K 52 | Puffin | K 99 | Gardenia |
| K 07 | Dianella | K 53 | Woodruff (RCN) | K 100 | Alysse (FRANCE) |
| K 08 | Spirella | K 54 | Marguerite | K 101 | Nanaimo (RCN) |
| K 09 | Candytuft/ | K 55 | Naomi (RAN) | K 102 | Rose |
| | Bogam (RAN) | K 57 | Sundew | K 103 | Alberni (RCN) |
| K 10 | Snapdragon | K 58 | Aconit (FRANCE) | K 104 | Dawson (RCN) |
| K 12 | Auricula | K 59 | Dahlia | K 105 | Loosestrife |
| K 14 | Primula | K 60 | Lavender | K 106 | Edmundston (RCN) |
| K 15 | Atholl (RCN) | K 61 | Pentstemon | K 107 | Nasturtium |
| K 16 | Geranium | K 62 | Widgeon | K 108 | Campion |
| K 17 | Amaranthus | K 64 | Hollyhock | K 110 | Shediac (RCN) |
| K 18 | Campanula | K 65 | Myosotis | K 111 | Pennywort |
| K 19 | Nigella | K 66 | Begonia/ | K 112 | Matapedia (RCN) |
| K 20 | Starwort | | Williamstown (RAN) | K 113 | Arvida (RCN) |
| K 21 | Dart | K 67 | Snowdrop | K 114 | Bellwort |
| K 22 | Gloxinia | K 68 | Jonquil | K 115 | Levis (RCN) |
| K 23 | Jasmine | K 69 | Heather | K 116 | Chambly (RCN) |
| K 24 | Hibiscus/ | K 70 | Kingfisher | K 117 | Ranunculus |
| | Campaspe (RAN) | K 71 | Pimpernel | K 118 | Napanee (RCN) |
| K 25 | Azalea | K 72 | Balsam | K 119 | Orillia (RCN) |
| K 27 | Honeysuckle | K 73 | Arabis (1) | K 120 | Borage |
| K 28 | Calendula | K 74 | Narcissus | K 121 | Rimouski (RCN) |
| K 29 | Tulip | K 75 | Celandine | K 122 | Fleur de Lys |
| K 30 | Kittiwake | K 77 | Delphinium | K 123 | Oxlip |
| K 31 | Camellia | K 78 | Rhododendron | K 124 | Cobalt (RCN) |
| K 32 | Coreopsis | K 79 | Petunia | K 125 | Kenogami (RCN) |
| K 33 | Kingcup | K 80 | Bluebell | K 126 | Burdock |
| K 34 | Ararat (RAN) | K 83 | Cyclamen | K 127 | Algoma (RCN) |
| K 35 | Violet | K 84 | Hyacinth | K 129 | Agassiz (RCN) |
| K 36 | Clematis | K 85 | Verbena | K 130 | Lotus |
| K 37 | Veronica | K 86 | Arbutus (1)/ | K 131 | Chilliwack (RCN) |
| K 38 | Mignonette | | Wimmera (RAN) | K 132 | Vetch |
| K 39 | Hydrangea | K 87 | Clarkia | K 133 | Quesnel (RCN) |
| K 41 | Sunflower | K 89 | Guillemot | K 134 | Clover |
| K 42 | Mallard | K 90 | Gentian | K 136 | Shawinigan (RCN) |
| K 43 | Freesia | K 91 | Primrose | K 138 | Barrie (RCN) |
| K 44 | Wallflower | K 92 | Exe | K 139 | Moncton (RCN) |
| K 45 | Convolvulus | K 94 | Columbine | K 140 | Coltsfoot |

| | | | | | | |
|---|---|---|---|---|---|---|
| K 141 | *Summerside* (RCN) | K 191 | *Mayflower* | K 245 | *Fredericton* (RCN) |
| K 142 | *Stonecrop* | K 192 | *Bryony* | K 246 | *Spey* |
| K 143 | *Louisburg* (RCN) | K 193 | *Buttercup.* | K 248 | *Waveney* |
| K 144 | *Meadowsweet* | K 194 | *Fennel* | K 250 | *Tweed* |
| K 145 | *Arrowhead* (RCN) | K 195 | *Chrysanthemum* | K 251 | *Ribble* |
| K 146 | *Pictou* (RCN) | K 196 | *Cowslip* | K 252 | *Helford* |
| K 147 | *Baddeck* (RCN) | K 197 | *Eglantine* | K 253 | *Helmsdale* |
| K 148 | *Amherst* (RCN) | K 198 | *Spikenard* | K 254 | *Ettrick* |
| K 149 | *Brandon* (RCN) | K 199 | *Fritillary* | K 255 | *Ballinderry* |
| K 150 | *Eyebright* (RCN) | K 200 | *Genista* | K 256 | *Bann* |
| K 151 | *Lunenburg* (RCN) | K 201 | *Gloriosa* | K 257 | *Derg* |
| K 152 | *Sherbrooke* (RCN) | K 202 | *Harebell* | K 258 | *Strule* |
| K 153 | *Sorel* (RCN) | K 203 | *Hemlock* | K 259 | *Lagan* |
| K 154 | *Camrose* (RCN) | K 207 | *Monkshood* | K 260 | *Moyola* |
| K 155 | *Windflower* (RCN) | K 209 | *Sweetbriar* | K 261 | *Mourne* |
| K 156 | *Chicoutimi* (RCN) | K 210 | *Thyme* | K 262 | *Aire* |
| K 157 | *Dauphin* (RCN) | K 211 | *Snowflake* | K 263 | *Braid* |
| K 158 | *Saskatoon* (RCN) | K 212 | *Hyderabad* | K 264 | *Cam* |
| K 159 | *Hepatica* | K 213 | *Poppy* | K 265 | *Dhanush* (RIN) |
| K 160 | *Lethbridge* (RCN) | K 214 | *Potentilla* | K 266 | *Fal* |
| K 161 | *Prescott* (RCN) | K 215 | *Nith* | K 267 | *Frome* |
| K 162 | *Sudbury* (RCN) | K 216 | *Tamarisk* | K 268 | *Lambourne* |
| K 163 | *Galt* (RCN) | K 217 | *Swale* | K 269 | *Meon* |
| K 164 | *Moosejaw* (RCN) | K 218 | *Brantford* (RCN) | K 270 | *Nene* |
| K 165 | *Battleford* (RCN) | K 219 | *Ness* | K 271 | *Plym* |
| K 166 | *Snowberry* (RCN) | K 220 | *Midland* (RCN) | K 272 | *Tavy* |
| K 167 | *Drumheller* (RCN) | K 221 | *Chelmer* | K 273 | *La Malbaie* (RCN) |
| K 168 | *The Pas* (RCN) | K 222 | *Tevoit* | K 274 | *Sind* (RIN) |
| K 169 | *Rosthern* (RCN) | K 223 | *Timmins* (RCN) | K 275 | *Buddleia* |
| K 170 | *Morden* (RCN) | K 224 | *Rother* | K 277 | *Comfrey* |
| K 171 | *Kamsack* (RCN) | K 225 | *Kitchener* (RCN) | K 278 | *Cornel* |
| K 172 | *Trillium* (RCN) | K 226 | *Godetia* | K 279 | *Dittany* |
| K 173 | *Weyburn* (RCN) | K 227 | *Itchen* | K 280 | *Smilax* |
| K 174 | *Trail* (RCN) | K 228 | *New Westminster* (RCN) | K 281 | *Statice* |
| K 175 | *Wetaskiwin* (RCN) | | | K 282 | *Linaria* |
| K 176 | *Kamloops* (RCN) | K 229 | *Dundas* (RCN) | K 283 | *Willowherb* |
| K 177 | *Dunvegan* (RCN) | K 230 | *Wear* | K 284 | *Flax* |
| K 178 | *Oakville* (RCN) | K 231 | *Calgary* (RCN) | K 285 | *Honesty* |
| K 179 | *Buctouche* (RCN) | K 232 | *Tay* | K 286 | *Rosebay* |
| K 180 | *Collingwood* (RCN) | K 223 | *Port Arthur* (RCN) | K 287 | *Mandrake* |
| K 181 | *Sackville* (RCN) | K 234 | *Regina* (RCN) | K 288 | *Milfoil* |
| K 182 | *Bittersweet* | K 237 | *Halifax* (RCN) | K 289 | *Musk* |
| K 184 | *Abelia* | K 238 | *Woodstock* (RCN) | K 290 | *Nepeta* |
| K 185 | *Alisma* | L 239 | *Test* | K 291 | *Privet* |
| K 186 | *Anchusa* | K 240 | *Vancouver* (RCN) | K 292 | *Torridge* |
| K 187 | *Armeria* | K 241 | *Kale* | K 293 | *Tees* |
| K 188 | *Aster* | K 242 | *Ville de Québec* (RCN) | K 294 | *Towy* |
| K 189 | *Bergamot* | K 243 | *Trent* | K 295 | *Usk* |
| K 190 | *Vervain* | K 244 | *Charlottetown* (RCN) | K 297 | *Annan* |

| | | |
|---|---|---|
| K 298 Barle | K 351 Duckworth | K 405 Alnwick Castle |
| K 299 Cuckmere | K 352 Duff | K 406 Barwon (RAN) |
| K 300 Evenlode | K 353 Essington | K 407 Beaconhill (RCN) |
| K 301 Findhorn | K 354 Gascoyne (RAN) | K 408 Culgoa (RAN) |
| K 302 Inver | K 355 Hadleigh Castle | K 409 Capilano (RCN) |
| K 303 Lossie | K 356 Odzani | K 410 Coaticook (RCN) |
| K 304 Parret | K 357 Rivière du Loup | K 411 Ribble |
| K 305 Shiel | (RCN) | K 412 Bamborough Castle |
| K 306 Assam (RIN) | K 358 Asbestos (RCN) | K 413 Farnham Castle |
| K 307 Mimico (RCN) | K 360 Forrest Hill (RCN) | K 414 Glace Bay (RCN) |
| K 310 Bayntun | K 362 Portchester Castle | K 415 Hawksbury (RCN) |
| K 311 Bazely | K 363 Hawkesbury (RAN) | K 416 Hurst Castle |
| K 312 Berry | K 364 Lachlan (RAN) | K 417 Halladale |
| K 313 Blackwood | K 365 Lochy | K 418 Joliette (RCN) |
| K 314 Bentinck | K 366 Ste Thérèse (RCN) | K 419 Kokanee (RCN) |
| K 315 Byard | K 367 Taff | K 420 Kenilworth Castle |
| K 316 Drury | K 368 Trentonian (RCN) | K 421 Loch Shin |
| K 317 Chebogue (RCN) | K 369 West York (RCN) | K 422 Loch Eck |
| K 318 Jonquière (RCN) | K 371 Wye | K 423 Largo Bay |
| K 319 Montreal (RCN) | K 372 Rushen Castle | K 424 Loch Achanalt (RCN) |
| K 320 New Glasgow (RCN) | K 373 St Thomas (RCN) | K 425 Loch Dunvegan |
| K 321 New Waterford (RCN) | K 374 Shrewsbury Castle | K 426 Loch Achray |
| K 322 Outremont (RCN) | K 375 Barcoo (RAN) | K 427 Luce Bay |
| K 323 Springhill (RCN) | K 376 Burdekin (RAN) | K 428 Loch Alvie (RCN) |
| K 324 Prince Rupert (RCN) | K 377 Diamantina (RAN) | K 429 Loch Fyne |
| K 325 St Catherines (RCN) | K 378 Hespeler (RCN) | K 430 Natal (SANF) |
| K 326 Port Colborne (RCN) | K 379 Carisbrooke Castle | K 431 Loch Tarbert |
| K 327 Stormont (RCN) | K 382 Longbranch (RCN) | K 432 Good Hope (SANF) |
| K 328 Swansea (RCN) | K 383 Flint Castle | K 433 Loch Insh |
| K 329 Valleyfield (RCN) | K 384 Leeds Castle | K 434 Loch Quoich |
| K 330 Waskesiu (RCN) | K 385 Arabis (RNZN) | K 435 Enard Bay |
| K 331 Wentworth (RCN) | K 386 Amberley Castle | K 436 Surprise |
| K 332 Belleville (RCN) | K 387 Berkeley Castle | K 437 Loch Lomond |
| K 333 Cobourg (RCN) | K 388 Dunver (RCN) | K 438 Derby Haven |
| K 335 Frontenac (RCN) | K 389 Knaresborough Castle | K 439 Listowel (RCN) |
| K 336 Ingersoll (RCN) | K 390 Loch Fada | K 440 Lachute (RCN) |
| K 337 Kirkland Lake (RN) | K 391 Loch Killin | K 441 Monnow |
| K 338 Lindsay (RCN) | K 393 Kincardine (RCN) | K 442 Murchison (RAN) |
| K 339 North Bay (RCN) | K 394 Thorlock | K 443 Maiden Castle |
| K 340 Owen Sound (RCN) | K 395 Mahratta (RIN) | K 444 Matane (RCN) |
| K 341 Parry Sound (RCN) | K 396 Hedingham Castle | K 446 Bowmanville (RCN) |
| K 342 Peterborough (RCN) | K 397 Launceston Castle | K 447 Humberstone (RCN) |
| K 344 St Lambert (RCN) | K 398 Arnprior (RCN) | K 448 Orkney (RCN) |
| K 345 Smiths Falls (RCN) | K 399 Tintagel Castle | K 449 Pevensey Castle |
| K 346 Whitby (RCN) | K 400 Levis (RCN) | K 450 Pembroke Castle |
| K 347 Burges | K 401 Louisburg (RCN) | K 452 Renfrew (RCN) |
| K 348 Gondhwana (RIN) | K 402 Toronto (RCN) | K 453 Petrolia (RCN) |
| K 349 Calder | K 403 Arbutus (RNZN) | K 454 St Stephen (RCN) |
| K 350 Cape Breton (RCN) | K 404 Annan | K 455 Strathroy (RCN) |

| | | | | | |
|---|---|---|---|---|---|
| K 456 | *St John* (RCN) | K 506 | *Cayman* | K 578 | *Narbrough* |
| K 457 | *Stellarton* (RCN) | K 507 | *Dominica* | K 579 | *Waldegrave* |
| K 458 | *Teme* | K 508 | *Byron* | K 580 | *Whittaker* |
| K 459 | *Thetford Mines* (RCN) | K 509 | *Conn* | K 581 | *Holmes* |
| K 460 | *Leaside* (RCN) | K 510 | *Cotton* | K 582 | *Hargood* |
| K 461 | *Huntsville* (RCN) | K 511 | *Cranstoun* | K 583 | *Hotham* |
| K 462 | *Affleck* | K 512 | *Cubitt* | K 584 | *Labuan* |
| K 463 | *Aylmer* | K 513 | *Curzon* | K 585 | *Tobago* |
| K 464 | *Balfour* | K 514 | *Lawford* | K 586 | *Montserrat* |
| K 465 | *Bentley* | K 515 | *Louis* | K 587 | *Nyasaland* |
| K 466 | *Bickerton* | K 516 | *Lawson* | K 588 | *Papua* |
| K 467 | *Bligh* | K 517 | *Loch Morlich* (RCN) | K 589 | *Pitcairn* |
| K 468 | *Braithwaite* | K 526 | *Awe* | K 590 | *St Helena* |
| K 470 | *Capel* | K 529 | *Hedingham Castle* | K 591 | *Sarawak* |
| K 471 | *Cooke* | K 530 | *Oakham Castle* | K 592 | *Seychelles* |
| K 472 | *Dacres* | K 531 | *Stonetown* (RCN) | K 593 | *Perim* |
| K 473 | *Domett* | K 532 | *Macquarie* (RAN) | K 594 | *Somaliland* |
| K 474 | *Foley* | K 533 | *Warburton* (RAN) | K 595 | *Tortola* |
| K 475 | *Garlies* | K 534 | *Murrumbidgee* (RAN) | K 596 | *Zanzibar* |
| K 476 | *Gould* | K 535 | *Shoalhaven* (RAN) | K 600 | *St Brides Bay* |
| K 477 | *Grindall* | K 538 | *Toronto* (RCN) | K 601 | *Loch Affric* |
| K 478 | *Gardiner* | K 550 | *Dakins* | K 602 | *Transvaal* (SANF) |
| K 479 | *Goodall* | K 551 | *Deane* | K 603 | *Loch Arkaig* |
| K 480 | *Goodson* | K 552 | *Ekins* | K 604 | *Start Bay* |
| K 481 | *Gore* | K 553 | *Fitzroy* | K 605 | *Tremadoc Bay* |
| K 482 | *Keats* | K 554 | *Redmill* | K 606 | *Bigbury Bay* |
| K 483 | *Kempthorne* | K 555 | *Retalick* | K 607 | *Loch Clunie* |
| K 484 | *Kingsmill* | K 556 | *Halsted* | K 608 | *Padstow Bay* |
| K 485 | *Mimico* (RCN) | K 557 | *Riou* | K 609 | *Loch Craggie* |
| K 486 | *Forrest Hill* (RCN) | K 558 | *Rutherford* | K 611 | *Herne Bay* |
| K 487 | *Longbranch* (RCN) | K 559 | *Cosby* | K 612 | *Loch Ericht* |
| K 488 | *St Thomas* (RCN) | K 560 | *Rowley* | K 613 | *Loch Erisort* |
| K 489 | *Hespeler* (RCN) | K 561 | *Rupert* | K 614 | *Hollesley Bay* |
| K 490 | *Kincardine* (RCN) | K 562 | *Stockham* | K 615 | *Widemouth Bay* |
| K 491 | *Orangeville* (RCN) | K 563 | *Seymour* | K 616 | *Wigtown Bay* |
| K 492 | *Leaside* (RCN) | K 564 | *Pasley* | K 617 | *Loch Garve* |
| K 493 | *Bowmanville* (RCN) | K 565 | *Loring* | K 619 | *Loch Glendhu* |
| K 494 | *Arnprior* (RCN) | K 566 | *Hoste* | K 620 | *Loch Gorm* |
| K 495 | *Coppercliff* (RCN) | K 567 | *Moorsom* | K 621 | *Loch Griam* |
| K 496 | *Tillsonburg* (RCN) | K 568 | *Manners* | K 622 | *Burghead Bay* |
| K 497 | *Humberstone* (RCN) | K 569 | *Mounsey* | K 623 | *Loch Harray* |
| K 498 | *Petrolia* (RCN) | K 570 | *Inglis* | K 624 | *Morecambe Bay* |
| K 499 | *Huntsville* (RCN) | K 571 | *Inman* | K 625 | *Loch Katrine* |
| K 500 | *Anguilla* | K 572 | *Spragge* | K 626 | *Loch Ken* |
| K 501 | *Antigua* | K 573 | *Stayner* | K 627 | *Mounts Bay* |
| K 502 | *Ascension* | K 574 | *Thornbrough* | K 628 | *Loch Killisport* |
| K 503 | *Bahamas* | K 575 | *Trollope* | K 629 | *Loch Kirbister* |
| K 504 | *Barbados* | K 576 | *Tyler* | K 630 | *Cardigan Bay* |
| K 505 | *Caicos* | K 577 | *Torrington* | K 631 | *Loch Linfern* |

| K 632 | Loch Linnhe | K 652 | Loch Tanna | K 672 | Longueil (RCN) |
|---|---|---|---|---|---|
| K 633 | Whitesand Bay | K 653 | Loch Tilt | K 673 | Magog (RCN) |
| K 634 | St Austell Bay | K 654 | Woodbridge Haven | K 675 | Poundmaker (RCN) |
| K 635 | Loch Lyon | K 655 | Loch Tralaig | K 676 | Penetang (RCN) |
| K 636 | Carnarvon Bay | K 656 | Loch Urgill | K 677 | Royal Mount (RCN) |
| K 637 | Loch Minnick | K 657 | Loch Vennacher | K 678 | Runnymede (RCN) |
| K 638 | Pegwell Bay | K 658 | Loch Veyatie | K 680 | St Pierre (RCN) |
| K 639 | Loch More | K 659 | Loch Watten | K 681 | Stettler (RCN) |
| K 640 | Thurso Bay | K 661 | Antigonish (RCN) | K 682 | Strathadam (RCN) |
| K 641 | Loch Nell | K 662 | Prestonian (RCN) | K 683 | Sussexville (RCN) |
| K 642 | Loch Odairn | K 663 | Cap de la | K 684 | Victoriaville (RCN) |
| K 643 | Loch Ossian | | Madeleine (RCN) | K 685 | Buckingham (RCN) |
| K 644 | Cawsand Bay | K 664 | Carlplace (RCN) | K 686 | Fergus (RCN) |
| K 645 | Loch Ruthven | K 665 | Eastview (RCN) | K 687 | Guelph (RCN) |
| K 646 | Loch Ryan | K 666 | Hallowell (RCN) | K 689 | Allington Castle |
| K 647 | Alert | K 667 | Incharran (RCN) | K 690 | Caistor Castle |
| K 648 | Loch Scavaig | K 668 | La Hulloise (RCN) | K 691 | Lancaster Castle |
| K 649 | Loch Scrivain | K 669 | Lanark (RCN) | K 692 | Oxford Castle |
| K 650 | Porlock Bay | K 670 | Fort Erie (RCN) | K 693 | Morpeth Castle |
| K 651 | Veryan Bay | K 671 | Lauzon (RCN) | | |

## Flag 'L' Superior

| L 03 | Badsworth | L 34 | Bicester | L 67 | Adrias (Greece) |
|---|---|---|---|---|---|
| L 05 | Atherstone | L 35 | Cattistock | L 68 | Eridge |
| L 06 | Avon Vale | L 36 | Eskdale | L 69 | Tanatside |
| L 07 | Airedale | L 37 | Hambledon | L 70 | Farndale |
| L 09 | Easton | L 39 | Rockwood | L 71 | Calpe |
| L 10 | Southwold | L 42 | Brocklesby | L 72 | Kujawiak (Poland) |
| L 11 | Fernie | L 43 | Blackmore | L 73 | Melbreak |
| L 12 | Albrighton | L 45 | Whaddon | L 74 | Middleton |
| L 14 | Beaufort | L 46 | Cleveland | L 75 | Haydon |
| L 15 | Eggesford | L 47 | Blean | L 76 | Brecon |
| L 16 | Stevenstone | L 48 | Holderness | L 77 | Grove |
| L 17 | Berkeley | L 50 | Bleasdale | L 78 | Cottesmore |
| L 18 | Talybont | L 51 | Themistocles (Greece) | L 79 | Brissenden |
| L 19 | La Combattante | L 52 | Cowdray | L 81 | Catterick |
| | (France) | L 53 | Canaris (Greece) | L 82 | Meynell |
| L 20 | Garth | L 54 | Cotswold | L 83 | Derwent |
| L 22 | Aldenham | L 56 | Holcombe | L 84 | Kriti (Greece) |
| L 24 | Blencathra | L 57 | Limbourne | L 85 | Heythrop |
| L 25 | Southdown | L 58 | Quantock | L 86 | Wensleydale |
| L 26 | Slazak (Poland) | L 59 | Zetland | L 87 | Eglinton |
| L 27 | Goathland | L 60 | Mendip | L 88 | Lamerton |
| L 28 | Hurworth | L 61 | Exmoor | L 89 | Penylan |
| L 30 | Blankney | L 62 | Croome | L 90 | Ledbury |
| L 31 | Chiddingfold | L 63 | Dulverton | L 91 | Miaoulis (Greece) |
| L 32 | Belvoir | L 65 | Pindos (Greece) | L 92 | Pytchley |

| L 95 | *Lauderdale* | L 99 | *Tetcott* | L 115 | *Krakowiak* (Poland) |
|---|---|---|---|---|---|
| L 96 | *Tynedale* | L 100 | *Liddesdale* | L 122 | *Wheatland* |
| L 98 | *Oakley* | L 108 | *Puckeridge* | L 128 | *Wilton* |

## FLAG 'T' SUPERIOR

| T 01 | *Cedar* | T 119 | *Rowan* | T 167 | *Hamlet* |
|---|---|---|---|---|---|
| T 02 | *Acacia* | T 120 | *Hornpipe* | T 168 | *Bute* |
| T 05 | *Ophelia* | T 122 | *Rumba* | T 169 | *Jura* |
| T 06 | *Arran* | T 123 | *Juniper* | T 170 | *Shiant* |
| T 09 | *Cypress* | T 124 | *Deodar* | T 171 | *Flotta* |
| T 10 | *Romeo* | T 125 | *Sarabande* | T 172 | *Islay* |
| T 12 | *Rampur* (RIN) | T 126 | *Olive* | T 173 | *Hildasay* |
| T 16 | *Hoxa* | T 127 | *Whitethorn* | T 174 | *Killegray* (RNZN) |
| T 18 | *Inchcolm* | T 128 | *Saltarello* | T 175 | *Scarba* (RNZN) |
| T 19 | *Holly* | T 129 | *Fir* | T 176 | *Shapinsay* |
| T 26 | *Lilac* | T 130 | *Veleta* | T 177 | *Sluna* |
| T 30 | *Mazurka* | T 131 | *Minuet* | T 178 | *Stronsay* |
| T 31 | *Magnolia* | T 132 | *Sword Dance* | T 179 | *Switha* |
| T 32 | *Hawthorn* | T 133 | *Quadrille* | T 180 | *Tiree* |
| T 37 | *Sycamore* | T 134 | *Celia* | T 181 | *Trondra* |
| T 38 | *Maple* | T 135 | *Rosalind* | T 182 | *Westray* |
| T 39 | *Ash/Pirouette* | T 136 | *Juliet* | T 200 | *Kerrera* |
| T 50 | *Balta* | T 137 | *Laertes* | T 201 | *Eday* |
| T 66 | *Willow* | T 138 | *Macbeth* | T 202 | *Fetlar* |
| T 76 | *Othello* | T 139 | *Polka* | T 203 | *Foula* |
| T 77 | *Bay* | T 140 | *Coriolanus* | T 204 | *Orfasy* |
| T 86 | *Redwood* | T 142 | *Twostep* | T 207 | *Coll* |
| T 93 | *Birch* | T 144 | *Pladda* | T 208 | *Damsay* |
| T 96 | *Larch* | T 145 | *Cava* | T 209 | *St Kilda* |
| T 99 | *Brora* | T 146 | *Tango* | T 210 | *Rousay* |
| T 100 | *Blackthorn* | T 147 | *Copinsay* | T 211 | *Ruskholm* |
| T 101 | *Pine* | T 149 | *Ronaldsay* | T 212 | *Filla* |
| T 102 | *Kiwi* (RNZN) | T 150 | *Stroma* | T 213 | *Unst* |
| T 103 | *Walnut* | T 151 | *Valse* | T 214 | *Bressay* |
| T 104 | *Cotillion* | T 153 | *Horatio* | T 215 | *Egilsay* |
| T 105 | *Elm* | T 154 | *Cumbrae* | T 216 | *Ensay* |
| T 106 | *Coverley* | T 155 | *Inchkeith* (RNZN) | T 217 | *Eriskay* |
| T 107 | *Fandango* | T 157 | *Fluellen* | T 218 | *Birdlip* |
| T 108 | *Hazel* | T 158 | *Burra* | T 219 | *Butser* |
| T 109 | *Foztrot* | T 159 | *Staffa* | T 220 | *Duncton* |
| T 110 | *Mull* | T 160 | *Sanda* (RNZN) | T 221 | *Portsdown* |
| T 112 | *Mangrove* | T 161 | *Canna* | T 222 | *Yestor* |
| T 113 | *Wistaria* | T 162 | *Fara* | T 223 | *Bredon* |
| T 114 | *Hoy* | T 163 | *Skye* | T 224 | *Dunkery* |
| T 115 | *Gavotte* | T 164 | *Rysa* | T 225 | *Inkpen* |
| T 116 | *Hickory* | T 165 | *Kintyre* | T 231 | *Bonito* |
| T 117 | *Morris Dance* | T 166 | *Inchmarnock* | T 232 | *Whiting* |

| | | | | | | |
|---|---|---|---|---|---|
| T 233 | *Moa* (RNZN) | T 288 | *Gateshead* | T 355 | *Gilstone* |
| T 234 | *Tui* (RNZN) | T 289 | *Herschell* | T 356 | *Steepholm* |
| T 236 | *Brurey* | T 291 | *Graemsay* | T 359 | *Caldy* |
| T 237 | *Scalpay* | T 292 | *Sheppey* | T 360 | *Grain* |
| T 238 | *Fiaray* | T 293 | *Whalsay* | T 361 | *Lindisfarne* |
| T 239 | *Gruinard* | T 294 | *Bern* | T 362 | *Minalto* |
| T 243 | *Grayling* | T 295 | *Mousa* | T 363 | *Rosevean* |
| T 246 | *Gweal* | T 296 | *Oxna* | T 365 | *Gulland* |
| T 247 | *Neave* | T 297 | *Earraid* | T 366 | *Longa* |
| T 248 | *Ulva* | T 298 | *Hunda* | T 368 | *Grilse* |
| T 249 | *Baroda* (RIN) | T 304 | *Bombardier* | T 373 | *Skokholm* |
| T 250 | *Shilling* (RIN) | T 305 | *Fusilier* | T 374 | *Mewstone* |
| T 251 | *Cuttack* (RIN) | T 306 | *Bream* | T 375 | *Oronsay* |
| T 252 | *Dacca* (RIN) | T 311 | *Mullet* | T 376 | *Ganilly* |
| T 253 | *Lahore* (RIN) | T 312 | *Travancore* (RIN) | T 377 | *Ailsa Craig* |
| T 254 | *Agra* (RIN) | T 313 | *Vizagapatam* (RIN) | T 378 | *Vatersay* |
| T 255 | *Patna* (RIN) | T 314 | *Trichinopoly* (RIN) | T 379 | *Benbecula* |
| T 256 | *Berar* (RIN) | T 315 | *Cochin* (RIN) | T 380 | *Crowline* |
| T 258 | *Nasik* (RIN) | T 317 | *Allahabad* (RIN) | T 381 | *Skomer* |
| T 259 | *Sholapore* (RIN) | T 318 | *Benares* (RIN) | T 382 | *Kittern* |
| T 260 | *Poona* (RIN) | T 319 | *Bareilly* (RIN) | T 383 | *Calvay* |
| T 261 | *Amritsar* (RIN) | T 320 | *Ambala* (RIN) | T 384 | *Colsay* |
| T 262 | *Karachi* (RIN) | T 321 | *Sialkot* (RIN) | T 385 | *Fuday* |
| T 263 | *Peshawar* (RIN) | T 322 | *Multan* (RIN) | T 386 | *Harris* |
| T 264 | *Ahmedabad* (RIN) | T 323 | *Jubbulpur* (RIN) | T 387 | *Gorregan* |
| T 265 | *Chittagong* (RIN) | T 324 | *Pachmari* (RIN) | T 388 | *Mincarlo* |
| T 266 | *Kolaba* (RIN) | T 325 | *Gaya* (RIN) | T 389 | *Hannaray* |
| T 267 | *Lucknow* (RIN) | T 326 | *Dinapore* (RIN) | T 390 | *Hascosay* |
| T 268 | *Madura* (RIN) | T 327 | *Monghyr* (RIN) | T 391 | *Hellisay* |
| T 269 | *Nagpur* (RIN) | T 328 | *Puri* (RIN) | T 392 | *Hermetray* |
| T 270 | *Barisal* (RIN) | T 329 | *Sylhet* (RIN) | T 393 | *Guardsman* |
| T 271 | *Hayling* | T 330 | *Kiamari* (RIN) | T 394 | *Home Guard* |
| T 272 | *Lundy* | T 331 | *Bannu* (RIN) | T 395 | *Royal Marine* |
| T 273 | *Bardsey* | T 332 | *Quetta* (RIN) | T 404 | *Biggal* |
| T 274 | *Anticosti* (RCN) | T 334 | *Grenadier* | T 423 | *Lingay* |
| T 275 | *Baffin* (RCN) | T 335 | *Lancer* | T 424 | *Sandray* |
| T 276 | *Cailiff* (RCN) | T 336 | *Sapper* | T 425 | *Scaravay* |
| T 277 | *Miscou* (RCN) | T 337 | *Coldstream* | T 426 | *Skillay* |
| T 278 | *Campobello* | T 339 | *Calcutta* (RIN) | T 427 | *Sursay* |
| T 279 | *Magdalen* (RCN) | T 341 | *Annet* | T 429 | *Ronay* |
| T 280 | *Manitoulin* (RCN) | T 342 | *Foulness* | T 431 | *Trodday* |
| T 281 | *Porcher* | T 344 | *Grassholm* | T 432 | *Vaceasay* |
| T 282 | *Prospect* | T 346 | *Cawnpore* (RIN) | T 434 | *Vallay* |
| T 283 | *Texada* | T 347 | *Pollock* | T 435 | *Wallasea* |
| T 284 | *Ironbound* (RCN) | T 350 | *Bryher* | T 441 | *Wiay* |
| T 285 | *Liscomb* (RCN) | T 352 | *St Agnes* | T 450 | *Orsay* |
| T 286 | *Dochet* | T 353 | *Farne* | T 451 | *Tocogay* |
| T 287 | *Flint* | T 354 | *Flatholm* | | |

## Flag 'U' Superior

| | | | | | |
|---|---|---|---|---|---|
| U 03 | *Erne* | U 33 | *Opossum* | U 64 | *Nereide* |
| U 05 | *Chanticleer/Waterhen* | U 37 | *Partridge* | U 66 | *Starling* |
| U 07 | *Actaeon* | U 38 | *Cygnet* | U 69 | *Redpole* |
| U 08 | *Woodpecker* | U 39 | *Hind* | U 71 | *Sparrow* |
| U 10 | *Cauvery* (RIN) | U 40 | *Narbada* (RIN) | U 73 | *Warrego* (RAN) |
| U 11 | *Lark* | U 42 | *Modeste* | U 74 | *Swan* (RAN) |
| U 16 | *Amethyst* | U 45 | *Wild Goose* | U 75 | *Egret* |
| U 18 | *Flamingo* | U 46 | *Kistna* (RIN) | U 82 | *Magpie* |
| U 20 | *Snipe* | U 49 | *Pheasant* | U 84 | *Nymphe* |
| U 21 | *Jumna* (RIN) | U 52 | *Godavari* (RIN) | U 86 | *Pelican* |
| U 23 | *Crane* | U 54 | *Nonsuch* | U 87 | *Kite* |
| U 28 | *Wren* | U 57 | *Black Swan* | U 90 | *Woodcock* |
| U 29 | *Whimbrel* | U 58 | *Hart* | U 95 | *Sutlej* (RIN) |
| U 30 | *Mermaid* | U 60 | *Alacrity* | U 96 | *Peacock* |
| U 31 | *Wryneck* | U 62 | *Lapwing* | U 99 | *Ibis* |

## Flag '5' Superior

| | | | | | |
|---|---|---|---|---|---|
| 5 01 | *Kilbirnie* | 5 06 | *Kildwick* | 5 11 | *Kilmarnock* |
| 5 02 | *Kilbride* | 5 07 | *Kilham* | 5 12 | *Kilmartin* |
| 5 03 | *Kilchattan* | 5 08 | *Kilkenzie* | 5 13 | *Kilmelford* |
| 5 04 | *Kilchrenan* | 5 09 | *Kilhampton* | 5 14 | *Kilmington* |
| 5 05 | *Kildary* | 5 10 | *Kilmalcolm* | 5 15 | *Kilmore* |

## Fishery Flag Superior

| | | | | | |
|---|---|---|---|---|---|
| FY 205 | *Buttermere* | FY 206 | *Thirlmere* | FY 239 | *Wastwater* |
| FY 204 | *Ellesmere* | FY 252 | *Ullswater* | FY 207 | *Windermere* |

One of the floating power stations, *Marsh* of the 'Buckley' type. Taken in Hawaii, this shows the power points in place of the torpedo tubes, a new type bridge and postwar radar aerials at the masthead. (*US Navy*)

# *Glossary*

| | |
|---|---|
| Admiralty | Royal Navy's central authority, now Ministry of Defence (Navy). |
| A/S | anti-submarine. |
| Asdic | RN name for anti-submarine detection equipment. Named after UK's Anti-submarine Detection Investigation Committee, formed after World War I, which developed this equipment. Later the RN followed the USN in renaming this equipment as Sonar. Control equipment was in a compartment on or near the bridge, and transmitter/receiver was lowered below bottom of the ship, in a streamlined dome, usually below B gun position. |
| ATW | ahead-throwing weapon, an A/S mortar, called Hedgehog or Squid during this period. |
| BHP | brake horsepower. |
| BL | breech-loading, an old term, still applied to some guns in this period. |
| Bofors | 40mm quick-firing close-range weapon, common to all Allied navies. |

| | |
|---|---|
| bp | between posts, the length of a ship between outermost perpendicular girders. |
| calibre | measurement of barrel diameter of gun. |
| Captain (D) | the senior officer of a destroyer flotilla in the RN and RCN. At large bases, such as Liverpool, he would be based ashore. |
| capstan | steam or electrically driven winch, with vertical drum. For handling anchor cables, wires and ropes, on the forecastle. |
| carley float | lifesaving raft, with rigid buoyancy ring, and net footropes. |
| CAT | USN/RCN codename for countermeasure gear used against acoustic torpedoes |
| CIC | combat information center—USN term for central control room, usually sited below bridge. |
| class lists | The following convention has been generally used; where gaps are found, this is due to the information not being available from official records: Ship's name, pendant number, builder, yard |

number, overall building time, completion date. Shipbuilders' names for the larger countries are repeated in full at the end of each navy. Launching dates have not been included, as being less relevant to this study, unless the other dates are not available, in which case the date is preceded by 'L'.

close-range    all armament, other than the main armament.

corvette    escort vessel, usually 175-275 feet in length.

CSA apparatus    chemical smoke-making apparatus, which produced dense white smoke. Mounted right at the stern.

CTL    constructive total loss—where a ship is badly damaged at sea, brought back to port by her crew, but is not worth repairing.

CVE    American designation for escort carrier.

DCT    director control tower, for directing the main armament, mounted at the back of the bridge.

DF    direction finding.

degaussing    electrical method of reducing a steel ship's field of magneticism against magnetic mines. Composed of an electrical cable running round the hull and energised from a generator.

department    Government Department, as 'of Defence'; usually post-war successor authority to 'navy' title.

depth charge    cylindrical or shaped steel drum filled with 300 pounds of explosive, and with a detonator set to fire by water pressure at the required depth.

destroyer escort    USN term for frigate, but see also the earlier term for the RN 'Hunt' class.

destroyer flotilla    a group of destroyers. This could vary from, say, 8 ships to all the destroyers based at one port, up to, say, 30 ships.

DP    dual-purpose, high angle or low angle (describing a gun).

endurance    distance in nautical miles which a ship can cover, at a given speed, within her fuel capacity.

escort    another early term for the RN's 'Hunt' class.

escort group    a number of escorts, operating together as a group, and trained to work closely in harmony as a unit. All RN and RCN close escort and support groups carried this title, with a distinguishing number.

escort vessel    a generic term, not a specific type.

fantail    USN term for after end of ship—RN equivalent is quarterdeck, or sweep deck on a minesweeper.

fleet minesweeper    a steel-hulled minesweeper, large and fast enough to operate ahead of a fleet, where necessary, and also fitted out as an A/S escort.

| | | | |
|---|---|---|---|
| forecastle deck | decks of escorts were variously described, but this was usually the deck extending aft from the stem. | IHP | indicated horsepower, of main machinery. |
| foredeck | usually the deck forward of the bridge. | kite | item of minesweeping equipment, also applied to small A/A balloon, flown from some escorts in the early war years. |
| Foxer | noisemaking antidote to German acoustic torpedoes; it was towed astern of the escort. Called CAT in the USN, and in the RCN at times. | knot | nautical mile (2,000 yards) per hour. |
| | | LCG | Landing Craft (Gun). |
| funnel | smoke uptake—stack in the USN. | L | denotes launching date in class lists when other dates not available. |
| F/D | Fighter Direction. | Lend-Lease | the US law which enabled new American-built warships to be transferred on loan to Allied navies. |
| gaff | small pole, slung at about 45 degrees angle from mast, to take flags and, specifically, the ship's ensign. | Loran | long-range navigation system. A US-developed radio navigational device, based on a number of shore transmitting stations with shipborne receivers. Effective in the North Atlantic, in the later years of the war. |
| Gnat | RN codename for German acoustic torpedoes—USN equivalent was Wren. | | |
| Hedgehog | A/S ahead-throwing mortar—the first ATW throwing 24 bombs in an elliptical pattern ahead of ship. | LL | the electric sweep against magnetic mines. Two buoyant cables were towed astern of the sweeper and electric impulses sent out through them. Diesel generators on board the sweepers supplied the energy. |
| H/F D/F | high-frequency direction finding, for monitoring U-boat radio transmissions, taking bearings, and then running down them to the quarry. | | |
| HH | Hedgehog. | LSH(S) | Landing Ship Headquarters (Small). |
| Huff Duff | Much-used colloquial term for H/F D/F q.v. | LST | Landing Ship, Tank. |
| IFF | identification friend or foe—a radar device, for identifying friendly warships. | MAC | merchant aircraft carrier, conversions usually manned by merchant navy crews, and still carrying oil or bulk grain below decks. |

main armament — the heaviest guns in a ship—in escorts, usually 5″, 4″, 3″, or 12 pounder.

manual twin — a twin 20mm Oerlikon mounting, usually only found in RN ships, and rarely then. It used the same mounting as the single gun, but doubled the firepower.

M/F D/F — medium frequency direction finding, the normal commercial radio network, for navigational purposes only. The range was limited to coastal areas under normal reception conditions.

Ministry of Defence — the successor authority to the Admiralty in the UK. The naval part of it has the suffix (Navy).

M/S — minesweeping.

MSF — minesweeping flotilla.

motor boat — a ship's main boat, propelled by a diesel or petrol (gas) engine. Usually some 25 feet long overall.

MTB — motor torpedo boat.

motor cutter — an alternative term for motor boat.

motor dinghy — usually a smaller boat, as RN trawler boats, or the skimming dish.

oa — overall length, the longest measurement of a ship.

Oerlikon — the standard 20mm automatic weapon of the Allied navies. It appeared in numbers from 1941 onwards.

Oropesa — the torpedo-shaped float, from which the wire sweep against moored mines is suspended, when towed astern of a minesweeper.

Otter — item of minesweeping equipment used against moored mines.

patrol craft — a USN class, largely equivalent to the RN's corvette.

patrol frigate — another USN class, the equivalent of the RN's frigates.

plot — RN equivalent of CIC.

pom pom — official, though onomatopaeic, term for RN's 2 pounder gun, in either single or quadruple mountings, in escort vessels.

pp — another sign for length between perpendicular.

PPI — plan position indicator—the horizontal presentation of the radar set's echoes. A circular tube, like a TV tube, with the bearing line sweeping round from the centre.

quarterdeck — the after deck in an RN ship, fantail in the USN.

QH3 — accurate, short-range position-fixing navigation set, developed in the UK. Position presented visually on a cathode ray tube.

QF — quick-firing.

radar — term produced by the USN, and later adopted by the RN, whose original term was RDF. A full description is included in this book.

| | | | |
|---|---|---|---|
| radar types | USN types carried letters, such as SG, SL. RN types carried numbers, as 271, 277. | SO | Senior Officer. |
| | | sonar | USN name for RN Asdic gear. |
| RAN | Royal Australian Navy. | specification | this is laid out as uniformly as possible for each class, but there are gaps in official information in this area, and some are therefore either incomplete or incorrect in detail. |
| RDF | radio-direction finding. See Radar. | | |
| RIN | Royal Indian Navy. | | |
| RN | Royal Navy. | | |
| RNZN | Royal New Zealand Navy. | spur | small horizontal metal or wood extension from a mast, to support a radar or radio-telephone aerial. |
| rocket flares | very efficient RN 2″ flares, with solid propellant. | | |
| R/T | radio-telephone. | squadron | USN term for group or flotilla of escorts or minesweepers. |
| SA | an air-warning radar set in the USN, and minesweeping gear against acoustic mines in the RN and RCN. | Squid | RN anti-submarine ATW mortar, 12″ bore, firing 3 or, in twin mounts, 6 large bombs of 385 pounds each, which fell in a triangular pattern 300 yards ahead of the ship, and were set to explode at a given depth; the mounting was fully gyro-stabilised. Only found during the war years in 'Loch' class frigates and 'Castle' class corvettes. |
| SANF | South African Naval Forces. | | |
| shp | shaft horsepower, in main machinery. | | |
| skimming dish | a pre-war RN fast planing motor dinghy, issued to 'Hunt' class destroyers, and 'Black Swan' class sloops—but not in all cases. | | |
| SL | USN surface warning radar set. | stack | USN term for 'funnel'. |
| | | support group | RN and RCN groups, usually of 6 ships, moving from one convoy to another to give additional protection, or to hunt down U-boats. |
| sloop | a pre-war RN escort type designation. During the war it was only applied to the 'Black Swan' class, among the war-built classes. | | |
| smoke floats | metal canisters containing white smoke-producing chemicals, carried on or near the quarterdeck of an escort and dropped overboard when smoke was required as a screen. | sweep deck | the 'quarterdeck', or 'fantail', of a fleet minesweeper. |

| | | | |
|---|---|---|---|
| task force | or task unit. A USN term for a group of ships often operating in the same way as an RN or RCN escort group. | whaler | RN and Commonwealth 27 foot long wooden open boat, propelled by oars, much used as a seaboat; in a number of photographs of ships at sea they can be seen turned out in their davits, ready for use. |
| topmast | the light mast fitted above the main mast structure. | | |
| trawler | fishing vessel towing trawl wires in deep water. | windlass | steam winch with horizontal drums on the forecastle, for handling anchors, wires and ropes. Installed in corvettes and frigates in RN, RCN, and USN PFs, where ships were following mercantile practice |
| TBS | talk between ships, a high-frequency radio telephone set, much used by escorts in the later years of the war. | | |
| upper deck | a term for the midships deck. | wl | waterline length. |
| USN | United States Navy. | Wren | USN codename for German acoustic torpedoes. |
| VH/F D/F | very high frequency direction finding, developed late in the war. | | |

*Below:* The 'Evarts' type frigate *Grindall*, of the RN 'Captain' class, just showing her forefoot as she closes a consort, on 12th April 1944. The cover has been removed from her Type SL radar aerial, and she has the extra two-tier depth charge racks aft. (*Ministry of Defence*)

# Index

1. There are approximately 50 instances in which exactly the same name was used by two or more Allied navies; and there are numerous instances in addition of names with minor differences.

2. Photographs are indexed under their ship class names, as shots of some ships appear throughout the book, away from their class chapters.

3. U.S. Navy ships are indexed under their proper names, and listed in pendant number order under their class chapters. Individual P.C.s are indexed separately, where they are mentioned away from their class chapter.